THE AMERICAN AGE

THE AMERICAN AGE

United States Foreign Policy at Home and Abroad

WALTER LAFEBER

Second Edition

1750 to the Present

W · W · NORTON & COMPANY · NEW YORK · LONDON

This book is dedicated to Michael Kammen, Larry Moore, Mary Beth Norton, Richard Polenberg, and Joel Silbey for being, over the years, friends, colleagues, and co-teachers of the U.S. Survey Course.

The text of this book is composed in Linotype Walbaum,
with display type set in Walbaum.
Composition and manufacturing by The Maple-Vail Book Manufacturing Group.
Book design by Antonina Krass

Second Edition

The poems "Dusty" and "Dear Smitty" from *Shrapnel in the Heart* by Laura Palmer copyright © 1987 by Laura Palmer. Reprinted by permission of Random House, Inc.

Library of Congress Cataloging in Publication Data
LaFeber, Walter.
    The American age : United States foreign policy at home and abroad /
Walter LaFeber. — 2nd ed.
        p.   cm.
    Includes bibliographical references and index.
    1. United States—Foreign relations. I. Title.
E183.7.L27   1994
327.73—dc20   93-14460

One Vol: ISBN 0-393-96474-4 (pa)
Vol 1: ISBN 0-393-96475-2 (pa)
Vol 2: ISBN 0-393-96476-0 (pa)

W. W. Norton & Company, Inc., 500 Fifth Avenue, New York, N.Y. 10110
W. W. Norton & Company Ltd., 10 Coptic Street, London WC1A 1PU

2 3 4 5 6 7 8 9 0

Contents

6 | Laying the Foundations for "Superpowerdom" (1865–1896)

7 | Turning Point: The McKinley Years (1896–1900)

8 | The Search for Opportunity: Rough Riders and Dollar Diplomats (1901–1913)

17 | JFK and LBJ: From the New Frontier through the Great Society to Vietnam (1961–1969)   580

18 | Coming to Terms with History: The Nixon-Kissinger Years (1969–1976)   633

19 | Back to the Future: The Carter-Reagan Years (1977–1988) 680

List of Maps

Preface to the Second Edition

Since the first edition of this book appeared in 1989, we and our world have gone through changes that are not merely memorable, but historic—the kinds of changes that occur only several times a century. Because of these transformations, and also because this book was fortunate in the kind of interest shown by teachers and scholarly reviewers, this new edition analyzes the 1989–1993 watershed in some detail while strengthening the features that students and teachers found useful in the first edition. Four additions are especially important:

- The end of the Soviet empire, the U.S. response as the sole remaining superpower, and Bill Clinton's election are discussed not only from the American perspective, but from other perspectives as well.
- The pre-1900 sections have been enlarged. *The American Age* was written especially for courses in the post-1914 history of U.S. foreign relations. It has been a pleasant surprise to learn that pre-1900 material is receiving increased attention in classrooms, and that teachers have found the book's early chapters useful—but they want more detail. So new discussions and graphics have been added, especially on the Jeffersonian era, the 1830s–1840s, and 1890s. (Perhaps one reason for the interest in the pre–World War I era is that it so eerily, and sometimes frighteningly, resembles the 1989–1993 years with their ethnic violence, disruptions in the Balkans and eastern Europe, the rise of a vigorous Japan and a united Germany, and the appearance of radically new—and politically disruptive—technology and communications.)
- Materials have been used from newly opened files and fresh research to rewrite the book's sections on the outbreak of the cold war, the causes of the Korean War, the Cuban missile crisis, and President Richard Nixon's policies and personality.
- Additional references are made to motion pictures and television, and new graphics of films have been used. Readers liked the book's use of these references, and the new material has been added in the belief that films do reflect large concerns of Americans and their foreign policies. (Sometimes this reflection is badly distorted and

dangerously misleading, even while being influential.) Television has increasingly shaped U.S. foreign-policy choices, not least in the Central American upheavals, the Persian Gulf War, and Somalia.

Virtually every chapter has had revisions and/or additions. All the bibliographies, especially the General Bibliography at the end of the book, are updated. For those interested in a more specific listing, the following are some of the topics discussed on the new pages: the beginnings of the secretary of state's office; Daniel Webster's Whig policies; the *Caroline* and *Creole* affairs, and the Maine boundary dispute; women's key role in the anti-imperialist movement after 1898; a new interpretation that frames the 1880s to 1913 era; the 1900–1913 revolutionary outbreaks in Latin America and Asia, with attention to the Chinese upheaval; the role of motion pictures in the 1915–1917 debates and again (with *Sergeant York*) in 1941; Truman's decisions to use the atomic bomb and to delay before accepting Japan's surrender; newly opened Soviet materials giving Moscow's perspective on the Marshall Plan and the Klaus Fuchs spy case; Stalin's and Mao's roles in the Korean War; John F. Kennedy's approach to the possibility of bombing China's nuclear facilities; Kennedy's views on Vietnam and the views of Oliver Stone's film, *JFK*; the post-1948 roots of U.S. policies on South Africa; the Chilean crises of 1973 and the film *Missing*; Reagan, Gorbachev, and breakthrough agreements; the end of the cold war, a growing disorder, and David Lynch's world on television and in films, 1989–1993.

In addition to the friends thanked in the Acknowledgments of the first edition, I am greatly indebted to Robert Beisner, Barton Bernstein, Tim Borstelmann, Philip Brenner, Kenton Clymer, Warren Cohen, Michael Doyle, Robert Hannigan, Alan Kraut, Fumiaki Kubo, Julius Milmeister, Martin Sklar, and Evan Stewart, as well as several outside readers, who provided criticism and materials for this edition. I am especially grateful to Steve Forman, History Editor of W. W. Norton's College Division, to Bonnie Hall and Kate Brewster, editorial assistants, and to a most helpful copy editor, Sandy Lifland, all of whom improved this edition considerably; and to long-time friends Ed Barber and Gerry McCauley. Lizann Rogovoy and Bob Rouse provided indispensable research help. Above all, I thank the students and teachers, as well as the general readers, who have used *The American Age* and found it helpful in understanding United States foreign policy.

Walter LaFeber
Spring 1993

Preface to the First Edition

This book has been written to provide a relatively brief (and, I hope, readable) overview of post-1750 U.S. foreign relations. Chapters' lengths increase markedly after 1890. The pre-1890 sections, however, include the material needed to understand the first century of those foreign relations; all or part of those chapters can be used as introductory assignments in a one-semester post-1890 class.

The title is taken seriously. As Professor Thomas A. Bailey once observed, the United States was a world power at the birth of its independence in 1776. Then, if not before, the American age began because the country already ranked with the great European nations in terms of territory, population, economic strength, and natural resources, not to mention ambition. This survey tries to develop several themes that tie 250 years together, make sense of them, and give students and teachers starting points for discussion. The most obvious theme is the landed and commercial expansion that drove the nation outward between 1750 and the 1940s. Then, resembling other living things that age, the country's power began a relative decline after the mid-1950s. Americans have yet to understand and come to terms with the causes and consequences of that decline, although presidents from Kennedy through Reagan have, in varying ways, shaped their policies so that the country could adjust to this new world.

The book's second theme is the steady centralization of power at home, especially in the executive branch of government after 1890. This centralization occurred not merely because of the normal quest of human beings for power, but also because the foreign policies that Americans have desired since the nineteenth century are most effectively carried out by a strong presidency. There are no recurring cycles in this book, only the long rise and the relative decline of U.S. power, and the steady accretion of authority by presidents because of the way Americans have wanted to exercise that power. U.S. diplomatic history has often been written as if constitutional questions ceased to be important after 1865; this volume tries in small part to rectify that neglect.

A third theme is "isolationism," which means in U.S. history not withdrawal from world affairs (a people does not conquer a continent and become the world's greatest power by withdrawal or by assuming it enjoys "free security"), but maintaining a maximum amount of freedom of action. Americans who have professed to believe in individualism at home not surprisingly have often professed the same abroad.

A fourth theme is the importance of the transitional 1850-to-1914 era, a time when Americans' attitudes toward democracy, the Monroe Doctrine, the Constitution, and, especially, revolution underwent profound change and ushered in modern U.S. foreign policy. It is perhaps the great irony—and dilemma—of the nation's experience that it became a great power and wanted either to preserve the political *status quo* or only gradually to effect change precisely when the world began to erupt in revolution. This book tries to note some of the results of that irony and dilemma.

Finally, in the belief that how Americans act at home reveals much about how they act abroad, the analysis often focuses on domestic events (including films and sports). Social and diplomatic history have too seldom been wedded; parts of this account attempt in a minor way to start, at least, the courtship.

THE AMERICAN AGE

If I should not be thought too presumptuous I would beg leave to add what is my idea of the qualifications necessary for an American foreign minister in general. . . .

In the first place, he should have an education in classical learning and in the knowledge of general history, ancient and modern, and particularly the history of France, England, Holland, and America. He should be well versed in the principles of ethics, of the law of nature and nations, of legislation and government, of the Civil Roman law, of the laws of England and the United States, of the public law of Europe and in the letters, memoirs, and histories of those great men who have heretofore shone in the diplomatic order and conducted the affairs of nations and the world. He should be of an age to possess a maturity of judgment, arising from experience in business. He should be active, attentive, and industrious, and, above all, he should possess an upright heart and an independent spirit, and should be one who decidedly makes the interest of his country, not the policy of any other nation nor his own private ambition or interest, or those of his family, friends, and connexions, the rule of his conduct.

—JOHN ADAMS (1783)

Domestic issues can only lose elections, but foreign policy issues can kill us all.

—PRESIDENT JOHN F. KENNEDY (1962)

The Roots of American Foreign Policy
(1492–1789)

The Beginnings: Gold, God, and Paradise

William Seward, a fascinating scholar and New York backroom politician as well as Abraham Lincoln's secretary of state during the Civil War, once called the story of American development "the most important secular event in the history of the human race."[1] Seward might well have been correct. Americans, however, have viewed their secular, or more earthly, successes (such as making money) as part of a higher purpose. This view goes back to the origins of their country. Portuguese explorer Vasco da Gama needed few words to explain why a new world was discovered in the late fifteenth century: "We come in search of Christians and spices."

Mission and money or, as some historians prefer to phrase it, idealism and self-interest have for nearly five hundred years been the reasons Americans have given for their successes. From their beginnings, they have justified developing a continent and then much of the globe simply by saying they were spreading the principles of civilization as well as making profit. They have had no problem seeing their prosperity—indeed, their rise from a sparsely settled continent to the world's superpower—as part of a Higher Purpose or, as it was known during much of their history, a Manifest Destiny.

The most spectacular chance taker of his time said it directly. "Gold is most excellent, Gold is treasure," Christopher Columbus observed, "and he who possesses it does all he wishes to in this world, and succeeds in helping souls into paradise." Columbus was the original self-made man in America. As historian Edward Bourne observes: "His hopes, his illusions, his vanity and love of money, his devotion to by-gone ideals, his keen and sensitive observation of the natural world, his lack of practical power in dealing with literary evidence, his practical abilities as a navigator, his tenacity of purpose and boldness of execution, his lack of fidelity as a husband and a lover, his family pride,"[2] all mark Columbus as an appropriate figure to start the story of America's place in the world.

Columbus is also a useful symbol and starting point in American foreign policy for another reason: he founded empires by going westward. Again, nature, perhaps even the supernatural, seemed to be guiding Americans. They simply had to follow the sun. "We held it ever certain," the explorer Cabeza de Vaca declared in 1535, "that going toward the sunset we would find what we desired." Two centuries later, George Berkeley captured this vision in his famous poem that has the line "Westward the course of empire takes its way."

ON THE PROSPECT OF PLANTING ARTS
AND LEARNING IN AMERICA

The Muse, disgusted at an age and clime
    Barren of every glorious theme,
In distant lands now waits a better time,
    Producing subjects worthy fame:

In happy climes where from the genial sun
    And virgin earth such scenes ensue,
The force of art by nature seems outdone,
    And fancied beauties by the true:

In happy climes, the seat of innocence,
    Where nature guides and virtue rules,
Where men shall not impose for truth and sense
    The pedantry of courts and schools:

There shall be sung another golden age,
    The rise of empire and of arts,
The good and great inspiring epic rage,
    The wisest heads and noblest hearts.

Not such as Europe breeds in her decay;
    Such as she bred when fresh and young,
When heavenly flame did animate her clay,
    By future poets shall be sung.

Westward the course of empire takes its way;
    The four first acts already past,
A fifth shall close the drama with the day;
    Time's noblest offspring is the last.

Berkeley set out a great theme in Americans' foreign policy as they settled a continent by crossing from the Atlantic to the Pacific, moved across the Pacific Ocean to become a great world power for the first time in 1900, and then fought three major wars on the Asian mainland in the twentieth century. This westward movement has shaped much of the nation's best literature (the novels of Mark Twain and Willa Cather, and Robert Penn Warren's *All the King's Men* come to mind), as it has U.S. foreign policy.

westward Movement [handwritten margin note]

Another key theme of American diplomacy also appeared during the era of discovery: the country's prosperity and success, sometimes its very existence, have depended on events thousands of miles away. The birth of Americans as a separate people came out of fourteenth- and fifteenth-century events. Religious crusades, scientific discoveries, attempts to find new routes to Asia so expensive Italian middlemen could be avoided—all led Portugal and Spain to undertake the expeditions that climaxed in the discovery of the New World. The Spanish finally built a three-century-old empire because they had succeeded in consolidating power at home (sometimes brutally, as expelling or enslaving Moors and some 100,000 Jews who would not join the Roman Catholic church) and seizing the money needed to pay for Columbus's voyages. This centralized power then set about discovering and colonizing parts of North America and most of South America, exploring the Pacific, circling the globe, and introducing the first black slaves into the New World as early as 1502, a full century before the British brought such slaves to their colonies. Aside from their "Christianizing" the New World's inhabitants, Spain so violently extracted gold and valuable minerals that Native Americans ("Indians") and black slaves who worked in the mines died in large numbers.

The political events in Spain and the economic opportunities in America combined to revolutionize world trade. From their beginnings, Americans formed part of a world economic system. Nor could they successfully isolate themselves from the upheavals of Europe. On the other hand, they also were pivotal in reshaping the globe's politics and economics. Their wealth and labor allowed Spain and then England and Holland to replace Italian and German cities as the world's trade centers. Furs, tobacco, sugar, and fish from North America replaced Asia's spices as the most valuable products in Europe's trade.

There is also another theme that links the five hundred years of America's relations with the rest of the world: the effect on those relations of new technology and scientific discoveries. Columbus depended on fresh calculations that indicated the world was round, not flat. He proved those calculations correct by using the latest compasses, astrolabe, and elaborate tables that measured longitude. From these first voyages of discovery through the Yankee clipper ship that conquered world trade, the Colt .44 revolver that conquered the West, the airplane that conquered distance, the atomic bomb, and the multistage rocket that conquered space, American foreign policy cannot be understood apart from the technology that transformed the world and made diplomacy ever more complex—and dangerous. Those technological conquests also help us to understand why Americans have too often believed that crises in foreign affairs might well be solved through new scientific breakthroughs.

The early quests for wealth, personal salvation, westward empire, control of the world's centers of political and economic power, and supremacy in technology led to both the settlement of America and its rise as the globe's superpower.

THE CITY ON A HILL—AND ON THE WATER

Throughout the 1500s, England watched Spain and Portugal explore the New World. But the British also shared in the profits by looting Spanish ships that carried precious metals back to Europe. England's settlements, however, failed disastrously until 1606–1607, when a group of wealthy investors established Jamestown, Virginia. Jamestown's founding and survival could be traced to its economic role in international trade. The founders were looking for the river system that supposedly provided entry into the fabled markets of Asia. They hoped that the James River might be such a system. Some 10,000 miles short of their goal, the settlers quickly discovered that they had to find an export crop to pay for their food and other imports from the home country. They tried silk and sassafras, but unfortunately neither was habit-forming. Then John Rolfe experimented in 1612 with Indian tobacco. In 1614, two barrels of cured tobacco left for England. Four years later, tobacco was a rage in Europe. Virginia shipped nearly 50,000 pounds abroad annually. The "hellish, devilish, and damned tobacco," as English critics called it, provided the settlement's lifeline to the world.[3]

Thus, hardly had America been settled than it transformed Europe's trade and personal habits. But tobacco also forced Virginia's foreign relations into surprising avenues. As growers discovered the profitability of importing black slaves to tend the fields, new trade routes extended southward to Africa. Westward the Virginians began seizing fresh land to replace the soil worn out by as few as three tobacco crops. The "hellish" weed had both locked America into Africa's history and had driven the settlers westward toward the sun—and the Native Americans.

To the north, another group of English men and women settled at Massachusetts Bay in 1630. Their leader, John Winthrop, uttered words that resounded nearly four hundred years later, when he urged the devout separatists: ["We must consider that we shall be as a city upon a hill, the eyes of all people are upon us.] Those are among the most famous words in American history and have been quoted repeatedly—from the founders in the 1780s to President Ronald Reagan in the 1980s—to define the U.S. mission in the world. Much less quoted are Winthrop's warnings in that famous utterance. "The care of the public must oversway all private respects," and "Wee must be knitt together in this work as one man." Or again: "Wee [should] be willing to abridge ourselves of superfluities for the supply of others' necessities."[4] Those words have been less popular in American history.

Indeed, from the start, the opportunities of foreign trade and landed expansion destroyed Winthrop's hope that "the city upon a hill" would be "knitt together . . . as one man." The city on a hill was actually a city on an ocean.[5] It had open to it world trade, especially the export of the famous Boston cod, which was exploited by adventurous individualists who cared more about profit margins than about Puritan restraints. From the start, fish were vital to American foreign relations because they brought in much-needed hard money (gold and silver) from Europe. The fisheries of the North Atlantic were the equivalent of the gold mines in South America—and the fish even reproduced. Moreover, one devout observer wrote at the time of settlement that the fisheries were so bleak that sailors would be tempted by neither "wine nor women."[6] It seemed a perfect combination of gold and God. No wonder that, as we shall see, three generations of the famous Adams family of Massachusetts devoted much of their distinguished diplomatic careers to keeping the fisheries in American hands. But the fisheries and other trade also shaped early foreign relations in another way: New Englanders invested their growing profits in western lands and thus pushed settlement toward the sunset until it collided with Native Americans and with Frenchmen who were settling Canada and exploring the Great Lakes region.

These first American foreign relations did nothing less than change American society. As one scholar has noted, the possibility of making fortunes in overseas trade and western territories made settlers "more interested in saving dollars than souls, more concerned with good land than compact villages, more excited about individual wealth than group welfare."[7] From their beginnings, Americans have never been able to separate their foreign relations from the way they carry on their lives at home.

THE FIRST AMERICANS

The settlers did not discover a vacant East Coast. For the next 350 years they did not move over an empty continent. A central theme of American diplomatic history must be the clash between the European settlers and the Native Americans between 1620 and 1890. That clash led the settlers to fight wars of conquest, create a unique military machine. to wage war, and nearly exterminate the Indian tribes.

Probably 8.5 to 10 million Native Americans populated all of North America in 1492. The first American immigrants had arrived well before the Europeans—in about 30,000 B.C. With as many as 600 different societies and over 200 languages, they had developed complex civilizations that carefully preserved—even as they lived from—the rivers, woods, land, and wild animals. By the time settlements of whites appeared in Virginia and Massachusetts, many Native Americans had already disappeared because of lack of immunity to the explorers' diseases, especially smallpox and measles which ravaged many tribes.

At the beginning of settlement, the Indians provided the food and agricultural know-how that allowed many of the whites to survive. But the Native Americans gradually began to fear the Europeans' growing numbers and different culture. Moreover, they were inflamed by internal divisions and fears of neighboring tribes. In 1622, on Good Friday, the Powhatans suddenly attacked and destroyed one-quarter of Virginia's white population. Thus began a series of wars between whites and Native Americans that soaked the rest of colonial history in blood. With British help and at great cost, the settlers not only won most of the conflicts, but virtually wiped out such tribes as the powerful Pequots in New England. The Indians had long been independent, were deeply divided among themselves, and could not cooperate in waging war. Some were easily bought off with money or European goods. Many even served as guides or raiders for the whites against other tribes. Although usually superior fighters individually, Native Americans did not fight for long periods with the intensity of the whites, nor—although they were highly skilled in making weapons—did they learn in the early decades how to make gunpowder.[8]

The settlers quickly drew several lessons from these seventeenth-century encounters. They developed a racism that provided an excuse to remove or kill Indians who blocked landed expansion. Native American cultures were not individualistic, Christian, or even monotheistic. It was, therefore, easy for the great Puritan divine, Cotton Mather, to believe that "Probably the Devil decoyed" the Indians to America "in hopes that the gospel of the Lord Jesus Christ would never come here to destroy or disturb his absolute empire over them."[9] The "noble savage" idea fascinated those in faraway British and French coffee shops, but it never interested American leaders such as Mather. The whites also learned that exploiting the environment—that is, destroying woods and killing large numbers of fur-bearing animals—not only was profitable for their overseas trade, but severely weakened the Native Americans. As colonial population grew, so many animals were killed and so many fields were cleared that the climate in North America changed.[10]

Finally, the settlers discovered from the Indian wars that they had to break with the European tradition of a professional army. Instead, they gave weapons to all able-bodied male settlers, who farmed part-time and fought part-time. Thus was born the militia system that formed the backbone for the American military over the next several centuries. Thus were also born the tactics for "Indian fighting"—guerrilla-type warfare instead of the traditional European armies-in-mass that slaughtered each other on open battlefields. These new tactics shaped U.S. military strategy in wars from the American Revolution through the interventions in the Caribbean–Central American region in the 1920s.

THE AMERICAN "MULTIPLICATION TABLE" AND THE EUROPEAN POWER STRUGGLE

The settlers sharply honed those military tactics in the century before 1776. The Indian wars diminished slightly by 1700, but the colonials then turned their rifles on other Europeans. From the beginning of their history, Americans lived not in any splendid isolation, far from the turmoil and corruption of the Europe many had hoped to escape. They instead had to live in settlements that were surrounded by great and ambitious European powers. France controlled the St. Lawrence River region through eastern Canada and down the Great Lakes to the Mississippi River. The French explorer La Salle had claimed Louisiana (that is, nearly all the vast lands whose rivers emptied into the Mississippi) as early as 1682. To the south, Spain moved out of Florida and consolidated its hold on the Caribbean region.

Perhaps the three great empires (British, French, and Spanish) might have lived at peace in the New World through much of the eighteenth century except for an incredible development: the American "multiplication table." This "table" referred to the high birth rate of colonials that produced families of five to ten children even as infant mortality rates dropped. The term itself was coined much later, in the 1840s by Representative Andrew Kennedy of Indiana. Kennedy told the House of Representatives that "our people are spreading out with the aid of the American multiplication table." He elaborated: "Go to the West and see a young man with his mate of eighteen; after a lapse of thirty years, visit him again, and instead of two, you will find twenty-two. That is what I call the American multiplication table."[11]

One result of the American "multiplication table" was almost continual war with France and Spain between 1689 and 1763. These struggles in the New World formed part of a larger European conflict among the three great imperial nations. But the wars also showed how Americans—whether they liked it or not—were part of European power politics even as they moved into the forests and fertile lands beyond the Appalachian Mountains. They could not separate their destiny from the destiny of those they had left behind in Europe. Their own imperial ambitions were not small. In 1745, William Shirley, the restless, imaginative governor of Massachusetts, captured the French fortress at Louisbourg in eastern Canada. He then set his sights on conquering the rest of Canada and all the French holdings in the Mississippi region. London officials, however, infuriated Shirley by making peace with the French (those hated Roman Catholics to the north) and restoring Louisbourg as part of an overall peace settlement.

Shirley and other colonial leaders impatiently waited for another opportunity they knew would soon arise. In the early 1750s, it happened. British settlers established forts in the central part of present-day Ohio. In 1752, the French retaliated by seizing a key fortress in the region. England's Indian allies swung over to support the French.

Benjamin Franklin (1706–1790), man of the world and Pennsylvania politician, colonial postmaster general, author of wise advice for a growing nation in Poor Richard's Almanack, *and member of the Continental Congress and the 1787 Constitutional Convention. He was also the original U.S. diplomat who combined worldly knowledge with the ability to play the New World "primitive" to charm both the salons as well as the foreign ministry in Paris in order to negotiate the crucial alliance with France.*

The Native Americans were coming to see that the French, who wanted the Indians' trade and Roman Catholic souls but not their territory, posed less danger than did the land-hungry British settlers. Virginia sent out a twenty-one-year-old surveyor-soldier, George Washington, to negotiate with the French. When talks failed, Washington attacked the French around the key strategic position of present-day Pittsburgh. Thus began the Seven Years' War—or the Great War for Empire, as it later became known. The struggle transformed the political face of North America and led directly to the American Revolution.

BENJAMIN FRANKLIN AND THE PROBLEMS OF A RISING PEOPLE

The conflict also brought Benjamin Franklin to the world stage. The first American diplomat, Franklin's life illustrated the ambition and intelligence of the settlers. His career also demonstrated how Americans created a landed empire, then broke with England so that they could themselves run and profit from that empire.

Born in 1706 as the tenth child of Josiah and Abiah Folger Franklin in Boston, Franklin, at the age of seventeen, fought with his family and moved to Philadelphia. There he became a printer, accumulating both personal wealth (especially with his *Poor Richard's Almanack*) and political power. Franklin paraded as an ordinary man, but his travels and contacts with leading figures in colonial life gave him unique knowledge about America. He set up profitable printing companies in Antigua, Connecticut, and New York. In that sense, Franklin was perhaps America's first multinational corporation.

In 1751, Franklin, drawing on his research and knowledge of colonial life, published a pamphlet that remains crucial for understanding American foreign policy. *Observations Concerning the Increase of Mankind* began with careful calculations showing that Americans were doubling their population approximately every twenty years. This unbelievable figure, Franklin argued, had far-reaching consequences. First, it meant that additional land would soon be needed for settlement or else the colonies would be dammed up and become stagnant. Second, it meant that Britain should help find the land because Britain's manufacturers and merchants would enjoy a most profitable market in the new settlements. Finally, it became apparent that finding the necessary room meant war against the French and their Indian allies.[12] Franklin seemed to welcome that conclusion.

In his 1751 pamphlet, Franklin thus helped explain the causes of both the Great War for Empire and the American Revolution. When the struggle began in 1754, Franklin immediately focused on the problem that henceforth haunted American officials: How could they govern the tremendous expanse of land they hoped to conquer? He answered with the Albany Plan of 1754, a scheme that concentrated power in a central colonial agency that could effectively deal with Native Americans and fight the French. Neither the British Crown nor the thirteen colonial governments, however, would surrender power to the agency, so Franklin's idea died. It was thirty-three years ahead of its time and the Constitutional Convention.

In 1757, the Pennsylvanian sailed to London to serve as the colony's official representative. British military victories over France led to heated discussions over peace terms. The major question was whether London should take the rich French sugar island of Guadeloupe in the Caribbean or the largely empty expanse of Canada. Franklin had no doubt. Using his 1751 pamphlet as a weapon, he argued that the population explosion and the resulting sales for British manufacturers dictated seizing Canada. But his argument did not go unchallenged. A British pamphleteer, William Burke, warned that if Franklin's advice were followed and the French were expelled, the Americans would rush into the vast region and become uncontrollable. Burke also touched a nerve that remained sensitive for the next two hundred years of American diplomacy. Noting Franklin's argument that "security" required removing the French from Canada, Burke argued that "to desire the enemy's whole country on no other principle but that otherwise you cannot secure your own, is turning the idea of mere defense into the most dangerous of all principles. It is leaving no medium between safety and conquest. It is to suppose yourself never safe, whilst your neighbor enjoys any security."[13]

Franklin won the argument. In 1763, the British took Canada and all the land that stretched southward and westward to the Mississippi River. Spain, a French ally, received Louisiana territory from Paris in return for agreeing to an immediate peace. The Spanish gave East and West Florida to England in exchange for Cuba, which the British navy had seized. France's long career as a New World power was over. But Burke had the last word: "What the consequences will be to have a numerous, hardy, independent people [loose in the Canadian wilderness]" he left to the reader's imagination.

Humiliated French officials plotted revenge for their losses in 1763. Delighted colonials prepared to find their fortunes by following the sun.

THE ROAD TO REVOLUTION (1763–1775)

But the colonials instead crashed into boundaries set by the British Empire. The empire's theory had for a century been "mercantilist"— that is, Great Britain had the right to operate the colonies for its own profit; in return, London protected the colonials from outsiders. Such was the theory. In reality, the colonials acted independently and largely protected themselves. By 1700, probably half of Boston's trade was illegal because it was with the French West Indies instead of with British merchants, as London's mercantile laws required. Few in London or Boston cared. Profits from the French trade went to London to pay for British goods. Prime Minister Sir Robert Walpole nicely, if insensitively, described colonial policy before the 1754 war as "Let sleeping dogs lie." But the dogs did not sleep. Merchants, settlers, and colonial legislators did as they pleased until they came to believe that they were the equal of London's Parliament in running colonial affairs.

From 1763 to 1765, Parliament decided to pay for the costs of the 1754–1763 war by taxing the colonies. London merchants, moreover, demanded that the illegal trade with France be stopped. The Stamp Act, taxing colonial newspapers and mail, raised the revenue. Other acts clamped down on smuggling. Americans responded with the revolutionary doctrine that they had been self-governing since the first

*North America, during the war of 1754 to 1763 (The Great War for Empire),
after the British drove the French from Canada and as the thirteen colonies
started down the road to revolution.*

settlements and that, consequently, Parliament had no right to regulate each colony's trade. Americans refused to import British goods.
London officials dismissed the claim of self-government. They and the
British merchants, however, could not dismiss the nonimportation policy. As trade declined, Parliament finally repealed most of the 1764–
1765 acts. But it then tried to raise revenue more subtly—such as
imposing a tax on tea. In late 1773, the colonials, led by a deeply religious revolutionary, Samuel Adams, dumped large amounts of tea in

Boston Harbor. The infuriated British lashed back with the Intolerable Acts (as the colonials termed them) of 1774: Boston port was closed, political power in Massachusetts was largely switched from the colonials to appointed British officials, and—in a related move that made Protestant land speculators of Massachusetts and Virginia furious— Canada's boundaries were extended to the Ohio River. The colonials could no longer follow the sun without running into the Roman Catholic Canadians who were now loyal to Great Britain.

Colonial legislatures convened a Continental Congress to discuss retaliation. Americans had suddenly learned that their foreign policy and individual freedoms were closely related. London's claim to regulate foreign trade struck at the heart of their political independence, which they had long taken for granted. The *Georgia Gazette* urged support in the South for the far-off Bostonians in 1774 by arguing that if the British claim to "have a right or power to put a duty on my tea," they "have an equal right to put a duty on my bread, and why not on my breath, why not on my daylight and smoke, why not on everything?"[14] The South also shared another grievance with the North. In 1763, the British had declared a "Proclamation Line" that prohibited colonials from settling west of the Appalachian Mountains. The purpose was to regulate settlement and avoid Indian wars. Treaties with Native Americans allowed some expansion after 1770, but the Quebec Act closed the door again in 1774. The door closed, moreover, just as frustrated Americans were turning westward to find the trade and profit that the British denied them in the French West Indies.

Colonial leaders concluded that they could no longer find help in London. British politics changed rapidly in the 1760s as new factions, created in part from profits from the colonies, moved to control Parliament. London's politics, as Franklin described it from the scene, were most corrupt: "This whole venal nation is now at market," he wrote in 1768.[15] Decent colonials had little hope for relief from such an indecent system. Such sentiments were returned by Londoners, who considered the colonials grasping and ungrateful. As England's most famous literary figure put it, "Sir, [Americans] are a race of convicts and ought to be thankful for anything we allow them short of hanging." Dr. Samuel Johnson continued: "You know I am willing to love all mankind, except an American."[16]

The links of British colonial policy were now being pulled apart from both sides of the Atlantic. Foreign-policy issues (trade, westward expansion) were in the middle of this pulling and hauling.

This 1774 cartoon of a woeful Great Britain, shorn of her badly needed colonial limbs, was by Benjamin Franklin. In addition to his other many talents, Franklin was one of the first important American political cartoonists. His view of the former British Empire (two years before the Revolution actually began) is indicated by the "Date Obolum Bellisario"—or "Give a Farthing to Belisarius," who was a general in Ancient Rome after the Roman Empire collapsed.

THE FOREIGN POLICY OF INDEPENDENCE (1776)

By early 1776, many of the 2.5 million white Americans thought of themselves as a separate people. As early as ten years before, a shrewd British observer told his nephew in North America that "you [in the colonies] wish to be an Empire by itself."[17] But revolution against the world's greatest power was not trivial. According to one British legal source, a convicted traitor was to be hanged and taken down while alive, then his entrails were to be removed and burned, his head to be chopped off, and his body divided into four parts.[18]

Despite the long shadows of British gallows, the First Continental Congress met in September 1774 to bring together twelve colonies and discuss the Intolerable Acts. The delegates pledged not to import or consume British goods until the acts were repealed. But the British were now determined to enforce their own law. They also ordered their troops to seize the powder and arms of the colonials at Concord, Massachusetts. On April 19, 1775, British forces and American militia clashed at Lexington and Concord. A Second Continental Congress, more radical than the first, convened. It learned that early military operations had gone badly. But Franklin, ever upbeat, urged his fellow rebels to consider the glories of the American "multiplication table":

"Britain, at the expense of three millions [pounds], has killed 150 Yankees this campaign, which is twenty thousand pounds a head. During the same time 60,000 children have been born in America."[19]

The rebels nevertheless rapidly needed other kinds of help as well. The Congress established a five-member Secret Committee of Correspondence to find allies abroad. Independence required an active, successful foreign policy. The committee marked the beginning of the later Department of State. Its members included Franklin and John Jay of New York. The committee sent three agents abroad to seek help, including the first official U.S. diplomat, Silas Deane of Connecticut, who was to sound out the French foreign minister, Charles Gravier, Count de Vergennes, about political aid and arms purchases. France had already decided to make a secret loan of $2 million to the colonials. Vergennes, who had been thirsting for revenge against the British since France's 1763 defeat, sent a secret agent to contact rebel leaders in late 1775, then moved to isolate Great Britain by forming alliances with Spain, Austria, and Prussia. The Dutch, whose ambitious traders clashed with British naval power, also helped by sending gunpowder and rifles badly needed by the colonial militias.

The Congress meanwhile decided to invade and annex Canada. It was one of the more amazing and disastrous decisions in American diplomatic history. Many colonials had lusted after Canada, and a number wanted to teach Roman Catholics a lesson. Resources for the invasion were scarce, but as Richard Henry Lee of Virginia put it in late 1775, "We must have that country with us this winter cost what it will."[20] The Congress, whose members had long damned Canadians, now switched tactics and begged the "fellow sufferers" to join the Revolution. When the Canadians refused, General Richard Montgomery's army moved from upper New York toward Montreal. Another force, commanded by General Benedict Arnold, marched on Quebec. Neither army reached its objective. Winter weather forced Montgomery's "half-naked" troops to retreat and join Arnold. Montgomery died, and Arnold was wounded in a brave but useless attack on Quebec on New Year's Eve. Arnold later distinguished himself in October 1776 by brilliantly blocking the British invasion from Canada. It was a significant but anticlimactic victory, given the original American desire of annexing their "fellow sufferers" in Canada.

Defeats in the north and second thoughts in the Congress threatened the Revolution. Then, in January 1776, appeared *Common Sense*, an incendiary, skillfully written pamphlet by Thomas Paine, whom Franklin had sent to America after Paine was fired from the British

Thomas Paine (1737–1809), born in England and author of Common Sense, *the incendiary pamphlet that helped push Americans to revolution. After serving as secretary of the Committee on Foreign Affairs, Paine moved to France, where he defended the French Revolution. He then returned to the United States but made the mistakes of attacking organized religion and criticizing George Washington. He lived out his life in poverty.*

government for demanding higher wages. *Common Sense* revitalized the revolutionary cause. Moreover, it directly stated themes that dominated U.S. foreign policy over much of the next two hundred years. Paine attacked the British king, George III, as an "ass" and disdained remaining subject to Great Britain: "There is something absurd, in supposing a continent to be perpetually governed by an island. In no instance hath nature made the satellite larger than its primary planet." The new United States had a higher calling: "The cause of America is in a great measure the cause of all mankind." As historian Reginald Horsman notes, Paine helped Americans "convince themselves that what was good for America was good for the world."[21]

How did Paine plan to achieve independence? By using trade as a diplomatic lever. Thus appeared one of the assumptions in U.S. history that Great Britain (and later Russia, Japan, Communist China, Cuba, and South Africa) could be tamed because, as Paine phrased it, American products "are the necessaries of life, and will always have a market while eating is the custom of Europe." Victory, moreover, could be won without political alliances. Because all Europe needed U.S. goods, "we ought to form no partial connection with any part of it. It is the true interest of America to steer clear of European contentions." Paine thus made a famous statement of U.S. "isolationism"—that Americans should maintain maximum freedom of action to protect their interests, which were distinct from, and purer than, Europe's.

Paine's pamphlet was electrifying not because it said much that was new, but because he so skillfully expressed the views of many revolutionaries. The timing was perfect. It appeared as the Congress faced its most fateful decisions on independence. Moreover, in those days Americans read. Literacy rates ran as high as 95 percent among white males in some states and was probably the highest in the world. (In the 1980s, by comparison, the United States ranked forty-ninth among 158 nations in rate of literacy.[22]) The 500,000 copies of *Common Sense* printed in 1776 are equivalent to 25 million copies in the 1990s, given the difference in population size. High literacy and a successful (and orderly) revolution coincided in American history.

French help, Paine's writing, and Britain's inability to score crushing military victories finally gave the Congress the courage to open American ports in April 1776 to the entire world. America had broken free of British mercantile laws. Two months later, Richard Henry Lee resolved that "these United Colonies are, and of right ought to be, free and independent states." He then proposed the necessary measure for independence: "That it is expedient forthwith to take the most effectual measures for forming foreign alliances." On July 2, the Congress accepted Thomas Jefferson's draft of the Declaration of Independence, but only after it was heavily rewritten. Even then, John Dickinson of Pennsylvania launched an attack to defeat the Declaration. He warned that Americans could never conquer and govern an empire that stretched beyond the Appalachian Mountains. He feared that the country would come apart in twenty or thirty years and believed that the Hudson River was "a proper boundary" for America's western limit. He warned that if Americans allied with France to win that empire, they would only exchange British for even more intolerable French masters.[23] Dickinson's arguments were prophetic, but Lee and John Adams had the votes. The United States declared its independence.

THE FRENCH TRAP

Two weeks later, John Adams gave the Congress his draft of a Model Treaty for alliances. It repeated some of Paine's principles but translated them into diplomatic tactics that shaped U.S. foreign policy long after 1776:

> What Connection may We safely form with [France]? 1st. No Political Connection. Submit to none of her Authority—receive no Governors, or officers from her. 2nd. No Military Connection. Receive no troops from her. 3rd. Only a Commercial Connection, i.e., make a Treaty to receive

her Ships into our Ports. Let her engage to receive our Ships into her
Ports—furnish Us with Arms, Cannon, Salt, Petre, Powder, Duck, Steel.[24]

Adams thus expected France to provide full economic aid and wage
war with Great Britain in return for no political payoff except the possible breakup of the British Empire. He also expected France to treat
Americans as commercial equals and help them conquer parts of North
America, including the rich fisheries of Newfoundland, while France
kept its hands off North American territory.[25] Congress accepted Adams's
dreams. It was doubtful that France would accept. The doubt grew as
Lord Howe's British troops won a major victory on Long Island that
nearly destroyed the American army under the command of General
George Washington. U.S. trade slowed, tobacco piled up on southern
docks. New England fishermen could not ply their trade because of
British warships.

In late December 1776, a frightened Congress remodeled the Model
Treaty. It offered France islands in the West Indies. If the French brought
into the war their Spanish allies, Spain (which most Americans despised
because it was Roman Catholic as well as in control of the immense
empire of Louisiana) could have the Floridas. Americans prepared to
pay a price, even bargain away some of their possible empire, for help
in obtaining independence. Paine's and Adams's belief in the power
of mere commercial ties had been proven wrong. The Congress dispatched Franklin to France, John Adams to Holland, and John Jay to
Spain to obtain alliances and money.

In France, Franklin described himself as "very plainly dress'd" among
"the Powder'd Heads of Paris." He was, however, hardly the "noble
savage" he liked to portray. In historian Tadashi Aruga's words, the
shrewd Franklin did nothing less than "call in the Old World to liberate the New World from the Old World."[26] The word *diplomacy* comes
from the Greek word for a message that is folded so that its contents
cannot be read. In that sense, Franklin superbly practiced diplomacy,
for the "noble savage" was more devious and sophisticated than he
seemed. The French once even caught him trying to collect one loan
from them twice. The twentieth-century poet, William Carlos Williams, summarized Franklin's achievements by writing, "He played
with lightning and the French Court."[27] Franklin did so, moreover,
despite his age (he was seventy-two in 1778); difficult ocean voyages;
a bad case of gout; the desertion of his beloved son, William, to Great
Britain; and a private secretary (Edward Bancroft) who, unknown to
Franklin, was a British spy.

When the Philadelphian landed in Paris late in 1776, the cause seemed lost. British armies were poised to take Philadelphia and Albany, while the U.S. Treasury was nearly empty. Franklin's great test arose in late 1777, when news arrived of the U.S. victory in October over General John Burgoyne's British army at Saratoga, New York. The French became worried, moreover, when British officials approached Franklin about possible reconciliation, talks that the American imaginatively enlarged upon for his French friends. Vergennes decided it was time to make a formal treaty. He and Franklin signed the deal on February 6, 1778. The commercial provisions provided for reciprocity, much as Adams's Model Treaty had requested. But the political provisions did not resemble Adams's scheme. Each nation pledged military cooperation. The United States had to guarantee French control of certain West Indian islands and promise not to sign a separate peace with the British. The Americans even had to pledge to remain France's partner "forever." Franklin had nevertheless played it well. "My dear papa," a beautiful French woman wrote him, why do people criticize "the sweet habit I have taken of sitting on your lap, and your habit of soliciting from me what I always refuse?" But Franklin had also been using the wife to form a friendship with her husband—who became a key agent for selling weapons to Washington's armies.[28]

No sooner did France promise to help, however, than Vergennes instructed his agents in the New World to keep the United States as small and weak as possible. If the Americans grew powerful, he feared, they would conquer the West Indies, then "advance to the Southern Continent of America . . . and in the end not leave a foot of that Hemisphere in the possession of any European power."[29] He had, moreover, finally convinced Spain to join the war effort. The Spanish cared most about reconquering Gibraltar from the British and seizing more land in the New World—not about helping Americans become independent. Thus, France held contradictory treaty obligations: to the Americans to fight until independence was won, but to the Spanish to fight until Gibraltar was won.

When Jay arrived in Madrid to obtain more Spanish help, he was snubbed and infuriated. Spain's officials had no desire to create an independent American giant on the boundaries of their New World empire. Adams fared better in Holland. He received financial and commercial help—indeed, so much that the British finally turned and destroyed much of Holland's fleet while sacking valuable Dutch islands in the West Indies. After those disasters, Dutch help was necessarily limited.

John Jay (1745–1829), a well-to-do gentleman lawyer in New York, was U.S. minister to Spain when he helped negotiate the 1783 peace treaty with Great Britain. For that he was honored, but was damned and hanged in effigy when he negotiated another treaty with the British twelve years later.

By 1779–1780, the Continental Congress seemed to be a slave to Vergennes. Its sad state was not due solely to the number of American politicians on the French payroll—although in Lawrence Kaplan's words, that payroll "was long, illustrious, and well-padded"[30]—but because U.S. survival seemed to depend on French help. The currency was so worthless that Washington complained "that a wagon-load of money will scarcely purchase a wagon-load of provisions." For a moment, the Congress hoped to get help from Catherine the Great of Russia. She worked with Vergennes to set up a League of Armed Neutrality to lay low England's commercial power. But she did so for Russian, not American, interests—she hated revolutionaries. When Francis Dana arrived as the first U.S. minister to Russia in 1781, he found the reception as frigid and desolate as the Russian winter. After two years of failure, Dana finally trudged back home.

But the news reaching the Congress was not all bad. Americans helped themselves in 1778–1779, when George Rogers Clark and his Kentucky militia braved a Midwest winter to surprise and capture key British posts in Wabash River country (the later states of Indiana and Illinois). The United States then signed its first treaty with an Indian tribe, the Delaware, who promised to help U.S. forces. In western New York, General John Sullivan attacked Indians who, with British aid, had massacred several settlements of whites. In 1779, Sullivan's troops virtually destroyed the great Iroquois nation that comprised many tribes. These victories, especially Clark's, helped establish the U.S. claim to the transappalachian West that the British, to the surprise of many, recognized in the 1783 peace treaty.

In the East, Washington's armies marked time in 1779–1780. The

```
┌──────────────────────────────────────────────────────────────────────┐
│                  CHRONOLOGY: 1774–1778                                 │
```

September 1774	First Continental Congress meets; twelve colonies represented.
October 1774	Colonies protest Quebec Act by pledging not to import British goods.
May 1775	Second Continental Congress meets; more radical membership than First.
August 1775	King George III declares colonies in rebellion.
November 1775	Secret Committees of Correspondence established.
December 1775	French secret agent arrives in America as King George III cuts off all trade into the colonies.
Winter 1775–1776	American attempt to conquer Canada fails disastrously.
January 1776	Thomas Paine publishes *Common Sense*.
March 1776	Continental Congress sends Silas Deane to France.
April 1776	Continental Congress opens American ports to the world.
May 1776	King Louis XVI of France accepts Vergennes's argument to aid Americans.
June 1776	Richard Henry Lee proposes resolutions to declare independence, form a confederation, and make foreign alliances.
July 2, 1776	Continental Congress accepts Declaration of Independence.
July 18, 1776	John Adams presents Model Treaty.
August 1776	General Howe leads British army into New York.
December 1776	Continental Congress revises Model Treaty's provisions; Benjamin Franklin arrives in France as U.S. representative.
December 1777	News of U.S. victory at Saratoga in October arrives in Paris.
December 1777– January 1778	British approach Franklin to discuss reconciliation.
February 6, 1778	U.S. and France sign treaties of alliance in Paris.

British decided to concentrate their forces in the South, where the largest number of pro-British Americans (the Loyalists) lived. The growing threat to the South between 1779 and 1781 led frightened Virginians to strengthen the new nation's government by ceding to it lands north of the Ohio River claimed by Virginia. Since 1776, the states had haggled bitterly over the question of western lands. Some of the landless states refused to ratify the Articles of Confederation, which formed the national government, until the wealthier landed states, such as Virginia, gave up their western claims. Now the logjam was broken, and all thirteen states prepared to join hands under a common constitution. But even under the Articles, the government would have little real power. Most important, the critical right to tax and regulate commerce remained in the hands of each state. The currency's value continued to sink.

In 1780, a nervous Congress instructed Franklin to surrender U.S. rights to the Mississippi River, if necessary, to obtain quick French and Spanish help. Jay, whose short-fused temper had already exploded in his dealings with the Spanish, and Franklin refused to follow instructions. The visionary but pragmatic Pennsylvanian wrote that he would rather buy more U.S. rights to the Mississippi, even at "a great price . . . than sell a Drop of its Waters. A Neighbour might as well ask me to sell my Street Door."[31]

After months of U.S. begging, the French fitted out 6 ships and 5,000 troops for warfare. This fleet was large enough to help save the colonies, but not large enough to conquer more land for the Americans. Before the French fleet could arrive in mid-1780, the British won a major battle at Charleston and prepared to move north to trap Washington's forces. But British General Lord Cornwallis's troops suffered heavy losses at the hands of Generals Nathanael Greene and Daniel Morgan at Guilford Courthouse, North Carolina, on March 15, 1781. Cornwallis withdrew to Yorktown, Virginia, to await orders for marching north. Washington's troops and the French army of Comte de Rochambeau had planned to attack New York, but when the French fleet drove British ships from Yorktown, the two commanders swung south and defeated Cornwallis's bottled-up forces on October 19, 1781.

Yorktown was the Revolution's decisive campaign. In the months that followed, a new British government under Lord Shelburne came to power. Shelburne reversed London's position of not recognizing American independence. He shrewdly understood that granting independence did not mean U.S. dependence on France. To the contrary, the double bait of independence and British trade could lure Americans back under England's control. For his part, Franklin initially demanded that, in return for peace, the British give the United States most of their holdings in North America, including Canada. Shelburne abruptly dismissed that demand, and the two sides sat down to hammer out more realistic terms. The boundaries of an independent United States were to be the Great Lakes on the North, the Mississippi on the

west, and the thirty-first parallel on the south. Americans received rights
to fish the rich Newfoundland banks. In return, the United States
promised not to hinder the British from collecting millions of dollars
of debts owed by colonials to London and Scottish merchants, and to
help restore the property of perhaps 200,000 Loyalists who had left the
country to join the British side. The Mississippi was to be open to both
the British and Americans.

The U.S. negotiators (Franklin, Jay, Adams, and Henry Laurens)
agreed to the terms on November 30, 1782. The first three negotiators
(especially Jay) handled the talks, and their major problem was whether
to obey the Congress's instructions to deal away the Mississippi, if necessary. Another complication was the promise of 1778 not to make
peace without Vergennes's participation. Franklin had no intention of
obeying such instructions and promises. And when he asked for Jay's
opinion, the angry New Yorker said that if they conflicted with U.S.
interests, "I would break them like this"—and he snapped the stem of
his clay pipe.[32] Vergennes, who actually had little choice in the matter,
allowed the talks to go on because they gave him an excuse not to
prolong the war simply for Spain's sake. The Spanish were insisting
on fighting until they regained Gibraltar. A major British naval victory
finally destroyed that dream, and Spain—bought off by the promise
that it could have the Louisiana Territory—allowed Vergennes to make
peace.

BITTERSWEET RESULTS OF PEACE

That the Americans ended the conflict with their independence and a
large landed territory is remarkable. That they did so with so little
bloodshed and class conflict is astonishing. Unlike the great revolutions that later struck France, Mexico, China, and Russia, the American Revolution did not become radical and kill off the class that started
the revolt. John Adams led the revolutionaries in 1776 and insisted
that maintaining order would be "the most difficult and dangerous
Part" for Americans in "this Mighty Contest."[33] Adams and his colleagues, however, maintained not only order, but, remarkably, their
own political power.

In this sense, the American Revolution was not revolutionary at all.
Instead, it was the first modern anticolonial war. With rich opportunities for landed settlement and money-making, and having decades of
experience in the art of self-government, Americans just wanted the

British to get out of the way. The legacy of this experience turned out to be momentous for U.S. foreign policy. Henceforth, Americans smiled on anticolonial wars but frowned on revolution—unless it resembled their own. Given their own unique history, no other revolution could be the same.

TO THE CONSTITUTION: "WHAT WILL RENDER US RESPECTABLE ABROAD?"

In September 1783, Franklin penned the famous phrase "There never was a good war or a bad peace." [34] But having won independence through war by 1783, Americans nearly lost it in peacetime within three years. Shelburne had been correct: the United States needed British markets and goods. Lord Sheffield's widely read pamphlet of 1784, *Observations on the Commerce of the United States,* laid out British policy. Because the United States depended on British trade, Sheffield argued, London could demand tough terms. It especially could do so because under the Articles of Confederation, the thirteen states were too weak and decentralized to fight back with a united policy. Parliament consequently decreed that U.S. ships could not trade with the British West Indies, certain goods could be carried only on British ships, and Canadian-U.S. trade would be severely limited. John Adams angrily condemned Parliament as "a parcel of sots" for passing such rules, but the British were succeeding in making Americans into mere providers of raw materials for British factories and then buyers of the finished British goods carried on British ships.

In 1783, the United States bought three times the amount of goods from the British that it sold to them. Prices fell, money grew scarce. Depression rocked the country between 1783 and 1786. Unpaid, disgruntled soldiers threatened rebellion until Washington personally intervened in 1783 with a resounding speech that condemned anyone "who wickedly attempts to open the floodgates of civil discord and deluge our rising empire in blood." [35] Searching desperately for economic help, the United States signed commercial treaties with France, Holland, Sweden, Prussia, and Morocco, but even combined they could not equal England's ability to provide markets and capital. In 1784, Boston investors fitted out the *Empress of China* for the first U.S. venture to exploit the legendary markets of Asia. It was a scene that would be repeated in such later postwar depressions as the 1820s, 1840s, 1890s,

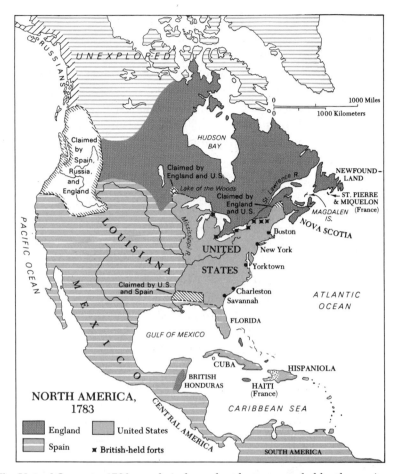

HUDSON BAY

UNEXPLORED

RUSSIANS

Claimed by Spain, Russia, and England

Claimed by England and U.S.

Lake of the Woods

Claimed by England and U.S.

St. Lawrence R.

NEWFOUND-LAND

ST. PIERRE & MIQUELON

MAGDALEN IS. (France)

NOVA SCOTIA

Boston

UNITED STATES

New York

Yorktown

Claimed by U.S. and Spain

Charleston
Savannah

ATLANTIC OCEAN

PACIFIC OCEAN

LOUISIANA

MEXICO

Mississippi R.

FLORIDA

GULF OF MEXICO

CUBA

HISPANIOLA

BRITISH HONDURAS

HAITI (France)

NORTH AMERICA, 1783

CENTRAL AMERICA

CARIBBEAN SEA

SOUTH AMERICA

| England | United States |
| Spain | ✱ British-held forts |

The United States in 1783, newly independent but surrounded by the navies and landed possessions of the great European powers.

and 1970s. Discovering the huge demand for ginseng, which the Chinese considered a stimulant for sexual activity, the first U.S. voyages carried over the herb, brought back tea, and made enormous profits. But the narrow, undeveloped China market—whose trade the Chinese tightly regulated so that they endured only slight personal contact with those they called the less civilized "New People"—could not replace British purchases.

The only solution was a unified, strong U.S. government able to discriminate against British goods and ships until London officials would open the West Indies and allow U.S. ships more rights. But such discrimination was impossible under the Articles of Confederation, which gave each state the right to control its own commerce. The British simply played off state against state.

This foreign-policy failure soon produced political crisis. In frontier Massachusetts, money virtually disappeared. Debtors, threatened with the loss of their land, organized under Daniel Shays to gain control of the courts through military force. The Massachusetts governor managed to put down Shays's Rebellion in 1786, but the effects of this near-revolution rippled as far away as Virginia. Washington, Jefferson (now U.S. minister to France), and James Madison all viewed Shays as the dangerous product of a bankrupt foreign policy. Other sections of the West seemed almost out of control as war veterans and other settlers rushed into the Ohio River territory. In 1779, Kentucky had about 200 white settlers. Six years later it contained 30,000. These Americans needed money and credit. They also needed protection against both Indians and the Spanish agents who sought to seduce them into Spain's empire—an empire that encircled Kentucky from the Mississippi around to the Floridas. George Washington visited the West, then warned that "the western settlers . . . stand as it were upon a pivot; the touch of a feather would turn them any way."[36] The individual states, however, could not coordinate an effective policy to deal with the Indians and Spain. In the background loomed British power. London officials refused to evacuate the northwest forts at Niagara, Detroit, and Oswego until the Americans settled their pre-1776 debt. British agents exploited the fur trade and encouraged Native Americans to drive back the settlers.

Washington's "rising empire" was fragmenting. The danger reached a peak when, in 1784, the Spanish sealed the Mississippi trade at New Orleans. Americans in Kentucky country suddenly faced the choice of losing their trade or joining the Spanish Empire. Spain then sent the smooth Don Diego de Gardoqui to strike a deal with the U.S. secretary of foreign affairs, John Jay. Spain knew that Americans needed markets and specie (gold and silver). Gardoqui offered new trade opportunities in Spain and its Canary Islands in return for Spanish control of the Mississippi for thirty years. An agonized Jay decided to accept. He concluded that Americans needed markets immediately. Anyway, he reasoned, the American multiplication table would soon swarm over the river to take possession of the trans-Mississippi. But Jay had chosen eastern merchant interests over western landed-commercial interests. The West rose in fury. The Congress accepted the Jay-Gardoqui Treaty 7 states to 5, but under the Articles of Confederation, 9 states were

James Madison (1751–1836), born in Virginia, educated at Princeton, deeply schooled in both the politics of a new nation and the political theory of the Western world. As the "Father of the Constitution," a founder of the American political party system, secretary of state between 1801 and 1809, and then president (1809–1817), the soft-spoken Virginian was perhaps the country's greatest political thinker, but also one of its least successful presidents.

needed to ratify a treaty. Thus, the West and South effectively blocked it. Westerners threatened to join the British in Canada and then, they warned the Congress, "Farewell, *a long farewell* to all *your* boasted greatness, [for we] will be able to conquer you."[37]

Jay and other nationalists tried to amend the Articles to give the Congress new power to deal with Spain, but under the Articles of Confederation any amendments required unanimous consent of the states. One state (usually Rhode Island or New York, whose trade prospered) could block Jay. In Virginia, Madison grew concerned about the growing crisis. Thirty-five years old in 1786, educated at Princeton (where he finished in three years by sleeping only two to five hours a night), and a young but powerful member of the Congress in 1781–1782, Madison knew intimately both national politics and political theory. Indeed, he remains the best and most influential political theorist the United States has produced. By late 1786, he had reached certain conclusions with which such friends as Washington, Jefferson, Jay, and Alexander Hamilton of New York agreed.

How, Madison asked, could America hope to survive? Only by having the power to retaliate against England and Spain. How could such power be obtained? "Only by harmony in the measures of the States," Madison responded. How could such harmony be obtained? Only by allowing a "reasonable majority" of states to make policy for all, instead of allowing a single state (such as Rhode Island) to block effective action. As Madison summarized the problem, "In fact most of our political evils may be traced to our commercial ones, as most of our moral [evils] can be traced] to our political."[38] Radical change was needed. Madison and his friends led a drive to have the states meet in Philadelphia.

Publicly, they indicated that they only intended to amend the Articles. But in reality, they intended to establish a new form of government, one that would allow the United States to survive in the brutal world of clashing empires.

THE "GRAND MACHINE" OF THE CONSTITUTION

During six months of secret debate in an intensely hot Philadelphia summer, the convention's delegates wrote a constitution that transformed the nation's ability to handle foreign-policy problems. First, under Madison's urging, the delegates gave Congress the power to regulate trade and pass commercial measures by a mere majority vote (not the two-thirds required by the Articles). Southerners, afraid that the more populous North could outvote and thus control their tobacco and cotton trade, fought the proposal. Madison observed "that the real difference of interests lay not between the large and small but between the N[orthern] and Southn. States. The institution of slavery and its consequences formed the line" between the two sections.[39] In one of the convention's major compromises, the South agreed that a mere majority vote could pass trade measures; in return, the North accepted the continuation of the slave trade until at least 1808.

Second, treaties with other nations could be made lawful when the president proposed them and "two-thirds of the Senators present concur." This provision not only protected the South and West against another Jay-Gardoqui treaty, but it also created a stronger central government because only the senators "present" had to agree. States could no longer threaten to kill treaties simply by not attending Congress, as some did before 1787. This provision also applied to treaties made with Indian tribes, whom the whites usually considered separate nations.

Third, a single-person executive, the president, was created. It had no counterpart in the Articles of Confederation. Congress, however, had the ultimate power: the appropriation of funds for the executive's use. The executive was to be "Commander in Chief of the Army and Navy," could negotiate treaties for Senate consideration, and might nominate ambassadors and "other public Ministers" with "the advice and consent" of the Senate. The Constitution thus established a new agency to conduct day-to-day foreign policy.

Fourth, Congress received an amazing series of powers that it could exercise through a mere majority vote. Congress, not the states, could now "regulate Commerce with foreign Nations, and among the several

States, and with the Indian Tribes." It could do so, moreover, through its new "Power To lay and collect Taxes, Duties, Imposts and Excises." Of equal importance, the convention, acting on Madison's proposal, gave Congress the sole power to "declare" war. The 1787 convention clearly did not want the president to have the power to "make" war without Congress "declaring" it first. As Jefferson later observed, it was only right that the power to involve the nation in conflict should be taken from those in the executive "who are to spend" and given to those in Congress "who are to pay." The delegates, moreover, viewed the president's right to repel sudden attacks as only a necessary exception to the general rule.[40]

Congress received the power to rule all territory outside state control. In another meeting also held in 1787, members of the old Confederation Congress drew up the Ordinance of 1787 that specified a three-stage process through which a territory (such as Kentucky or Ohio in the 1780s) would have to pass to become a state. To ensure that the frontiersmen and -women behaved themselves, the ordinance gave Congress virtual dictatorial power in the first stage so that the territory could be run as a colony. After 1787, a new Congress had the money and ability to operate the ordinance and keep the restless West under control. Overall, the founders clearly wanted Congress to make general laws and rules for foreign policy. The president was to carry out these measures and conduct detailed diplomacy.

Finally, Madison provided a brilliant political theory on which these powers rested. He argued that the national government could be given great powers to defend the United States against other empires (such as the British and Spanish), but also protect individual freedom within America. This seemingly impossible job could be done, he believed, by placing checks and balances within the government itself. As he nicely phrased it, "Ambition must be made to counter ambition." Thus, the states retained significant authority to counter the national government. Thus, three branches of the federal government—the executive, Congress, and the Supreme Court—checked each other. Thus, the two parts of Congress itself, the House and the Senate, checked one another. With these devices and the vast powers in the hands of the new government, Madison felt that he and the other founders had solved a 2,500-year-old problem that the greatest minds—Aristotle, Montesquieu, Hume—had believed could not be solved: how to maintain a just and democratic system over an area as vast as the United States. Aristotle and the others had feared that selfish, individual interests would tear apart a large empire and lead to either anarchy or dictatorship.

Madison disagreed. He believed that dangerous "factions" could be neutralized by spreading them across a vast territory and then having the new government—with its federalism and its checks and balances—rule the territory.[41] Madison thus reversed the beliefs that had governed political theory. In doing so, he explained the new constitutional system and justified the creation of a new American Empire stretching over vast distances.

GREAT LOSERS: THE ANTIFEDERALISTS

The detailed proceedings of the Constitutional Convention remained secret until the 1830s, but Madison publicly outlined his reasoning that undergirded the new government in *The Federalist*, a series of eighty-five essays, written with Jay and Hamilton and published anonymously in 1787–1788. The essays were needed because "Antifederalists" were determined to kill the Constitution in the ratifying conventions that each state convened to accept or reject the document.

The Antifederalists powerfully argued that Aristotle was right: republics must be small so that rulers and other dangerous factions could be closely watched. Other critics warned that the president would be of "the most dangerous kind too—an *elective* King." Elbridge Gerry of Massachusetts had quit the convention in disgust because he feared the new Congress could "raise armies and money without limit." Such power would ruin the people's liberties. Gerry was furious that Madison and Hamilton had succeeded in creating such centralized power and then had the nerve to call themselves "Federalists." Gerry suggested it would be more accurate to call the two sides "rats and anti-rats."[42]

The pivotal battle occurred in Virginia, where Madison's group opposed Governor Patrick Henry's. Head of a strong state machine, Henry did not want to surrender his powers. He was a talented politician and orator. (A poll in 1958 revealed that Henry's "Give me liberty or give me death" had become the second best-known quote in American history. Only "Come up and see me sometime," seductively uttered by movie actress Mae West, was more famous.)[43] Henry charged that the new government would sell out the transappalachian region, suppress liberty within the states, glorify the few who controlled the national government, and destroy the Articles of Confederation, which had pulled the country through the war. Madison responded that the Articles made up a "contemptible system," disdained by the world's powers. He then struck at the core of the problem: Americans had to govern themselves better at home so that they could protect themselves abroad. Madison summarized this in a classic phrase: "Does [Henry] distinguish between what will render us secure and happy at home, and what will render us respectable abroad? If we be free and happy at home, we shall be respectable abroad."[44]

Successful foreign policy, Madison argued, grew from the inside out. But Americans could survive as a people only if they could effectively fight the other great world empires. The United States has never been isolated or outside the world's political struggles. It was born in the middle of those conflicts, and its great problem was—and has always been—how to survive those struggles while maintaining individual liberty at home. Madison believed that he and his colleagues had gone far in solving that central problem. They devised a system that Franklin termed "the grand machine." Madison defeated Henry in the Virginia ratifying convention because of the promise of that "machine," because George Washington threw his great prestige back of the Constitution, and because the Federalists shrewdly agreed to add a bill of rights that would explicitly protect certain personal and state rights.

The Antifederalists lost the argument. They nevertheless raised the pivotal questions that plagued Americans over the next two hundred years. The more immediate problem, however, was to see whether the "machine" would work and the "course of empire" continue to move westward.

Notes

1. William H. Seward, *Life and Public Services of John Quincy Adams* (Auburn, N.Y., 1849), p. 362.
2. Edward G. Bourne, *Spain in America, 1450–1580* (New York, 1904), pp. 82–88.
3. D. A. Farnie, "The Commercial Empire of the Atlantic, 1607–1783," *The Economic History Review*, 2d ser., 15 (December 1962): 205–208.
4. The quote and useful analysis are in Samuel Eliot Morison, *Builders of the Bay Colony* (Boston, 1930), pp. 73–74.
5. Daniel Boorstin, *The Americans: The National Experience* (New York, 1965), p. 3.
6. Louis B. Wright, *The Dream of Prosperity in Colonial America* (New York, 1965), pp. 27–29.
7. Harold U. Faulkner, *Economic History of the United States* (New York, 1937), p. 93.
8. Allan R. Millett and Peter Maslowski, *For the Common Defense: A Military History of the United States of America* (New York, 1984), pp. 2, 9–18.

9. William T. Hagan, *The Indian in American History* (Washington, D.C., 1971), p. 8; Frederic E. Hoxie, "The Indians versus the Textbooks," *American Historical Association Perspectives* 23 (April 1985): 18–22.

10. Pauline Maier, "Second Thoughts on Our First Century," *New York Times Book Review*, 7 July 1985, p. 20.

11. Thomas R. Hietala, *Manifest Design: Anxious Aggrandizement in Late Jacksonian America* (Ithaca, N.Y., 1985), p. 111; an earlier citation is in Thomas A. Bailey's *A Diplomatic History of the American People*, 7th ed. (New York, 1964), p. 224.

12. Benjamin Franklin, *Observations Concerning the Increase of Mankind . . .* , in *The Papers of Benjamin Franklin*, ed. Leonard W. Labaree *et al.* (New Haven, 1959–   ), IV, pp. 233–234.

13. Franklin's Canada pamphlet is in *The Writings of Benjamin Franklin*, ed. Albert Henry Smyth, 10 vols. (New York, 1905), IV, pp. 55–57; Burke's argument can be found in Gerald Stourzh, *Benjamin Franklin and American Foreign Policy* (Chicago, 1954), pp. 70–74.

14. *New York Times*, 4 July 1976, p. F2; a key analysis of Sam Adams and these events is in William Appleman Williams, *The Contours of American History* (Cleveland, 1961), p. 112.

15. Benjamin Franklin to William Franklin, 13 March 1768, in *The Writings*, ed. Smyth, V, p. 117. A fine analysis of this crucial change in British politics is in Michael Kammen, *Rope of Sand* (Ithaca, N.Y., 1968), esp. pp. 314–318.

16. *Boswell's Life of Johnson*, ed. R. W. Chapman (New York, 1953), pp. 590, 876, 946.

17. Richard Van Alstyne, *Empire and Independence* (New York, 1976), p. 28.

18. Curtis P. Nettels, "The Origins of the Union and of the States," *Proceedings of the Massachusetts Historical Society* 72 (1957–1960), p. 71.

19. Benjamin Franklin to Joseph Priestly, October 1775, in *The Writings*, ed. Smyth, VI, p. 430.

20. Richard Henry Lee to George Washington, 26 September 1775 and 22 October 1775, in *The Letters of Richard Henry Lee*, ed. James C. Ballagh, 2 vols. (New York, 1911–1914), esp. I, p. 153.

21. Reginald Horsman, *The Diplomacy of the New Republic, 1776–1815* (Arlington Heights, Ill., 1985), p. 7; Thomas Paine, *Common Sense* (New York, 1942), pp. 23, 26–27, 31–32.

22. See Neil Postman's review of Jonathan Kozol's *Illiterate America* in *Washington Post Book World*, 31 March 1985, p. 5.

23. J. H. Powell, ed., "Speech of John Dickinson," *Pennsylvania Magazine of History and Biography* 65 (October 1941): 458–481.

24. John Adams, *Diary and Autobiography*, ed. Lyman H. Butterfield *et al.*, 4 vols. (Cambridge, Mass., 1961), II, p. 236.

25. Worthington C. Ford, ed., *Journals of the Continental Congress* (Washington, D.C., 1906), V, pp. 768–778.

26. Tadashi Aruga, "Revolutionary Diplomacy and the Franco-American Treaties of 1778," *Japanese Journal of American Studies* no. 2 (1985): 60. The Franklin quotes are in Benjamin Franklin to Mrs. Thompson, 8 February 1777, in *The Writings*, ed. Smyth, VII, p. 26.

27. William Carlos Williams, *In the American Grain* (New York, 1957), p. 153.

28. Recounted in *New York Times*, 3 January 1987, p. 11; the "forever" clause and the

treaties themselves are conveniently found in *The Record of American Diplomacy*, ed. Ruhl J. Bartlett, 4th ed. (New York, 1964), pp. 24–27.

29. Van Alstyne, pp. 92–93.

30. *The American Revolution and "A Candid World,"* ed. Lawrence Kaplan (Kent, Ohio, 1977), p. 141.

31. Benjamin Franklin to John Jay, 2 October 1780, in *The Writings*, ed. Smyth, VIII, pp. 143–144.

32. Robert Calhoon, *Revolutionary America: An Interpretive Overview* (New York, 1976), p. 153.

33. John R. Howe, *The Changing Political Thought of John Adams* (Princeton, 1966), pp. 8–9.

34. Benjamin Franklin to Josiah Quincy, 11 September 1783, in *The Writings*, ed. Smyth, IX, p. 96.

35. Richard Van Alstyne, *The Rising American Empire* (Chicago, 1960), esp. pp. 1–20.

36. Merrill Jensen, *The New Nation* (New York, 1950), p. 171. The best overview now is Frederick W. Marks III, *Independence on Trial: Foreign Affairs and the Making of the Constitution* (Baton Rouge, 1973, 1986).

37. *The Revolutionary Diplomatic Correspondence of the United States*, ed. Francis Wharton, 6 vols. (Washington, D.C., 1889), VI, pp. 223–224.

38. James Madison to James Monroe, 7 August 1785, in *The Writings of James Madison*, ed. Gaillard Hunt, 9 vols. (New York, 1901), II, pp. 155–157, 228–229; Irving Brant, *James Madison*, 6 vols. (Indianapolis, 1944–1961), III, pp. 55–56.

39. *The Records of the Federal Convention of 1787*, ed. Max Farrand, 4 vols. (New Haven, 1937), II, pp. 9–10. I am greatly indebted here to Professor Diane Clemens of the University of California, Berkeley, who is preparing a major monograph (to be published by Oxford University Press) on executive powers.

40. Abraham Sofaer, *War, Foreign Affairs, and Constitutional Power* (Cambridge, Mass., 1976), pp. 31–32.

41. *The Federalist*, ed. Clinton Rossiter (New York, 1961), p. 325; Sofaer, pp. 42–43.

42. Merrill Jensen, *The American Revolution within America* (New York, 1974), pp. 213–214; *The Anti-Federalist Papers*, ed. Morton Borden (East Lansing, Mich., 1965), esp. pp. 27–28, 37–39, 213; *Records of the Federal Convention*, ed. Farrand, II, p. 633.

43. Bernard Mayo, *Myths and Men* (Athens, Ga., 1959), pp. 1–24, has the poll and a good analysis of Henry.

44. *The Writings of James Madison*, ed. Hunt, V, p. 146.

For Further Reading

Most of the bibliographical references given in these sections specify post-1980 publications. For pre-1981 materials, no textbook can hope to compare with *Guide to American Foreign Relations since 1700*, ed. Richard Dean Burns (1983), which, with three indexes and more than 1,200 pages of references, is the necessary starting place for any student who wants to read more on the first three centuries of U.S. foreign policy. See also the notes to this chapter and the General Bibliography at the end of this book.

A stimulating account, much influenced by the U.S. experience in Vietnam during the 1960s and the 1970s, is Robert W. Tucker and David C. Hendrickson, *The Fall of the First British Empire: Origins of the War of American Independence* (1982), which should be used with Alison Gilbert Olson, *Making The Empire Work: London and American Interest Groups 1690–1790* (1992). Of special importance on the development of the American view of empire are Douglas Edward Leach, *Roots of Conflict: British Armed Forces and Colonial Americans, 1677–1763* (1966), and Francis Jennings, *Empire of Fortune* (1988), on the Seven Years' War. For a "realist" perspective, see the readable essays in Norman Graebner, *Foundations of American Foreign Policy* (1986), especially those on Franklin and Adams. Jonathan Dull has written on the first American diplomat in "Benjamin Franklin and the Nature of American Diplomacy," *International History Review* 5 (August 1983) and in "Franklin the Diplomat: The French Mission," *Transactions of the American Philosophical Society* 72, pt. 1 (1982) and has examined the larger picture in *A Diplomacy of the American Revolution* (1985). A fascinating account of Silas Deane's escapades is in James West Davidson and Mark H. Lytle, *After the Fact* (1982), and of an opponent of the Declaration of Independence in Milton E. Flower, *John Dickinson* (1983), while Louis W. Potts delves into U.S.-French diplomacy in *Arthur Lee: A Virtuous Revolutionary* (1981), and Lynne Withey presents a fresh perspective on the Revolution and its diplomacy in *Dearest Friend: A Life of Abigail Adams* (1981), as does Edith B. Gelles, *Portia: The World of Abigail Adams* (1992).

Encounters with Native Americans are covered in important essays in *The American Indian and the Problem of History*, ed. Calvin Martin (1986), from the Indians' viewpoint. Superb accounts have opened new perspectives on the military experience: *Arms at Rest*, ed. Joan R. Challinor and Robert L. Beisner (1987), especially the essays by Harold D. Langley and James A. Field, Jr., on the pre-1815 years; *Arms and Independence*, ed. Ronald Hoffman and Peter J. Albert (1984), especially the Royster, Higgenbotham, and Buel essays on foreign-policy aspects; Reginald C. Stuart, *War and American Thought: From the Revolution to the Monroe Doctrine* (1982); and Lawrence D. Cress, "Republican Liberty and National Security: American Military Policy as an Ideological Problem, 1783 to 1789," *William and Mary Quarterly* 38 (January 1981). George Washington deserves a special place: Don Higginbotham's excellent *George Washington and the American Military Tradition* (1985); Edmund S. Morgan's succinct *The Genius of George Washington* (1980); and *The Papers of George Washington: Revolutionary War Series*, Vol. I: *June–September 1775*, ed. Philander D. Chase (1985), with more volumes scheduled to appear soon.

Special topics are well handled in *Diplomacy and Revolution: The Franco-American Alliance of 1778*, ed. Ronald Hoffman and Peter J. Albert (1981); Lawrence S. Kaplan, "The Treaty of Paris, 1783: A Historiographical Challenge," *International History Review* 5 (August 1983); and the key sources in *The United States and Russia: The Beginning of Relations, 1765–1815*, ed. Nina N. Bashkina, Nikolai N. Bolkhovitinov, *et al.* (1980). On the years 1783 to 1789, begin with Frederick W. Marks III, *Independence on Trial*, 2d ed. (1986), which sees foreign policy as the major reason for the 1787 convention. Note *Beyond Confederation: Origins of the Constitution and American National Identity*, ed. Richard Beeman, Stephen Botein, and Edward C. Carter II (1987). A deserved examination of the "losers" is given in *The Anti-Federalist: An Abridgment of the Seven-Volume Set of the Complete Anti-Federalist*, ed. Herbert J. Storing (1985), and of the "winners" in *The Papers of James Madison,* ed. Robert A. Rutland *et al.* (1973, 1975), whose volumes are now up to the 1793–1795 years. Marks, *Independence on Trial,* has a useful bibliography on the foreign-policy implications of the decisions leading to the adoption of the Constitution. See also the important perspective in Jonathan Marshall, "Empire or Liberty: The Antifederalists and Foreign Policy, 1787–1788," *Journal of Libertarian Studies* 4 (Summer 1980).

2

A Second Struggle for Independence and Union (1789–1815)

LIBERTY AND EMPIRES

Americans were doubly blessed at the time of their independence. They had before them a vast, fertile territory that strained even the pioneers' wild imagination. A Pennsylvanian proudly wrote that the trees were taller, the soil richer than anywhere else in the world, while the Mississippi was "the prince of rivers, in comparison of whom the Nile is but a rivulet, and the Danube a mere ditch."[1] But Americans were also given a unique federal form of government by founders who were unique. The generation that gave Americans their independence and Constitution was the only generation in U.S. history that combined the nation's political leaders and its intellectual leaders in the same people.[2] The theoretical and the practical met, fortunately for Americans, at the moment their Constitution was written.

But even James Madison, the "father of the Constitution," as he later became known, was unsure whether the first government under the new laws could survive. "We are in a wilderness without a single footstep to guide us," he wrote to Jefferson in 1789. Madison quickly learned that the survival of individual freedom at home was related to the course of policy abroad. As he observed in the late 1790s, "The management of foreign relations appears to be the most susceptible of abuse of all the trusts committed to government."[3] Between 1789 and 1814, the United States struggled both to survive within the world of

Thomas Jefferson (1743–1826) wrote the original draft of the Declaration of Independence, served as governor of Virginia and U.S. minister to France, became the nation's first secretary of state under the new Constitution, and, as president, bought the Louisiana Purchase in 1803. He hoped to obtain the rest of North America in 1812, when he unfortunately thought that conquering Canada would be a mere matter of marching.

the titanic Napoleonic Wars, and to keep alive the union that had been formed in 1787–1788.

There was irony here. The person who was to run foreign policy for the new system was originally entitled "secretary for foreign affairs," but it turned out that the official seemed to have so little to do in the late 1780s that the job was renamed "secretary of state" and given the responsibility of guarding the nation's Great Seal, publishing laws, and taking the census. Thomas Jefferson thought so little of the position that he wanted to remain in Paris rather than join Washington's cabinet. But the Virginian finally accepted the post that paid $3,500 annually and had a staff of five for copying and translating messages. The War and Treasury departments were much larger and also worked in rather stately buildings, while the original State Department building was a small house on Broadway in New York City, where Washington's first government gathered before moving to Philadelphia in 1790.[4] But the irony was that the State Department, for all its lack of glamor, was to be the very center of the debate over the next quarter-century on whether the new nation, surrounded by great empires, could conduct a foreign policy that would allow the survival of the constitutional experiment. As was to be the case so often over the next several centuries, American domestic politics were crucial, but foreign policies involved matters of life and death.

THE FRAMEWORK: THE UNITED STATES (1789–1814)

When John Quincy Adams traveled as U.S. minister to Prussia in the mid-1790s, he had to wait outside the Berlin city gates while an officer tried to discover if a place called the United States actually existed. No such uncertainty was found in the Western Hemisphere. With astounding speed, Americans moved to conquer the land and commerce of the New World. The "multiplication table" continued to double the population approximately every twenty-two years. In Connecticut (the seedbed for populating much of New York and the Midwest), couples could brag of a dozen children, five times that number of grandchildren, and two hundred to three hundred great-grandchildren.[5] In the South, onrushing population put great pressure on Native Americans and the relatively few Spaniards who tried to hold on to the vast territories of Florida and the trans-Mississippi.

Not only the Constitution, but literature and technology shaped the nation. Noah Webster, an ardent nationalist (and Federalist), wrote his famous speller, reader, and dictionary to make Americans aware and proud of their distinct language, as well as to make them literate. Soon after the steam engine began to revolutionize British industries, it started replacing animal and human muscle in America. John Fitch may have been ugly, bad-mannered, and a wife deserter, but he also ran a newly invented steamboat on the river in Philadelphia, where the founders could see it in 1787. By 1790, the vessel was coming into regular use. Three years later, Eli Whitney perfected the cotton gin, which separated fiber from seed with such speed that the new machine fastened a cotton culture on the South. Cotton exports rocketed from 2 million pounds in 1794 to 18 million pounds in 1800 to 128 million pounds by 1820.[6] In 1798, Whitney devised the radical process of making rifles rapidly and cheaply out of interchangeable parts in an assembly-line process. American expansion was increasingly linked to its people's genius for machinery and technology.

Native Americans felt the brunt of this expansionism. Since many had fought alongside the British between 1775 and 1782, the settlers had no qualms about pushing them aside after the Revolution. The Indians fought effectively against the badly organized Americans. The new Constitution, however, gave the government the needed authority to raise armies, oversee settlement, and make treaties with the tribes. With this new power came a new philosophy: instead of being destroyed, the Indians were to be "civilized" and made to act like white farmers.

Thomas Jefferson best exemplified this approach. As president in 1808, he told a group of Indians that they should become small capitalist landowners. Then "you will mix with us by marriage. Your blood will run in our veins and will spread with us over this great land." If they did not follow his advice, Jefferson later commented, the alternative was not pretty: "They will relapse into barbarism and misery . . . and we shall be obliged to drive them, with the beasts of the forests into the Stony [Rocky] Mountains."[7]

The region between the Appalachian Mountains and the Mississippi (an area bordering the British Empire on the north and the Spanish Empire on the south and west) was becoming extremely productive, politically complex, and quickly populated. By 1795, Tennessee exported cast iron as well as whiskey and bacon. The West was not being filled by idyllic, self-sufficient Daniel Boones, but by settlers whose multiplying commercial interests produced so many farm and manufacturing goods that they thought of themselves as part of an international trading network. As the new Constitution took effect, moreover, Europe lost much of its ability to feed itself. The quarter-century agony of the French Revolution and Napoleonic Wars began. U.S. farm prices rose as foreign markets blotted up American cotton, tobacco, grain, meat, and fish. In the North as well as in the plantation South, as a Philadelphia orator put it, "the Star-bespangled Genius of America . . . points to agriculture as the stable Foundation of this rising mighty Empire."[8]

U.S. exports leaped from $19 million in 1791 to $108 million in 1807. But the country remained a debtor as imports shot up from $19 million in 1791 to $138 million in 1807. The debt was often paid for by the success of U.S. merchants and shipowners. They not only carried American trade, but the trade of others—especially the commerce generated by the rich British and French West Indies. As the European wars grew bloodier, this trade grew greater and the U.S. traders grew richer even as they became in reality parts of the British or French empires rather than the American system. As these traders came to care more about European than U.S. interests, they caused major problems for Washington officials between 1805 and 1814. Indeed, some northeastern merchants almost destroyed the new Union in 1814. But in the earlier years, they acted as a cutting edge for the expansion of American power in some unusual places. For example, they helped undermine Spain's control of Latin America by dominating the Spanish-American carrying trade.

The Yankees also targeted Russia's colonies in Alaska and the present American Northwest until they monopolized the rich fur trade between Alaska and China. That trade produced as much as 500 percent annual profit. In historian Howard Kushner's words, the supposedly Russian-controlled areas actually "depended on Yankee traders" for both supplies and exports.[9] The Russian tsar Alexander I tried to retaliate by giving a trading monopoly to John Jacob Astor's American fur company, which, the tsar hoped, would undercut other Americans and allow him to control Astor. Alexander next sent a mission into California to take over the San Francisco region so food from the area could replace supplies provided by Americans. Neither policy worked. By 1820, the Yankees were handsomely, if illegally, growing rich from the Russian Empire. A Bostonian, Captain Robert Gray, in 1792 found the magnificent river that he named after his ship, the *Columbia*. Gray's discovery gave the United States strong claim to the vast Oregon territory. Other American traders exploited the coasts for furs and, in three-year expeditions, grew rich selling them to China. They sometimes stopped for rest in Hawaii, thus giving them an early interest in those strategic islands as well. Before it was ten years old, the new United States was becoming a power in the Pacific region.

Americans also were proving that they could govern their growing continental empire. Shays-type rebellions were no longer to be tolerated. When William Blount (a leading politician in Tennessee) and James Wilkinson (a well-known scoundrel and schemer) renewed earlier plots to sell parts of the new West to Spain, Washington used his power simply to buy Blount and Wilkinson by giving them political jobs and military commissions. Washington became the central figure who held together the nation's domestic and foreign affairs. The first president set many of the precedents that later chief executives had to follow. He had "neither the quickness nor the brilliance of genius," the British minister reported to London, perhaps because of "his natural shyness and reserve." But, the minister granted, the president had "sound sense and . . . excellent judgement."[10] Jefferson noted that Washington was tall, "his deportment easy, erect, and noble; the best horseman of his age."[11] His long military career, the leadership of the revolutionary forces, and his service as chair of the Constitutional Convention gave him unequaled experience. He knew the West intimately, largely as a result of his own extensive land speculation. The first president believed that the Constitution's success depended not only on its words, but on its citizens' character. "A good general government," he wrote to one of his several intimate women admirers, "without good morals and good habits, will not make us a happy People."[12]

Jefferson agreed about the need for good morals, but he had fewer doubts than Washington. In designing a national seal, Jefferson suggested that it show the children of Israel led by a pillar of light from the heavens. He was confident that Americans were the new chosen people of God. Returning from France in 1790 to become the first secretary of state under the Constitution, his confidence was put to the test.

CHOSEN PEOPLE, THE BRITISH EMPIRE, AND THE FRENCH REVOLUTION

Washington understood his most important foreign-policy problem: "That we avoid errors in our system of policy respecting Great Britain."[13] The British continued to hold forts on U.S. territory and encouraged Indians to oppose American settlement. London also tightened its control on U.S. trade. To break that control, Madison rose in the first session of the First Congress to propose a series of measures that would utilize the new powers of the Constitution as a club to smash the British hold. His approach was direct: threaten other nations with commercial retaliation unless they treated American trade fairly. As the Virginian phrased it, "We possess natural advantages which no other nation does; we can, therefore, with justice, stipulate for a reciprocity in commerce. The way to obtain this is by discrimination."[14] Congress passed bills levying tonnage duties eight times higher on foreign vessels than on U.S. ships in American ports, and also imposed import taxes on foreign goods entering the country. Americans wanted freer trade, but they were prepared to play rough mercantilist trading games if necessary.

Madison nevertheless wanted more. He sought to favor French trade (because France bought more than it sold to Americans) and discriminate against the British. His proposals quickly encountered opposition from Secretary of the Treasury Alexander Hamilton. The illegitimate son of a Scottish merchant, at twenty Hamilton had been a brilliant pamphleteer for the Revolution and at twenty-six a hero at Yorktown. After practicing law and marrying into a powerful New York family, he had joined Madison to push through the Constitution. Only thirty-four in 1789 (Madison was thirty-eight), Hamilton split with the Virginian and Jefferson over foreign policy. The Treasury secretary put together a program that gave the new nation sound, centralized finances. His program promised to pay the large national debt and to establish a national bank to oversee the country's economy. But these schemes required a great deal of money, and those sums had to come from land sales or import taxes on goods that were mostly British. Hamilton, therefore, feared any measure that threatened Great Britain and that might lead to a cutting off of British capital or, worse, another devastating conflict. Thus, he opposed Madison's every attempt to get tough with the British. He even worked secretly with the British minister to undercut Madison's influence.

Jefferson and Madison were furious. Hamilton is "panic-struck if we refuse our breeches to every kick which Gr. Brit. may choose to give us," Jefferson fumed.[15] Nor did it lessen the Virginians' fear when Jefferson told Hamilton that the leading men in history were Francis Bacon, Isaac Newton, and John Locke, only to have the secretary of the Treasury reply dryly that he personally preferred Caesar.

In 1790, a cabinet crisis erupted when Spanish naval officers stupidly seized British ships in Nootka Sound off the northwest coast. London quickly planned to retaliate by marching troops from Canada to conquer Spanish lands along the Caribbean, a march that would take the troops through the Mississippi Valley. The British could end by surrounding the new nation on all four sides. Jefferson advised Washington that the British must never be allowed to make that march. Hamilton, however, warned that nothing should be done to alienate Great Britain, and, he added, it would help to have the Spanish thrown off the continent. Before Washington had to take action, however, the Spanish wisely apologized for the ship seizures, and the crisis passed.

It was quickly replaced by an even graver problem. In 1789, the French Revolution had begun. By 1793, it became an international struggle as France declared war on England, Holland, and Austria. Jefferson sympathized with the French. They seemed to be following the example of 1776. Madison was less starry-eyed about the upheaval, but for his own reasons he also favored the French. A great opportunity opened for U.S. commerce. As Jefferson phrased it, the United States wanted no part of the Europeans' problems except "we have only to pray that their soldiers may eat a great deal."[16] Hamilton agreed.

But the two men sharply divided over U.S. obligations to France under the 1778 alliance, a pact that remained in effect between the two nations, even though the 1778 governments had changed. Hamilton argued that U.S. national interests rose above any vague obligations under the treaty. Washington took his advice and issued a Neutrality Proclamation. Madison blasted the president's announcement for disregarding U.S. "duties to France," ignoring "the cause of liberty," and—of special concern—exercising a power that Madison believed belonged to Congress: the power to declare neutrality could also decide whether and against whom the United States might declare war.[17] But Washington stuck to his policy and established a constitutional precedent that claimed important power for the president. Nor did it help Jefferson when a new French minister, Edmond Charles Genêt, arrived and immediately began breaking U.S. laws by fitting out French privateers in U.S. ports to seize British ships. He then enlisted American boys to fight in France. Washington refused to deal with "Citizen" Genêt. As the Frenchman grew unpopular, Jefferson "saw the necessity of quitting a wreck which could not but sink all who should cling to it."

The French Revolution soon got out of hand. Dr. J. I. Guillotin's device for separating heads from bodies worked more frequently until King Louis XVI became a victim. After Genêt's supporters in Paris fell to a more radical faction, even he recoiled at the thought of returning. (He married into a wealthy American family and lived in the United States for the rest of his life.) Jefferson was sickened. The French were not following the moderate example of 1776. Two centuries later, one can see that the French Revolution, not the American, was more the model for such great upheavals as those in Russia, China, Iran, and Vietnam. As the British foreign minister Lord Grenville sniffed to an American in 1798, "None but Englishmen and their Descendents know how to make a Revolution." That belief became a central assumption in U.S. diplomacy.

In 1793–1794, Madison pushed his campaign to destroy British control of U.S. commerce. He received help from the British themselves in late 1793, when they seized 250 U.S. vessels that were carrying goods between France and the West Indies. Madison arose in the House of Representatives in March 1794 and bitterly attacked the action. He observed that the British sold the United States twice as much as they bought, while the French bought seven times more than they sold to the United States. It was time to cut British trade and shipping until London officials treated Americans fairly. Madison gained support from many who were outraged by the ship seizures. As Hamilton's program seemed about to collapse, the Treasury secretary brilliantly gained time and undercut Madison by convincing Washington to send Chief Justice John Jay to London to negotiate a settlement in order to avert possible war with the British.

A TURN: FROM JAY TO X Y Z

Jay had one high card to play: he could threaten to join the new League of Armed Neutrality formed by several European nations to check British naval power. Hamilton, however, undercut his own diplomat by secretly telling London that the United States had no intention of joining the league. This deviousness left Jay to sign a treaty that sharply limited U.S.–West Indian trade. The pact gave Americans nothing on the issues of neutral rights (such as the valued U.S. principle that "free ships make free goods"), or impressment (the hated British practice of seizing their own—and sometimes American—citizens from U.S. ships on the grounds that they had deserted His Majesty's fleet). The British repeated their 1783 pledge that the Mississippi was opened to both nations. On the other hand, the British did agree to leave the northwest forts, and they opened Great Britain and the British East Indies to U.S. merchants. American trade with Asia consequently boomed. By 1801, Yankee ships carried 70 percent of all foreign trade with India.

But even this opportunity did not stop anti-Jay riots from erupting throughout the East. Mobs in Philadelphia threatened Vice-President John Adams's house and stoned the windows of the British minister's office. Americans were incensed at the limits placed on the West Indies trade. Westerners threatened to leave the Union if the British used the treaty to try to control the Mississippi. Madison was deeply angered. He argued that the House of Representatives had an equal right with the Senate to act on the treaty because the House had to appropriate money to put treaties into effect. Washington set another crucial constitutional precedent by invoking executive privilege and refusing to release the documents of the Jay mission. Then he denied that anything more than a two-thirds vote of the Senate was needed to ratify treaties. The president faced down the House, but his growing concern was over those he called "the restless and impetuous spirits of Kentucky," who threatened in the West to take matters into their own hands.

Since 1789, he had tried to protect the settlers from Indian attacks that were at least winked at by the British. In 1791, about a hundred miles north of Cincinnati, the Miami chief Little Turtle inflicted one of the worst defeats in history on a U.S. military force. Nine hundred whites were killed. The rest broke and ran. In 1793–1794, Washington finally placed General "Mad Anthony" Wayne in command of 3,000 men. After careful preparation, Wayne defeated the Shawnee in 1794 at the Battle of Fallen Timbers in the Ohio territory. The general leveled every Indian settlement he could reach, built forts (including Fort Wayne, now in Indiana), and opened the region to settlement.

Washington then enjoyed another well-timed success. The Spanish had joined Great Britain against France in 1793, but within a year they were ready to rejoin their traditional ally in Paris. To do so, however, created the danger that the British would retaliate by sweeping down on Spanish possessions in America. Those possessions were indeed already slipping away. Several years earlier, Spain had tried to seduce American settlers by encouraging them to settle in the Floridas. Jefferson was elated that the doors would be open: "We may complain of this seduction of our inhabitants just enough to make [the Spanish] believe it very wise policy for them & confirm them in it."[18] By 1794, Spain had lost control of most of those settlers and much of the Indian trade. When Madrid ordered the situation to be brought under control, a beleaguered Spanish official responded: "You cannot lock up an open field." Beset in both Europe and America, the Spanish were ready to talk. Washington sent Thomas Pinckney to Madrid. In late 1795, he signed a pact that pledged mutual cooperation to stop Indian attacks in the South and, most important, to open Spanish-held New Orleans to tax-free use for three years to the hundreds of thousands of Americans whose prosperity now depended on Mississippi trade.

The Pinckney Treaty was a godsend to Washington. In it, Spain promised the West the use of the Mississippi just as the Jay Treaty gave the East's merchants peace with the British fleet. Moreover, those who continued to oppose the Jay Treaty in Congress were quickly sobered by threats of losing the Union. New Jersey, for one, said it would dissociate itself from the South if the Jay pact were not ratified. As one Federalist wrote, "The conversation of a separation is taking place in almost every company."[19] Washington also threw his immense prestige behind Jay's agreement. The Senate barely accepted it by a 20-to-10 vote. Madison complained that "banks, the British merchants, the insurance companies" had won through bribery and threats. More accurately, however, the new nation had been saved in 1795–1796 by "Mad Anthony" Wayne, Pinckney, and Washington.

Americans now made a major turn. U.S.-British relations rapidly improved, while the French—embittered that the United States would accept the Jay Treaty but not honor the 1778 alliance—turned against Washington's administration. The French minister to Philadelphia, Pierre Adet, first tried to block the Jay Treaty, then worked vigorously to have Jefferson win the 1796 presidential election over Federalist candidate John Adams. That interference influenced Washington to

John Adams (1735–1826) was dour, brilliant, a leader of the revolutionary movement, and a co-negotiator of the 1783 peace treaty. The nation's first vice-president, then president (1797–1801), he demonstrated courage and skill in making peace instead of war with France in 1799–1800 and, as a result, decisively lost re-election in 1800.

issue (in a newspaper) his Farewell Address that warned Americans against tying themselves to the fortunes of any "foreign influence." In words that have not lost their importance nearly two hundred years later, the president observed that "the nation which indulges toward another an habitual hatred or an habitual fondness is in some degree a slave." If such "slavery" could be avoided, he held out a magnificent vision: the growth of their power until Americans could virtually do whatever they wished. The Farewell Address remains significant because it argued that if Americans were restrained in the 1790s, they would have to suffer few restraints later. Of equal importance, the Farewell Address remains the major statement of the need for American freedom of action, a central theme in the first two centuries of U.S. foreign policy.[20]

Adams won the election, but Jefferson's triumph would have produced much the same foreign policy, Adet believed:

> [Jefferson, Adet reported to Paris,] seeks to draw near to us because he fears us less than England; but tomorrow he might change his opinion about us if England should cease to inspire his fear. . . . Jefferson, I say, is an American, and as such, he cannot sincerely be our friend. An American is the born enemy of all the peoples of Europe.[21]

John Adams led a rapidly developing but still primitive country—so primitive that when his wife Abigail took a coach from Philadelphia to join him in the new capital city of Washington, she became lost in the wilderness south of Baltimore. "You find nothing but a forest and woods on the way," she complained. But the city's location revealed great insight into the country's future, because it had been placed on the Potomac River in the belief that the waterway was to become a major route westward.[22]

With usual American sensitivity to events beyond the mountains, Adams quickly heard of Spanish and French plots to win over the distant settlements. George Rogers Clark, hero of the American Revolution, even became involved in some of the schemes, despite—or because of—a severe drinking problem. The president seized the initiative by sending three diplomats to France for talks. They were to terminate the 1778 alliance, make the French promise to behave in the West, and win France's recognition of wide-ranging U.S. trading rights. Three French agents, code-named "X," "Y," and "Z," countered with simpler proposals: Adams must apologize for his past criticism of the French, then give Paris a large loan as well as a $250,000 bribe to grease the negotiations. They also expected help in the ongoing war against the British. An astounded Adams broke off the talks. The cry was born, "Millions for Defense, but not one Cent for Tribute!"

The president had to fight a two-front struggle. An "undeclared war" broke out with France, which seized more U.S. ships between 1797 and 1800 than did the greater British fleet. On the home front, Hamilton, now a powerful lawyer in New York City, worked through his informants in Adams's cabinet to seize the opportunity and strike at the crumbling Spanish Empire in the South and West—preferably with British help. Adams and Hamilton, despite being fellow Federalists, had become bitter political enemies. Their personalities clashed, and the president strongly disagreed with Hamilton's pro-British views. Closer to Madison on the trade question, Adams wanted a vigorous, independent U.S. commerce. He called Hamilton "the bastard brat of a Scots peddler." Hamilton, in turn, had tried to block Adams's victory in 1796. Now Hamilton not only hoped to break ties with France, but personally to lead an army that would conquer the Floridas and trans-Mississippi—and even "take a squint at Mexico." Adams, who knew about Hamilton's admiration for Caesar, concluded that "this man is stark mad or I am."

Meanwhile, the Federalists pushed the Alien and Sedition Acts through Congress. These measures gave the government power to arrest aliens as well as newspaper editors who were suspected of being pro-French. In reality, the Federalists used the acts to persecute Jeffersonians. Not for the last time in American history was the threat of conflict abroad used to justify a witch hunt at home. Jefferson and Madison responded with resolutions passed in the Virginia and Kentucky state legislatures. These measures defied the two acts and implied that disunion would occur if the Federalists did not retreat.

The danger thus arose of both a full-scale war with France and a constitutional crisis at home. Adams commissioned three fighting ships and established the United States Navy Department to oversee operations. George Logan, a Pennsylvania Quaker, took it upon himself to sail to France and work out a peace settlement. His mission failed, and the Federalists passed the Logan Act, which made it illegal for any private citizen to negotiate with a foreign government. (In the 1960s through 1980s, the government threatened to invoke the law—for example, against actress Jane Fonda, who traveled to Vietnam—but the law was not applied.)

As U.S.-French relations reached a critical point, Adams took a politically dangerous but statesmanlike step. He overruled Hamilton and dispatched a peace mission to Paris. The president believed that France posed less of a danger ("There is no more prospect of seeing a French army here, than there is in heaven," Adams thought) than did Hamilton. Adams worried more about the probability of becoming involved in the Napoleonic Wars and the possibility of a severed Union. The French were now ready to deal. They needed U.S. trade, especially after the British fleet had nearly destroyed their navy. The Convention of 1800 ended the 1778 alliance. In return, the United States agreed to assume claims against France (although these were never fully honored). Each side agreed to grant the other most-favored-nation rights in trade and—not surprisingly—declared that neutrals (such as the United States) should have extensive rights to trade during wartime.

The United States thus ended the last European alliance it would have for nearly a century and a half. The experience had been bitter. The costs even touched the possibility of disunion. In 1801, Jefferson recalled how the western and eastern states had preserved the new constitutional system by balancing each other in the Jay Treaty and undeclared war crises. He concluded that those experiences provided "a new proof of the falsehood of Montesquieu's doctrine, that a republic can be preserved in only a small territory. The reverse is the truth. Had our territory been even a third only of what it is, we were gone."[23]

JEFFERSON AND LOUISIANA

To the astonishment of many, the United States managed a peaceful transition of power in the 1800 election from Adams's Federalists to

"The Providential Detection" is a superb American graphic drawn for the bitter 1800 election fight by an artist who clearly hated Jefferson and his supposed ties to revolutionary France. As the Virginian kneels at the burning altar of French "despotism," a powerful (and beautifully sketched) American eagle stops Jefferson from throwing the Constitution into the flames. Note the all-seeing eye (in the upper right corner) watching out for the United States.

THE PROVIDENTIAL DETECTION

Jefferson's Republicans. The campaign had been brutal. The pro-Adams president of Yale, Timothy Dwight, warned that if Jefferson won, "we may see the Bible cast into a bonfire, the vessels of the sacramental supper borne by an ass in public procession," and "our wives and daughters the victims of legal prostitution." The reality was less exciting. Historian William Stinchcombe has noted that Adams was actually beaten by the backlash against the Federalist war scare—"the greatly increased defense spending, particularly on the army, and the notorious Alien and Sedition Acts," which Jefferson turned to his political advantage. The news of peace with France arrived too late to save Adams. In any case, years later he wrote that "I desire no other inscription on my gravestone than: 'here lies John Adams, who took upon himself the responsibility of peace with France in 1800.'" The new president moved quickly to build a consensus. "We are all Republicans, we are all Federalists," he declared in his 1801 inaugural address.[24]

He appointed his close friend James Madison secretary of state. Their foreign-policy assumptions were few but direct. As Jefferson wrote in 1801, American expansion should be thought of as virtually unlimited:

> However our present situation may restrain us within our own limits, it is impossible not to look forward to distant times, when our rapid multiplication will expand itself beyond those limits, and cover the whole northern, if not the southern continent, with a people speaking the same language, governed in similar forms, and by similar laws; nor can we contemplate with satisfaction blot or mixture on that surface.[25]

To achieve these goals, Americans had to protect their freedom of action: "Peace, commerce, and honest friendship with all nations, entangling alliances with none," as he announced in his inaugural address. In a rephrase of Paine's *Common Sense* and Washington's Farewell Address, Jefferson told a friend that "we have a perfect horror of everything connecting ourselves with the politics of Europe," but because Americans are "daily growing stronger," if they can have a few more years to build their power, they can tell others how the United States must be treated, "and we will say it."[26] Power abroad, as Madison had told Patrick Henry in 1788 (see p. 35), depended on effective rule at home. In this sense, Jefferson became the first chief executive to manage Congress through well-disciplined party leaders who followed the president's wishes. His foreign policies were often effective because he was able to whip Congress into line to support them. Jefferson successfully centralized power in the new Executive Mansion.[27]

Nor was Jefferson reluctant to build and use military power. However, he kept a sense of proportion. He never believed that the young United States could build a navy to challenge the British fleet, but he built a small flotilla of gunboats to fight the Barbary States between 1801 and 1805. Operating out of the North African Islamic states of Tripoli, Algiers, Tunis, and Morocco, the raiders demanded large tributes from ships plying the Mediterranean or the ships would be seized and sailors brutalized. Washington and Adams had paid tribute to these robbers. Jefferson refused and sent four warships to protect U.S. commerce. One ship ran aground, and Tripoli seized the crew. It was the first overseas hostage crisis in American history.

Jefferson went to war. Scoring several sensational victories on both sea and land, the president nevertheless had to pay $60,000 to obtain Tripoli's pledge not to capture other U.S. ships. During the War of 1812, the plundering of U.S. ships began again, but in 1815 President Madison dispatched a small fleet that forced the Barbary States to retreat. The U.S. Navy then leased a port on the island of Majorca in the Mediterranean so it could move quickly against future plundering. The American war with Barbary, however, was over.[28]

These characteristics of Jefferson's foreign policy—expansionism, freedom of action, centralization of power, and the willingness to use force in selected situations—appeared in his greatest triumph, the purchase of Louisiana in 1803. But the affair could have been a diplomatic catastrophe. Jefferson and Madison found themselves facing a crisis in 1801 when they learned that the weakened Spanish had finally

Toussaint L'Ouverture (1743–1803), the black revolutionary who led the fight to drive the French from Haiti, inadvertently helped the United States to purchase the Louisiana Territory from France.

surrendered to Napoleon's demands and sold him the Louisiana Territory. His war with Great Britain had stopped (temporarily, it soon turned out), and Napoleon turned to developing a New World empire. He especially wanted to find a food supply in Louisiana for the black slaves who produced highly profitable sugar crops in Haiti and Santo Domingo. In 1802, the crisis intensified when Spanish officials (who still controlled New Orleans) suddenly shut off the Mississippi to U.S. trade. Madison had long understood that whoever controlled that great river controlled the rapidly multiplying Americans settling in the West: "The Mississippi is to them everything," he wrote privately in late 1802. "It is the Hudson, the Delaware, the Potomac, and all the navigable rivers of the Atlantic States formed into one stream."[29]

In 1802, Jefferson and Madison devised a brilliant series of policies that finally forced Napoleon to sell not only New Orleans (the primary American objective), but most of the immense area between the Mississippi and the Rocky Mountains. First, Madison sent secret help to black revolutionaries, led by Toussaint L'Ouverture, who were fighting to overthrow French rule in Haiti. The secretary of state knew that without the sugar island of which Haiti was a part, Napoleon would not need Louisiana as a granary. The French finally captured Toussaint. But his followers fought on, and their successes—together with malaria, which devastated the French troops—led Napoleon to blurt out in frustration in early 1803, "Damn sugar, damn coffee, damn colonies."

Second, Jefferson used his Indian policy to pressure the French. Having long hoped to "civilize" the Native Americans, Jefferson suddenly ordered the removal of tribes into the trans-Mississippi region. This order forced Napoleon to worry about them, while turning the Midwest into a secure all-white base from which Jefferson could attack New Orleans. The greatest historian of the Jeffersonian era, Henry Adams, graphically summarized the effect on the Native Americans: "No acid ever worked more mechanically on a vegetable fibre than the white man acted on the Indian. As the line of American settlements approached, the nearest Indian tribes withered away."[30] Some tribes, however, finally fought bitterly in 1810–1811 before retreating.

Third, the president obtained authority from Congress to build 15 gunboats and raise 80,000 men for an assault on the lower Mississippi. Napoleon learned of this in early April 1803, just as he was pondering the failure of a large French force to sail to the New World because a late winter had frozen over European ports. Since Jefferson had sent James Monroe and Edward Livingston to purchase New Orleans and the Floridas for $10 million, they were in Paris (where Livingston was the U.S. minister) when Napoleon decided to unload all of his mainland holdings. About to start the war against Great Britain once more, he needed freedom from New World malaria, slave revolts, and possible war with the United States, as well as the money the sale would bring. He asked, and Jefferson finally agreed to pay, $15 million for all of Louisiana. Luck had helped give Jefferson and Madison the opportunity, but they had seized upon it to double the size of the United States.[31]

But the crisis was not over. Nothing in the Constitution provided for such an acquisition. When Louisiana developed into numerous new states, the balance of political power and the nature of American society could be radically changed. Federalists in New England were especially fearful. "We rush like a comet into infinite space," proclaimed Fisher Ames of Massachusetts. "Our country is too big for union, too sordid for patriotism, too democratic for liberty." Ames and other Federalists began planning to pull New England out of the Union. They apparently received encouragement from, of all people, Aaron Burr, vice-president of the United States. By 1803–1804, Burr and Jefferson had become bitter political enemies. The Ames Federalists, however, remained a small, if dangerous, minority. More representative was his-

The Louisiana Purchase of 1803 doubled the size of the United States and later provided thirteen of the fifty states. The map also shows exploration that led to further settlement and expansion. When Napoleon sold the territory and was told that the boundaries were vague, he observed, correctly, that he supposed the Americans would make the most of vague territorial claims.

torian David Ramsay's oration of 1804 on the theme "What territory can be too large for a people, who multiply with such unequalled rapidity?"[32]

With that kind of support, Jefferson construed the Constitution liberally and assumed the United States could acquire and rule large new areas. He received backing from Gouverneur Morris, who had written a draft of the Constitution for the convention's debates in 1787. Morris pointed to Article IV, Section 3: "New States may be admitted . . . into this Union. . . . The Congress shall have Power to dispose of and make all needful Rules and Regulations respecting the Territory or other

Property belonging to the United States." In 1803, Morris added, "I always thought that when we should acquire Canada and Louisiana it would be proper to govern them as provinces and allow them no voice in our Councils."[33] Jefferson followed Morris's advice. He had little hope that the Indians, French, Spaniards, Creoles, and runaway Americans who had fled to New Orleans (often to escape a U.S. jail) were capable of self-government. Consequently, he obtained legislation that allowed him to rule Louisiana as a virtual dictator until it was peopled by responsible Anglo-Saxons. Meanwhile, order and security were to be maintained through force, if necessary.[34]

Thus, strong national power secured Louisiana. But arguments over who was to exert this power did lead to civil war in 1861, although not in the way Ames had envisioned. Meanwhile, Jefferson and Madison so disregarded Federalist fears that from 1804 to 1806 they tried through diplomacy, bribery, and covert pressures to pry the Floridas out of Spanish hands. These efforts stalled, especially as the two men suddenly faced a major conflict with the British Empire on the Atlantic sea lanes.

THE SECOND WAR FOR INDEPENDENCE AND UNION

In 1805, prospering U.S. trade with both warring nations, Great Britain and France, came under attack from British author Sir James Stephen, who, in his *War in Disguise; or, The Frauds of the Neutral Flags*, argued that England should use its naval superiority to stop U.S. trade that aided Napoleon. That same year, British courts issued the *Essex* decision. It declared illegal and subject to seizure those U.S. ships that picked up goods in the French West Indies, off-loaded them briefly in the United States so that they would appear to be American goods, and then carried them to France. As the British began seizing U.S. ships, Napoleon retaliated by announcing a blockade of Great Britain, a blockade he could not enforce. Any ship entering European ports after stops in England, he declared, would be seized.

After "fattening upon the follies" of the Old World, as Jefferson had phrased it, Americans were becoming victims trapped between the two European giants. In a brilliant pamphlet of 1806, Madison attacked the new British regulations and warned that "all history" proved that war results from "commercial rivalships" of nations. He and Jefferson tried to counter not with military force, but with a Nonimportation Act of 1806 that threatened to exclude imports, especially British, until the Europeans promised to respect U.S. neutral rights. In compiling the list of excluded goods, however, the two men made a frightening discovery: Americans were more dependent on British textiles, iron, and steel than the British were on American goods. Jefferson believed that he could not afford to exclude those badly needed products. U.S. economic power was turning out to be quite different than Paine, Madison, and others had assumed it would be.

While he delayed putting the Nonimportation Act into effect, Jefferson confronted a more immediate problem. Great Britain had intensified its impressment searches of deserters from its fleet. Tens of thousands of British sailors had escaped from the poor pay, unspeakable food and conditions, and brutality (lashings were frequent) at a moment when England was locked into a battle to the death with Napoleon. A large number—perhaps as many as eight out of every ten men seized—were Americans who were then impressed into the dangers of British service. In June 1807, a British warship, the *Leopard*, boarded the U.S. ship *Chesapeake* just ten miles off Chesapeake Bay, killed three Americans, wounded eighteen, then carried off four men, of whom only one was a British citizen. Americans demanded revenge. At this moment, Jefferson could have taken a near-united nation into war against Great Britain. He realized, however, his relative military weakness and believed that economic pressure could force the British to behave. In November 1807, London announced orders in council tightening control over neutral shipping. Napoleon responded with a similar decree affecting ships dealing with the British.

When the president raised the possibility of war, his able secretary of the Treasury Albert Gallatin warned that the British could "land at Annapolis, march to [Washington]," and return to England before Jefferson could even raise a militia to fight. Meanwhile, as Federalist senator John Quincy Adams noted, the British orders struck "at the very root of our independence."[35] Jefferson finally responded with an Embargo Act that closed U.S. ports and made exports illegal. Unintentionally, the president helped the British, who could handle their own commerce, by cutting off French trade. He also infuriated American merchants and producers of exports, whose survival depended on trade. When smuggling intensified, Jefferson made arbitrary arrests and seizures of goods. As historian Burton Spivak argues, Jefferson faced a terrible choice between his belief in democratic ideals and his belief in the commercial destiny of Americans.[36] The president's political party as well as his ideals were threatened. In 1808, Madison won the Executive Mansion, but the Federalists, using the embargo as a whip against him, tripled their 1804 electoral vote.

Leaving office in early 1809, Jefferson proudly told his successor that, with Louisiana and after Florida, Cuba, and Canada were annexed, the United States would be "such an empire for liberty as [the world] has never surveyed since the creation; and I am persuaded no constitution was ever before so well calculated as ours for extensive empire and self-government."[37] Both his vision and his confidence in the Constitution, however, were to be tested in the next five years.

Jefferson, under strong congressional pressure, was forced to end the embargo as he left office. Congress replaced it with the Nonintercourse Act of 1809 that prohibited both British and French ships and goods from U.S. ports but pledged to restore normal commerce with any country that repealed its restrictions on American trade. When this measure brought no good result, Congress, in 1810, passed Macon's Bill Number 2, which reopened U.S. ports to all peaceful commerce but promised commercial nonintercourse against one country (for example, Great Britain), if the other (France) repealed its anti-U.S. trade laws. It was a law heaven-sent to a manipulator like Napoleon. He declared the restrictions lifted, then added conditions that meant that they were not lifted at all. A desperate, if suspicious, Madison foolishly accepted the emperor's assurance and cut off trade with England in early 1811. The British were furious, Madison humiliated, once Napoleon's scheme became clear. U.S. economic pressures were not working.

As early as 1809, the president had wondered whether war might be the only real alternative; by 1811, it was his firm conviction. He was not alone. The South and West were emerging from a severe three-year economic depression caused, in the view of the brilliant young South Carolina congressman John Calhoun, not by Madison's actions, but by "foreign injustice" committed by the British, who aimed to enslave Americans again into a "colonial state." The sharp decline of southern cotton exports from 93 million pounds in 1809 to 62 million pounds in 1811 allowed Calhoun to conclude that if the British continued to control U.S. trade, "the independence of this nation is lost. . . . This is the second struggle for our liberty."[38] The young Speaker of the House of Representatives in 1811–1812, Henry Clay of Kentucky, loudly agreed. Born in Virginia, trained in the law as well as in the dueling ritual and the gambling and drinking halls of frontier Kentucky, the tall, dynamic thirty-four-year-old Clay was rightly described by one political oppo-

Henry Clay (1777–1852) was born in Virginia and became a plantation owner in Kentucky. A power in the House of Representatives (1811–1825), he led the war hawks into the War of 1812. Later, as a U.S. senator, he championed commercial expansion and, as "the Great Pacificator," helped craft the compromises of 1820 and 1850 that temporarily preserved the Union from the strain of expansionism.

nent as "bold, aspiring, presumptuous, with a rough overbearing eloquence."[39] Running the House with a firm hand and working closely with Madison, Clay and Calhoun led a group of "War Hawks" elected in 1810 who were determined to force the British to behave.

Their determination turned to fury when news arrived in Washington during late November 1811 that a battle with Indians at Tippecanoe in Indiana territory resulted in the deaths of sixty-eight white men, including some well known to Clay and other war hawks. Evidence also arrived that the British had incited the Indians.[40] War hawks wore black armbands and charged London with "inciting the savages to murder." In truth, territorial governor William Henry Harrison's sharp practices had cheated the Native Americans of most of Indiana for a few dollars. Led by two great leaders, Tecumseh (a statesman and orator who preached that all land belonged to all Indians) and his brother Tenskwatawa the Prophet, the Native Americans had warned Harrison that they wanted no part of the white man's version of private property. "Sell a country!" Tecumseh exclaimed. "Why not sell the air, the clouds and the great sea, as well as the earth? Did not the Great Spirit make them all for the use of his children?"[41] Tecumseh hoped to avoid war—at least until he organized tribes as far south as Florida. But when Harrison marched close to the Prophet's town, the Winnebago tribe attacked. Suffering fewer casualties than Harrison's forces, the Native Americans nevertheless retreated, meanwhile scalping isolated white settlers on the way.

The war hawks and Madison prepared for battle. The president took the opportunity to order a secret operation to seize West Florida from

Tecumseh (1768–1813), a Shawnee leader who tried to stop the expansionism of the whites by allying Indian tribes from the Great Lakes to Florida. When the War of 1812 erupted, he fought with the British and was killed at the Battle of the Thames in Canada during the autumn of 1813.

the Spanish. He organized a coup, after which the plotters asked for U.S. annexation. The president nicely reasoned that the seizure was necessary to prevent the British from taking the area first. West Florida formally became a part of the Union in 1811. Madison then tried to repeat the operation in East Florida. That attempt, however, became an embarrassment when his secret agents botched the scheme. The president and Congress nevertheless declared in 1811 that henceforth they would not tolerate the transfer of New World territory owned by a foreign power to another foreign country. This "nontransfer principle" later became a part of the Monroe Doctrine.

Madison next named fellow Virginian James Monroe, who had close ties with the West, to replace Robert Smith as secretary of state. Smith, a Marylander, came from a mercantile group that hated Madison's economic policies. Moving toward war, the president then proposed to build a larger navy. But that measure lost 62 to 59 in the House. Clay and Calhoun voted for it, but every westerner except Clay voted "nay" on the grounds that the bill would, in the words of a Kentucky journal, "give an overwhelming influence to the commercial interest" in eastern cities. It was an odd way to prepare for war against the world's greatest naval power. The West, however, along with Madison and Jefferson, thought that the war would actually be decided beyond the Appalachians, especially in an invasion of Canada.

On June 1, 1812, Madison sent his war message to Congress. He charged the British with impressment, spilling "American blood" within American territory (a reference to the *Chesapeake* affair), "pretended blockades" and orders in council that allowed the British to have "plundered" U.S. shipping, and the "warfare just renewed by the savages" in the West. In reality, since 1807, the British had seized only 389 U.S. ships, while Napoleon had taken at least 460. But those numbers did not move Madison. The British threatened U.S. interests globally because of their naval power, their avowed competition for markets in such newly opening areas as Latin America (a region now breaking away from Spain), and their ties to the Native Americans. The House voted for war 79 to 49, the Senate 19 to 13. Voting was along party lines. The pro-war vote stretched through all geographical sections, including the coastal cities, whose merchants worked closely with British mercantile interests. Some of these merchants apparently preferred war to continued halfway measures such as embargoes. (Moreover, once war began, many of them grew rich smuggling and supplying British forces.) There can be no doubt, however, that, in the words of historian Ronald Hatzenbuehler, it was Madison, Monroe, and Clay who were "primarily responsible for directing war preparations."[42]

In July 1812, Americans were stunned to learn that on June 16 the British had repealed their orders in council. An economic depression, demands from British merchants, and a change in government in London led to the repeal. Historians have since speculated whether, if a transatlantic telegraph had existed in 1812 to speed the news of the repeal, the war would have been avoided. Probably not, for the impressment and Indian issues remained. The opportunity to conquer Canada was irresistible. Madison refused to reconsider the war declaration. Since 1789, he had determined to free U.S. commerce from British control. Now he had a chance to do it.

FROM NEAR-CATASTROPHE TO NEAR-VICTORY

No sane American hoped for victory on the high seas (the British fleet had three fighting *ships* for every U.S. *cannon*).[43] Instead, Madison hoped to take advantage of Great Britain's preoccupation with Napoleon and believed that Canada could be seized as a hostage (as well as turned into a future U.S. state).

However, when U.S. forces drove into Canada, they were met by determined resistance—which included many Loyalists who had left the United States during the Revolution—and suffered a series of humiliating defeats. Tecumseh, in late 1812, seized the opportunity to unite tribes and join the British to capture both Detroit and an entire

THE WAR OF 1812:
Major Northern Campaigns

⟵ American forces   ⟵ British forces

✸ Battle site

LAKE SUPERIOR

Ft. Michilimakinac

LAKE HURON

LAKE MICHIGAN

MICHIGAN
TERRITORY

York
(Toronto)

CANADA

Quebec

Montreal

Plattsburgh
Lake
Champlain

VT.

N.H.

LAKE ONTARIO

BROCK, JULY 1812

Ft. Niagara
Queenstown Heights
RENSSELAER
OCT. 1812

N.Y.

MASS.

CONN.

Ft. Dearborn

Detroit

The Thames

LAKE ERIE

Presque Isle
(Erie)

PERRY,
SEPT. 1813

Put-in-Bay

HULL, AUG. 1812

HARRISON, OCT. 1813

Maumee

INDIANA
TERRITORY

Wabash R.

OHIO

Ohio R.

PENN.

Pittsburgh

Susquehanna R.

N.J.

Hudson R.

BRITISH BLOCKADE

KY.

MD.

Ft. McHenry

Washington, D.C.

Baltimore

DEL.

Potomac R.

Chesapeake
Bay

VIRGINIA

ROSS,
AUG. 1814

St. Lawrence R.

0   200 Miles
0   200 Kilometers

MISSOURI
TERRITORY

TENN.

Huntsville

JACKSON
1813

MISSISSIPPI

Tuscaloosa

TERRITORY

Horseshoe
Bend

GA.

Alabama R.

1814

Ft. Mims

JACKSON, 1814

Mobile

Pensacola

Perdido R.

FLORIDA
(Spanish)

Mississippi R.

LOUISIANA

New Orleans

PAKENHAM, 1814

GULF OF MEXICO

THE WAR OF 1812: Major Southern Campaigns

⟵ American forces   ✸ Battle site
⟵ British forces

0   100 Miles
0   100 Kilometers

*The War of 1812, which the United States lost on land but finally battled the
British to a draw because of U.S. victories on the lakes and rivers.*

American army. The Potawatomi tribe took the occasion to massacre everyone at Fort Dearborn (now Chicago). William Henry Harrison finally killed Tecumseh in 1813 after a series of brilliant U.S. naval victories on the Great Lakes sealed off British aid and isolated the Indian leader. Harrison held the Old Northwest, but Canada could not be conquered.

In the South, General Andrew Jackson of Tennessee, aided by Cherokees, defeated Creek Indians (the "Red Sticks") and then dictated a peace that opened much of Alabama to whites. Jackson was suddenly a national hero. He soon became a household word in January 1815, when his troops squashed a British invasion at the Battle of New Orleans. That triumph helped propel Jackson to the White House in 1828, although it occurred two weeks after the peace treaty was signed in Europe.

Otherwise, the war was notable because it nearly destroyed the new constitutional government. British ships controlled the coast. Their troops landed in Washington, burned the city in 1814, and forced James and Dolley Madison to escape into the hills across the Potomac River. Even Calhoun was dispirited: "Our executive officers are most incompetent men. . . . We are literally boren [*sic*] down under the effects of errors and mismanagement."[44] New England's (especially Boston's) merchants openly traded with, and loaned money to, Great Britain. In late 1814, some of these New Englanders met at Hartford, Connecticut, and threatened to leave the Union unless constitutional amendments gave them veto power over such issues as commercial questions and the admission of new western states into the Union. Only the peace treaty negotiated at Ghent, Belgium, in late 1814 ended this threat of possible secession.

Actually, within two weeks after war began, Madison had sought peace talks. By late 1813, the British were ready to deal: the wars with Napoleon seemed to be ending, so impressment could be stopped. London military officials had no stomach for dispatching the huge, costly force and fighting the long war required to conquer the United States. Sharp changes in Europe's diplomatic situation demanded British attention as well. As historian Donald Hickey summarizes, the British wanted peace because "of the lack of military progress in America [especially on the Great Lakes], unfavorable diplomatic developments in Europe, and domestic discontent over taxes."[45] The distinguished U.S. diplomatic team consisted of Henry Clay, John Quincy Adams, and Albert Gallatin (Jefferson's brilliant former secretary of the Treasury, who spent much of his time keeping peace between the ram-

As part of their major land offensive, the British landed in Maryland in August 1814, then marched on and burned the capital at Washington, D.C. President and Dolley Madison fled the city, and then a tornado hit the capital to complete the destruction. The British were finally beaten at Baltimore, and peace terms were signed in December 1814.

bunctious Clay and the dour Adams). They stopped a British demand for the annexation of Maine and parts of New York. The two sides then worked out the Treaty of Ghent (or the Peace of Christmas Eve). Both countries simply accepted the prewar territorial boundaries. Nothing was included about neutral rights.

Given the disastrous military situation around Washington and the disastrous political situation in New England, the United States won a remarkable diplomatic victory. The War of 1812 would be remembered less for Madison's embarrassed rush from a burning capital than for producing "The Star Spangled Banner," Uncle Sam (an actual person who provided supplies to beleaguered U.S. troops), and Jackson's postwar triumph at New Orleans. Because of the end of the Napoleonic Wars in Europe, impressment and orders in council no longer troubled relations. Hartford Federalists and their demands evaporated in the warm light of peace.

But it had been a brush with tragedy. The Jay Treaty, the X Y Z affair, the Alien and Sedition Acts, New England's anger over political power moving toward Louisiana, and Hartford's last-gasp attempt to remain within the rich British trading system even if it meant leaving the American one—all had threatened to destroy the Union. The nation had survived—if barely—and Americans were free for the first time since their independence forty years before to turn west and seize the incredible opportunities of a continental empire. It was to be a turn, however, that again nearly destroyed their Union in civil war.

NOTES

1. Merrill Jensen, *The New Nation* (New York, 1950), pp. 88–92.
2. Edmund S. Morgan, "The American Revolution Considered as an Intellectual Movement," in *Paths of American Thought*, ed. Morton White and A. M. Schlesinger (Boston, 1963), pp. 32–33.
3. Richard B. Morris, *Seven Who Shaped Our Destiny* (New York, 1973), p. 1; Arthur M. Schlesinger, Jr., *The Imperial Presidency* (Boston, 1973), p. 15.
4. Bradford Perkins, *From Sea to Sea, 1776–1865*, in *The Cambridge History of U.S. Foreign Relations*, ed. Warren Cohen (New York, 1993), ch. III.
5. Rowland A. Berthoff, *An Unsettled People* (New York, 1971), pp. 136–137.
6. U.S. Bureau of the Census, *Historical Statistics of the United States: Colonial Times to 1957* (Washington, D.C., 1960), p. 547.
7. Reginald Horsman, "American Indian Policy and the Origins of Manifest Destiny," *University of Birmingham Historical Journal* 11, no. 2 (1968): 131–134.
8. Joyce Appleby, "Commercial Farming and the 'Agrarian Myth' in the Early Republic," *Journal of American History* 68 (March 1982): 840–841.
9. See Howard Kushner's review of N. N. Bashkina *et al.*, *The United States and Russia* in *Journal of American History* 68 (June 1981): 125; Irby C. Nichols, Jr., "The Russian Ukase and the Monroe Doctrine: A Re-evaluation," *Pacific Historical Review* 36 (February 1967): 13–26.
10. Bradford Perkins, *The First Rapprochement: England and the United States, 1795–1805* (Philadelphia, 1955), p. 24.
11. Saul Padover, *Jefferson* (New York, 1942), p. 182.
12. *Washington Post*, 22 February 1985, p. E1; Marcus Cunliffe, *George Washington, Man and Monument* (Boston, 1958), p. 129.
13. Arthur B. Darling, *Our Rising Empire, 1763–1803* (New Haven, 1940), p. 130.
14. Irving Brant, *James Madison*, 6 vols. (Indianapolis, 1944–1961), III, pp. 246–254.
15. William P. Cresson, *James Monroe* (Chapel Hill, N.C., 1946), pp. 120–121.
16. J. Fred Rippy and Angie Debo, *The Historical Background of the American Policy of Isolation* (Northampton, Mass., 1924), pp. 148–149.
17. Brant, III, pp. 375, 382.
18. Joseph E. Charles, *The Origins of the American Party System* (New York, 1961), p. 85.

19. *Ibid.*, p. 113.
20. Burton I. Kaufman, "Washington's Farewell Address: A Statement of Empire," in *Washington's Farewell Address: The View from the Twentieth Century*, ed. Burton I. Kaufman (Chicago, 1969), a fine selection; Victor Hugo Paltsits's *Washington's Farewell Address* (New York, 1935) remains the best study that includes the various drafts.
21. The quote and an analysis are in Samuel Flagg Bemis, "The Farewell Address: A Foreign Policy of Independence," *American Historical Review* 39 (January 1934): 267.
22. Alfred Kazin, "In Washington," *New York Review of Books*, 29 May 1986, pp. 11–12.
23. Thomas Jefferson to Nathaniel Niles, 22 March 1801, in *The Writings of Jefferson*, ed. Paul Leicester Ford, 10 vols. (New York, 1892–1899), IX, p. 221.
24. William Stinchcombe, *The XYZ Affair* (Westport, Conn., 1980), p. 129; Albert Jay Nock, *Jefferson* (Washington, D.C., 1926), pp. 237–239; Perkins, *From Sea to Sea*, ch. IV.
25. Thomas Jefferson to James Monroe, 24 November 1801, in *The Writings of Thomas Jefferson*, ed. Andrew A. Libscomb, 20 vols. (Washington, D.C., 1903), X, p. 296.
26. Thomas Jefferson to William Short, 3 October 1801, in *The Writings*, ed. Ford, VIII, p. 98.
27. Good discussions of Jefferson's use of presidential powers are Abraham D. Sofaer, *War, Foreign Affairs, and Constitutional Power: The Origins* (Cambridge, Mass., 1976), pp. 167–227, and Robert M. Johnstone, Jr., *Jefferson and the Presidency* (Ithaca, N.Y., 1978); on Madison's role, Richard E. Ellis, *The Jeffersonian Crisis* (New York, 1971), pp. 236–237.
28. An interesting post-1979 perspective is Forrest McDonald, "The Hostage Crisis of 1803," *Washington Post*, 20 May 1980, p. A19; also Reginald Horsman, *The Diplomacy of the New Republic, 1776–1815* (Arlington Heights, Ill., 1986), pp. 84–86.
29. James Madison to Thomas Pinckney, 27 November 1802, in *The Writings of James Madison*, ed. Gaillard Hunt, 9 vols. (New York, 1901), VI, p. 462.
30. Henry Adams, *History of the United States during the Administrations of Jefferson and Madison*, 9 vols. (New York, 1889–1891), VI, 69.
31. The best account is Alexander DeConde, *This Affair of Louisiana* (New York, 1976); see also E. Wilson Lyon, *Louisiana in French Diplomacy, 1759–1804* (Norman, Okla., 1934), pp. 195–202; James Madison to Edward Livingston, 18 January 1803, in *The Writings*, ed. Hunt, VII, p. 7.
32. William H. Goetzmann, *When the Eagle Screamed* (New York, 1966), p. 9; Julian P. Boyd, "Thomas Jefferson's 'Empire of Liberty,'" *Virginia Quarterly Review* 24 (Autumn 1948): 553.
33. Drew McCoy, *The Elusive Republic* (Chapel Hill, N.C., 1980), p. 203; Gouverneur Morris to Robert Livingston, 4 December 1803, quoted in *Congressional Record*, 55th Cong., 3d sess., 19 December 1898, p. 294.
34. James Madison to Robert R. Livingston, 31 January 1804, in *The Writings*, ed. Hunt, VII, pp. 114–116. Jefferson's constitutional problems set historical precedents and are examined in Walter LaFeber, "An Expansionist's Dilemma," *Constitution* 5 (Fall 1993):5–13.
35. Gilbert Chinard, *Thomas Jefferson . . .* (Boston, 1926), pp. 420–421.
36. Bradford Perkins, *Prologue to War: England and the United States, 1805–1812* (Berkeley, 1961), p. 77; Paul A. Varg, *Foreign Policies of the Founding Fathers* (East Lansing,

Mich., 1963), pp. 190–192; Burton Spivak's *Jefferson's English Crisis* (Charlottesville, Va., 1984) is a fine analysis.

37. Boyd's "Thomas Jefferson's 'Empire of Liberty' " gives the context.

38. John Calhoun's reply to John Randolph, 12 December 1811 and defense of 29 November, House Foreign Affairs Report, in *John Calhoun, Papers*, ed. Robert L. Meriwether (Columbia, S.C., 1959–), I, p. 83; Perkins, pp. 434–435; U.S. Bureau of the Census, *Historical Statistics of the United States . . .* , p. 547. Madison's aggressive policies were pushed by a small but powerful group labeled "the militants of 1809" by Reginald C. Stuart in his important article "James Madison and the Militants," *Diplomatic History* 6 (Spring 1982): 145–167.

39. Edmund Quincy, *Life of Josiah Quincy* (Boston, 1868), p. 255.

40. Henry Clay to ____, 18 June 1812, in *The Papers of Henry Clay*, ed. James F. Hopkins (Lexington, Ky., 1959–), I, p. 674.

41. Angie Debo, *A History of the Indians of the United States* (Norman, Okla., 1970), pp. 90–93.

42. Ronald L. Hatzenbuehler, "The War Hawks and the Question of Congressional Leadership in 1812," *Pacific Historical Review* 45 (February 1976): 1–22; the best book-length study on the subject is now J. C. A. Stagg, *Mr. Madison's War . . .* (Princeton, 1983).

43. Brant, VI, p. 39.

44. John Calhoun to Dr. James MacBride, 25 December 1812, in *Papers*, ed. Meriwether, I, p. 146.

45. Donald R. Hickey, "American Trade Restrictions during the War of 1812," *Journal of American History* 68 (December 1981): 517–538.

For Further Reading

In addition to the notes to this chapter, most of whose references are not repeated here, consult the General Bibliography at the end of this volume. For pre-1981 materials, one must examine *Guide to American Foreign Relations since 1700*, ed. Richard Dean Burns (1983). The best recent overview with excellent bibliography is Bradford Perkins, *From Sea to Sea, 1776–1865*, in *The Cambridge History of U.S. Foreign Relations*, ed. Warren Cohen (1993). A brilliant examination of the context is *Capitalism and a New Social Order: The Republican Vision of the 1790s* by Joyce Appleby (1984), especially important for commercial policies. Other accounts examining the framework of the era are *The American and European Revolutions, 1776–1848*, ed. Jaroslaw Pelenski (1980), conference papers on comparative aspects; Peggy K. Liss, *Atlantic Empires: The Network of Trade and Revolution 1713–1826* (1983), key on post-1800 Western Hemisphere relationships; Javier Cuenca Esteban, "Trends and Cycles in U.S. Trade with Spain and the Spanish Empire, 1790–1819," *Journal of Economic History* 44 (June 1984); Daniel C. Lang, *Foreign Policy in the Early Republic: The Law of Nations and the Balance of Power* (1986); Dorothy V. Jones, *License for Empire* (1982), beautifully arguing that post-1776 Indian policy was a form of "containment"; Reginald Horsman, *Race and Manifest Destiny: The Origins of American Racial Anglo-Saxonism* (1981), indispensable; Ralph Ketcham, *Presidents above Party: The First American Presidency, 1789–1829* (1984); and Steven Watts's superb *The Republic Reborn . . . 1790–1820* (1987).

For the 1790s specifically, a succinct treatment is Frank T. Reuter, *Trials and Triumphs: George Washington's Foreign Policy* (1982); Jacob E. Cooke's biography, *Alexander Hamilton* (1982); Paul D. Nelson, *Anthony Wayne: Soldier of the Early Republic* (1985), on both the military and Indian campaigns. Lawrence Kaplan is a leading scholar of the era, as is demonstrated in his *"Entangling Alliances with None": American Foreign Policy in the Age of Jefferson* (1987); and a useful essay is Burton Spivak, "Thomas Jefferson . . . ," in *Traditions and Values: American Diplomacy, 1790–1865*, ed. Norman Graebner (1985), as is Spencer C. Tucker, "Mr. Jefferson's Gunboat Navy," *American Neptune* 43 (April 1983). A new overview is Robert W. Tucker and David C. Hendrickson, *Empire of Liberty: The Statecraft of Thomas Jefferson* (1990). And for the most colorful—and dangerous—opponent to Jefferson, see *Political Correspondence and Public Papers of Aaron Burr*, ed. Mary-Jo Ryan and Joanne Wood Ryan, 2 vols. (1983). The 1807 debacle is examined in several centuries of context in Richard J. Ellings's *Embargoes and World Power* (1985), while Clifford L. Egan's *Neither Peace nor War; Franco-American Relations, 1803–1812* (1983) provides important counterpoint; J. C. A. Stagg, *Mr. Madison's War* (1983), superbly examines Canada and the West Indian trade as causes of the 1812 war, but within the entire 1783–1830 framework; Ronald L. Hatzenbuehler and Robert L. Ivie, *Congress Declares War* (1983), skillfully dissects congressional voting behavior; Robert Rutland, "James Madison . . . ," in *Traditions and Values*, ed. Graebner, is by a leading scholar who is also the lead editor of *The Papers of James Madison, Presidential Series* (1984–　); C. Edward Skeen, *John Armstrong, Jr., 1758–1843* (1981), has important material on French diplomacy and the mismanagement of the 1812 war; Lawrence D. Cress, *Citizens in Arms* (1982), has written a superb social history of the 1812 conflict. An excellent account of expansionism is *Astoria and Empire* by James P. Ronda (1990), on the U.S.-British rivalry on the Pacific to 1812. For extensive recent sources, consult Dwight L. Smith *The War of 1812: An Annotated Bibliography* (1985).

3

The First, the Last: John Quincy Adams and the Monroe Doctrine (1815–1828)

WINDMILLS, CLIPPER SHIPS, AND GOOD FEELINGS

Soon after the peace of 1814, Lord Castlereagh, the British foreign minister, shrewdly observed that Americans won their wars not on the battlefield but "in the bedchamber." He could have made much the same observation about how Americans won much of the North American continent between 1815 and 1850. Freed of European quarrels for the first time in their history, Americans burst westward. Sixteen states existed in 1800, but there were twenty-four by 1824. As early as 1820, as many people lived in the new states formed after 1789 as had inhabited the original thirteen states before the Revolution. These new states formed the springboard for the drive across the continent.

The doubling of the population every twenty to twenty-five years fueled the search for new land, as did basic changes in the economy. Since their early history, Americans had prospered from the carrying and re-export trade—that is, carrying anyone's goods (not just American products) in the efficient ships that worked out of such ports as Salem, Boston, New York, Philadelphia, Alexandria, and Charleston. The profits had grown so fat in carrying British goods worldwide that between 1807 and 1814 some New England merchants cooperated more with London's laws than with Jefferson's and Madison's wishes. After 1815, these merchants began to disappear. With peace, British ships were free to carry British goods.

The U.S. merchant, moreover, found a more profitable investment in a new home-grown industrial complex. That complex remained in its infancy until the Civil War, but a major first step was taken in 1813–1815 when a group of wealthy merchants established the Waltham textile works. For the first time, this factory efficiently brought under one roof the various processes of spinning and weaving. Waltham's profits soon demonstrated that Americans could begin to compete with British manufacturers. But that success came much later. Between 1815 and 1819, the British dumped so many goods on the United States that Americans suffered a severe economic panic in 1819. New Englanders demanded a tariff wall to protect them from the dumping. By 1820, about $50 million was invested in U.S. manufacturing. (By 1860, that figure was to amount to $1 billion.)

These twists and turns of the 1815-to-1820 economy bankrupted many Americans, who then moved west to find their fortune. The country seemed to be in perpetual motion as people flooded over the Appalachians and the Mississippi. A German visitor wondered how Americans could survive while acting as if they were always "tied to the wing of a windmill." Events occurred so rapidly, he said, that "ten years in America are like a century in Spain."[1] One of those broken by the 1819 panic was Moses Austin, an Illinois lead miner. Austin decided to start anew by leading a small band of Americans into Mexico's province of Texas. Thus began the U.S. conquest of the region. Other victims of the economy turned farther west to search out land and trading opportunities in Oregon, although the 1837 depression sent the major flood of settlers into the Northwest. By 1825, American geography texts showed Texas already having closer ties with the United States than with Mexico. By 1834, a widely used geography primer already showed Texas, California, and Oregon as parts of the United States, even though they were not to be annexed for a decade or more.[2]

Not that everyone moving west had given up on the carrying trade. Indeed, the U.S. merchant fleet was entering its greatest era. These years ushered in the period of the magnificent Yankee clipper ship, admired on the world's oceans. As early as 1820, U.S. consuls watched over American interests in such exotic spots as French Mauritius, Java, the Philippines, and Hawaii. Treaties to protect Americans were signed in the 1820s with Tahiti and Hawaii. In the 1830s, the first official U.S. diplomat to Asia, Edmund Roberts, sailed west to the Far East and made treaties with Siam (later Thailand) and Zanzibar.[3] The U.S. ships that explored these corners of the globe carried not British (or French) goods, but American exports. They also transported to Europe the cotton and tobacco grown on the South's slave plantations. Cotton allowed Americans to dominate European markets and obtain the capital needed to buy new lands and build needed roads and canals. Between 1815 and 1860, cotton accounted for more than half the value of all U.S. exports. Its importance began to slide after 1840, when western grain crops started to capture foreign markets.[4] But by then, the system was fixed: the Northeast possessed much of the nation's capital, ships, and manufacturing, while the South was wedded to cotton and the slave labor that produced it.

Thus, precisely at the moment U.S. landed expansion accelerated westward, two systems—a northern free-labor industrial and commercial complex, and a southern slave-agricultural complex—began to struggle over which system would control the course of the nation's foreign policy. The struggle demonstrated again how domestic developments molded foreign policy, and how foreign policy, in turn, influenced the everyday lives of Americans—until the Civil War that the foreign policy helped bring about took 600,000 of those lives.

That horror was in the future. Between 1815 and 1825, optimism, not fear, guided U.S. expansion. For example, in an 1824 cabinet meeting, President James Monroe declared that he was afraid that the distant Oregon settlements would become a separate nation. Instantly, his secretary of state, John Quincy Adams, and secretary of war, John Calhoun, disagreed. Although Adams hated slavery and Calhoun justified it, both fully agreed, in Adams's words, that the Constitution's federal system "would be found practicable upon a territory as extensive as this continent."[5] Oregon might be three thousand miles away and claimed by the Russian and British empires, but these men had no doubt about the future. The nation was entering the 1815-to-1860 era of "manifest destiny"—that is, the belief that God had created North America for exactly the kind of white farmers and merchants that the American settlers happened to be.

They had such confidence despite (or was it because of?) the virtual disappearance of political parties by 1820. As the Federalists committed political suicide at the 1814 Hartford Convention, James Monroe managed to establish one major party, the Jeffersonian Democrat-Republican, that removed much of the two-party competition. The nation headed into the so-called "era of good feelings." The name was most misleading. Even if formal political-party competition had disappeared, factions and individuals attacked each other so bitterly inside Monroe's cabinet and in Congress that at times the government came to a halt. Monroe nevertheless bragged that with his one general party

John Quincy Adams (1767–1848) became the nation's greatest secretary of state because of his vast experience (minister to Russia, the Netherlands, and Prussia, as well as U.S. senator from Massachusetts), education, intelligence, and sense of history. He was also possessed by a discipline and an intensity that clearly appear in this photograph.

in control, the nation's government had "approached . . . perfection; that in respect to it we have no essential improvement to make."[6] Such beliefs also generated confidence in their manifest destiny as Americans moved west and across the oceans. The "era of good feelings" also made possible virtual miracles: the re-election of Monroe in 1820 to a second term with only one electoral vote opposing him, and—more significantly—the rise to power of John Quincy Adams.

Adams

The years 1816 to 1824 marked one of the most successful eras in American diplomatic history. Without doubt, John Quincy Adams remains the nation's greatest secretary of state because of his accomplishments during those years.

No one was ever better trained to guide the nation's foreign policy.

Born in 1767, he was the son of two of the most talented Americans, Abigail and John Adams. At the age of eleven, he traveled with his father to Europe and in his teens served as secretary to the first U.S. mission to Russia. Meanwhile, he mastered five languages, French literature, ancient as well as modern history, European and American theater, and began to learn the often-fatal intricacies of Europe's power politics. From both his father and mother, he inherited a strong American nationalism, intense suspicion of British politics, and stern Calvinist discipline. The nationalism appeared when he won election from Massachusetts to the U.S. Senate in 1802, after returning from serving as U.S. minister to the Netherlands and Berlin. Although representing a strong Federalist state, Adams supported Jefferson's and Madison's purchase of Louisiana and the embargo. For such political treason, the Federalists threw Adams out of office. Madison named him minister to Russia in 1809. In St. Petersburg, his dislike of Great Britain was not hidden. As an English observer vividly described Adams in 1812:

> Of all the men whom it was ever my lot to accost and to waste civilities upon, [Adams] was the most doggedly and systematically repulsive. With a vinegar aspect, cotton in his leathern ears, and hatred to England in his heart, he sat in the frivolous assemblies of Petersburg like a bull-dog among spaniels; and many were the times that I drew monosyllables and grim smiles from him and tried in vain to mitigate his venom.[7]

Adams's view of England was not in doubt, but his personality was more complex than this observer wanted to admit. Adams loved parties and was an expert on wines. He also loved the theater, so much so that at age fourteen he decided he must leave actresses alone if he were to discipline himself to be a statesman. In 1795, he had such a fine time in London that he wrote in his diary, "There is something so fascinating in the women I meet in this country that it is not well for me. I am obliged immediately to leave it."[8] At age thirty, he married the talented Louisa Catherine Johnson. Her spouse's dedication to protecting U.S. interests carried her into a special kind of hell. She suffered twelve pregnancies, with eight ending in miscarriages, as she followed her husband throughout Europe and the United States. Louisa buried their only daughter in Russia, where her husband took the family without consulting his wife.[9] One son later committed suicide.

Throughout, John Quincy Adams never doubted his country's destiny. In a cabinet meeting, one of Monroe's advisers declared that Americans must not be so openly ambitious, because the British were criticizing U.S. expansionism. Adams shot back that nothing should be done: "Nothing we could say or do would remove this impression until the world shall be familiarized with the idea of considering our proper dominion to be the continent of North America." It would only be a matter of time before the "law of nature" led to the annexation of Spain's holdings in the south, and Canada in the north. Until Europeans understood "that the United States and North America are identical," the secretary of state lectured the cabinet, any denial of U.S. ambition "will have no other effect than to convince them that we add to our ambition hypocrisy."[10]

He could utter such spread-eagle, manifest-destiny statements, but Adams never believed that Americans would always be on God's side regardless of what they did. When he heard that naval hero Stephen Decatur had cried the famous words "Our country, right or wrong," Adams disagreed. "May our country be always successful," his version went, "but whether successful or otherwise always right. I disclaim as unsound all patriotism incompatible with the principles of eternal justice."[11] His faith in "eternal justice" was strong, although Adams's religious beliefs were complex. He did believe that the Creator worked according to fixed, scientific laws and that with discipline and education these laws could be discovered. Thus, Adams arose each morning at 5:00 A.M. to read the Bible for an hour in the belief that because God had especially blessed the United States, the proper course of U.S. foreign policy could be discovered by studying God's word.[12] And, thus, he wrote the historic and still used *Report on Weights and Measures* that provided scientific standards for the use of—and to tie together—the continent. Adams wrote the *Report* during his busiest days as secretary of state by arising an hour or two earlier each morning—that is, 3:00 A.M.

Adams studied diplomacy as carefully as he studied his science and Latin. He understood the first principle: the greatest threat to the United States came from the British, for they occupied Canada, could control the seas, and were moving to dominate the newly independent Latin American states that were breaking away from Spain. But there was a second principle: if the British could be contained in Canada, over the long run the American "multiplication table" and U.S. commercial ambition would occupy and control the rest of the continent and, perhaps, such choice Latin American areas as Cuba. The key to his policy was containment, a policy famous in dealing with the Soviet Union after World War II, but which Adams brilliantly created to block the British 125 years earlier. A third principle was his understanding that the Americans and British had certain common interests that he could exploit. Most important was London's interest in having the Spanish Empire break up so that London merchants could develop Latin American markets. The United States also wanted Spain out of the New World. Thus, Adams saw that the powerful British fleet would actually protect U.S. interests by keeping Spain and other Old World powers out of Latin America—without Americans having to pay for it. To reap such benefits, however, he understood that Great Britain and the United States had to be at peace. It was a well-conceived diplomatic strategy that soon gained historic victories.

SETTING THE STAGE

Adams helped ensure peace with Great Britain by overseeing two agreements, the first signed by Acting Secretary of State Richard Rush. The Rush-Bagot pact of 1817 was an executive agreement made between the U.S. and British governments that demilitarized the Great Lakes and helped prevent accidental clashes along the U.S.-Canadian border. Many Canadians were not pleased. Having been invaded twice by the United States within forty years, they preferred to keep their defenses fully armed. When they pulled their cannons off the Great Lakes, they nevertheless kept them aimed at the Americans. London officials, however, wanted no border outbreaks. They had enough problems in Europe and Latin America. Consequently, they sacrificed Canadian wishes to make a deal with the United States. It was not the last time they would sacrifice Canadian interests. The Rush-Bagot deal was historically important for another reason. Instead of submitting it to the Senate as a treaty that would require a two-thirds vote for ratification, Monroe put it into effect by merely announcing it to Congress in his annual message. The usual straight-arrow Monroe, however, knew he was stretching his constitutional powers, so he asked Congress whether the executive was constitutionally competent to put such a pact into effect. The Senate never gave a direct reply, but it did approve this "agreement" without voting on it as a treaty. Thus the major constitutional precedent was set that allowed presidents to make such agreements with other governments without asking for Senate ratification. By the mid-twentieth century, such "executive agreements" were to replace treaties as the most numerous form of agreements with other nations.[13]

A second historic pact with the British was the Convention of 1818.

Adams obtained the perpetual U.S. right to fish along the Newfoundland coast, settled outstanding disputes over slaves that the British had taken from southern states, and opened new opportunities for each nation in the other's commerce. More important, Adams established the forty-ninth parallel as the U.S.-Canadian boundary from Lake of the Woods to the Rockies. This boundary shut the British off from northern access to the Mississippi River. He thus unknowingly obtained most of the present states of Idaho, Montana, and North Dakota, as well as parts of the incredibly rich Mesabi iron-ore range that was to help create the U.S. steel industry sixty years later. Finally, and of equal importance, the convention provided that the disputed region of Oregon would remain "free and open" to both nations. Adams believed the provision would allow the American population explosion to seize Oregon peacefully.

He next tried to open the British West Indies to U.S. trade. After Adams threatened economic retaliation against London shipping, the British opened several ports. But Adams wanted more. He demanded that the British charge a U.S. ship no higher tariff than they charged their own vessels. That demand was too much. London officials closed the West Indies to teach Adams (now president) a lesson, and it was left to Adams's hated political opponent, Andrew Jackson, to use diplomatic politeness and regain access again in 1830.

The West Indies episode revealed Adams's belligerence and ambition. He assessed himself in 1817 as "a man of reserved, cold, austere, and forbidding manners; my political adversaries say a gloomy misanthropist, and my personal enemies, an unsocial savage." A friend was more complimentary: "Mr. Adams is in person short, thick, and fat . . . and neither very agreeable nor very repulsive. . . . He is regular in his habits, and moral and temperate in his life."[14] By 1821, Spanish officials doubtless thought Adams's own view was more accurate.

THE TRANSCONTINENTAL TREATY

With the British contained, Adams, in 1818, began negotiations to obtain East Florida from Spain. The Spanish Empire was gasping its last breath in most of Latin America, but its minister to Washington, Luís de Onís y Gonzalez, used every diplomatic trick he knew to stall the U.S. advance. "I have seen slippery diplomats . . . ," Adams complained, "but Onís is the first man I have ever met with who made it a point of honor to pass for more of a swindler than he was."[15]

Andrew Jackson (1767–1845) gave his name to an entire age (the Jacksonian Age of the 1820s to the 1850s) and, after becoming president in 1828, had a bitter personal feud with John Quincy Adams. But in 1818–1820, the two men were the perfect pair for American expansionism—General Jackson as the ruthless frontier fighter who seized key parts of Florida, Adams as the tough diplomat who parlayed Jackson's victory into a treaty that gave the United States not only Florida, but a continent.

In 1817–1818, drama in Florida radically changed the context of the Adams-Onís talks. Monroe had ordered General Andrew Jackson to the Florida border to stop attacks by the Seminole Indians on the advancing white settlements. Jackson, who was seldom moderate when dealing with Indians or the British, decided to attack the problem's root. He marched into East Florida, destroyed Indian villages, captured and promptly hanged two British citizens who he claimed were egging on the tribes against Americans, and took the region for the United States. Monroe and most of his cabinet were horrified. Hanging British citizens could cause the second burning of Washington in just five years. Adams alone defended Jackson. The secretary of state argued that London would not retaliate because the two British subjects were in the wrong. Besides, England wanted no war with the United States. Adams wrote a blistering public paper condemning the two victims and the Seminoles. As historian Richard Drinnon notes, the paper "was a virtuoso performance that added luster and reach to the theme of merciless savages and outside agitators."[16] Adams carried the day. The cabinet decided to support Jackson, who had become, after all, enormously popular for killing Englishmen and Indians at New Orleans and now East Florida.

Adams put it to Onís directly: if Spain did not give up Florida immediately, "Spain would not have the possession of Florida to give us." The British had refused to move against Jackson. The Spanish were isolated. The secretary of state now demanded more. Negotiating the 1818 convention had reopened Adams's long interest in Oregon and the Pacific coast. He asked for Spain's claims to that region. Onís

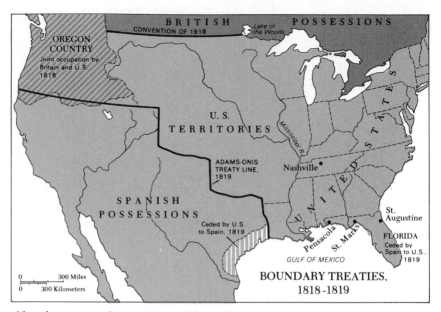

After three years of negotiations, Adams obtained a treaty continental in scope but whose boundaries turned out to be vague—so vague that Americans could later use them in the Texas region to make further landed claims.

responded by asking for Adams's promise not to recognize the Latin American nations that were rebelling against Spain, and for the U.S. recognition that Spain owned Texas. Adams flatly refused to make the promise. He also objected to giving up rights to Texas; but on this issue, the Monroe cabinet overruled him. Thus, the deal was struck: Spain turned over Florida and its rights to the Pacific coast in return for the United States dropping certain monetary claims against Spain and recognizing Spanish claims to Texas. For virtually no money and the surrender of no actual U.S. interest, Adams obtained all of Florida and the first U.S. formal rights to the Pacific coast. When the Senate finally ratified the Transcontinental Treaty in 1821, Adams bragged in his diary that he had first proposed the Pacific-coast part of the pact and had almost single-handedly carried the talks through to victory. The treaty, he observed, "forms a great epocha in our history."[17]

OPENING "A GREAT TRAGIC VOLUME"—AND JULY 4, 1821

It was ominous that at the same moment Adams was expanding the United States to the Caribbean in the south and to the Pacific in the west, he and the country suddenly had to confront the deadly issue of slavery. Adams quickly understood that it was the issue that could destroy the Union he was creating.

The struggle began in 1819, when Missouri applied for admission to the nation as a slave state. Northerners responded by proposing to exclude slavery from all the former Louisiana Purchase Territory, of which Missouri was a part. Southerners condemned the proposal for bottling up their own expansion of cotton lands. The slave system depended on continual expansion, not least because without the possibility of shipping young slaves west, southerners in the older states could find themselves (as one warned) "dammed up in a land of slaves." Congressional business stalled as the debate grew bitter. Adams initially paid little attention to it, but he came to see that slavery threatened the future of U.S. foreign policy. He had always believed that God intended Americans to rule all of North America as a land of freedom, but by 1820 he concluded, "The greatest danger of this Union was the overgrown extent of its territory, combining with the slavery question." Even Adams now wanted neither Texas nor Florida unless slavery was excluded from them. He understood earlier than most that

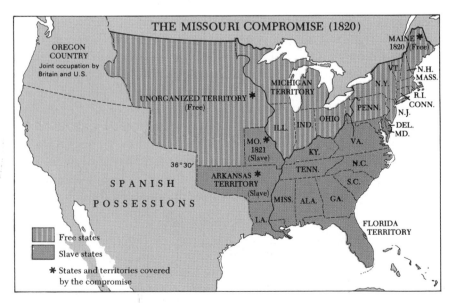

The furor and sectional bitterness that led to the great debate of 1819–1820 were not quieted by the 1820 Missouri Compromise, but only blunted until further expansion in the 1840s resurrected the issue of slave expansionism and led to the Civil War.

American expansion could no longer be discussed without having to decide whether slave or free states would benefit from expansion. In this respect, he confided to his diary, the Missouri debate "is a mere preamble—a title-page to a great tragic volume."[18] In 1820, Congress struck a compromise: Missouri entered as a slave state, Maine a free state—thus maintaining the balance—and slavery was prohibited in northern Louisiana Territory but allowed in the southern. Adams doubted that the compromise would settle the problem.

For the first time, Adams began seriously to wonder whether God was blessing or condemning the United States. He began rethinking his nation's and his own ambitions. Adams wanted quiet and no more debates over slavery. He certainly wanted no wars for conquest to the south that could enlarge slave territory and increase the power of the South. Adams's views clashed with those of Henry Clay, the powerful Kentucky senator who was openly challenging Adams and Jackson for the presidency in 1824. Clay pushed to recognize the new Latin American nations, regardless of relations with Spain. The Kentuckian even urged helping the revolutionaries "by all means short of actual war." Adams condemned immediate recognition. It could destroy his deal with Onís. He believed, moreover, that the United States had little in common with the monarchical Roman Catholic governments appearing to the south. Adams had no illusion they were following the example of 1776. The great South American liberator, Simón Bolívar, actually agreed with Adams. Bolívar admired how North Americans made their "weak and complicated" Constitution work. But he thought that applying the political, civil, and religious system of the "English-American" to the "Spanish-American" was an impossibility.[19]

Adams was especially afraid that any U.S. involvement, even in supposed wars for liberty and independence, could destroy the United States. In an address on July 4, 1821, Adams answered Clay by warning—in words that would be repeatedly quoted 150 years later by those opposing the U.S. war in Vietnam—about certain American commitments:

> Wherever the standard of freedom and independence has been or shall be unfurled, there will her [the United States'] heart, her benedictions, and her prayers be. But she goes not abroad in search of monsters to destroy. She is the well-wisher to the freedom and independence of all. She is the champion and vindicator only of her own. . . . She well knows that by once enlisting under other banners than her own, were they even the banners of foreign independence, she would involve herself beyond the power of extrication, in all the wars of interest and intrigue, of individual avarice,

envy, and ambition, which assume the colors and usurp the standard of freedom. The fundamental maxims of her policy would insensibly change from *liberty* to *force*. . . . She might become the dictatress of the world. She would no longer be the ruler of her own spirit.[20]

Adams continued to oppose recognition of new Latin American nations, but in 1822 Monroe overruled him. The president wanted to reap the economic benefits of recognizing the new governments before the British. Adams gave in but made it clear that the United States recognized only governments that controlled their country and that promised to respect that country's international obligations (such as protecting U.S. citizens). No moral approval, he emphasized, was involved. Adams's recognition policy (which followed Jefferson's policy set in 1793) was followed by all future presidents until Woodrow Wilson changed it nearly ninety years later.

THE MONROE DOCTRINE

In his annual message to Congress in December 1823, Monroe climaxed six years of successful foreign policy by announcing a historic set of principles. Later (after 1844) called "the Monroe Doctrine," the message was largely shaped by Adams. It summarized the secretary of state's containment policy in the Western Hemisphere. The message told Europeans to stay out of American developments, thus leaving the United States as potentially the strongest power in the hemisphere. Moreover, as Adams had long since realized, a delicious part of the policy was that the British, for their own interests, would actually keep other Europeans out of the New World while the United States developed its own strength.

The belief that the Americas were for Americans had deep roots. It at least went back to Paine's *Common Sense* (see p. 19). But more immediate events triggered the 1823 declaration. One was the rapid development of U.S. trade with Latin America that gave Washington officials good reason for preventing the reconquest of South America by Spain or her European friends, especially France and Russia. U.S. exports to Latin America rose from $6.7 million in 1816 to nearly $8 million in 1821, despite a slump caused by the 1819 economic panic. Latin America took 13 percent of U.S. exports, and if the Spanish could be kept out—and British economic competition cut out—the Southern

Hemisphere promised to be a rich market for North American producers.

In 1821, the problem of possible European intervention moved closer to home. The Russian tsar, Alexander I, notified the world that in order to protect his claims stretching from the Aleutians and Alaska down to San Francisco, all land north of 51 degrees latitude would be sealed off, and no non-Russian ship was to be allowed within 100 miles of the northwest coasts. The tsar thus directly excluded both U.S. claims to parts of the Northwest that Adams obtained from Spain, and the right of American merchants to trade in the vast region. The United States and Great Britain protested. Adams bluntly told the Russians in July 1823 that "the American continents are no longer subjects for *any* new European colonial establishments."[21] Nor would the secretary of state recognize the 100-mile limit. He passionately believed that U.S. merchants should be able to buy and sell wherever they wished. Adams condemned European colonialism not only because it politically sealed off pieces of land, but also because it closed down trade. He had already told the British government in late 1822 of his feelings about these central issues: "The whole system of modern colonization is an abuse of government and it is time that it should come to an end." He had aimed that barrage specifically against London's claim to Oregon.

These problems of trade and Russian-British ambitions arose in an explosive political atmosphere. In 1821, the Greeks had revolted against the brutalities of Turkish control. Americans jumped to the conclusion that it was 1776 again. They raised thousands of dollars (especially among idealistic college students who knew their Greek), and such names as Syracuse and Athens came into vogue as city names. Monroe searched for a way to help the Greeks but was cut short by Adams, who warned that it was a European quarrel over which the United States had no control. When Adams received a request for a personal contribution to help Greece, he flatly refused. Not only would such a contribution break U.S. neutrality, he replied, but "we had objects of distress to relieve at home more than sufficient to absorb all my capacities of contribution."[22] He was practicing what he had preached in his July 4, 1821, address.

The shrewd British foreign secretary, George Canning, carefully watched Adams's performance. Although he disliked being lectured about his country's colonialism, Canning understood that U.S. and British interests coincided. Both nations wanted Spain, France, and Russia out of the New World. British merchants were busily profiting from trade with the newly independent Latin Americans. Canning,

James Monroe (1758–1831), although president between 1817 and 1825, was not so much the author of the Monroe Doctrine (1823) as was his secretary of state, John Quincy Adams. But Monroe had been an early and a successful U.S. diplomat himself. The Virginian had helped negotiate the Louisiana Purchase while serving in Paris during 1803 and was Madison's secretary of state between 1811 and 1817 as well as secretary of war part of that time.

moreover, wanted the Quadruple Alliance, led by the tsar and including other European monarchies who opposed British foreign policies, to gain no dramatic victory by restoring Latin America to Spain. He, therefore, sent a most attractive offer to Adams: the United States could make a joint announcement with the world's greatest power, Great Britain, that no more colonial rule would be allowed in Latin America. Both nations would then show their own good faith by promising to take no more territory in the region.

Flattered, Monroe asked Jefferson and Madison for advice. Both former presidents recommended accepting Canning's offer. Adams, however, single-handedly stopped the move for the joint declaration. He saw that the second part of the deal (a mutual promise to take no more territory) would prevent the United States from someday annexing Texas and Cuba. He had no doubt that both areas were to become parts of his country, although not necessarily through armed conquest. As he instructed the U.S. minister to Spain in April 1823:

> There are laws of political as well of physical gravitation; and if an apple severed by the tempest from its native tree cannot choose but fall to the ground, Cuba, forcibly disjoined from its own unnatural connection with Spain, and incapable of self-support, can gravitate only towards the North American Union, which by the same law of nature cannot cast her off from its bosom.[23]

Nature's will, the secretary of state argued, must not be blocked by the pledge suggested by Canning. Adams, moreover, had long argued that any such deal was unnecessary because the British would keep out other Europeans anyway. Nor did he want to join the British so openly against Russia. It was in the U.S. interest to play off those two European powers in the Northwest, to neutralize both, and then to move in itself. Adams thus convinced Monroe to announce the policy by himself and maintain complete freedom of action: "It would be more candid, as well as more dignified . . . , than to come in as a cock-boat in the wake of the British man-of-war."[24]

In his annual address to Congress on December 2, 1823, the president announced the Monroe Doctrine's substance in three principles. First, he reviewed the exchanges with the tsar, exchanges which had been friendly. The Russians were willing to discuss their claims in the Northwest. Making no threats, Monroe issued the noncolonization principle that Adams had carefully crafted: "The American continents . . . are henceforth not to be considered as subjects for future colonization by any European powers." Historian Edward Crapol has discovered a letter of 1831 in which Adams stated that this principle was aimed not only at Russia, but was "a warning to Great Britain herself."[25] All the Europeans were to be contained—then expelled.

Next, Monroe discussed the Greek crisis, then used it to introduce the doctrine's second principle: the so-called two-spheres policy. But in declaring that the affairs of the Old and New Worlds should not become entangled (or what some historians have called a policy of "isolationism"), Monroe carefully chose his words: "In the wars of the European powers in matters relating to themselves we have never taken any part, nor does it comport with our policy to do so." The president— note—did not say that the United States would remain out of all foreign quarrels, only those involving "matters relating" solely to Europeans. He and Adams fully understood that as a budding world power, U.S. interests might have to become involved in European quarrels— as in 1812–1814.

Third, Monroe announced a general hands-off policy: "We should consider any attempt on [the Europeans'] part to extend their system to any portion of this hemisphere as dangerous to our peace and safety." The president quickly added that "with the existing colonies or dependencies of any European power we have not interfered and shall not interfere." But no further European expansion or influence could be tolerated. These phrases were directed against Spanish and French hopes of restoring Spain's influence in Latin America, but they could also be applied to British activities in the Northwest.

Although supposedly aimed at the Russians, the Spanish, and the

French, Adams's policies, in historian Ernest May's phrase, were "particularly hard on the British."[26] London officials posed the greatest threat to the United States, especially to continued American landed and commercial expansion. Monroe's 1823 message took that expansion for granted—indeed, it was viewed as a requirement for the country's survival. In a rephrase of Madison's argument in *The Federalist* Numbers 10 and 14 (see p. 34), Monroe recounted proudly the American population explosion and the creation of new states:

> It is manifest that by enlarging the basis of our system and increasing the number of States the system itself has been greatly strengthened in both its branches. Consolidation [that is, centralized government] and disunion have thereby been rendered equally impracticable. Each government [the states and the national], confiding in its own strength, has less to apprehend from the other.[27]

Adams must have read those words with mixed emotions. He fully understood after the Missouri Compromise debate of 1820 that continued expansion might not render disunion "impracticable," but instead bring on fresh threats of disunion.

The Monroe Doctrine set up the ground rules for the great game of empire that was to be played in the New World. European colonization was to stop, European influence to be contained. The Old World and the New World were to be increasingly separated, unless U.S. interests forced it to become involved in Old World struggles. Especially notable was the Adams-Monroe view of Latin American revolution. The two officials did not praise it for being in the U.S. tradition, for it was not. They nevertheless refused to interfere in those revolutions, nor did the two men hope to guide the outbreaks (or, as Adams put it in his 1821 speech, to go abroad "in search of monsters to destroy"). Monroe demanded that Europe follow this example.

Meanwhile, the Latin Americans were to be on their own. When they soon made five direct requests to Washington for U.S. guarantees of their independence, the North Americans refused to act. France sent a fleet to make demands of Haiti, and in 1833 the British seized the Malvinas (Falkland Islands) over Argentina's protests, but the United States did nothing. The Monroe Doctrine's importance for North America was immediate, especially in the Northwest; but for Latin America, its impact was to be felt in the more distant future.

It had been a remarkable eight years in American foreign policy: settlement of explosive Canadian boundary questions, the containment of the world's greatest power, annexing Florida, the first claims to the Pacific coast, and the announcement of the Monroe Doctrine principles. If he had not been overruled by the president, Adams might also have successfully laid claim to Texas, and not only annexed another empire, but averted the Texas question that helped push the United States into civil war. Remarkably, Adams had accomplished all this with brains, not brawn, for the United States military power paled in comparison with the British. Historian William Earl Weeks has noted that "the gap between relative power and relative accomplishment is the true measure of statesmanship. Surely no other statesman in American history accomplished as much as Adams did with so little economic and military power."[28]

GREAT LOSERS: ADAMS THE PRESIDENT

During the 1817–1825 "era of good feelings," Adams acted without having to worry too much about an opposing political party sniping at him. But an absence of parties did not mean an absence of politics. Quite the contrary. Without the controls and understood procedures of a political-party system, politics turned individualistic and vicious. As historian Joel Silbey has argued, the American democratic system worked best when two strong institutional political parties competed against each other in that system, and worked worst when those parties were weak.[29] The Monroe administration proved Silbey's argument. While Adams conducted his brilliant, lone-wolf diplomacy, Monroe accomplished little at home. Nor could the president control the personal ambitions and hatreds that tore his administration apart. Adams was even accused (falsely) of appearing in church barefoot and tie-less.[30] (It was true, however, that the secretary of state regularly swam nude in the Potomac River.)

In this political confusion, Adams outmaneuvered three other opponents to win the presidency in 1824. Andrew Jackson obtained the largest number of popular votes, but because no candidate won a majority of electoral ballots the decision was thrown into the House of Representatives, as the Constitution provides. At a crucial moment, Henry Clay threw his support to Adams, who then triumphed. Clay's action was not unnatural: he disliked Jackson personally and agreed with Adams's strong nationalist program for creating roads, canals, and a higher tariff. The new president, however, then made Clay secretary of state. Jacksonians cried that they had been victimized by a "corrupt bargain." No such "bargain" has been documented by historians, but obviously Adams and Clay understood each other. The accusation, in any case, destroyed whatever chance the new president might have had to pass his political program or win re-election in 1828. Clay and Adams were ruthlessly attacked by the brilliant and eccentric John Randolph of Virginia, a long-time power in Congress. When Randolph called the two men a combination of "the puritan with the blackleg," Clay challenged him to a duel. In the famous encounter on the Virginia side of the Potomac in April 1826, Clay's second shot pierced Randolph's coat, while the Virginian fired in the air. (Critics claimed that Randolph took pains to wear an extra-large coat that day.) Randolph so hated Clay that when the Virginian died in 1833 he ordered that he be buried with his face to the West—so he could keep his eyes on Henry Clay.

With this kind of political dirt flying around him, Adams had little chance of realizing his great dream: uniting and developing the empire he had acquired as secretary of state. His presidency is important because it marked the last attempt by a chief executive to tie North and South together through a nationally supervised program of roads, tariffs, canals, and with such scientific projects as a national university, naval academy, and exploring expeditions. Adams saw what most failed to see: that the nation was sharply dividing along the lines of a free-labor, rapidly growing North and West that were commercial, wheat-growing, and increasingly industrial, and a slave South that was becoming locked into a one- or two-crop economy and could not keep up with the North's population gains. As he became president, however, Americans were fanning out across a continent, states were rewriting constitutions to decentralize and democratize their politics, and Jacksonians were accusing Adams of wanting to centralize power because "all Adamses are monarchists." Andrew Jackson rode this democratic wave into the presidency in 1828. Believing in the centralization of Madison, Hamilton, and John Adams, John Quincy Adams was, in this sense, the last important figure of the revolutionary generation. He was also largely isolated. Nor did his dislike of mass democracy and his lack of talent and sensitivity for public politics help him.

While he did uncomfortably live at the Executive Mansion, Adams's major foreign-policy problem arose in 1826, when delegates from newly independent Latin America planned to meet in Panama to discuss cooperation and mutual protection. They invited the United States to participate. At first, Adams was not enthusiastic. He feared the delegates wanted to involve the United States in their revolutions. When he was assured that the Panama congress planned to discuss other topics, the president agreed to send delegates, but only to work for more liberal trade, for an agreement to the noncolonization principle announced in the Monroe Doctrine, and—most interestingly—for the end of an "exclusive" (that is, Roman Catholic) church that he believed held back religious liberty. Secretary of State Clay, long an advocate of North-South cooperation, wanted to embody these principles in what he called "good neighborhood" treaties. The U.S. Congress, however, refused to appropriate money to send the two delegates. Southerners feared that Adams secretly planned to use the conference to oppose the slave trade and work with black revolutionaries in Haiti. Adams finally laid these worries to rest, but it was too late. While the debate roared on, one of the two delegates had died. The other never reached the meeting. The episode revealed not only the deep divisions between North and South America, but also within U.S. politics.[31]

In 1825–1827, Adams unsuccessfully attempted to acquire Texas. He believed that the area could be annexed as a free territory. Within ten years, as Texans became independent and slaveholding, Adams turned violently against any plans for annexation. In 1826, he also renewed the joint-occupation pledge with England in regard to Oregon territory. In doing so, he beat back proposals that would have surrendered U.S. claims to fine harbors in the present state of Washington. The renewal was Adams's only major achievement as president. The nation's greatest secretary of state, he was also one of its least successful presidents.

Defeated overwhelmingly in 1828, Adams despised his conqueror. When Adams's own alma mater gave Jackson an honorary degree in 1833, he refused to attend "to see my darling Harvard disgrace herself by conferring a Doctor's degree upon a barbarian and savage who could scarce spell his own name."[32] Adams at first decided to retire, "as much as a nun taking the veil." But he missed Washington and was determined to fight, alone if necessary, against the Jacksonians. Ralph Waldo Emerson caught him perfectly at this point: "He is no literary old gentleman, but a bruiser, and he loves the melee."[33] Elected by his home district in 1830, Adams spent the last seventeen years of his life in the House of Representatives fighting for the rights of free speech of antislave groups and working tirelessly against expansion of any slave territory. "Old Man Eloquent," as he was called, died on the floor of the House in 1848 as he attacked the U.S. attempt to conquer much of Mexico. He had long since concluded that because Jackson had defeated his national programs of 1825 to 1828, the Union was doomed to split between North and South.

Poet Walt Whitman wrote in 1848 that "John Quincy Adams was a virtuous man—a learned man—and had singularly enlarged diplomatic knowledge; but he was not a man of the People."[34] More than a century later, however, a superb historian of the era, Bradford Perkins, concluded that Adams's "new American generation vindicated the aspirations of their fathers in 1776."[35] No greater compliment could be paid to the statecraft of 1817 to 1828.

Notes

1. Marvin Meyers, *The Jacksonian Persuasion* (Stanford, 1957), pp. 122–127.
2. Laurence M. Hauptmann, "Westward the Course of Empire: Geography Schoolbooks and Manifest Destiny, 1783–1893," *The Historian* 40 (May 1978): 430–431.
3. William H. Goetzmann, *When the Eagle Screamed* (New York, 1966), pp. 95–96.
4. Douglass C. North, *Growth and Welfare in the American Past* (Englewood Cliffs, N.J., 1966), ch. VI.
5. *Memoirs of John Quincy Adams*, ed. Charles Francis Adams, 12 vols. (Philadelphia, 1874–1877), VI, pp. 250–251.
6. Richard Hofstadter, *The Idea of a Party System . . . 1780–1840* (Berkeley, 1969), pp. 192–197.
7. George Dangerfield, *The Era of Good Feelings* (New York, 1952), p. 7.
8. Samuel Flagg Bemis, *John Quincy Adams and the Foundations of American Foreign Policy* (New York, 1949), p. 8.
9. Jack Shepherd, *Cannibals of the Heart: A Personal Biography of Louisa Catherine and John Quincy Adams* (New York, 1981), is especially useful on this relationship.
10. *Memoirs of John Quincy Adams*, ed. Adams, IV, pp. 438–439.
11. John Quincy Adams to John Adams, 1 August 1816, in *The Writings of John Quincy Adams*, ed. Worthington C. Ford, 7 vols. (New York, 1913–1917), VI, p. 61.
12. Henry Adams, *The Degradation of the Democratic Dogma* (New York, 1919), pp. 28–31.
13. Frederick Merk, *The Oregon Question* (Cambridge, Mass., 1967), pp. 122–124; Bradford Perkins, *From Sea to Sea, 1776–1865*, in *The Cambridge History of U.S. Foreign Relations*, ed. Warren Cohen (New York, 1993), ch. III.
14. Quoted in *Writings of Adams*, ed. Ford, VI, p. 519n; Bemis, p. 253.
15. On Onís, 7 August 1821, in *Writings of Adams*, ed. Ford, VII, p. 167.
16. Richard Drinnon, *Facing West: The Metaphysics of Indian-Hating and Empire-Building* (Minneapolis, 1980), pp. 108–111.
17. *Memoirs of John Quincy Adams*, ed. Adams, IV, p. 275.
18. *Ibid.*, IV, pp. 502–503, 524–525, 530, 531; V, pp. 3–12, 68.
19. *Selected Writings of Bolívar, vol. I: 1810–1822*, ed. Harold A. Bierck, Jr. (New York, 1951), p. 179.
20. The text is in *John Quincy Adams and American Continental Empire*, ed. Walter LaFeber (Chicago, 1965), pp. 42–46. Italics in original.

21. *Memoirs of John Quincy Adams*, ed. Adams, VI, pp. 157, 163.
22. *Ibid.*, VI, pp. 324–325.
23. John Quincy Adams to Hugh Nelson, 28 April 1823, in *Writings of Adams*, ed. Ford, VII, pp. 372–373.
24. *Memoirs of John Quincy Adams*, ed. Adams, VI, p. 179.
25. Edward P. Crapol, "John Quincy Adams and the Monroe Doctrine: Some New Evidence," *Pacific Historical Review* 48 (August 1979): 414.
26. Ernest May, *The Making of the Monroe Doctrine* (Cambridge, Mass., 1975), pp. 181–182.
27. *A Compilation of the Messages and Papers of the Presidents, 1789–1897*, ed. James D. Richardson, 10 vols. (Washington, D.C., 1900), II, pp. 219–220.
28. William Earl Weeks, "New Directions in the Study of Early American Foreign Relations," *Diplomatic History* 17 (Winter 1993): 88–89; William Earl Weeks, *John Quincy Adams and American Global Empire* (Lexington, Ky., 1992), especially its discussion of the 1819–1821 treaty talks; Kenneth M. Coleman, "The Political Mythology of the Monroe Doctrine," in *Latin America, the United States and the Inter-American System*, ed. John D. Martz and Lars Schoultz (Boulder, Col., 1980), pp. 98–99. There is a good overview from the French perspective and an interesting thesis about the split between official and public opinion in Réne Rémond, *Les États-Unis devant l'opinion française, 1815–1852*, 2 vols. (Paris, 1962), II, pp. 606–611. For the quite different U.S. policy on the Malvinas in 1982, see p. 706.
29. Joel H. Silbey, *The Partisan Imperative* (New York, 1985 and 1987), especially chs. III and IV.
30. James Sterling Young, *The Washington Community* (New York, 1966), pp. 186–188, 236–238.
31. *Compilation of the Messages and Papers of the Presidents*, ed. Richardson, II, p. 319; an excellent survey is Andrew R. L. Clayton, "The Debate over the Panama Congress and the Origins of the Second American Party System," *The Historian* 47 (February 1985): 219–238; also Bemis, pp. 537–561.
32. Samuel Flagg Bemis, *John Quincy Adams and the Union* (New York, 1956), p. 250.
33. Gore Vidal, *Matters of Fact and of Fiction* (New York, 1979), p. 169.
34. Walt Whitman, *The People and John Quincy Adams* (Berkeley Heights, N.J., 1961), p. 17.
35. Bradford Perkins, *Castlereagh and Adams* (Berkeley, 1964), p. 347.

FOR FURTHER READING

Consult the notes to this chapter and the General Bibliography at the end of this book; most of those references are not repeated here. Most important, begin with *Guide to American Foreign Relations since 1700*, ed. Richard Dean Burns (1983), whose thoroughness in listing pre-1981 materials cannot be matched by any textbook.

In addition to the Weeks, Dangerfield, North, May, and—above all—Bemis and Perkins volumes listed in the notes, the following provide important interpretations and superb contexts for understanding this era of Adams: Ronald E. Seavoy, *The Origins of* the *American Business Corporation, 1784–1855* (1982), good on the interchange between economics and politics; the essays on the 1815-to-1861 era in William H. Becker and Samuel F. Wells, Jr., *Economics and World Power: An Assessment of American Diplomacy since 1789* (1984); Ralph Ketcham, *Presidents above Party* (1984), which discusses the political framework; and Peter D. Hall, *The Organization of American Culture, 1700–1900* (1982), which stresses how the northeastern elites maintained their power through the new corporation.

Harry Ammon, Monroe's leading biographer, summarizes his views in "James Monroe and the Persistence of Republican Virtue," in *Traditions and Values: American Diplomacy, 1790–1865*, ed. Norman Graebner (1985); and in the same volume Graebner analyzes "John Quincy Adams and the Federalist Tradition." The sad, sometimes comic, and most instructive story is told in Mary Hargreaves, *The Presidency of John Quincy Adams* (1985); while the key Latin American view is examined in David Bushnell, "Simon Bolívar and the United States: A Study in Ambivalence," *Air Force University Review* 37 (July–August 1986); and there is overlapping material on Adams's nemesis in John M. Belohlavek, *"Let the Eagle Soar!": The Foreign Policy of Andrew Jackson* (1985). Especially revealing is Vivien Green Fryd, *Art and Empire: The Politics of Ethnicity in the U.S. Capitol, 1815–1860* (1992).

4

The Amphibious Expansion of a Sixty-Five-Hundred-Thousand-Horsepower Steam Engine (1828–1850)

THE CONTEXT: MANIFEST DESTINY AND RAILROADS IN RUSSIA

During the 1830s, increasing numbers of Americans moved into Texas and Oregon. In the 1840s, these two areas plus one-third of Mexico were annexed to the United States. The nation's territory increased by more than 50 percent to about three million square miles. At the same time, the amphibious Americans, who were moving on sea as well as land, sealed their first formal trade and diplomatic agreements with China. Henry David Thoreau, the philosopher of Walden Pond, observed Americans spreading out over continents and ocean as if "we have the Saint Vitus dance." Half a century later, at the height of British power, Lord Salisbury advised students who wished to understand England's history to use very large maps. The same advice could have been given in the 1830s and 1840s to observers of American history.

These decades mark the zenith of U.S. Manifest Destiny. The term appeared, appropriately, in mid-1845, when a Democratic editor, John

L. O'Sullivan of New York, summarized the feelings of most Americans: any European attempt to prevent the U.S. annexation of Texas was an act against God, for opposition might check "the fulfillment of our manifest destiny to overspread the continent allotted by Providence for the free development of our yearly multiplying millions."[1] Two years later, Secretary of the Treasury Robert J. Walker explained both history and the American future by declaring in a government report that "a higher than any earthly power" had guided American expansion and "still guards and directs our destiny, impels us onward, and has selected our great and happy country as a model and ultimate centre of attraction for all the nations of the world."[2]

But there also existed a darker side to Manifest Destiny. O'Sullivan's newspaper, the *Democratic Review*, warned in 1848 that Americans had no choice: "A State must always be on the increase or the decrease," for this was "the law of movement."[3] Expand or die became the shadowy underside of American thinking, especially as the population continued to double each generation and as millions of immigrants—including those driven out in the late 1840s by Irish famine and German revolutions—flooded into American cities. The threat perhaps appeared most dangerous to the South's slaveholders. They demanded more land to replace worn-out soil in southeastern states, to provide more room for blacks who were outnumbering whites in the older states, and to increase representation in Congress so that the South could breathlessly try to keep up with rampaging northern growth. O'Sullivan himself, although from the North, ended his career by supporting the South's attempts to seize new lands in the Caribbean. He finally declared himself proslavery, claimed that in the Civil War the South fought for "American liberty," and urged American blacks to erect a monument to the first slave trader.[4]

O'Sullivan and the other Manifest Destiny faithful believed that God had given them a special sign of His favor in the 1830s and 1840s. At the moment the United States grew by half, it also began to experience a transportation and communication revolution. That revolution enabled Americans to tie their vast land together with links undreamed of just a generation earlier. If Americans believed in the supernatural aspect of Manifest Destiny, they could also trust in the hard realities—the iron and steel—that made Manifest Destiny possible. Editor Thomas Ritchie noted in 1847 that James Madison had believed that the United States, under the new Constitution, could expand indefinitely, but not even Madison understood how new inventions made expansion possible. The railroad, new ships, the "magnetic telegraph had not entered

into the dreams of the most enthusiastic philosophers." In 1844, just
five days after a telegraph sent the first message, its inventor, Samuel
F. B. Morse, received in Washington the news, via wireless from a
partner in Baltimore, that James K. Polk had received the Democrats'
presidential nomination. Polk's war with Mexico was the first American conflict covered by war correspondents. They used telegraph and
pony express to speed reports published in the new "penny press" that
quickly reached tens of millions of Americans.[5]

U.S. engineers even supervised 30,000 Russians building railroads
in the tsar's empire. In 1847, an overinspired author prophesied the
results when U.S. know-how encountered Europe's downtrodden:

> Who knows but in a few years the now Russian serf may stand a free man
> at his own cottage door, and as he beholds the locomotive fleeting past,
> will take off his cap . . . and bless God that the mechanics of Washington's
> land were permitted to scatter the seeds of social freedom in benighted
> Russia.[6]

Asa Whitney, who had made his fortune in the China trade, lobbied
in the 1840s for a transcontinental American railroad that would attain
two historic objectives at once: link together the sections of the United
States and enable U.S. producers to ship their products cheaply so that
they could capture Asian markets. The railroad, Whitney believed, would
"revolutionize the entire commerce of the world; placing us directly in
the centre of all." He preached that the American Empire need not go
the way of all past empires that were now dust: "They had not the
press, nor the compass, nor the steam-engine."[7] Whitney and other
believers, led by Democratic senator Stephen A. Douglas from Illinois,
soon obtained federal funds to build railways, but southerners—content with their waterways and fearful that the new iron horse would
most benefit northern merchants—prevented building the transcontinental railway system until they left the Union in 1861.

The pull of Manifest Destiny and new technology was so strong that,
O'Sullivan argued, Americans would never have to kill for conquest:
"It will never be the forcible subjugator of other countries."[8] Poet
Walt Whitman phrased it best as he caught the new power and confi-
dence of an expanding, industrializing America:

> While the foreign press . . . is pouring out ridicule on this Republic and
> her chosen ones—Yankeedoodledom is going ahead with the resistless
> energy of a sixty-five-hundred-thousand-horsepower steam engine! It is

carrying everything before it South and West, and may one day put the Canadas and Russian America in its fob pocket! Whether it does these things in a conventionally "genteel" style or not, isn't the thing: but that it will tenderly regard human life, property and rights, whatever step it takes, there is no doubt.[9]

John Winthrop's seventeenth-century dream of an American community of virtue was giving way to a fragmented, spread-out society that cared more about wealth than virtue and more for individual freedom than community. During this era, the acute French observer, Alexis de Tocqueville, studied America and coined the word "individualism" for the first time. Tocqueville feared that unless it were controlled, individualism would isolate Americans and lead to the destruction of their society and freedom.[10] The remarkable limited liability company, or the corporation, developed at this time. Many states happily issued charters to individuals, which gave them the right to raise money through public sale of stock to build railways, and telegraph and steamship lines.

Two forces tried to pull Americans back and keep them under some control. The first was a new political party system that grew from the grass roots in the 1820s and 1830s. It cut across state lines to bring Americans together.[11] The Democratic party of Jackson and Polk believed in a passive federal government that largely left the states and individuals to conduct their own affairs. The Democrats thus favored low tariffs, a decentralized Treasury system, and state-built internal improvements. In foreign policy, their party contained such ardent landed expansionists as Polk, Douglas, and Walker. It also included many who favored mercantile expansion, especially if it came at the expense of the British, whom the Democrats—notably the growing number of their Irish members—feared and despised. The Whig party leadership, on the other hand, tended to come from commercial, manufacturing, and wealthier slaveholding classes. These groups wanted government support as they tried to create an orderly, regulated society at home and to find more overseas markets. They worked for higher tariffs, and national banking and internal improvement systems. In foreign policy, Whigs lined up consistently against landed expansion. They were afraid that its inevitable warfare and unpredictability could pull apart American society. But they did favor mercantile expansion. Whigs feared any conflict with the British that might upset their trade routes.

Leading Whigs included Daniel Webster and Henry Clay. Webster embodied Whig foreign-policy principles in the 1840s. The political power of mercantile, industrializing Massachusetts, he also acted as the U.S. agent for the Baring Brothers banking house of London. The Barings financed much of the new U.S. merchant fleet and manufacturing complex. They had even lent the money for the Louisiana Purchase. Always in need of cash, Webster naturally wanted no wars with the British, nor did he and Clay want to lose the cotton markets and Whig votes in the South that might result from such a war. They led in forging political compromises, especially in 1850, that kept the Union together. Moreover, it was Webster who sent the historic U.S. mission to China in 1842–1844, which formally opened that country to Americans, and it was Webster who was responsible for opening Japan to the West in the 1850s. For all their caution, concern for pocketbook commercial issues, and desire for quiet, however, not even Whigs were immune to certain virulent forms of Manifest Destiny that were sweeping through the United States. They, like most Americans then and long after, strongly believed that Manifest Destiny would bring the blessings of American democracy to many other peoples. "Do we deceive ourselves," Webster proclaimed in 1832, "or is it true that at this moment that love of liberty and that understanding of its true principles which are flying over the whole earth, as on the wings of all the winds, are really and truly of American origin?"[12] Nature seemed to be spreading the "principles" of American democracy as nature's winds spread the smell of sweet blossoms.

Nature, however, received considerable help from an increasingly powerful presidency. The Jacksonian era's political system contributed much to the development of the modern presidency, especially as democracy spread and popular votes for the president gained importance over the old, elitist electoral-college system. Elections focused more and more on the presidential vote. A shrewd winner, in turn, could dominate both his party and Congress, especially on foreign-policy questions. Jackson and Polk, both masters of the new politics, became such powerful chief executives that they could ram through their foreign policies despite strong congressional opposition.

The U.S. system thus began to resemble an hourglass: large at the top with a strong presidency, large at the bottom with an expanding population and state powers, but narrow in the middle where congressional and federal powers were located. The question became whether that slim middle could hold the hourglass together, especially as expansionism and Manifest Destiny exerted tremendous pressure on the system.

Removing Native Americans

After the War of 1812, the government's policy toward the Indians changed for the worse. Jefferson had hoped that they could be turned into farmers and assimilated into white society. After 1815, Native Americans were not to be assimilated, but removed—if necessary, by force—to unwanted lands beyond the Mississippi. The warfare of 1811 to 1814 shaped the new policy, but so did the belief of Clay, Jackson, and others that Indians could not be "civilized." As Jackson declared in 1830, "What good man would prefer a country covered with forests and ranged by a few thousand savages to our extensive Republic, studded with cities, towns, and prosperous farms . . . , occupied by more than 12,000,000 happy people, and filled with all the blessings of liberty, civilization, and religion?"[13]

During the 1820s and 1830s, the five great Indian tribes in the South were forced to move westward. The Choctaws went into Oklahoma territory. After brief resistance, the Creeks' men were put in chains by Alabama forces and moved to Oklahoma with neither weapons nor cooking utensils. The Chickasaws moved out peacefully, but the Seminoles hid in the Florida Everglades until the U.S. Army used bloodhounds to track them down. Forty percent of the Seminole population died in that struggle and in the final march west.

Most notable was Cherokee resistance. The Cherokees lived, unluckily, in an area of Georgia where gold was discovered. In 1830, state authorities began evicting the Indians. Jackson fully supported Georgia. The Cherokees, however, took their case to the United States Supreme Court. In the famous *Cherokee Nation* decision of 1831, Chief Justice John Marshall ruled that an Indian tribe was not a "foreign state." But it was "a distinct political society," and tribes were "domestic dependent nations." The next year, the Court ruled that U.S. law and the Constitution, not state law, controlled Indian-white relations. Jackson, however, refused to carry out the decision. The president allegedly declared, "John Marshall has made his decision; now let him enforce it." Georgia, then the U.S. Army, arrested and sent the Indians on a terrifying forced march. One observer estimated that 4,000 of the 18,000 Cherokees forced out after 1835 died on the journey westward.[14]

In the North, the Native Americans were also driven across the Mississippi. After being cheated by a fraudulent treaty, the Sauk and Fox tribes fought back in the short-lived Black Hawk War of 1831–1832.

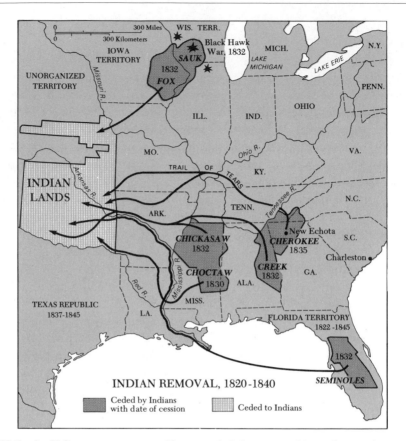

INDIAN REMOVAL, 1820-1840

Ceded by Indians with date of cession

Ceded to Indians

While the U.S. government steadily expanded the national boundaries after 1800, it also used force to remove large numbers of Native Americans from their lands. U.S. foreign policy and policy toward American Indians have been closely related.

That conflict is better remembered because of a young, nervous Illinois militiaman, Abraham Lincoln, who served patrol duty. Otherwise, the tribes moved out peacefully, if unwillingly. The removals confirmed the whites' view that the Indians were inferior, could be brutalized whenever necessary, and were not under the protection of the national government but were at the mercy of local authorities. These views could be transferred to other peoples. As the United States prepared to annex parts of Mexico, O'Sullivan's *Democratic Review* declared, "The Mexican race now see, in the fate of the aborigines of the north, their own inevitable destiny." The *New York Evening Post* neatly combined Manifest Destiny and Indian policy to justify the killing: "Providence has so ordained it. . . . The Mexicans are aboriginal

Indians, and they must share the destiny of their race."[15] The Indian removals and wars of the 1830s provided racial beliefs and battlefield experience that helped prepare Americans for their war of 1846–1848.

THE ROAD TO CHINA

American expansion moved on both land and sea. It thus reflected the needs of both agrarians who sought new lands, and producers (both agrarian and industrial) and merchants who required foreign markets. U.S. officials had to take such needs into account. Polk, for example, carefully tried to balance his policies for landed and overseas expansion. Often the two nicely meshed, as in the drive for Oregon and California. But above all, the history of the 1830s and 1840s shows how Americans thought of Asia not as the Far East (which was a British term), but the Far West, the natural extension of their movement across the continent.

The maritime wing of U.S. expansionism rapidly gained momentum in the 1830s. In 1832, growing U.S. trade with the western Pacific led Jackson to send Edmund Roberts to make commercial treaties with Siam, Southeast Asia, and Japan. Roberts succeeded in Siam and Muscat, but failed at Hue—not the last time U.S. diplomacy was to have problems in the area later known as Vietnam. He died before reaching Japan. In 1839, President Martin Van Buren played to mercantile interests by ordering Captain Charles Wilkes to explore the Pacific. Wilkes gave the nation its first claim to Antarctica (which he was the first also to recognize as a separate continent) and the strategic port of Pago Pago in Samoa. As historian Thomas McCormick observes, the Wilkes mission of 1839–1842 helped make the United States "the most knowledgeable power in the world as far as the great Pacific basin was concerned."[16]

Americans also staked out claims to the way station of Hawaii. U.S. traders and missionaries had been settling on the beautiful islands for more than a generation. The settlements created replicas of Protestant Boston society, even to the extent of restricting native and Roman Catholic religious practices. When British and Canadian claims threatened the newcomers, President John Tyler publicly warned in December 1842 that non–United States governments were to keep their hands off the islands. It marked the first time that Hawaii was brought under a Monroe Doctrine–type of policy.

The double column of U.S. traders and missionaries also marched into the much larger arena of China during these years. The United States had no formal treaties with the Chinese but instead depended on, and cooperated with, British power—even to the point of working with English traders to develop the highly profitable opium traffic. Chinese called the Americans "second chop Englishmen."[17] U.S. exports of furs, ginseng, and—of all things—ice chopped from ponds around Boston were exchanged for imports of tea, hides, and gunnysacks. Nevertheless, of the fifty-five foreign firms in the great trading city of Canton in 1836, only nine were American. U.S. businessmen had difficulty understanding the Orient's customs. In one story, an ignorant trader learned to his distress that he was eating not a "quack quack," but a "bow-wow-wow."[18] Even missionaries, who adjusted to strange ways better than most merchants, met major problems. Between 1814, when the first Chinese was baptized in a Protestant ceremony, and 1839, the dozen Protestant missions (of which seven were American) each averaged less than one convert per year.[19]

Missionaries and traders alike began to push for formal U.S. treaties so that they could better compete for their China markets. Then, between 1839 and 1842, the Chinese and British engaged in the Opium War. The conflict resulted from European demands for continued use of Canton as part of the rich, illegal opium trade. When the British won those rights in the 1842 Treaty of Nanking, they also seized Hong Kong, opened four other Chinese ports to the West, and assumed power over China's ability to fix tariff and customs rates. The Americans now realized that they had to win equal trading privileges on their own.

Their new interest in Asia also resulted from internal U.S. pressure. The intense economic depression of 1837–1841 severely struck merchants and New England–southern textile manufacturers. In 1842, President Tyler flatly declared that "the greatest evil which we have to encounter is a surplus of production beyond the home demand, which seeks, and with difficulty finds, a partial market in other regions."[20] The president's Whig administration, led by Secretary of State Daniel Webster, appointed Caleb Cushing as the first U.S. minister to China. Cushing came from an old Massachusetts merchant family. Tyler's quaint personal letter to the emperor of China began: "I hope your health is good. . . . The Chinese are numerous. You have millions and millions of subjects. . . . The Chinese love to trade with our people, and to sell them tea and silk, for which our people pay silver, and sometimes other articles. But if the Chinese and the Americans will trade, there should be rules."

Webster then laid down the rules. These were incorporated in the

1844 Treaty of Wangxia (i.e., Wanghia). The United States received most-favored-nation status in China's trade—that is, it automatically received any trade rights the Chinese gave others (such as the British). Americans also received extraterritorial rights, meaning that all U.S. citizens and their property were to be free of Chinese law and instead regulated and protected by U.S. officials and law. The British and Americans congratulated themselves for forcing extraterritoriality out of the Chinese. In truth, the practice had begun with medieval China's decision to let foreign "barbarians" and their queer ways stay to themselves so that they would not disturb the superior Chinese civilization.

Americans, ignorant of that nation's traditions and convinced of their own unselfish desire to help the Chinese, entered into a "special relationship." That relationship rested for the next century on most-favored-nation and extraterritorial privileges. Later in the nineteenth century, it would become known as the "open door" and would be defined in the 1890s by Secretary of State John Hay as "a fair field and no favor" for all the nations involved in trying to exploit the China market. The open-door policy attempted to protect China from European or Japanese colonization so all of it would be open to U.S. traders. Americans soon prided themselves as being the only anti-imperialists who dealt with the Middle Kingdom. The Chinese quickly sensed this misplaced self-satisfaction. They played off Americans against the other foreign nations in an attempt to keep all of them at bay.

U.S. trade developed well after the Treaty of Wangxia. So did the work of Roman Catholic and Protestant missionaries. They became interpreters for U.S. diplomats and merchants, the cutting edge of American influence that penetrated the nation's interior, and, in all, the eyes and ears through which most Americans saw and heard about China. The emperor continued to fight Christianity. The vast and bloody Taiping Rebellion of 1850–1864, in which perhaps as many as 20 million people died, was aimed at destroying foreign influences as well as the Manchu dynasty. But the missionaries remained. They soon justified the use of force to bring the Chinese to God. One popular book, *Hand of God in American History*, argued that "war is the sledgehammer of Providence" to open China to "the family of nations and the benign influence of Christianity."[21] Thus, when France and Great Britain made war on China in 1857–1858 to obtain new trade rights, Americans refused to join the conflict. In 1858, however, they signed with China the Treaty of Tianjin (i.e., Tientsin) that gave them the spoils won by the Europeans. Nearly all of China was opened to U.S. trade, the emperor finally accepted Western diplomats at his capital of

Beijing (i.e., Peking), and he now had to tolerate openly the work of the missionaries. The Wangxia and Tianjin treaties formed the legal and diplomatic base on which U.S.-China relations rested for the next ninety years.

TEXAS, MARIA CHILD, AND JAMES K. POLK

The Americans' movement into China between 1830 and 1860 coincided with their annexation of the immense Pacific-coast strip that stretched from Oregon territory to San Diego. China, like California and Oregon, formed part of the great westward movement that shaped and shook American society during the mid-nineteenth century. But it was the Texas question that triggered the U.S. seizure of the West Coast during the climactic years 1844 to 1848.

The three hundred American families led by Moses Austin into Texas during 1819–1821 had become 15,000 Americans by 1830. The Mexican province turned into another part of the American frontier as immigrants, lured by the possibility of obtaining 4,400 acres of land for a mere $200, flocked in to find their fortune. In addition to accepting Mexican citizenship, Mexico required the settlers to be Roman Catholic and have no slaves. The Americans ignored the last two rules. In 1830, Mexico City officials realized that Texas was being swamped by the multiplying Americans, some of whom ranked among the most uncontrollable gunslingers on the frontier. Santa Anna, who ruled Mexico, finally abolished all state legislatures, centralized power in Mexico City, and moved an army into Texas to control the settlers. Instead of obeying, the Texans replayed 1775–1776: they demanded full restoration of their rights, set up Committees of Correspondence to coordinate resistance, and finally, in 1836, declared their independence. Texas won a short, bloody war. The new government was helped by thousands of Americans who rushed in for glory, action, and land. Some of the emigrants died when the Texas garrison at the Alamo was wiped out in early 1836, but others helped win the pivotal battle of San Jacinto. Meanwhile, Stephen Austin, Moses' son, borrowed most of his funds from the United States to fight the war.

President Andrew Jackson soon recognized Texas independence. He wanted to annex the country, but he and his successor, Martin Van Buren, knew that the time was not ripe. Annexation could lead to an unpopular U.S. war with Mexico. Moreover, after the 1837 depression struck, Americans concentrated on their economic problems at home.

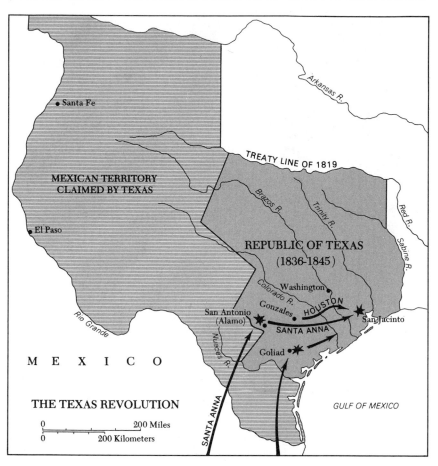

The Texas revolution of 1836 not only ended Mexico's rule of the region, but helped trigger the massive U.S. expansionism of the 1840s. Texas was independent between 1836 and 1845, when, amid bitter debate, it joined the Union as the twenty-eighth state.

Most important, any move to take Texas triggered a vicious debate within the United States. Annexation would mean that the South had a vast new area for slavery. John Quincy Adams led the opposition in Congress, but he enjoyed support from the rising antislave movement.

Anti-Texas voices reverberated throughout the North. None was clearer than Lydia Maria Child's. By the 1830s, this remarkable woman was a widely read novelist and publisher of the first children's magazine in the United States. She concluded that women's rights could be won only in a society that first repudiated black slavery. In 1833, she published *An Appeal in Favor of That Class of Americans Called Afri-*

Lydia Maria Child (1802–1880) was a pioneer in publishing and women's rights, then but made a special mark on U.S. diplomatic history as a vigorous opponent of American—especially slave—expansion.

cans, apparently the first book by a white American to call for immediate emancipation of the slaves. It also laid out the explosive argument that slaveowners controlled the U.S. government. The *Appeal* angered many of Child's readers and nearly bankrupted her. Child did not retreat. When the wife of a Virginia senator argued that southern women helped slave women, especially during childbirth, Child shot back that in the North, "after we have helped the mothers, *we do not sell the babies.*" In the words of historian Edward Crapol, "For more than forty years as writer, petitioner, organizer, pamphleteer, and editor, she fought slavery, sought racial and sexual equality, and decried [what she called] 'the insane rage for annexation in this country.' "[22] Child, Adams, and other antislave advocates stalled the Texas annexation movement until early 1844. Then, President Tyler and his new secretary of state, John Calhoun, pushed for a Senate vote on the issue. Calhoun publicly used proslavery arguments to justify annexation. Needing a two-thirds vote of approval, the treaty went down to an overwhelming 35-to-16 defeat in June 1844.

Within eleven months, however, the United States annexed Texas and was about to declare war on Mexico. The remarkable turnaround was brought about by James K. Polk. One of the most successful presidents in achieving his goals, especially in foreign policy, Polk is usually rated by historians as one of the half-dozen "great" presidents. Born in North Carolina in 1795, Polk soon moved to frontier Tennessee. When he was seventeen years old, Polk was strapped to a table, given a large amount of whiskey, and then suffered through a gallstone operation that broke his health. Unable to farm and fascinated by books, he went to the University of North Carolina, where he won honors in mathematics and classics. He studied law, entered politics, and was elected to the House of Representatives. Polk quickly made his reputation as a Jacksonian who opposed nearly everything John Quincy Adams stood for. The Tennessean attacked "consolidation" of government, ideas favoring national universities or internal improvements, "expensive and unnecessary foreign missions," and "European etiquette."[23] Polk showed little interest in political theory or history. Adams caustically remarked that Polk had "no wit, no literature . . . , no philosophy," but Adams had to grant that Polk possessed immense determination and will. He also was blessed with uncommon political instinct. His ability as an open-air orator won him the title "Napoleon of the stump." In 1839, he became governor of Tennessee. In 1841 and 1843, however, he was defeated in the governor's race. But in 1844, he was elected president of the United States.

That this first "dark horse" candidate in American history won the presidency owed much to Texas and the power of Manifest Destiny. As the Texas issue heated up in early 1844, the two leading presidential candidates, Democrat Martin Van Buren of New York and Whig Henry Clay of Kentucky, publicly declared they did not want to annex Texas. Both preferred the issue to die down so that they could discuss less dangerous, but politically attractive, issues such as tariff and banks. Polk, however, came out for annexation. Already close to Andrew Jackson, who, with his dying breath, now worked to take Texas, Polk won support from powerful politicians in the South and West who wanted a spread-eagle foreign policy. These operators manipulated the Democratic nominating convention's rules and, when it deadlocked,

James K. Polk (1795–1849) of Tennessee (shown in an early daguerrotype by Mathew Brady) is often considered one of the strongest of all presidents. Polk added more land to the nation than any president except Jefferson. But the Tennessean also presided over a disintegrating political party system that had helped hold the Union together, and his foreign policy was a cause of the Civil War.

pushed Polk forward as a compromise candidate. The nominee's platform called for strict construction of the Constitution, but also "the reoccupation of Oregon and the re-annexation of Texas at the earliest
practicable period." (The "re-" prefixes alluded to the Democrats'
mistaken claim that John Quincy Adams had happily given away U.S.
claims to Texas and Oregon in the 1820s.) The 1844 campaign was
close and bitterly fought. One Whig claimed that Polk's supporters
called Whig candidate Clay such awful names that one could conclude
"he was more suitable as a candidate for the penitentiary than President of the United States."[24] The Whigs returned the name-calling in
kind, but Polk won by a paper-thin margin.

John Tyler, the outgoing president, decided to leave his mark on
history by annexing Texas not through the usual constitutional method
of a two-thirds Senate vote (which remained unobtainable), but through
the unusual tactic of a joint resolution that required only a majority of
the House and Senate. The House passed the measure. The Senate,
however, balked when several powerful members feared that claims
over the vague Texas-Mexico boundary would lead to war. Polk, preparing for his inauguration, won these key votes by apparently promising to send a mission to negotiate the boundary issue peacefully. The
Senate then voted for annexation 27 to 25. Texas became part of the
Union on December 29, 1845, as Tyler set a constitutional precedent
by acquiring empire through a simple majority of both houses. But
Polk then somehow neglected to settle the boundary issue. He instead
attempted to use it and other claims to force Mexico to sell California.
Although weak and divided, the Mexican government refused to deal
on Polk's terms. Meanwhile, the new president alienated pivotal Democrats, including Van Buren, with his appointments and positions on
domestic issues. Even Vice-President George Dallas became angry:
Polk's "most devoted friends [complained] . . . with bitter grief and
shame, of his crooked politics. His defeats, they said, gave them less
pain than his intrigues."[25]

WEBSTER, POLK, AND LOOKING JOHN BULL IN THE EYE

After his election as president in 1968, Richard Nixon told his speech-
writers to study James Polk's 1845 inaugural address, because the
Tennessean, in Nixon's words, promised to be "president of all the
people."[26] Regardless of their promises, however, both Polk and Nixon
soon came to preside over a nation tragically divided by their foreign

Daniel Webster (1782–1852) was elected to Congress from New Hampshire at age twenty-nine, and in 1827 became a senator from Massachusetts. For the next quarter-century, he, along with Henry Clay, embodied Whig foreign policy that emphasized commercial expansion (especially in Asia); peace with Great Britain; and the 1850 Compromise that, temporarily saved the Union. Historian Kenneth Shewmaker concludes that the Webster-Ashburton Treaty of 1842 not only "possibly averted a third Anglo-American war, it laid the basis for a rapprochement with England that has endured to the present." (Daniel Webster: The Complete Man *[Hanover, N.H., 1990], p. xxiii.)*

policies. In Polk's case, that division began with Texas and nearly exploded into war with Great Britain over Oregon.

Polk's (and the Democratic party's) sometime recklessness in twisting the British Lion's tail can be better understood by comparing his policy with the Whig party's approach fashioned by Daniel Webster just a few years before in the early 1840s. A host of U.S.-British confrontations were erupting, but Webster—who, as a good Whig wanted peaceful commercial expansion, no clashes with the world's great economic power (Great Britain), and no jarring political debates that would threaten the Union—took a distinctly different approach to these confrontations than did Polk.

The crises began in 1837 when some Canadians rebelled against British rule. Ever willing to help their neighbors in such efforts, a few Americans used the vessel *Caroline* to send supplies to the small band of revolutionaries. Pro-British Canadians attacked the *Caroline* in U.S. waters, killed a U.S. citizen, and spectacularly sunk the boat in flames just above Niagara Falls. Outraged Americans south of the border prepared for war, in part by exhibiting in Buffalo, New York, the body of their slain countryman (his "pale forehead mangled by the pistol ball, and his locks matted with his blood!" according to one hard-breathing New York newspaper). President Martin Van Buren cooled passions by sending General Winfield Scott, who warned that any attack on Canada would have to be "over my body."

The issue festered for two years until 1840, when a Canadian, Alexander McLeod, made the serious mistake of drinking too much in a

Buffalo tavern and then bragging that he had done the killing in the *Caroline* raid. He was immediately jailed on charges of arson and murder. The British demanded McLeod's release on the grounds that he had not been near the *Caroline* and, anyway, the attack had been ordered by the government in Canada and was not the act of a single man. As New Yorkers (and other anti-British voices) angrily demanded McLeod's execution, Webster became secretary of state in early 1841. Publicly, Webster took a hard line. Privately, he worked with New York to free the prisoner before another clash broke out. The jury finally freed McLeod for the good reason that he had proven he had been miles away from the *Caroline* on the night of the attack. Webster and his good friend, Lord Ashburton, the British minister to the United States, then tied up loose ends. Ashburton essentially apologized for the *Caroline* attack, and Webster apologized for McLeod's long detention. The secretary of state also had Congress pass a law in 1842 that henceforth brought under federal (not state) jurisdiction any foreigners charged with criminal acts who were acting under orders of their government.

Having solved the international problems caused by drunkards in Buffalo, Webster and Ashburton then had to contend with a more serious crisis: slavery. In 1839, slaves aboard the Spanish slave ship, the *Amistad*, mutinied and tried to force their white captives to take them back to Africa. Instead, the whites steered the ship north until, finally, a U.S. ship captured the *Amistad* off Long Island. Abolitionists instantly demanded freedom for the Africans. In 1841 the Supreme Court indeed granted their freedom on the grounds that the *Amistad* had broken treaties between Great Britain and Spain that prohibited the slave trade. The Spanish, in turn, demanded indemnity in cash. Webster flatly refused, and the Africans returned to their home in 1842.

The slave-trade question refused to go away. In late 1841, slaves took over a U.S. ship, the *Creole*, sailing from Virginia to New Orleans, and piloted it to the British possession of Nassau. There officials freed the slaves on the grounds that the king had ended slavery in all his possessions a decade earlier. Webster bitterly opposed slavery, but as secretary of state he had to listen to southern slaveholders who warned that the *Creole* mutiny could not be allowed to stand without either punishment or indemnity (or, preferably, both). Again Webster and Ashburton worked out a solution. The British did not return the Africans, but they did promise no future interference with U.S. vessels driven into British ports by "accident or by violence." In 1853, a claims commission awarded the United States $110,000 for the property in humans lost in the *Creole* affair.

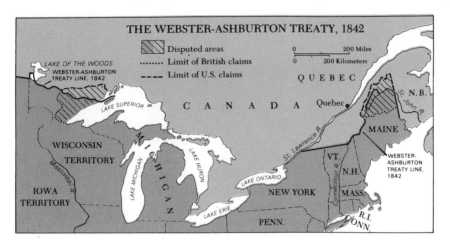

The Webster-Ashburton Treaty of 1842 settled the disputed boundaries of Maine (although not to the satisfaction of everyone in Maine) and gave the United States land between Lake Superior and Lake of the Woods, on which were later found the rich Mesabi iron deposits—a base for the nation's iron and steel industries several generations later.

Webster and Ashburton had narrowly avoided two potential catastrophes in the *Caroline* and *Creole* affairs. Perhaps their success was not too surprising since Ashburton had married an American woman and was head of the great banking institution, the House of Baring (his family name had been Alexander Baring), which poured money into U.S. investments—and which over the years had paid handsomely for legal advice from Daniel Webster. The two men understood each other perfectly. But that understanding was strained to a near-breaking point in the most dangerous U.S.-British problem of the early 1840s: an argument over the boundary between Maine and Canada. That boundary had been fuzzy ever since the 1783 peace treaty (see pp. 26–27) failed to make clear which country owned some 12,000 square miles of highly strategic and rich (especially because of lumber) territory. Webster secretly held two old maps that seemed to put most of the land inside Canada. He kept these from his good friend, Ashburton, while using secret funds controlled by President John Tyler to send an agent to Maine and explain to the local citizens why a compromise was necessary with the British. That compromise was worked out between Webster and Ashburton in July 1842. The sixty-seven-year-old British aristocrat was ready to deal—in part to escape the "oven," as he accurately called summertime Washington, D.C.

The United States received about 7,000 of the disputed 12,000 square miles, and also obtained territory in New York, Vermont, and in the Lake Superior region (an area soon discovered to have rich iron-ore deposits). Webster then told Ashburton of the old maps upholding much of the British claim. The minister was not unhappy; he valued good relations with the United States over the acreage (and Canadians) in question. But his British critics unleashed a blistering attack on Ashburton's diplomacy—only, in a melodramatic turn in a series of U.S.-British melodramas—to have *another* map suddenly turn up in London that upheld the most extreme U.S. claim to the territory. Thus, Ashburton's high reputation as a diplomat was preserved. So which of these various maps was correct? Which nation deserved some of the richest lumber and mineral resources in the Western Hemisphere? The answer, as historian Howard Jones suggests, is that "no map was both authentic and valid" because they either had not been used at Paris in 1783 or boundary questions had been delayed, to be decided later. But the Webster-Ashburton Treaty was both a tribute to the skill of the two negotiators and a signal that differences between Americans and the British no longer had to be resolved with war.[27]

Unfortunately, that historic lesson was almost lost on President Polk in 1845–1846. Granted, the stakes in his struggle with the British were enormous. The Oregon contest was fought over an empire that contained nearly half a million square miles—or an area larger than France, Germany, and Hungary combined. U.S. merchants dominated the region's commerce. Word had spread rapidly after one shipowner had traded several dollars of trinkets to Indians for $20,000 worth of otter pelts. The Native Americans soon called all white men "Bostons" because every white person seemed to come from the Massachusetts port.[28] Few permanent white settlers lived in Oregon by 1830, but that changed rapidly after missionaries came to believe that the Indians wanted to learn about Christianity. With Samuel Parker and the intrepid Marcus and Narcissa Whitman in the foreground, during 1835–1836 the missionaries followed a pathway along the Oregon Trail out of Independence, Missouri. They moved their wagon trains through plains and desert, across the Rockies, and then down into the lush Willamette Valley. The economic troubles of 1837–1841 also pushed out-of-luck farmers along the Oregon Trail. In 1845, some 3,000 Americans arrived in Oregon to double the white population. The new technologies, moreover, were now cutting distances. If you had represented Oregon in the U.S. Congress before the mid-1840s, you would have had to spend about twenty-five weeks going to Washington and another twenty-five weeks returning home, leaving about two weeks to spend in the capital. After the mid-1840s, the railroad, telegraph, and steamship rapidly reduced travel time.

At first, Polk handled the growing problem with the British over Oregon carefully and wisely. In mid-1845 he offered the king's minister to Washington, Richard Pakenham, a deal that divided the Oregon territory along the forty-ninth parallel. The proposal placed both banks of the Columbia River in U.S. territory, even though no American settlements existed north of the great waterway. Faced with a grave political crisis in London at that moment, the British government would probably have accepted Polk's offer just to resolve the distant Oregon question. But Pakenham foolishly rejected the deal without consulting London. Polk, angry and believing that the British had now put themselves at a disadvantage, then demanded all the land to the northernmost U.S. claim, 54°40′. The British flatly rejected the demand. They were not about to surrender much of their northwestern territory and virtually all of the region's best harbors.

Polk received vibrant support from Democrats in the Midwest, where land hunger and faith in God-directed expansionism was strongest. The cry of "Fifty-four forty or fight" soon resounded, encouraged by John L. O'Sullivan, who at this point coined the term "manifest destiny." Northern and many southern Whigs, however, wanted no war with their best customers in England. The U.S. Army, which numbered only 6,000 in 1830 (and one-quarter of those deserted within the year), had grown to 11,000 by the early 1840s, but it was both highly undependable and too small to fight the British Empire in such a faraway place. With Americans divided and his military unprepared, Polk nevertheless whipped up feelings over Oregon. In his annual message of December 1845, he resurrected the Monroe Doctrine (which had slept peacefully and largely forgotten since 1823). He used it to warn Great Britain that "no future European colony or dominion shall with our consent be planted or established on any part of the North American continent."

The president then urged Congress to terminate the 1827 joint-occupation agreement that had regulated Oregon affairs. When a timid congressman expressed the fear that this meant war, Polk retorted "that the only way to treat John Bull was to look him straight in the eye." Behind those overly defiant words was Polk's belief that the British needed U.S. trade—notably cotton (especially since the British Parliament was just then committing itself to a radically new free-trade policy). "We hold England by a cotton string," a Virginia Democrat bragged.[29]

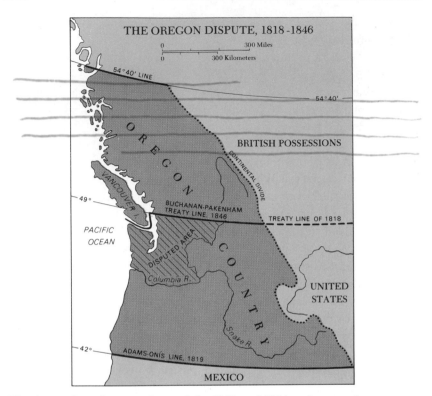

THE OREGON DISPUTE, 1818-1846

The disputed northwest region and the 1819 and 1846 settlements that pre-served peace with Great Britain, and also preserved the U.S. hold on invaluable land and ports.

The "string" proved to be more fragile than John Bull's eye. The British told Polk that they would not retreat beyond the forty-ninth parallel. They next mobilized thirty warships for possible action. Polk, a devout Presbyterian who seldom conducted business on the Sabbath, quickly called a cabinet meeting on Sunday to discuss the crises. Already facing a war with Mexico, he decided to send the Oregon issue to the Senate for resolution. This decision shifted responsibility, and the president no doubt assumed that the Senate, with Webster (now returned to represent Massachusetts) and Calhoun in the lead, would accept the forty-ninth-parallel compromise. Webster gloated that the Oregon treaty reversed the Constitution's procedure: "Here is a treaty negotiated by the Senate, and only agreed to by the President." Polk had neverthe-less turned possible war and his own humiliation into a victory. The United States obtained the Oregon territory, including both banks of the Columbia River. The agreement came none too soon, for the president had meanwhile maneuvered the country into war with Mexico.

THE "FIRE-BRAND IN THE BODY": THE MEXICAN WAR AND SLAVERY

In his inaugural address of 1845, Polk stressed that U.S. expansionism meant extending "the dominions of peace. . . . The world has nothing to fear from military ambition in our Government. . . . Our Government can not be otherwise than pacific." Within fifteen months, Polk took the country into a war for conquest. The reason was his determination to obtain California.

Americans had sailed along California's coast for generations. As early as 1829, they controlled its cattle-hide and provision exchanges as surely as they monopolized Russian America's trade to the north. Richard Henry Dana's famous account, *Two Years before the Mast*, popularized the romance of the California coast. By 1845, about a thousand Americans, many pushed out by the 1837 panic, had trekked across the continent to settle the region. There was, however, no popular cry to annex California in 1845. The settlers were outnumbered by at least 7,000 Spanish and Mexican natives. Most Americans knew or cared little about the area. The issue of California never arose in the 1844 presidential campaign. Only Polk seemed to care, but he cared a great deal.

An astute politician, the Tennessean wanted California not only for its land, but especially for its fine ports. Owning the harbors of San Francisco and San Diego could magnificently enhance the mushrooming U.S. trade in the Pacific and—as Polk fully appreciated—greatly please American merchants. The president, moreover, suspected that the British were using their financial control over Mexico's debt to force the Mexicans to sell, or at least to mortgage, their province of California to London financiers. It was for that reason, as he privately told a friend, that "in reasserting Mr. Monroe's doctrine [in the 1845 message] I had California and the fine bay of San Francisco as much in view as Oregon."[30]

In late 1845, Polk sent John Slidell (a U.S. congressman and influential lawyer from New Orleans) to make Mexico a series of offers, including one of $25 million and the U.S. assumption of its claims against the Mexicans in return for much of California, New Mexico

CHRONOLOGY, 1844–1848

June 1844	Secretary of State John Calhoun's treaty for annexing Texas overwhelmingly defeated 35–16 in Senate.
November 1844	James K. Polk wins presidential race over Henry Clay.
February 1845	Polk secretly makes deal with Senate leaders for Texas.
March 1, 1845	President John Tyler signs joint resolution to annex Texas.
March 4, 1845	Polk inaugurated.
July 1845	Polk proposes division of Oregon at 49°; British minister rejects proposal without submitting it to his superiors in London.
October 1845	Polk sends Thomas O. Larkin to stir up demands in California for annexation.
November 1845– March 1846	Polk sends John Slidell to Mexico to obtain California and New Mexico. Slidell mission fails.
December 1845	Polk revives Monroe Doctrine to demand the "whole" of Oregon.
January 1846	Polk sends General Zachary Taylor's troops into disputed territory of Rio Grande.
February 1846	Rise of "Manifest Destiny" and "Fifty-Four-Forty-or-Fight" cries in Congress over Oregon issue.
May 8, 1846	Polk learns of Slidell mission's failure; prepares for war.
May 9, 1846	Polk learns that Mexican forces attacked Taylor's troops in disputed territory.
May 11, 1846	Polk sends war message to Congress.
June 1846	Treaty with Great Britain to settle Oregon passes Senate.
July 1846	Walker tariff, lowering rates significantly, passes Congress.
August 8, 1846	David Wilmot proposes the Wilmot Proviso in House.
August 18, 1846	U.S. Army occupies Sante Fe.
February 1847	After bitter debate, House passes Wilmot Proviso; Senate kills it.
September 1847	General Winfield Scott's forces capture Mexico City.
January 1848	Discovery of gold sets off California gold rush.
February 1848	Nicholas Trist signs Treaty of Guadalupe Hidalgo to end war.
November 1848	Zachary Taylor wins presidency over two candidates of divided Democratic party.

territory, and the Rio Grande as the Texas-Mexico boundary. To the
Mexico City government, this was but one more in a continual stream
of political crises. It refused to deal with Slidell, nor could it have negotiated Polk's terms without falling from power. A change in early 1846
brought an even more ardent anti-U.S. regime into office. Polk turned
to other alternatives. He had earlier instructed the U.S. consul in California, Thomas O. Larkin, to watch for both British activities and any
opportunity to start a revolt against Mexican rule. Larkin could find no
opportunity to play the role of Thomas Jefferson in California. But in
June 1846, American settlers in the Sacramento area took advantage
of the looming U.S.-Mexican war to declare their own independent
"Bear Flag" state. The Republic of California survived less than a month,
for, by July 1846, Polk was embarked on his main policy: conquest of
all of California by force.

The president's policy was both simple and devious. He slowly
squeezed Mexico militarily until it struck back. He then misrepre-
sented the evidence for the attack to obtain Congress's declaration of
war. In July 1845, ten months before war began, Polk instructed the
U.S. military commander in Texas, Zachary Taylor, to move across the
Nueces River into territory (between the Nueces and the Rio Grande)
that was hotly disputed between Texas and Mexico. In January 1846,
the president told Taylor to encamp on the Rio Grande itself. In April,
the Mexican army demanded that Taylor move back. He responded by
blockading the Mexicans and threatening them with starvation. On
April 24, they tried to break the blockade, and blood was spilled. Back
in Washington, Polk was becoming frustrated by Mexico's refusal to
deal with Slidell. On May 9, he and his cabinet decided to settle the
claims against Mexico and block British influence by declaring war.
Later that day, Polk received word of the attack on Taylor's forces.

The president immediately sent a war message to Congress that was
as historically inaccurate as it was politically potent. "The cup of for-
bearance had been exhausted" even before the news of the fighting
arrived in Washington, Polk declared. "But now . . . Mexico . . . has
invaded our territory and shed American blood upon the American
soil." Doubting Whigs, even some Democrats, demanded evidence.
The key documents, Polk's followers responded, were at the printer's
and not available. Besides, they added, Congress should trust the president. The House of Representatives voted for war 174 to 14 (with John
Quincy Adams in the small minority, as usual). In the Senate, John
Calhoun—who now had acquired Texas for the South and wanted no
war for Mexican territory that probably could not support slavery—and

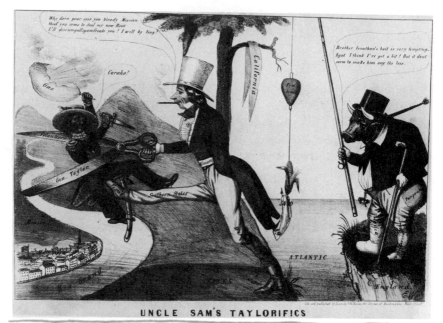

UNCLE SAM'S TAYLORIFICS

E. W. Clay's 1846 cartoon is a classic example of good American graphic art as well as of rampant American Manifest Destiny and anti-British feelings in 1846. The "Union," or an early "Uncle Sam" figure, is cutting up Mexico for trying to steal his "boot" of Texas. Note the early "John Bull" figure of the British Empire fishing for all of Oregon while Uncle Sam's back is turned.

a few others tried to slow down the rush to battle. They failed. The war declaration passed 40 to 2, with Calhoun abstaining.[31]

Polk finally had his war, but he also faced a terrible dilemma. He had called the war merely a defensive response to a Mexican attack, but in reality he wanted a war for conquest. Such a war could require high and politically unpopular expenses, as well as a large army that would have to be paid for by an already suspicious Congress. He discovered, moreover, that his two top military commanders, Generals Winfield Scott and Zachary Taylor, were both Whigs. If they covered themselves with glory, they could become leading presidential nominees. Polk had already declared that he would not be a candidate in the 1848 race, but he coldly disliked Whigs (whom he often condemned as "Federalists") and especially feared Scott and Taylor.

The two generals made real the president's nightmare. Attacking across the Rio Grande, Taylor won a series of victories at Monterey and Buena Vista, although at Buena Vista, Taylor's 5,000 troops had been surprised by a 20,000-man Mexican force. At Monterey, the

Americans won despite the absence of one of their top officers, who had taken a strong laxative the night before. (Nevertheless, Congress later gave the officer a jeweled sword for his "gallantry at Monterey.")[32] Meanwhile, Scott landed at Vera Cruz in a brilliant amphibious operation, for which he had designed the first landing crafts in U.S. military history. He then began a march toward Mexico City that no less an authority than the Duke of Wellington (conqueror of Napoleon) said could not be done. In a careful campaign that kept his casualties low, Scott reached Mexico City in late summer 1847 and prepared to wait for the government's surrender. He had even avoided costly battles with the Mexican army in the hope that patience would bring about a political settlement.

Polk had neither the time nor the temperament for such a campaign. As soon as war was declared, he asked Congress for $2 million to purchase peace (and California) from Mexico. His request set off an

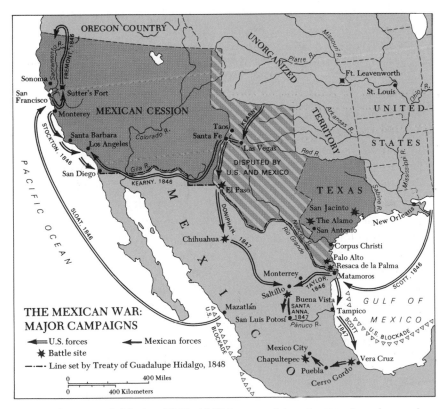

The U.S. war with Mexico (1846–1848) increased American territory by nearly 50 percent, gained valuable California ports, and helped lead to the Civil War.

explosion that reverberated for the next twenty years. When he asked Congress to legislate the funds, Democrats—who had become angered by Polk's political appointments and proslavery foreign policy in Texas—attached an amendment to the legislation that became known as the Wilmot Proviso. It was named after a Pennsylvania Democrat, David Wilmot, who belonged to Van Buren's Free Soil wing of the party. The proviso required that the money not be used to purchase any territory that would allow slavery. Democrats and Whigs from the South immediately condemned the measure. In the House vote, Polk's Democratic party splintered, but the proviso passed. Fifty-two northern free-state Democrats supported, and all fifty southern Democrats opposed, the measure. The Senate, where free- and slave-state representation was in balance, prevented the Wilmot Proviso from becoming law. Nevertheless, everyone involved understood that a political monster had appeared, one that could not be easily killed.

Polk could not understand what he had done. He denied that the great domestic issue had anything to do with foreign policy: slavery "was purely a domestic question" and "not a foreign question." In reality, of course, slavery had everything to do with foreign policy. Expansion, the central theme of the American experience since 1607, now raised the possibility of one side—either slave or nonslave—controlling vast new territories and, thus, soon controlling the government itself. Polk did see that "the slavery question . . . is a fire-brand in the body,"[33] but he also believed that because slavery could not exist on the poor soils of northern Mexico, Congress was raising the issue simply to embarrass him. The president proposed to settle the rising argument by extending the 1820 Missouri Compromise line of 36°30′ to the Pacific. But that compromise was no longer adequate. It could leave the vast Mexican territories south of the line open to slavery. Foreign policy and domestic concerns were so intertwined that each now threatened to strangle the other.

Congress quarreled and Democrats split while Whig generals triumphed. Those were not the results for which Polk had bargained. Despite the battlefield victories, however, Mexico refused to surrender. By the summer of 1847, even John L. O'Sullivan had doubts about Manifest Destiny: "I am afraid it was not God that got us into the war, but that He may get us out of it is the constant prayer of yours very truly."[34] The president finally decided to send Nicholas Trist to discuss peace with the Mexicans. A State Department clerk, Trist had mostly made his political fortune by marrying Thomas Jefferson's favorite granddaughter. He believed ardently in Manifest Destiny but now feared that the war threatened to destroy the Union. Trist wanted a quick peace. His early talks with Mexico, however, collapsed. Polk began to wonder whether Trist wanted peace so badly that he might even be willing to give up claims to much of California to achieve it. Almost as bad, the president learned that Trist and Scott had become fast friends. Polk told the diplomat to return immediately.

Mexico's refusal to surrender then produced another crisis for the president. An "All-Mexico" movement appeared. It demanded that U.S. claims and loss of life could only be satisfied by seizing the entire country. The movement had its most feverish supporters among northern Democrats, both among the sensationalistic press in cities such as New York and the agrarian–Manifest Destiny expansionists of the Midwest. Polk fueled the All-Mexico drive by leaving open the possibility of more war and more conquest if Mexico did not immediately give him what he wanted. As the All-Mexico mania intensified, however, Trist killed it in a single stroke. He ignored Polk's orders to return after he heard that Mexico might be prepared to discuss peace terms. Scott's plan to wait out his opponents had finally worked. Trist obtained all that Polk had originally demanded: California, New Mexico, and the Rio Grande boundary.

Infuriated that Trist had disobeyed his order to return, Polk nevertheless had little choice but to accept the peace treaty of Guadalupe Hidalgo. It was either accepting what he had initially wanted or facing a profound political crisis generated by the All-Mexico and Wilmot Proviso zealots. Polk chose peace. After all, as he told Congress on July 6, 1848, California and the New Mexico territory "constitute of themselves a country large enough for a great empire."

Two Near-Misses and a Near-Settlement

Polk had apparently learned little from the experience. His passion for expansion and his inability to understand the links between domestic and foreign policy forced him to face two more potential crises.

In April 1848, Yucatán—a province of Mexico—asked for U.S. aid against an Indian revolt. Yucatán also asked Spain and Great Britain for aid. Polk immediately requested permission from Congress to intervene. Waving once again the Monroe Doctrine, he warned that the United States would occupy Yucatán before allowing it to come under European influence. Americans were tired of hearing about Mexico, none more so than John Calhoun. The South Carolina sena-

John C. Calhoun (1782–1850) of South Carolina defended slavery and slave expansionism almost literally until his dying breath. But Calhoun disliked the War with Mexico and bitterly fought Polk's attempt to use the Monroe Doctrine as a tool to obtain more territory.

tor unleashed an attack on the request that not only finally killed the plan, but raised fundamental questions for Americans in the future.

Calhoun, who had been in Monroe's cabinet in 1823, denied that the original doctrine had anything to do with occupying such places as Mexico. It only said that North America would keep its hands off Latin American problems and expected Europeans to do the same. The South Carolinian observed that if the United States occupied Yucatán, a most dangerous precedent would be established: other Latin American countries (such as Yucatán) will have obtained the power "to make us a party to all their wars" on their terms and according to their own, not United States', interests. "We shall be forever involved in wars" to save Latin Americans from themselves, Calhoun warned. It was one of the most powerful attacks ever made on the Monroe Doctrine. Fortunately for both Polk and Calhoun, Yucatán resolved its problem, and Polk withdrew the request.[35]

Even though the debate had been an embarrassment, Polk next set his sights on Cuba. In May 1848, John L. O'Sullivan and Democratic senator Stephen A. Douglas from Illinois privately urged Polk to buy Cuba from Spain. Americans had long coveted the island. In 1848, moreover, France had freed its West Indian slaves. England had freed its bondsmen in 1833. Cuba now remained as the major slave society in the Caribbean. American slaveholders believed that the island had to be saved from the building pressure for emancipation. They were joined by northern merchants who profited from Cuban routes and even from the secret, but highly lucrative, trade in black men and women—a trade that had been outlawed forty years before. Cuba exemplified slavery at its worst. About 324,000 slaves and 425,000 whites lived on the island, bound together in a decaying and brutal system.

Polk nevertheless pushed for annexation. He believed that it would ease the fears of southerners who felt that they were becoming a minority section. The island, moreover, "would speedily be Americanized [with whites] as Louisiana had been," as Secretary of State James Buchanan phrased it. Perhaps nothing could have more aroused and divided American society in 1848 than a debate over Cuban annexation. Fortunately, Polk's plan never reached that point. Despite U.S. pressure, Spain refused to sell. Buchanan had used the occasion, however, to warn Spain that Cuba must never pass into the hands of any other power.

Polk's proposals on Yucatán and Cuba occurred amid a wild U.S. political scene. In mid-1848, the Democrats split. The regular party nominated Lewis Cass of Michigan, a zealot for Manifest Destiny who had fought to take Texas and opposed the Wilmot Proviso. Antislave Democrats quit the convention and nominated Martin Van Buren of New York on the Free Soil ticket. The Whigs countered with Zachary Taylor. The Mexican War hero was such a strong believer in traditional values that he acknowledged his nomination late because the notification letter arrived with postage due and he refused to pay it. After Taylor won and assumed the presidency, he moved to settle the central question of how to govern the vast territory conquered by Polk.

In one of the great debates in U.S. history, the Compromise of 1850 was hammered out in the Senate. A dying Calhoun warned that "the cords which bind these states together" were snapping under "the agitation of the slavery question." He intimated the need for constitutional amendments to protect the rights of slaveholders in the new territories. But the aged Henry Clay and Daniel Webster carried the day for the more moderate forces. They argued that local conditions and climate should settle the issue. The final compromise, therefore, brought in California as a free state (as its inhabitants desired). It allowed citizens in New Mexico and Utah territories to work out their own policy on the slave question. This approach became known as popular sovereignty. The slave trade (but not slavery) was finally abolished in the District of Columbia, where humans had been traded for cash and crops in the shadows of U.S. government buildings for half a century. In return, the federal government promised, in a Fugitive Slave Law, to help southerners capture and return runaway slaves. This "businessman's peace," as the compromise was called, postponed the war over the Union for ten years.

MANIFEST DESTINY IN CENTRAL AMERICA

The Senate also passed another historic measure in 1850: the Clayton-Bulwer Treaty gave Americans their first formal right to realize a dream of centuries—an isthmian canal in Central America to link the Atlantic and the Pacific. The treaty was an appropriate act with which to climax the U.S. trade and territorial conquest of the 1840s.

Until this time, Great Britain dominated Central American affairs. Growing U.S. interest in Asian trade, the annexation of Oregon and California, then the dramatic discovery of gold in California during 1848 transformed the Central American power balance. Adventurers and entrepreneurs from the United States profited from turning the region into a passageway for Americans who traveled from the East to the West Coast or to the far Pacific. Newly arrived Americans discovered that the British controlled several strategic areas on the Atlantic-coast side of a possible canal (the Mosquito Coast in Nicaragua, and Belize, bordered by Guatemala) and had been eying the Panamanian area of New Granada. U.S. diplomats neatly played on the fears of the Latin Americans to checkmate the British. The U.S. minister to New Granada, Benjamin Bidlack, signed a treaty in 1846 that gave the United States transit rights across Panama. In return, the United States guaranteed transit rights in the area for other parties. The Senate, realizing that this deal amounted to an entangling alliance, delayed ratification until 1848. The Bidlack pact enabled Americans to build the first transcontinental railway (of 48 miles) in Panama during the 1850s and provided the excuse, in 1903, for Theodore Roosevelt's seizure of Panama to build the present canal. Nicaragua and Honduras, also fearful of British imperialism, next signed treaties giving the United States transit rights. The Americans and British were on a collision course.

To avoid possible war, British minister Sir Henry Bulwer and Secretary of State John Clayton worked out a pact providing that (1) neither nation would build an isthmian canal in Central America without the consent or cooperation of the other, (2) neither would fortify or found new colonies in the area, and (3) if a canal were built, both powers would guarantee its neutrality. It was a handsome victory for Zachary Taylor's administration. The British had recognized the United

States as an equal in Central America. Whigs were delighted with both the isthmian rights and the dodging of war with Great Britain. Democrats, led by Stephen A. Douglas, not surprisingly condemned the treaty for compromising with the hated John Bull.

THE LEGACIES OF MANIFEST DESTINY AND JAMES K. POLK

The importance of 1840s expansionism in American history goes far beyond the new influence in Central America or even the conquest of the million-square-mile empire in the West. Ralph Waldo Emerson compared the Mexican War to a dose of arsenic for the Union. The military hero of the Civil War, General Ulysses S. Grant, recalled in his memoirs that he had "bitterly opposed" invading Mexico and wanted to obtain the southwest territory through peaceful means. "The Southern rebellion [the Civil War] was largely the outgrowth of the Mexican War," Grant believed.[36] More than a century later, historian Thomas Hietala would look back over Polk's systematic expansionism and conclude that it "was not manifest destiny. It was manifest design."[37]

Polk also left another historic legacy. The way in which he led the United States into the Mexican War set precedents for later powerful chief executives—indeed, provided an early preview of the so-called "imperial presidency" of the twentieth century. Abraham Lincoln, then a young Illinois Whig strongly opposed to Polk's policies toward Mexico, attacked these new presidential powers in a now-famous letter written to a friend in 1848:

> Allow the President to invade a neighboring nation, whenever *he* shall deem it necessary to repel an invasion, and you allow him to do so, *whenever he may choose to say* he deems it necessary for such purpose—and you allow him to make war at pleasure. Study to see if you can fix *any limit* to his power in this respect, after you have given him so much as you propose. . . . You may say to him, "I see no probability of the British invading us" but he will say to you, "be silent; I see it, if you don't."
>
> The provision of the Constitution giving the war-making power to Congress, was dictated, as I understand it, by the following reasons. Kings had always been involving and impoverishing their people in wars, pretending generally, if not always, that the good of the people was the object. This, our Convention [of 1787] understood to be the most oppressive of all Kingly oppressions; and they resolved to so frame the Constitution that *no one* man should hold the power of bringing this oppression upon us.[38]

Polk never lived to see the Civil War that his own use of presidential power had helped bring about. As chief executive, he worked long hours to supervise every act of his administration. While other officers fled Washington's summer heat, the president remained. Polk grew to believe, moreover, that his administration was the victim of petty politics and the presidential ambitions of others. "I now predict that no President of the U.S. of either party will ever again be re-elected" to a second term, he said.[39] The self-discipline and the politics and passions of U.S. foreign policy killed him. Within four months of leaving the presidency, Polk died at the age of fifty-four.

NOTES

1. Julius W. Pratt, "The Ideology of American Expansion," in *Essays in Honor of William E. Dodd*, ed. Avery Craven (Chicago, 1935), p. 343.
2. *Ibid.*, p. 342.
3. Albert K. Weinberg, *Manifest Destiny* (Baltimore, 1935), pp. 192–223.
4. Arthur M. Schlesinger, Jr., *The Age of Jackson* (Boston, 1945), pp. 496–497.
5. The Ritchie quote is in Thomas R. Hietala, *Manifest Design: Anxious Aggrandizement in Late Jacksonian America* (Ithaca, 1985), p. 198; good background can be found in John Holenberg, *Foreign Correspondents: The Great Reporters and Their Times* (New York, 1964), pp. 28–29.
6. Leo Marx, *The Machine in the Garden* (New York, 1964), is a superb analysis.
7. Charles Vevier, "American Continentalism: An Idea of Expansion, 1845–1910," *American Historical Review* 65 (January 1960): 324–327, a small classic; Hietala, pp. 198–199.
8. Frederick Merk, *Manifest Destiny and Mission in American History: A Reinterpretation* (New York, 1963), pp. 107–108.
9. Walt Whitman, *The Gathering of the Forces*, 2 vols. (New York, 1920), I, pp. 32–33.
10. "What's So Bad about Feeling Good?" *Public Opinion* 8 (April/May 1985): 3, is an update and evaluation of Tocqueville's insight.
11. Joel H. Silbey, "The Election of 1836," in *History of American Presidential Elections, 1789–1968*, ed. Arthur M. Schlesinger, Jr., 4 vols. (New York, 1971), I, pp. 577–583, 598–599; *The American Party System*, ed. William N. Chambers and William Dean Burnham (New York, 1975), p. 112.
12. Robert W. Tucker and David C. Hendrickson, *The Imperial Temptation* (New York, 1992), p. 173.
13. Reginald Horsman, "American Indian Policy and the Origins of Manifest Destiny," *University of Birmingham Historical Journal* 11, no. 2 (1968): 138.
14. Angie Debo, *A History of the Indians of the United States* (Norman, Okla., 1970), pp. 101–111.

15. Pratt, p. 344.
16. Thomas McCormick, "Liberal Capitalism . . . ," in Lloyd Gardner *et al.*, *Creation of the American Empire*, 2d ed. (Chicago, 1976), pp. 120, 130.
17. Stuart C. Miller, "The American Trader's Image of China, 1785–1840," *Pacific Historical Review* 36 (November 1967): 381.
18. Mira Wilkins, *The Emergence of Multinational Enterprise: American Business Abroad from the Colonial Era to 1914* (Cambridge, Mass., 1970), p. 9; Miller, 384–385.
19. Peter W. Fay, "The Protestant Mission and the Opium War," *Pacific Historical Review* 40 (May 1971): 145–149.
20. Hietala, pp. 60–63.
21. John R. Bodo, *The Protestant Clergy and Public Issues, 1812–1848* (Princeton, 1954), pp. 230–231.
22. Edward P. Crapol, "Lydia Maria Child: Abolitionist Critic of American Foreign Policy," in *Women and American Foreign Policy*, ed. Edward P. Crapol (Westport, Conn., 1987), pp. 1–18, and Crapol's superb essay, "The Foreign Policy of Antislavery, 1833–1846," in *Redefining the Past: Essays in Diplomatic History in Honor of William Appleman Williams*, ed. Lloyd C. Gardner (Corvallis, Ore., 1986).
23. Charles G. Sellers, *James K. Polk, Jacksonian: 1795–1843* (Princeton, 1957), p. 112.
24. James T. Hathaway, *Incidents in the Campaign of 1844* (New Haven, 1905), p. 26.
25. Norman A. Graebner, "James K. Polk," in *America's Ten Greatest Presidents*, ed. Morton Borden (Chicago, 1961), p. 135.
26. William Safire, "Second Inaugural Address," *New York Times*, 14 January 1985, p. A19.
27. Howard Jones, "Daniel Webster, the Diplomatist," in *Daniel Webster: "The Completest Man,"* ed. Kenneth E. Shewmaker (Hanover, N.H., 1990), pp. 204–218, provides an especially good summary of these episodes; Howard Jones, *To the Webster-Ashburton Treaty; A Study in Anglo-American Relations, 1783–1843* (Chapel Hill, N.C., 1977), is excellent on the background and standard on the negotiations, especially pp. 88–102; Howard Jones, *Mutiny on the Amistad* (New York, 1987), tells the story of the mutiny by the slaves and negotiations for their freedom, especially pp. 204–219 on Webster.
28. Ray Allen Billington, *Westward Expansion* (New York, 1949), pp. 509–511.
29. *The Diary of James K. Polk during His Presidency*, ed. Milo M. Quaife, 4 vols. (Chicago, 1910), I, p. 155; Hietala, p. 74.
30. *Diary of Polk*, ed. Quaife, I, p. 71.
31. Charles Sellers, *James K. Polk, Continentalist: 1843–1846* (Princeton, 1966), pp. 416–421, has a good account of the debate and Polk's springing of the war declaration preamble on Congress.
32. *Parade Magazine*, 8 April 1984, p. 17.
33. *Diary of Polk*, ed. Quaife, II, pp. 289, 305.
34. Frederick Merk, *The Monroe Doctrine and American Expansion, 1843–1849* (New York, 1966), p. 253.
35. *Ibid.*, p. 231; Dexter Perkins, *The Monroe Doctrine, 1826–1867* (Baltimore, 1933), pp. 182–183.
36. Gore Vidal, *Matters of Fact and of Fiction* (New York, 1977), p. 179, for context.
37. Hietala, ch. II, has a good discussion.
38. *The Political Thought of Lincoln*, ed. Richard N. Current (Indianapolis, 1967), pp.

43–44. Lincoln, of course, used those presidential powers to the utmost just thirteen years later.

39. *Diary of Polk*, ed. Quaife, II, p. 314.

FOR FURTHER READING

Consult the notes of this chapter and the General Bibliography at the end of this book (most of whose references are not repeated below), but especially note *Guide to American Foreign Relations since 1700*, ed. Richard Dean Burns (1983), light-years ahead of anything else on pre-1981 sources and helpfully organized as well.

A sweeping cultural overview on Manifest Destiny is Vivien Green Fryd's *Art and Empire: Ethnicity in the U.S. Capitol, 1815–1860* (1992). The earlier years are covered in Robert Remini's prize-winning biography *Andrew Jackson and the Course of American Empire* (1981) and in John H. Schroeder's fine *Shaping a Maritime Empire* (1985), which covers the U.S. Navy's activities from the 1830s to the Civil War. Four superb books make westward expansion come alive: Sandra L. Myres, *Westering Women and the Frontier Experience, 1800–1915* (1982), and Annette Kolodny, *The Land before Her: Fantasy and Experience of the American Frontiers, 1630–1860* (1984), Julie Ray Jeffrey, *Converting the West: A Biography of Narcissa Whitman* (1991), which are vivid on the horrors that confronted women in the westward trek; and Bill Gilbert, *Westering Man: The Life of Joseph Walker* (1983).

The best and most complete overview remains David M. Pletcher, *The Diplomacy of Annexation: Texas, Oregon, and the Mexican War* (1973), with excellent sources noted; specific areas are well covered in Wilbur D. Jones, *The American Problem in British Diplomacy, 1841–1861* (1985); Michael H. Hunt's pathbreaking *The Making of a Special Relationship: The United States and China to 1914* (1983); Curtis T. Henson, Jr., *Commissioners and Commodores: The East India Squadron and American Diplomacy in China* (1982); and the readable Arthur P. Dudden, *The American Pacific* (1992); while key figures are analyzed in Frederic A. Greenhut, "Edmund Roberts: Early American Diplomat," *Manuscripts* 35 (Fall 1983), and in three superb works by Kenneth Shewmaker: "Daniel Webster and American Conservatism," in *Traditions and Values: American Diplomacy, 1790–1855*, ed. Norman Graebner (1985); "Forging the 'Great Chain': Daniel Webster and the Origins of American Foreign Policy toward East Asia and the Pacific, 1841–1852," *American Philosophical Society* 129 (September 1985); and *The Papers of Daniel Webster: Diplomatic Papers* (1983–   ), of which Shewmaker is chief editor. The South's leading figure tells his story in *The Papers of John C. Calhoun*, ed. Clyde N. Wilson *et al.* which, by 1991, had reached 1844 documents and Calhoun's more intense involvement in foreign policy; and John Niven, *John C. Calhoun and The Price of Union: A Biography* (1992). Deborah Pickman Clifford, *Crusader for Freedom: A Life of Lydia Maria Child* (1991), is an important biography.

On the Mexican War, aside from the Pletcher volume (and its bibliographical references) noted above, the following are important: Paul H. Bergeron, *The Presidency of James K. Polk* (1987); Carlos Bosch Garcia, "The Mexican War," in *Diplomatic Claims: Latin American Historians View the United States*, trans. and ed. Warren Dean (1985), an important Latin American perspective; Neal Harlow, *California Conquered: War and Peace on the Pacific, 1846–1850* (1982); Ernest M. Lander, Jr., *Reluctant Imperialists: Calhoun, the South Carolinians, and the Mexican War* (1984); four essays on the 1840s in *Foundations of American Foreign Policy*, ed. Norman Graebner (1986); and two works by Graebner himself: "The Mexican War: A Study in Causation," *Pacific Historical Review* 49 (August 1980), and the reprint of his 1955 book, *Empire on the Pacific* (1983), with an important interpretation and an updated bibliography.

Especially useful is Norman E. Tutorow, *The Mexican-American War, an Annotated Bibliography* (1981).

5

The Climax of Early U.S. Foreign Policy: The Civil War (1850–1865)

American expansion accelerated after 1815. It seemed out of control by 1850. The new Democratic president, Franklin Pierce, candidly declared in his 1853 inaugural address that "my administration will not be controlled by any timid forebodings of evil from expansion." Pierce had been elected on a platform that embodied Manifest Destiny. It termed the Mexican War "just and necessary." George Sanders, a Kentucky politician, caught perfectly the spirit of the age: Americans "are booted and spurred, and are panting for conquest."[1]

The Civil War logically climaxed post-1815 expansionism and the fragmentation of the United States. But it was also part of larger changes in the Western world. Europe endured an era of revolution between 1789 and 1850. Modern industrial capitalism and middle-class society were born amid the rubble of old classes overwhelmed by the new forces. This birth, moreover, was made more painful because large numbers of common people became active political participants for the first time, both in the United States and in western Europe. Many of these people were also caught up in mass migrations that shocked and transformed many parts of the world.[2] The United States especially experienced the astonishing effects of the immigration. Between 1820 and 1840, about 700,000 newcomers entered the country; but between 1840 and 1860, some 4.2 million flooded over eastern cities and western lands. In Europe, communism first began to appear as a movement to be reckoned with; in the United States, the first important labor unions emerged. The United States could not escape the crosscurrents that rocked the Western world.

Amid this rapid change and the promise of indefinite expansion in the post-1815 era, two factions emerged in the United States to struggle over the question of who would control the foreign policies and benefit from the expansion. They were the same two that James Madison had observed were the main opponents in the 1787 Constitutional Convention: the slave and the nonslave states (see p. 32). Since 1787, the Union had been kept in precarious balance by equally dividing the new territories between the two. After 1850, however, the balance began to disappear when California entered the Union and the free states gained a majority in the U.S. Senate. The North, with its much larger population, already could control the House of Representatives. In addition, the North was becoming wealthier faster than the South. By 1859, the value of the former's manufacturing alone was ten times greater than that of the latter's cotton. People discussed King Cotton, but the real rulers were iron, leather, and wheat. Per-capita income in the industrial Northeast was double that of the South.

Power created power. Railroad mileage in New England and the Midwest outstripped the South's. Western farmers were linked to the Northeast's merchants by bands of iron. The new rail system neutralized the Mississippi and other north-south waterways. Chicago, nonexistent in 1800, became a railroad hub and saw its population jump from 30,000 in 1850 to 110,000 in 1860—an amount larger than the South's Charleston, Memphis, Mobile, and Atlanta combined. Southerners found themselves trapped in a one-crop slave economy. They were dependent on northeastern bankers and shippers. They were at the mercy of world cotton markets over which they had little control. They lived in the middle of a growing black population that had already set off slave revolts. They were unable to increase the number of white or immigrant inhabitants to keep pace with the North. And now they were in a minority in both houses of Congress.

These developments directly shaped U.S. foreign policy: southerners believed that the survival of their society relied on acquiring new land. Cuba and Central America were the areas most frequently targeted. Only expansion could give the South new soil to replace worn-out land in the older states. Only expansion could give southerners hope to bal-

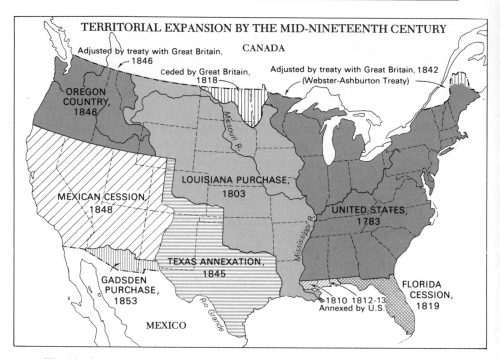

The United States in the 1850s, after expansion rounded out the continental boundaries and just before the Civil War nearly tore it in half.

ance once again the North's power in Congress. Northerners, for their part, had no intention of losing their newly found power. And northern farmers certainly had no intention of allowing the South to block them from settling their free-labor system in new territories.

In the 1850s, therefore, two explosive forces collided. A great debate erupted over the direction of American expansion. In 1860, the election of Abraham Lincoln (a free-soil Republican who gained fame and income as a sharp lawyer for the new railroads) convinced the South that it had finally lost control of U.S. foreign policy. It could no longer hope to obtain fresh lands for slavery, cotton, and political power. So the southerners left the Union. The bloodiest event in their history demonstrated how Americans could not escape the intimate relationship between their foreign and domestic affairs.

YOUNG AMERICA: SOUTH, NORTH, AND AT HOME

More than a century later, it is difficult to recapture the ferocity, even violence, with which Americans conducted this foreign-policy debate in the 1850s. In the Democratic party, an extreme group, Young America, used popular racist arguments to put down those who urged restraint ("the old fogies") and instead insisted on "sympathy for the liberals of Europe, the expansion of the American republic southward and westward, and the grasping of the magnificent purse of the commerce of the Pacific." Young America's leading politician, Stephen A. Douglas of Illinois, believed his country too great to have silly "disputes about boundaries" or to "suffer mere 'red lines' on maps." Douglas and his friends condemned their "unnatural mother," Great Britain, for trying to contain U.S. expansion.[3] Young America's idea was to expand both north and south, then worry about the political problems later—although some, such as Douglas, believed that the problem of which section was to govern the newly acquired regions could be resolved through "popular sovereignty," that is, allowing the settlers to decide whether they wanted a slave or free society.

Young America was more than rhetoric and bombast. Its favorite presidential candidate in 1852, Franklin Pierce of New Hampshire, won the election and promptly gave diplomatic posts to the group's members. The appointments included minister to France (John Mason of Virginia) and minister to Spain (Pierre Soulé of Louisiana). Young America, however, then ran into a series of difficulties. Expanding southward meant dealing with black and other nonwhite races in Cuba and Latin America, an encounter that most Americans hoped to avoid. In 1854, for example, a crisis arose when Spain illegally seized a U.S. ship. Then rumors flew that the Spanish were about to free the slaves in Cuba. The Pierce administration used the opportunity to order Soulé

Franklin Pierce (1804–1869) from New Hampshire had never made a mark as a member of Congress or the Senate, and was even accused of being the sad "hero of many a well-fought bottle." But his expansionism, identification with the Young America movement, and hatred of abolitionists surprisingly gained him the Democratic party's nomination, then the presidency in 1853. Over the next four years, the expansionism of this untalented man further dragged the nation down the path toward civil war.

to buy Cuba for $130 million. If Spain refused, the minister was to plan "to detach" Cuba from Spain.

Soulé, Mason, and James Buchanan (U.S. minister to Great Britain) met in Ostend, Belgium, to coordinate their moves. The three were not the calmest of diplomats (Soulé had already shot the French minister in Madrid during a duel after someone in the French Embassy had publicly commented on Mrs. Soulé's breasts). The ministers now sent a secret message to Washington—the Ostend Manifesto—that urged "wresting Cuba from Spain" if the island could not be purchased. Both Europeans and northerners in the United States instantly condemned the "manifesto." Pierce beat a hasty retreat. The clumsiness of Young America deepened free-soilers' suspicions of a slave-power conspiracy to control U.S. foreign policy. The episode and the reaction to it also ruined any chance to annex Cuba during the 1850s.

Another setback to Young America occurred in the North. Few believed that Canada could simply be seized; after all, it was owned by the world's greatest power. But Canadians were growing restless under British rule. They especially wanted more trade with the growing market to their south. In 1854, the United States made a significant reciprocity agreement by signing the Marcy-Elgin Treaty. (Trade reciprocity means lowering U.S. tariffs to a nation in return for that country making reciprocal, or similar, concessions.) Young Americans viewed the treaty as a first step toward annexation of Canada. In reality, however, the pact helped quiet Canadian unrest. The British also promised Canada greater independence, and in 1867 Canada gained control over many of its own affairs.

Ardent expansionists suffered a major setback at home between 1854 and 1857. Douglas brought a bill before Congress to organize Nebraska Territory into two states, Kansas and Nebraska, where a key section of the proposed transcontinental railroad was to be built. Southerners refused to support Douglas unless the Missouri Compromise of 1820 (which prohibited slavery north of 36°30') was explicitly repealed. Douglas successfully worked for the repeal of the prohibition. All of Kansas-Nebraska opened to slaveowners. Free-soilers were furious. They used the North's superiority in money and population to flood the region with antislave advocates. Violence erupted. As the southern part of the territory became known as "bleeding Kansas," free-soilers turned bitterly against Douglas and his idea of popular sovereignty. But so did many slaveholders who now realized that they could no longer compete with the North's power.

Both sides began to demand government guarantees and protection for their own cause. Popular sovereignty became discredited. When Douglas insisted on retaining the idea, southern Democrats, who wanted Washington to protect slavery in all territories, disavowed him. The Democratic party split in 1857–1858. An adhesive that had kept the Union together, the two-party system (which contained in each party both northerners and southerners), now became a three-party system: northern Democrats, southern states-rights Democrats, and the new Republican party. Political affiliations began to divide more and more along sectional lines.

No longer could Americans conquer new lands and assume that the question of who was to control the area could be worked out peacefully and democratically. Now foreign-policy expansionism could mean war at home in the form of a "bleeding Kansas." But Americans were not about to stop doing what they had been doing for centuries. They continued to try to carry out a vigorous expansionist foreign policy. Three case studies—the first involving Japan, the second revolving around the ambitions of William Henry Seward, and the third focusing on Central America—are especially revealing. The first two give a glimpse into the future. The third attempted to recreate a past that, as southerners and Young America boosters learned to their sorrow, was not to be repeated.

WHIGS AND ASIA

In 1850, Millard Fillmore moved up to the presidency after Zachary Taylor's sudden death. Fillmore appointed Daniel Webster as secretary of state. The nation was still recovering from the bitter 1850 Compromise debate (see p. 123), and Webster set out to use bombastic pronouncements (but little action) on foreign policy as a means of making Americans proud and bringing them back together. A superb opportunity arose after Hungary revolted against Austria. Tsarist Russia, Austria's conservative ally, quickly smashed the rebellion and restored the monarchy. When Austria discovered that the United States had planned to recognize the revolutionaries, it shot off a strong protest to Washington. Webster responded with the so-called Hülsemann letter (sent to Austria's chargé in Washington, Chevalier Hülsemann) in which he told Austria in grand terms how Americans would support freedom anywhere they pleased. For good measure, Webster added that compared with the United States, Austria was nothing more than "a patch on the earth's surface." As historian Kenneth Shewmaker observes, the Hülsemann letter was a "classic example of tailoring foreign policy to the needs of domestic politics."[4]

Webster and the Whigs also stirred hearts when they loudly welcomed Louis Kossuth, the Hungarian revolutionary leader, to the United States in 1851. Kossuth, however, mistakenly believed that when Webster and other Americans praised his revolution, they also were offering to help it directly. No U.S. political leader, especially among Whigs, considered challenging the Russian use of force in Hungary. As historian Donald S. Spencer has shown, Young America Democrats more strongly supported Kossuth's cause than did the Whigs, but not even these Democrats offered their bodies to ensure that Hungary could enjoy the blessings of 1776.[5] The disillusioned Kossuth left the United States in 1852 virtually unnoticed.

Other than fine, if empty, declarations, the Whigs offered one other outlet for expansionist-minded Americans in the 1850s: the promise of new opportunities in Asia. China had been opened to Americans by the last Whig administration. Webster now focused on Japan. As the London *Times* understood, once Americans took San Francisco, "the course lies straight and obvious to Polynesia, the Philippines . . . and China, and it is not extravagant to suppose that the merchants of this future emporium may open the commerce of Japan."[6] The commerce had largely been closed to the West. U.S. businessmen, as well as politicians such as John Quincy Adams, had long believed that it was against the laws of nature for countries to close themselves off from commerce and "civilization." "We do not admit the right of a nation of people to exclude themselves and their country from intercourse with the rest of the world," declared a group of U.S. merchants who eyed the Japanese market.[7] Hating iron curtains and colonial powers that shut them out of some markets, Americans have long looked at trade as a natural and an inalienable right. Japan needed to be opened as well to protect shipwrecked U.S. sailors. They had often been brutally treated when washed up on Japanese shores.

But above all was the lure of profit—a profit that came from the new technology of steamships and the growing trade they carried to and from Asian ports. President Fillmore's May 10, 1851, letter to the Japanese emporor (a letter written by Webster) stressed the importance of this technology and trade in the opening of the historic relationship. Having acquired "the great countries of Oregon & California," Fillmore told the emporor, Americans with their new steamships can suddenly reach Japan "in less than twenty days. . . . Our object is friendly commercial intercourse, and nothing more. . . . Your empire has a great abundance of coal . . . which our Steamships, in going from California to China, must use." When Commodore Matthew C. Perry learned in 1852 that he was to head a mission to open Japan, he rushed up and down the Boston-Washington region to collect new American inventions and information from businesses so he could instruct the Japanese how to become industrialized. He later gave them their first telegraph as well as a miniature railroad that delighted Japanese officials who rode on it with gowns flying in the wind.[8]

Americans, however, also planned to "civilize" Japan. Until that happened, the Asians would resemble Native Americans who insisted on living outside the law. "You have to deal with barbarians as barbarians," a Whig senator from North Carolina declared, because Japan could not be expected to act like "the civilized portion of mankind." That view gained popularity after the Japanese acted rudely toward Perry during his first visit in 1853; but they then became cooperative a year later, when he returned with a much larger fleet. The U.S. secretary of the navy concluded that triumphs such as Perry's were "but an extension of popular virtue, republican simplicity and world-teaching example." A less enthusiastic senator from Florida, however, wondered whether Americans should only "take one continent at a time."[9]

The Japanese learned quickly. After intense internal debate, they followed the principle of jujitsu—that is, use the opponent's strength to control him. Soon after Perry departed, Japan set up an Institute for the Investigation of Barbarian Books so that it could learn how the West had become so strong technologically and militarily. On the other hand, Western philosophy and religion were clearly inferior and disruptive, so they were to be ignored.[10] By 1858, the Japanese willingly dealt with the American consul, Townsend Harris, more openly than they had with Perry. The 1858 treaty first opened five major ports to foreign trade and affirmed extraterritoriality rights. Diplomatic representatives were exchanged. In 1864, a small fleet of foreign warships, including a single U.S. vessel, shot their way back into Japan after foreigners were mistreated. But the Japanese adjusted rapidly. In 1868, the emperor returned to power. Under his rule the people resumed learning from foreigners while also playing them off against each other. The small, disciplined nation of islands learned the lessons so well that within a generation it challenged the West for supremacy on the Asian mainland.

Many Americans saw their successes in Japan as simply Manifest Destiny. A popular magazine caught the spirit and gave it proper historical perspective. "Twenty years ago the 'far west' was a fixed idea

Walt Whitman (1819–1892) of New York is perhaps the greatest American poet and is certainly one of the nation's most original voices. He explored especially what he termed "the new empire" of the mid-nineteenth century that reached across the continent and toward Asia.

resting upon a fixed extent of territory," the journal wrote in 1852. But now "President Fillmore finds a 'far west' on the isles of the Japanese Empire and on the shores of China."[11] Poet Walt Whitman best expressed the belief that although U.S. territorial expansion had hit the wall of the Pacific Ocean, that was no reason to stop expanding. As Whitman said in his 1860 poem "The New Empire" (written to celebrate the first visit of Japanese diplomats to New York City), the Pacific could become a vast highway that opened to Americans an incredible future.

> I chant the world on my Western Sea; . . .
> I chant the new empire, grander than any before—as in a vision it comes
>   to me;
> I chant America, the Mistress—I chant a greater supremacy;
> I chant, projected, a thousand blooming cities yet, in time, on those groups
>   of sea-islands;
> I chant commerce opening, the sleep of ages having done its work—
>   races, reborn, refresh'd. . . .[12]

SEWARD: PROPHET OF U.S.-RUSSIAN RELATIONS

No politician of the era better exemplified its spirit or more dominated its foreign policy than William Henry Seward of New York. "A slouching, slender figure; a head like a wise macaw, a beaked nose; shaggy eyebrows; unorderly hair and clothes; hoarse voice; offhand manner;

free talk, and perpetual cigar" was the firsthand description of Seward by Henry Adams.[13] Appearances could deceive. Despite the informality, Seward had one of the best-stocked minds of his time. His foreign policies, in the words of historian Ernest Paolino, "anticipated the direction of American foreign policy for the next generation and beyond."[14] Those policies arose from a deep, although not original, reading of history. As one of his biographers remarked, "He made the past his servant." When Seward first visited Washington in the 1840s, he was amazed at "how little study and how little learning men who have ambition on this great stage are content to arm themselves."[15]

A graduate of Union College in New York (at the age of nineteen in 1820), Seward was a lawyer and then the highly successful governor of New York before he entered the Senate as a Whig in 1849. He immediately opposed slave expansion. The New Yorker declared that "a higher law than the Constitution" should guide antislavery actions, a phrase that seemed to hint of revolution to many nonsoutherners as well as to slaveholders. By 1858, he warned of an "irrepressible conflict" that would continue until either slavery or freedom triumphed. These words did not come easily, for Seward, like his hero John Quincy Adams, believed in the nation's Manifest Destiny. But also like Adams, he opposed slave expansion so his own free-soil region could control the western lands—and Congress. Seward coveted Cuba, Central America, Mexico, and Canada. He even believed that, ultimately, so many Americans would live in the Southwest, the nation's capital should be moved from Washington to the Mississippi Valley—or perhaps even Mexico City. Realizing the political price of such expansion in the 1850s, however, he switched his expansionist enthusiasm to commerce and the Pacific trade.

Seward was the first U.S. official who developed a coherent Asian policy. It rested on a bedrock assumption: that the first step toward controlling Asia's markets required the spread of industry, railroads, and canals through the American heartland. "Open up a highway through your country, from New York to San Francisco," he proclaimed to the Senate in 1853. "Put your domain under cultivation and your ten thousand wheels of manufacture in motion. The nation that draws most materials and provisions from the earth, and fabricates the most, and sells the most of productions and fabrics to foreign nations, must be, and will be, the great power of the earth."[16] He was convinced that the Monroe Doctrine was already largely fulfilled. The United States was well on its way to dominating the Western Hemisphere. It was now "the Pacific Ocean . . . and the vast regions beyond" that were

William Seward (1801–1872) had been a brilliant lawyer and governor of New York before moving to the U.S. Senate in 1849, where he became the leader of the Whig and, later, Republican parties. Lincoln defeated the outspoken antislave New Yorker for the White House, but Seward left his mark as the prophet (and later, between 1861 and 1869 when he served as secretary of state, as the diplomat) for American expansionism into the Caribbean and, especially, the vast Pacific Ocean regions.

to "become the chief theatre of events in the world's great hereafter."[17]

An ambitious politician, a student of history, Seward was also a Whig who urged the creation of a federal program of internal improvements (such as national railroads) so that future Americans could use the most efficient transportation. His radical antislave statements prevented him from capturing the Whig and then Republican party presidential nomination. But Abraham Lincoln appointed Seward to head the Department of State in 1861, and in that post the New Yorker was able to carry out some of his dreams. He worked out the tactics for protecting both U.S. interests and freedom of action in Asia. The tactics included working for the territorial integrity of all Asian nations (that is, not allowing Japanese or Europeans to colonize mainland markets). He aimed at avoiding any political alliances but cooperated with any nation that also wanted to maintain the open door.

Seward then drew a startling conclusion. The Americans' westward push put them on a collision course with Russia. He hoped that the meeting would be friendly. As secretary of state in 1861, he instructed the new U.S. minister to St. Petersburg, Cassius Clay of Kentucky, that "Russia, like the United States, is an improving and expanding empire. Its track is eastward while that of the United States is westward." Seward believed that "Russia and the United States may remain good friends until, each having made a circuit of half the globe in opposite directions, they shall meet and greet each other in the region [Asia] where civilization first began, and where, after so many ages, it has now become lethargic and helpless."[18]

Such a breathtaking perspective was not new. Thirty years before, Alexis de Tocqueville, the acute French visitor, had prophesied that Americans and Russians, although "their starting point is different and their courses are not the same," seemed "marked out by the will of heaven to sway the destinies of half the globe."[19] In 1856, Commodore Perry, fresh from his triumph in Japan, warned that American and Russian expansion would continue until "the Saxon and the Cossack will meet once more" in Asia. "Will it be friendship? I fear not! I think I see in the distance the giants that are growing up for that fierce and final encounter: In the progress of events that battle must sooner or later inevitably be fought."[20] Seward was perhaps more optimistic than Perry. More important, the New Yorker could help control the growing relationship with Russia because of his power as secretary of state. Before Seward could realize his plans in Asia, however, he had to face a crisis at home that arose out of slavery and three centuries of imperial dreams.

CENTRAL AMERICA AND CUBA

An observer in the 1850s wondered why Americans fought each other so fiercely over such an issue as slavery in the desert regions of the southwest United States. It was a debate over "an imaginary Negro in an impossible place," this observer concluded. But he missed the context of the debate, for it occurred amid rampant expansionism. It seemed that it would be only a matter of time before regions north and south would fall to the irresistible magnet of U.S. Manifest Destiny.

In late 1853, the U.S. minister to Mexico, James Gadsden, following President Pierce's orders, approached Mexico to discuss the purchase of territory so that a U.S. railroad could have a clear southern route to the Pacific. The Mexican government, in need of money, agreed to sell a smaller area than Gadsden requested, some 45,000 square miles, in return for $15 million. The Gadsden Purchase ran into fierce antislave opposition in the Senate. The revised treaty then provided paying $10 million for 29,670 square miles, which included part of present-day Arizona and New Mexico. It marked the first time the Senate refused to accept land offered to it. Nevertheless, no one would have then guessed that the deal rounded out the boundaries of the continental United States. It marked the end of the conquest of an ocean-to-ocean empire.

At the time, however, it seemed one more step southward, with many more to follow. Just the first six months of 1854 exemplified how the aggressive Americans were on the move. During those months (the

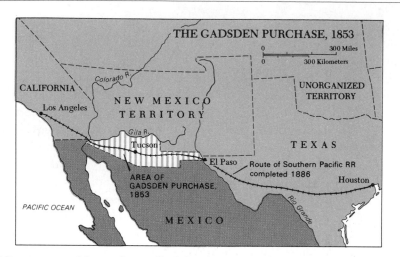

U.S. minister to Mexico, James Gadsden (a native of South Carolina) bought for $10 million what was finally an area of 29,670 square miles so that the southern states could have a transcontinental railway route. The Gadsden Purchase, accepted by the U.S. Senate despite violent northern opposition, rounded out the nation's continental boundaries in 1853–1854.

time when the bitter Kansas-Nebraska debates were shattering the Democratic party), Gadsden sent his treaty to the Senate; an American, William Walker, announced his plans to seize part of Mexico; the possibility of war with Spain over Cuba loomed; the Ostend Manifesto became public; the U.S. Navy shelled Nicaragua; and southerners launched new "filibustering" expeditions aimed at seizing Cuba and other Latin American territories for slavery.[21]

Americans seemed to be taking over Central America. Slaveholders hoped to acquire new territory and possibly even states. Merchants coveted control of the profitable, short isthmian passageways through Nicaragua and Panama that linked the two oceans. Even Republican free-soilers eyed Central America as the place in which free African Americans could be settled in a colonization scheme. Such resettlement would quiet the racial question at home—"Keep our Anglo-Saxon institutions as well as our Anglo-Saxon blood pure and uncontaminated," as a Republican declared—and would spread U.S. influence and values to Latin America.[22] The colonization plans finally collapsed because some Republicans did not want to lose cheap black labor. Moreover, the colonizers discovered that the cost and time needed to ship out all African Americans far exceeded the nation's available resources. In the 1850s, however, colonization remained a much-discussed solution to growing racial problems.

Nicaragua attracted special attention. The British had seized control of the eastern entry to a possible interocean canal route in the 1840s. One of the great U.S. adventurers, Cornelius Vanderbilt, appeared in 1848 to acquire from Nicaragua the right to monopolize transportation on the country's waters. U.S. power dramatically appeared in 1854. One of Vanderbilt's officials killed a Nicaraguan. Anti-American feelings ran high. The U.S. minister attempted to restore calm, only to have a bottle thrown at him. He asked Washington to teach the Nicaraguans a lesson. Commander George Nichols Hollins appeared at the Atlantic coast port of Greytown. Hollins demanded an apology and an indemnity from the Nicaraguans. The commander then loaded his ship's cannon and leveled the port's huts and buildings.

Hollins had scarcely sailed off before William Walker appeared. About five feet tall, very thin, a man consumed by the idealistic reform movements of the time (such as women's rights and the abolition of slavery), Walker had been a lawyer, then a journalist in New Orleans. By 1855, he had unsuccessfully tried to use a small private army to spread the blessings of democracy to parts of Mexico. Nicaraguan political factions asked him to help them fight their opponents. This "gray-eyed man of destiny," as he came to be known, assembled sixty men and, with Vanderbilt's help, conquered Nicaragua in 1855. The U.S. government moved to recognize Walker's regime officially. The self-styled disciple of democracy, however, made a fatal mistake. He allowed Nicaraguan land and mineral rights to be stolen by American business interests. Nicaraguans merely objected. Vanderbilt, whose interests were threatened, was not as passive. He set out to destroy Walker. The British gladly joined the crusade. In 1857, Walker fell. He could conquer Nicaragua but not Vanderbilt. The adventurer tried three more times to capture parts of Central America. In 1860, Honduran troops captured and shot him. The first U.S. clash with Nicaraguans had not been a happy occasion, as Nicaraguan school children forever after learned.

Cuba also became a target of U.S. expansionists. Southerners led the charge. "With Cuba and St. Domingo," the Charleston *Southern Standard* trumpeted, "we could control the productions of the tropics, and, with them, the commerce of the world, and with that, the power of the world."[23] A colorful and dangerous example of the South's determination was a secret society, the Knights of the Golden Circle, that pledged to extend slavery throughout the Gulf of Mexico. By 1860, the Knights claimed 65,000 members, three state governors, and several of President Buchanan's cabinet. But northerners also set their sights on the Caribbean. Some—particularly in New York City—especially desired Cuban trade. By 1855, U.S. commerce with the island had doubled in a decade until it was seven times greater than Great Britain's and even four times larger than Spain's—which owned Cuba. For their part, abolitionists wanted Cuba in order to open new markets for northern farmers and to end the slave trade in the region. The North's primary motive for coveting Cuba, however, was increased trade.

After the fiasco over the Ostend Manifesto in 1854, the issue died down, then revived with a rush in 1858. The Democratic party had suffered a severe blow. In 1857, the Supreme Court ruled in the *Dred Scott* decision that slavery could be taken into U.S. territories. (A territory was the stage just before a region reached statehood.) The Court added that the federal government had to protect the slaves, because they were property. Southern Democrats rejoiced. Northern Democrats, led by Stephen A. Douglas, opposed the Court's decision: they urged that the issue be settled in the territories through popular sovereignty. Southerners roundly condemned Douglas. Desperate Democratic leaders, led by inept, but expansion-minded President Buchanan, tried to use foreign policy to reunite the party. Polk's former secretary of the Treasury, Robert Walker, told the president: "Cuba! Cuba! (and Puerto Rico, if possible) should be the countersign of your administration, and it will close in a blaze of glory."[24]

Buchanan responded in 1858 by urging Congress to appropriate money to buy Cuba. Douglas and southerners came together to back the measure. But free-soilers blasted it. They were part of a rapidly growing Republican party that had come unexpectedly close to winning the presidency in 1856 and appeared to be in a position to take the House of Representatives in 1858. Seward, newly converted to the Republicans from the dying Whig party, helped lead the attack. In one of the more unique claims in American history, Seward announced that Cuba must some day become part of the United States because "every rock and every grain of sand in that island were drifted and washed out from American soil by the floods of the Mississippi, and the other estuaries of the Gulf of Mexico."[25] Some day—but not in 1858. The slave controversy, Seward believed, first had to be resolved. He received support from other Republicans, who argued that most Cubans were Roman Catholic and that the U.S. constitutional system could "only be maintained . . . on the principle of Protestant liberty."[26]

There was also the possible obstacle of the British fleet. London officials believed that Cuba would fall naturally into American laps, much as John Quincy Adams had predicted thirty-five years earlier. But they were determined not to allow the United States to conquer the island, because it would allow southern slave expansionists to threaten British holdings in the West Indies. In 1857, the British minister to Washington secretly suggested to London that Americans should have Cuba. His superiors replied that he must have lost his senses. Giving Cuba to the United States would resemble pleasing "an animal of Prey by giving him one of one's traveling companions. It would increase [the animal's] desire for similar food and spur him to obtain it."[27]

Out of the smoke and excitement of American expansionism in the 1850s, only the Gadsden Purchase actually emerged, although Cuba, Central America, Canada, and Hawaii were heatedly discussed. In 1859, the United States even made the McLane-Ocampo Treaty in which, in return for a $4 million loan, the Mexicans would give their neighbor extensive railroad routes and the right to intervene with force to provide police protection over all of Mexico. But the U.S. Senate rejected the deal; and in other questions as well, the antiexpansionists carried the day. These foreign-policy issues nevertheless shaped many of the great debates and hopes of the decade as well as intensified southern frustration and fears. Foreign-policy issues were a central cause of the Civil War, for, while relatively few Americans urged total abolition of slavery in all southern states, many determined never to allow slaveholders to establish their "peculiar institution" in the newly acquired territories. Nor were the southerners to be allowed to conquer new regions for their slave system. Foreign-policy issues had combined with domestic controversy to form the combustible mixture that blew the United States apart.

LINCOLN AND THE FOREIGN-POLICY DREAMS OF 1860–1861

The Cuban issue resembled a monster in a science-fiction story that repeatedly had knives driven through its heart but refused to die. Left for dead by Seward and other Republicans in Congress during 1859, the issue arose again a year later. This time Abraham Lincoln decided to kill it once and for all. His decision helped drive the South out of the Union.

Lincoln was a supreme politician who had carefully thought through the central problem of the relationship between foreign policy and slavery. Born in the slave state of Kentucky (and married into a slave-holding southern family), Lincoln moved to Indiana and then Illinois, where he ran successfully for office within seven months of his arrival. Only between 1849, when he returned to Illinois after serving a term in the U.S. House of Representatives, and 1854 did he not run for elected office. A lawyer for the new Illinois Central Railroad and a devout political follower of Henry Clay, Lincoln understood the industrializing corporate America that was transforming the nation's economy. As for slavery, he condemned all abolitionists "who would shiver into fragments the Union of these states" and "tear into tatters its now venerated Constitution." He also condemned, however, any measure that hinted of allowing slavery into the territories or newly acquired foreign areas. These lands were to be preserved for white men without slaves.

In 1858, Lincoln challenged Stephen A. Douglas in the Illinois Senate race. In their famous debates, Lincoln outlined his own views (expansion for none but free white men), then asked the "Little Giant" if he favored taking new territory regardless of how such a conquest might affect the slavery controversy. Douglas's amazing answer revealed his Young America expansionism:

> This is a young and growing nation. It swarms as often as a hive of bees, and . . . there must be hives in which they can gather and make their honey. . . . I tell you, increase, and multiply, and expand, is the law of this nation's existence. You cannot limit this great republic by mere boundary lines. . . . Any one of you gentlemen might as well say to a son twelve years old that he is big enough, and must not grow any larger, and in order to prevent his growth put a hoop around him to keep him to his present size. What would be the result? Either the hoop must burst . . . or the child must die. So it would be with this great nation.[28]

Lincoln barely lost the 1858 election. But by forcing Douglas to separate himself from many northern moderates and southern radicals, the loser became a national figure. In the 1860 Republican convention, he triumphed as a moderate over Seward. The 1860 election became a four-way race among Lincoln; Douglas, who gained the Democratic party nomination; John Bell of Tennessee, whose Constitutional Union party included remaining Whigs who hoped to find some compromise; and John Breckinridge of Kentucky, the nominee of the South's pro-slavery Democrats. Lincoln won a plurality of the popular vote and a

majority of the electoral ballots to gain the presidency. The South prepared to secede. Congress met in short session during January–February 1861 to try to hold the Union together. John Crittenden of
Kentucky fashioned a compromise that provided federal protection to
slavery where it existed. Then, in the crucial clause, he proposed that
"slavery or involuntary servitude" would be prohibited north of the old
Missouri Compromise line of 36°30' but protected in all territory "now
held, or *hereafter acquired*" (italics added).

Lincoln flatly rejected the Crittenden Compromise. "A year will not
pass till we shall have to take Cuba as a condition upon which [the
South] will stay in the Union," he warned friends. "There is in my
judgment but one compromise which would really settle the slavery
question, and that would be a prohibition against acquiring any more
territory."[29] With those words, Lincoln not only separated himself from
Douglas's belief that the American "bees" had to have new "hives"
from which to swarm. He temporarily stopped four centuries of Amer-

*Abraham Lincoln (1809–1865) was considered a mere "prairie statesman" by
leading Republicans. But he outmaneuvered them to win the presidency in
1860, then named some of them to his cabinet, where he could both watch and
use them to restore the Union. Secretary of State Seward is seated in the right
foreground. It took Seward awhile before he could accept his subordinate position.*

ican territorial expansion. No American with his authority had ever taken such a position. Madison, Monroe, Polk, and Douglas, among many others, had argued that the preservation and prosperity of the American system depended on continued landed expansion. Lincoln took another tack. He believed that no expansion was preferable to expansion that enriched slavery and discriminated against freeholding whites.

The Crittenden Compromise never passed Congress. Lincoln took office in March 1861 as southern congressmen left Washington. The new cabinet debated the issue of trying to maintain the Union. The lead was taken by Secretary of State Seward, who had looked down on Lincoln as a "prairie statesman" and believed only he, Seward, could prevent a civil war. The New Yorker had urged compromise and moderation. He feared war. So did his supporters in the New York City mercantile community who acted as bankers and shippers for the great southern cotton crop. As early as January 1861, Seward thought he had hit upon a scheme to save the Union. As he privately told the British minister to Washington, he could unite America by declaring war against foreign powers who threatened to interfere with U.S. interests in the Caribbean. This scheme had one beneficial result. British officials decided to wait before trying to interfere in, or trying to gain benefits from, the growing sectional crisis.

But Lincoln continued to refuse to compromise on the territorial issue. The president then decided to force the question by overruling Seward and sending provisions to Fort Sumter, a Union-held island in Charleston Harbor. Lincoln's move would surely lead South Carolina to fire on the fort and start civil war. The desperate Seward then took a final gamble. On April 1, 1861, the secretary of state told Lincoln that Spain and France seemed to be threatening Santo Domingo and other areas in the Caribbean. Seward suggested that explanations be "demanded" from both European nations. If their answers were unsatisfactory, Lincoln should "convene Congress and declare war against them." Seward perhaps had in mind the conquest of Cuba. He then told the president that he (the secretary of state) should have all necessary power to conduct the diplomacy as well as the war that might result. Seward was convinced that the South would re-enter the Union to help fight such a conflict.[30]

Lincoln quietly buried the astonishing proposal. But Seward's idea was not new. He had been warning the British and others for months that a war for territorial expansion could resolve the domestic crisis. Americans, moreover, had gone to war in 1812 and 1846 to resolve internal as well as external problems. What was new in 1861 was Lincoln's determination not to use foreign policy as a salve for the temporary relief of the burning issue of slavery.

The Diplomacy of the Civil War

As the North's blue- and the South's gray-uniformed armies prepared for battle in the spring of 1861, their leaders prepared to battle for European support. The Confederate nation's president, Jefferson Davis of Mississippi, had extensive political connections. He had been a U.S. Army officer, then married Zachary Taylor's daughter against Taylor's wishes. Davis also was experienced; during the 1850s he had led the South's fight in the Senate for landed expansion. A moderate among the secessionists, Davis had not at first sought the presidency. His wife recalled that when he received the telegram notifying him of the election, "he looked so grieved that I feared some evil had befallen our family."[31] Davis knew that the North's larger population and greater resources could grind down the South unless he obtained European aid. Russia and France, however, might neutralize each other's help. The tsar's government favored the North because Russia might need Union ports and support in case of possible war with Great Britain. Louis-Napoléon's France had nearly 700,000 textile workers dependent on southern cotton. Napoleon, moreover, had imperial dreams of his own for Latin America. He hoped to divide and contain North American expansion southward.

The key to Europe's response was, therefore, Great Britain. Economically, it was divided in its sentiments. The country's gigantic textile industry imported 80 percent of its cotton from the South. But the 1860 bumper crop had provided British mills with a two-and-a-half-year supply of the fiber. That breathing space allowed England to develop alternative supplies in India and Egypt. Moreover, a historic turn in Anglo-American trade had occurred in the mid-1840s. Lower British tariffs combined with spectacular new U.S. wheat crops (brought about in large part by such new technology as the McCormick reaper) to make England increasingly dependent on North American grain. King Corn began to checkmate King Cotton. Poor European grain harvests in 1860, 1861, and 1862 helped Lincoln by enriching U.S. farmers, who were becoming so efficient that they could feed both the giant Union armies and hungry Europeans. The British, in turn, found a vast market in the booming North for their manufactures. As Seward privately observed in early 1861, his section provided the "chief consumption of European productions," and more than a southern rebellion would be needed to "change these great features of American commerce."[32]

Aside from these economic magnets, powerful British liberals favored the North's battle to end slavery, especially after Lincoln's Emancipation Proclamation in September 1862. Because of their own self-interest, the British did not support the South. Divided economic and political opinion did not allow London officials to form a strong, united position. War with the Union could gravely endanger British shipping and, of course, Canada. Intervention might play into the hands of Louis-Napoléon, of whom the British were deeply suspicious as he constantly begged them to take the lead in helping the South. Moreover, with the humiliating northern military defeat at the first and second battles of Bull Run (near Manassas, Virginia) during 1861–1862, many Europeans believed a Union defeat was only a matter of time.[33]

Especially important in the British calculation was the issue of precedent. In April 1861, Davis, who had virtually no navy, commissioned privateers (privately owned ships that operated like pirates in preying on northern merchantmen). Lincoln retaliated with a blockade of the South. That act trapped Lincoln, for a blockade indicated an actual state of war. He had previously insisted that the South was not in a state of war with the North, but only in a state of rebellion. If a state of war was recognized, it could allow Europeans to deal with both sides equally. In May, London declared its neutrality, an act that also recognized the South's belligerent status. Seward and Lincoln, who had warned Europeans against such action, were angered. Seward severely warned France not to deal further with the South, or he would cut off all food exports that Frenchmen were "likely to need most and soonest." (While the crisis was building, however, Seward maintained close personal relations with the French minister to Washington by sending him fine cigars.)

The secretary of state also drafted a tough, even threatening, note (Dispatch Number 10) to the British. Lincoln calmed down Seward's rhetoric, and the new U.S. minister to Great Britain, Charles Francis Adams (John Quincy's son), watered down the wording before giving it to the British government. Adams's intelligence, calmness, and well-timed toughness made him one of the most successful diplomats in American history. A single major mistake in London could have changed the course of the Civil War.

Adams and Seward especially appealed to precedent and British self-interest. When the U.S. government intercepted neutral vessels en route to a neutral port and searched them for contraband, it committed an act that the British had repeatedly committed from 1793 through 1812. The British now did not strongly object as Lincoln repeated their earlier acts. In both the Revolutionary War and the War of 1812, the United States had depended on privateering, much to British displeasure. When Lincoln declared the South's privateering illegal, the British, who had considered it illegal years earlier, happily agreed. Finally, London honored Lincoln's loose blockade (the North did not have the ships needed to throw a tight blockade around the South's 3,500-mile-long coastline) because the British had used such a blockade in the past and would no doubt need to use it in the future.

After mid-1861, Seward settled down to conduct such successful diplomacy that historians have ranked him as the second greatest secretary of state in American history, just behind Seward's idol, John Quincy Adams. The New Yorker met and mastered four spectacular tests. The first occurred in November 1861, when hot-tempered Captain Charles Wilkes of the Union's navy learned that two Confederate diplomats, John Slidell and James Mason, had sailed for London on the British ship *Trent.* Wilkes stopped the ship, seized Slidell and Mason, then allowed the vessel to continue. The British protested and dispatched an ultimatum for the release of the two men. Seward knew that Wilkes had acted illegally. The Confederates had to be freed. But northern feelings ran high. Wilkes became a hero. Seward decided to release Slidell and Mason but, in a brilliant note to Great Britain, argued that Wilkes had been in the right. The secretary of state next neatly expressed gratefulness to the British for finally recognizing that their own acts of impressment before 1812 had been wrong. Seward thus averted war with Great Britain while stroking northern feelings. Journalist Richard Henry Dana wrote, "Seward is not only right, but sublime."[34]

A second crisis occurred in 1862, during the worst Union military setbacks. In March, the Confederate ironclad *Virginia* (formerly the *Merrimac*) fought a more powerful Union warship, the *Monitor,* to a standstill. The battle marked the first time that armored naval vessels had fired on one another. The stand-off demonstrated that the Confederate navy might not be as weak as many had assumed. On land, General Robert E. Lee's forces scored such impressive victories that Seward refused to discuss the Union's humiliations in his diplomatic correspondence.[35] Europeans, led by France, threatened to intervene and mediate a peace. Seward wrote the tsar, who was friendly to the

Union's cause, that Europe could "commit no graver error" than to become involved in the war.[36] A similar but toned-down version of this message also went to London.

Union general George McClellan, who had been overly cautious in fighting Lee, dramatically stopped the South's advance at Antietam, Maryland, in September. Lincoln meanwhile gained support in late 1862 by issuing the Emancipation Proclamation that freed all slaves in areas controlled by the Confederacy. Over the winter and early spring of 1863, a bolder general, Ulysses S. Grant, took great risks but succeeded in cutting off the Confederate force at Vicksburg, Mississippi. Grant's victory split the Confederacy and gave Lincoln control of the lower Mississippi. The triumph occurred, moreover, at the same time (July 1863) that northern troops won a bloody but decisive victory at Gettysburg, Pennsylvania. Concern over European intervention quickly declined in the North. Seward's diplomacy had gained time until the Union's greater resources could be mobilized to wear down Lee's brilliantly directed but undermanned forces. The Union's victories, especially at Antietam, Lincoln's well-timed Emancipation Proclamation, and Adams's shrewd use of these events were critical in forcing the British to pull back from any thought of helping the South.

Seward and Adams faced a third crisis in 1862–1863, when the Confederacy contracted with a British firm, the Laird Brothers, to build several ships. Before Adams could stop the construction, the *Alabama* and *Florida* slipped out of the shipbuilding yards and began attacking northern commerce. Insurance costs in the North rose as merchant shipping sank. A greater danger appeared when Laird began building armored rams that could break the North's blockade and attack northern coastal cities. Adams warned the British foreign secretary, Lord Russell, that if the Laird rams sailed, "it would be superfluous in me to point out to your Lordship that this is war." Aware that allowing the ships to leave was both bad policy and bad law, Russell had already stopped their launching. After the war, the British realized that outfitting these vessels set bad precedent; if the British themselves became involved in a war, their enemy could contract with U.S. shipbuilders to build such ships. To remove the precedent and improve tattered Anglo-American relations, the British paid the United States $15.5 million in 1872 to settle the *Alabama* claims.

A fourth crisis occurred in Mexico. In 1855, Santa Anna, who had tormented and teased both Texans and James K. Polk, finally lost power in Mexico City. He was replaced by Benito Juárez, whose ardent nationalism led him to suspend debts owed to Europeans. In 1861, a joint Spanish, British, and French force appeared to collect the debts, but the first two nations stopped cooperating when they learned that the French intended to control all of Mexico. In 1863, Napoleon III found another tool to achieve his plans for seizing Mexico, establishing a vast New World empire, and finally blocking the expansion of North American Protestants. The tool was an Austrian archduke, Maximilian, who, with his beautiful wife, Carlotta, was persuaded by Louis-Napoléon to lead a French force into Mexico. Seward strongly protested the Austrian's establishment of a monarchy during 1864, but he could do little else. With Lee's surrender at Appomattox Courthouse in Virginia on April 9, 1865, however, a huge, seasoned Union army was suddenly available to move south. General Philip Sheridan, who had trapped Lee at the final battle, led 50,000 soldiers to the Mexican border. Then, Seward again demanded that Maximilian leave Mexico. He carefully never mentioned the Monroe Doctrine, which Europeans refused to recognize, and instead rested his case on U.S. security interests—and, of course, on Sheridan's troops. But Seward only had to wait and watch as Juárez's guerrillas destroyed Maximilian's depleted army. Louis-Napoléon, concerned about the rise to power of Germany in the center of Europe, lost interest in Mexico and reneged on his earlier pledge not to desert the hapless archduke. In June 1867, a Mexican firing squad ended Maximilian's dreams. Carlotta spent most of the next sixty years insane and rambling around Europe in search of help to revive her empire.

Union armies, overwhelming northern resources, Lincoln's shrewdness and determination, Seward's diplomacy, and Adams's skill won the war. Ninety years after an independent United States had set out to settle a continental empire, the territory had been obtained, but at the cost of a civil conflict that took 600,000 lives. With the continent conquered and the issue of slavery decided, a new era opened. A different nation and a different foreign policy emerged. In historian Thomas Schoonover's words, "dollars not dominion" were to spread America's blessings.[37]

NOTES

1. Reginald Horsman, *Race and Manifest Destiny* (Cambridge, Mass., 1981), p. 228; David Potter, *The Impending Crisis, 1848–1861* (New York, 1976), pp. 181–182.

2. Eric Hobsbawm, "The Crisis of Capitalism in Historical Perspective," *Socialist Revolution* 6 (October–December 1976): 82–83. A superb analysis of this background is Kinley J. Brauer, "Diplomacy of American Expansionism," in *Economics and World Power . . .* , ed. William Becker and Samuel F. Wells, Jr. (New York, 1984), esp. pp. 56–58, 112–114.

3. Horsman, pp. 284–286.

4. Kenneth E. Shewmaker, "Daniel Webster and the Politics of Foreign Policy," *Journal of American History* 63 (September 1976): 314.

5. Donald S. Spencer, *Louis Kossuth and Young America* (Columbia, Mo., 1977), pp. 136–183.

6. David M. Pletcher, *The Diplomacy of Annexation: Texas, Oregon, and the Mexican War* (Columbia, Mo., 1973), p. 577.

7. Quoted in Akira Iriye, "America Faces a Revolutionary World," manuscript, in author's possession (1976), p. 2.

8. Eugene S. Ferguson, "The American-ness of American Technology," *Technology and Culture* 20 (January 1979): 18–19; Kenneth Shewmaker and Kenneth Stevens, eds., *The Papers of Daniel Webster. Diplomatic Papers, Volume 2, 1850–1852* (Hanover, N.H., 1987), pp. 255, 289.

9. William Neumann, "Religion, Morality, and Freedom: The Ideological Background of the Perry Expedition," *Pacific Historical Review* 23 (August 1954): 247–257.

10. John Paton Davies, "America and East Asia," *Foreign Affairs* 55 (January 1977): 368–394.

11. William Neumann, "Determinism, Destiny, and Myth in the American Image of China," in *Issues and Conflicts*, ed. George L. Anderson (Lawrence, Kan., 1959).

12. Walt Whitman, "A Broadway Pageant," in *Drum-Taps*, ed. F. DeWolfe Miller (Gainesville, Fla., 1959), pp. 62–64.

13. Henry Adams, *The Education of Henry Adams, an Autobiography* (Boston, 1918), p. 104.

14. Ernest N. Paolino, *The Foundations of the American Empire: William Henry Seward and U.S. Foreign Policy* (Ithaca, N.Y., 1973), p. 212.

15. Frederic Bancroft, *The Life of William H. Seward*, 2 vols. (New York, 1900), I, p. 153.

16. *Ibid.*, I, p. 469.

17. William H. Seward, *The Works of William H. Seward*, ed. George Baker, 5 vols. (Boston, 1853–1883), I, pp. 247–250.

18. *Ibid.*, V, p. 246.

19. Alexis de Tocqueville, *Democracy in America*, 2 vols. (New York, 1948), I, p. 434.

20. Hans Kohn, *American Nationalism, an Interpretive Essay* (New York, 1957), p. 175.

21. Potter, pp. 177–178.

22. Eric Foner, *Free Soil, Free Labor, Free Men* (New York, 1970), pp. 272–280.

23. Kohn, p. 117.

24. Bancroft, I, pp. 472–478.

25. Albert K. Weinberg, *Manifest Destiny* (Baltimore, 1940), p. 66.

26. Foner, p. 228.

27. Gavin B. Henderson, ed., "Southern Designs on Cuba, 1854–1857, and Some European Observations," *Journal of Southern History* 5 (August 1939): 385.

28. Harry Jaffa, *Crisis of the House Divided* (Seattle, 1973), p. 406.

29. David Potter, *Lincoln and His Party in the Secession Crisis* (New Haven, 1942), p. 223.
30. Bancroft, II, ch. 29. There are important comments and bibliography offered by Professors Kinley Brauer and Norman Ferris on Seward's proposal in *The Society for Historians of American Foreign Relations Newsletter* 13 (September 1982): 12–15.
31. Nathaniel W. Stephenson, "Jefferson Davis," in *Dictionary of American Biography*, ed. Allen Johnson and Dumas Malone, 21 vols. (New York, 1930–   ), V, p. 127.
32. Seward, V, pp. 210–211.
33. Brian Jenkins, *Britain and the War for the Union*, 2 vols. (Montreal, 1974–1980), II, pp. 61–105.
34. Foster Rhea Dulles, *Prelude to World Power: American Diplomatic History, 1860–1900* (New York, 1965), p. 11.
35. William H. Seward to Simon Cameron, 6 September 1862, Instructions, Russia, Record Group 59, National Archives, Washington, D.C.
36. Norman A. Graebner, "Northern Diplomacy and European Neutrality," in *Why the North Won the Civil War*, ed. David Donald (Baton Rouge, 1960), pp. 65–75.
37. T. D. Schoonover, *Dollars over Dominion* (Baton Rouge, 1978), p. 283.

For Further Reading

Consult the notes of this chapter and the General Bibliography at the end of this book; these materials are not repeated below. Above all, use the unparalleled *Guide to American Foreign Relations since 1700*, ed. Richard Dean Burns (1983), for pre-1981 materials. The following mostly deal with post-1981 publications. The best recent overview, with excellent bibliography is Bradford Perkins, *From Sea to Sea, 1776–1865*, in *The Cambridge History of U.S. Foreign Relations*, ed. Warren Cohen (1993).

K. Jack Bauer's *Zachary Taylor* (1985), sets the stage, especially with its examination of the 1850 debates that began under Taylor's presidency. Other major biographies are Larry Gara, *The Presidency of Franklin Pierce* (1991); and William C. Davis, *Jefferson Davis* (1991). The South's drive for expansion is interestingly and well told in Charles H. Brown, *Agents of Manifest Destiny* (1980), and Robert E. May, *John A. Quitman* (1985). The scene in the West and conflict with Native Americans can be explored in Robert M. Utley's *The Indian Frontier of the American West, 1846–1890* (1984), which also has a fine bibliography. James T. Wall, *Manifest Destiny Denied* (1982), is especially good on Nicaragua in the 1850s. Key is *The Papers of Daniel Webster: Diplomatic . . . 1850–1852*, ed. K. E. Shewmaker and K. R. Stevens (1987).

The entire era, and especially 1861–1868, is beautifully explored in James M. McPherson, *Ordeal by Fire: The Civil War and Reconstruction* (1982), with a superb bibliography. Herman Hattaway and Archer Jones, *How the North Won: A Military History of the Civil War* (1983), is detailed and focuses on Grant; Richard Current's *Speaking of Abraham Lincoln* (1983) is a series of important essays by a foremost Lincoln scholar; William Appleman Williams's *Empire as a Way of Life* (1980) is a stimulating analysis that is especially important for its original view of Lincoln. Also provocative and important are Norman Ferris, "William Seward and the Faith of a Nation," in *Tradi-*

tions and Values, ed. Norman Graebner (1985), and Gordon H. Warren, *Fountain of Discontent: The Trent Affair and the Freedom of the Seas* (1981). Warren F. Spencer has provided the definitive account on the title's subject and also much on the diplomacy in *The Confederate Navy in Europe* (1983), and interesting views by scholars in India are given in T. C. Bose's "The Diplomacy of the Civil War" and Dwijendra Tripathi's "Indian Cotton and Cotton Diplomacy," both in *American History by Indian Historians*, ed. Giri S. Dikshit, 2 vols. (1969), especially volume 2. On the Mexican crisis, the leading scholar is Thomas D. Schoonover, whose *Dollars over Dominion* (1978) should now be supplemented with his edition of *Mexican Lobby: Matías Romero in Washington, 1861–1867* (1986), a fascinating account of Washington politics during the Civil War as well as of U.S.-Mexican and U.S.-European relations. Another important foreign view is in Martin Crawford, *The Anglo-American Crisis of the Mid-Nineteenth Century: "The Times" of London and America, 1850–1862* (1987).

6

Laying the Foundations for "Superpowerdom" (1865–1896)

Americans emerged from the dark shadows of the Civil War as a reluctantly united nation and, in the North, as a supremely confident people. Lincoln and Seward had exerted immense military power to force the South into unconditional surrender. At the same time, they had successfully managed the most delicate of foreign policies. These triumphs consolidated U.S. power and, in the words of historian David P. Crook, allowed the nation "to continue its headlong rush into superpowerdom."[1]

But something more than northern power triumphed. An incredible new industrial and communications complex also emerged from the conflict. This complex formed the launch pad for that "rush into superpowerdom" over the next thirty years. Many of the North's businesspeople had not wanted civil war, but once the South seceded, they moved quickly to pass probusiness legislation through Congress. They also took advantage of the nearly bottomless needs of the huge northern armies to make immense profits. When the North's humiliation at the first Battle of Bull Run in mid-1861 indicated that the war would be long, one northern financier confidently predicted a fortune for every person on Wall Street "who is not a natural idiot."[2] A young U.S. businessperson of 1860 lived in a nation that produced hardly any steel and little petroleum. Just forty years later, that person lived in the land that was the world's largest steel manufacturer and dominated the world's oil markets.

The Civil War provided the running start for such triumphs. Andrew Carnegie, the greatest iron and steel baron of the era, entered business during the war. Soon after oil pools were initially found in Pennsylvania during 1859, young John D. Rockefeller began combining his first five refineries during the Civil War. As early as 1865, oil ranked sixth on the list of U.S. exports. Rockefeller had begun the Standard Oil (later Exxon) global empire. The war spurred the same dramatic development in the businesses of carriages, sugar refining, and canning.

These businesses laid the foundations on which was built the world's economic superpower of the twentieth century. Such dominance resulted in part from considerable governmental aid. For example, Carnegie reaped huge profits partly because his steel business was protected against cheaper British steel by high tariff walls. From the 1840s until 1861, low tariffs had prevailed, but once the southerners left Washington, a series of tariff measures whipped through Congress. At first, the tariffs were to produce revenue to pay for the war effort, but by 1862, business lobbyists descended on the Capitol to bribe and cajole Congress into passing tariffs that protected their businesses from foreign competition. After the war, government expenses dropped, but the tariff walls remained high. By the 1890s, U.S. business had become so powerful that it could even vault over these walls to sell abroad and thus dominate world as well as American markets.

The manufacturers could move their goods on a rail system that had amounted to 31,000 miles in 1860, but 259,000 miles in 1900. Again, war and government action accelerated growth. In acts of 1862 and 1864, Congress gave railroad companies huge chunks of public land and easy credit to build transcontinental as well as shorter rail systems. By 1872, Washington had given private railroad builders 150 million acres, or an area equal to Maine, New Hampshire, Vermont, Massachusetts, Rhode Island, Connecticut, New York, and part of Pennsylvania combined. The Union Pacific Railroad doubled its original land grant by spending almost half a million dollars to bribe Congress. But few cared about the costs, either financial or moral. One industrialist pointed out the meaning of all this for U.S. foreign policy. Because of the vast rail system, he observed, "the drills and sheetings of Connecticut, Rhode Island, and Massachusetts and other manufacturers of the United States may be transported to China in thirty days; and the teas and rich silks of China, in exchange, come back to New Orleans, to Charleston, to Washington . . . to Boston in thirty days more."[3]

Despite the millions who served in the armies, labor remained cheap for the industrialists because of increased immigration. About 800,000 immigrants arrived between 1861 and 1865. Again, the government played a crucial role in helping private business. The 1864 contract labor law allowed business firms to send agents to Europe and Asia for laborers who were willing to sail to the New World. Seward had argued that Americans were happily following the example of other great empires: "The intermingling of races always was, and always will be, the chief element of civilization . . . [and] we emulate the sway of ancient Rome."[4] As secretary of state, Seward was able to encourage the entry of cheap Chinese labor to work on his favorite project, the transcontinental railroad. In 1868, he and Anson Burlingame (a former Massachusetts congressman and U.S. minister to China who now represented the Chinese government itself) wrote the so-called Burlingame Treaty that allowed the free immigration of each country's citizens.

With the cheap labor, great rail system, government grants, low taxes, and protected market, the number of industrial establishments rocketed upward some 80 percent during the 1860s until they hit 252,000. The number of industrial laborers soared 56 percent, to over 2 million. A new United States of factories and urban areas appeared. But despite the growing number of businesses, new concentrations of power also emerged. In key industries, giant corporations such as Standard Oil, Carnegie Steel, and Singer Sewing Machine began to swallow up small, individually owned businesses. The government gave corporations the right to raise large amounts of money through sale of stocks, but each investor had only limited liability if the business went sour. This almost magical power allowed a concentration of capital unimagined before the Civil War. As the *New York Commercial and Financial Chronicle* observed in 1866, "There is an increasing tendency in our capital to move in larger masses than formerly. Small business firms compete at more disadvantage with richer houses, and are gradually being absorbed into them."[5] These "larger masses" made the U.S. economy both highly efficient and a tough new competitor for the great banking and business combines of Europe. An industrializing America moved out to fight with the old giant empires in a prizefight ring that was global.

THE CONTEXT OF THE ERA: TRIUMPH AND TRAGEDY

The United States became a great world power between 1865 and 1900. It did so even as Americans endured severe economic depressions and

GETTING JEALOUS

In 1901, the Minneapolis Tribune *cartoonist caught the U.S. confidence that Americans were about to replace Europeans as the great world trading power. That confidence had begun to appear a generation earlier as the incredibly productive U.S. industrial and agricultural complexes came to dominate world markets—even in the middle of one of the worst economic depressions in history.*

widespread violence at home. Charles Dickens's opening for his novel, *A Tale of Two Cities,* perfectly applied to the United States of the post–Civil War era: "It was the best of times, it was the worst of times." It was the best of times because of the growing internal market (U.S. population more than doubled to 71 million between 1860 and 1900), the near-tripling of wheat production, the eightfold increase in coal production, the fivefold rise in steel and rail manufacturing, and the gushing of oil production by some twenty times to 55 million barrels in 1898. Total exports of all goods jumped from $281 million to $1.2 billion between 1865 and 1898, while imports rose from $239 million to $616 million. U.S. iron and steel products moved up the export list rapidly to threaten the traditional leaders—cotton and wheat.[6] Americans thus challenged Europeans for the world markets for highly profitable processed goods.

Beginning in 1874, moreover, U.S. exports regularly exceeded imports to produce a favorable balance of trade. With few exceptions (as during the economic panic of 1893–1894), the efficient Americans continued to sell more than they bought abroad—until 1971, when their comparative efficiency plummeted and they returned to their unfavorable merchandise trade balances of a century earlier. The profits gained from these post-1874 trade balances created even more efficient machines at home and fresh U.S. investments overseas.

But it was also the worst of times. In 1873, financial panic struck the country. Americans settled into a twenty-three-year-long depression that, with only a few brief upturns in the 1880s and early 1890s, became one of the most tragic in their history. Some twenty-three years of "boom" were nearly hidden in twenty-three years of "bust." For the depression was caused by the same production of U.S. factories and farms that raised the nation to the top of the slippery pole of international economic competition. Americans produced far more than they could consume. Prices consequently fell. But the increasingly mechanized industries continued to churn out more goods. Finally, laborers were put out of work in growing numbers. Strikes and riots gripped Chicago, Brooklyn, San Francisco, Cleveland, and other large cities. A perceptive British observer, Goldwin Smith, declared that "the youth of the American Republic is over; maturity, with its burdens, its difficulties, and its anxieties, has come."[7]

But even worse lay ahead. Nearly 24,000 labor strikes hit the United States between 1881 and 1900. One evolved into the Haymarket Riot of 1886, in which both strikers and police were killed in Chicago. Four supposed "anarchists" were hanged; another committed suicide. In 1894, President Grover Cleveland sent federal troops into Chicago to break up a railroad strike that had paralyzed much of the city. Not coincidentally, in 1886, the term *capitalism* had entered the American vocabulary as meaning "the concentration of wealth in the hands of the few; the power or influence of large or concentrated capital."[8]

The United States thus became a great world power as its system came under harsh attack at home. But the system was under attack because its productivity was so stunningly successful. Even with the doubling of U.S. population, certain businesses needed more and more overseas markets. The new iron and steel industry exported 15 percent of its goods by the turn of the century, sewing-machine makers 25 percent, oil refiners 57 percent of their illuminating oil. Farmers depended on volatile, unpredictable foreign markets to take as much as one-quarter of their wheat production. Between 70 and 80 percent of the cotton crop went abroad. As Russian and Argentine wheat fields enlarged in the late nineteenth century, and Egyptian and Indian cotton competed in world markets, Americans found out the hard way

"Home, Sweet Home! There's no place like home!"
Destroyer of All: "Home ties are nothing. Family ties are nothing.
Everything that is—is nothing."

Thomas Nast did most of his drawings in the 1860s and 1870s, but he continues to rank as one of the greatest and most influential of political cartoonists. This powerful work of 1878 (just as Americans endured economic crises and a general labor strike) has two special characteristics: the depiction of a good American family trying to get along honestly, and the ghostly figure of "Communism" (with a "Free Love" button in his hat) cynically praising the home before he tries to destroy it. After the appearance of communism in the Paris Commune of 1871, most Americans hated the ideology and the social breakdown and violence associated with it. Anti-communism, as Nast shows, has deep roots in American society, especially during eras of great change.

how developments overseas directly affected their daily lives. Wheat prices received by U.S. farmers fell from $1.90 a bushel in 1860 to 57 cents in 1895. Cotton dropped below the 10-cents-a-pound break-even point to half that amount. Farmers went bankrupt, endured the agonies of moving west to find a new life, or moved their families into city tenements—all because they could not sell enough overseas.

These victims found little sympathy from their representatives in Washington. As the Civil War tariff and railway legislation vividly demonstrated, the political as well as economic system was coming under the control of the new corporate leaders. The officials who made foreign policy usually shared the views—and sometimes even the pocketbooks—of those who ruled the business community. Seward had observed that a political party was "in one sense a joint stock company in which those who contribute the most, direct the action and management of the concern." The politics were often not highly moral. But in terms of consolidating the power of the industrialists and others who shaped the new postwar United States, the politics were spectacularly effective. When Benjamin Harrison, a Republican, learned that he won the 1888 presidential election, he declared: "Providence has given us the victory." A Republican Pennsylvania political boss complained to a friend, "Think of the man. He ought to know that Providence hadn't a damn thing to do with it." Harrison "would never know how close a number of men were compelled to approach the gates of the penitentiary to make him President."[9]

The terrible shaking of the entire U.S. system between 1873 and 1897 even took some of the winners to the brink of a breakdown. John D. Rockefeller later recalled "how often I had not an unbroken night's sleep. . . . All the fortune I have made has not served to compensate for the anxiety of that period." Theodore Roosevelt, along with many others, turned for relief to "the strenuous life," as TR termed it in a famous speech of the 1890s. He urged Americans to "boldly face the life of strife" through "hard and dangerous endeavor. Oversentimentality, oversoftness . . . , and mushiness are the great danger of this age and this people," Roosevelt warned. "Unless we keep the barbarian virtues, gaining the civilized ones will be of little avail."[10] Americans took TR's advice and churned into furious activities during the 1880s and 1890s, especially in the new sports of baseball, football, and basketball. A rage for bicycle riding found men and women pedaling onto the roads. Indeed, a "new woman" appeared, one who rode bicycles, played tennis, and even attended golf clubs and racetracks. Bernarr Mac-Fadden's *The Power and Beauty of Superb Womanhood* (1901) displayed exercises so women could have the "muscular strength" to equal the hyperactive American male.[11] Thus, many Americans found outlets in feverish activities at home—and overseas.

Much of their energy focused on finding overseas markets for the U.S. glut of goods. Business needed an efficient global foreign policy to match industry's efficient global sales networks. A leading manufacturer was quoted in 1885 as saying that business most of all needed "an intelligent and spirited foreign policy" that would "see to it" that enough overseas markets were obtained, even if the use of military force was necessary.[12] Some Americans disagreed. Led by William Jennings Bryan in the 1890s, these dissenters argued that prices and employment could be improved by coining more silver (and not just gold) so that more money would be in circulation. But even these silverites accepted the common view that more foreign markets were required. They only shrewdly added that by using more silver, Americans would be able to capture those markets in areas where silver was widely used—as in China and Latin America. When the silverites and Bryan went crashing down to defeat in the 1896 presidential election, the all-purpose solution of more overseas markets continued to dominate American thought. Four years before, in 1892, U.S. foreign trade had already exceeded that of every country in the world except Great Britain. But it was not enough.

Some businesses found a new way to capture overseas markets. In the 1880s, it became possible for the first time to speak of U.S. multinational corporations. Such leading companies as Singer Sewing Machine, McCormick farm machinery, Standard Oil, and Kodak Camera directly invested overseas so they could more easily sell their products abroad. The 1890s economic depression spurred this movement. Sherwin-Williams Paint almost literally made good on its slogan "We Cover the Earth." By 1890, worried European officials warned of an "American invasion" into their economies. Articles appeared with the titles "The Americanization of the World" and "The American Invaders" to discuss the new multinationals. The largest firms did not require government help. But smaller companies did need support from the State Department. Consequently, a revitalized U.S. Consular Service and such business groups as the National Association of Manufacturers (formed during the depths of the 1894–1895 depression) appeared to work for the ambitious multinational corporations.[13]

The largest firms often handled their own foreign policy. By the 1890s, for example, John D. Rockefeller's Standard Oil controlled 70 percent of the world's oil markets. It quadrupled its sales abroad during the 1880s. William Herbert Libby, who directed Rockefeller's overseas invasion, bragged that petroleum had "forced its way into more nooks and corners of civilized and uncivilized countries than any other product in history emanating from a single source." But the Russian oil industry, with financial support from the great Rothschild banking house of France, rose to challenge Standard Oil. Rockefeller successfully fought back. A U.S. State Department consul in the Russian oil-producing area carefully kept Standard up-to-date on the competition's movements. Rockefeller opened new refineries in central Europe. And Standard set up a subsidiary that specifically targeted its efforts to undercut Russian moves in western Europe and the Far East. Long before other Americans fought a cold war with Russia, Standard Oil executives were engaged in their own bitter conflict.[14]

A CHRONOLOGY OF POSTWAR EXPANSION:
THE ALASKA PURCHASE AND A BACKLASH

The U.S.-Russian confrontation, however, lay out of sight in a clouded future when Secretary of State Seward laid plans for an ambitious, post–Civil War foreign policy. Indeed, Russia, of all the major powers, seemed in 1865 to be the United States' best friend. Part of the tsar's fleet had made a dramatic, highly popular visit to the Union's ports during the Civil War—although Americans later learned (as Seward believed at the time) that the Russians actually cared less about the North's cause than finding refuge for their own ships in case of a war with the British. That war nearly occurred in the wake of a Polish uprising against Russia's rule in 1863. But Russian-American relations received a real boost in 1867, when the tsar decided to sell Alaska.

Alaska's fate had been decided by U.S. traders and merchants as early as the 1820s. By that date, the Russian Trading Company, charged with ruling and exploiting Alaska for the tsar, actually depended on U.S. sources—not Russian—for most of its necessities. By 1865–1866, the U.S. minister to St. Petersburg, Cassius Clay of Kentucky, pushed for Alaska as a route through which a U.S.-built telegraph line would link the two great countries. (The energetic fifty-six-year-old Clay worked for this project, that is, when he was not fighting off protective mothers of young girls he admired or when he was not challenging Russian nobles to duels with bowie knives.) The telegraph project was never completed, but Clay used information obtained from it to help persuade Russian officials to sell Alaska. Seward concluded the deal in Washington during March 1867. The United States agreed to buy the great expanse for $7.2 million.

But congressional opposition quickly arose. The price seemed extravagant for a frozen wasteland ("Walrussia" or "Seward's Ice Box," as Alaska became known). Seward and President Andrew Johnson, moreover, were hated by radical Republican leaders because the president wanted to bring the South back rapidly into the Union on easy terms. Seward finally triumphed for five major reasons. First, he and

OUR NEW SENATORS.

Seward's purchase of Alaska from Russia turned out to be one of the all-time real-estate bargains, but he was ridiculed in 1867. Here a cartoonist has Seward telling the Alaskan representative to "bring . . . Mr. Seal along with you [to Washington]."

the Republican Senate leader, Charles Sumner from Massachusetts, emphasized the rich Alaskan mineral and animal resources awaiting exploitation by ambitious Americans. Second, they and others stressed that the purchase meant that the United States would partially block Great Britain's and Canada's access to the Pacific—would "cage the British Lion on the Pacific Coast," in one congressman's words—and perhaps make the annexation of Canada easier. Third, Alaska and the Aleutian Islands would serve, in the phrase of Republican House leader Nathaniel P. Banks of Massachusetts, as the "drawbridge between America and Asia." The rich China and Japan trade could be reached and protected more easily by the great circle route passing from San Francisco to Alaska to Asian markets. Fourth, Russia was a good friend. By working with her, Americans could remove a possible future source of conflict and cooperate with the friend against their common enemy— Great Britain. Finally, when the House of Representatives hesitated to appropriate the $7.2 million, the Russian minister in Washington apparently distributed about $73,000 as bribes to grease the passage. Seward, moreover, had already run up the Stars and Stripes over Sitka, Alaska—which allowed one congressman to proclaim: "Shall that flag which waves so proudly there now be taken down? Palsied be the hand that would dare remove it."[15]

Seward thus added 586,000 square miles, or an area nearly two and a half times the size of Texas, to the Union. The editor of *U.S. Railroad and Mining Register* crowed that the purchase ensured American greatness in the Pacific. But more, he added, both Americans and Russians "believe that in time not far remote Washington and St. Petersburg will be the political poles of the earth. . . . Never was international friendship deeper than between America and Russia."[16] Little could the ecstatic editor imagine what lay ahead for that "friendship."

Nor, in the flush of victory, could Seward and other expansionists imagine that Alaska was to be the last U.S. landed conquest for more than a generation. Seward had been able to annex the Midway Islands (about 1,200 miles west of Hawaii) in 1867 for possible use as a way station and cable point in the Asia trade. But he failed in efforts to obtain bases in Santo Domingo, Haiti, the Central American isthmus (for a future ocean-to-ocean canal), Hawaii, Greenland, and the Danish West Indies (Denmark's Virgin Islands) in the Caribbean. Congress was more interested in questions of the South and newly freed blacks than in distant territories. Such bases, moreover, could cost money, and the nation already was burdened with a huge Civil War debt. The House of Representatives actually passed a resolution in late 1867 opposing "any further purchases of territory" because of the country's "financial condition." Many also believed the nation already had enough land. As the *Chicago Tribune* phrased it, in the vast western regions "we have already more territory than we can people in fifty years."[17]

Americans, for the first time in their history, even lost interest in immediately annexing Canada. Radical Irish-Americans—Fenians— hoped to free Ireland from British rule by moving out of Buffalo, New York, to attack Canadian territory and thus stir up a U.S.-British war. Even Seward, who long lusted after Canada, disavowed the Fenians' bloody raids. After the 1867 North America Act, in which England granted autonomy to the new Dominion of Canada, some disgruntled western Canadians rebelled against the new regime and flirted with the idea of attaching their region to the United States. But Washington officials had lost their passion for such a romance. Their attention turned inward and then focused on the critical problem of finding overseas markets for their overproductive farmers and industrialists.

A CHRONOLOGY OF POSTWAR EXPANSION:
WINNING THE WEST

Americans obviously did not lose interest in foreign policy between the Civil War and the 1898 war. They only went about dealing with foreign policy differently. U.S. officials realized that they faced a new set of problems. The most immediate problem was settling the vast western territories that had been conquered since 1803. Such settlement was crucial for two reasons: to find new agricultural lands for the growing population and to develop the routes for the transcontinental railroads that would carry U.S. goods to Pacific ports, from which the goods could find markets in Asia.

But settlement meant that tribes of Indians had to be moved or destroyed. In this sense, the wars against the Native Americans between 1870 and 1890 marked the last step needed to unify and consolidate the United States before Americans could go abroad to become the superpower of the twentieth century. About 360,000 Indians lived west of the Mississippi in 1850. They included the powerful Sioux, Cheyennes, and Comanches. White and black Americans numbered about 20 million. In 1860, 1.5 million whites lived in the West, but by 1890

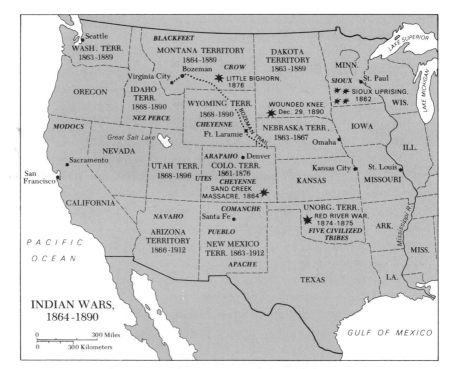

Between the Civil War and 1890, white Americans fought a seemingly continual war against the Indians to control land seized before 1848. Far from being a quiet period in American settlement, it was one of the most active—especially for the U.S. Army.

*George Armstrong Custer (1839–1876)
graduated at the bottom of his West
Point class but fought bravely in the
Civil War before leading two hundred
of his troops into an Indian ambush in
which he and his men were massacred.
His name became synonymous with one
of the few failures in nineteenth-century
American expansion.*

that number had multiplied six times. Native Americans had no idea
that so many white people existed.

Many of the new settlers doubtless agreed with Theodore Roosevelt's view in his popular book, *The Winning of the West* (published in
several volumes between 1889 and 1896), that "this great continent
could not have been kept as nothing but a game preserve for squalid
savages. . . . The man who puts the soil to use must of right dispossess
the man who does not, or the world will come to a standstill."[18] In the
early nineteenth century, Indians had been treated as "separate nations,"
but by 1871 Congress no longer viewed them as separate nations or
made lasting treaties with them. Instead, U.S. officials simply passed
laws to push Native Americans off desirable lands, created isolated
reservations for the tribes, and—in the Supreme Court's words—saw
the Indians not as "nations," but as "local dependent communities."

These views of Roosevelt and the government justified driving the
Native Americans off their rich western lands. The victims not surprisingly struck back. Most notably they did so in 1876 at Little Bighorn
in Montana, when 2,500 Sioux warriors, some with 16-shot repeating
rifles, surrounded and slaughtered 260 men of George Custer's Seventh Cavalry. As later accounts described the horror, the cavalrymen
were "bawling in terror, shooting themselves and each other." Then
the "discovery of Custer's obliterated force: hills strewn with bloated
pink, stripped, mutilated corpses and dead horses. Eyeballs and brains
extracted and laid out on rocks, hearts impaled on poles."[19]

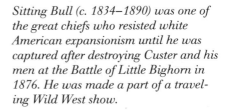

Sitting Bull (c. 1834–1890) was one of the great chiefs who resisted white American expansionism until he was captured after destroying Custer and his men at the Battle of Little Bighorn in 1876. He was made a part of a traveling Wild West show.

Between 1877 and 1890, however, such victims were usually red, not white. News of Custer's defeat reached the East as Americans celebrated the centennial of their independence. In the words of one popular magazine, they swore revenge by the time the next anniversary arrived in 1976, when nothing would remain of the "red man but a case of flint arrow-heads, stone hatchets, and moth-eaten trappings at the Smithsonian [a museum in Washington, D.C.]." Native Americans were systematically killed, starved by the extermination of the buffalo herds on which they depended for food and other needs, or pushed into desolate reservations. General Nelson A. Miles (who, in the 1898 war, headed the U.S. Army in its fight against Spain) tracked down Sitting Bull, who had destroyed Custer's forces, and the great Indian chief became an exhibit in the popular Buffalo Bill's Wild West Show. Sitting Bull later returned to his people, but a confrontation with white authorities developed, a gun discharged accidentally, and U.S. officials quickly killed the chief and seven Sioux, while the Indian's old circus horse mistook the gunfire for the Wild West Show and did tricks. The U.S. Army then surrounded another Sioux chief, Big Foot, and some 350 followers at Wounded Knee, South Dakota, reservation in 1890. Again, an accidental gunshot apparently set off full-scale firing. The U.S. troops lost 25 men (many of them victims of their own crossfire) but killed Big Foot and 150 others, including women and children.[20]

In historian Robert M. Utley's words, "The Indian frontier of the American West vanished in the smoke of Hotchkiss shells bursting over the valley of Wounded Knee Creek."[21] With the Native Americans crushed, whites settled more land in the thirty years after 1870 than they did in the previous three hundred years. Such settlement at once formed an immensely productive landed empire and a route from the East Coast to Asian markets. The U.S. Army meanwhile used the Indian wars as training for conflicts overseas. British observers thought the 25,000-man U.S. Army and its 2,000 officers one of the world's toughest fighting forces because of its battles with the Indians. Scholar Walter L. Williams has found that of the 30 U.S. generals who fought against Philippine rebels between 1898 and 1902, 26 (or 87 percent) had earned their spurs fighting Indians. Williams has also noted that the new legal terms devised after 1870 to control the Native Americans and take away many of their rights were simply transferred to Cuban, Philippine, and Puerto Rican affairs after 1898.[22] The post-1870 Indian wars were a key link between the whites' landed expansion to 1860 and their new overseas empire taken in 1898 and after.

A CHRONOLOGY OF POSTWAR EXPANSION: AFRICA AND LATIN AMERICA

U.S. overseas expansion had two main characteristics after 1870: it was almost entirely interested in markets (not in land), and it moved along not one but many routes to all corners of the earth. In Africa, for example, American interests had been almost nonexistent, except for the U.S.-sponsored colonization of free African Americans in Liberia that had occurred in the 1830s and 1840s. Even in Liberia, however, Washington officials refused to recognize the new nation, which declared its independence in 1847, until 1862. The slave controversy and antiblack feelings prevented recognition of the U.S.-created colony until that time. After 1862, relations remained slight.

In the 1870s, however, Commodore Robert Shufeldt led a pioneering voyage that gained new U.S. rights to coaling stations and trade in Africa and along the Persian Gulf. In 1884, private citizens who sought markets in Africa, and diplomat John Kasson, who well understood the need of fresh markets for U.S. goods, pushed Washington officials to send a delegation (led by Kasson) to participate in the Berlin Conference. This conference was called by the German government to resolve growing problems in the Congo. In that African region, the ambitions of the Belgian king, Leopold II, seemed on a collision course with other European colonial powers. The United States only wanted—and indeed obtained—a pledge by all the powers to an "open door" so that its goods could enter the Belgian Congo on fair terms. The U.S. delegation then helped Leopold block his European rivals, although the Belgian king was enforcing one of the most brutal colonial policies in all of Africa. Kasson's work at Berlin was strongly supported by the powerful Democratic senator from Alabama, John T. Morgan. Historian Joseph A. Fry, after studying Morgan's passionate expansionism, concludes that the Alabaman believed "the Congo's throngs of unclad natives seemed to offer an unlimited market" for the South's textile industry. Morgan also saw the region "as an ideal dumping ground for the South's surplus blacks."[23]

But not even Morgan's influence was enough. The new U.S. president, Grover Cleveland, took power in 1885 and disavowed Kasson's agreement because it could possibly become an entangling alliance. Five years later, U.S. opinion against Belgium was shaped by an extraordinary man. George Washington Williams had fought in the Civil War, had been a popular preacher, editor of a major black newspaper, the first African American ever elected to the Ohio legislature, and the first major black historian in the United States. After a trip to the Congo, his *Open Letter* of 1890 detailed twelve specific charges against Leopold's brutality, including enslaving "women and children" while neither educating nor economically developing the society. But even Williams could do little more than slow the growing belief of some Americans that a rich African market awaited them. By 1890, historian Milton Plesur relates, U.S. newspapers even predicted "that the whites would in time swallow up the African Negro in the same way the North American Indian had all but disappeared."[24]

The road to Latin American markets and bases seemed clearer and was certainly a more traditional path for U.S. expansion. In 1870, President Ulysses S. Grant tried to annex Santo Domingo partly at the request of several friends who had some highly corrupt business projects in that Caribbean country. Grant also wanted to ensure that no other power could control the country. He justified annexation in part by arguing that it would help quiet racial problems at home: Santo Domingo could support "the entire colored population of the United States, should it choose to emigrate." Americans' racism had usually restrained their expansionist impulses into the Caribbean, but the president now tried to turn racism into a reason for expansionism. He ran into a buzz saw of opposition. The powerful Sumner (who before the Civil War had been an Abolitionist on the slave issue), argued that as "an Anglo-Saxon Republic" the United States must not take in "colored communities" where the "black race was predominant." Secretary of State Hamilton Fish also opposed annexation in part for racial reasons. Maria Child, for forty years a vigorous opponent of U.S. expansionism (see p. 105), fought the president with quite different arguments. Child compared Grant's grab to a pre–Civil War "filibustering project." She feared that "this Republic will sink rapidly to degeneracy and ruin if we go on thus seizing the territory of our neighbors by fraud or force."[25] Grant finally gave up his plans, but he announced in 1870 that henceforth the Monroe Doctrine contained a new principle: "Hereafter no territory on this continent shall be regarded as subject to transfer to a European power." This "nontransfer" principle had appeared as early as 1811, when President James Madison applied it to Florida. But Grant's declaration first made the principle a formal part of the Monroe Doctrine.

Another, more promising chance to seize new territory occurred in Cuba. The Cubans had begun a revolution against decaying Spanish control in 1868. Some U.S. lives and property were lost in the fighting, but the major crisis arose in 1873, when Spain seized the *Virginius*, a ship under the U.S. flag that was carrying weapons to the rebels. The Spanish executed fifty-three crew members. Cries went up in the United States for revenge—that is, for taking Cuba. But Grant's cool-headed secretary of state, Hamilton Fish, knew that the ship had been breaking the law. Fish and other officials, moreover, wanted no part of the multiracial Cuban population. When one cabinet member raised the possibility of annexing Cuba, Fish squashed the idea by noting the terrible racial problems already existing in "South Carolina and Mississippi." Spain paid an $80,000 indemnity for the lives of the crew members. By 1878, it had been able to stop the revolution, but it had been a close call. Maria Child concluded, "I do believe if we could annex the whole world, we should [then] try to get a quarrel with Saturn, in order to snatch his ring from him."[26]

U.S. attention next turned to Central America. It focused on a new grave danger: in the late 1870s, the French began building an isthmian canal in Panama (a province of Colombia). The project directly threatened the 1850 Clayton-Bulwer agreement between the United States and Great Britain for joint construction of such a passageway. More pointedly, the French enterprise endangered the growing determination of Americans to build the canal by themselves. Seward had nearly obtained such a right from Colombia in 1869, only to have the Colombian legislature reject the treaty. When the French began their digging, the U.S. government warned sharply that it would never "consent to the surrender of this control [over an isthmian canal] to any Euro-

"The Plumed Knight from Maine" (nicely caught in this portrait), James G. Blaine (1830–1893) was secretary of state twice (1881 and 1889–1892), a defeated Republican presidential candidate (1884), and—of special importance—a skilled politician who understood the needs of the new American industrial complex and preached the need for U.S.–Latin American economic ties. Blaine foresaw U.S. relations with the Latin nations much as Seward foresaw U.S. relations with Asia in the twentieth century.

pean power or combination of powers." Secretary of State James G. Blaine entered office in 1881 and opened talks about building a canal in Nicaragua—as if the 1850 treaty did not exist. For most Americans the Clayton-Bulwer Treaty indeed did not exist. As one phrased it, Americans refused "to be bound hand and foot" by that "covenant of national disgrace." The French effort finally failed in the 1880s, a victim of enormous engineering problems as well as of the deadly mosquito-carried yellow fever. It was only a matter of time before Americans would try on their own. Indeed, during these year: U.S. military forces landed in Panama half a dozen times to restore order and protect American citizens threatened by armed uprisings against the Colombian government. The turn toward an ocean-to-ocean canal owned and operated by the United States occurred in the 1870s and 1880s, long before it was realized in Panama in 1903.[27]

Blaine personally exemplified the new U.S. approach to Latin America. A power in the Republican party (he was its presidential nominee in 1884), the "Plumed Knight from Maine" understood the needs of the fast-developing U.S. industrial system and the business leaders who built it—and who also contributed handsomely to his Republican party. As secretary of state, in 1881 he declared that his foreign policy must bring peace to, then increase U.S. trade in, Latin America. "To attain the second object the first must be accomplished," Blaine concluded. That conclusion meant more vigorous American intervention to ensure a secure marketplace. In 1890, again serving as secretary of state, Blaine spelled out his policy. His statement, which is a lesson in American history as well as diplomacy, serves as a summary of U.S. economic policy toward Latin America from 1865 until the late twentieth century:

> I wish to declare the opinion that the United States has reached a point where one of its highest duties is to enlarge the area of its foreign trade. Under the beneficent policy of [tariff] protection we have developed a volume of manufactures which, in many departments, overruns the demands of the home market. In the field of agriculture, with the immense propulsion given in it by agricultural implements, we can do far more than produce breadstuffs and provisions for our own people. . . . Our great demand is expansion. I mean expansion of trade with countries where we can find profitable exchanges. We are not seeking annexation of territory. At the same time I think we should be unwisely content if we did not seek to engage in what the younger Pitt so well termed annexation of trade.[28]

In 1889, the year before that speech, Blaine had called and then presided over the First International American Conference. He sought a customs union (a kind of vast, inter-American common market) and even a common currency to expedite U.S. exports southward. Blaine obtained neither objective, but the meeting did lead to the building of the Pan-American Highway system, linking the United States to nations in South America. The gathering also marked the beginning of the Pan-American movement that brought North and South Americans closer culturally and economically. Blaine's success helped lead, in 1890, to the first significant "reciprocity" tariff passed by the U.S. Congress. This legislation allowed certain Latin American products (especially coffee, hides, and sugar) to enter the United States freely as long as the nations that produced them allowed U.S. exports into their countries equally free from tariff restrictions. Under the 1890 reciprocity treaties, trade immediately boomed with Cuba and Brazil, among others.

Indeed, U.S. exports to Brazil rose $500,000 in three years, while imports from that country increased by an amazing $17 million. Then, in 1893, the friendly republican government in Brazil was threatened by an uprising led by promonarchical Brazilian naval units and encouraged by the British and other European powers. The U.S. administration of President Cleveland at first tried to remain neutral. But when U.S. exporters (including the Standard Oil Company) warned Cleveland that their trade could be endangered by a rebel victory, the president ordered naval units to protect U.S. shippers who wanted to unload goods in Brazilian ports. This order directly aided the government in the capital of Rio de Janeiro, because the government depended on revenue paid on the unloaded goods. Cleveland's action thus broke the back of the rebellion and protected the growing North American trade. When one rebel vessel challenged the U.S. warships escorting American merchantmen to the harbors, a U.S. warship fired a shell across the Brazilian vessel's bow and warned that any further challenge would result in the sinking of the rebel ship. The rebellion quickly ended. The grateful Brazilian government erected a statue to James Monroe, celebrated the Fourth of July, and even organized a serenade for the U.S. minister in Rio de Janeiro.[29]

Thus, the U.S. need to find more markets abroad had led to direct interference in internal Brazilian affairs. The story was less happy, but the conclusion much the same, when a rebellion threatened the pro-U.S. government in Chile during 1891. The U.S. minister, Patrick Egan, was a rambunctious Irishman who had the touch to be a successful politician in the United States but not a suave diplomat in Chile. His public support of the Chilean government led a mob to kill two U.S. sailors who were on shore leave in Valparaíso from the USS *Baltimore*. President Benjamin Harrison, a former Civil War hero, took a tougher line than even Egan and demanded an apology and indemnity. But Chile refused to pay for the mob's acts. As Harrison's anger grew, the two countries edged toward war. Some worried U.S. observers noted that Chile's navy was actually larger than the U.S. fleet, which had been allowed to rot after the Civil War. Blaine, in one of his last acts, and a new Chilean government then moved to cool the crisis. Chile finally paid an indemnity of $75,000 for the killing of the sailors.

The Chilean and Brazilian affairs displayed the new, active interventionism of the United States in Latin America. But nowhere did this vigorous policy appear more dramatically than in Venezuela during 1895–1896. For in that crisis, Washington officials challenged Great Britain, the world's leading power.

The showdown had begun long before, in the 1840s, when British policy makers claimed disputed territory lying between Venezuela and their colony of British Guiana. Little more happened, however, until the 1890s, when the British began to reassert their claim. Worried U.S. officials noted that the disputed land controlled the entry into the Orinoco, a vast waterway that could provide access to trade for a large section of South America. Rumors of rich mineral wealth in the region also appeared. President Cleveland especially focused on the British threat to the Monroe Doctrine. In 1895, he demanded that the London government of Lord Salisbury arbitrate the claim. Salisbury, one of Europe's great statesmen, was busy with Germany's threat to British interests in South Africa. He ignored Cleveland's message.

Infuriated, the president ordered his secretary of state, Richard Olney, to restate the U.S. position forcefully so that Salisbury would pay attention. Olney did so in a historic note of July 20, 1895. It claimed that the United States could enforce the Monroe Doctrine because the nation was now supreme in the Western Hemisphere. A surprised Salisbury became aware that his country and Cleveland's were rushing toward a conflict. He refused to recognize the legality of the Monroe Doctrine but did implicitly recognize Olney's spread-eagle claim that the "infinite resources [of the United States] combined with its isolated position render it master of the situation and practically invulnerable as against any or all other powers," as Olney had stated it in the note.[30] Salisbury agreed to arbitrate the dispute, and Venezuela indeed received the land controlling the Orinoco. The British prime minister finally bowed to U.S. demands because the gravest threat to his nation's interests came not in the New World, but from a rising Germany (especially the growing German fleet) and from explosive imperialistic rivalries with the French and Germans in Africa. Faced with those dangers, Salisbury shrewdly laid a foundation for Anglo-American friendship by agreeing to arbitrate the less important Venezuelan boundary.

For their part, Americans also replaced long-held British interests in Nicaragua during the 1890s. Indeed, throughout Central America—a region that London's power had shaped for half a century—U.S. companies and military power became overwhelming. By 1900, the United Fruit Company of Boston dominated Costa Rica's and Guatemala's economies. Soon, United Fruit's control of Central American affairs reached a point where the company was simply called "The Octopus." Sam "The Banana Man" Zamurray of New Orleans gained control of Honduras's economy after 1900, until that country became known as a banana republic. As early as the 1880s, a Guatemalan official recognized that the United States had become "the natural protector of the integrity of Central American territory."[31] But these moves into Central America only formed part of a larger expansionism that transformed the United States into the dominant power in the hemisphere between 1865 and 1896. Even Lord Salisbury had to admit the new extent of that power.

A CHRONOLOGY OF POSTWAR EXPANSION:
THE PACIFIC AND ASIA

When U.S. naval officers claimed the Midway Islands (so named because they were halfway between California and Japan) for the United States in 1867, they triggered a thirty-three-year surge of westward expansion over the Pacific Ocean. In 1867, Americans were trying to rebuild from the ruins of their civil war. By 1900, they had an army on the Asian mainland and had conquered a string of bases across the broad Pacific that linked that mainland to the United States.

The magnificent Hawaiian Islands were the first stop. As early as 1843, so many U.S. traders and missionaries worked there that wary British and French officials asked the United States to sign a treaty guaranteeing Hawaii's independence. The Americans not only refused, but a decade later tried to annex the islands—a move foiled by British opposition as well as by the growing division in Washington over the slavery and expansion issues. In 1867, Seward reopened the campaign to annex by shrewdly trying to seduce Hawaii into the U.S. orbit through a reciprocity treaty. Again, internal U.S. political fighting stopped Seward's move, but in 1875 Grant and Fish did negotiate such a trade treaty. The results were all that expansionists such as Seward and Grant could have desired. With the rich U.S. market at their disposal, Hawaiian planters, between 1876 and 1885, raised their sugar production from 26 million pounds to 171 million pounds. The planters utterly depended on the mainland as their exports to the United States quadrupled to $8.9 million in those ten years. By 1881, Blaine could call the islands "a part of the productive and commercial system of the American states."[32]

President Cleveland, mistakenly labeled by some historians as an antiexpansionist, worked hard to renew the reciprocity treaty in 1885. But domestic U.S. sugar interests hated Hawaiian competition and so opposed the agreement. The Hawaiians further sweetened the deal by giving the United States a lease on Pearl Harbor, an undeveloped but potentially spectacular naval base. Cleveland termed the islands "the stepping-stone to the growing trade of the Pacific." That phrase captured exactly how he and other officials saw Hawaii as a gateway to the great Asian commerce.[33] The Hawaiians, however, were soon shocked by the 1890 reciprocity treaties that allowed cheap Cuban sugar into U.S. markets. The islands' economy began sinking. By this time, the Americans who controlled the plantations also controlled the poli-

Queen Liliuokalani (1838–1917) was a determined and shrewd leader of her Hawaiian peoples. But in the early 1890s, she was unable to reverse the growing U.S. power on the islands, and in 1893 a coup, supported by the U.S. Navy, in effect ended her power despite President Cleveland's refusal to annex Hawaii at that point.

tics. They had demanded a constitution in 1887 that recognized their power. By the early 1890s, however, a strong-minded native monarch, Queen Liliuokalani, moved to neutralize the Americans' influence. Her attempt to reclaim power for the Hawaiians combined with the economic troubles to produce an American-led rebellion against her in January 1893. Washington's minister to Hawaii, John L. Stevens, actively helped by landing U.S. naval units to aid the rebels.

But now, Cleveland (just returned to the White House for a second term of 1893–1897) rejected the plea by the Americans in Hawaii for annexation. He knew the native Hawaiians had been coerced by U.S. force. Moreover, the president doubted that the U.S. Constitution could work when stretched across thousands of miles of water and imposed on such a non-Caucasian society. Cleveland also had enough problems at home. The 1893 stock-market collapse marked the lowest and most dangerous point in the twenty-five-year depression that had begun in 1873. But time was on the side of the pro-annexation group. Hawaii depended on U.S. markets. That dependence was tightened by an 1894 tariff bill restoring a favored place for the islands in the U.S. market. A new administration and new chance for a Pacific empire in 1898 finally allowed for the annexation of the islands. The annexation climaxed the expansionist drive that had begun more than half a century before.

The next stepping stone across the Pacific was Samoa. These beautiful islands, populated by Polynesians, had long served as an important stopping place for whaling vessels and traders (hence their early name, Navigators Islands). By the 1870s, their strategic location had attracted British and German attention. Into that rivalry stepped U.S. Naval Commander R. W. Meade. In 1871, Meade took the initiative to give Samoan chiefs American protection in return for their giving him a lease on the fine harbor of Pago Pago. The U.S. Senate did not accept that pact, but it ratified a similar treaty in 1878. Within a decade, the three Western powers were bitterly immersed in conflict over Samoa. By 1887, Cleveland's secretary of state, Thomas F. Bayard, asked for a conference before war possibly erupted. Bayard, a Delaware patrician with long political experience in an industrializing America, actually saw Samoa as an extension of the U.S. transcontinental railroad that carried U.S. goods to Asian markets. German Foreign Office officials angrily muttered that Bayard was extending the principles of "the Monroe Doctrine as though the Pacific Ocean were to be treated as an American lake."[34]

In 1887, Germany and Britain attempted to cut a deal over Samoa that threatened U.S. claims. Bayard refused to recognize the deal. At the same time, Germany began to bar U.S. meat imports (especially pork) on the grounds that they were tainted by a dangerous parasite. German-American relations, hardly in existence a generation before, suddenly became an intense rivalry over trade rights and access to the distant Pacific islands. The great German chancellor, Otto von Bismarck, had enough worries maintaining the new Germany that he had pieced together since 1860 through conquests and diplomacy. Wanting no war with Great Britain or the United States, in 1889 he called a conference in Berlin to discuss Samoa. Just before the meeting, a hurricane destroyed German and U.S. lives and vessels on the islands. Against this somber background, the Germans, British, and Americans agreed to divide the islands among themselves into a tripartite protectorate. They merely paid lip service to the Samoans' independence.

In 1899, the United States again found itself in a struggle with Germany and Great Britain over control of Samoan politics. British attention, however, was soon drawn off to that country's war in South Africa. London officials finally gave up all claims to Samoa. Germany and the United States then divided the islands between themselves, with the Americans retaining Pago Pago. The ending was peaceful, but, as historian Manfred Jonas observes, Germany, while giving in to U.S. claims, now viewed America as a rival. The Americans feared that German expansionism in Samoa might spread to the Caribbean. During this era, therefore, a "great transformation"[35] (as Jonas calls it) of the normally friendly U.S.-German relations began to strain the ties between Washington and Berlin. Within another generation, that strain would lead to war.

With the 1899 agreement on Samoa, the United States had added another key section in its bridge to Asia. The final destination was the Asian mainland itself, the quest of U.S. traders and missionaries for more than a century. Again, Seward had pointed the way. Since the 1840s, Americans had worked for an "open door" (that is, equality) for their trade in Asia. They did so, however, largely through "scavenger diplomacy"—coming behind the British Lion and taking from Asians whatever the Lion had left behind after its conquests. Seward dramatically changed that approach. In 1863 in Japan, and again in 1866 in Korea, the secretary of state worked alongside the British and French in their attempts to gain concessions. Thus, Seward added two new tactics to U.S. diplomacy in Asia: a willingness to use force, and a willingness to work with European powers to expand Western interests in Asia. These tactics shaped Washington's Asian diplomacy for the next eighty years.

Seward's policy, however, also created a problem—indeed, a contradiction—that bedeviled U.S. policy toward China over those next eighty years. For, in 1868, he signed with China's representative, Anson Burlingame, a treaty that allowed free immigration between the two nations. The agreement also pledged the United States not "to intervene in the domestic administration of China in regard to the construction of railroads, telegraphs, or other material internal improvements." Seward thus recognized China's control over its own internal development. But he refused to give up any claims on China's trade that might be made by the Western powers. While the United States thus recognized China's control of certain domestic affairs, it refused to recognize China as a fully sovereign country in control of its foreign commercial affairs. A month before he died in 1870, Burlingame wrote, "Let us try once, at least, to see what the Chinese will do if let alone by those who would Christianize them with gunpowder." Burlingame's hope was not to be realized. As his biographer, David L. Anderson, writes, Burlingame hoped to use the 1868 treaty to "replace coercion with cooperation" in U.S.-Chinese relations.[36] Instead, the United States merely mentioned Chinese sovereignty while working ever more closely with European powers to control Chinese affairs.

Seward especially got tough with Korea, the "Hermit Kingdom," over which China tried to claim control. Korea was strategically important, for it was at the gateway to the markets and raw materials of

Manchuria and northern China, as well as to eastern Russia itself. When the crew of the U.S. ship *General Sherman* mistakenly made its way into a Korean river, it was slaughtered by outraged Koreans. Seward quickly used his two new tactics. He prepared a U.S. naval attack, and asked the French to cooperate. But France, which had also lost citizens to Korean retaliation, refused to go along. In 1871, the Grant administration finally dispatched a fleet of five U.S. ships up the Han River. When Koreans fired on the ships, the Americans destroyed forts and killed more than two hundred people. Twelve Americans were killed, and the United States remained without any treaty with the tough Koreans. In 1876, Japan entered the scene by recognizing Korean independence from China. Korea now became a prize to be fought over by Japan and the Western powers.

The United States again took up the fight in 1882, when Commodore Robert Shufeldt forced Korea to sign a treaty opening itself to the Western world. An ardent expansionist, Shufeldt colorfully expressed his vision for American destiny in the Pacific:

> The Pacific is the ocean bride of America—China and Japan and Corea— with their innumerable islands, hanging like necklaces about them, are the bridesmaids, California is the nuptial couch, the bridal chamber, where all the wealth of the Orient will be brought to celebrate the wedding. Let us as Americans—let us determine while yet in our power, that no commercial rival or hostile flag can float with impunity over the long swell of the Pacific sea. . . . It is on this ocean that the East and the West have thus come together, reaching the point where search for Empire ceases and human power attains its climax.[37]

But the "bridesmaids"—Korea and China—were soon violated by Japan. The United States could do little about it. Americans certainly were concerned as Japanese power grew. Led by an extraordinary U.S. diplomat, Horace Allen, American interests in Korea temporarily increased. Allen, who nicely combined his Presbyterian missionary dedication with a robber-baron passion for making money, helped Americans develop Korean gold mines (perhaps the richest in Asia) and bribed authorities to obtain streetcar construction contracts.[38] But the U.S. attempt to split Korea from China backfired. Japan was the region's developing power, and it rightly saw Korea as vital to its own security.

As tension built between the rising Japanese and the declining Chinese empires, war finally erupted in 1894. Japan quickly forced China to quit Korea as well as give in to other demands. The Asian balance of power had shifted. Allen's and other U.S. enterprises were endangered by Japan. A prophetic U.S. senator, Anthony Higgins of Delaware, warned that when China "shall have arisen out of her defeat," she was likely to become the dominant military force of the globe. But most U.S. officials agreed with Secretary of State Walter Quintin Gresham in 1894: Japan was "the most civilized country" in Asia and, as such, could be trusted to respect the United States "as her best friend."[39] The friendship seemed to be reinforced strongly by trade. U.S. exports to China jumped from $3 million in 1890 to $7 million in 1896, but exports to Japan grew from $5 million to $8 million in those years. (The $22 million of imports from China in 1896 and $26 million of goods imported from Japan that year far outstripped U.S. exports to those two nations.)

THE 1865-TO-1896 ERA: A CONCLUSION

The race for the riches of Asia was accelerating. The race for dominance in Latin America, however, had ended. The United States had won that contest by 1896. This historic victory and the growth of American power in Asia signaled fundamental changes in U.S. diplomacy between 1865 and 1896, changes that shaped diplomacy throughout the twentieth century.

Most notably, the friends and enemies of 1865 exchanged places by the 1890s. During the century after 1776, the United States and England had fought two wars. Another conflict threatened during and after the Civil War, when the British built several ships, including the *Alabama*, for use by the Confederacy. After the war, infuriated Americans, led by Senator Charles Sumner, demanded that London pay millions for the damages that the ships had caused—or, as some Americans indicated, the annexation of Canada, which would be equally satisfactory as payment. As Anglo-American relations grew tense in the late 1860s, President Grant, who had come to despise the pompous Sumner, maneuvered the senator off the chairmanship of the powerful Foreign Relations Committee and made a deal with England. In the 1872 Washington Treaty, the British essentially apologized for releasing the *Alabama* and agreed to pay $15.5 million in the so-called *Alabama* claims. The United States, in turn, agreed to submit other disputes to arbitration. As a result of this agreement and long-held British claims against Americans, the United States finally paid England $7.4 million. Both U.S. and Canadian citizens gained free access to the St. Lawrence, St. John, and Yukon rivers, and also to Lake Michigan.[40]

In 1893, U.S. and British diplomats settled a long-festering dispute over the killing of female seals in the Bering Sea. The slaughter was destroying herds that provided rich, highly profitable furs. The United States, moreover, claimed control over the Bering Sea itself. Washington officials finally had to drop that claim, but in 1892–1893 Russians and Japanese, as well as Canadians, agreed with the American demand to protect the seals.

With these agreements of 1872 and 1892–1893, the air cleared between London and Washington. U.S.-British relations also were built on marriages of the children of American robber barons, who sought respectability, to those of British aristocrats, who sought dollars. But of special importance, in the Venezuelan crisis of 1895–1896, the British in fact recognized U.S. dominance in the Western Hemisphere, while in Asia the two English-speaking peoples shared a common commitment to the "open door" to China. Theodore Roosevelt caught this historic turn in 1898 when he wrote a friend: "I feel very strongly that the English-speaking peoples are now closer together than for a century and a quarter . . . ; for their interests are really fundamentally the same, and they are far more closely akin, not merely in blood, but in feeling and principle, than either is akin to any other people in the world."[41]

At the same time, however, relations with Russia, a long-time U.S. ally, turned worse. The tsars and the British monarchs were rivals, especially in the Near and Far East. As U.S.-British relations warmed, U.S.-Russian relations cooled. In Asia, the Russians, lagging far behind British and American industrial development, could not survive in an open-door type of economic competition. They favored outright colonization, which was precisely the policy the open-door approach opposed. Of special importance to many Americans, the tsar launched vicious attacks on Russian Jews in the 1880s. These pogroms, which had deep roots in the nation's history, occurred just as millions of European Jews migrated to seek opportunities in the United States. The attacks also appeared as many U.S. businessmen, including Jews, suffered discrimination when they tried to do business in Russia. U.S. opinion changed radically. "Russia's ambition is sleepless and insatiable," a Baltimore newspaper editor proclaimed in 1886. "It goes ahead step by step, through intrigue, through treachery, through diplomatic mendacity," and she cares not if "her people remain poor." The powerful Louisville newspaper publisher, Henry Watterson, put it simply: the

Russian had "proven his ability to fight like the European, and to deceive like the Asiatic."[42]

This historic switch in their international friendships was mirrored at home, when Americans realized in the 1890s that they had reached a turning point in their domestic life. The 1890 Census announced that the frontier line had finally disappeared. A young University of Wisconsin historian, Frederick Jackson Turner, explored the meaning of the Census finding. He did so in perhaps the most influential essay ever written on American history. In 1893, Turner argued that the U.S. economy and politics had been vigorous and successful because of the frontier. ("Economic power," Turner stated, in fact "secures political power.") The frontier had also produced "individualism" in the American character. Turner then had to conclude with a dramatic warning: "And now, four centuries from the discovery of America, at the end of a hundred years of life under the Constitution, the frontier has gone, and with its going has closed the first period of American history."[43]

To many Americans, the question now became: What can we find to replace the frontier so our economy, politics, and individualism can remain strong? That question took on a special urgency as strikes, riots, political radicalism, and bankruptcy struck the United States during the economic depression of the 1890s. Turner himself argued in 1896 that the frontier's disappearance created "demands for a vigorous foreign policy . . . and for the extension of American influence to outlying islands and adjoining countries."[44]

That conclusion had already been reached by Captain Alfred Thayer Mahan, who became perhaps the most influential military strategist in U.S. history. In 1886, Mahan was a bored, middle-aged naval officer. Then in a Lima, Peru, library he read that ancient Rome's control of the sea had secured its empire. Over the next quarter-century, in a series of widely read books and in lectures at the Naval War College in Newport, Rhode Island, Mahan built on that insight into Rome to construct a global foreign policy for the United States. He assumed that American surplus production required overseas markets. In order to obtain and protect those markets, the United States needed a great navy and fueling bases as rest stops for that navy. Beginning in 1886— and especially in 1890, when the first modern U.S. battleship was commissioned (and also the year when Mahan's first great book *The Influence of Sea Power upon History, 1660–1783,* appeared)—Americans built the Great White Fleet that fought the 1898 war and formed the basis of the twentieth-century U.S. Navy. Mahan pushed hard to annex an isthmian canal area, as well as bases in the Caribbean, Hawaii, and

Alfred Thayer Mahan (1840–1914) was a friend of presidents and emperors because he knew how to use history to justify expansionism and the building of great navies. His seriousness, stiffness, discipline, and self-esteem are indicated in this portrait.

the distant Pacific to serve the fleet. He focused on the markets of Asia as the supreme prize.

To conquer that prize, he advised the United States to work with Great Britain and Japan (other seagoing powers who wanted the open door), and oppose Russia (a land-based power who opposed the open door). As a devout Christian, he believed that the seeking of this empire was "the calling of God." To do God's work, Mahan demanded a centralized government and powerful president. He blasted the democratic legacy of Thomas Jefferson, who "made a hideous mess in his own day, and yet has a progeny of backwoodsmen and planters who think what he taught a great success." Force was to be used freely, especially force in the form of large battleship fleets. The mere threat of such force, Mahan believed, prevented war. Anyway, he wrote, war had become merely "an occasional excess, from which recovery is easy."[45] Mahan enormously influenced U.S. officials, especially Presidents William McKinley and Theodore Roosevelt.

Other U.S. naval officers worked for a great navy because, in historian Peter Karsten's words, of "rank, discipline, and boredom."[46] Needing ships and action to gain personal promotion, they lobbied hard in Congress to build a new fleet with the most modern weapons. In 1883, the U.S. Navy was a pitiful collection of 90 woeful ships, 38 made of wood. Mahan and other officers, such as Mahan's mentor at the Naval War College, Stephen B. Luce, worked with Congress and such industrial giants as Bethlehem Steel and Andrew Carnegie to construct a great navy. It marked the success of the first military-industrial complex.[47] U.S. government dollars put laborers to work during the depression. Carnegie and other builders profited from highly subsidized government contracts.

The navy's officers obtained their fleet. And, in 1898, the United States moved to obtain what historian Frederick Drake calls "the empire of the seas."[48]

NOTES

1. David P. Crook, *Diplomacy during the American Civil War* (New York, 1975), p. 9.
2. Arthur C. Cole, *The Irrepressible Conflict, 1850–1865* (New York, 1934), p. 345.
3. Charles A. Beard and Mary Beard, *The Rise of American Civilization*, 2 vols. (New York, 1927), II, pp. 128–129.
4. William H. Seward, *The Works of William H. Seward*, ed. George Baker, 5 vols. (Boston, 1853–1883), III, pp. 498–499.
5. Thomas C. Cochran and William Miller, *The Age of Enterprise* (New York, 1942), p. 116.
6. David M. Pletcher, "Growth and Diplomatic Adjustment," in *Economics and World Power*, ed. William H. Becker and Samuel F. Wells (New York, 1984), pp. 120–124. For the agricultural side, the pioneering account is William Appleman Williams, *The Roots of the Modern American Empire* (New York, 1969).
7. Robert V. Bruce, *1877: Year of Violence* (Indianapolis, 1959), pp. 312–314.
8. Henry Nash Smith, *Mark Twain's Fable of Progress* (New Brunswick, N.J., 1964), pp. 8–9.
9. Cochran and Miller, p. 157.
10. David Healy, *U.S. Expansionism: The Imperialist Urge in the 1890s* (Madison, Wis., 1970), p. 115.
11. John Higham, "The Reorientation of American Culture in the 1890s," in *The Origins of Modern Consciousness*, ed. John Weiss (Detroit, 1965), pp. 26, 28.

12. Ralph Dewar Bald, Jr., "The Development of Expansionist Sentiment in the United States, 1885–1895, as Reflected in Periodical Literature" (Ph.D. diss., University of Pittsburgh, 1953), 266–267.

13. Mira Wilkins, *The Emergence of the Multinational Corporation* (Cambridge, Mass., 1970), pp. 68–69, 71.

14. Ralph W. Hidy and Muriel E. Hidy, *Pioneering in Big Business, 1882–1911: A History of Standard Oil* (New York, 1955), pp. 122–154.

15. Ronald Jensen tells the story well in *The Alaska Purchase and Russian-American Relations* (Seattle, 1975); see also Foster Rhea Dulles, *Prelude to World Power: American Diplomatic History, 1860–1900* (New York, 1965), pp. 53–56, and Fred H. Harrington, *Fighting Politician: Major General N. P. Banks* (Philadelphia, 1948), pp. 182–185.

16. *U.S. Railroad and Mining Register*, 6 April 1867, in "Alaska, 1867–1869" file, Papers of William H. Seward, University of Rochester, Rochester, New York.

17. Donald M. Dozer, "Anti-Expansionism during the Johnson Administration," *Pacific Historical Review* 12 (September 1943): 255–256; Charles S. Campbell, *The Transformation of American Foreign Relations, 1865–1900* (New York, 1976), p. 17. Seward and U.S. investors nevertheless moved significantly into Mexican affairs. Their important story is well told in Thomas Schoonover, *Dollars over Dominion* (Baton Rouge, 1978), pp. 252–254, 282–283 esp.

18. A superb analysis is Walter L. Williams, "U.S. Indian Policy and the Debate over Philippine Annexation," *Journal of American History* 66 (March 1980): 816; also Robert M. Utley, *The Indian Frontier of the American West, 1846–1890* (Albuquerque, 1984), p. 14.

19. Quoted in *Washington Post Book World*, 18 November 1984, p. 14; *Washington Post*, 29 December 1986, p. A3. A classic account is Stanley Vestal's *War-Path and Council Fire* (New York, 1948) on the Plains Indians.

20. Utley, pp. 186, 201, 251–257.

21. *Ibid.*, p. 261.

22. Williams, "U.S. Indian Policy," 828; Vestal, p. xi, quotes the British expert.

23. Joseph A. Fry, "John Tyler Morgan's Southern Expansionism," *Diplomatic History* 9 (Fall 1985): 329–346.

24. *The Gilded Age, a Reappraisal*, ed. H. Wayne Morgan (Syracuse, 1963), p. 167; Williams's story is beautifully told in John Hope Franklin, *George Washington Williams, a Biography* (Chicago, 1985), esp. pp. 202–203, 234–241.

25. Alexander DeConde, *Ethnicity, Race, and American Foreign Policy* (Boston, 1992), p. 46; Edward P. Crapol, "Lydia Maria Child: Abolitionist Critic of American Foreign Policy," in *Women and American Foreign Policy*, ed. E. Crapol (Westport, Conn., 1987), p. 13.

26. Richard H. Bradford's *The Virginius Affair* (Boulder, Col., 1980) is a fine account.

27. David Pletcher, *The Awkward Years* (Columbia, Mo., 1962), p. 105; Dulles, pp. 37–38; Campbell, pp. 15–18; Robert A. Friedlander, "A Reassessment of Roosevelt's Role in the Panamanian Revolution of 1903," *Western Political Quarterly* 14 (June 1961): 538–539.

28. James G. Blaine, *Political Discussions, Legislative, Diplomatic, and Popular, 1856–1886* (Norwich, Conn., 1887), p. 411; *New York Tribune*, 30 August 1890, p. 1.

29. The story is told and footnoted in Walter LaFeber, *The New Empire* (Ithaca, N.Y., 1963), pp. 210–218.

30. Richard Olney to Thomas F. Bayard, 20 July 1895, in *Foreign Relations of the United States, 1895,* 2 vols. (Washington, D.C., 1896), I, pp. 545–562; the classic account is Dexter Perkins's *The Monroe Doctrine, 1867–1907* (Baltimore, 1937), pp. 153–168.

31. Pletcher, *Awkward Years,* pp. 35–36.

32. *Foreign Relations of the United States, 1881* (Washington, D.C., 1882), pp. 635–639; Donald M. Dozer, "Opposition to Hawaiian Reciprocity, 1876–1888," *Pacific Historical Review* 14 (June 1945): 157–183.

33. *A Compilation of the Messages and Papers of the Presidents, 1789–1897,* ed. James D. Richardson, 10 vols. (Washington, D.C., 1900), VIII, pp. 500–501.

34. Quoted in LaFeber, p. 55.

35. Manfred Jonas, *The United States and Germany* (Ithaca, N.Y. 1984), pp. 48–49.

36. David L. Anderson, "Anson Burlingame: American Architect of the Cooperative Policy in China, 1861–1871," *Diplomatic History* 1 (Summer 1977): 239–256.

37. Quoted, with excellent analysis, in Frederick G. Drake, *The Empire of the Seas: A Biography of Rear-Admiral Robert N. Shufeldt* (Honolulu, 1984), p. 116.

38. The extraordinary story of Horace Allen is superbly told in Fred H. Harrington's *God, Mammon, and the Japanese* (Madison, Wis., 1944). Harrington published a reconsideration forty-two years later: "An American View of Korean-American Relations, 1882–1905," in *One Hundred Years of Korean-American Relations, 1882–1982,* ed. Yur-Bok Lee and Wayne Patterson (University, Ala., 1986).

39. Jeffrey M. Dowart, "The Pigtail War: The American Response to the Sino-Japanese War of 1894–1895" (Ph.D. diss., University of Massachusetts, 1971), 111–112.

40. Adrian Cook's *The Alabama Claims: American Politics and Anglo-American Relations, 1865–1872* (Ithaca, N.Y., 1975) tells this story well.

41. Theodore Roosevelt, *The Letters of Theodore Roosevelt,* ed. Elting E. Morison *et al.,* 8 vols. (Cambridge, Mass., 1951–1954), II, pp. 889–890.

42. Thomas A. Bailey, *America Faces Russia* (Ithaca, N.Y. 1950), pp. 147–148.

43. Frederick Jackson Turner, *The Frontier in American History* (New York, 1947), esp. pp. 32–37.

44. Frederick Jackson Turner, "The Problem of the West," *Atlantic Monthly* 78 (September 1896): 289–297.

45. Alfred Thayer Mahan, *Letters and Papers of A. T. Mahan,* ed. Robert Seager II and Doris D. Maguire, 3 vols. (Annapolis, 1975), II, pp. 506, 662; III, pp. 80, 484; William L. Livezey, *Mahan on Sea Power* (Norman, Okla., 1947), p. 263.

46. Two books by Peter Karsten are crucial here: *The Naval Aristocracy* (New York, 1972) and *Soldiers and Society* (Westport, Conn., 1978).

47. See especially B. F. Cooling, *Gray Steel and Blue Water Navy: The Formative Years of America's Military-Industrial Complex, 1881–1917* (Hamden, Conn., 1979).

48. Drake, p. xi.

For Further Reading

Begin with the well-organized pre-1981 references in *Guide to American Foreign Relations since 1700,* ed. Richard Dean Burns (1983); the notes of this chapter and the General Bibliography at the end of this book; the up-to-date bibliography in Robert L. Beisner, *From the Old Diplomacy to the New, 1865–1900* (1986); Walter LaFeber, *The American Search for Opportunity, 1865–1913*, in *The Cambridge History of U.S. Foreign Relations*, ed. Warren Cohen (1993); and the exhaustive list of works in Charles S. Campbell's *The Transformation of American Foreign Relations, 1865–1900* (1976). The Beisner and Campbell are also most helpful and provocative overviews, as is Richard Welch, Jr., *The Presidencies of Grover Cleveland* (1988).

For the context and perspectives on the "imperialist" debate, especially helpful are *Imperialism and After: Continuities and Discontinuities*, ed. Wolfgang J. Mommsen and Jurgen Osterhammel (1986); Tony Smith, *The Pattern of Imperialism: The U.S., Great Britain and the Late Industrializing World since 1815* (1982); Eric Hobsbawm, "The Crisis of Capitalism in Historical Perspective," *Socialist Revolution* 6 (October–December 1976): 77–96, especially on 1873–1896; William H. Becker, *The Dynamics of Business-Government Relations* (1982), for a more benign view of the relationship; Joseph A. Fry, *Henry S. Sanford: Diplomacy and Business in Nineteenth-Century America* (1982), for a fine case study; Tom E. Terrill's important analysis, *The Tariff, Politics and American Foreign Policy* (1973); and Edward Crapol's readable, significant study, *America for Americans* (1973), on Anglophobia.

Ideological and cultural influences are well analyzed in Michael H. Hunt, *Ideology and U.S. Foreign Policy* (1987), especially chapter III, tying internal and external racism together; Stuart Anderson, *Race and Rapprochement: Anglo-Saxonism and Anglo-American Relations, 1895–1904* (1981); Frank A. Cassell, "The Columbian Exposition of 1893 and U.S. Diplomacy in Latin America," *Mid-America* 67 (October 1985): 109–124; Robert W. Rydell, *All the World's a Fair: Visions of Empire at American International Expositions, 1876–1916* (1985), a fascinating account; and Donald C. Bellomy, "Social Darwinism Revisited," *Perspectives in American History* New Series, I (1984): 1–129, the best analysis. The frontier's impact is also noted in Brian W. Dippie, *The Vanishing American: White Attitudes and U.S. Indian Policy* (1982).

On specific geographical areas, the Latin American problems are explored in the Anderson and Cassell accounts noted above; Craig T. Dozier, *Nicaragua's Mosquito Shore* (1985); Joseph Smith, *Unequal Giants . . . 1889–1930* on U.S.-Brazil relations; Thomas Schoonover, "Imperialism in Middle America," a superb overview, in *Eagle against Empire*, ed. Rhodri Jeffreys-Jones (1983); Joyce S. Goldberg, *The Baltimore Affair: U.S. Relations with Chile, 1891–1892* (1986), now the standard account; and James F. Vivian, "U.S. Policy during the Brazilian Naval Revolt, 1893–1894: The Case for American Neutrality," *American Neptune* 41 (October 1981), a defense of U.S. policy. For Asia, see Phillip Darby, *Three Faces of Imperialism: British and American Approaches to Asia and Africa, 1870–1970* (1987), a fine comparative study; David L. Anderson, *Imperialism and Idealism: American Diplomats in China, 1861–1898* (1986); Yur-Bok Lee, *Diplomatic Relations between the United States and Korea, 1866–1887* (1970), which is the best on the subject, and also Lee's "Establishment of a Korean Legation in the United States, 1887–1890," *Illinois Papers in Asian Studies* 3 (1983). On Africa, begin with Darby's book noted above, and also Peter Duignan and L. H. Gann, *The United States and Africa: A History* (1984).

For individual administrations, Paul S. Holbo's *Tarnished Expansion: The Alaska Scandal, the Press, and Congress, 1867–1871* (1983) is most revealing; Clifford W. Haury, "Hamilton Fish and the Conservative Tradition," in *Studies in American Diplomacy*,

1865–1945, ed. Norman Graebner (1985), an interesting interpretation; Justus D. Doenecke, *The Presidencies of James A. Garfield and Chester A. Arthur* (1981), important on Latin America and Korea especially; Michael J. Devine, *John W. Foster: Politics and Diplomacy in the Imperial Era, 1873–1917* (1981), a good analysis of a key figure; and Charles W. Calhoun, *Gilded Age Cato: The Life of Walter Q. Gresham* (1988), the standard biography.

7

Turning Point: The McKinley Years (1896–1900)

THE SIGNIFICANCE OF THE LATE 1890s

As the twentieth century dawned, the United States stepped onto the world stage as a great power. Because of the triumphs scored between 1898 and 1900, it strode confidently now with Great Britain, France, Russia, Germany, and Japan—nations that possessed immense military strength and had used that strength for conquest. Never had a newly independent nation risen so far so fast as did the United States between 1776 and 1900.

Historians have argued not over whether the United States deserved great-power status by 1900 (all agree that it did), but whether Americans consciously intended to follow the expansionist policies after 1896 that projected them into such distant regions. Historian Ernest May believes that the United States had "greatness thrust upon it." But another scholar, Albert K. Weinberg, concludes that U.S. officials were no more passive at key moments than "is the energetic individual who decides upon, plans, and carries out the robbery of a bank."[1] The years 1896 to 1900 thus become critical for the student of U.S. foreign policy in the twentieth century. For if the nation entered the ranks of great world powers at this time, it is of central importance to know how it did so. By accident? Because of a few elite officials who pushed reluctant Americans overseas? Because of the U.S. system's domestic needs that forced that system to assume global responsibilities? The well-known saying "Just as the twig is bent, the tree's inclined" might have meaning for U.S. diplomatic history. The reasons why the United States moved outward so rapidly in the late 1890s help us understand why it grew from these roots (or twig) into a twentieth-century superpower.

McKINLEY AND McKINLEYISM

Americans living in the late 1890s understood that they were witnessing a historic turn. After the triumph over Spain in 1898 brought the United States new holdings in the Caribbean and the western Pacific, Assistant Secretary of State John Bassett Moore observed that the nation had moved "from a position of comparative freedom from entanglements into the position of what is commonly called a world power. . . . Where formerly we had only commercial interests, we now have territorial and political interests as well."[2]

Moore's boss, President William McKinley, presided over these changes. McKinley won the 1896 election over the highly popular Democrat, William Jennings Bryan. The affection Americans felt for McKinley ranked with the feelings they later had toward the popular Theodore Roosevelt, Franklin D. Roosevelt, and Dwight D. Eisenhower. A gentle, soft-spoken, highly courteous man, McKinley had long been known for the love and care he had lavished on his wife, an invalid who required much of his attention. Born in Niles, Ohio, in 1843, Major McKinley had been a Civil War hero, then parlayed his reputation and uncanny political instincts into a career in the House of Representatives between 1876 and 1890. By the end of his stay, no one on Capitol Hill better understood the new industrialized America. He dominated debates on the central issues of tariffs and taxes because he had mastered the facts and understood the powerful industrialists who made the country run. Moving on to the governorship of Ohio, he maintained order in an economically depressed state while nearby regions were wracked by riots. He was not reluctant to use state forces to control strikers, but he somehow did so while keeping the good will of the labor leaders. With the help of fellow Ohioan and millionaire steel industrialist Marcus Hanna, who ran a superbly organized campaign, McKinley moved to the White House. The new president named Ohio senator John Sherman as secretary of state and then rewarded Hanna by having him appointed to the empty Senate seat. The United States thus obtained a secretary of state who was aged, sometimes incapacitated, and too often senile; but in Hanna, McKinley enjoyed a

William McKinley (1843–1901) of Ohio was the last Civil War veteran to be president (enlisting at age seventeen, he had been a hero) but the first modern American chief executive. He also appointed a modern cabinet—that is, one made up of administrators who owed allegiance to the president. He is at far left. John Hay is at McKinley's right.

trusted power broker in the Senate who followed the president's every wish.

Anyway, McKinley intended to control foreign policy himself. An accomplished negotiator and an experienced politician whose antennae could instantly detect an opponent's weakness, the president knew how to conduct back-room talks and keep secrets. His State Department depended especially on Alvey A. Adee, a long-time professional who served in the department for fifty-five years until his death in 1924. Adee personally wrote or approved nearly every outgoing message. When he once bicycled past, a Washingtonian said, "There goes our State Department now." Though hard-of-hearing, Adee seemed to have learned everything that the president needed to know about international law and diplomatic history. The closed-mouth president, deaf Adee, and senile Sherman led to the complaint that "the President says nothing, the Assistant Secretary hears nothing, and the Secretary of State knows nothing."

Controlling foreign policy in the way that he did, McKinley became not only the first twentieth-century president, but the first modern chief executive. He developed new powers, especially in maneuvering and controlling Congress, while he kept the control of foreign policy in his own hands (and used the new devices of the telephone and typewriter while doing so). McKinley expanded the Constitution's commander-in-chief powers until, without congressional permission, he used it to dispatch U.S. troops to fight in China. His action set a precedent for the "imperial presidency" of the 1960s and 1970s.

McKinley and Hanna, moreover, cleverly used the backlash caused by the 1893–1897 economic crisis that had driven the Democrats from power in 1894 and 1896. The two men built a political coalition so powerful that only one Democratic presidential nominee would be elected between 1896 and 1932. The new politics had profound influence on presidential power. As a result of the 1890s political realignment, Republicans dominated the North and Democrats controlled the South. This division meant that contests between Republicans and Democrats declined in individual states, voters grew less interested, and many (especially black people in the South) were disfranchised.[3] The president thus broke free of the hard-fought party rivalry that had marked the 1876–1896 years. He enjoyed more freedom and a more dependable political base from which to conduct foreign policy. McKinley exploited these opportunities by becoming the first chief executive to appoint a staff member who dealt with newspaper reporters and prepared press handouts that publicized the administration's case. The Ohioan was even the first president whose inauguration was put on film.

The great Kansas journalist, William Allen White, observed that McKinley survived twenty years in the jungles of Ohio politics, "where survival values combined the virtues of the serpent, the shark, and the cooing dove." White believed that the president was too much "cooing dove," "too polite," for McKinley's "Prince Albert coat was never wrinkled, his white vest front never broken. . . . He weighed out his saccharine on apothecary scales, just enough and no more for the dose that cheers but does not inebriate." White further perfectly caught McKinley's genius for handling people, especially those in Congress. After rejecting one visitor's request for a favor, the president took the carnation he always wore in his coat and told the man to "give this to your wife with my compliments and best wishes." He did it so graciously that the visitor declared, "I would rather have this flower from you for my wife than the thing I came to get."[4]

At the same time, the president understood the brute truths of politics. Historian Henry Adams watched the president closely and described "what might be called McKinleyism; the system of combinations, consolidations . . . , realized at home, and realizable abroad."[5] Under McKinley, an industrialized America moved to Americanize new parts of the world.

Two Crises, One War

McKinley took the presidential oath in March 1897 as a revolution raged just ninety miles from U.S. shores. In 1894–1895, the U.S. tariff policy had kept out Cuban sugar from mainland markets. The island went into an economic tailspin. A revolution against Spanish colonialism had broken out between 1868 and 1878. It now re-emerged with greater force. By late 1895, the rebels claimed to have established a provisional government. Support for their cause swelled in the United States, but neither Cleveland nor McKinley would recognize the revolutionaries. To do so would have released the Spanish government from its responsibility for protecting $50 million of U.S. property in Cuba. Washington officials preferred to hold Spain fully responsible for protecting U.S. lives and property, while pushing the Madrid government to give Cuba enough autonomy so that the revolutionaries would stop fighting.

Spain, however, refused to move the island toward autonomy. Its once-great, four-hundred-year-old empire had rotted away until it amounted to little more than Cuba, Puerto Rico, a few scattered islands in the Pacific, and the Philippine Islands. No government in Madrid could surrender these last holdings and expect to remain in power. The Spanish instead took a tough approach. They dispatched 150,000 soldiers, who, under the command of General Valeriano Weyler (soon nicknamed "Butcher" Weyler by U.S. newspaper editors), tried to destroy rebel support by rounding up thousands of Cubans and placing them in barbed-wire concentration camps. The revolution nevertheless continued to spread. The insurgents burned U.S. property in the hope of forcing McKinley's intervention.

Nineteenth-century Americans had little respect for Spain. They had seized its North American empire piece by piece between 1800 and 1821. The Spanish, wrote one of the first American historians, the Reverend Jedidiah Morse, are "naturally weak and effeminate," and "dedicate the greatest part of their lives to loitering and inactive pleasures." "Their character," he sniffed, "is nothing more than a grave and specious insignificance."[6] In the 1890s, leading U.S. newspapers picked up Morse's views and demanded that the more civilized Americans help Cuba. The publishers were not unselfish. Technological breakthroughs in making paper and setting type had driven newspaper prices down to a penny or two a copy. These changes opened the possibility for mass distribution and the rich advertising fee that came with such a market. Two giants of the trade, William Randolph Hearst and Joseph Pulitzer, led the struggle to gain more newspaper readers. Each man sought subscribers through sensational front-page stories, and nothing was more sensational than events in Cuba—unless, of course, it was a U.S. war against Spain. Hearst especially promoted such a conflict. Congress picked up his beat and, in 1897, pressured McKinley to recognize the rebels.

The new president was moved by neither congressional demands nor the sensationalist "yellow journal" press. He feared that U.S. recognition would lead to war, a war whose costs could drag the United States back into the economic crises from which it was finally emerging in 1897. Businessmen and conservative politicians, both Republican and Democrat, warned that such a war could be paid for only by coining more silver. But more silver would cheapen the dollar and threaten U.S. credit overseas. McKinley, moreover, opposed war because it could lead to demands for annexing Cuba. Annexation would raise constitutional problems (for example, Can the Constitution safely stretch across water to take in new states without tearing apart?). Bringing Cuba into the Union would also incorporate a multiracial society at a

José Martí (1853–1895) was the father of the Cuban revolution that erupted in 1895, but he feared U.S. intervention as much as Spanish colonialism: "And once the United States is in Cuba," he asked, "who will drive it out?" A journalist in New York during the 1880s, he returned to Cuba in early 1895 to start the final phase of the uprising but was killed a month later by Spanish troops. Half a century later, he became a great hero of Fidel Castro.

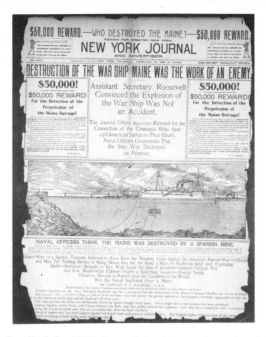

"Yellow journalism" of the 1890s fanned the flames of war by giving Americans immediate news of foreign-policy crises, especially if that news could be sensationalized to sell more newspapers.

time when white Americans were already having problems dealing with black Americans and millions of newly arrived immigrants. McKinley, therefore, pressed Spain to grant enough reforms to undercut the revolutionaries. Madrid began to do so, even recalling "Butcher" Weyler and offering the first steps toward autonomy. The president, however, criticized the response as too little too late.

Spain had lost control. In late 1897, riots erupted in the Cuban capital of Havana. McKinley moved a warship, the *Maine*, into Havana Harbor to protect U.S. citizens and property. In early February 1898, a pro-war group in New York captured a letter in which the Spanish minister to Washington, Dupuy de Lôme, called McKinley "weak and a bidder for the admiration of the crowd." The minister also downplayed the importance of Spain's reforms. The little trust that Americans had in the Spanish evaporated. Six days later, on February 15, an explosion shook the *Maine*. Settling into the muck of Havana Harbor, the ship took more than 250 U.S. sailors to their deaths. In 1976, a thorough investigation of the tragedy concluded that the vessel had probably been destroyed by an internal explosion (perhaps in the engine room) and not by some external device set by Spanish agents.[7] In 1898, however, Americans quickly concluded that a bomb had taken those lives, and the yellow journals and congressmen screamed for war. McKinley played for time by asking for an investigation. He feared, as he told a friend, that "the country was not ready for war." Military preparations had only begun. Economic dangers still loomed. He worried about the possible results of a victory: "Who knows where this war will lead us," he told a congressional leader. "It may be more than war with Spain."[8]

When making that remark, McKinley may have had in mind a second foreign-policy crisis that emerged in March 1898. It had begun with Japan's victory over China in 1894–1895 (see p. 182). In 1897, Germany blocked Japan from grabbing further territorial spoils. Using as an excuse the murder of two German missionaries, Berlin officials demanded as indemnity from China the port of Kiaochow (now Chiao Hsien). Located at an entrance to the rich Chinese province of Manchuria, Kiaochow controlled a trade route used by an increasing number of Americans. Other European powers and Japan then clamored for important parts of China's territory. The traditional U.S. open-door policy to all of China faced extinction. Great Britain, which shared much of Washington's concern about the open door, asked McKinley for help in stopping the other Europeans. The president sympathized with the British position, but he could not help. China was too far away, Cuba too close. McKinley had to deal with revolution before he could help protect the open door. Meanwhile, worried U.S. exporters and business newspapers began chanting a warning that, in the *Journal of Commerce*'s words, the Far East crisis threatened "the future of American trade."[9]

One possible escape from the dilemma had, however, already appeared. Rebels in the Philippines had begun war against Spanish rule. The islands could become a key military base from which to protect U.S. interests in Asia. McKinley, Captain Alfred Thayer Mahan, and Assistant Secretary of the Navy Theodore Roosevelt closely watched the Philippine struggle in early 1898. On February 25, when his superior was out of the office, Roosevelt sent a series of cables that ordered U.S. naval commanders to prepare their ships for fighting. The next day, the astonished secretary of the navy, John D. Long, rushed to the White House with the news that his assistant had single-handedly tried to push the country to the brink of war. McKinley ordered that all of Roosevelt's cables be recalled—except the order to Admiral George Dewey that his Pacific fleet prepare to attack the Philippines in case of war with Spain.[10] In actuality, Dewey had earlier received orders to attack the Philippines in case of war with Spain. The president, meanwhile, had been reinforcing Dewey's squadron. McKinley later softsoaped critics of his Philippine policy by assuring them that he had involuntarily been pushed into conquering "those darn islands," which he could not even quickly locate on a map. His statement was good politics but bad history. The president knew very well before he went to war with Spain how much the Philippine base could mean to preserving the open door in China. The crisis caused by German and Japanese grabs of China's territory left him no alternative—unless he wanted to quit the century-long U.S. quest for Asian markets. And the president had no intention of doing that.

McKinley carefully prepared his policy to deal with the Cuban and Asian crises at once. After the *Maine*'s destruction, he moved rapidly to prepare the country for war. On March 9, he acquired $50 million from Congress to begin mobilization of the army and navy. On March 17, Republican senator Redfield Proctor of Vermont, one of McKinley's close friends, returned from a visit to Cuba and electrified Americans by announcing that he had changed his anti-war stand. A strong conservative, Proctor declared that his business contacts in Cuba had told him that Spain's reforms had failed. Property was being destroyed. Conservative Cubans wanted autonomy or U.S. annexation. Proctor's fears were underlined when State Department officials in Cuba warned McKinley that unless the fighting was stopped, "there might be a revolution within a revolution."[11] This meant that the rebellion threatened to take a sharp leftward turn that could threaten conservative property holders if the revolutionaries won. McKinley thus not only had to stop the fighting, but control the revolution itself.

On March 25, the president received a telegram from a close political adviser in New York City: "Big corporations here now believe we will have war. Believe all would welcome it as a relief to suspense."[12] This cable revealed that eastern business groups, long afraid of war, now felt that battle was preferable to the fears generated by Proctor's speech and the other events of February and March. New York business leaders had concluded that the United States could safely pay for a war without having to coin silver. Many midwestern and western business groups, as well as nationwide commercial journals who were frightened over the threat to the open door in Asia, had long supported war. The business community was uniting behind McKinley's military preparations.

Between March 20 and 28, the president sent a series of demands to

Spain. The Spanish would have to pay indemnity for the *Maine*, promise not to use the *reconcentrado* policy, declare a truce, and negotiate for Cuban independence through U.S. mediation, if necessary. In the end, Spain surrendered to all the demands except the last. No Madrid government could promise Cuban independence and remain in power. Spain stalled, no doubt hoping that once the rainy season began in Cuba during early summer, McKinley would ease the pressure until the weather cleared for fighting in the autumn. But the president decided to move quickly. On April 11, he sent his message to Congress. He asked for war on the grounds that the three-year struggle on the island threatened Cuban lives, U.S. property, and tranquillity in the United States itself.

The president did not want war. But he did want results that only war could bring: protecting property in Cuba, stopping the revolution before it turned sharply to the left, restoring confidence in the U.S. business community, insulating his Republican party from Democratic charges of cowardice in safeguarding U.S. interests, and giving himself a free hand to deal with the growing Asian crisis. For these reasons, McKinley took the country into war in April 1898.

"A SPLENDID LITTLE WAR . . ."

McKinley's war message triggered a bitter debate in Congress. Since 1895, many congressmen had supported the Cuban junto, which raised millions of dollars in the United States to support the rebels. A number of Americans invested heavily in Cuban bonds to purchase arms for the revolution. These pro-Cuban groups now insisted that McKinley recognize Cuban independence as part of the war declaration. The president instantly rejected the deal. Mistrusting the revolutionaries, he insisted on keeping his freedom of action in handling the island once the fighting ended. The Senate tried to impose the junto's policy on the president, but he blocked the measure in the House. Then, in a week of intense political infighting (during which the usually calm McKinley had to take sleeping potions so that he could rest), he forced the Senate to retreat. The president received exactly what he wanted: only a declaration of war. Theodore Roosevelt, angry because McKinley refused to rush into war, privately complained that the president had "no more backbone than a chocolate eclair" and added that the gentle Ohioan was a "white-livered cur." But as historian Paul Holbo notes, the central question by early April was not whether the country was going to war, "but who was to direct American policy." [13] The Senate fight demonstrated that the president could dominate Roosevelt, the Congress, and the powerful interests behind the Cuban junto.

Congress included in the war resolution the Teller Amendment. This provision declared that the United States was not entering the war to conquer territory. The Teller Amendment eased some consciences, but it actually aimed to protect American sugar producers from cheap Cuban sugar. (Senator Henry Teller, a Republican, came from the sugar-beet state of Colorado.) Historians later discovered, moreover, that Cuban leaders handed out $1 million in payment to lobbyists and perhaps to members of Congress who voted for the amendment. McKinley accepted the provision. He had no intention of annexing Cuba.[14] But he did want Hawaii—and quickly. The mid-Pacific islands could be vital bases for U.S. ships heading toward the Philippines. Wartime need, however, by no means explained why the United States annexed Hawaii in June 1898. The story begins earlier.

After 1893, when President Cleveland rejected requests from Americans in Hawaii for annexation, the United States paid little attention to the islands. That lack of interest dramatically disappeared in mid-1897, when McKinley received urgent messages that the Japanese were sending several warships to Hawaii. The Tokyo government was angry that its citizens who were attempting to enter the islands were being turned away. The reason for the rejection lay in numbers: in 1884, only 116 Japanese lived in Hawaii; but by 1897, their 25,000 people accounted for one-quarter of the entire population. The Japanese even outnumbered the Americans, Europeans, and native Hawaiians. If they obtained the vote, the power of the white planters who ruled the islands could be shattered. Hawaii could become a Japanese colony.

When Tokyo's two warships appeared in Hawaiian waters during early 1897, McKinley, who had long wanted to annex the islands, ordered U.S. vessels prepared for action. Captain Alfred Thayer Mahan privately warned Roosevelt in the Navy Department to be aware of "the very real present danger of war" with Japan.[15] To the delight of Roosevelt, Mahan, and other expansionists, the president sent a treaty for Hawaiian annexation to the Senate in June 1897. But he moved too quickly. The president could not line up the necessary 60 Senate votes for the two-thirds approval needed to ratify the pact. Americans wanted to think carefully before extending their Constitution that far into the Pacific. Domestic sugar producers especially assailed the pact; they feared Hawaiian sugar imports.

On May 2, 1898, a telegram reached Washington that Admiral George

In the far west, the sailing of Dewey's fleet from Hong Kong to Manila made Americans a Pacific power. But U.S. interests had been growing in the region for a century.

Dewey's ships had destroyed the Spanish fleet in the Philippines. Two days later, McKinley again asked the Senate for Hawaiian annexation. He still did not have the needed 60 votes, so he resorted to the device of annexation through joint resolution of the House and Senate. (That same device had been used in 1846 to take Texas, see p. 108.) The majorities needed for passing the joint resolution were easily found in both houses. On August 12, 1898, Hawaii became a U.S. territory.

By then, the islands fit within a grander plan developing in McKinley's mind: "We need Hawaii just as much and a good deal more than we did California. It is manifest destiny," he had declared earlier in 1898.[16] The U.S. Minister to Siam, John A. Barrett, believed that "we need Hawaii to properly protect our cotton, flour, and richly laden ships which . . . will one day ply on the Pacific like the Spanish galleons of old," as they make themselves "masters of the Pacific seas." Mahan chimed in with his influential arguments about the need for mid-Pacific coaling stations on the route to Asia. The shortest route from California to China's markets was via the Alaskan coast. But, as historian Alan Henrikson has noted in a fascinating analysis, Mahan used Mercator, flat-world maps, not maps viewing the earth from the North and South Poles. Thus, the main U.S. Pacific base was developed at Pearl Harbor in Hawaii rather than on the more direct Alaskan–Aleutian Islands route.[17]

By early August, when Hawaii became a U.S. territory, Americans had already won the easiest conflict in their history. With the declaration of war in April, Dewey had set out from Hong Kong to engage the Spanish fleet in the Philippines. His small squadron appeared so weak that British officers at the Hong Kong Club observed sorrowfully: "A fine set of fellows, but unhappily we shall never see them again." When Dewey arrived at Manila Bay, however, he discovered seven armorless Spanish vessels. The Spanish commander was so certain of his fate that he simply moved his ships to the bay's shallowest waters so his men would not drown when their vessels were shot out from under them. Dewey then destroyed the Spanish flotilla, killing or wounding 400 men. No U.S. ship was badly hit, and only several Americans received scratches. After four hours of cannon fire, the United States had become a power in the western Pacific. "Our crews are all hoarse

The 1898 meeting of empire, movies, and public education immediately after the "splendid little war" against Spain. Early, quite primitive motion pictures and slides brought home to Americans the thrill of the new overseas empire, as U.S. technology both won a war and then celebrated the winning.

from cheering," a U.S. official cabled Washington from Manila on May 4, "and while we suffer for cough drops and throat doctors we have no use for liniment or surgeons."

Washington officials also believed that Cuba would be captured by sea power. They, therefore, used much of the $50 million appropriated by Congress in March to prepare the navy, not the army, for action. As a result, the War Department bought few modern weapons or tropical clothing until after the fighting began. When McKinley ordered troops to prepare to invade Cuba and Puerto Rico, they had to wear heavy uniforms designed for northern climates. They ate provisions so badly prepared that one mainstay was accurately called "embalmed beef." Field weapons dated from the Civil War. As 180,000 volunteers trained to join the regular 30,000-man army, scandals rocked the War Department. Despite these disasters, in late May, General William R. Shafter began moving 16,000 troops from Tampa, Florida, to Cuba. His army traveled on 32 transports that could move no faster than 7 miles an hour. They sailed for 5½ days, much of it in well-lit vessels just off the Cuban coast, while the U.S. flagship crew enjoyed a band on deck that played ragtime.[18]

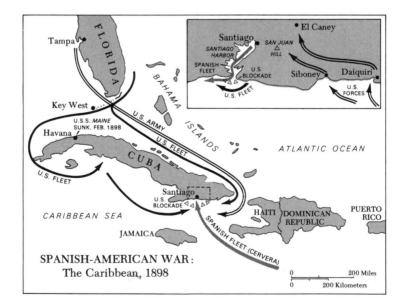

SPANISH-AMERICAN WAR:
The Caribbean, 1898

In the Caribbean, the war removed Spain from the region, made the United States the hemisphere's leading power, and opened an era of turbulent U.S.-Cuban relations.

The main U.S. fleet, including the three 10,000-ton battleships authorized in 1890, prepared to fight the Spanish fleet that was steaming across the Atlantic to Cuba. An important U.S. warship, the *Oregon*, arrived only after a highly publicized 68-day voyage from the Pacific around Cape Horn on the tip of South America to the Caribbean. It was a remarkable feat of seamanship that made Americans understand why they needed an isthmian canal cut through Central America. During the *Oregon*'s voyage, inhabitants of New York, Boston, and other coastal cities feared that their homes would be blasted by Spanish shells. They demanded protection, so McKinley sent a few broken-down Civil War coastal defense vessels, although he knew that the danger was nonexistent. The real question was whether the dilapidated Spanish squadron could even make it safely across the Atlantic. When it did, the U.S. fleet quickly cut off the four most respectable vessels in Santiago Harbor. As U.S. troops moved into Santiago by land, the Spanish ships tried to escape.[19] The twelve American vessels destroyed the entire fleet at the cost of one U.S. life. As Americans took target practice, one U.S. officer had to shout the famous order: "Don't cheer, men! Those poor devils are dying."

For nearly all Americans, the conflict gave war a good name. Fighting seemed easy and nearly cost-free. Journalist Richard Harding Davis concluded that "war as it is conducted at this end of the century is civilized."[20] No one benefited more from the conflict than Theodore Roosevelt. He left the Navy Department to organize friends (especially men he had met while living as a cowboy in South Dakota's Black Hills a decade earlier) into the "Rough Riders." Finally getting his long-sought chance to kill, TR determined to do it as a gentleman. For example, he ordered from Brooks Brothers clothiers an "ordinary Cavalry lieutenant Colonel's uniform in blue Cravenette" so that he would be properly outfitted. When he finally reached Cuba, he nearly destroyed his Rough Riders by leading them up the steep Kettle's Hill directly into hostile gunfire. Fortunately for TR, the Spanish weapons could not shoot accurately at slowly moving targets. Roosevelt emerged a national hero. He made certain his heroism was appreciated by publishing in 1899 *The Rough Riders*—a book that humorist Finley Peter Dunne ("Mr. Dooley," as he was known to newspaper readers) suggested could be entitled "Alone in Cubia."[21] But Richard Harding Davis's sarcasm at the time applied to the U.S. war effort as well as Roosevelt's: "God takes care of drunken men, sailors, and the United States."

Table 1
Principal Wars in Which the United States Participated: U.S. Military Personnel Serving and Casualties

War/conflict	Branch of service	Number serving	Casualties		
			Battle deaths	Other deaths	Wounds not mortal
Revolutionary War	Total		4,435	—	6,188
(1775–1783)	Army	—	4,044	—	6,004
	Navy	—	342	—	114
	Marines	—	49	—	70
War of 1812	Total	286,730	2,260	—	4,505
(1812–1815)	Army	—	1,950	—	4,000
	Navy	—	265	—	439
	Marines	—	45	—	66
Mexican War	Total	78,718	1,733	11,550	4,152
(1846–1848)	Army	—	1,721	11,550	4,102
	Navy	—	1	—	3
	Marines	—	11	—	47
Civil War (Union forces only)	Total	2,213,363	140,414	224,097	281,881
(1861–1865)	Army	2,128,948	138,154	221,374	280,040
	Navy	—	2,112	2,411	1,710
	Marines	84,415	148	312	131
Spanish-American War	Total	306,760	385	2,061	1,662
(1898)	Army	280,564	369	2,061	1,594
	Navy	22,875	10	—	47
	Marines	3,321	6	—	21

Source: Department of Defense.

... For Control of Cuba and Puerto Rico

America's mood and future were better caught by the U.S. ambassador to France, Horace Porter. He wrote McKinley in November 1898 that European officials "express the opinion that we did in three months what the great powers of Europe had sought in vain to do for over a hundred years." These accomplishments included, Porter observed,

> having secured a chain of island posts in the Pacific, secured the Philippines, captured their trade, paved the way for a Pacific [telegraph] cable of our own, virtually taken possession of that ocean, and occupied a position at Manila ... only a couple of days in time from the Chinese coast with no fear of Chinese or Russian armies at our back yet near enough to protect our interest in the Orient.[22]

It all seemed miraculous. At the cost of 2,900 lives (with approximately 2,500 the victims of disease, not enemy gunfire) and only $250 million, the United States became a great world power. But if Americans were dreaming big dreams, McKinley refused to be carried away. He had only certain limited diplomatic objectives. In his first public statement on possible terms of peace, McKinley wrote in June 1898 that Cuba, Puerto Rico, and a Philippine naval base had to end up in U.S. hands. By late summer, he had actually rejected the opportunity to take control of Caroline Island and the Marianas, which Spain held in the Pacific.

In Cuba, the question became whether the island should be independent, annexed, or come under informal U.S. control. McKinley quickly ruled out immediate independence. His mistrust of the Cuban revolutionaries increased. Their ill-equipped, barefoot forces proved to be superb guerrilla fighters when working alongside U.S. troops but, in American eyes, became racial inferiors and thieves of U.S. food supplies when the fighting stopped. The U.S. forces "despise" the Cubans, one journalist reported. When General Shafter was asked about possible self-government, he retorted, "Why those people are no more fit for self-government than gun-powder is for hell."[23] McKinley also refused to annex the island. That solution could bring too many unpredictable mixed races into the Union. Moreover, annexation was not needed. Because Cuba was so close to U.S. shores, it, unlike the Philippines, could be controlled informally. The United States could use the island for its own purposes, but Cubans could have the headaches of day-to-day governing.

This imaginative policy was finally formulated by McKinley and his top military commander in Cuba, General Leonard Wood. The general convened a Cuban constitutional convention in late 1900 and instructed the delegates to establish their own internal laws. Washington required, however, that they include in their new constitution certain foreign-policy provisions: (1) the United States had the right to intervene as it wished to protect Cuba's independence; (2) the Cuban debt had to be limited so that European creditors could not use it as an excuse to use force to collect it—and perhaps take Cuban territory as compensation; (3) the United States demanded a ninety-nine year lease of the naval base at Guantánamo; and (4) an extensive sanitation program was to protect the Cuban people and make the island more attractive to U.S. investors. These provisions, drawn up by McKinley and his advisers, became known as the Platt Amendment after Republican Senator Orville Platt from Connecticut formally proposed them in Congress. Furiously attacking the proposals, the Cuban delegates refused to vote on them. Wood warned that he would keep them meeting until they did vote. He knew, moreover, that the Cubans needed immediate access to the American market for their sugar. Under intense U.S. pressure, the Cuban Constitutional Convention finally accepted the Platt Amendment in 1901 by a vote of 15 to 11. "There is, of course, little or no independence left Cuba under the Platt Amendment," Wood wrote Roosevelt.[24]

The McKinley and Roosevelt administrations then overcame tough opposition from high-tariff Republicans and sugar producers to negotiate and finally ratify a reciprocity treaty in 1903. The pact thoroughly integrated the U.S. and Cuban economies. Cuba's sugar and mineral wealth moved north, as American farm and industrial products flowed south. The U.S. sugar producers lost their fight when the giant American Sugar Refining trust, which wanted cheap sugar to refine for the home market, moved into Capitol Hill and bribed the necessary number of senators.[25] U.S.-Cuban trade skyrocketed from $27 million in 1897 to over $300 million in 1917.

The United States restored order to Cuba but assumed few responsibilities. "When people ask me what I mean by stable government, I tell them money at six percent," General Wood wrote to McKinley in 1900. That kind of "order," however, proved to be dangerous. As historian Lloyd Gardner notes, the Platt Amendment built into Cuba "a revolutionary impetus," because later critics of Cuban poverty could not effectively attack the island's own government, which had little control over the economy, but had to attack the United States.[26] As early as 1906, U.S. officials had to land troops to maintain order. The Platt Amendment continued to be the basis of U.S. policy in Cuba until 1934.

McKinley also took Puerto Rico away from Spain in 1898. The conquest was a surprise. Few Americans knew or cared about that island when war began. For that reason, however, McKinley's decision to annex it (as partial indemnity from Spain for U.S. war costs) raised little debate. The Puerto Ricans were not pleased. In a rare moment of Spanish colonial wisdom, Madrid officials had given Puerto Rico a large amount of autonomy, including its own elected legislature. McKinley destroyed that autonomy. General Nelson Miles, the U.S. military commander, conquered the country without opposition, then announced that the United States intended to give "the immunities and blessings of the liberal institutions of our government." But instead of granting such blessings, Congress passed the Foraker Act of 1900, which made Puerto Rico an "unincorporated territory" subject to the whim of Congress. For one of the few times since the 1787 Ordinance (see p. 33), the United States annexed a large territory with no intention of making the inhabitants U.S. citizens. Puerto Ricans had no guaranteed rights. As one of their newspapers complained in 1901, "We are and we are not a foreign country. We are and we are not citizens of the United States. . . . The Constitution . . . applies to us and does not apply to us."[27]

The U.S. Supreme Court proved the newspaper correct when it handed down a series of judgments between 1901 and 1904. In these historic decisions, known as the Insular Cases, the Court ruled that the Foraker Act was constitutional. The United States could annex an area, make it an "unincorporated" territory, and refuse to grant its people citizenship. Thus, the Constitution did not automatically "follow the flag," as many Americans had long believed. The territory's people were at Congress's mercy. The U.S. attorney general told the Court that the government had to have such power. In the future, he prophesied, a Puerto Rico–like situation might arise in Africa or even China, given the course of U.S. expansionism. The Constitution had to be interpreted to fit that expansionism. Later, the Insular Cases did provide a legal justification for the U.S. rule of Guam and other Pacific territories.[28]

Congress, meanwhile, passed tariff legislation that integrated Puerto Rico—and especially its increasing number of sugar plantations—into the U.S. economy. In 1850, the country's landholding had been fair

A cartoonist, who captioned this work "Find the Constitution," portrays in 1901 his belief that Americans were paying a high price to acquire overseas possessions. This is from the Philadelphia North American.

and equitable when compared with other countries in the Caribbean and Central America. By 1917, the best lands had fallen into the hands of a few wealthy owners who grew crops for export. In that year, the United States finally gave Puerto Ricans citizenship through the Jones Act. In 1947, the country won the right to elect its own governor. After that, Third World and Soviet-bloc countries in the United Nations regularly proposed resolutions condemning Washington's "colonial" policy. Puerto Ricans, meanwhile, divided among a small group demanding independence, a larger faction wanting U.S. statehood, and the largest number who preferred the tax and trade preferences obtained from the United States because of their commonwealth status. But Puerto Rico remained a poor country whose people increasingly sought work in the United States. Nearly a century after the 1898 conquest, Washington officials have not been able to devise a workable policy for development.[29]

. . . AND THE CONQUEST OF THE FILIPINOS

The best-known version of how McKinley decided to annex the Philippine Islands came from the president himself, when he talked with a group of Methodist church leaders in 1899:

I walked the floor of the White House night after night until midnight; and I am not ashamed to tell you, gentlemen, that I went down on my knees and prayed Almighty God for light and guidance more than one night. And one night it came to me in this way—. . . . (1) that we could not give [the Philippines] back to Spain—that would be cowardly and dishonorable; (2) that we could not turn them over to France or Germany—our commercial rivals in the Orient—that would be bad business and discreditable . . . ; . . . that there was nothing left to do but take them all, and educate the Filipinos, and uplift and civilize them, and by God's grace do the very best by them as our fellow-men for whom Christ also died. And then I went to bed, and went to sleep and slept soundly.[30]

It is a dramatic story, but few historians believe it. Recent scholarship reveals that the president's reasons were both more complex and fascinating. From the moment he had heard of Dewey's smashing victory in Manila Bay, the president wanted at least to annex that port for the use of U.S. commerce and warships. Indeed, he ordered troops to leave for the Philippines even before he received official word that Dewey won. It marked the first time a president had ever ordered U.S. soldiers outside the Western Hemisphere to fight. McKinley delayed deciding whether to annex all the Philippine islands, which stretched over 115,000 square miles. McKinley did not want the responsibility for governing them, especially since a strong Filipino revolutionary army, which had been effectively fighting Spain before 1898, intended to govern its own homeland. Nevertheless, as fighting continued in the summer of 1898, McKinley kept his options open: "While we are conducting war and until its conclusion we must keep all we get; when the war is over we must keep what we want."[31] On October 25, 1898, the president finally instructed the U.S. commissioners in Paris, who were negotiating peace terms, to demand all the islands. In return, the United States offered Spain $20 million.

McKinley made the decision for a number of reasons. He concluded that the Filipinos could not run their own country. Dewey had cabled him in mid-October that "the natives appear unable to govern." The problem was similar to the Cuban situation: the revolutionaries were divided among themselves, and one radical faction threatened property holdings. That difficulty led to a second reason for McKinley's decision: a civil war could allow those whom he termed "our commercial rivals in the Orient" (France, Germany, and Great Britain) to seize the islands. McKinley, moreover, had to make his decision just as the China cauldron began boiling again. Russia threatened to close Chinese ports, including Port Arthur, that were vital for U.S. commerce. Great

Britain considered quitting the open-door policy and joining the race for Chinese loot. To protect U.S. interests, the president needed a secure base. To use Manila for that purpose, however, required control of Luzon, Manila's home island. But to protect Luzon, McKinley learned, meant controlling the adjoining islands. As one U.S. army officer testified in mid-October, with "over 400 islands in the group . . . a cannon shot can be fired from one to another in many instances." Thus, the final and most important reason for McKinley's decision: to protect the naval base at Manila, he had to take all the islands.[32]

American public opinion had little to do with his decision. That opinion, as usual, was sharply divided. The *Presbyterian Banner* declared in August 1898 that the religious press, almost without exception, agreed oh "the desirability of America's retaining the Philippines as a duty in the interest of human freedom and Christian progress." Three months later the same journal announced: "We have been morally compelled to become an Asiatic power. . . . America and Great Britain will see to it that China is not Russianized."[33] On the other side, many Americans, especially Democrats, feared extending the Constitution across the Pacific. Even McKinley's own cabinet was divided. His wartime secretary of state (and close friend from Ohio days), William R. Day, opposed annexation.

During a congressional campaign swing through the Midwest in October, the president decided he would test opinion on the annexation question. But he did so in an odd fashion. McKinley repeatedly brought crowds to their feet with rousing, patriotic speeches, such as one in Hastings, Iowa: "We want new markets, and as trade follows the flag, it looks very much as if we are going to have new markets." The president nevertheless seemed struck by how hard he had to work to arouse his audiences. As historian Ephraim Smith concludes, McKinley "seemed more concerned about the public's apprehension about accepting new responsibilities."[34]

Proof of that apprehension appeared on February 6, 1899, when the Senate accepted McKinley's peace treaty 57 to 27, a mere one vote more than the two-thirds needed to ratify. Until the final twenty-four hours, victory was in doubt. McKinley, aided by Republican Senate leaders, lobbied hard and distributed patronage plums with a free hand to obtain votes. Oddly, the president received unneeded last-minute help from his old Democratic opponent, William Jennings Bryan. The Democrat had fought annexation, then suddenly switched to urge Democratic senators to vote for the treaty. Bryan later argued that he wanted ratification so that the war would officially end, lives would be

Richard Jordan Gatling stands by his Gatling Gun, the parent of the machine gun. Samuel Colt and others had developed a repeating rifle before the Civil War, but Gatling's 1862 patent led to the most famous rapid-fire weapon. Not used in the Civil War, the Gatling Gun was used to quell riots in New Orleans during 1868, to kill Indians during the 1870s–1880s campaigns, and, most famously, to help win the battle of Santiago, Cuba, against Spain in 1898, and to put down the Philippine revolt.

saved, and the Philippine mistake would then be corrected through diplomacy.[35] It was, however, one of Bryan's many unrealized dreams. Of even greater importance than Bryan's turn was the news that reached Washington on the evening before the vote: Filipino rebels had attacked U.S. soldiers. The revolt against American control had begun. McKinley immediately understood that he had won: a vote against his treaty could now be seen as a vote against supporting the U.S. soldiers embattled by the Filipinos.

The insurrection marked the first of many antirevolutionary wars fought by the United States in the twentieth century. The rebels were led by Emilio Aguinaldo (a moderate who had executed the more radical opponent within the revolutionary movement, Andres Bonifacio). They had originally welcomed the U.S. force that defeated Spain. Welcome turned to hostility when they learned that the Americans intended to remain. McKinley paid little attention to Aguinaldo until the rebel declared the creation of a Philippine republic in January 1899. The war that erupted the next month continued for three years. At first, U.S. officers believed that they could subdue the barefoot opponents with 20,000 or 30,000 men. Soon, the commanders asked McKinley for 40,000, then 60,000 regulars. In all, 120,000 U.S. troops finally fought in the Philippines. Nearly 4,200 were killed and 2,800 wounded. In turn, they killed outright 15,000 rebels, and estimates run as high as 200,000 Filipinos dying from gunfire, starvation, and the effects of

U.S. troops had to fight a vicious four-year war to defeat the Filipino resistance and consolidate the American hold over Manila's valuable port, where this picture of street fighting was taken.

concentration camps into which the United States crowded civilians so that they could not help Aguinaldo's troops.[36]

Viewing the Filipinos as they had viewed Native Americans, U.S. soldiers coined the term "gooks" to describe them. These racial views allowed the war to be fought even more savagely. As a young infantryman from New York reported home: "Last night one of our boys was found shot and his stomach cut open. Immediately orders were received . . . to burn the town and kill every native in sight. . . . About 1,000 men, women, and children were reported killed. . . . I am in my glory when I can sight my gun on some dark skin and pull the trigger."[37] When rebels massacred a squad of U.S. troops, an American commander ordered the killing of every male over the age of ten—an order, fortunately, that was quickly countermanded by his superiors.

The revolution was finally quelled after McKinley moved General Arthur MacArthur to top command in 1900. The new leader (father of General Douglas MacArthur, who governed the Philippines in the 1930s and was U.S. commander in the Pacific during World War II) took a different tack. He fought the war vigorously but also offered amnesty to rebels who surrendered. MacArthur worked closely with the islands' wealthy elite, who prospered by cooperating with the Americans. In 1901, U.S. troops captured Aguinaldo. The back of the revolt was broken, although fighting continued at reduced levels until 1913. After that, U.S.-trained and -directed Filipino forces fought a continual series of wars against rebels, wars that lasted from 1913 until at least the 1990s.[38] The Philippines have never remained pacified for very long. For his part, Aguinaldo finally had revenge by collaborating with Japanese forces, who drove the United States out of the Philippines in World War II.

Warriors such as Theodore Roosevelt argued that Americans had to remain in the Philippines to develop their own character and teach the natives self-government. Democratic senator Edward Carmack from Tennessee acidly observed that Roosevelt admitted that it had taken Anglo-Saxons one thousand years to learn self-government. Thus, "we are not to hold [the islands] permanently," Carmack quipped, "we want to experiment with them for only a thousand years or so." Famed sociologist William Graham Sumner was more pointed: "We talk of civilizing lower races, but we have never done it yet. We have exterminated them." Despite such criticisms, Carmack and Sumner could not slow McKinley's and Roosevelt's policies for taking the Philippines. After all, as Assistant Secretary of the Treasury (and banker) Frank Vanderlip observed, the Philippines were to be the U.S. Hong Kong so Americans could "trade with the millions of China and Korea, French Indo-China, the Malay Peninsula and the islands of Indonesia."[39]

McKINLEY'S TRIUMPHS IN CHINA

In 1899–1900, the president vividly demonstrated why the Philippines were vital for his foreign policy. At long last, he was free to fight the threat to the open door in China. The crisis had begun in 1897–1898 (see p. 200). By mid-1899, the Russians and Germans threatened to colonize and close off strategic areas of China. Meanwhile, the British, French, Japanese, and Americans scrambled to protect their trade and other interests. None of the powers was primarily concerned about the Chinese themselves. As Americans, for example, pressed for greater rights in China, they closed off Chinese rights of immigration obtained in the 1868 Burlingame Treaty.

By 1882, so many Chinese had found work in the United States that Americans were fearful. In that year, Congress passed the first anti-immigration measure in U.S. history when it stopped Chinese immigration for ten years. Anti-Chinese outbreaks nevertheless spread. In 1885, a mob killed twenty-eight Chinese in Wyoming. Observers feared even worse bloodshed would occur in California, where many Asian immigrants had settled. By the 1880s and 1890s, Americans were increasingly discriminating against immigrants just as the Americans themselves were moving out into other countries such as China and the Philippines. This historic turn was dramatized in 1886, when, in magnificent ceremonies, the United States dedicated the Statue of Liberty, placed in New York City Harbor as a gift from France. Not one speech in the ceremonies mentioned the lines Emma Lazarus had written for the statue: "Give me your tired, your poor, / Your huddled masses yearning to breathe free." Instead, the speakers stressed how Americans must go forth to spread liberty throughout other lands.[40]

In China, however, Americans seemed less interested in liberty for the Chinese than the liberty to sell goods for profit and save souls for Christianity. Economically, U.S. exports to China nearly quadrupled to $15 million between 1895 and 1900.[41] The Chinese took only 1 percent to 2 percent of total U.S. exports, but Americans focused on the potential (hundreds of millions of Chinese) and that market's rapid growth since 1895. Certain industries and sections in the United States depended utterly on the China market. No producers needed it more than those making textiles. That product ranked first among exports, with petroleum second, iron and steel products third. New England textile plants had overexpanded, then were badly stung by the 1873–1897 economic depression. Some moved to the South, but, as one spokesman warned, it was better to avoid "destructive competition" at home by developing markets abroad. "We want the open door," a Georgia senator exclaimed, "and a big one at that."[42] Historian Patrick Hearden concludes that by 1899, "the New South's rapidly growing China trade promised to keep the entire American cotton industry in a healthy condition."[43]

But no group surpassed the Christian missionaries' involvement in China. It was an era of extraordinary growth: between 1870 and 1900, Americans increased their Protestant overseas missions by 500 percent. In the single decade of the 1890s, U.S. missionaries in China doubled in number to over one thousand. This great movement arose in part out of the churches' determination to defy threats to their beliefs posed by new science and Darwinian challenges. The movement also sprang from colleges, where religious revivalism on such campuses as Oberlin, Cornell, and Yale produced the Student Volunteer Movement for Foreign Missions in 1887. By 1900, the Student Volunteers, who marched under the proud banner proclaiming "The Evangelization of the World in This Generation," had chapters in nearly every Protestant college. These groups reflected the profit seeking as well as soul seeking of the late nineteenth century. Some missionaries invested in foreign land and minerals; others preached morality and profit at once by asking that saved souls wear North Carolina textiles.[44] The missionaries patriotically represented their country as well as their religion. They also became more interested in mass conversion than in the slower saving of individual sinners from the fires of hell. Thus, they looked increasingly to the U.S. government for help and protection, especially as the other foreign powers crowded into Asia. This new approach was exemplified in 1896, when the U.S. government ordered a commission to travel to the Chinese government and insist on American rights. As Professor Thomas McCormick explains, "The commission consisted of the American Consul at Tientsin, a missionary, and a naval officer—the expansionist trinity."[45]

Women, especially a rising feminist movement, became an important source of missionary expansionism both at home and abroad. In 1880, about twenty women's foreign missionary societies existed. The number doubled by 1900. By 1915, 3 million women belonged to these forty societies. Some of the groups aimed to carry abroad the values of middle-class America. As one leader wrote, "The aim of this woman's work we conceive to be *in heathen lands*— . . . in bringing the women into His Kingdom, in the creation of Christian mothers." The "fathers and brothers" were to "strike vigorous blows at the brains of heathendom, to superintend large educational and evangelistic enterprises." But "to woman belongs the quiet, patient labour in the homes of the people." Women also understood, however, how they were to bring creature comforts and new values of an industrialized America to the "heathen." As one woman declared, foreign missionary work "should appeal to every broad-minded Christian woman who is interested in education, civics, sanitation, social settlements, hospitals, good literature, the emancipation of children, the right of women to health, home and protection; and the coming of the Kingdom of our Lord." As historian Patricia R. Hill observes, by this time, it seems, the Lord's kingdom tended to come at the end of the list.[46] American goods and social values went into China with the missionaries, both male and female.

The belief grew, as Secretary of State John Hay noted in 1900, that whoever understood China "has the key to world politics for the next five centuries."[47] No one tried harder to understand, or—after Seward—contributed more to U.S. policy in China than did Hay, the author of

John Hay (1838–1905) was born in Indiana and had a distinguished career as secretary to Lincoln, an official in the Department of State, industrialist in Ohio, and U.S. ambassador to Great Britain before becoming a powerful secretary of state (1898–1905). A poet and novelist as well, Hay drafted the historic "open-door" notes of 1899–1900.

the 1899–1900 open-door notes. Nor did anyone better understand how U.S. business and politics related to policy in China. Born in Indiana in 1838, Hay went to Brown University, then used his midwestern political contacts to become Abraham Lincoln's secretary at the age of twenty-three. Hay grew to fear the mass, urbanized, industrialized society that developed after 1865. His fear multiplied when he entered the steel business in Cleveland and had to deal with the rising labor movement. He anonymously published a novel, *The Bread-Winners*, that remains one of the bitterest attacks ever made on the labor movement, especially the movement's foreign members. But he also worried that "the rich and intelligent" were so busy making money, they ignored the dangers: they "hate politics" and so "fatten themselves as sheep which could be mutton whenever the butcher was ready." Hay had no intention of becoming mutton. He supported McKinley in 1896, and the new president named him U.S. ambassador to Great Britain in 1897. Hay greatly admired England. He believed passionately that the British and Americans could save themselves and the best parts of their societies only by fighting Russia's, France's, and Germany's attempts "to divide and reduce China to a system of tributary provinces." McKinley knew Hay well and recalled him in 1898 to lead the fight for China as secretary of state.[48]

Hay's first initiative was an open-door note of 1899 that asked the other powers (especially Russia and Germany) to charge foreigners no more than their own citizens paid for shipping and railway privileges within so-called "spheres of interest" in China that each power claimed.

Hay's note also insisted that the general Chinese tariff apply to all the spheres of interest, and that China collect the duties itself. Chinese territorial integrity was to be reinforced. No other power rushed to agree with Hay's note, but none directly defied it either. Russia did not as yet believe that it had sufficient power to challenge the Americans, who were supported to some degree by Great Britain and Japan. Hay finally gained assent through an ingenious diplomatic tactic. He first gained agreement from the British and Japanese, who he knew were closest to his position, then obtained France's assent. Germany and Russia then had to agree or defy the other powers. The two nations did go along, but with considerable grumbling. With no U.S. military force in China and without making any political alliance with other powers, Hay had maneuvered them into declaring their agreement with U.S. open-door policy—a policy, as Hay neatly defined it, of "fair field and no favor" for anyone who wanted to compete in the China market. He and other knowledgeable Americans knew that with such ground rules, they could use their growing industrial power to undersell nearly any-

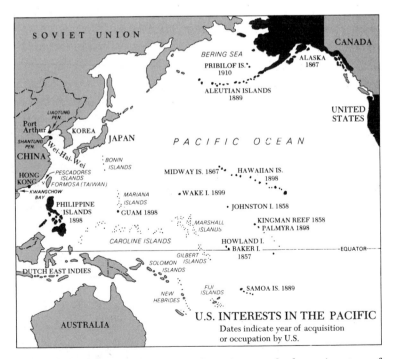

By 1900, the new U.S. economic and military interests had stepping stones for crossing the Pacific to reach Asia. The dates indicate when the United States acquired its possessions.

one and capture much of China's market. That was, indeed, another sign of the high stakes for which McKinley and Hay played: they wanted to sell to all of China, not just a sliver or a sphere they might annex.

But the Chinese themselves refused to stand still while the powers exploited them. In early 1900, the empress dowager, head of the collapsing Manchu dynasty, encouraged a radical antiforeign and militaristic society known as the Boxers to attack foreigners and their property. By May, foreign compounds in Chinese cities were besieged. On May 29, U.S. minister Edwin Conger captured the terror when he cabled Washington from the capital of Beijing (Peking): "Boxers increasing. Nine Methodist converts brutally murdered at Pachow. The movement has developed into open rebellion. Chinese government is trying but apparently is unable to surpress it. Many soldiers disloyal."[49] The foreign powers, including the United States, sent in troops to protect their citizens. It became clear, however, that Russia, Germany, and even Japan were using the Boxers as an excuse to seal off parts of China into their own spheres of interest.

After McKinley ordered 5,000 U.S. troops to move from Manila into China, Hay used the force as a bargaining chip. He tried to pressure the other powers to agree to a policy of July 3, 1900, that became known as the second open-door notes. He asked all powers to declare directly that they promised to preserve "Chinese territorial and administrative integrity." This key point had only been implied in the 1899 notes. With the powers nervously eying each other as well as the Boxers, all of them fell into line behind Hay. McKinley and his secretary of state had pulled off a remarkable victory. By 1901, Russia seemed checked. The president had greatly increased his executive power by sending thousands of U.S. troops onto the mainland of China without bothering to consult Congress. And the foreign powers maintained the Manchu dynasty as the ruler of China, although that victory was short-lived. In 1911, internal conflict again erupted, and this time the dynasty disappeared amid the beginnings of the Chinese Revolution.

Hay understood both sides of U.S. policy in China: the American need for markets both commercial and religious, and the relatively little power the United States could exert in the region. In August 1900, a crisis flared when Russia again made threatening moves. This time, the British indicated that they might join the Russians. McKinley, in the middle of a tough re-election fight against Bryan, uncharacteristically panicked. He seriously considered carving off an area of China for the United States—that is, giving up the open-door policy and joining the other colonial powers. From a sickbed in New Hampshire, Hay

FOREIGN INFLUENCE IN CHINA

Areas colonized or occupied by foreign powers

RUSSIA

RUSSIA 1896-1898

Amur R.

MANCHURIA

JAPAN

JAPAN 1876-1910

KOREA

Port Arthur
Peking • Weihaiwei •
Kiaochow •

BRITAIN 1898

GERMANY 1897-1898

JAPAN 1895

Yellow R.

C   H   I   N   A

Yangtze R.

FORMOSA

BRITAIN 1842

Kwangchowan

Hong Kong
Macao (Portugal)

INDIA
(BRITISH)

BURMA
(BRITISH)

INDOCHINA

Mekong R.

SIAM

FRANCE 1898

FRANCE 1858-1895

PHILIPPINE
ISLANDS
(U.S. 1898)

0   500 Miles
0   500 Kilometers

*China became an object of big-power competition and colonialism—"the bone"
amid the dogs, as a later U.S. official called China.*

convinced the president not to surrender the open-door approach. He
did so by giving McKinley a lesson in power politics:

> The inherent weakness of our position is this: we do not want to rob China
> ourselves, and our public opinion will not permit us to interfere, with an
> army, to prevent others from robbing her. Besides, we have no army. The

talk of the papers about "our preeminent moral position giving the authority to dictate to the world" is mere flap-doodle.[50]

Hay concluded that McKinley had no alternative but to remain in China and try to keep the powers *voluntarily* lined up behind the open-door policy. This could be accomplished not through U.S. military force, but only by playing power off against power, as Hay had done in 1899 and again in 1900. The secretary of state himself weakened only once. In late 1900, the U.S. War Department insisted that the navy needed a base in China. No doubt with some embarrassment, Hay asked the Chinese for a lease at Samsah Bay. Japan, which had plans of its own for China, quickly objected by throwing Hay's policy back at him: the U.S. request violated the open-door policy. The secretary of state dropped the request.

. . . AND A FINAL TRIUMPH AT HOME

By November 1900, the crisis in China had apparently passed—and none too soon. Throughout 1899–1900, Bryan and the Democrats had planned to club McKinley's re-election hopes with the issues of the bloody Philippine campaign and the volatile China crisis. Throughout the summer of 1900, both sides hotly debated foreign policy. The Democrats termed it "the paramount issue" in the election fight.

An "anti-imperialist" movement had grown rapidly after mid-1898 to oppose McKinley's policies. This movement was led by wealthy and upper-middle-class professionals (especially lawyers), mostly from the Northeast and Midwest. But it also included an increasing number of women. Historian Judith Papachristou estimates that in the five years after 1898 tens of thousands of women became foreign-policy activists: "Never before had American women involved themselves in foreign affairs in such a way and to such an extent." When the Anti-Imperialist League began to form at a meeting in Boston's Faneuil Hall during June 1898, more than half the audience was female. Women determined to have voting rights easily identified with Filipinos who were to be governed without their consent. Some anti-imperialists, both female and male, feared that extending the Constitution to the Philippines, Puerto Rico, and even Hawaii might change the basic provisions of the document and bring into the system certain races who were considered dangerous to traditional American values. Many anti-imperialists argued that these peoples were not ready for self-government; but if the United States tried to rule them, it would turn into an imperialist power and thus destroy its own democratic values. A South Carolina senator warned against "the incorporation of a mongrel and semibarbarous population into our body politic."[51]

That warning hit home in the North as well as the South. About 150 black people were lynched each year in the United States during the early 1890s. Race riots erupted in New York City in 1900, as well as earlier in southern states. It was not the time, Bryan and other anti-imperialists argued, to try to teach democracy to Filipinos with the tips of bayonets. Henry Blake Fuller caught the spirit with his anti-imperialist poetry of 1899. He dealt with the president of the United States as follows:

> G is for Guns
> That McKinley has sent,
> To teach Filipinos
> What Jesus Christ meant.

Fuller also provided a self-portrait of McKinley's vice-presidential running mate, Theodore Roosevelt, as anti-imperialists painted it:

> I'm a cut and thrusting bronco-busting
> Megaphone of Mars,
> And it's fire I breathe and I cut my teeth
> On nails and wrought-iron bars.[52]

Such extreme rhetoric could be discounted, but McKinley could not disregard Andrew Carnegie's large bankroll which financed many anti-imperialist activities.

The president directly challenged the anti-imperialists by naming Theodore Roosevelt to the Republican ticket. No one was more identified with, or more loudly defended, U.S. expansionism. Governor of New York in 1900, Roosevelt at first did not want to be only a vice-president. ("I would rather be professor of history in some college," he wrote a friend.) But he finally gave in, rightly noting that "it was believed that I would greatly strengthen the ticket in the West, where they regard me as a fellow barbarian and like me much."[53] While McKinley remained in Washington or in his hometown of Canton, Ohio, Roosevelt spun across the country, giving as many as ten speeches a day until he finally lost his voice on the eve of the election.

He blasted the anti-imperialist arguments. Because "the Philippines are now part of American territory," the only question was whether the Democrats planned "to surrender American territory." He attacked the anti-imperialists as antiexpansionist and thus, he charged, they had deserted the ideals of their own father—Thomas Jefferson—who had taken all of Louisiana. Dealing with the Indians, TR argued, established the needed precedents for dealing with the Filipinos, who were also "savages." If whites were "morally bound to abandon the Philippines, we were also morally bound to abandon Arizona to the Apaches." Bayonets were needed because "the barbarian will yield only to force." Other Republicans mocked Democrats who urged self-government in the Philippines or Hawaii by asking when the Democrats planned to extend the Declaration of Independence to southern black people. One observer commented on "Democrats howling about Republicans shooting negroes in the Philippines and the Republicans objecting to Democrats shooting negroes in the South. This may be good politics, but it is rough on the negroes."[54]

McKinley and Roosevelt decisively won the argument. By September, the president's policy in China and TR's attacks from the stump forced Bryan to reverse his campaign strategy. The Democratic nominee dropped foreign policy and began to emphasize Republican economic policy. His decision turned out to be politically fatal. The United States had emerged from its twenty-five-year depression to bask in prosperity in 1900. McKinley ran on the slogan "Let Well Enough Alone." He defeated Bryan more decisively in 1900 than he had four years before and even captured Bryan's home state of Nebraska. In the end, many anti-imperialists, including Andrew Carnegie, found that they could not tolerate Bryan's more radical economic program (especially after he dropped foreign-policy issues) and joined McKinley.

The president had led the United States into the small, select circle of great world powers. He did so not by following those powers and conquering large colonies. Between 1870 and 1900, Great Britain added 4.7 million square miles to its empire, France 3.5 million, and Germany 1.0 million. Americans, however, added only 125,000 square miles. They wanted not land, but more markets to free them of the horrors that had resulted from the post-1873 depression. Louisville newspaper publisher and Democratic party boss Henry Watterson explained what had occurred in 1898:

> From a nation of shopkeepers we became a nation of warriors. . . . We
> escape the menace and the peril of socialism and agrarianism, as England
> escaped them, by a policy of colonization and conquest. It is true that we

exchange domestic dangers for foreign dangers; but in every direction we multiply the opportunities of the people. We risk Caesarism certainly; but even Caesarism is preferable to anarchism.[55]

In September 1901, Watterson's "Caesar" traveled to Buffalo, New York, to explain to Americans the new world in which they lived. The president was greeted by a spectacular fireworks display that climaxed with the exclamation in the sky: "WELCOME MCKINLEY, CHIEF OF OUR NATION AND EMPIRE." As historian Edward Crapol summarizes, Americans were—finally—the equal of the British, and rapidly becoming more than equal.[56] The United States, McKinley told the Pan-American Exposition in Buffalo, now had "almost appalling" wealth. Consequently, "isolation is no longer possible or desirable." Americans had to frame new tariff and other policies to conquer world markets.

The next day, a deranged man shot and mortally wounded McKinley. That "wild man," as Marcus Hanna had called Theodore Roosevelt, suddenly became president of the United States. Once again, historian Robert Beisner notes, Americans were to test whether "a republic can prosper in a career of empire."[57] They would have to do so under the leadership of a person more flamboyant—and unpredictable—than McKinley.

NOTES

1. Ernest R. May, *Imperial Democracy* (New York, 1961), p. 270; Albert K. Weinberg, *Manifest Destiny* (Baltimore, 1940), p. 273.
2. Robert L. Beisner, *From the Old Diplomacy to the New, 1865–1900* (Arlington Heights, Ill., 1986), p. 89.
3. V. O. Key, "A Theory of Critical Elections," *Journal of Politics* 17 (February 1955): 12–15.
4. William Allen White, *The Autobiography of William Allen White* (New York, 1946), p. 292; Paul Boller, Jr., *Presidential Anecdotes* (New York, 1981), p. 189.
5. Henry Adams, *The Education of Henry Adams, an Autobiography* (Boston, 1918), p. 423. The best recent study of McKinley's extensive use of presidential powers is Lewis Gould, *The Presidency of William McKinley* (Lawrence, Kans., 1980).
6. Frances Fitzgerald, "Rewriting American History," *New Yorker*, 26 February 1979, p. 66. A Latin American view of the evolving U.S.-Cuban relationship is Manuel Moreno Fraginals, "Cuban-American Relations and the Sugar Trade," in *Diplo-*

matic Claims: Latin American Historians View the United States, ed. and trans. Warren Dean (Lanham, Md., 1985).

7. *Washington Post*, 21 July 1983, p. A23.

8. L. White Busbey, *Uncle Joe Cannon* (New York, 1927), p. 187.

9. *Journal of Commerce*, 14 March 1898, p. 1.

10. Theodore Roosevelt to George Dewey, 25 February 1898, Ciphers Sent, 1888–1898, Record Group 45, National Archives, Washington, D.C.; Charles S. Campbell, *The Transformation of American Foreign Relations, 1865–1900* (New York, 1976), pp. 279–280. Campbell's is the best-detailed analysis of the entire era and has a superb bibliography.

11. Fitzhugh Lee to William R. Day, 27 November 1897, Consular, Havana, and Hyatt to William R. Day, 23 March 1898, Consular, Santiago, Record Group 59, National Archives, Washington, D.C.

12. W. C. Reick to J. R. Young, 25 March 1898, Papers of William McKinley, Library of Congress, Washington, D.C.

13. Paul S. Holbo, "Presidential Leadership in Foreign Affairs: William McKinley and the Turpie-Foraker Amendment," *American Historical Review* 72 (July 1967): 1322–1334.

14. A superb analysis of the literature on McKinley and the war is Joseph Fry, "Essay Review: William McKinley and the Coming of the Spanish-American War," *Diplomatic History* 3 (Winter 1979): 77–97; John L. Offner, *An Unwanted War* (Chapel Hill, N.C., 1992), p. 189.

15. William Michael Morgan, "The Anti-Japanese Origins of the Hawaiian Annexation Treaty of 1897," *Diplomatic History* 6 (Winter 1982): 25–34.

16. *Washington Evening Star*, 11 January 1898, p. 1; 13 January 1898, p. 4; 19 January 1898, p. 14; also William Adam Russ, Jr., *The Hawaiian Republic, 1894–1898* (Selinsgrove, Pa., 1961), p. 240.

17. Alan K. Henrikson, "Maps, Globes, and 'The Cold War,' " *Special Libraries* 65 (October–November 1974): 445–454.

18. Frank Freidel, "Dissent in the Spanish-American War," in Samuel Eliot Morison *et al., Dissent in Three American Wars* (Cambridge, Mass., 1970), pp. 74–75; the May 4 cable from Manila is in U.S. Senate Document no. 62, *A Treaty of Peace . . .* , 55th Cong., 3d sess. (Washington, D.C., 1899), p. 326.

19. Russell Weigley, *The American Way of War* (New York, 1973), pp. 183–184.

20. Frank Freidel, *The Splendid Little War* (Boston, 1958), p. 46.

21. Theodore Roosevelt, *The Letters of Theodore Roosevelt*, ed. Elting E. Morison *et al.*, 8 vols. (Cambridge, Mass., 1951–1954), II, p. 1099n.

22. Thomas J. McCormick, *The China Market* (Chicago, 1967), p. 224.

23. David F. Healy, *The United States in Cuba, 1898–1902* (Madison, 1963), pp. 34–36.

24. Leonard Wood to Theodore Roosevelt, 28 October 1901, Papers of Leonard Wood, Library of Congress, Washington, D.C.

25. Healy, pp. 204–205.

26. Lloyd Gardner, "From Containment to Liberation," in *From Colony to Empire*, ed. William Appleman Williams (New York, 1972), p. 220.

27. Richard M. Morse, "Embarrassing Colony," *New York Review of Books*, 6 December 1984, p. 17.

28. Louis Henkin, *Foreign Affairs and the Constitution* (Mineola, N.Y., 1972), pp. 268, 330.

29. The best analysis on post-1898 is now Raymond Carr, *Puerto Rico, a Colonial Experiment* (New York, 1984).

30. Lazar Ziff, *America in the 1890s* (New York, 1966), p. 221. The original account appeared after McKinley's death in the *Charleston Advocate* 68 (22 January 1903): 137–138; I am indebted to R. H. (Max) Miller for this citation.

31. H. Wayne Morgan, *America's Road to Empire: The War with Spain and Overseas Expansion* (New York, 1965), esp. chs. IV, V.

32. McCormick, pp. 168–187; Ephraim K. Smith, " 'A Question from Which We Could Not Escape': William McKinley and the Decision to Annex the Philippine Islands," *Diplomatic History* 9 (Fall 1985): 363–388; John Offner, "The U.S. and France: Ending the Spanish-American War," *Diplomatic History* 7 (Winter 1983): 1–22.

33. Julius W. Pratt, *Expansionists of 1898* (Baltimore, 1936), pp. 297–298.

34. Smith, 373.

35. William Jennings Bryan to Mrs. U. S. Wissler, 20 May 1900, Papers of William Jennings Bryan, Library of Congress, Washington, D.C. A fine discussion of this point and the context is given by Richard H. Miller in his edition of *American Imperialism in 1898* (New York, 1970), pp. 10–12.

36. Freidel, "Dissent in the Spanish-American War," p. 93.

37. A most compelling account, which includes this story, is David Haward Bain, *Sitting in Darkness: Americans in the Philippines* (Boston, 1984).

38. Russell Roth's *Muddy Glory: America's "Indian Wars" in the Philippines, 1899–1935* (West Hanover, Mass., 1981) is a good account of the post-1902 battles.

39. David Healy, *U.S. Expansionism: The Imperialist Urge in the 1890s* (Madison, 1970), pp. 237–238; Emily Rosenberg, *Spreading the American Dream* (New York, 1982), p. 43.

40. John Higham, *Strangers in the Land* (New Brunswick, N.J., 1955), pp. 14, 63.

41. U.S. Bureau of the Census, *Historical Statistics of the United States: Colonial Times to 1957* (Washington, D.C., 1960), p. 55.

42. Patrick J. Hearden, *Independence and Empire: The New South's Cotton Mill Campaign, 1865–1901* (DeKalb, Ill., 1982), pp. 127, 133.

43. *Ibid.*, p. 128.

44. Beisner, p. 83.

45. McCormick, p. 65.

46. Patricia R. Hill, *The World Their Household: The American Woman's Foreign Mission Movement and Cultural Transformation, 1870–1920* (Ann Arbor, 1985), pp. 3, 54, 112, 164; a fine case study is Joan Brumberg's *Mission for Life: The Story of the Family of Adoniram Judson* . . . (New York, 1980).

47. William Neumann, "Determinism, Destiny, and Myth in the American Image of China," in *Issues and Conflicts*, ed. George L. Anderson (Lawrence, 1959), p. 1.

48. This account is drawn from Walter LaFeber, "John Hay," in *Encyclopedia of American Biography*, ed. John A. Garraty and Jerome L. Sternstein (New York, 1974), pp. 502–503.

49. Edwin Conger to John Hay, 29 May 1900, Papers of William McKinley, Library of Congress, Washington, D.C.

50. John Hay to Alvey A. Adee, 14 September 1900, Papers of William McKinley.

51. Judith Papachristou, "American Women and Foreign Policy, 1898–1905: Exploring Gender in Diplomatic History," *Diplomatic History* 14 (Fall 1990), esp. pp. 493–500; *Congressional Record*, 55th Cong., 3d sess., 13 January 1899, p. 639.

52. Fred H. Harrington, "American Anti-Imperialism," *New England Quarterly* 10 (December 1937): 654–655.
53. Roosevelt, II, pp. 1244, 1291, 1358.
54. *Ibid.*, pp. 1404–1405; Walter L. Williams, "U.S. Indian Policy and the Debate over Philippine Annexation," *Journal of American History* 66 (March 1980): 819–826, 830–831; Martin Ridge, *Ignatius Donnelly* (Chicago, 1962), pp. 394–397.
55. Richard Hofstadter, *The Paranoid Style in American Politics and Other Essays* (New York, 1965), pp. 180–181.
56. Edward Crapol, "From Anglophobia to Fragile Rapprochement," unpublished paper in author's possession, p. 21.
57. Beisner, p. xviii.

FOR FURTHER READING

No text can hope to match the references for pre-1981 material in *Guide to American Foreign Relations since 1700*, ed. Richard Dean Burns (1983). Also consult this chapter's notes and the General Bibliography at the end of this volume. The bibliography that follows, as in all the bibliographies in this book, concentrates on post-1981 works.

Cultural influences are well explored in Stuart Anderson, *Race and Rapprochement: Anglo-Saxonism and Anglo-American Relations, 1895–1904* (1981), and Gary Marotta, "The Academic Mind and the Rise of U.S. Imperialism: Historians and Economists as Publicists for Ideas of Colonial Expansion," *American Journal of Economics and Sociology* 42 (April 1983). McKinley and the march toward war are nicely analyzed in John Offner, *An Unwanted War* (1992); Richard E. Welch, Jr., "William McKinley: Reluctant Warrior, Cautious Imperialist," in *Studies in American Diplomacy, 1865–1945*, ed. Norman Graebner (1985); Robert C. Hilderbrand, *Power and the People: Executive Management of Public Opinion in Foreign Affairs, 1897–1921* (1981), a pioneering account; Tennant McWilliams, *Hannis Taylor: The New Southerner as an American* (1978); David R. Contosta and Jessica R. Hawthorne, "Rise to World Power: Selected Letters of Whitelaw Reid, 1895–1912," in *Transactions of the American Philosophical Society* (1986), key on a major figure; Carl Parrini, "Charles A. Conant," in *Behind the Throne*, eds. T. McCormick and W. LaFeber (1993), essays in honor of Fred Harvey Harrington; and a superb study of Reid's influential newspaper in Richard Kluger, *The Paper: The Life and Death of the New York Herald Tribune* (1986). The best one-volume study of the war itself is David F. Trask, *The War with Spain in 1898* (1981).

Michael H. Hunt, "Resistance and Collaboration in the American Empire, 1898–1903: An Overview," *Pacific Historical Review* 48 (June 1979), provides interesting case studies of Cuba, China, and the Philippines; Hawaii is analyzed in Thomas J. Osborne, *Empire Can Wait: American Opposition to Hawaiian Annexation, 1893–1898* (1981), especially good on commercial interests; Cuba's revolt is seen as a prototype of later national wars for liberation in Louis A. Perez, Jr., *Cuba between Empires, 1878–1902* (1983); the Philippines are well explored in three key works: Stuart Creighton Miller, *"Benevolent Assimilation": The American Conquest of the Philippines, 1899–1903* (1983), which stresses racism; Kenton J. Clymer, *Protestant Missionaries in the Philippines, 1898–*

1916: An Inquiry into the American Colonial Mentality (1985); and *The Anti-Imperialist Reader: A Documentary History of Anti-Imperialism in the United States*, Vol. I: *From the Mexican War to the Election of 1900*, ed. Philip S. Foner and Richard C. Winchester (1984). For affairs in China, see James J. Lorence, "Organized Business and the Myth of the China Market: The American Asiatic Association, 1898–1937," in *Transactions of the American Philosophical Society* (1984); James Reed, *The Missionary Mind and American East Asia Policy* (1985); and the fascinating case study by Jane Hunter, *The Gospel of Gentility: American Women Missionaries in Turn-of-the-Century China* (1984).

New overviews include Jules R. Benjamin, *The United States and the Origins of the Cuban Revolution* (1990); Ivan Musicant, *The Banana Wars* (1990); Joseph A. Fry, *John Tyler Morgan and the Search for Southern Autonomy* (1992), a significant study of the South's expansionism; H. W. Brands, *Bound to Empire: The United States and the Philippines* (1992), a highly useful synthesis; Paul Gordon Lauren, *Power and Prejudice: The Politics and Diplomacy of Racial Discrimination* (1988); and Walter LaFeber, *The American Search for Opportunity, 1865–1913*, in *The Cambridge History of U.S. Foreign Relations*, ed. Warren Cohen (1993), which has additional bibliography.

8

The Search for Opportunity:
Rough Riders and Dollar Diplomats
(1901–1913)

THEODORE ROOSEVELT AND TWENTIETH-CENTURY U.S. FOREIGN POLICY

William McKinley was the first twentieth-century president, but no chief executive has better caught, exemplified, and gloried in the spirit of modern America than Theodore Roosevelt. As *Time* magazine wrote in 1979, "He was America." At the 1984 Republican convention in Dallas, a young follower of Ronald Reagan explained:

> People sometimes ask me who was the last great President. Some say Kennedy. I don't think so. . . . I say Teddy Roosevelt. He was a fighter, he was stubborn. He was almost a salesman for America. America was the greatest country in the world and he was willing to go to any lengths to prove it. And he had the qualities I was brought up on—that you do the best you can, whatever it is. . . . He *loved* life. And he loved America.[1]

No president has been more colorful. "Cowboy, crime-fighter, soldier, and explorer . . . ," David Healy writes, "he fulfilled as an adult the ambitions of every small boy."[2] Roosevelt, however, was also as complex as the nation he led. Raised in New York City by private tutors, a graduate of Harvard, having traveled abroad extensively, he came from America's aristocratic class. The author of a dozen books, an avid naturalist, a lover of art (if it was traditional), he better combined the scholar-in-politics than anyone since John Quincy Adams. But he had also been a cowboy in South Dakota's Black Hills in the 1880s (where he went to mourn after his first wife had died in childbirth), worked as a lowly ward politician amid the rank corruption of New York City, and became uncommonly popular with mass America.

An aristocrat, a scholar, and a politician, Roosevelt also loved killing. After an argument with a girl friend, the twenty-year-old vented his anger by shooting a neighbor's dog. When he killed his first buffalo in the West, Roosevelt danced wildly around the carcass while his Indian guide watched in amazement. As noted in earlier chapters, TR justified slaughtering Indians, if necessary; their life, he wrote, was only "a few degrees less meaningless, squalid, and ferocious than that of the wild beasts." But he had little more use for certain whites. In his history of New York City, he approved of the killing of thirty men who had joined antidraft riots during the Civil War. TR called the shooting an "admirable object-lesson to the remainder" of New Yorkers.[3]

Perhaps Roosevelt's inclination for war and killing was part of a common racism at the time that justified the removal of "inferior" peoples. Perhaps it arose from the belief that when a "civilized" people used force, it would be limited and improve human character: "No triumph of peace is quite so great as the supreme triumphs of war," TR believed. In this case, however, he meant war against less industrialized nations: "In the long run civilized man finds he can keep the peace only by subduing his barbarian neighbor." As for possible conflict between more "civilized" nations, however, "we have every reason . . . to believe that [wars] will grow rarer and rarer."[4] Perhaps TR's urge to subdue others simply came out of his legendary energy. France's distinguished ambassador to the United States, Jean Jules Jusserand, told Paris officials about hiking with the president through Washington's Rock Creek Park:

> At last we came to the bank of a stream, rather too wide and deep to be forded. . . . But judge of my horror when I saw the President unbutton his clothes and heard him say, "We had better strip, so as not to wet our things in the creek." Then I, too, for the honor of France removed my apparel, everything except my lavender kid gloves. . . . "With your permission, Mr. President, I will keep these on; otherwise it would be embarrassing if we should meet ladies."

Theodore Roosevelt (1858–1919), born into an elite New York family (and also having experienced the life of a cowboy in the badlands of the Dakotas), became chief executive in 1901. He loved the presidency and the exercise of the new American power around the globe as much as most Americans loved him. Understanding that the U.S. mission often required the strenuous life of military force, Roosevelt declared that "I do not like to see young Christians with shoulders that slope like champagne bottles."

Other diplomats endured much the same experience in order to talk with the president of the United States. He once entertained a formal White House luncheon by using a judo hold to throw the Swiss Minister to the floor several times. An awed British official declared that Roosevelt was a combination of "St. Vitus and St. Paul . . . a great wonder of nature."[5]

Most of all, Roosevelt used force to bring about and maintain his central objective: order. Born in 1858, he grew to manhood amid the chaos of the Civil War and the post-1873 economic depression. He feared the danger posed by both the right ("the dull purblind folly of the very rich men," the "malefactors of great wealth"), and left-wing socialist and populist movements. He understood the need for reform;

but change had to evolve slowly, preferably under the guidance of a farseeing, honest broker with an aristocratic background. Roosevelt once said that he had become a modest reformer because "I intended to be one of the governing class." Only in that position could he preserve the best of American values by maintaining order and stability. A devotion to order especially explains TR's diplomacy. His policies abroad mirrored his politics at home. He opposed those whom he believed were reactionary (as tsarist Russia and, later, Kaiser Wilhelm's Germany), because by clinging to outdated beliefs they threatened to bring about catastrophic, radical change. But Roosevelt as strongly stood against those in Russia, China, and especially Latin America who worked for revolutionary change. TR, like the America of the Progressive Era that he led, sought a middle way.

He believed in the superiority of certain races, especially the Anglo-Saxon, because, in his view, they had organized, democratized, and especially industrialized and subdued "barbarians" more effectively than had other races. Roosevelt did not have great faith in Social Darwinism. (Social Darwinism enjoyed much popularity in his era and was used then and since to help explain why "lesser" peoples had to be controlled by the more "civilized." By applying Charles Darwin's studies on the evolution of lower animals to the evolution of human society, the Social Darwinians concluded that such "superior" races as the Anglo-Saxon resulted from unrestrained competition and individualism, and that the results were scientifically inevitable.) Roosevelt believed not in the Social Darwinians' inevitability, but in free will and an individual's (especially his own) ability to change society. He did not like rampant competition and individualism, for they too often had produced economic chaos, general disorder, and revolution.[6] He, instead, believed in regulating such competition so that disorder could be avoided. Roosevelt wanted order and peace, and for that he was prepared to go to war.

TR thus personally exemplified central themes of post-1890 U.S. foreign policy—a willingness to use force to obtain order, an emphasis on a special U.S. responsibility to guarantee stability in Latin America and Asia, and a belief that Anglo-Saxon values and successes gave Americans a right to conduct such foreign policy. He also hit upon a key theme of twentieth-century U.S. foreign policy when he declared in 1905: "The United States has not the slightest desire for territorial aggrandizement at the expense of any of its southern neighbors."[7] Americans wanted no more land.

After four hundred years, their quest for territorial expansion had ended in the twentieth century. Now they needed markets abroad. As Roosevelt's brilliant secretary of state, Elihu Root, announced in 1906, Americans had "for the first time accumulated a surplus of capital beyond the requirements of internal development."[8] Statistics bore out Root's announcement. Americans had invested overseas $0.7 billion in 1897, $2.5 billion in 1908, and, by 1914, $3.5 billion. Nearly half of those amounts went into Latin America, about 23 percent into Canada, 22 percent into Europe, and 5 percent to Asia (including the Philippines). William McKinley, almost until his dying breath, had preached the need for overseas markets to absorb products from American factories and farms. Roosevelt and Root agreed, but they now added the need for capital markets as well. They also believed that imaginative leadership could use this economic power to prevent disorder and revolution. American goods and capital could create happier, more stable societies in the Caribbean and Central America—even in distant Asia. Their successors, President William Howard Taft (1909–1913) and his secretary of state, Philander C. Knox, called this policy "dollar diplomacy."

THE AMERICAN SEARCH FOR OPPORTUNITY: A NEW PRESIDENCY FOR A NEW FOREIGN POLICY

Roosevelt bragged that he used the White House " as a bully pulpit." He led Americans and made them love it. But he also inherited a position whose powers had already multiplied during the post-1860 era. Roosevelt admired Lincoln's expansion of presidential powers during the Civil War. Even without a Civil War, however, TR believed that presidents had to follow what he termed the "stewardship" theory: "Occasionally great national crises arise which call for immediate and vigorous executive action." The president must then act "upon the theory that he is the steward of the people." It is "not only [his] right but his duty to do anything that the needs of the Nation demanded unless such action was forbidden by the Constitution or the laws."[9]

In 1890, the Supreme Court had almost accidentally moved to support this theory of large presidential powers. Deciding a case (In re Neagle) that actually had nothing to do with foreign policy, the Court declared that the president was not limited to carrying out congressional laws and treaties. His duty included enforcing "the rights, duties, and obligations growing out of the Constitution itself, our international relations, and all the protection implied by the nature of the govern-

UNCLE SAM: "Now I can do what I please with 'em."

This cartoonist not only portrays the liberty that Uncle Sam took with the Constitution in order to control his new possessions, but catches as well some of the era's racism.

ment under the Constitution."[10] These were extraordinarily general, open-ended words, and they were obiter dicta—not binding or essential to the decision. But they were to be used later to justify the most vigorous presidential power, especially in "our international relations."

It was almost as if some members of the Supreme Court had looked into a crystal ball and had foreseen that a new foreign policy would soon require a new presidency. As late as 1897, some close observers wondered whether the Constitution could be adapted to a U.S. government that might soon have worldwide responsibilities. Captain Alfred Thayer Mahan warned that any projection of U.S. power overseas could smash up against constitutional restraints—"the lion in the path" of empire, as he vividly phrased it.[11] Apparently unfamiliar with the *Neagle* decision, Mahan believed that the ambitious president might simply have to ignore the Constitution in order to protect U.S. interests overseas. McKinley proved Mahan wrong. The president's handling of the 1898 war, the annexation of the Philippines, and the 1899–1900 China crises demonstrated the tremendous power a shrewd politician could exercise as chief executive of American foreign policy. The more Americans supported a vigorous foreign policy, the more they were going to get a vigorous presidency.

A young but already well-known political scientist best explained the effect of end-of-the-century foreign policy on presidential powers. The post-1898 "ownership of distant possessions and [the] many sharp struggles for foreign trade," Woodrow Wilson wrote in a widely used textbook, meant that "the President can never again be the mere domestic figure he has been throughout so much of our history." As the United States "has risen to first rank in power and resources," so the president "must stand always at the front of our affairs, and the office will be as big and as influential as the man who occupies it." Wilson prophesied:

> Men of ordinary physique and discretion cannot be Presidents and live, if the strain be not somehow relieved. We shall be obliged always to be picking our chief magistrates from among wise and prudent athletes—a small class.[12]

Roosevelt, the disciple of "the strenuous life," seemed perfect for the role. He believed that only the president could conduct foreign policy. Congress was too large and unwieldy. Public opinion, TR privately declared, was "the voice of the devil, or what is still worse, the voice of a fool." But he went to great lengths to ensure that public opinion was with him—or at least not against him. He, indeed, used the White House as a "bully pulpit," went on frequent speaking engagements, and carefully cultivated powerful journalists in Washington. When a New York State Supreme Court justice once tried to limit the president's power, TR dismissed him as an "amiable old fuzzy-wuzzy with sweetbread brains."[13]

More directly, Roosevelt used the president's power as commander in chief of the armed forces to dispatch U.S. troops as he saw fit in Latin America. Once when Congress refused to accept a treaty he had made, Roosevelt circumvented Congress with an "executive agreement." Such an agreement could be one of two types: authorized by congressional legislation, or—as became too common—made by a president on his own authority. A little-known device until the 1890s, presidents have used it since far more than treaties because an executive agreement is not submitted to Congress, as a treaty must be. It is an agreement between the president and another government. The real difference between the two is that treaties are binding on all parties as long as they are in force, but an executive agreement is technically binding only as long as the president who signed it is in power. That was good enough for Roosevelt. He judged (correctly) that future presidents would uphold his agreements—in part because they would want their successors to uphold their deals. Most notably, TR ignored Senate opposition by taking over the Caribbean country of Santo Domingo between 1905 and 1907. One angry congressman exclaimed that Roosevelt had "no more use for the Constitution than a tomcat has for a marriage license."[14]

But that was not entirely accurate. As a student of American history, Roosevelt had great respect for the Constitution. As a politician as well as student of his nation's history, however, he also had great respect for the need for American expansionism. And that turned out to be the problem. Americans, historian Robert Wiebe has argued, embarked on a "search for order" between 1865 and 1920. That well might have been so at home; given the long economic depression, general strikes, and social upheavals that struck the United States during those years, they understandably wanted peace and quiet. But it was not the case abroad. In their foreign policies, Americans valued a search for opportunity over the search for order. In Cuba, Hawaii, the Philippines, China, and Central America—and especially during the 1901–1913 years, in Cuba, Panama, the Dominican Republic, Nicaragua, China, and Mexico—Americans demanded opportunity for their trade, investment, and security needs. In every instance noted, the result in these countries was upheaval and, in several instances, revolution. But U.S. officials did not back off. They continued to demand economic and other rights, even if the demands climaxed in massive disorder. They valued those rights over the disorder the demands helped cause. At that point, Americans then demanded a new, more vigorous presidency to guarantee continued opportunities for their growing economic machine—and, if possible, to restore order in these foreign countries. The presidents, led by McKinley, Taft, and—most flamboyantly—Roosevelt, used military force to guarantee continued opportunity and, they hoped, order. Thus was born the twentieth-century "imperial presidency."[15]

In this new world for U.S. opportunity, Roosevelt was determined to use his considerable energy and powers to the limit. Thanks to Lincoln, the Supreme Court, McKinley, executive agreements, and the worldwide quest of Americans for opportunity, those limits stretched far. Roosevelt colorfully demonstrated Woodrow Wilson's insight: an aggressive foreign policy created a strong president. And vice versa.

East, North, and South to an Isthmian Canal

TR knew what he wanted to do with his new powers. He immediately moved to realize the American dream of a U.S.-controlled isthmian canal in Central America. First, however, he had to break the 1850 Clayton-Bulwer Treaty that made Great Britain a full partner in any canal project. Roosevelt and his first secretary of state (and close friend), John Hay, terminated that treaty. They did so while actually strengthening U.S.-British relations, despite events that tested the relationship. The tests occurred in South Africa, Alaska, and then Central America.

In South Africa, the British had become bogged down in a bloody struggle with the Boers between 1899 and 1902. The Boers (a Dutch word for "farmers") had settled at the southern tip of black Africa in 1652. The British seized the South African cape in 1795 and instantly clashed with the austere, Calvinist, isolated, and fiercely nationalistic Boers. In the 1830s, the Boers undertook the great trek north to escape British control. They created their own independent nation. Then, as diamonds and other mineral wealth were found in the 1870s, the Boers' region became a focal point for European colonial power rivalry, and the British moved in to reassert control. At that point, U.S. economic interests rapidly increased in the region. Between 1895 and the outbreak of the Boer War in 1899–1900, for example, U.S. exports to South Africa tripled to $20 million. Americans also believed that the British were more progressive and better able to "civilize" the black Africans, who represented the large majority of South Africans.

All-out war between the British and the Boers erupted in 1899. To everyone's astonishment, during "Black Week" of December, the Boer troops inflicted the worst military defeat on the powerful British forces in living memory. Most Americans, remembering 1776, sided with the Boers. But U.S. officials, while remaining officially neutral, strongly sided with the British. American bankers floated loans to pay one-fifth of England's war costs. Roosevelt and Hay were shaken by the British defeats. "It certainly does seem to me that England is on the downgrade," the president wrote privately. But he understood the need to champion Anglo-Saxon values. Roosevelt quietly supported the British and refused to send any aid to the Boers until London's armies turned the tide and won victory between 1900 and 1902. TR received few rewards for his help in South Africa. As historian Thomas Noer concludes, the United States supported Great Britain to ensure the entry of American goods through an open-door policy in South Africa, a policy that Roosevelt thought the British supported. But despite U.S. pressure and the growing interest of American blacks in South Africa after 1900, "this policy failed: British domination resulted in a decline of American economic influence and did little to improve the lot of the black African."[16]

British problems in Africa, however, did allow Roosevelt to score two victories closer to home. The first involved a disputed boundary between Alaska and Canada that became enflamed after gold was found in 1896. TR was furious at the Canadians for advancing what he considered to be an empty claim. "I'm going to be ugly," he warned his British friends. The president finally agreed to allow "six impartial jurists" to arbitrate the dispute. He showed his determination to have his way by dispatching troops to Alaska. Then he appointed three Americans who were neither "impartial" nor "jurists," but U.S. politicians who completely shared TR's views. The Canadian prime minister, Sir Wilfrid Laurier, rightly denounced the appointments as "an outrage." He named two Canadian members, and the British named their own lord chief justice—who promptly voted with the Americans and handed Roosevelt most of the land. The Canadians cried that they had been double-crossed. To the Americans and the British, however, maintaining their improving relationship was worth giving away what was a small, if valuable, slice of Canada. For not the first or last time, Canadian interests were sacrificed for the sake of U.S.-British friendship.[17]

The most significant victory over the British came after "Black Week" in South Africa. London officials reversed themselves and agreed to discuss doing away with the Clayton-Bulwer Treaty. The U.S. Senate, never reluctant to kick the British Lion as long as it was already badly wounded, pushed events along by introducing measures to build an American-owned canal regardless of the 1850 pact. In early 1900, Hay and the British ambassador to Washington signed the Hay-Pauncefote Treaty, which allowed the United States to build and own—but not fortify—an isthmian canal. The U.S. Senate indignantly rejected the treaty and told Hay to obtain the right to fortify as well. The secretary of state was furious with the Senate and especially with Democratic presidential nominee William Jennings Bryan, who led the opposition: "He struck at [the treaty] in mere ignorance and malice," Hay wrote a friend, "as an idiot might strike at a statue because he happened to have a hammer in his hand."[18] Hay nevertheless had no alternative, especially after the new president agreed with the Senate. A second Hay-Pauncefote Treaty was signed in November 1901. The United States gained the right to fortify the canal.

But where was the canal to be located? Official U.S. commissions between 1876 and 1901 recommended Nicaragua as the cheapest and most efficient route. Its rival, Panama (a province of Colombia), might have been cheaper, but the French company that owned rights to that route (Compagnie Universelle du Canal Interocéanique) demanded over

$100 million. By 1901–1902, however, as the second Hay-Pauncefote Treaty took effect, the company fell under the control of two shadowy, skilled lobbyists who changed the course of isthmian history. Philippe Bunau-Varilla was a Frenchman with extensive contacts in Panama and Washington. William Cromwell was senior partner in the influential New York law firm of Sullivan and Cromwell; he enjoyed access to powerful leaders in Washington politics and New York finance. The two men reduced their company's asking price to $40 million. Then, in June 1902, they pushed through Congress the Spooner Amendment, giving Roosevelt the right to pay $40 million to the company and purchase a six-mile zone in Panama from Colombia. The lobbying of the two men had received heaven-sent help when a Nicaraguan volcano suddenly erupted and endangered the proposed route. Bunau-Varilla quickly put a picture of the volcano (which the Nicaraguans had, unfortunately for themselves, printed on their postage stamps) on the desk of everyone in Congress.

The secretary of state negotiated the Hay-Herrán Treaty that gave Colombia $10 million plus $250,000 annually for the six-mile zone. The Colombian legislature, however, rejected the pact and demanded more money. In truth, the Colombians hoped to stall until 1904, when the French company's charter was to revert to Colombia. The Latin American country would then gain—and Bunau-Varilla and Cromwell lose—$40 million. Roosevelt blew up. All his considerable racism appeared. He refused to have those "banditti" in Latin America publicly humiliate and rob the United States. In truth, as Richard L. Lael observes in his important study of U.S.-Colombian relations, U.S. officials seemed ignorant of Colombia's deep problems as it emerged from a costly civil war, and "none of them seemed to realize, or seriously consider, the possibility that U.S. actions, as seen from Colombia, could legitimately be perceived as interventionist, dangerous, and imperialistic." Roosevelt instead spread the word that he would not be displeased if Panama revolted against Colombia. The Panamanians needed little encouragement. Since at least the 1880s, they had developed a strong nationalist movement that repeatedly tried to obtain independence. As Panama grew more restless, U.S. armed forces had become extraordinarily active. One estimate concludes that those forces had spent a total of about 200 days ashore in Panama in various forms of intervention during the second half of the nineteenth century. It was the longest U.S. occupation of any foreign area until 1898.[19]

Under Bunau-Varilla's guidance and with Washington's support, the Panamanians again revolted in November 1903. This time, the U.S.

"Man's greatest liberty with nature," the cutting of the Panama Canal, was a crucial step in building twentieth-century U.S. military and economic power. In the photo, the battleship Ohio *sails through the passageway that opened in 1914.*

warships prevented Colombian troops from landing in Panama to quell the revolt. Roosevelt recognized the new nation two days after the rebellion started. He signed a treaty giving Panama $10 million plus $250,000 a year for rights to a ten-mile-wide strip that cut the country in half. The United States fully guaranteed Panama's independence. U.S.-Colombian relations did not return to normal until a treaty gave Colombia $25 million in 1921, two years after Roosevelt's death removed the loudest objection to making the pact.

Roosevelt and Hay found ingenious excuses for their actions in November 1903. They claimed that the 1846 treaty with Colombia gave the United States the right to maintain freedom of transit across the isthmus. The treaty did so, but certainly not against Colombia, which owned Panama and with whom the United States had made the 1846 pact. Nor did the treaty require Colombia to allow a canal to be built. Another rationale for the action was offered by TR's close friend, Oscar Straus, who claimed that the 1846 treaty was "a covenant running with the land"—regardless of whether Panamanians or Colombians owned

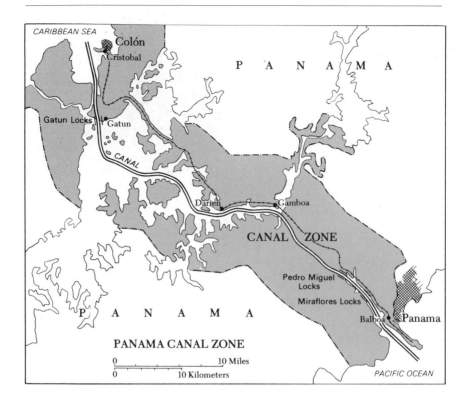

CARIBBEAN SEA

Colón

Cristobal

P A N A M A

Gatun Locks Gatun

CANAL

Darien Gamboa

CANAL ZONE

Pedro Miguel
Locks

Miraflores Locks

P A N A M A

Balboa Panama

PANAMA CANAL ZONE

0 ————————— 10 Miles
0 ————————— 10 Kilometers

PACIFIC OCEAN

the land. A State Department lawyer dismissed Straus's interpretation with the joke that it turned out to be a "covenant running (away!) with the land." The real reasons for Roosevelt's action were his determination to build a canal and the U.S. naval power that enforced his will. As for the Panamanians, they gained independence but lost part of their country. They soon claimed title over the ten-mile-wide strip, but the United States effectively closed it off and controlled the territory. John Hay justified U.S. rights with the phrase "titular sovereignty," a claim so vague that Washington officials could not define or defend it when Panamanians demanded the return of their land (and the canal) in the 1960s and 1970s.[20]

At a cabinet meeting, TR vigorously gave his reasons for taking the canal zone, then loudly challenged his advisers: "Have I defended myself?" Elihu Root answered, "You certainly have Mr. President. You have shown that you were accused of seduction and you have conclusively proved that you were guilty of rape." Roosevelt, of course, would never admit to having doubts about his act. He had overcome Colombia's opposition. He also overcame domestic opposition. But leading newspapers, led by the *New York Times* and the Hearst journals, claimed (in Hearst's words) that the "Panama foray is nefarious. Besides being a rough-riding assault upon another republic over the shattered wreckage of international law and diplomatic usage, it is a quite unexampled instance of foul play in American politics."[21]

Most Americans, however, overwhelmingly approved Roosevelt's actions. They cared about the canal, not about the means he used to acquire it. TR made "the dirt fly," as he put it, and in 1906 paid a personal visit to witness the construction. It marked the first time a president had ever left the United States while in office. Roosevelt saw miraculous engineering feats being performed as the waterway cut through Panama's mountains and lakes. The United States was completing the biggest construction job in history. He also watched medical history being made as American scientists discovered how to find and kill the mosquito that caused malaria and yellow fever, diseases that had destroyed the French effort in the 1880s. With the opening of the canal in 1914—"the greatest liberty Man has ever taken with Nature," in the words of British ambassador James Bryce—the distance between New York and San Francisco by boat shrank from 13,615 miles to 5,300 miles. U.S. merchants and warships now moved easily between the Atlantic and Pacific oceans. And Americans grew even more sensitive about disorder in the region surrounding their canal.

A Great Departure: The Roosevelt Corollary

Long before he obtained the canal area, TR understood the importance of the most hallowed of U.S. foreign policies, the Monroe Doctrine, and how it had to be enforced. "There is a homely adage that runs 'speak softly and carry a big stick; you will go far,' " he told the Minnesota State Fair audience in 1901. "If the American nation will speak softly and yet build and keep at a pitch of the highest training a thoroughly efficient navy, the Monroe Doctrine will go far."[22]

The danger to the doctrine no longer was British expansionism. London officials were preoccupied with Africa and Europe. The danger came from two other sources. The first, Germany, was not obvious and worried mainly U.S. military planners. Modern U.S. military planning began in 1900, when McKinley established the navy's General Board. (It was created largely so that war hero Admiral Dewey could occupy himself with war games instead of running against McKinley for the presidency.) In 1903, Secretary of War Elihu Root created the

Don't forget that in the mild Dr. Jekyll
there lurks the unsafe Mr. Hyde
—*Milwaukee News*

This cartoon of 1904 from the Milwaukee News—*"Don't forget that in the mild Dr. Jekyll there lurks the unsafe Mr. Hyde"—is not only critical of Roosevelt the campaigner, but also indicates why cartoonists loved to draw the always active, colorful president.*

Army General Staff. That year, an interservice planning group, the Joint Army and Navy Board, was also set up. A global foreign policy needed sophisticated military planning. In the most sensitive region, the Caribbean, the planners grew to fear the growing navy and imperial ambitions of Kaiser Wilhelm's Germany. The kaiser was getting at cross-purposes in Europe, Africa, and Asia with England, TR's closest ally. Historians later discovered that in 1899, the kaiser actually ordered plans drawn up for possible war against the United States. A lack of ships forced him to stop the planning.[23]

The second danger to the Monroe Doctrine was well known, even blatant. Frequent revolutions in the smaller Caribbean–Central American nations were an open invitation for Germany and other powers to intervene to protect their citizens—and perhaps to stay indefinitely. Much as the United States feared Soviet involvement in Latin American revolutions after 1960, so Americans feared the European presence in the area long before the Russian Revolution of 1917. At first, in 1901–1902, Roosevelt thought that the Europeans were justified in intervening to protect their citizens and property and to collect just debts, as long as they did not remain. Then in 1902–1903, Germans, French, and British took TR at his word and used force to collect debts owed to them by Venezuela.[24]

An uproar ensued in the United States. It grew when the International Court of Justice at The Hague ruled that the Europeans acted within their rights. The U.S. State Department warned Roosevelt that the ruling put "a premium on violence" and undermined the Monroe Doctrine.[25] The Europeans had been careful not only to keep the president informed of their plans, but even to indicate their recognition of the Monroe Doctrine. Roosevelt nevertheless knew he was in a tight spot. He could not tolerate major European intervention in the region, but if he opposed it, the Europeans would demand that he make the Latin Americans behave properly. "These wretched republics cause me a great deal of trouble," he lamented.[26]

His moment of decision came in 1904. In Santo Domingo, whose harbors and customshouse Americans had been eying since at least 1870, U.S. business groups came into conflict with German and French interests. The U.S. minister to Santo Domingo, William F. Powell, used the threat of Germany to convince the U.S. government to intervene directly on behalf of American bankers and shipping companies. These foreign rivalries in turn triggered internal disorders. In late 1904, TR declared that he intended to stop the threat of possible revolution. He arranged the payment of debts to Europeans by seizing the customshouses. The president announced his policy to Congress in December 1904. Reviewing major themes of post-1865 as he gave a history lesson to Congress, TR stressed his belief in the obligations— and rights—of "civilized" nations as he outlined what became known as the Roosevelt Corollary to the Monroe Doctrine:

> It is not true that the United States feels any land hunger or entertains any projects as regards the other nations of the Western Hemisphere save such as are for their welfare. All that this country desires is to see the neighboring countries stable, orderly, and prosperous. . . . Chronic wrongdoing, or an impotence which results in a general loosening of the ties of civilized society, may in America, as elsewhere, ultimately require intervention by some civilized nation, and in the Western Hemisphere the adherence of the United States to the Monroe Doctrine may force the United States, however reluctantly, in flagrant cases of such wrongdoing or impotence, to the exercise of an international police power. . . . We would interfere with [Latin Americans] only in the last resort, and then only if it became evident that their inability or unwillingness to do justice at home and abroad had violated the rights of the United States or had invited foreign aggression to the detriment of the entire body of American nations.[27]

Roosevelt's action pleased U.S. businesses in the country as well as the president, Carlos Morales, whom they supported. But many Santo Domingans disliked the idea of the United States having a blank check to interfere in their affairs. Morales finally had to sign the treaty while

This Argentine cartoon, published in a Buenos Aires newspaper in early 1905, provides a growing Latin American view of U.S. foreign policy. An Uncle Sam figure, with the head of Theodore Roosevelt, reaches throughout the hemisphere with the heavy hand of the Monroe Doctrine. Santo Domingo is depicted as the small island below Cuba and between Uncle Sam's hands.

U.S. warships protected him from his own people. That, however, turned out to be the least of TR's problems, for next the treaty was rejected by the U.S. Senate: it refused to throw an American protectorate over the restless country. Roosevelt effectively thumbed his nose at the Senate by signing an executive agreement with Morales. U.S. government agents and bankers, led by J. P. Morgan and Kuhn, Loeb and Company, took over control of Santo Domingo. They paid off the debt owed the Europeans.

Roosevelt saw his action not as imperialism, but as work that a "policeman" must do to maintain order among less civilized people. As he privately wrote a friend in 1904:

> I want to do nothing but what a policeman has to do in Santo Domingo. As for annexing the island, I have about the same desire to annex it as a gorged boa constrictor might have to swallow a porcupine wrong-end-to. . . . I have asked some of our people to go there because, after having refused for three months to do anything, the attitude of the Santo Domingans has been one of half chaotic war towards us.[28]

The gorged-boa-constrictor analogy was appropriate, given that the United States was trying to digest Hawaii, the Philippines (which TR was beginning to see as "our Achilles heel" because it was so vulnerable to such powers as Japan), Puerto Rico, Cuba, and Panama. All had been brought within the American orbit within just six years.

But a gorged boa constrictor also wants peace and quiet. Roosevelt's corollary marked a historic break from Monroe's doctrine and anticipated U.S. policy toward Latin America for the rest of the twentieth century. It did so for five reasons. First, Monroe's message had supported Latin American revolutions, but TR's opposed them. Second, Monroe had urged nonintervention in those revolts by all outside parties, including the United States. Roosevelt, however, declared that he would directly intervene to maintain "civilized" order. Third, Monroe had seen U.S. economic power acting in a traditional marketplace—that is, buying and selling according to rules set by the home country. But Roosevelt used his economic power to control that marketplace and bring it under U.S., not home-country, control. (One senator who bitterly opposed TR's action sarcastically observed that the U.S. Navy rallying cry had been that of a commander in the War of 1812: "Don't give up the ship boys"; now, however, a U.S. naval officer could cry: "We have met the enemy and they are ours. Advance the bid on Dominican bonds.")[29] Fourth, because Monroe had argued for keeping out of internal Latin American affairs, he had no need for the use of military power. But Roosevelt's policy depended on force. Between 1898 and 1920, U.S. troops entered Latin American countries no fewer than twenty times. Those nations were seen less as neighbors in the hemisphere than problems to be managed militarily. Finally, because Monroe's policy had urged abstention, Congress had no role and the president did not have to be concerned about constitutional problems with the legislature. Roosevelt, however, followed a course that constitutionally required obtaining Congress's assent (to pursue such policies, for example, as making war on foreign nations or making treaties to operate their customshouses). But he simply ignored Congress when it opposed him. His actions drew power out of the legislative branch and pulled it into the executive.

The Roosevelt Corollary opened a new era in hemispheric relations. Latin Americans fully understood. They moved to curb TR's claims. In 1907, the so-called Drago Doctrine (named after Argentina's foreign minister Luis María Drago) became accepted international law. It declared that no nation could use force to collect debts. TR strongly opposed the Drago dictum and finally acquiesced only after it was radically weakened. In 1911, the United States even expanded its new version of the Monroe Doctrine. Republican senator Henry Cabot Lodge from Massachusetts, a close friend of Roosevelt's, learned that a Japanese company was angling to buy strategic Mexican territory. The Lodge Corollary, passed in a Senate resolution, declared U.S. opposition to the sale of any strategic area to a nonhemispheric company that might be an agent for a foreign government. The Japanese firm had earlier lost interest anyway, but the State Department used the resolution to discourage similar ventures after 1911. The Monroe Doctrine resembled U.S. industry and the president's powers: it grew larger all the time.

THE FATEFUL TRIANGLE: THE UNITED STATES, CHINA, AND JAPAN, 1900–1908

Roosevelt fervently believed that the American future rested on events in Asia—the new Far West—as well as on those in the Western Hemisphere. He had led the fight to take the Philippines and completely supported the open-door policy. His beliefs were bolstered by his close friend, Brooks Adams. Grandson of John Quincy Adams, Brooks was a brilliant eccentric who believed that he had discovered a historical "law" proving that the world's money center had moved ever westward over a thousand years. Following the sun, it had jumped from the Mediterranean to Paris and then to London. Now, he believed, it was poised once again to bestow greatness and wealth on a people. The only question was whether it would turn west to New York, or lurch east toward Germany and Russia. Brooks Adams saw the 1898–1900 triumphs "as the moment when we won the great prize. I do believe that we may dominate the world, as no nation has dominated it in recent time."[30]

But to reach, then remain at, the peak of world power, Americans had to conquer the world's greatest market and cheapest labor supply: China. And to do that, Adams told Roosevelt, the United States had to use its vast resources—but also strong government involvement—to build the cheapest, most efficient transportation system to carry its goods to Asia. "We must have a new deal . . . , we must suppress the states, and have a centralized administration, or we shall wobble over," Adams declared. Or, as he told TR, Americans "must command the terminus in Asia—if we fail in this we shall break down."[31] The president responded in July 1903 that he agreed: "We must do our best to prevent the shutting to us of Asian markets. In order to keep the roads to these terminals we must see that they are managed primarily in the interest of the country."[32] Out of such ideas emerged laws, pushed especially by Progressives such as TR, that created new central-government agencies to regulate the railroads and make the society more efficient.

In foreign policy, such ideas led Roosevelt, Hay, and Adams to try to guarantee an open door to the China market by supporting Japan (who seemed to agree with U.S. aims) and opposing Russia's attempts to colonize Manchuria and control Korea. Secretary of State Hay believed that if TR gave the Japanese "a wink," they would "fly at the throat of Russia in a moment." When some Americans feared such a "wink" might make Japan supreme in Asia and perhaps create disorder inside Russia, Hay dismissed the critics as members "of that highly respected family, the common or barnyard ass." Roosevelt warmly supported the historic 1902 alliance between Japan and Great Britain, which further isolated Russia in the Far East. And as the rivalry between Tokyo and St. Petersburg grew hot, TR sided with Japan.

In 1904, the Japanese launched a surprise attack that destroyed most of Russia's Pacific fleet. Americans supported Japan. Leading Jewish bankers who had vivid memories of Russia's recent anti-Semitic attacks provided war loans to Tokyo. The Japanese government worked through these bankers to float the first major foreign-government loan ever offered to American investors.[33] In the bright glow of Japan's early victories and TR's Latin American triumphs in 1903–1904, few doubted his policies. One who did, however, was Henry Adams. The brother of Brooks, a close friend of the president's, and perhaps the greatest of all American historians, Henry Adams eerily prophesied in 1904 that Americans—and the world—had stumbled down the wrong road:

> Everybody is interested, and excited, and all are anti-Russian, almost to a dangerous extent [he wrote privately]. I am the only—relative—Russian afloat, and only because I am half-crazy with the fear that Russia is sailing straight into another French revolution which may upset all Europe and us too. A serious disaster to Russia might smash the whole civilized world.[34]

In 1905, Henry Adams's prophesy began to come true. Revolution erupted in Russia. The tsar smashed it, but other European monarchs grew worried. They had asked Roosevelt to try to mediate a peace, and TR agreed, in part because he feared that Japan lacked the resources to fight a long war against Russia. He called the two sides to meet at

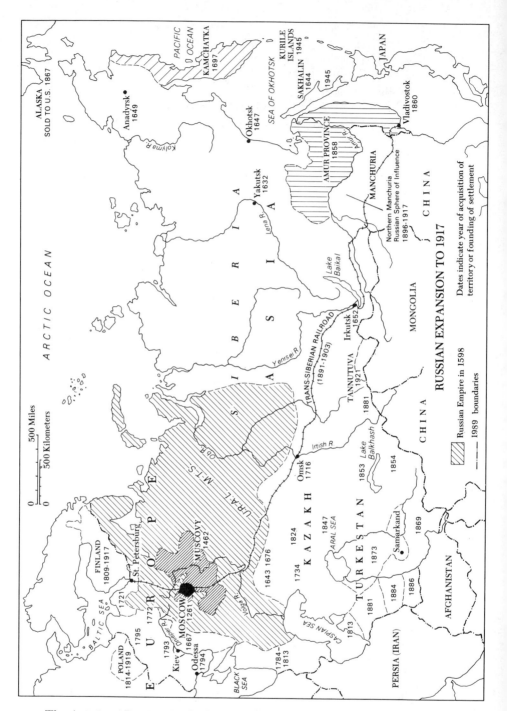

The American-Russian rivalry has deep roots. Early twentieth-century presidents mistrusted the Russians not only because of the tsars' autocratic system, but because of the history of Russian expansionism, shown on this map.

Portsmouth, New Hampshire, in late summer 1905. Although China's interests lay at the center of the talks, no Chinese were invited to participate. After the Japanese finally dropped their demand of a huge indemnity from the tsar, the two sides hammered out a peace treaty in September. Both nations agreed to respect China's territorial integrity (thus honoring the open door). But Japan emerged with controlling interest in Korea, key Chinese ports formerly belonging to Russia, the main railway in southern Manchuria, and the southern half of Sakhalin Island, formerly claimed by the tsar. The next month, Tokyo forced Korea to become a Japanese protectorate. Japan would remain in control until 1945. The Koreans appealed to TR for help, but he now refused to become involved.[35]

Instead, the president made a secret deal—the Taft-Katsura Agreement—in which Japan promised to keep hands off the Philippines, and TR recognized Tokyo's domination of Korea. He emerged from Portsmouth more anti-Russian than ever. "Bad as the Chinese are, no human being, black, yellow or white, could be as untruthful, as insincere, as arrogant—in short as untrustworthy in every way—as the Russians under their present system," he complained privately.[36]

But the Russo-Japanese War brought U.S. officials into a dangerous new world. The Chinese observed how an Asian people had humiliated a white race in conflict. Fresh antiforeign tendencies appeared when China stunned Roosevelt in 1905 by protesting U.S. immigration policy with a highly effective boycott of American goods.

A fascinating case study revealed some of the causes and results of the boycott. In the 1880s, James B. Duke learned about the invention of a machine that rolled cigarettes at high speeds. He decided—after glancing at an atlas's population chart—that only China had the population to buy so many cigarettes. By 1902, he was selling 1 billion cigarettes a year through his British-American Tobacco Company (BAT). He undercut both Chinese and Japanese competitors by using the newest technology and advanced sales techniques. When the boycott began in 1905, however, Chinese students and merchants alike targeted Duke's operation as a way of striking back at foreign control. The protestors turned BAT's advertising around by publishing posters showing a dog (which the Chinese considered a low form of life) smoking a BAT cigarette and saying, "Those who smoke American cigarettes are of my species." BAT, Standard Oil, and other U.S. firms urged TR to force the Chinese to end the boycott. But Roosevelt (who called people he deemed especially inefficient "Chinese") was bewildered by the boycott's efficiency. Finally, with its point made and pressure building, the

James Buchanan Duke (1856–1925) began working at the family's Durham, North Carolina, tobacco company in 1874. Some fifteen years later, the company controlled 50 percent of U.S. cigarette production, thanks to "Buck's" genius with machinery and marketing. He renamed it the American Tobacco Company, bought or drove off competitors, exploited the vast China market— until Chinese nationalism checked the company and the U.S. Supreme Court in 1911 dissolved Duke's monopoly. He gave generously to his hometown college, Trinity, which was renamed Duke University.

Chinese government ended the boycott. BAT quickly crushed its Chinese competitors who had appeared during the boycott, then set prices so high that by 1916 it enjoyed an 18 percent profit.[37] Three years later, in 1919, the Chinese Revolution began in earnest. The 1905 boycott, resembling the 1905 Russian revolt, had been a warning sign.

Roosevelt next had to confront a challenge from Tokyo. Japan closed off Korea to U.S. interests, then began moving into Manchuria itself. These direct threats to the open door were compounded by an uproar in the United States over Japanese immigration. In 1890, some 2,000 Japanese had lived in California. In 1900, the number reached 24,000 and the governor called the influx the "Japanese menace." The state prepared to pass an Asian exclusion bill, and in San Francisco, a city ordinance segregated Oriental children. Anti-Asian riots erupted. Fear of a U.S.-Japanese war spread. Tokyo officials were deeply angered at the discrimination, but Roosevelt could calm California only by stopping Japanese immigration. In a "gentlemen's agreement" of 1907, Japan said that it would no longer allow laborers to emigrate to the

United States provided that California stopped discriminating against Japanese.

A temporary calm set in, but TR knew that he was confronting an aggressive Japan. To show his resolve, he determined in 1907 to send the entire fleet of sixteen U.S. battleships around the world, with a special stop in Japan. Congressmen, anxious that the Japanese would sneakily attack the fleet as they had the Russian navy in 1904, threatened to withhold needed funds. Roosevelt responded that he had enough money to send the ships halfway around the world. If Congress wanted to bring them back, it could give him the funds. Congress surrendered. The fleet's visit to Japan was a huge popular success. Roosevelt, moreover, had dramatically shown the global reach of the new U.S. battle fleet.

But the trip's diplomatic effect was slight. Japan continued its pressure on Korea and Manchuria. In 1907–1908, a colorful twenty-seven-year-old U.S. consul in Manchuria, Willard Straight, set out to block Japan on his own. Raised on turn-of-century racism, Straight had turned against the Japanese after the Russo-Japanese War. "I now find myself hating the Japanese more than anything in the world," he wrote to a friend. Perhaps, he thought, it was due to the "strain of having to be polite and to seek favors from a yellow people." Straight worked with the great U.S. railroad builder, E. H. Harriman, to plan a railroad in Manchuria that would compete directly with the Japanese-held railway. The project was to be part of Harriman's round-the-world transportation scheme through which he hoped to obtain a stranglehold on global commerce. The Chinese naturally encouraged the Straight-Harriman scheme. China was following the traditional policy of playing off "barbarian against barbarian." But in 1905, the Japanese had secretly forced China to agree that no such competing rail line would be built in Manchuria. Straight, a close friend of Roosevelt's dashing daughter Alice, went to Washington to plead his case personally with the president.

Unfortunately for Straight (and the Chinese), the Japanese delegation arrived first and convinced Roosevelt (who actually needed little convincing) that it was no use challenging them. Instead of accepting the Straight-Harriman dream, TR agreed to a deal. In the Root-Takahira Agreement of 1908, he recognized Japan's pre-eminence in southern Manchuria. In return, Tokyo pledged to uphold the open door and independence of China, but carefully refused to agree to Chinese *territorial* integrity. (After all, southern Manchuria was supposedly a part of China.)[38]

In reality, Roosevelt had given up the open door in much of Manchuria. He had, however, avoided war with Japan and reached a shaky agreement with Asia's rising power. For a man who so loved war and killing, he had shown extraordinary sensitivity to the limits of U.S. power. This preacher of "the strenuous life" and the use of force against the "uncivilized" even won the Nobel Peace Prize for his efforts to end the Russo-Japanese War. In dealing with the Indians and Latin Americans, TR did use force to deal with weaker peoples. In Asia and Europe, however, he knew that the United States was outgunned. He, therefore, followed advice he had learned in the North Dakota frontier saloons: "Never draw unless you mean to shoot." Whether Roosevelt's successors in the White House could afford to follow this advice became a central question of twentieth-century American diplomacy.

TAFT, KNOX, AND DOLLAR DIPLOMACY

TR's successor in the White House between 1909 and 1913, William Howard Taft, did not follow his example in Asia. The result was near-catastrophe for both Chinese and U.S. interests. Taft's failure was not due to lack of experience. He had been Roosevelt's secretary of war, headed the commission governing the Philippines, and traveled extensively in the Far East (including one venture during which he came to know Willard Straight). Nor was the failure due initially to Taft rebelling against Roosevelt. The Rough Rider hand-picked his successor, and one wit observed that TAFT stood for "Take-Advice-From-Theodore." But their relations cooled by 1911 as they clashed over a number of issues. TR even prepared to run against Taft for the presidency in 1912. Differences over foreign policy were major reasons for the cooling.

Part of Taft's failure was due to lack of energy. He weighed 300 to 320 pounds. And since his eating increased when his policies were in trouble, by 1911–1912 he was eating a great deal. He liked playing golf, sitting on the White House front porch and listening to the "music machine" (the new phonograph), and taking naps. Taft's real love was the law and the courts—their predictability, logic, and set of rules in which he had been trained. Foreign affairs (usually neither predictable nor logical) seemed messy. Five of his nine cabinet members were lawyers. Resembling the president, they thought cautiously, believed in following precedent, and admired tradition—even as the world rapidly changed around them. Taft was no moss-backed conservative. His

William Howard Taft (1857–1930) was a distinguished lawyer and jurist, a valued assistant and adviser to Theodore Roosevelt. But, contrary to the impression left by this photo, as president between 1909 and 1913 he was a weak politician and leader, although a famous advocate of building U.S. power in Asia and Latin America through what he termed "dollar diplomacy."

administration produced the amendment to the Constitution creating the income tax; created a Department of Labor; and successfully argued a series of antitrust cases against Standard Oil, U.S. Steel, and other giants that far surpassed TR's record as a "trust buster." Aware of the legal and economic complexities of American society, Taft had no similar understanding of foreign affairs. He only clung to certain principles: the open door in Asia, order in Latin America, and the belief that enough money (dollar diplomacy) could secure both.[39]

His secretary of state, Philander C. Knox, was a much thinner version of the president. A leading Pittsburgh corporation lawyer, Knox knew little about foreign policy. A British diplomat complained that Knox thought foreign relations resembled law practice: "To him a treaty is a contract, diplomacy is litigation, and the countries interested are parties to a suit." One advantage·to this approach was Taft's and Knox's reorganization of the State Department so that it worked more like a corporation. They created a neat organization chart with specialists reporting upward to the secretary of state. The specialists were arranged along separate geographical divisions (Straight became head of the Far East Division for a short time) so that they could focus on the complexities of being a great world power. Neither Knox nor some of his specialists, however, did enough homework. Many days, the secretary worked at home until late morning, spent several hours at his office, enjoyed a leisurely lunch, and then played golf much of the afternoon. During one golf match, a partner suggested that Knox should travel to China and see the growing crisis firsthand. "I'm just starting to learn this game," he replied, "and I'm not going to let anything as unimportant as China interfere." Knox soon paid for such a schedule.

He and Taft believed more constructive foreign affairs could be achieved by using the nation's rapidly growing capital resources and downplaying Roosevelt's emphasis on military force. Branded at first by critics as "dollar diplomacy," by 1912 the president himself took credit for "substituting dollars for bullets. It . . . appeals alike to idealistic humanitarian sentiments, to the dictates of sound policy and strategy, and to legitimate commercial aims."[40] Dollar diplomacy, Taft argued, could create orderly societies by helping develop the unindustrialized nations and, happily, make a nice profit for American investors.

DOLLAR DIPLOMACY IN ASIA

The Taft administration believed in the need to maintain the Asian open door for U.S. goods and investment. U.S. officials understood that because of this need, the Japanese and Russian domination of Manchuria had to be checked. In 1907, the old enemies had made a deal in which Russia and its Chinese Eastern Railroad effectively controlled northern Manchuria, and Japan and its South Manchurian Railroad dominated southern Manchuria. Knox, however, refused to surrender. The stakes were too high. He believed that whoever financed the Chinese railway system would be the major voice in developing all of the immense China market. Knox's most notable effort came in 1910. He tried to break the Japanese-Russian hold on Manchuria by proposing a "neutralization" scheme. All the major foreign powers, he suggested, should pool their resources, buy the railroads, then operate them in accordance with the open-door principle. The response was cold. The British and French, who increasingly needed Russia's and Japan's cooperation in protecting interests in Europe and southern Asia, pulled away. The Russians and Japanese moved closer together to fend off

Knox. On July 4, 1910, the two nations signed a fresh treaty of friendship. Seven weeks later, Japan formally annexed Korea. As historian Michael Hunt notes, "By their own standards," the Taft-Knox policy "was bankrupt." Even the once-dominant U.S. cotton textiles were replaced in Manchuria by Japanese goods.[41]

U.S. dollar diplomacy came to the same sad end in China's heartland. In that region, British, French, and German capitalists planned to build the 563-mile-long Hukwang Railway between the capital of Beijing (Peking) and the great port of Canton. Knox demanded that U.S. bankers be included. J. P. Morgan, the Rockefeller-owned National City Bank, Kuhn, Loeb, E. H. Harriman, and other U.S. investors with previous involvement in China set up a group with State Department encouragement. The Chinese government, however, pulled back. It did not want the plan reopened and Americans—and then, no doubt, Japanese and Russians—brought in. Antiforeign riots again broke out. But the collapsing Chinese government could not hold off the United States. Much as China feared, Japan and Russia next forced their way into the deal. The Chinese government signed the contract, sold bonds it could never redeem, and soon disappeared in revolution.

His hopes to become an empire-builder in Asia destroyed, Willard Straight bitterly blamed the Chinese. The power of the Manchu dynasty is gone, he wrote a friend; "he [the Manchu emperor] didn't have his wings clipped," but instead the Chinese people "just naturally pulled out the feathers, and found that it was only a jack-daw with eagles' plumage after all. . . . Verily this is a nation of skunks." Straight, however, missed the main point. Foreign demands, including U.S. demands for increased economic opportunity, had fanned antiforeign feelings in China to a boiling point and had helped create the upheaval that drove the corrupt Manchu dynasty from power in 1912. Indeed, the Manchus, who had entered China from Manchuria in 1644, and in 1909 finally claimed full power, were themselves the targets of Chinese antiforeignism. The great China Revolution was underway. (The Taft demands for an open door for foreign opportunity cast long shadows. The new Nationalist government paid interest on the Hukwang Railway bonds until 1939. In 1983, nine Americans who still held the bonds won a $41.3 million claim in an Alabama court. The infuriated Communist government in Beijing (Peking) warned President Reagan that the claim, if pushed, could severely harm U.S.-Chinese relations. The legacy of the Hay-Taft policies in Asia lived on.)[42]

Roosevelt watched Taft's bumbling with growing alarm. He suggested that his successor make the best of a terrible situation by proposing that Japan develop Manchuria in return for California's right to exclude unwanted Japanese immigrants. When Taft showed no interest, TR warned that the president must not push too hard. The only way to maintain the open door in Manchuria, he wrote, was to fight Japan, and that would require a fleet as large as Great Britain's and an army as powerful as Germany's.[43] But Taft continued to believe that he had found a better way. During 1912, Knox tried to lead U.S. bankers into a six-nation consortium that was to provide a $300 million loan to the new Chinese republic. The bankers were not enthusiastic. Knox insisted. It was a last chance to prevent other powers, and perhaps Chinese nationalism itself, from closing the door. Taft's successor, Woodrow Wilson, pulled the Americans out of the consortium in 1913. It remained to be seen whether Wilson had a better plan for propping open the door.

DOLLAR DIPLOMACY IN LATIN AMERICA AND CANADA

Revolutions also threatened in Latin America. But here, as one U.S. Navy officer boasted, the Monroe Doctrine and American force held "this hemisphere in check against Cosmic Tendencies."[44] In 1906, Secretary of State Elihu Root declared that the United States had reached the point where it both needed Latin American markets and possessed the necessary "surplus of capital beyond the requirements of internal development" to develop in the hemisphere "the peaceful prosperity of a mighty commerce." South and North Americans, he argued, were made for each other. The South had the raw materials, the North the manufacturers. The South's people were "polite, refined, cultivated"; the "North American is strenuous, intense, utilitarian." Perhaps best of all, "Where we accumulate, they spend."[45] The United States thus had other reasons than the Panama Canal to insist on order in Latin America.

In 1906, for example, TR feared that the Cubans were acquiring "a revolutionary habit." He sent in U.S. troops to oversee elections that firmly established an orderly regime. In 1906–1907, Nicaraguan dictator José Santos Zelaya intensified a long-running feud with Guatemala by invading neighboring states. Partly because Zelaya introduced the machine gun to Central Americans, record numbers of people died each day of the war. Roosevelt and the Mexican dictator, Porfirio Díaz, twice intervened to stop the carnage and, on a U.S. warship, to arrange peace terms. In 1907, the United States also helped establish a historic

Elihu Root (1845–1937) of New York was probably the nation's top corporate lawyer during the era of the robber barons, secretary of war between 1899 and 1905 (when he made reforms that, in turn, made him "the father of the modern army"), and secretary of state (1905–1909). Root well understood, and described in his speeches, how the new U.S. economic power shaped the nation's overseas needs.

institution, the Central American Court. It was charged by the Central Americans to resolve outstanding regional problems peacefully. The court worked surprisingly well until 1914–1916, when Costa Rica won a decision against the United States. The Wilson administration disregarded the decision and effectively killed the court.[46]

In several Central American countries, U.S. investors themselves had for some years maintained order. Costa Rica was the most democratic nation in the region, in part because of its more equitable landholding. In 1872, a railroad builder from Brooklyn, New York, Minor Keith—described by one journalist as "an apple-headed little man with the eyes of a fanatic"—succeeded in building a major rail system in Costa Rica. He then developed banana plantations so that the trains would have cargo. Thus began the United Fruit Company of Boston, or "The Octopus," as Central Americans came to call it. By World War I, United Fruit controlled not only the banana market, but the rail systems, shipping, banking, and governments in Costa Rica and Honduras. The Roosevelt Corollary was not needed in those countries.[47]

Other countries were not as calm, however. Haiti was temporarily pacified in 1910 by an infusion of U.S. bank loans. In several Central American nations, TR's policies seemed to have had little good effect. Taft privately complained that he needed "to have the right to knock their heads together." Nicaragua's Zelaya was the worst offender. His persistent challenges to U.S. policies climaxed when rumors spread that he was going to give a non-American power the right to build an isthmian canal. In 1909, a revolutionary movement appeared on Nicaragua's east coast. It was helped along by U.S. diplomatic officials and U.S. Marines, who landed to protect the rebels. Zelaya caught two North Americans who were trying to blow up a boatload of his troops. Despite Knox's grave warning, the dictator executed both captives. Knox and U.S. naval commanders then pressured Zelaya to resign. Several changes of government later, U.S. bankers, with Knox's encouragement, were acquiring Nicaraguan banks and railroads in return for loans that kept the government afloat.

A new president, Adolfo Díaz (who had been a clerk in an American company in Nicaragua), finally offered to make his country a U.S. protectorate in return for more loans. Angry Nicaraguans revolted. Some 2,600 U.S. troops landed in 1912 to protect Díaz. The forces remained, reduced in number, until 1925, then had to return in 1926 for another seven-year stay.[48] Modern revolutionary Nicaragua began to arise out of Knox's dollar diplomacy.

The same approach led Taft into quite another kind of problem in U.S.-Canadian relations. Those ties had been quiet since the Alaskan boundary dispute of 1902–1903. The two countries enjoyed mostly prosperous years, and, consequently, the long-present interest on both sides of the boundary in possible annexation had declined. In 1909, Taft unintentionally stirred that interest again by proposing reciprocity treaties. Correctly analyzing the needs of an industrializing United States, he hoped through the reduced tariffs to lower costs of imported raw materials. Taft made the proposal only to have the powerful high-tariff wing of the Republican party rise in revolt. Roosevelt had refused to deal with the issue ("God Almighty could not pass a tariff and win the next election," he believed). But Taft waded in, compromised with the high-tariff interests in order to obtain a bill, and was promptly branded a traitor by low-tariff politicians.

The new tariff heavily discriminated against Canadian imports. Taft and Prime Minister Wilfrid Laurier quickly moved to avoid a trade war by signing a fresh U.S.-Canadian tariff agreement. From Washington's view, the deal could serve a stunning long-range goal: integrate Canada (and, through a similar treaty, Mexico) into a vast hemispheric industrial complex controlled by the United States. Between 1901 and 1908, U.S. investment in Canada had already increased four times to nearly $750 million, mostly in minerals, lumber, and other raw materials. Historian Robert Hannigan aptly calls the emerging U.S. policy "the new continentalism." It aimed, moreover, at changing Canadian-British trade to north-south trade. Careless U.S. politicians, however, began to spell out the probable result: the annexation of Canada. Infuriated and frightened Canadian Conservatives, fully supported by the British, killed the agreement. Dollar diplomacy failed in the north as well as the Far East, although President Ronald Reagan, seventy years later, would again push the idea of "the new continentalism" for many of the same reasons.[49]

The Irony of 1900–1913

After the easy triumphs of 1898–1901, U.S. officials encountered severe setbacks in Asia and the Western Hemisphere over the next dozen years. American power nevertheless continued to push outward, even in China and Canada. The United States also became involved in European affairs, an area it had largely bypassed since 1815.

These affairs centered on European attempts to colonize more of Africa. In two episodes, U.S. officials intervened to protect what they believed were threats to an open door in Africa. The first occurred in 1904–1906 in Morocco. In that country, where France claimed a sphere of influence, Germany challenged Paris officials by recognizing Moroccan independence. As war threatened, the European powers asked Roosevelt to repeat his success as mediator at Portsmouth. He hesitated, then agreed, rationalizing that an 1880 U.S.-Moroccan trade treaty gave the United States a strong economic interest in the country. Of at least equal importance, TR feared a possible European war. He convened the Algeciras Conference in 1906 at the Spanish port city. When the meeting protected French claims, Roosevelt, who strongly favored the growing British-French alliance, was secretly pleased.

Five years later, Taft won a more resounding victory for the open door in Liberia. That African country had been colonized, and was now controlled, by descendants of black slaves from the United States. After the Civil War, the U.S. government had shown no interest in the country. In dire financial straits, Liberia's land was being seized by surrounding colonies controlled by France and Great Britain. In 1910, Taft asked Congress to provide financial help and military protection. When the Senate rejected his plea, the president—following McKinley's and Roosevelt's examples—organized financial aid through private banks. The British and French were checked. The U.S.-supported black elite continued to rule. Historian Judson M. Lyon has placed the episode in perspective: Taft's proposals for Liberia were "almost identical" to those the president offered to Nicaragua and China. As a top State Department official believed, dollar diplomacy would bring order to these nations, while "extending the Open Door to as many regions of the world as possible."[50]

Taft's luck, such as it was, ran out in 1911, when he tried to negotiate arbitration treaties with France and Great Britain. The arbitration movement had gained popularity a decade earlier as it became apparent how brutal the next conflict among industrialized powers might be. The Hague Peace Conferences of 1899 and 1907 were one result. They produced the Permanent Court of Arbitration at The Hague as well as a set of rules for fighting wars, but little on how to avoid them.[51] Roosevelt supported the 1907 conference, although he had pointedly refused to submit the Alaskan boundary question to the court. In 1911, he became deeply angry when Taft made two bilateral arbitration pacts. TR was preparing to fight Taft for the 1912 presidential nomination, so his opposition was not dispassionate. Roosevelt's friends in the Senate carved up the treaties until Taft withdrew them. Nevertheless, between 1899 and 1911, the United States for the first time signed treaties with European and other nations that provided for peaceful resolution of disputes. Twenty-two pacts went into effect under Roosevelt, another twenty-one under Woodrow Wilson.

But the arbitration movement could not grow fast enough to stop World War I or even to prevent great powers such as the United States from using force to put down revolutions. In this sense, the American entry onto the world stage between 1898 and 1914 produced a most ironic result. For just as McKinley, Roosevelt, Taft, and, later, Wilson demanded order in Latin America, Africa, Asia, and even Europe, the world began to explode into revolution. Japan's victory over a white race in 1905 helped trigger anticolonial revolts in places as far apart as Vietnam, Persia, Turkey, and China. Russia experienced an ominous uprising in 1905. Mexico erupted in 1911–1913.

An understanding of twentieth-century U.S. foreign policy requires learning one central theme: just as Americans began to claim Great

Britain's title as the globe's greatest power and, at the same time, to demand an orderly world, the globe burst into revolution. The American claim was to be realized, but the demand was never met nor the revolutions ended.

NOTES

1. V. S. Naipaul, "Among the Republicans," *New York Review of Books*, 25 October 1984, p. 17.
2. David Healy, *U.S. Expansionism: The Imperialist Urge in the 1890s* (Madison, Wis., 1970), p. 110.
3. The quotes and stories are found in Edmund Morris, *The Rise of Theodore Roosevelt* (New York, 1979), the best biography of TR's life until 1901, although weak on the historical context of 1895 to 1901; see especially pp. 98, 224, 463.
4. Healy, pp. 151–153.
5. Anne H. Oman, "Past and Present," *Washington Post Weekend*, 18 January 1985, p. 6; *Time*, March 3, 1958, p. 16; Nathan Miller, *Theodore Roosevelt, A Life* (New York, 1992) p. 387.
6. David Burton, *Theodore Roosevelt: Confident Imperialist* (Philadelphia, 1969), p. 137.
7. Albert K. Weinberg, *Manifest Destiny* (Baltimore, 1940), pp. 464–465.
8. Carl P. Parrini and Martin J. Sklar, "New Thinking about the Market, 1896– 1904 . . . ," *Journal of Economic History* 48 (September 1983): 559–578, analyze, in a pioneering essay, the effects of surplus capital on U.S. foreign policy, especially in Asia from 1900 to 1904.
9. Arthur M. Schlesinger, Jr., *The Imperial Presidency* (Boston, 1973), p. 83.
10. Louis Henkin, *Foreign Affairs and the Constitution* (Mineola, N.Y., 1972), p. 309.
11. Alfred Thayer Mahan, *The Interest of America in Sea Power, Present and Future* (Boston, 1898), pp. 256–257, 268.
12. Woodrow Wilson, *Constitutional Government in the United States* (New York, 1908), pp. 78–80.
13. Lawrence Martin, *The Presidents and the Prime Ministers* (Toronto, 1982), p. 58.
14. Quoted in Morris, p. 3.
15. This argument is spelled out in Walter LaFeber, *The American Search for Opportunity, 1865–1913*, in *The Cambridge History of U.S. Foreign Relations*, ed. Warren Cohen (New York, 1993).
16. Howard K. Beale, *Theodore Roosevelt and the Rise of America to World Power* (New York, 1962), pp. 85–102, discusses the turn in TR's thinking toward England; see also Stuart Anderson, "Racial Anglo-Saxonism and the American Response to the Boer War," *Diplomatic History* 2 (Summer 1978): 219–236; Thomas J. Noer, *Briton, Boer and Yankee: The U.S. and South Africa, 1870–1914* (Kent, Ohio, 1978), pp. 5– 20, 135, 186.
17. Martin, pp. 58–61.

18. John Hay to William McKinley, 23 September 1900, Papers of William McKinley, Library of Congress, Washington, D.C.

19. Richard L. Lael, *Arrogant Diplomacy: U.S. Policy Toward Colombia, 1903–1922* (Wilmington, Del., 1987), esp. p. xiv; Michael L. Conniff, *Panama and the United States* (Athens, Ga., 1992), pp. 33–34.

20. Dana G. Munro, *Intervention and Dollar Diplomacy in the Caribbean, 1900–1921* (Princeton, 1964), pp. 57–58; David S. Patterson, *Toward a Warless World: The Travail of the American Peace Movement, 1887–1914* (Bloomington, Ind., 1976), pp. 124–125.

21. Richard W. Leopold, *Elihu Root and the Conservative Tradition* (Boston, 1954), p. 178; *Public Opinion* 35 (19 November 1903): 645.

22. J. Bartlett, *Familiar Quotations* (Boston, 1981), p. 687.

23. Healy, pp. 112–113.

24. Dexter Perkins, *The Monroe Doctrine, 1867–1907* (Baltimore, 1937), p. 394.

25. *Ibid.*, pp. 419–421.

26. *Ibid.*, pp. 408–409.

27. The document is available in *The Record of American Diplomacy*, ed. Ruhl J. Bartlett, 4th ed. (New York, 1964), p. 539.

28. Theodore Roosevelt, *The Letters of Theodore Roosevelt*, ed. Elting E. Morison *et al.*, 8 vols. (Cambridge, Mass., 1951–1954), IV, p. 734.

29. Perkins, p. 440.

30. Daniel Aaron, *Men of Good Hope* (New York, 1961), p. 268.

31. Brooks Adams to Theodore Roosevelt, 17 July 1903, Papers of Theodore Roosevelt, Library of Congress, Washington, D.C.

32. Theodore Roosevelt to Brooks Adams, 18 July 1903, *ibid.*

33. This loan is analyzed in Grosvenor Jones, Chief, Investment and Financial Division, Bureau of Foreign and Domestic Commerce, to Herbert Hoover, 7 August 1926, Commerce, Off. Files, Box 130, Herbert Hoover Library, West Branch, Iowa.

34. Henry Adams to Elizabeth Cameron, 10 January 1904, in Henry Adams, *Letters of Henry Adams (1892–1918)*, ed. Worthington Chauncey Ford (Boston, 1938), pp. 419–420.

35. John Edward Wiltz, "Did the United States Betray Korea in 1905?" *Pacific Historical Review* 54 (August 1985): 243–270.

36. Paul A. Varg, *The Making of a Myth: The U.S. and China, 1897–1912* (East Lansing, 1968), pp. 83–88.

37. This fascinating story is told in Sherman Cochran, "Commercial Penetration and Economic Imperialism in China . . . ," in *America's China Trade in Historical Perspective: The Chinese and American Performance*, ed. John K. Fairbank and Ernest R. May (Cambridge, Mass., 1985), pp. 190–194, esp. for the boycott.

38. Michael H. Hunt, *The Making of a Special Relationship: The United States and China to 1914* (New York, 1983), pp. 204–208.

39. These paragraphs on Taft (and the ones on Knox that follow) are drawn from three good accounts: Walter Scholes and Marie Scholes, *The Foreign Policies of the Taft Administration* (Columbia, Mo., 1970), esp. pp. 1–31; Donald F. Anderson, *William Howard Taft: A Conservative's Conception of the Presidency* (Ithaca, N.Y., 1968); James Barber, *Presidential Character* (Englewood Cliffs, N.J., 1972), pp. 174–190, which has an interesting section on Taft.

40. Quoted in Lloyd Gardner *et al.*, *The Creation of the American Empire*, 2d ed. (Chicago, 1976), p. 280.

41. Michael H. Hunt, *Frontier Defense and the Open Door: Manchuria in Chinese-American Relations, 1895–1911* (New Haven, 1973), p. 228.

42. *Ibid.*, p. 241; Straight to Calhoun, 7 November, 1911, in Papers of Willard Straight, Cornell University, Ithaca, N.Y.; *New York Times*, 20 March 1983, p. E5.

43. Henry Pringle, *Theodore Roosevelt, a Biography* (New York, 1931), pp. 684–685.

44. Richard D. Challener, *Admirals, Generals, and American Foreign Policy* (Princeton, 1973), p. 20.

45. *Foreign Relations of the United States, 1906*, 2 pts. (Washington, D.C., 1909), pt. II, pp. 1457–1461.

46. The best account is Thomas L. Karnes, *The Failure of Union: Central America, 1824–1975* (Tempe, Ariz., 1976), pp. 200–202.

47. Thomas P. McCann, *An American Company*, ed. Henry Scammell (New York, 1976), pp. 15–30; William H. Durham, *Scarcity and Survival in Central America . . .* (Stanford, 1979), pp. 115–118; Mitchell Seligson, "Agrarian Policies in Dependent Societies: Costa Rica," *Journal of Interamerican Studies* 19 (May 1977): 218–224.

48. Walter LaFeber, *Inevitable Revolutions: The United States in Central America*, 2nd ed. (New York, 1993), pp. 47–51.

49. Robert Hannigan, "Reciprocity 1911: Continentalism and American Weltpolitik," *Diplomatic History* 4 (Winter 1980): 1–18.

50. Judson M. Lyon, "Informal Imperialism: The U.S. in Liberia, 1897–1912," *Diplomatic History* 5 (Summer 1981): 221–243.

51. The standard account remains Calvin D. Davis's prize-winning *The United States and the First Hague Peace Conference* (Ithaca, N.Y., 1962), esp. pp. 54–102, on the peace movement, and 207–212, on Roosevelt and the court.

FOR FURTHER READING

Pre-1981 references are most easily found in *Guide to American Foreign Relations since 1700*, ed. Richard Dean Burns (1983). Also see the notes to this chapter and the General Bibliography at the end of this book; those references are usually not repeated here.

Fresh overviews of Roosevelt and presidential power during these years can be found in Richard H. Collin, *Theodore Roosevelt, Culture, Diplomacy, and Expansion* (1985); John Milton Cooper, Jr., *The Warrior and the Priest: Woodrow Wilson and Theodore Roosevelt* (1983); Frederick W. Marks III, "Theodore Roosevelt and the Conservative Revival," in *Studies in American Diplomacy, 1865–1945*, ed. Norman A. Graebner (1985); Kathleen Dalton, "Theodore Roosevelt and the Idea of War," *Theodore Roosevelt Association Journal* 7 (Fall 1981), an interesting cultural perspective; Lawrence Margolis, *Executive Agreements and Presidential Power* (1985), a historical framework for TR's acts in 1904–1905; George Juergens, *News from the White House: The Presidential-Press Relationship in the Progressive Era* (1981).

Three recent economic-historical analyses are pathbreaking: Paul Wolman, *Most*

Favored Nation (Chapel Hill, N.C., 1992), on the tariff battles, 1897–1912; Emily S. Rosenberg, "Foundations of U.S. International Financial Power: Gold Standard Diplomacy, 1900–1905," *Business History Review* 59 (Summer 1985); and Vivian Vale, *The American Peril* (1984), on J. P. Morgan versus Great Britain. For Latin America, Lester Langley's *The Banana Wars* (1983, 1988) is a starting point for the Caribbean–Central American region; Louis A. Pérez, Jr.'s *Cuba under the Platt Amendment, 1902–1934* (1986) is now a standard account; Thomas Schoonover's "Imperialism in Middle America," in *Eagle against Empire*, ed. Rhodri Jeffreys-Jones (1983), places the U.S. drive for an isthmian canal amid the international scramble in a pioneering essay; J. Michael Hogan's *The Panama Canal in American Politics* (1986) is excellent on Roosevelt; Terence Graham's *The "Interests of Civilization": Reaction in the United States against the Seizure of the Panama Canal Zone, 1903–1904*, Lund Studies in International History (1983), well tells a story long needed to be told; Ivan Musicant's *The Banana Wars* (1990) provides an important overview; Leslie Manigat's "The Substitution of American for French Preponderance in Haiti, 1910–1911," in *Diplomatic Claims: Latin American Historians View the United States*, ed. and trans. Warren Dean (1985), is a critical view of a critical turn. On Canadian relations, R. A. Shields's "Imperial Policy and Canadian-American Commercial Relations, 1880–1911," *Bulletin of the Institute of Historical Research* 59 (May 1986), supplements the Hannigan essay listed in the notes.

Three good overviews of U.S.-Asian relations have been recently published: Michael H. Hunt's *The Making of a Special Relationship: The U.S. and China to 1914* (1983), especially important for its analysis of the Chinese side; James C. Thomson, Jr., Peter W. Stanley, and John Curtis Perry, *Sentimental Imperialists: The American Experience in East Asia* (1981), for its controversial view of U.S. motives; and Daniel M. Crane and Thomas A. Breslin, *An Ordinary Relationship: American Opposition to Republican Revolution in China* (1986), which puts the years 1911 to 1914 within a century of U.S. opposition to revolutions. The nonofficial dimension is studied in Key Ray Chong, *Americans and Chinese Reform and Revolution, 1898–1922: The Role of Private Citizens in Diplomacy* (1984), with emphasis on Sun Yat-sen's links to Americans. Raymond A. Esthus, *Double Eagle and the Rising Sun: The Russians and Japanese at Portsmouth in 1905* (1988), should become a standard account of the conference. A good overview of the entire era is Joseph A. Fry, "In Search of an Orderly World: U.S. Imperialism, 1898–1912," in *Modern American Diplomacy*, ed. John M. Carroll and George C. Herring (1986).

9

Wilsonians, Revolutions, and War (1913–1917)

THE WORLD OF WOODROW WILSON

It was Woodrow Wilson's fate to be the first U.S. president to face the full blast of twentieth-century revolutions. Wilson's responses made his policies the most influential in twentieth-century American foreign policy. "Wilsonian" became a term to describe later policies that emphasized internationalism and moralism and that were dedicated to extending democracy. Critics described them as unrealistic and especially unaware of power (by which the critics usually meant military power). Wilson's policies, however, now appear to be more complex and instructive than either his supporters or critics claimed. Many later presidents, including Lyndon Johnson, Richard Nixon, and Jimmy Carter, looked back to Wilson as the chief executive who had the largest vision of the nation's future and who had first confronted challenges that continued to plague them.

Born in Virginia in 1856, Wilson was the first native southerner to reach the White House since 1849. He had trained as a lawyer but failed miserably in his practice. The failure tended to make him mistrustful of lawyers and turned him toward an academic career. By 1912, Wilson had become a national figure. A respected political scientist and lecturer, he was president of Princeton and then the highly successful Progressive governor of New Jersey. His success came not only from his speaking ability, but also from a sharp, analytical mind that was as able to place problems in a historical context as any president's in the American experience.

A stern Calvinist, devout Presbyterian, Wilson believed he was guided by God's will. Wilson often appeared cold even to those whose support he needed. A leading Progressive journalist complained that the president's handshake was "like a ten-cent pickled mackerel in brown paper." The new chief executive even refused to attend his own inaugural dance. Privately, another Wilson sometimes appeared. This one loved vaudeville, baseball, told jokes in excellent dialect, wrote limericks, and loudly sang "Oh, You Beautiful Doll" when he courted his second wife in 1915; it now appears that he had an affair in Bermuda with a married woman during 1908. The tensions that resulted from such a background not only made him highly complex, but also caused him, starting in 1896 (when he was not yet forty), to suffer a series of small strokes. By 1916, he had to restrict his work time in the White House, and by 1919—during the critical days of the peace conference—he had to spend much time in bed recovering from flu and exhaustion.[1]

Wilson was not only a politician, but a scholar who developed policies out of an understanding of the nation's history. He knew that the large corporation was a staggering new fact of national life, but he nevertheless wanted to use government to reinforce traditional political and moral values. In his first inaugural address, Wilson repeatedly emphasized that "our duty is . . . to restore" and, again, "our work is a work of restoration." He demanded that the new corporate system be opened up so that "the little man on the make," as Wilson proudly called him, could have a chance along with the rulers of U.S. Steel. His view of history, especially his understanding that the nation's landed frontier had closed, nevertheless forced Wilson to conclude that "the days of glad expansion are gone, our life grows tense and difficult." The president had learned this directly from the great historian of the frontier, Frederick Jackson Turner. The two had met during the 1880s at Johns Hopkins University. Wilson believed that with the frontier "lost," a "new epoch will open for us."[2]

The implications for foreign policy seemed endless. U.S. producers, Wilson warned in 1912, "have expanded to such a point that they will burst their jackets if they cannot find a free outlet to the markets of the world."[3] A frontier of world markets had to be found to replace the lost landed frontier. The government, led by a strong president, must open and order those new frontiers. "The truth is that in the new order," Wilson announced, "government and business must be associated."[4]

Woodrow Wilson's power as chief executive (1913–1921) arose in part from his oratorical ability. Here in white trousers, Wilson speaks in Washington during 1913 while at the far right his young assistant secretary of the navy, Franklin D. Roosevelt, and on the left his secretary of state, William Jennings Bryan, look on.

The young political scientist had been one of the first to understand the impact of the 1898 war on presidential power: "Foreign questions became leading questions again," and "in them the President was of necessity leader." Even before 1898, Wilson believed that at critical times, "the pleasure of the people" had to give way to presidential power: "He *exercises* the power, and *we obey.*"[5]

He followed this principle in the White House. At times it worked. Between 1913 and 1916, he pushed through Congress a significant series of reform measures, including the 1913 Underwood Tariff that lowered rates significantly for the first time since 1894. At other times, however (as in the 1919 fight over the peace treaty), Americans refused to "obey" the president. As a student of British politics, he admired the parliamentary system in which the prime minister, as the leader of the majority party, almost automatically was assured victory. Wilson grew short-tempered with the more cumbersome American system. Until

1918, he nevertheless dealt effectively with Congress. One reason was his decision to appear before Congress (somewhat like the British prime minister) and deliver his annual and other special messages personally. Since the time of Jefferson, who knew he was not an orator, presidents had merely sent their messages to Capitol Hill via courier. Wilson changed all that, and as he was able to whip Congress into line, he sometimes paid little attention to public opinion. Public-opinion polls did not exist. He seemed to have read newspapers unsystematically. The man in charge of the White House mail room recalled that the president apparently cared little about incoming letters. During several diplomatic crises in 1914–1916 (such as the *Sussex* episode), Wilson almost totally isolated himself, then emerged to issue a policy—often personally pecked out on his own typewriting machine. Robert Lansing, his second secretary of state, noted that Wilson's "very nature resisted outbursts of popular passion. . . . He had the faculty of remaining impervious to such influences, which so often affect the minds of lesser men."[6]

His reading of history shaped foreign policy in yet another way. Wilson feared revolutionary change. He wanted order—or at least slow reform. The president believed that the American system had prospered because it avoided radical change. In 1889, he wrote that the year marked the centennial of both the U.S. Constitution and the French Revolution. "One hundred years ago," he concluded, "we gained, and Europe lost, self-command, self-possession." A people could not be "given" democracy, Wilson argued. It required "long discipline" and "a reverence for law."[7] Thus, for example, he doubted that Filipinos were fit for self-government. American ideas and goods, however, could prepare others for democracy—and could do so while making profits:

> Lift your eyes to the horizons of business [he told a U.S. business group visiting the White House] . . . let your thoughts and your imaginations run abroad throughout the whole world, and with the inspiration of the thought that you are Americans and are meant to carry liberty and justice and the principles of humanity wherever you go, go out and sell goods that will make the world more comfortable and more happy, and convert them to the principles of America.[8]

The landed frontier had closed, but, luckily, the world frontier now spread out before Americans. With some government help, ambitious, hard-working Americans ("the little man on the make") could find opportunities abroad. The president, in leading these efforts, wanted that world to be a safe and an orderly place in which Americans could compete equally—perhaps even a place in which all people, with enough time and help, would become much like Americans.

Wilson's views were reinforced by the few foreign-policy advisers he consulted. He first named William Jennings Bryan secretary of state not because Bryan knew much about foreign policy (he did not), but for his long service to the Democratic party. Bryan agreed with Wilson's emphasis on the need to help others with U.S. goods and values. Taft's dollar diplomacy, Bryan complained, tried to "till the field of foreign investment with a pen knife; President Wilson intends to cultivate it with a spade."[9] Bryan also shared many of Wilson's traditional values, although Bryan's came from a nineteenth-century rural America that seemed quaint to some. The secretary of state was "irresistably funny," young journalist Walter Lippmann wrote, "because he moves in a world that has ceased to exist."[10] But at a critical moment in 1915, Bryan resigned as a matter of principle because he believed that Wilson was no longer truly neutral in the European war. He was replaced by Robert Lansing, a New York lawyer who was well connected (his uncle had been a secretary of state in the 1890s; his nephew, John Foster Dulles, was to occupy the office during the 1950s). Lansing was pro-British and as worried as Wilson over revolutionary outbreaks.

The president's closest adviser never held a formal office. Colonel Edward M. House, born in Texas, educated in the Northeast, and reared in smoke-filled rooms of Democratic party bosses, befriended Wilson in 1911–1912 to ride his coattails into power. Independently wealthy, he traveled abroad to talk with the powerful. House was as stealthy and secretive as a cat. One official who thought he was a close friend only years later learned that House had tried to ruin him. The colonel "was an intimate," the official's son noted, "even when he was cutting a throat."[11] Wilson appreciated House's discretion as well as the colonel's large view of policy.

Much of that view appeared in a remarkable novel, *Philip Dru: Administrator*, which House published anonymously in 1912. Dru, as House portrayed him, was a West Point graduate who all Americans demanded had to assume near-dictatorial powers to save them from rich, short-sighted interests that were driving the people to revolution. By issuing brilliant decrees (note that Congress was not to be consulted), Dru saved the country and made it prosperous and happy again. He then turned to foreign policy. Here Dru and his creator began to converge. In both the novel and real life, House urged that a U.S.-British partnership had to be developed into which Germany would be

Politician, strategic thinker, and world-class flatterer, Edward M. House (1858–1938) came out of Texas politics and eastern drawing rooms to become Wilson's closest foreign-policy adviser, although he never held office. House's shrewdness and slyness come through in this portrait.

drawn. The three would then destroy the great threat to the West by driving "Russia back" (as the novel put it). Once Russia was properly contained, House believed that the three powers could then divide up, develop, and stabilize the rest of the world.[12] Such cooperation could halt the senseless fight over colonial areas as well as stop the growing militarization that threatened to bankrupt, if not destroy, Great Britain and Germany.

Wilson came to the White House with no direct experience in foreign policy. But with House close by and his own sense of history, the new president quickly developed strong, well-thought-out views to guide his decisions.

WILSON AND REVOLUTION: CHINA

In his first major diplomatic action, Wilson ditched Taft's dollar diplomacy in Asia. He pulled U.S. bankers out of the six-power consortium set up to stabilize China. Wilson withdrew not because he feared that the consortium would exploit the new Chinese republic that had arisen in 1911 from the ashes of the Manchu dynasty. Nor did he have any intention of deserting the open door. He fully understood that China was "the market to which diplomacy, if need be power, must make an open way," as he had written a decade earlier.[13]

Wilson rejected the consortium because he understood that the Russians and Japanese, who showed little regard for the open door, controlled the group. Moreover, while the United States was in the consortium, his hands would be tied. Wilson wanted to use growing U.S. economic power and go it alone in China. He also planned to bring in smaller U.S. bankers (those "little men on the make") and not depend on the few giants who had joined the original group. As historian Jerry Israel summarizes the president's policy, "Rather than a rejection of the open door goals, the American withdrawal . . . was an effort to speed up their attainment by the United States alone."[14]

The president was willing to pay a price. In a cabinet meeting, Wilson ordered that the U.S. Navy be on alert for a possible challenge from Japan, then reported one expert's advice that U.S. financial power by itself could build 10,000 miles of railroads in China. In May 1913, he recognized the new Chinese ruler, Yüan Shih-k'ai. Yüan had seized the revolution from its father, Sun Yat-sen, and then set about destroying its republicanism and making himself a monarch. Wilson never protested. He wanted only to work with any Chinese leader who promised stability and cooperation.

Fifteen months later, Wilson's dreams shattered as World War I erupted. Suddenly the British, French, Germans, and Russians—who Wilson assumed would check each other and the Japanese in China—were absorbed in Europe. Virtually alone, Japan swiftly moved to seize the exposed German colonies, including the key entry point at Shantung. Only the United States could possibly check Japanese power, but Wilson was preoccupied with European and Mexican affairs. U.S. bankers sent vast sums to both sides fighting in Europe and had none to spare for China. The president, moreover, deeply mourned when his first wife died in 1914, then quickly became involved in a passionate courtship with Edith Galt that led to marriage the next year. Willard Straight watched his hard work for the open door disappear in the wake of Japan's advance and privately cursed the president for making love, not war. Wilson seemed "somewhat similar to the white rabbit," Straight remarked to a friend, "with the sex instinct strongly developed but unwilling to protect its young."[15]

On January 18, 1915, Japan secretly pressed China to accept a document that became known as the Twenty-one Demands. Wilson found out about most of the demands, but because they largely involved areas in which Japan was already dominant, he did little. The Chinese, however, told Bryan that a final, secret set of the demands would give Japan influence in China's military and police as well as in the vital Yangtze River region of central China. When the Japanese ambassador blandly denied the accusation, Bryan believed him. But American missionaries

The president and his soon-to-be second wife, Mrs. Edith Galt, attend baseball's 1915 World Series. After Wilson's illness in 1919, she became a powerful figure who greatly influenced White House decision making.

in China and U.S. ambassador Paul Reinsch obtained evidence that Bryan had been lied to. In two tough notes in March and May 1915, Wilson told Japan to back down from the secret demands. Tokyo officials did so, but not because of U.S. pressure. Their own internal politics and British opposition forced them to retreat. Wilson had nevertheless repeated the historic U.S. commitment to Asia. As historian Noel Pugach observes, "In the historically important note of May 11, 1915, the United States declared to China and Japan that it would not recognize any agreement which impaired the right of the United States, the political or territorial integrity of China, or the Open Door." [16]

Wilson had hoped to enjoy both the open door and freedom of action in China. Now, with Japan on the loose, his policy was endangered. A century of U.S. policy in the region hung in the balance. Ambassador Reinsch urged the president to work with China against the Japanese. But Colonel House and Secretary of State Lansing (who replaced Bryan in June 1915) wanted Wilson to control Japan through cooperation— to work with, rather than fight, Tokyo. As the United States itself prepared to go to war in early 1917, Wilson believed that he had no choice.

The United States took two steps to cut a deal with Japan. First, in November 1917, the secretary of state negotiated the Lansing-Ishii Agreement. In it, the United States recognized that "territorial propinquity creates special relations between countries." This meant that the United States recognized Japanese dominance in such areas as southern Manchuria. But Japan, in turn, reaffirmed the open door. Lansing and Ambassador Kikujiro Ishii also agreed on a protocol that remained secret until 1938. It stipulated that neither side would use the war to gain privileges in China at the expense of other states. The protocol attempted to short-circuit anything more like the Twenty-one Demands.

Wilson's second step was to control Japan by repudiating his 1913 policy and, instead, creating a second consortium. The United States, Japan, Great Britain, and France would cooperate in investment projects in China. Japanese financiers could thus be more closely watched. Wilson was not coy about government-business relations. He promised "complete support" to U.S. bankers as he asked them to join the new group. That a revolutionary China might soon try to control its own affairs worried few officials in Washington.

WILSON AND REVOLUTIONS: MEXICO
(OR, PAINTING THE FENCE POST WHITE)

Until World War I demanded his attention, Wilson was immersed in the problems of revolutions in China, Mexico, and the Caribbean region. He understood that the upheavals arose out of such internal problems as poverty, oppression, and the failure of government to protect its citizens. He also realized that foreign intervention seldom cooled revolutionary fervor; the fervor only became more intense and antiforeign. But along with these views about internal causes, he concluded that revolutions could be caused by foreign corporate and banking interests that exploited smaller nations. By checking such interests and by cleansing a country's internal politics, revolution could be avoided. No better way existed to cleanse those politics and create a legitimate government, he reasoned, than democratic elections.

Determined to help other peoples become democratic and orderly, Wilson himself became the greatest military interventionist in U.S. history. By the time he left office in 1921, he had ordered troops into Russia and half a dozen Latin American upheavals. To preserve order in some countries, Wilson learned, required military intervention. He was not unwilling to use force. Journalist Walter Lippmann recalled

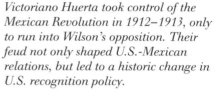

Victoriano Huerta took control of the Mexican Revolution in 1912–1913, only to run into Wilson's opposition. Their feud not only shaped U.S.-Mexican relations, but led to a historic change in U.S. recognition policy.

"one metaphor [Wilson] used to like to use a great deal illustrating his idea of how a progressive attitude was really conservative. He said 'If you want to preserve a fence post, you have to keep painting it white. You can't just paint it once and leave it forever. It will rot away.' "[17]

Some people, however, had concluded that their "fence posts" no longer served a useful purpose. They wanted the posts pulled up, not repainted. The Mexicans began reaching this conclusion in 1910–1911, when they rallied to Francisco Madero's attempt to overthrow the thirty-four-year-old dictatorship of Porfirio Díaz. Many U.S. interests were not pleased. Under Díaz's regime, U.S. investment in Mexico had skyrocketed to nearly $2 billion, much of it in rich oil wells. Americans owned 43 percent of all the property values in Mexico—10 percent more than the Mexicans themselves owned.[18] Madero overthrew Díaz (who was rapidly becoming senile) but found that he had let loose forces he could not control. A number of armed groups tried to claim power. Unable to restore order, Madero was captured by a band led by Victoriano Huerta. The U.S. ambassador to Mexico, Henry Lane Wilson, was deeply involved in pushing Madero out of power, but he declared his surprise when Huerta's men killed Madero.

At this point, Woodrow Wilson entered the White House. Huerta not only had blood on his hands, but rumors circulated that he was supported by British oil interests that had long been in bitter competition with U.S. companies. London and other capitals soon recognized

Huerta's government. Wilson, however, refused. The president objected to Huerta's use of force to gain power. He feared that if the Mexican leader remained in power, other Latin American revolutionaries would follow his example. Wilson demanded that Mexico hold democratic elections. The president thus transformed U.S. recognition policy that went back to Jefferson's time. The United States had usually recognized any government that maintained internal order and agreed to meet foreign obligations (such as debts). Wilson added a third requirement: the new government had to come to power through a process acceptable to the United States. Most governments, of course, did not have America's democratic tradition. Indeed, he did recognize certain regimes (such as China's or Peru's) that made no pretense to being democracies. The belief grew that, in Mexico, the president used his demand for democratic elections only to get rid of the Huerta regime he so disliked.

The president began supporting Huerta's enemies, especially Venustiano Carranza, who led well-armed forces. Wilson sent a personal agent, John Lind, to tell Huerta that if he held an election in which he was not a candidate, a large loan might be available from U.S. oil, railway, and copper interests in Mexico.[19] Lind, a Minnesota politician who knew little about diplomacy, did not handle his mission well. Huerta turned down the attempt to bribe him and, with British support, conducted an election he handily won. (The election was so open, moreover, that even Lind reported he had cast a ballot.) Deeply angered, Wilson began to turn the screws on Huerta. He was determined, he said, that the Mexican government "be founded on a moral basis." Sir Edward Grey, the British secretary of state for foreign affairs, privately remarked that "it would require about 200,000 soldiers to put Mexico on a 'moral basis.' " Grey stepped back, however, after Wilson assured London that British interests in Mexico would be protected.[20]

Then, on October 27, 1913, Wilson warned, in a speech at Mobile, Alabama, that exploitative foreign "concessions" were no longer to be tolerated in Latin America. Claiming that his own nation's motives were pure ("the United States will never again seek one additional foot of territory by conquest"), the president said that Americans only wanted to be "friends" of other nations on terms "of equality and honor." He would oppose "foreign interests" that tried to "dominate" Latin America and so create "a condition . . . always dangerous and apt to become intolerable."[21] As the British and other foreign governments understood, the Mobile Address was Wilson's declaration that he now would try to throw out any foreign "concessions" that in his view created "intolerable" conditions. The British also began to realize that Huerta's days were numbered.

The president's opportunity arose suddenly in April 1914, when Huerta's agents arrested seven U.S. sailors who, while on shore leave, had wandered into a forbidden area. Huerta quickly apologized, but Wilson made a series of demands to satisfy American "honor." When Huerta rejected them, Wilson appeared before Congress to ask for the use of U.S. military force against Mexico. As Congress stalled and investigated the charges, the president learned that a German ship planned to unload arms for Huerta at Vera Cruz. Wilson ordered U.S. vessels to occupy the port. Firing broke out that killed 19 Americans and over 300 Mexicans. Latin American nations intervened to help restore peace and meet Wilson's real objective: Huerta's removal. In August 1914, Carranza assumed power. Wilson had apparently won— but only apparently. An ardent nationalist, Carranza refused to bargain with Wilson. The frustrated president now turned to aiding anti-Carranza forces, including Pancho Villa.

Carranza responded with one of the most momentous acts in the revolution. He announced plans for agrarian reform and, most notably, for Mexico's claim to all its subsoil mineral rights. In a stroke, the revolution had turned sharply to the left and threatened U.S. oil companies.[22] Wilson intensified his pressure on Carranza, but the Mexican leader succeeded in destroying most of Villa's forces. The president, involved in a continual series of crises arising out of the world war, most reluctantly recognized Carranza's government *de facto* in late 1915.

Villa responded by terrorizing Arizona and New Mexico in the hope that Wilson's military retaliation would undermine Carranza. When Villa murdered seventeen Americans in Columbus, New Mexico, and eighteen U.S. engineers in Mexico itself, Wilson demanded that Carranza allow U.S. troops to track down the killers. Carranza reluctantly agreed, but imposed limits on the movements of U.S. forces. In March 1916, 6,000 men under the command of Major-General John J. ("Black Jack") Pershing rode across the border. Pershing never captured Villa, but his forces did clash with Carranza's army when it tried to restrict Pershing's men. Forty Mexican and two U.S. troops died. Wilson was trapped. He knew the mission was failing. Carranza was firmly in power. But Wilson was determined to remove Carranza, and his determination was strongly reinforced by U.S. Roman Catholics, who feared the growing anticlericalism in the revolution. In early 1917, however, Wilson realized that he would have to enter the European struggle. He pulled out Pershing's forces and began coming to terms with Carranza.

The president had tried to stabilize and democratize the Mexican Revolution. Eighty percent of the people had never had a "look-in," he declared. "I am for that 80 percent!" He believed he knew what to do: "They say the Mexicans are not fitted for self-government," he had declared in early 1914, "and to this I reply that, when properly directed, there is no people not fitted for self-government." In "properly" directing the Mexican Revolution, however, Wilson twice invaded the country and killed Mexicans. Trying to repaint the old fence post proved expensive.

WILSON AND REVOLUTIONS:
CENTRAL AMERICA AND THE CARIBBEAN

Upon entering office, Wilson declared that he wanted "orderly processes" in Latin America as well as stability in "the markets which we must supply."[23] But frequently, maintaining order meant maintaining the *status quo*. In much of Latin America, the *status quo* meant maintaining small elites who (as had Porfirio Díaz in Mexico) worked with foreign interests and exploited their own people. Only revolution or foreign intervention could overthrow such elites. "Democracy" often meant the continued power of those elites because they controlled elections. Wilson wanted elections, real change, order, and no foreign interventions—all at once. He never discovered how to pull off such a miracle. When he then chose order, Wilson and Bryan had to send troops into Haiti, Santo Domingo, and Cuba, as well as Mexico. Latin Americans began to call the U.S. Marines "State Department troops."

In 1913, the marines already were protecting the U.S.-created government in Nicaragua (see p. 262). President Adolfo Díaz's bankrupt regime needed money quickly. Bryan, who had made his political career by attacking bankers, had a novel idea. Why not, he asked Wilson, have the U.S. government lend the money to Nicaragua? The bankers and their exorbitant claims would be bypassed, banks and railways would remain in Central American hands, and it could "prevent revolutions, promote education, and advance stable and just government." Wilson rejected the plan. Substituting government funds for private bank loans would be too "novel and radical."[24] Bryan then resorted to the bankers, who already owned 51 percent of Nicaragua's national bank and railways. The bankers loaned Díaz another $1 million in return for the rest of the railways.

Díaz next asked that Nicaraguan (by which he meant his own) stability be guaranteed by extending the Platt Amendment's principles to the country. Bryan agreed to extend the protectorate, but the U.S. Senate rejected the plan. The secretary of state did sign the Bryan-Chamorro Treaty (finally approved in 1916) that gave Washington exclusive rights to build an isthmian canal through Nicaragua. In return, Díaz's regime received $3 million. The U.S. banks, U.S. government, and U.S. Marines controlled Nicaragua.

Wilson next ordered the marines to Haiti. That country, about the size of Maryland, had defeated the French colonials in 1804 to become the world's first black republic. Between 1843 and 1915, however, twenty-two dictators ruled Haiti in a highly corrupt version of a political revolving door. The last rulers in the line worked closely with German and French interests. Wilson disliked that connection. Moreover, the United States coveted the harbor of Môle St. Nicolas. When another revolt broke out in 1914, Bryan mentioned the Monroe Doctrine, told the Germans and French to stand aside, and asked Haiti for a treaty that handed over the country's vital interests to U.S. bankers. When the Haitians refused, Bryan landed marines, who carried $500,000 from the Haitian treasury back to New York City to protect, in the secretary of state's words, "American interests which were gravely menaced." With little financial support, the Haitian government began to collapse. Bryan demanded that elections be held. The Haitians refused. He then demanded that U.S. bankers be allowed to buy out the French interests and asked Wilson to have a U.S. warship available to obtain Haiti's attention.

The Haitians, meanwhile, were turning on President Vilbrun G. Sam, who thought he had assured himself a presidency for life by slaughtering over 160 of his imprisoned political opponents. A mob pulled Sam out of his hiding place in the French legation, hacked his body into pieces, placed parts on poles, then dragged the remaining trunk of the body through the dusty streets. Intent on teaching such mobs the meaning of democracy and order, Wilson dispatched the marines. A new government signed a treaty in August 1915 that granted the United States control over the country's foreign and financial affairs, and also the right to intervene whenever Washington officials thought it necessary. The marines remained for nineteen years.

The other part of Haiti's home island, Hispaniola, is occupied by the Dominican Republic. After 1904, when U.S. officials controlled its customshouses through the grace of the Roosevelt Corollary (see p. 247), the Dominican Republic remained stable until 1911. Renewed

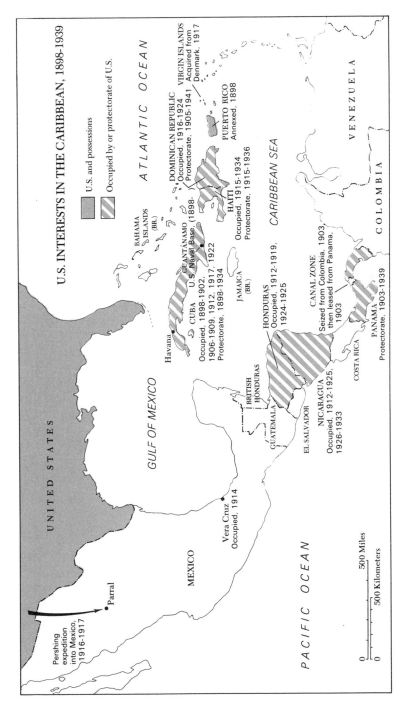

U.S. INTERESTS IN THE CARIBBEAN, 1898-1939

■ U.S. and possessions

▨ Occupied by or protectorate of U.S.

UNITED STATES

MEXICO

Parral

Pershing expedition into Mexico, 1916-1917

Vera Cruz Occupied, 1914

GULF OF MEXICO

PACIFIC OCEAN

ATLANTIC OCEAN

BAHAMA ISLANDS (BR.)

Havana

CUBA
Occupied, 1898-1902, 1906-1909, 1912, 1917, 1922
Protectorate, 1898-1934

GUANTANAMO
U.S. Naval Base, (1898-

JAMAICA (BR.)

CARIBBEAN SEA

DOMINICAN REPUBLIC
Occupied, 1916-1924
Protectorate, 1905-1941

HAITI
Occupied, 1915-1934
Protectorate, 1915-1936

VIRGIN ISLANDS
Acquired from Denmark, 1917

PUERTO RICO
Annexed, 1898

VENEZUELA

COLOMBIA

BRITISH HONDURAS

GUATEMALA

EL SALVADOR

HONDURAS
Occupied, 1912-1919, 1924-1925

NICARAGUA
Occupied, 1912-1925, 1926-1933

COSTA RICA

CANAL ZONE
Seized from Colombia, 1903, then leased from Panama, 1903

PANAMA
Protectorate, 1903-1939

500 Miles

500 Kilometers

The United States was active in the Caribbean throughout the post-1890s era, but, as the dates indicate, Wilson's administration was the most active.

disorder led Wilson in 1914 to demand the usual remedy: U.S.-sponsored elections. The government agreed to elections but not to the president's next demand—that U.S. bankers oversee the country's finances. In 1916, the government threatened to default on its debt. Eager to protect strategic routes in the Caribbean as well as to stop possible instability, Wilson landed the marines in May of that year. The U.S. military tried to rule the capital city of Santo Domingo, but guerrilla warfare tore the country apart between 1917 and 1922. U.S. investors took over large sugar and real-estate holdings. Racism fueled the anti-U.S. rebellion. (In a typical incident, a black shopkeeper brushed a U.S. soldier who screamed, "Look here, you damned Negro! Don't you know that no damned Negroes are supposed to let their bodies touch the body of any Marines?") By 1922, President Warren G. Harding's administration searched for an escape from the mess. The marines pulled out in 1925. A series of dictators again took over the country's affairs. As historian Kendrick Clements summarized, "Benevolent motives, backed by seemingly unlimited force, tempted the Americans to intervene where they were not wanted and where they did not understand the situation."[25] It would not be the last time in the twentieth century, unfortunately, that such a judgment could be made.

In June 1916, Wilson prepared a message to send to Congress. "It does not lie with the American people," he wrote, "to dictate to another people what their government shall be or what use shall be made of their resources." Secretary of State Lansing read the draft, then wrote in the margin: "Haiti, S. Domingo, Nicaragua, Panama." Wilson never sent the message. He did, however, keep U.S. troops in those places.[26]

THE UNITED STATES AND WORLD WAR I: LEGALITY VERSUS NEUTRALITY (1914–1916)

World War I began in August 1914. No one thought of it as a world war at first. The conflict seemed to resemble other crises that had arisen in the restless Balkans during 1908 and 1911–1913. These crises had been brought about by the slow collapse of the Austro-Hungarian and Ottoman empires. Circling the empires like vultures were two alliance systems—the Central Powers of Germany and Austria-Hungary itself, and the Entente (or Allied) powers of Great Britain, France, Russia, and, later, Italy. U.S. officials paid little attention to Balkan events. Nor, at first, did U.S. policy change in June 1914, when Archduke Francis Ferdinand of Austria was assassinated by a Serbian gunman.

When Austria tried to avenge itself against Serbia, however, Russia came to Serbia's side. Armies were mobilized, war declared, and bloodshed followed. Even then, many experts agreed with Captain Alfred Thayer Mahan's view that modern war was only an "occasional excess" from which recovery was easy. The huge arms build-up on both sides, these experts concluded, would deter either side from trying to push too hard.

By the autumn of 1914, it was clear that Mahan had been tragically wrong. As conflict expanded, all of Europe organized for war. Wilson issued a public statement urging Americans to be "neutral in fact as well as in name," "impartial in thought as well as in action." In reality, few could be neutral. Many recent Irish and German immigrants, for example, were anti-British. Many other Americans favored the Entente because of common language, the growth of economic ties, and the post-1895 warmth that cheered Anglo-American diplomats. That warmth rose considerably after British propagandists swamped the United States with stories of how the German "Huns" committed such atrocities as destroying the great library of Louvain when they invaded Belgium, killed in cold blood the famed British nurse Edith Cavell (who had, in truth, been acting as a spy), or, later, dispatched clumsy espionage agents to the United States itself.

Wilson's closest advisers quickly took sides. Colonel House had long hoped to work out U.S.-British-German cooperation. During the summer of 1914, House had been in Europe to sell these ideas to German and British leaders. As the war's shadows descended, the colonel feared that Wilson would have to choose between two evils: if the Central Powers won, German militarism would triumph; if the Allies won, then Russia could end up controlling central Europe. House chose to support the British and hoped that somehow the tsar could be held in check. Robert Lansing, then counselor in the Department of State, agreed. He was perhaps the most pro-British official in the administration's top echelons. Bryan took a more neutral position, although he was appalled by the German atrocities. Above all, the secretary of state did not want the United States to enter the war on either side.

It fell to Lansing to shape some of the first U.S. responses. When the war began, Wilson was recovering from the death of his first wife. The initial decisions, moreover, involved the U.S. response to the British naval blockade of German ports. As the administration's expert on international law, Lansing had some responsibility for drafting the proper response. By the end of 1914, he had strongly asserted U.S. neutral rights. But he had also gone far in recognizing the British right to stop

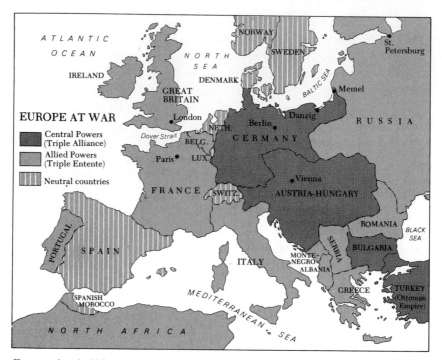

Europe divided bloodily between 1914 and 1918 as Americans (especially Wilson and House) had qualms about joining either the Central Powers or the Allies.

and search neutral (including U.S.) ships carrying munitions and other contraband (that is, weapons or other articles used to wage war) to the Central Powers. His position was good international law, but it also worked to Great Britain's advantage, especially when London officials began to expand the list of what they considered to be contraband.[27] The United States frequently protested British actions, but as Lansing later admitted, "I . . . prepared long and detailed replies" to complicate and prolong the controversies with London. Lansing hoped that as time passed, "the American people [would] perceive that German absolutism was a menace to their liberties."[28]

Lansing's tactics paid off. In February 1915, the Germans retaliated against the tightening British blockade with a submarine campaign aimed at Allied and neutral ships. The submarine (U-boat) was a shocking new weapon that brought sudden, unexpected death from the invisible depths of the Atlantic. There existed no body of international law to guide American responses to the U-boats. Wilson warned that he would hold Germany to "strict accountability" if U.S. ships were destroyed—although no one, including the president, knew exactly what this meant. The Germans took the position they had held for two years: they would call off their submarines if the British stopped trying to starve the Central Powers. Neither the British nor Wilson accepted that deal. Both believed that surface blockades were legal and traditional, but sudden submarine attacks illegal and uncivilized. In March 1915, the British passenger liner *Falaba* was sunk and one American life lost. In early May, the United States protested when one of its merchant ships was attacked and three lives lost.

Then, on May 7, a submarine sank the British liner *Lusitania.* Nearly 1,200 died, including 128 Americans. U.S. anti-German opinion grew white hot. Later investigation proved what the Germans claimed in 1915: the *Lusitania* was carrying a large cargo of munitions to Great Britain. Before it sailed, Germany had publicly warned that the ship was fair game. Wilson nevertheless prepared a note demanding that Germany pledge never again to attack a passenger liner. He insisted on the right of Americans to travel on any passenger ship they pleased. Bryan agreed on the need to protest but worried that the United States was moving slowly but surely into the Allied camp. He demanded that Wilson send an equally strong note to London protesting the British blockade. The president wavered and then, after discussing the problem with House (who was in London), refused Bryan's request. The secretary of state resigned.

In his parting words, he not only questioned U.S. policy, but complained that Wilson had always allowed House to act as the real secretary of state. Louisville newspaper editor Henry Watterson expressed the popular reaction when he blasted Bryan's resignation: "Men have been shot and beheaded, even hanged, drawn, and quartered, for treason less heinous." Germany responded to Wilson's demand by apologizing for the *Lusitania* sinking and offering an indemnity. But the episode marked a turning point. Wilson had now decided to separate, openly and formally, British and German sea warfare. His demands of Germany were not to be related to his policies toward Great Britain's blockade. Bryan's resignation removed the most neutral member of the cabinet. Robert Lansing moved up to be secretary of state.[29]

In August 1915, a German submarine commander sank the British liner *Arabic* and killed two Americans. Berlin immediately disavowed the attack and apologized for the commander's action. Lansing warned that if Germany did not promise to stop attacking passenger liners (unless the passenger ships tried to escape or attack the subs), the United States "would certainly declare war." The kaiser's government finally made such a promise in the so-called "*Arabic* pledge." Merchant ships were not covered by the pledge; but in due time, Wilson would also have to close that loophole if he hoped to protect U.S. rights to travel and sell to both belligerents.

Wilson's decided tilt toward the Allies became especially notable when he had to decide whether U.S. bankers should be allowed to grant credits and loans to the belligerents. The stakes were high, for they involved nothing less than the health of the American economy. When the war began in mid-1914, the economy was entering a severe slump. The two key exports, wheat and cotton, depended on British and German markets. As the war demand shot upward, especially for these exports, the Allies and Central Powers discovered that they were quickly exhausting their cash reserves. They needed financial help, preferably loans from the Americans, who were—as Jefferson had put it a century before—"fattening upon the follies" of Europeans.

The administration at first decided against allowing loans. As Bryan declared, "Money is the worst of all contrabands because it commands everything else." But without money, the Europeans could not buy, and without their buying, the United States faced economic bad times. Wilson and Bryan decided to compromise. They quietly allowed bankers to offer credits (a transaction limited to a bank's own resources, in which the borrower usually uses the money only to buy specified goods).

They would not allow the bankers to float loans—that is, to offer securities on the public market to raise huge amounts of dollars to lend to the belligerents. The Americans who subscribed to the loans would then have to rely on British (or German) securities for repayment, a dependence that could make the lender exceptionally interested in having his or her borrower win the war.

By mid-1915, however, the bank credits proved inadequate to finance the multiplying trade in food and munitions. U.S exports by mid-1915 had more than doubled since mid-1914. The Allies and the Central Powers alike appealed for outright loans. After agonizing over the decision for a month, Wilson quietly reversed himself in September 1915 and allowed loans to be floated. (Bryan, it will be remembered, had resigned three months earlier.) The president changed his mind not only because he believed that both Germany and the Allies would have equal access to U.S. money markets, but above all because—as his secretary of the Treasury wrote—"our foreign commerce is just as essential to our prosperity as our domestic commerce."[30]

It turned out to be a pivotal decision. Bankers immediately floated the first Allied loan for $500 million. Although the amount was found only with difficulty, it opened the floodgates. The Allies, with their stronger links to U.S. banks, borrowed $2.5 billion over the next two years. (These loans were secured by British investments in American companies.) The Central Powers received less than one-tenth that amount. War-related U.S. exports doubled in the last half of 1915 to $2 billion (with most going to England and France), then doubled once more in 1916. Again, as Wilson's first major biographer observed, the president's decision to allow loans retreated from a position of " 'the true spirit of neutrality' to one based upon 'strict legality.' "[31] The decision also helped transform the United States from being one of the world's greatest debtors (it owed the world about $3.7 billion in 1914) to a creditor of $3.8 billion by the end of the war. This huge, quick movement of money between 1914 and 1918 helped turn the United States into the world's economic superpower of the twentieth century.

Wilson's dilemma was intense. He understood how U.S. submarine and financial policies were pushing him into the Allied camp. He certainly did not want a total German victory, but neither did he want an Allied triumph that destroyed the European balance of power and left Russia astride much of the continent. From the start of the conflict, he believed that he alone was in the best position to mediate a fair settlement and stop the bloodshed. Like a virtuoso, House played on Wilson's vision of himself as the great peacemaker. He convinced the president to allow him to act as Wilson's agent in Europe.

In early 1915, House sailed across the Atlantic to try to mediate an end to the war. He believed that a proper settlement would include German payment of reparations for invading Belgium and a general European disarmament. But it was too late. Too much blood had already been shed. The war aims on both sides had escalated. The Allies, moreover, had been negotiating secret treaties with Italy and Japan in which those powers promised to help the French and British in return for territory after the war. The stakes for victory were rising even as an entire generation of young Europeans was being slaughtered.

House, who seldom hid his pro-Allied biases, signed the so-called House-Grey Memorandum in February 1916 with British foreign secretary Sir Edward Grey. It attempted to seduce the Allies to a peace conference by promising that if they accepted, and if Germany refused to accept terms the Allies liked, the United States would then join the war with the Allies. When House reported his deal back to Washington, Wilson inserted the condition that Americans would "probably" join the war. Grey then rejected the proposal. He believed that it would be only a matter of time before Wilson would enter the war on London's side anyway.

The president was beginning to fear the same thing. In 1915, Wilson responded to this concern with his "preparedness campaign." Camps were set up to train American males for possible combat. Naval appropriation measures were readied. Wilson gave speeches warning his listeners that the nation had to be prepared to defend itself. Theodore Roosevelt, who had damned the president's every move because he would not take the nation into war against Germany, finally found a Wilsonian act he liked. TR justified preparedness on the grounds that it would firm the fiber of American men, especially the apparently more effete northeasterners, who responded to the call with unusual enthusiasm. Wilson, however, had other objectives. Although he wanted to counter Roosevelt's growing criticism, the president also wanted to show Germany that he meant business, as well as appease growing anti-German sentiment in the United States. Perhaps most important, he wanted to begin building military power so that he would have a strong base from which to mediate an end to the conflict. When he sat down at the peace conference, he hoped to have military leverage against both sides. In reality, as historian John W. Coogan concludes, Wilson, by late 1915, "had become a partner, and not always a silent partner, in the Allied economic campaign to strangle Germany."[32]

The Battle Cry of Peace, *one of the first movie spectaculars, was hugely popular in 1915–1916 and helped shape the debate over the preparedness campaign and U.S. neutrality. It was powerfully pro-war: foreign invaders (thinly disguised Germans) destroy New York City and Washington, kill the pacifists, and lead the women to commit suicide before they are ravaged. Theodore Roosevelt and Admiral George Dewey, among many others, strongly recommended the film. It was based on a book by Hudson Maxim, a munitions-maker and inventor of the Maxim Gun. As the picture shows, Maxim also starred in the film.*

THE DECISIONS FOR WAR (1916–1917)

On March 24, 1916, a German U-boat sank the French passenger liner *Sussex* and injured several Americans. Lansing and House urged that this violation of the *Arabic* pledge be met with a severing of diplomatic relations. Wilson refused. The president continued to believe that only as the great neutral could he end the war and establish a just peace. He did, however, take one more step toward Lansing's position by sending a note to Berlin demanding that the submarines not attack merchant ships (as well as passenger liners). If Berlin officials would not agree, Wilson threatened, the United States would sever relations. After intense internal debate, the Germans agreed, but they implied that Wilson must put equal pressure on the British blockade. Angry at the response, the president again separated the two issues. Berlin's *Sussex* pledge nevertheless gave the initiative—a diplomatic "blank check"—

to the Germans. If they decided that it was in their interest to launch an all-out submarine attack to win the war, Wilson would have little alternative but to join the conflict. He had lost even more of his freedom of action.

The president realized that his room for maneuver had rapidly shrunk. In the summer of 1916, he tried to balance his policies by vigorously protesting against Great Britain's interception of U.S. mail and its blatant discrimination against some 800 American companies that had dealt with the Central Powers. On the other hand, when both the House of Representatives and the Senate threatened to pass the McLemore Resolution, which prohibited Americans from traveling on belligerent ships, Wilson pulled out all stops to defeat the measure. The president refused to give in on the thorny neutral-rights issue. He insisted on the rights of U.S. citizens to move on the high seas as they wished. Because of Britain's control of those seas, however, his victory also required increased U.S.-Allied cooperation.

Wilson's hopes for creating a stable and open postwar world received their greatest jolt in May 1916, when the Allies met secretly in Paris to plan economic policies. They clearly foresaw that after the war, the United States would be the world's strongest and most competitive economic power. The British, French, Russians, and Italians, therefore, drafted a program to seal themselves off from the effects of that power. The Allies planned to use government subsidies, higher tariffs, and controlled markets to fight U.S. competition. Wilson and Lansing were stunned when they learned of the Paris economic conference. The president concluded that "our businessmen ought to organize their wits in such a way as to take possession of foreign markets." He told one business group that he very much favored the "righteous conquest of foreign markets."[33]

Clearly, however, White House pep rallies were not enough. The U.S. government would have to enter the contest by directly helping the business community to neutralize the weapons developed by the Paris conference. Wilson approached the problem from two directions. In the long run, he planned to insist on a peace that provided open marketplaces, competition, and the minimum of government involvement. In such an arena, he knew that U.S. business could more than hold its own. But this meant that it was all the more important that he attend the peace conference. More immediately, he sponsored legislation to allow U.S. business to gear up for the "righteous conquest." The Webb-Pomerene Act freed corporations from anti-trust laws, thus allowing them to combine legally to conquer foreign markets. The Edge

Act removed government restraints so that U.S. banks could rapidly set up overseas operations. Wilson thus refused to join the Allies in using government power to close off and protect markets. Instead, he aimed to release government controls so that U.S. businesses could more efficiently compete abroad. But he still needed to get to the peace conference to ensure that world markets remained open.[34]

By the autumn of 1916, the president had become so determined to beat down British maritime and economic power that he sponsored a huge appropriations bill to enlarge the navy. He aimed at nothing less than the world's greatest fleet within a decade. "Let us build a navy bigger than [Great Britain's] and do what we please," he told House in September.[35] At the same time, however, the United States continued to be drawn to the British side. The Allies were now spending $10 million a day in the United States for war goods. "There is a moral obligation laid up on us to keep out of this war if possible," Wilson believed. "By the same token there is a moral obligation laid up on us to keep free the courses of our commerce and our finance." The president was snared in an ugly trap.

When the Democrats nominated him for a second term in 1916, they coined the slogan "He Kept Us Out of War." Wilson knew, however, that the days of peace were probably numbered. In his acceptance speech, he grimly announced that Americans could not long remain neutral in a war-torn world. He began to discuss a postwar "universal association of nations" (an idea mentioned earlier by such Republicans as Roosevelt, Taft, and Lodge). Such an association could establish a just world and protect U.S. interests. After he defeated Republican nominee Charles Evans Hughes in the 1916 elections, Wilson made one more attempt to mediate an end to the war. Both the Allies and Central Powers finally rejected his offer. Each side had now enlarged its war aims—for territory, bases, indemnities—that only a total victory could provide. Wilson's hopes of acting as a neutral, honest broker had been dashed.

In January 1917, Germany decided to launch all-out submarine warfare. The debate had raged in Berlin since the *Sussex* crisis. Now the kaiser was convinced by his advisers that only a military victory could obtain his war aims of new territory, a neutral Belgium, naval bases in the Atlantic and Pacific, and perhaps even war indemnities from the Allies. The moment seemed right: war-torn Russia bloodily stumbled toward collapse, and German armies seemed on the point of victory on the eastern front. Now was the time to put full pressure on the West as well. The German naval command boasted that "England will lie on the ground in six months, before a single American has set foot on the continent." Civilian advisers were not so optimistic. Berlin military experts believed that, in any case, Americans could hardly do more to help the Allied side than they were already doing.[36]

Wilson realized that the United States was about to enter the war. But he remained torn between his belief that only as a neutral could he mediate a just peace and his fear that only if the United States became a belligerent could he be assured of a seat at the peace table. It was a terrible dilemma. On January 22, 1917, he appeared on Capitol Hill to announce U.S. postwar objectives. Wilson tried to cut through his growing dilemmas by pleading for "peace without victory"—that is, a peace in which neither side could dictate terms to the other. Equally important, he announced that the postwar settlement must protect U.S. interests. He directly attacked the old European balance of power that had failed to prevent the war and now, he feared, threatened to undermine the peace: "There must be not a balance of power, but a community of power; not organized rivalries, but an organized common peace."

Such a peace, he continued, had to include certain principles: (1) self-determination for all nations, large or small; (2) freedom of the seas—"the *sine qua non* of peace, equality and cooperation," as Wilson called it when he lashed out at both British and German maritime practices; (3) no more "entangling alliances" that created "competitions of power" instead of an open world. "These are American principles, American policies," the president declared. He thus announced that the United States was entering the blood-soaked conflict not out of the goodness of its heart, not out of mere idealism, but to protect its own self-interest. He drove this point home: "I am proposing as it were, that the nations should with one accord adopt the doctrine of President Monroe as the doctrine of the world: that no nation should seek to extend its polity over any other nation or people."[37]

The speech marked Wilson's last attempt as a neutral to define peace terms that he believed necessary for both U.S. interests and "every enlightened community." But the war-shocked Europeans could no longer afford to be so enlightened. One important British observer, Sir George Otto Trevelyan, privately dismissed the president's appeal: "The man is surely the quintessence of a prig." How dare he, Trevelyan argued, come in after three years of "this terrible effort" and ask both sides to put down their arms and meekly agree to American principles. French author Anatole France compared Wilson's "peace without victory" to "bread without yeast" or "a camel without humps" or "a town without brothel . . . in brief, an insipid thing" that would be "fetid, ignominious, obscene, fistulous, hemorrhoidal."[38] Germany responded by beginning total submarine warfare on February 1, 1917. All ships in war zones were now fair game. Two days later, Wilson broke diplomatic relations with Berlin.

But even as U.S. merchant ships were torpedoed in February and early March 1917, Wilson refused to walk his last mile to war. He knew that a strong anti-war group in Congress, led by powerful Progressives such as Republican senators Robert La Follette from Wisconsin and William Borah from Idaho, posed an obstacle. On the other hand, he did not want to appear to be giving in to his bitterest critics, Theodore Roosevelt and Henry Cabot Lodge, who had urged war since 1915. (Even after Wilson asked for war, TR dismissed the president's foreign policy as "nauseous hypocrisy.")

More important, Wilson worried that U.S. involvement in Europe would allow Japan to run wild in Asia. He told Lansing that " 'white civilization' and its domination in the world rested largely on our ability to keep this country intact."[39] The secretary of state, who wanted war, began to devise tactics to keep the Japanese in check so that Wilson could fight Europeans in better conscience (see p. 277). Above all, the president feared that becoming a belligerent would ruin his chance to broker a "peace without victory." On February 2, he told his cabinet that "probably greater justice would be done if the conflict ended in a draw." He feared that joining the Allies meant "the destruction of the German nation"[40] and the creation of a dangerous political vacuum in the middle of Europe.

By early March, however, Wilson knew he had no alternative. U.S. merchant ships were being sunk. On March 1, the news broke that British intelligence had intercepted the Zimmermann telegram. In the cable, dated January 16, the German foreign minister asked Mexico to ally with Berlin in return for getting back the Texas-to-California region after the United States was defeated. Wilson did not take the telegram too seriously (fortunately for him, neither did Mexico), but the British scored a major propaganda victory. Despite the telegram, however, the Senate killed Wilson's request of March 1 to arm U.S. merchant ships. He went ahead and armed them anyway on the basis of an almost forgotten eighteenth-century law.

On March 15, the Russian front nearly collapsed, and the tsar, Nicholas II, abdicated his throne. A more liberal provisional government took power. Americans were elated, not least because the new regime promised (foolishly, as it soon turned out) to continue to fight

Germany. The United States was the first government to recognize the new regime. Roosevelt, that caustic critic of things Russian, now told a New York audience that "Russia, the hereditary friend of this country," had chosen "enlightened freedom." Wilson even announced that Russia was "a fit partner" because it had been "always in fact democratic at heart." The liberal journal *New Republic,* long a critic of the autocratic tsar, went into rapture: "The war which started as a clash of empires in the Balkans will dissolve into democratic revolution the world over."[41] As historian Peter G. Filene writes, "Americans . . . imposed American terms" on Russia, which was, "in effect, to be a Slavic version of the United States."[42]

The dramatic turn in Russia did not convince Wilson to go to war on behalf of "democratic revolution." It did allow him, however, to argue that now all Allies were "fit" partners for Americans. On March 18, three U.S. ships were torpedoed and went to the bottom of the Atlantic. On March 20, Wilson met with his cabinet to make the decision for war. Public pressure had little to do with the decision. Most important, the president concluded that U.S. rights on the high seas had to be protected and that only by becoming a full belligerent could he attain his great objective: to be a full participant at the postwar peace conference. As he told the famed Progressive reformer Jane Addams (who opposed going to war), he had to fight or otherwise be content, when the peace conference gathered, merely to "shout" at the participants "through a crack in the door."[43]

On April 2, 1917, he asked Congress to declare war. Despite strong opposition from Borah and Republican congresswoman Jeanette Rankin of Montana, on April 6 the war resolution was approved by the Senate 82 to 6 and by the House 373 to 50. Most of the opposition came from the Midwest and the Rocky Mountain states, especially areas with heavy German immigrant populations. But Borah spoke for many when he declared: "I join no crusade; I seek or accept no alliances."

Wilson had learned that in such a conflict, the United States could no longer be both neutral and prosperous. Nor could it be neutral and hope to have a decisive voice in constructing the postwar peace. To practice peace, he had to wage war. Tragic choices had to be made. And they had to be made amid bloodshed and chaos that not even the wildest imagination had conceived in 1914. "We are living and shall live all our lives now in a revolutionary world," pro-Wilson journalist Walter Lippmann declared. In that world, Wilson led Americans onto the charred fields of Europe, where 50,000 would die so that the president could try to replace revolution with a democratic world based on

Jeanette Rankin (1880–1973) was a suffragist and then the first woman member of Congress in 1917. Raised on a Montana ranch, she voted against war in 1917, lost her election campaign because of her pacifism in 1918, then was re-elected in time to vote against war again in 1941—the only person who cast a vote against entering each world war.

American principles. It was a gamble for the highest stakes. The brilliant anti-war voice of Randolph Bourne cut to the core of Wilson's dilemma: "If the war is too strong for you to prevent, how is it going to be weak enough for you to control and mold to your liberal purposes?"[44]

NOTES

1. Edwin A. Weinstein, *Woodrow Wilson: A Medical and Psychological Biography* (Princeton, 1981); Paul F. Boller, Jr., *Presidential Anecdotes* (New York, 1981), p. 218.
2. David W. Noble, *The Progressive Mind, 1890–1917* (Chicago, 1970), p. 171.
3. William Diamond, *The Economic Thought of Woodrow Wilson* (Baltimore, 1943), pp. 132–133.

4. William Appleman Williams, *The Contours of American History* (Cleveland, 1961), p. 410.

5. Woodrow Wilson, *The Public Papers of Woodrow Wilson*, ed. Arthur S. Link *et al.* (Princeton, 1966–   ), VII, p. 352, italics in original; Woodrow Wilson, *Constitutional Government in the United States* (New York, 1908), pp. 58–59.

6. Robert Lansing, *War Memoirs of Robert Lansing, Secretary of State* (Indianapolis, 1935), p. 349.

7. Wilson, *Constitutional Government*, pp. 52–53; Lloyd Gardner, "The Cold War," manuscript, in the author's possession, has quote on 1889.

8. Diamond, pp. 136–139.

9. Lloyd Gardner, "A Progressive Foreign Policy, 1900–1921," in *From Colony to Empire*, ed. William Appleman Williams (New York, 1972), p. 225.

10. Paolo E. Coletta, *William Jennings Bryan* (Lincoln, Neb., 1964), p. 93.

11. Arthur Link, *Wilson*, 5 vols. (Princeton, 1947–   ), II, p. 95.

12. N. Gordon Levin, Jr., *Woodrow Wilson and World Politics* (New York, 1968), pp. 24–25, 37–38; [Colonel Edward M. House], *Philip Dru, Administrator: A Story of Tomorrow, 1920–1935* (New York, 1912), pp. 275–276.

13. Diamond, p. 133.

14. Jerry Israel, *Progressivism and the Open Door: America and China, 1905–1921* (Pittsburgh, 1971), p. 108.

15. Willard Straight to Henry P. Fletcher, 24 February 1916, Papers of Willard Straight, Cornell University Library, Ithaca, New York; excellent background for the U.S.-China relationship is in Daniel M. Crane and Thomas A. Breslin, *An Ordinary Relationship: American Opposition to Republican Revolution in China* (Miami, 1986), pp. 163–177.

16. James Reed, *The Missionary Mind and American East Asian Policy, 1911–1915* (Cambridge, Mass., 1983), is now a standard account; also, Link, III, pp. 269–270, 275–278, 280–285; Noel H. Pugach, *Paul S. Reinsch, Open Door Diplomat in Action* (Millwood, N.Y., 1979) p. 157.

17. Walter Lippmann Oral History, Columbia University Oral History Project, New York, p. 35.

18. Howard F. Cline, *The United States and Mexico*, 3d ed. (Cambridge, Mass., 1963), pp. 117–123, 130–134; Lloyd Gardner *et al.*, *The Creation of the American Empire*, 2d ed. (Chicago, 1976), p. 305.

19. Cline, pp. 144–146.

20. Peter Calvert, *The Mexican Revolution, 1910–1914* (Cambridge, Eng., 1968), p. 238.

21. *The Record of American Diplomacy*, ed. Ruhl J. Bartlett, 4th ed. (New York, 1964), pp. 540–541.

22. Lloyd C. Gardner, *Safe for Democracy* (New York, 1984), pp. 65–68. Mark T. Gilderhaus provides an important interpretation in "Wilson, Carranza, and the Monroe Doctrine: A Question in Regional Organization," *Diplomatic History* 7 (Spring 1983): 103–115.

23. Raymond Leslie Buell, "The United States and Central American Stability," *Foreign Policy Reports* 7 (8 July 1931): 177; Diamond, p. 151.

24. Wilson *Papers*, ed. Link *et al.*, XXVIII, p. 48; Diamond, p. 153.

25. Bruce J. Calder, *The Impact of Intervention: The Dominican Republic during the U.S. Occupation of 1916–1924* (Austin, Tex., 1984), is especially important on the anti-

U.S. guerrilla war; Kendrick Clements, *The Presidency of Woodrow Wilson* (Lawrence, Kans., 1992), p. 106.

26. Diamond, p. 154n.

27. Link, III, pp. 105–129.

28. Lansing, p. 112.

29. Two excellent analyses are Link, III, pp. 390–401, and Ernest R. May, *World War and American Isolation, 1914–1917* (Cambridge, Mass., 1959), chs. 6–7.

30. Diamond, p. 156; Link, III, pp. 62–64, 133–136, 606–625.

31. Ray Stannard Baker, *Woodrow Wilson: Life and Letters*, 8 vols. (Garden City, N.Y., 1935–1939), V, p. 187.

32. John W. Coogan, *The End of Neutrality: The U.S., Britain, and Maritime Rights, 1899–1915* (Ithaca, 1981), p. 193; John Garry Clifford, *The Citizen Soldiers* (Bloomington, Ind., 1972); Michael Pearlman, *To Make Democracy Safe for America* (Urbana, Ill., 1984). Clifford's and Pearlman's accounts are standard on prepardness.

33. Lloyd Gardner, "Commercial Preparedness, 1914–1921," manuscript (1966), in the author's possession.

34. Carl P. Parrini, *Heir to Empire: United States Economic Diplomacy, 1916–1923* (Pittsburgh, 1969), pp. 15–39.

35. Link, IV, p. 337.

36. May, ch. 18.

37. Link, V, pp. 265–274.

38. *Ibid.*, pp. 273–274.

39. Entry of 4 February 1917, in Diaries of Robert Lansing, Box #2 (Microfilm ed., reel #1).

40. Edward H. Buehrig, *Woodrow Wilson and the Balance of Power* (Bloomington, Ind., 1955), p. 144.

41. Christopher Lasch, *The New Radicalism in America, 1889–1963* (New York, 1965), pp. 198–199.

42. Peter G. Filene, *Americans and the Soviet Experiment, 1917–1933* (Cambridge, Mass., 1967), pp. 10, 12–14.

43. Link, V, ch. 9, has the full account. A fine brief discussion of the context is Lawrence E. Gelfand, "The Mystique of Wilsonian Statecraft," *Diplomatic History* 7 (Spring 1983): 87–101.

44. Ronald Steel, "Revolting Times," *Reviews in American History* 13 (December 1985): 588; David Green, *Shaping Political Consciousness* (Ithaca, N.Y., 1987), p. 83.

For Further Reading

Start with the well-indexed pre-1981 references in *Guide to American Foreign Relations since 1700*, ed. Richard Dean Burns (1983), and consult the notes to this chapter and the General Bibliography at the end of this book; these references are not usually repeated below. Good recent sources are David R. Woodward and Robert F. Maddox, *America and World War I: A Selected Annotated Bibliography of English-Language Sources* (1985), and Kendrick A. Clements, *Woodrow Wilson: World Statesman* (1987).

On Wilson, start with Kendrick Clements, *The Presidency of Woodrow Wilson* (1992); Akira Iriye, *The Globalizing of America, 1914–1945* in *The Cambridge History of U.S. Foreign Relations,* ed. Warren Cohen (1993). *Woodrow Wilson and a Revolutionary World, 1913–1921,* ed. Arthur S. Link (1982), has superb essays written by experts on the era, especially in regard to Mexico, Russia, Poland, and collective security. Link's magisterial *The Public Papers of Woodrow Wilson* (1966–   ) is nearly completed; while Link and Robert C. Hilderbrand have edited a special volume, *The Public Papers of Woodrow Wilson,* Vol. 50: *The Complete Press Conferences* (1985). Important documents, a fine introductory essay, and an excellent bibliographic essay are in *Wilson and Revolutions: 1913–1921,* ed. Lloyd C. Gardner (1982). Important interpretations are in Frederick S. Calhoun, *Power and Principle: Armed Intervention in Wilsonian Foreign Policy* (1986), a useful overview; Lloyd Ambrosius, "Woodrow Wilson and the Quest for Orderly Progress," in *Studies in American Diplomacy, 1865–1945,* ed. Norman A. Graebner (1985); Norman A. Graebner, *America as a World Power: A Realist Appraisal from Wilson to Reagan* (1984); Michael H. Hunt, *Ideology and U.S. Foreign Policy* (1987), for placing Wilson in the context of a U.S. ideology and an antirevolutionary framework; William H. Becker, *The Dynamics of Business-Government Relations: Industry and Exports* (1982), which de-emphasizes the role of government, as opposed to the thesis found in Burton I. Kaufman, *Efficiency and Expansion: Foreign Trade Organization in the Wilson Administration 1913–1921* (1974), a pathbreaking study. Wilson's particular genius is featured in Robert C. Hilderbrand, *Power and the People: Executive Management of Public Opinion in Foreign Affairs, 1897–1921* (1982). See Ernest C. Bolt, Jr., *Ballots before Bullets* (1977), on the war-referendum idea. Important studies of film include Michael T. Eisenberg, *War on Film* (1981); and Craig W. Campbell, *Reel America and World War I* (1985).

Specific studies on the entry into the war have recently included Melvin Small, "Woodrow Wilson and U.S. Intervention in World War I," in *Modern American Diplomacy,* ed. John M. Carroll and George C. Herring (1986); John W. Coogan, *The End of Neutrality: The U.S., Britain, and Maritime Rights, 1899–1915* (1981); Kendrick A. Clements, *William Jennings Bryan: Missionary Isolationist* (1982), using Bryan to point up larger themes in U.S. diplomacy; Paolo E. Coletta, "A Question of Alternatives: Wilson, Bryan, Lansing, and America's Intervention in World War I," *Nebraska History* 63 (Spring 1982), by Bryan's biographer; and Kathleen Burk, *Britain, America and the Sinews of War, 1914–1918* (1985), which uses J. P. Morgan as a focal point of the U.S.-British competition. The anti-war groups are superbly studied by Charles DeBenedetti, *The Peace Reform in American History* (1985), which sees World War I as a turning point; Sandi E. Cooper, *Patriotic Pacifism . . . 1815–1914* (1992); and *Peace Heroes in Twentieth-Century America,* ed. Charles DeBenedetti (1986), especially the chapters on Jane Addams and Eugene Debs.

In addition to the Calhoun book, noted above, the following are important for Wilson's interventionism in Latin America: Lester Langley, *The Banana Wars* (1983), with a helpful bibliography; Brenda Gayle Plummer, *Haiti and the United States: The Psychological Moment* (1992), now the standard overview; Lester Langley, *Mexico and the United States* (1991); Friedrich Katz, *The Secret War in Mexico: Europe, the U.S. and the Mexican Revolution* (1981), an exhaustive account; Berta Ulloa, "Tampico and Vera Cruz," in *Diplomatic Claims: Latin American Historians View the United States,* ed. and trans. Warren Dean (1985); Bruce J. Calder, *The Impact of Intervention: The Dominican Republic during the U.S. Occupation of 1916–1924* (1984); David Healy, "Admiral William B. Caperton," in *Behind the Throne,* eds. T. McCormick and W. LaFeber (1993), essays in honor of Fred Harvey Harrington; and, for a rather stunning contemporary view, Hiram Bingham, *The Monroe Doctrine, an Obsolete Shibboleth* (1913).

The relations with China are studied in Daniel M. Crane and Thomas A. Breslin, *An Ordinary Relationship: American Opposition to Republican Revolution in China* (1986); John Allphin Moore, Jr., "From Reaction to Multilateral Agreement: The Expansion of America's Open Door Policy in China, 1899–1922," *Prologue* 15 (Spring 1983); and most of the accounts listed in the second paragraph of this bibliography.

10

Victors without Peace
(1917–1920)

WILSON'S APPROACH TO WAR AND PEACE

President Wilson, as he informed Congress in his war message of April 2, 1917, intended to smash the "autocratic governments backed by organized force which is controlled wholly by their [the autocrats'] will, not by the will of the people." He emphasized, "We have no quarrel with the German people. We have no feeling towards them but one of sympathy and friendship."[1]

It seemed an odd way to go to war—that is, to express "friendship" for the people Americans were about to kill in large numbers. The words, nevertheless, fit Wilson's approach to the conflict. He believed that once the kaiser and other "autocrats" were destroyed, the "people" of Germany (and elsewhere) would create happier, democratic governments. Thus, he urged Americans to fight "to make the world safe for democracy." Once the "autocrats" disappeared, the mass of people would want to be democratic. Then, as he phrased it in his January 22, 1917, speech, the world could be rebuilt on "American principles."

There was idealism here, certainly, but also realism. Indeed, Wilson has become the most influential architect of twentieth-century U.S. foreign policy in part because he so eloquently clothed the bleak skeleton of U.S. self-interest in the attractive garb of idealism. Nothing, after all, could be more self-interested for Americans than to have the rest of the world act according to their principles. But the president also understood that Americans had little choice. They could no longer withdraw from world affairs. "Neutrality is no longer feasible or desirable" for the United States, he declared in his war message, "where the peace of the world is involved and the freedom of its peoples." The nation had learned this lesson the hard way between 1914 and 1917, when it mistakenly believed that it could have both neutrality and the freedom to sell anywhere it pleased. Wilson consequently hoped to make the competition play the game according to American rules. Making the "world safe for democracy" was the necessary first step.

The president, however, well understood the hurdles in his way. Most important, his closest allies disagreed with him. They wanted total victory, not "peace without victory," as he had asked. They made no distinction between the German people and their rulers. The French, who were losing one out of every two of their young men between the ages of fifteen and thirty to German machine guns, wanted vengeance. They saw little difference between the Germans who shot the weapons and the officials who gave the orders. Nor did the British intend to recognize "American principles" if one of them was freedom of the seas. London officials placed their trust in their great fleet, not in American principles. They and the French, moreover, depended on their far-flung colonial empires in Africa and Asia too much to agree to "democracy." The two European powers were not destroying an entire generation of their young men to give democracy to their imperial holdings in India or Indochina. Outspoken Americans such as Theodore Roosevelt and Henry Cabot Lodge wanted total Allied victory and total German defeat. Then, they argued, the victors could create a peace that suited them. They assumed that American and Allied war aims would be much the same. Wilson fought such views. He believed that such an approach could only produce more colonialism, more autocracy, and more wars.

The president, therefore, swept the United States into war not as an "Allied" power, but as an "Associated" power. He was doing what little he could to separate himself from the European conservatives who wanted total victory and a division of the spoils. When the president discovered that one U.S. government agency was trying to whip up war spirit by using slogans that included "Our Allies," Wilson sharply ordered the phrase changed to "our Associates . . . because we have no allies."[2]

OVER THERE: THE WESTERN FRONT

The president's military policy fit this diplomatic approach. Wilson and his top military officials, led by General John J. ("Black Jack") Pershing, refused throughout 1917–1918 to allow the American Expeditionary Forces (AEF) in Europe to be integrated into Allied armies. Wilson insisted that they remain separate and under U.S. command. American armies were to be used for American, not necessarily British and French, war aims. One exception turned out to be the 200,000 African Americans who went to Europe. U.S. officers segregated and discriminated against them, to the displeasure of both the French and the black Americans. Finally, a large number of these troops were sent to fight with French forces, and they compiled a brilliant war record.

General John J. Pershing (1860–1948) led American troops in the bloody trench warfare of 1917–1918. A veteran of Indian wars and the war of 1898, and the leader of the U.S. military march into Mexico in 1916, Pershing quickly developed the American Expeditionary Force to fight on the western front. He became the nation's first general of the armies, a position that Wilson created to honor him.

Wilson insisted that U.S. forces fight on the single front of western Europe. The Allies also had to carry on campaigns in the east, where Russian troops fought with waning enthusiasm, and in Italy. Wilson cared little at first about these two fronts. In his view, they involved European imperial quarrels. He asked for a declaration of war against Austria-Hungary only in late 1917, after the Russian front had finally collapsed. Congress never did declare war against Bulgaria and Turkey, Germany's other two allies. Wilson wanted to focus on the kaiser's divisions, teach him not to sink U.S. ships, then create a democratic Germany.

The western European front, moreover, was closest to the United States and easiest for U.S. troops to reach. It was, however, a front on which British and French armies were approaching a critical point by early 1917. The carnage of trench warfare had long since become unfathomable. One young Frenchman had been unable to report for duty in August 1914 because of illness. By Christmas 1914, he was the only person still alive from his school class of twenty-seven boys. In early 1917, the British and French launched one more major offensive in the teeth of German machine guns and artillery to break through the kaiser's defenses before the Americans arrived. By late summer, the Allies had suffered 1 million casualties in this single offensive—which completely failed. Generals waited for fresh American troops to sacrifice on the battlefields. "We want men, men, men," French marshal Joseph Joffre proclaimed.

Wilson was able to place only half a million Americans under arms in 1917. U.S. officials aimed at a 2-million-man army but felt that they would need eighteen months to equip it. The Allies did not have that much time. Starvation was haunting France and Russia. Both eastern and western fronts were weakening. Under great pressure, a U.S. command under General Pershing was quickly set up in Europe during May 1917. By December, 200,000 Americans were in Europe but still in training. Nevertheless, they had to go into battle. The eastern front had collapsed, and, as the new Soviet government seized power, Russian armies evaporated. In the south, the Italians suffered a disastrous defeat at Kobarid (i.e., Caporetto), a village in Yugoslavia (later made famous by Ernest Hemingway in his novel, *A Farewell to Arms*), and were in headlong retreat toward Venice.

German commanders moved their troops from these collapsed fronts to France, where they launched a major assault on Allied positions in March 1918. By April, each side had suffered a quarter of a million casualties, but the kaiser's forces were just 40 miles from Paris. In

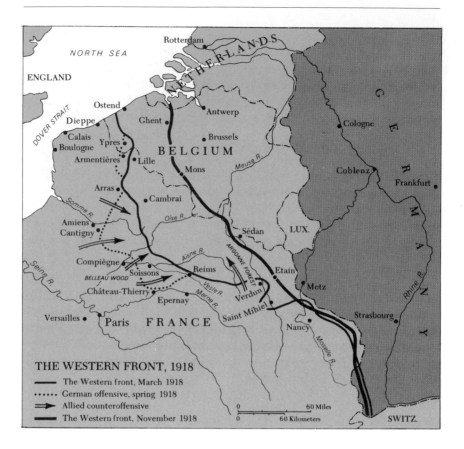

THE WESTERN FRONT, 1918

— The Western front, March 1918
····· German offensive, spring 1918
⟹ Allied counteroffensive
▬ The Western front, November 1918

May, the Americans entered combat in force. Their successful coun-
terattacks were critical in turning back the Germans along the Marne
River. Allied armies, moving along a broad front, were now spear-
headed by a new weapon—the tank—which at last gave troops mobility
and some protection. By September, 600,000 American troops launched
a decisive campaign that broke through German lines. The U.S. and
Allied armies continued to roll until the Germans asked for peace on
November 11. The offensive was the largest military effort in U.S. history. Overall, during about a year of heavy fighting, 53,402 Americans
had been killed, 204,000 wounded. Over 57,000 died from disease,
especially from the 1918 influenza epidemic that ravaged Europe and
the United States.[3]

U.S. naval policy also was fit into Wilson's broader diplomatic aims.
The navy's mission was to carry troops to Europe and defeat German
armies. To accomplish this mission, the command emphasized smaller,

submarine-hunting ships that could efficiently work together in "convoys" (a new idea) that accompanied troopships through U-boat–infested waters. This policy flew in the face of traditional military beliefs, formulated by Mahan and other naval planners since the 1890s, that the navy should depend on huge battleships capable of winning major battles by destroying the opponent's surface fleet. The core problem in 1917 was not the German battleship fleet, but submarines. On the Atlantic, unlike in European trenches, Americans worked more closely with the British to establish the convoy system. The U.S. assembly lines, meanwhile, performed miracles. Philadelphia's Hog Island could produce a 7,500-ton ship every seventy-two hours, although, as historian Warren Kimball notes, "its most long-lasting significance may be the addition of a new word . . . —'hogie,' describing a sandwich popular among the Hog Island workers."[4]

Certainly, much of the prewar American planning turned out to be useless, given Wilson's diplomatic objectives. As late as 1915, U.S. war plans included invading Canada and protecting New York City from British naval attack. Americans had mostly prepared to fight defensively.[5] In 1917–1918, they instead had to ship huge armies across thousands of miles of dangerous water so that they could go on the offensive and make the world safe for democracy.

OVER THERE: IN SOVIET RUSSIA

When Wilson inserted that famous phrase "make the world safe for democracy" in his 1917 war message, Colonel House objected. He feared some people might take it literally: "It looked too much like inciting revolution."[6] Some Russians did, indeed, incite revolution, but it had little to do with Wilson's message. Instead, the immediate cause of the Russian government's collapse in early 1917 was the breakdown of its war effort and the collapse of its ruling elite. The country could no longer marshal the resources needed to fight a three-year all-out war. Tsar Nicholas II, a weak, besieged man, retreated into seclusion, where not even his military commanders could reach him. The Duma (Parliament) demanded that the tsar surrender his power so that a more popular and liberal government could wage the war. The tsar—or, more accurately, his strong-willed wife—refused. They were then swept from power by bread riots and an army mutiny. In July 1918, revolutionary forces executed them and their children.

The Duma established a provisional government that, by July 1917, was led by Aleksandr Kerensky, a moderate socialist. Wilson and Lansing liked Kerensky because he insisted on fighting Germany despite the continued disintegration of Russian armies. The whirl of revolutionary politics worried and confused U.S. officials. They received infrequent help from their ambassador to Russia, David R. Francis, an elderly Missouri politician who had no diplomatic experience but, according to rumor, considerable romantic experience with a beautiful woman who was a suspected German spy.

In mid-1917, Wilson decided to send a special mission to Russia. It was led by Elihu Root, Roosevelt's former secretary of state and a strong conservative who found little to like in the chaos and dirt of revolution. His major pleasure came from a case of Haig & Haig Scotch Whisky that he had had the foresight to take on the journey. When Kerensky pleaded for more money, Root responded tartly, "No fight, no loan." Kerensky's fighting days, however, were quickly winding down. After reading Root's report, Secretary of State Lansing feared the worst. Kerensky, Lansing believed, was caving in to "the radical element." The secretary wanted to help Russia, if possible, but concluded that it was heading straight into a "hideous state of disorder," comparable to the great French Revolution.[7]

Kerensky's regime was finally destroyed when one of his own generals tried to overthrow him. The Russian army had so decomposed, however, that its soldiers would not obey the general. At that point, on October 24 (according to the old Russian calendar, November 7 according to the new), the Bolsheviks, or radical socialists, seized power. They were led by V. I. Lenin. Months earlier, the Germans had allowed him to cross their lines when he was on a train traveling from Switzerland to Russia. German officials bet that if he gained power, Lenin would effectively take Russia out of the war. The Bolshevik leader and his military commander, Leon Trotsky, first consolidated their power by destroying the moderate socialists. Kerensky escaped, living much of the next half-century in Stanford, California.

The Bolsheviks destroyed landed estates and distributed the land to peasants, nationalized banks, placed factories under the workers' control, and, in an all-out attack on the church, confiscated its property. To Wilson's discomfort, Lenin published the Allies' secret treaties of 1915 that parceled out the conquests of war. Wilson had tried to ignore these agreements because they undercut his own plans for an open postwar world shaped by self-determination. The president grew even more alarmed as the Bolsheviks called for world revolution and mass opposition to fighting the war.

Wilson suddenly found himself trapped. The French and British conservatives, with their colonialism and secret treaties, were on one side. Now Lenin was on the other. The Russian leader, moreover, offered a radical program that directly challenged Wilson's liberal agenda and threatened to end the war effort, especially on the eastern front. The president's closest advisers were divided over how to escape the trap. Lansing believed that Lenin and Trotsky were "German agents" who had to be destroyed by force. Colonel House, however, wanted Wilson to try to keep the new Soviet regime in the war—and undercut Lenin's growing appeal to Europe's war-ravaged peoples—by declaring fresh, liberal war aims. Wilson had instantly despised and feared Lenin's radical government, but, as historian N. Gordon Levin notes, the president's inability to choose between Lansing's and House's advice soon "gave a somewhat erratic quality to Wilsonian efforts to contain Russian Bolshevik influence."[8]

The president confided to House that he really wanted to tell the Russians to "go to hell," but he initially accepted the colonel's advice to woo the Russians and the wobbling European liberals.[9] The result was the Fourteen Points speech to Congress on January 8, 1918. The president offered a more detailed vision of a Wilsonian postwar world. But it was specially shaped to answer Lenin's demands for revolution and an end to the war without territorial annexations on either side. The points included:

1. "Open covenants of peace, openly arrived at, after which there shall be no private international understandings of any kind." This directly struck at the Allies' secret treaties.
2. "Absolute freedom of navigation upon the seas . . . alike in peace and in war."
3. A worldwide open door: "The removal, so far as possible, of all economic barriers and the establishment of an equality of trade conditions among all the nations."
4. Reduction of armaments.
5. An "adjustment of all colonial claims," with the people in colonial areas having "equal weight" in deciding their fate with the colonial powers.
6. "The evacuation of all Russian territory and such a settlement of all questions affecting Russia as will secure the best and freest co-operation of the other nations of the world in obtaining for her an unhampered and unembarrassed opportunity for the independent determination of her own political development." Russia was to be welcomed "into the society of free nations under

institutions of her own choosing" and receive "assistance." "The treatment accorded Russia by her sister nations in the months to come will be the acid test of their good will." . . .

14. "A general association of nations must be formed under specific covenants for the purpose of affording mutual guarantees of political independence and territorial integrity to great and small states alike."

The president also demanded that Germany leave Belgian and French territory. He wanted territorial problems in Italy, the collapsing Austro-Hungarian Empire, the Turkish Empire, and "an independent Polish state" to be largely taken care of by the people in the regions—or, what he called in one case, "along clearly recognizable lines of nationality."[10] During the remainder of the war, he added thirteen more points to his plan, but the original fourteen proved to be the most important in the debate over peace terms that soon raged in Europe and the United States.

Lenin was not moved by Wilson's appeal. Looking first to his own and his country's survival, the Bolshevik was unswerving in his determination to make peace with Germany. On March 3, 1918, he signed the Treaty of Brest Litovsk, and did so despite German terms that in a moment destroyed centuries of Russian expansion. Poland, Finland, and the Baltic States were taken from the new government. Even the rich Russian breadbasket, the Ukraine, became independent. Russia had left the war—or, more accurately, had exchanged one conflict for another; for anti-Bolshevik forces, led by conservative White Russian armies, launched a civil war to overthrow Lenin's regime.

Wilson now faced another stark decision: whether to ignore the civil war or help the White armies. For the most part, the American public was savagely anti-Lenin and showed considerable confusion about Russian affairs by calling him and Trotsky "willing German tools." Russians, who had been "democratic at heart" a year before, now became mere "children" unfit for self-government. The New York Times reflected the frustration by predicting ninety-one times between 1917 and 1919 that the Bolsheviks must surely be ready to collapse.[11] Wilson shared the anger and frustration, but he knew that any direct attempt to overthrow Lenin would be difficult, if not impossible, especially since the Russian people would cluster around the Bolsheviks to fight foreign invaders. In April 1918, however, Japanese forces moved into Siberia. Tokyo officials claimed that they only wanted to ensure the operation of the Trans-Siberian Railroad and help anti-German forces in the region. The Japanese received support from the British and

French. The Europeans also pressured Wilson to intervene. The president turned down six such requests between January and May 1918.

The turn came in mid-1918. In May and June, 20,000 Czech soldiers, who had been fighting the Germans on the collapsed eastern front, began to move east to find transportation and fight elsewhere. When Soviet troops tried to disarm them, fighting broke out. The Czechs reached and occupied the Russian eastern port of Vladivostok, then asked the Allies for help. A State Department officer quickly saw the request as a " 'God-send.' " Lansing used it to convince the president to move into Russia. On July 6, Wilson surrendered. He agreed to send several thousand U.S. troops to Vladivostok to help the Czech soldiers and to guard Allied military stores. But Wilson also wanted it both ways: on the one hand, he announced that the forces must stay out of Russia's internal affairs and that he would have nothing to do with British or French intervention; on the other hand, the president planned to use the move as an excuse to send in a political mission that would test Lenin's "intentions."[12]

At almost the same time (July 1918), Wilson agreed to send several U.S. battalions to intervene in the northern Russian port of Murmansk. Working under British command and with British troops, this intervention was originally aimed at saving large amounts of Allied military supplies that had been landed to help the prerevolutionary Russian armies and to prevent a German takeover of the surrounding region. But the U.S. and British troops soon found themselves pressured by Soviet, not German, forces. All the while claiming that he did not want to interfere in Russia's internal affairs, Wilson intervened with U.S. troops not once, but twice—in eastern as well as in northern Russia.

In September 1918, three U.S. battalions arrived at Vladivostok. Wilson's motives were complex. He helped the Czechs, but he also moved the 10,000 U.S. soldiers into eastern Russia to watch Japanese ambitions in the region. By participating, the president believed that he could also moderate British and especially French plans to become more deeply involved in the Russian civil war. But he was clearly working with the anti-Bolshevik forces in that war himself. Wilson dispatched his army not only to help the Czechs, but to help determine internal Russian affairs—one major reason why U.S. troops remained in the country until 1920, long after Germany's surrender in November 1918. In 1918–1920, 222 Americans lost their lives in this intervention.

Wilson had ringed his intervention with many conditions so that he would not be seen as a political bedfellow of the British and French.

But at this point (January–July 1918), Wilsonian liberals and Leninist communists joined a battle that was to rage through most of the twentieth century. Lenin challenged the liberals' view of how the world worked and was to work. He argued that, contrary to Wilson's belief, socioeconomic classes could not coexist but were fated to fight to the death. To prove the evil intent of Wilson's "associates," Lenin published the secret treaties that made a mockery of self-determination. He asked for immediate self-determination, regardless of the effect on the war effort of the colonial empires. As historian Lloyd Gardner observes, Lenin had "absconded with the biggest piece of liberal theory: the principle of self-determination. Liberals were never able afterwards . . . to reclaim nationalism for their own. . . . Little wonder Wilson sweat blood over Russia."[13]

The president even began to lose young liberals in his own government. Russian experts in the State Department unsuccessfully opposed the growing antibolshevism in the administration.[14] They were led by William Christian Bullitt, a wealthy Main Line Philadelphian who was close to Colonel House. By September 1918, as the Allied intervention was clearly failing to weaken Lenin, Bullitt outlined the dilemma that would repeatedly face U.S. officials. The number of Allied troops, he argued, was not enough to overthrow the Bolsheviks, but enough to scare the Russians—perhaps, God forbid, even to drive them "into military alliance with Germany" against the Allies. What could be done? Perhaps, Bullitt wrote House, Japan should send in half a million men "to overthrow the Soviets," or, on the other hand, the United States could open relations with Lenin. The point was, he concluded, that affairs were so bad that "I do not know [what to do]. And you do not know. And the President does not know."[15]

But the president had let slip one conclusion after he heard that Lenin had made peace with Germany. The only way to deal with the kaiser, Wilson exclaimed, was "Force, Force to the utmost, Force without stint or limit, the righteous and Triumphant Force which shall make Right the law of the world, and cast every selfish dominion down in the dust."[16] It certainly was not "peace without victory." Trapped between the European conservatives who wanted to return to their 1913 world (without the German military) and the Russian Bolsheviks who rushed to create a classless world regardless of cost, Wilson tried to break free by using unilateral U.S. force, both in western Europe and in Russia. In Mexico's revolution five years earlier, Wilson had intervened twice with U.S. forces but had failed to put his own "good men" in office. Now it was to be seen whether he could succeed in another such venture—this time on a global scale, in a world torn between the "forces of order" and the "forces of movement," as Arno Mayer terms them.[17] Against his will and contrary to his intentions when he took Americans into war, Wilson had already been compelled to choose one of those sides as he traveled to the Paris peace conference of 1919.

Preparing for Paris

Despite his twists and turns forced by Lenin's challenge, Wilson knew what he wanted to accomplish at the peace conference. His general objective was to reconstruct the world along the lines of the Fourteen Points. He hoped to reach that new world through self-determination, free trade, and a league of nations that would be able to oversee and make necessary adjustments in the cumbersome mechanism of global power politics.

This neat package began to come undone as soon as the Germans approached Wilson in October 1918 and offered to surrender on the basis of the Fourteen Points. On close examination, many of the points were maddeningly general. Wilson had ordered a group of advisers, called The Inquiry, to elaborate his peace plan, but when it did produce specific proposals, the president often ignored them and went off on his own.[18] Colonel House, suddenly faced with the need to negotiate with Germany, desperately tracked down young Walter Lippmann in Paris and said: "You helped write these points. Now you must give me a precise definition of each one. I shall need it by tomorrow morning at ten o'clock."[19] Lippmann worked all night to produce a draft, but given the incredible complexity of the problems facing the victors, it was an ominous sign of how ill-prepared Wilson was to enter into tough, lengthy talks.

He had, moreover, already compromised two of the Fourteen Points. The British flatly refused to accept Point 2 on freedom of the seas. They would not endanger their fleet's ability to control their strategic water routes. Prime Minister David Lloyd George pointed out, moreover, that Wilson had fully cooperated with British maritime restrictions after the United States entered the war. The president backed down. On Point 6—the evacuation of Russia and the self-determination of its future—Wilson had failed his own "acid test" by intervening and maintaining U.S. forces in Russia.

The president hoped to overcome these problems through the force of his own personal popularity and eloquence, and also through the

This painting by Johansen, Signing of the Treaty of Versailles, *not only pictures the Big Four in front, but catches the grandeur and historical significance of an occasion that would soon become the center of a heated debate in the United States.*

new, extraordinary power of the United States. Without doubt, Wilson did emerge from the war as the world's most popular and powerful individual. When he arrived in Europe in late 1918, millions of people greeted his triumphal tour by throwing flowers in his path. But his major opponents at Paris were to be not the German diplomats, but Lloyd George of Great Britain and the crusty, aged premier of France, Georges Clemenceau. Those two victors immediately realized that Wilson had made a near-fatal mistake in the 1918 U.S. congressional elections. He had asked Americans to give him a Democratic Congress to help him make the peace. Republicans struck back by crying that he impugned their patriotism and, after all they had done for the war effort, was accusing them of being un-American. The Republicans won the election and were able to put Wilson's archenemy, Henry Cabot Lodge, in control of the Senate Foreign Relations Committee that would have to accept or reject Wilson's work at Paris. The president then compounded his defeat by naming a peace commission, which he personally headed, that included not a single senator or Republican leader. In his defiance of Lodge, in his determination to dominate the commission, Wilson made a tactical blunder. If no Republican leader was to be involved as an architect, then the Republicans felt no responsibility for protecting the structure of the peace that Wilson brought back from Paris.

Meanwhile, Lloyd George's government won re-election by one of the largest margins in British history. In Paris, Clemenceau was given an overwhelming vote of confidence in the French Chamber of Deputies. Lloyd George suspected that Theodore Roosevelt better represented American, especially congressional, views, but the prime minister had to deal with Wilson. When the president threatened to appeal over Lloyd George's head to the British people on the freedom-of-the-seas issue, the prime minister called his bluff and dared him to try. Wilson dropped the challenge. Lloyd George called the president's threat an "unloaded blunderbuss" that intimidated neither him nor Clemenceau.[20]

The president also planned to use his country's new economic power as a weapon. During the war, he had held off pressing his postwar vision on the Allies because it would have led to disputes, perhaps even a crippling of the war effort. But Wilson did not mind. As he told Colonel House in mid-1917: "When the war is over, we can force [England and France] to our way of thinking, because by that time they will be financially in our hands."[21] And they were. By 1918, the Allies owed the United States over $3.5 billion. New York City was surpassing London as the world's financial center. But Wilson could never discover how magically to turn this power against the British and French (or the Bolsheviks).

The president did not help himself when, with the war's last shot, he pulled U.S. government representatives out of all the councils that had been established during the conflict to plan and finance the Allied war effort cooperatively. True to his pledge to build an open world, he refused to make any "special arrangements" to help Europeans rebuild their countries.[22] If they wanted help, they, like everyone else, had to go to New York private banks—not to Washington. Wilson was going to get the government out of the marketplace as rapidly as possible. That decision weakened his own economic leverage against Lloyd George and Clemenceau. Moreover, Wilson (and later presidents) learned that there were certain policies that just could not be purchased. Clemenceau's determination to ensure French security by crippling Germany had no price tag attached to it. Most nations do not place a purchase price on policies that they believe are required for their survival.

Such feelings were especially rampant in Europe after the horrors it had just experienced. Eight million soldiers and sailors had died. Over 1 million French soldiers had perished. Approximately 20 million civilians had died during the war and its immediate aftermath. More than 4,000 towns had been wiped off the map of France. Great Britain had suffered 900,000 troops killed and 2 million wounded. As Lloyd George put it, "Not a shack" had been destroyed in the United States. Americans, instead, had gotten much richer, even as the Europeans sacrificed millions of men and billions in treasure. "See that little stream?" novelist F. Scott Fitzgerald had a character say as he visited the site of the bloody Somme Valley battle. "We could walk to it in two minutes. It took the British a whole month to walk to it—a whole empire walked very slowly backward a few inches a day, leaving the dead behind like a million bloody rugs."[23]

Against that background of corpses and collapsing civilization, Clemenceau determined to protect French interests not with vague Wilsonian principles, but with boundary and economic agreements that protected France and crippled Germany. The Russian Revolution increased Clemenceau's concern. Not only did Lenin's victory threaten to radicalize much of Europe, but it destroyed France's valued prewar partner, tsarist Russia. Clemenceau had to find a new alliance arrangement. Wilson, meanwhile, sought agreement to his principles for an open, democratic world. While Clemenceau was driven by centuries of French history, Wilson believed, "If I didn't feel that I was the personal instrument of God I couldn't carry on."[24] After the peace conference, Lloyd George remarked, "I think I did as well as might be expected, seated as I was between Jesus Christ and Napoleon Bonaparte."[25] If it were true, moreover, that God helps those who help themselves, then even Wilson was in trouble. He failed to think through his own policies and suffered from severe, self-inflicted political wounds as he approached the conference table.

THE "BLACK CLOUD" OVER PARIS

Colonel House looked at war-devastated Europe, sized up the attractiveness of Lenin's message to millions of Europeans, then concluded, "We are sitting upon an open powder magazine and some day a spark may ignite it."[26] Sparks were everywhere. After the kaiser fled Germany in November 1918, the country came under a moderate Socialist government. In January 1919, Karl Liebknecht and Rosa Luxemburg tried to imitate Lenin's success. A Communist Germany was narrowly averted as right-wing troops smashed the attempted coup and killed Liebknecht and Luxemburg. Wilson had believed that Germany

TABLE 2
PRINCIPAL WARS IN WHICH THE UNITED STATES PARTICIPATED: U.S. MILITARY PERSONNEL SERVING AND CASUALTIES

War/conflict	Branch of service	Number serving	Casualties		
			Battle deaths	Other deaths	Wounds not mortal
World War I (6 Apr. 1917–11 Nov. 1918)	*Total*	4,734,991	53,402	63,114	204,002
	Army	4,057,101	50,510	55,868	193,663
	Navy	599,051	431	6,856	819
	Marines	78,839	2,461	390	9,520
World War II (7 Dec. 1941–31 Dec. 1946)	*Total*	16,112,566	291,557	113,842	670,846
	Army	11,260,000	234,874	83,400	565,861
	Navy	4,183,466	36,950	25,664	37,778
	Marines	669,100	19,733	4,778	67,207

Source: Department of Defense.

required major social change before it was ready for democracy, but communism was certainly not what he had in mind.

Radical Socialists did gain power in Hungary. In March 1919, moreover, Lenin established the Third International of the Socialist parties in an attempt to destroy the Second International, which moderate Socialists controlled. Western officials understood that the new organization was nothing less than Lenin's attempt to create a worldwide Communist party network under his control. In September, two Communist parties even appeared—with few members but much noise—in the United States.

The Big Three (i.e., Lloyd George, Clemenceau, and Wilson) had to work out a settlement amid spreading revolution. They also had to deal with the collapsing European empires in Asia, Africa, and the Middle East as nationalist leaders turned to Lenin as a model. While the victors met in Paris, Asians and Africans met in another part of the city to prepare their own demands. (One participant was young Ho Chi Minh, who between 1930 and 1969 led Vietnam against French, Japanese, and U.S. military forces to complete the task he had set upon in 1919.)

Ray Stannard Baker, Wilson's first major biographer and the president's friend, caught the picture. As the Big Three tried to reorder the world, there arose this "black cloud of the east, threatening to overwhelm and swallow up the world." Baker concluded that "Paris cannot be understood without Moscow." Lenin was never invited to the conference, but "the Bolsheviki and Bolshevism were powerful elements at every turn. Russia played a more vital part at Paris than [Germany]! For the Prussian idea had been utterly defeated, while the Russian idea was still rising in power."[27] As Lloyd George admitted, he found it nearly impossible to discuss Germany without mentioning Russia.

The French proposed to make the "black cloud" disappear through direct military action. Lloyd George objected. He had neither the finances nor the political support at home to embark on a crusade to overthrow Lenin. He confided, moreover, "I dread wild adventures in lands whose conditions are unknown, and," he added in a pointed reference to the last French army of Napoleon's that had marched on Moscow, "where nothing but catastrophe has awaited every Empire and every Army that has ever invaded them."[28] Wilson sided with Lloyd George on this point, but he refused to go along when the prime minister suggested recognizing Lenin's regime as a first step to dealing with it.

Wilson and Clemenceau only agreed to have their agents meet Lenin at the island of Prinkipo (now Büyükada), a site off the coast of Turkey, to discuss terms. The leaders in Paris chose the island so that Bolshevik diplomats could reach it without traveling through any European country in which they might spread their germs of revolution. Lenin agreed to talks and even offered to repay pre-1917 loans and give up territory if the Big Three would pledge not to interfere in Soviet affairs. He promised noninterference in other nations' domestic politics, but added that he could not control revolutionaries or propaganda in those countries. Clemenceau and Wilson disliked Lenin's response. Moreover, Russian exiles in Paris and agents of the White Russian Army lobbied hard to kill the Prinkipo talks. The meeting was never held.

Wilson, under great pressure from Colonel House and young liberals in the U.S. delegation, finally agreed to send William Bullitt to sound out Lenin in Moscow. Bullitt returned in April 1919 with terms that he believed held promise. Wilson, pleading that he was ill, refused to see him. The French ignored the young American. Bullitt and the other liberals began to move into opposition to the president. In reality, it was too late for Wilson to try to work out an agreement with Lenin. The president had chosen to try to contain Bolsheviks, not talk with them. He allowed his food administrator, Herbert Hoover, to help bring down the Hungarian Communist government by manipulating food supplies. When the Communists threatened Austria, Hoover again helped stop them by posting notices that such action would "jeopardize" Vienna's food supply.[29]

In 1920, Wilson announced that the United States would not officially recognize the Soviet government because the latter preached revolution and refused to honor international obligations. But Lenin refused to disappear. By late 1920, Trotsky's Red Army had smashed counter-revolutionary forces and had even driven into Poland before being pushed back. Lenin set up a deadly efficient secret police, the Cheka, to destroy internal opposition. Marxist-Leninist revolutionary ideology had been wedded to the power of the Russian state. The "black cloud of the east" was casting long shadows.

AT PARIS: THE PRICE OF THE COVENANT

Twenty-seven Allied and Associated nations began deliberations in Paris on January 12, 1919. The major decisions, however, were made by the most powerful: Wilson, Lloyd George, Clemenceau, and Italian Premier Orlando. This Big Four shrank to a Big Three after Orlando stalked out because of a dispute with Wilson over Italian claims.

The Big Four first tackled the question of the losers', especially Germany's, colonies. In the secret Treaty of London in 1915, the Allies had already divided many of these areas among themselves. Wilson, however, refused to agree. He urged that smaller nations be responsible for the former colonies under a League-of-Nations mandate. He ran into a stone wall of opposition from Japan (which wanted Germany's colonies in the Pacific north of the equator), Great Britain (which had its eyes on the Pacific colonies south of the equator as well as on oil-producing regions in the Middle East), and France. General Jan Christiaan Smuts of South Africa offered a compromise: the great powers would take over the colonies but under a League mandate. Wilson accepted this "mandate" principle.

Liberals quickly attacked him for allowing the victors to seize the spoils and even gain moral approval by doing it under the proposed League's banner. They also complained that Germany had nothing to say about these decisions, nor was it to be in any way compensated for these heavy losses. The policy certainly had nothing to do with self-determination. It seemed more like glorified imperialism. Even Smuts's South Africa emerged with control over the former German colony of South-West Africa. (Under the name of Namibia, the region would continue to be fought over more than half a century later.) Wilson wanted nothing for the United States, but the Allies insisted. He ended with a mandate over chaotic, starving Armenia and Constantinople in the disintegrated Ottoman Empire. Lansing estimated that it would take 50,000 U.S. troops to control this mandate. In 1920, the U.S. Senate disdainfully rejected the responsibility.

The president accepted the unfortunate mandate policy in part because he was intent on rushing on to discuss his League-of-Nations proposal. Lloyd George, Clemenceau, and most others disagreed. They urgently wanted to deal with Germany, which had been in limbo and had been threatened by a Communist takeover since the armistice two months earlier. Wilson persisted and won his point. Germany had to wait nearly four more months for a peace treaty that was written hurriedly and badly. The president, however, had convinced himself that the final treaty might, indeed, have problems, but that a properly created League of Nations could correct those problems over time.

Working largely on his own and with too little consultation with The Inquiry or other advisers, Wilson wrote out a covenant for the League in just ten days. He then left Paris on February 14, 1919, for a month of business in Washington. Wilson lobbied hard at home for his Covenant, including a lengthy, tough, give-and-take evening session with congressional leaders at the White House. He learned that the Monroe Doctrine had to be explicitly protected if the Senate were to accept the Covenant. Even then, a number of Republicans warned that they would accept the peace treaty, but not the Covenant. Wilson shot back that he intended to tie together the treaty and Covenant so tightly that the senators would have to accept both if they wanted cither. On March 4, Senator Henry Cabot Lodge dropped his bombshell. He had circulated a Republican round robin, declaring the League, "as now proposed," unacceptable. Thirty-nine senators—well over the one-third needed to defeat Wilson's pact—signed Lodge's challenge.

With his hatred for Lodge refreshed, the president returned to Paris in March determined to undercut the round robin. He insisted that the Paris delegates specifically protect such U.S. interests as certain domestic issues (including immigration, tariff, and racial policies) and, above all, the Monroe Doctrine. They did so, but only after Wilson was reduced to making a series of trades that weakened both his moral authority and the principles in the Fourteen Points. He had already surrendered Point 2 (freedom of the seas) at British insistence. Perhaps, however, his most notable and costly decision was allowing Japan to remain in Shantung. Formerly under German authority, Shantung was part of China and included some 30 million Chinese. Japan was already bitter because Wilson and the European leaders had refused to agree to include a clause in the Covenant that would uphold racial equality. When Wilson also rejected their claim to Shantung, the Japanese threatened to leave both Paris and the proposed League. The president surrendered. He felt that it was more important to have Japan in the League than to uphold self-determination. It was a horrible dilemma, and his choice further alienated liberals (such as Bullitt) in the American delegation.

Wilson called Article 10 the "heart of the Covenant." It provided that each member pledge "to respect and preserve as against external aggression the territorial integrity and existing political independence of all Members of the League." This article, aiming at orderly change in the world community (and even then only when League members consented), became the center of Wilson's later struggle with the U.S. Senate. To enforce Article 10, the delegates accepted Article 16, which provided that if members were attacked, all other nations in the League would economically isolate the aggressor. The League could also recommend the use of military force.

AT PARIS: A "SANITARY CORDON"
INSTEAD OF A "SANITARY EUROPE"

The president obtained his Covenant, but the more important question was what kind of a world the new League would have to oversee. The answer to that depended on how the conference dealt with the traditional center of world power, Europe, and, specifically, how it treated Germany. Wilson and Clemenceau sharply differed. The "Tiger," as Clemenceau was appropriately known, wanted to dismember Germany so that its southwestern coal and iron regions would fall under French control. He also demanded that the Germans be held guilty for all the war's destruction and be made to pay reparations—hundreds of billions of dollars of reparations—for those damages. Such incredible payments would obviously cripple Germany's economy for decades. That was just fine with most French.

Wilson warned that Clemenceau's policy could only produce a sick, unbalanced Europe and more wars. The president had no hope of obtaining his healthy, open-trading world without a healthy and viable Europe at its center. Nor could Germany be dismembered without the principle of self-determination being made a total mockery. Above all, as he had earlier warned the British, "the spirit of the Bolsheviki is lurking everywhere." Germany was Lenin's prime target: "If we humiliate the German people and drive them too far, we shall destroy all form of government, and Bolshevism will take its place. We ought not to ground them to powder or there will be nothing to build up from."[30] The struggle with Clemenceau became so consuming that in early April, Wilson became seriously ill. Exhausted, he was confined to bed with a temperature of 103 degrees. The Tiger had little compassion. As the president stood his ground, Clemenceau bitterly accused him of being "pro-German." Wilson immediately ordered his ship, the *George Washington*, to prepare to sail back to the United States. He was ready to break up the conference. Cooler heads then prevailed, both men backed down, and deals were struck.

Clemenceau gave up his demand for French annexation of much of the German Rhineland and control of the remainder. In turn, Wilson and Lloyd George agreed that French armies could occupy the Rhineland for fifteen years. Most surprisingly, Wilson signed a security treaty with France that guaranteed its borders with Germany. Against the advice of many of his advisers, he thus signed the most entangling of alliances. But it was the price he willingly paid to keep western Ger-

A cartoonist depicts a critical view of the "Tiger," Georges Clemenceau of France, who is saying that he thinks he hears a child crying. The "child" is the generation who would fight World War II. Wilson is at far right.

many in German hands. The defeated Central Powers were to be demilitarized and any necessary German military forces sharply limited. On the critical reparations issue, Germany was forced to sign a "war guilt" clause, but the total amount of payments was to be left to a reparations commission. Thus, Clemenceau won his principle, but Wilson believed the commission of experts would scale down the actual figure. The bill turned out to be $33 billion, far more than Germany was able to pay (especially after being effectively stripped of its colonies and parts of the Rhineland) but far less than Clemenceau had demanded.

With Germany's western boundaries settled, the Big Three turned to the highly sensitive question of its eastern regions—that is, the areas touching eastern and southern Europe where the distintegration of the Russian and Austro-Hungarian empires left only near-chaos. Wilson, of course, had a formula to propose. The boundaries of such new, independent nations as Poland and Czechoslovakia were to be settled by self-determination. But two problems plagued Wilson's approach. First, victors such as Japan and Italy cared more about acquiring nearby territory for their security and economic needs than about upholding vague principles. When Italy claimed a strip that was inhabited by

The victors at Versailles had pieced Europe back together after the devastation of World War I but, in doing so, sacrificed the principle of self-determination in order to create a Europe that they hoped could hold back bolshevism.

Yugoslavs (Croats), Wilson, operating on his belief that the masses were more moral than their governments, went over Italian Premier Orlando's head and appealed directly to the Italian people. For Wilson, however, this Orlando had no dawn. The Italian leader angrily walked out of Paris. The Italians not unnaturally chose their own government's position over the American president's. Wilson backed off. Orlando finally returned. After the peace conference concluded, the Italians and Yugoslavs settled the dispute themselves.

Wilson's second problem was more general. If the principle of self-determination was applied to eastern Europe, the nations might embrace bolshevism. Hungary was already coming under the control of native Communists. Wilson was forced again to choose between his principle and European security. The result was a compromised eastern Europe. Poland, for example, received special access to the Baltic Sea through Danzig, which was made a free port although it was wholly German. Only Lloyd George's and Wilson's determination prevented Clemenceau from giving Danzig to Poland directly. An area with several million Germans also came under Czechoslovakia's control so that with this region—the Sudetenland—the Czech borders could be made more secure.

France brilliantly turned these arrangements to its advantage. It negotiated a series of pacts with the new nations in eastern and southern Europe to tie them into a security system dominated by Paris. But France's paper diplomacy—making treaties with Wilson to fix Germany's western boundary and with the smaller nations to contain Germany to the east—deceived. In reality, the Big Three placed the new, weaker states of Poland and Czechoslovakia between the two outcasts, Germany and Russia. The smaller states, thus, had to carry an enormous burden: containing both Russian and German ambitions as well as acting as a buffer to prevent bolshevism from moving westward to Germany. It, indeed, turned out to be a crushing burden. These states were too weak economically and politically to carry out such a policy.

Walter Lippmann, once an ardent Wilsonian but, by 1920, bitterly disillusioned by what he had witnessed in Paris, defined the problem when he returned to the United States: the Big Three had created a "sanitary cordon" to block Germany and Russia militarily, when they should have created a "sanitary Europe."[31]

In Washington: The Defeat of the Covenant

Wilson came home determined to obtain Senate approval of his work at Paris. His determination seemed to rise as he was forced to compromise his original plans and as opposition gathered on Capitol Hill. Perhaps a majority of Americans wanted to join the League in 1919–1920. No one will ever know. It is certain, however, that two major groups of opponents awaited to attack Wilson's handiwork, and he played into their hands.

The first group of opponents earned the name "Irreconcilables." Numbering about twelve, they were led by old Progressive Republican senators such as William Borah of Idaho and Hiram Johnson of California. They opposed U.S. membership in any kind of organization resembling the League. This group especially feared being drawn in to defend the interests of such colonial powers as Great Britain and France. Instead, most Irreconcilables wanted to focus on problems at home and, when they did act abroad, to show sympathy for revolutions in Russia and China. They did not want to withdraw from the world, but, as Johnson declared, "I am opposed to American boys policing

Hiram Johnson (on the left) was a powerful Progressive Republican senator from California. William Borah of Idaho led the opposition to war in 1917 and to the Versailles Treaty in 1919–1920. Borah, also a Progressive Republican, and Johnson led the Irreconcilables, who most bitterly fought Wilson's policies—including the president's refusal to recognize the Soviet Union.

Europe and quelling riots in every new nation's back yard."[32] Refusing to guarantee the badly drawn European borders, the Irreconcilables also condemned the Covenant, especially Article 10.

They were joined in that condemnation by a second group of opponents, the "reservationists," led by Senator Henry Cabot Lodge, the powerful Republican chairman of the Foreign Relations Committee. This group included such leading figures outside the Senate as Hughes, Taft, and Hoover. Lodge and Roosevelt had grown to hate Wilson personally; especially for what they believed to be the president's weak-kneed response to the Mexican Revolution and German submarine attacks. TR suddenly died in January 1919 at age sixty (he had never recovered from the death of his son, Quentin, on a European battlefield), and Lodge redoubled his opposition to Wilson's grand plan. But the senator also objected to the peace treaties on grounds of substance.

Along with the Irreconcilables and many liberals, the reservationists hated the deal on Shantung. When Lodge's committee considered the treaty, he pointedly substituted "China" in every spot in which Wilson had put "Japan" in dealing with the former German colonies in China. Wilson was furious. American missionaries and businessmen in China were delighted. The Lodge group also continued to believe that internal U.S. issues and especially the Monroe Doctrine were not adequately protected.

Above all, the reservationists feared Article 10. It locked the United States into having to act with the weakening European colonial powers. It also threatened Congress's power to declare war. When Wilson was asked directly whether the United States would have to act automatically if the League put Article 10 into effect, he tried to wiggle free: the commitment "constitutes a very grave and solemn moral obligation. But it is a moral, not a legal obligation, and leaves our Congress absolutely free. . . . It is binding in conscience only, not in law." His response was not good enough. Most of the Senate, as well as Wilson, took a "moral obligation" seriously. Under Article 10, the United States might—as Lansing had to admit before a congressional committee— support Japan's control of Shantung against valid Chinese claims, and Congress would have to go along with this "moral obligation." The famed economist, Thorstein Veblen, condemned the provision directly: it seemed "in effect to validate existing empires." Wilson vehemently denied that Article 10 opposed revolution, but he was never able to explain why. As historian William Widenor concludes, Article 10 was "*the* obstacle to ratification," because "the nature of the obligation assumed by Member States would determine what kind of organization the League would be."[33]

Neither the Irreconcilables nor the reservationists wanted to undertake that kind of obligation. But Lodge, who was certainly more sympathetic to British and French interests than was Borah, offered a compromise. He added fourteen points of his own to modify Wilson's Covenant. They aimed at removing any automatic U.S. commitment to the League's principles. Not surprisingly, the president refused such a compromise. He decided to go to the people. In September 1919, the president embarked on a cross-country speaking tour to whip up support for the League. Frustrated with the politics of Washington, he once again resorted to speechmaking so that his cause could transcend the grimy political arena. Working day and night, the sixty-three-year-old Wilson—already in questionable health from his angry encounters with Clemenceau—delivered thirty-six formal speeches in just twenty-three days. On September 26 at Pueblo, Colorado, he suffered a para-lytic stroke. The broken president immediately returned to Washing-ton. But assisted by his strong-willed wife, who rigidly controlled access to her husband, Wilson fought every attempt to compromise with Lodge. He received little help from House, with whom Wilson had broken after arguments in Paris. Lansing soon moved over to agree with many of Lodge's reservations. Disillusioned with Wilson (Lansing said that the president's mind was as clear as a pool ball), the secretary of state, in historian Dimitri Lazo's words, "encouraged" the Senate opposition with his "sarcastic commentary" about the treaty. In February 1920, Wilson fired him.[34] Such young liberals as Bullitt and Lippmann had already left the U.S. peace delegation and now actively opposed the president.

Historian Thomas Knock has noted that Wilson tried to put together a "progressive internationalist coalition"—a group of liberals who believed in self-determination, anti-imperialism, and even democratic socialism. But by November 1919, due in part to Wilson's own actions, hope for such crucial political support lay in ruins as the Senate pre-pared to vote on the Covenant.[35] The fear of bolshevism had spread to the United States, especially after a bomb exploded outside the home of Attorney General A. Mitchell Palmer in June 1919. Between November 1919 and January 1920, Palmer issued 3,000 arrest war-rants and deported more than 500 aliens suspected of Bolshevist sym-pathies. The country was gripped by the "Red Scare." Wilson was not innocent of blame. During the war, his administration had helped inflame nationalist passions by passing an espionage act and a sedition act that allowed the government to arrest newspaper editors and others who were merely suspected of being critical of the war effort. Passions were out of hand. In Collinsville, Illinois, for example, a mob had decided that a town resident was a German spy and had then seized him, wrapped him in a U.S. flag, and murdered him. When Socialist party leader Eugene V. Debs condemned the war, he was jailed. Wilson kept him in prison until 1921, when President Warren G. Harding finally par-doned Debs. The administration's propaganda committee, directed by George Creel, played to fears of conspiracy and loudly protested Len-in's treachery in making peace with Germany. With few exceptions (historian Charles A. Beard of Columbia University was one), Ameri-can intellectuals joined in the crusade.

Thus, the atmosphere was already poisoned when Wilson turned to Palmer in 1919 and ordered him not "to let this country see Red." In his 1919 tour, the president tried to gather support for his cause by

Captioned "Refusing to Give the Lady a Seat," this cartoon caricatures the three leading senators who opposed Wilson's handiwork at Paris and warns about the consequences of their opposition.

arguing that "there are apostles of Lenin in our own midst" and by warning about "the poison of disorder, the poison of revolt" that may actually have entered "into the veins of this free people." Wilson was trying to make the case that only his League could provide the antidote to this "poison." But, as historian Lloyd Gardner writes, Americans most feared that "the League would mean an increase in contacts with the poison-infected areas of the world." Or as Wilson himself cried, "This thing reaches the depths of tragedy."[36]

On November 19, in this supercharged environment, the Senate defeated the treaty containing Lodge's reservations 39 to 55. On Wilson's orders not to compromise, loyal Democrats joined the Irreconcilables to vote down the measure. Over the winter, however, public pressure built for reconsideration. Lodge's own opposition moderated. He was probably moving toward a deal with the Democrats when the Irreconcilables pulled him back, and Wilson once again refused to discuss such a deal. On March 19, 1920, the Senate again voted on the treaty that contained Lodge's reservations. This time a majority was in favor (49 to 35), but the number was short of the necessary two-thirds. Twelve Irreconcilables lined up with twenty-three diehard Wilsonian

Democrats to kill the measure, which again had a series of fifteen reservations attached. In 1921, the United States officially ended its role in the war by signing separate peace treaties with Germany and Austria.

Wilson actually hoped to recover from his paralysis and win an unprecedented third term in 1920 so that he could renew and win the fight for the League. Democratic party bosses never seriously considered his candidacy, throwing him a sop only by agreeing to make the campaign a "solemn referendum" on the Covenant. A U.S. presidential election is never a referendum on a single issue, however. Both the Republican ticket, led by Senator Warren G. Harding of Ohio, and the Democrats, headed by Ohio governor James Cox (with young New Yorker Franklin D. Roosevelt as the vice-presidential nominee), fudged the League issue until voters could not tell exactly where the candidates did stand.

Harding won an overwhelming victory by 7 million votes. The problem of restoring war-torn Europe and revolutionary Asia now fell to the Republicans. The League became a secondary issue, as well it might, for the central problem in 1919–1920 and after was not the Covenant, but the specific terms of boundaries, reparations, and mandates that the Paris peace conference produced. Historian Kendrick Clements believes that it is "perfect nonsense" to assume that U.S. membership in the League could have prevented the horrors of the 1930s.[37] Those catastrophes were rooted in the 1919 peace terms, not in the Covenant. Wilson bequeathed to Harding those treaties, a policy of containing (but not formally recognizing) the Soviet Union, and a world threatened with revolution. But the broken president was convinced that he only failed in part: "The world has been made safe for democracy. . . . But democracy has not yet made the world safe against irrational revolution."[38] It was up to Harding and, as it turned out, to all of his successors to deal with this more difficult problem of "revolution," both irrational and rational.

NOTES

1. *The Record of American Diplomacy*, ed. Ruhl J. Bartlett, 4th ed. (New York, 1964), pp. 456–457.
2. Dean Acheson, "The Eclipse of the State Department," *Foreign Affairs* 49 (July 1971): 598.

3. Allan R. Millett and Peter Maslowski, *For the Common Defense* (New York, 1984), pp. 344–346, 350–352, 356–358.
4. *Churchill and Roosevelt: The Complete Correspondence*, ed. Warren Kimball, 3 vols. (Princeton, 1984), I, p. 88. A useful short analysis on naval strategy is David F. Trask, "Woodrow Wilson and World War I," in *American Diplomacy in the Twentieth Century*, ed. Warren F. Kimball (St. Louis, 1980), pp. 7–10.
5. J. A. S. Grenville and George B. Young, *Politics, Strategy, and American Diplomacy, 1873–1917* (New Haven, 1966), pp. 330–336.
6. Christopher Lasch, *The New Radicalism in America, 1889–1963* (New York, 1965), pp. 200–201.
7. Robert Lansing, *War Memoirs of Robert Lansing, Secretary of State* (Indianapolis, 1935), pp. 337–338.
8. N. Gordon Levin, Jr., *Woodrow Wilson and World Politics* (New York, 1968), pp. 50–51; Lansing, pp. 343–345.
9. Edward M. Bennett, *Recognition of Russia: An American Foreign Policy Dilemma* (Waltham, Mass., 1970), p. 26.
10. *Record of American Diplomacy*, pp. 459–461.
11. Peter G. Filene, *Americans and the Soviet Experiment, 1917–1933* (Cambridge, Mass., 1967), pp. 24–25, 59.
12. Lloyd C. Gardner, *Safe for Democracy* (New York, 1984), pp. 186–191.
13. Lloyd C. Gardner, *A Covenant with Power: America and World Order from Wilson to Reagan* (New York, 1984), pp. 20–27. A noted account is George Kennan, *Russia and the West under Lenin and Stalin* (Boston, 1960), chs. 5–8.
14. Linda Killen, *The Russian Bureau: A Case Study in Wilsonian Diplomacy* (Lexington, Ky., 1983), chs. 3–4, especially tells an interesting story.
15. William C. Bullitt to Edward M. House, 20 September 1918, Papers of Colonel Edward M. House, Yale University, New Haven, Connecticut.
16. Arthur S. Link, *Woodrow Wilson: Revolution, War, and Peace* (New York, 1979), p. 85.
17. Arno Mayer's two seminal books on the subject are *Political Origins of the New Diplomacy, 1917–1918* (New Haven, 1959), and *Politics and Diplomacy of Peacemaking . . . 1918–1919* (New York, 1967).
18. The standard study is Lawrence E. Gelfand, *The Inquiry: American Preparations for Peace, 1917–1919* (New Haven, 1963).
19. Ronald Steel, *Walter Lippmann and the American Century* (New York, 1981), pp. 149–150.
20. David Lloyd George, *War Memoirs*, 6 vols. (London, 1933–1936), I, pp. 40–48.
21. William L. Langer, "Peace and the New World Order," in *Woodrow Wilson and the World of Today*, ed. Arthur P. Dudden (Philadelphia, 1957), p. 71.
22. Woodrow Wilson, *The Public Papers of Woodrow Wilson*, ed. Ray Stannard Baker and William E. Dodd, Jr., 6 vols. (New York, 1925–1927), V, p. 569; Michael J. Hogan, "The United States and the Problem of International Economic Control . . . 1918–1920," *Pacific Historical Review* 44 (February 1975): 93–94.
23. F. Scott Fitzgerald, *Tender Is the Night: A Romance* (New York, 1948), p. 117; and also Gordon A. Craig, "The Revolution in War and Diplomacy," in *World War I: A Turning Point in Modern History*, ed. Jack Roth (New York, 1967), p. 8, for the Fitzgerald reference. A fine, brief background on the war's costs is in Paul Dukes, *A History of Europe, 1648–1948* (London, 1985), pp. 362–364.

24. Felix Frankfurter, *Felix Frankfurter Reminisces* (New York, 1960), p. 161. A provocative analysis is Lloyd E. Ambrosius, "Woodrow Wilson's Health and the Treaty Fight," *International History Review* 9 (February 1987): 82.

25. Paul F. Boller, Jr., *Presidential Anecdotes* (New York, 1981), p. 220.

26. Geoffrey Barraclough, *Introduction to Contemporary History* (New York, 1964), pp. 213–214.

27. Ray Stannard Baker, *Woodrow Wilson and the World Settlement*, 3 vols. (Garden City, N.Y., 1922), I, p. 102; II, pp. 63–64.

28. Gardner, *Safe for Democracy*, p. 262.

29. Herbert C. Hoover, *The Ordeal of Woodrow Wilson* (New York, 1958), pp. 134–137, 140–141. The contradictions in Wilson's overall policy are superbly captured in Betty Miller Unterberger, "Woodrow Wilson and the Bolsheviks: The 'Acid Test' of Soviet-American Relations," *Diplomatic History* 11 (Spring 1987): esp. 87–90.

30. John L. Snell, "Document: Wilson on Germany and the Fourteen Points," *Journal of Modern History* 26 (December 1954): 366–368.

31. Walter Lippmann, "The Political Scene," in *New Republic*, "Supplement," 22 March 1919.

32. Filene, pp. 52–53.

33. Thomas J. Knock, *To End All Wars* (New York, 1992), p. 253; William C. Widenor, *Henry Cabot Lodge and the Search for an American Foreign Policy* (Berkeley, Calif., 1980), p. 338.

34. Dimitri D. Lazo, "A Question of Loyalty: Robert Lansing and the Treaty of Versailles," *Diplomatic History* 9 (Winter 1985): 52–53; also Henry W. Brands, Jr., "Unpremeditated Lansing: His Scraps," *Diplomatic History* 9 (Winter 1985): 25–33.

35. Knock, *To End All Wars*, esp. pp. 227–270.

36. Gardner, *Safe for Democracy*, pp. 258–260; Knock, *To End All Wars*, p. 245.

37. Clements is quoted in Luther Spoehr, "Films for Classroom Reviewed," *OAH Newsletter* 14 (May 1986): 17.

38. Ronald Steel, "Revolting Times," *Reviews in American History* 13 (December 1985): 591.

FOR FURTHER READING

The extensive list of pre-1981 publications can best be found in the well-annotated chapters 18 and 19 of *Guide to American Foreign Relations since 1700*, ed. Richard Dean Burns (1983). Those references and the sources in the notes to this chapter and the General Bibliography at the end of this book are not usually repeated below. Also important is David R. Woodward and Robert F. Maddox, *America and World War I: A Selected Annotated Bibliography of English-Language Sources* (1985); and Linda Kallen and Richard Lael, *Versailles and After: An Annotated Bibliography* (1983).

Useful overviews, with excellent bibliographical references, are Kendrick A. Clements, *The Presidency of Woodrow Wilson* (1992); Thomas J. Knock, *To End All Wars* (1992); and Lloyd E. Ambrosius, *Woodrow Wilson and the American Diplomatic Tradition* (1987). Important for the war at home are Charles DeBenedetti's several important books on the peace movement, especially *Peace Heroes in Twentieth-Century America* (1986), which he edited and which has good chapters on Debs and Addams; Nick Salvatore's prize-winning biography, *Eugene V. Debs* (1983); Stephen L. Vaughn, *Holding Fast the Inner Lines: Democracy, Nationalism and the Committee on Public Information* (1980). For the war abroad, Edward M. Coffman, *The War to End All Wars: The American Military Experience in World War I* (1987), is a standard by a distinguished military historian; Lester H. Brune, *The Origins of American National Security Policy: Sea Power, Air Power and Foreign Policy 1900–1941* (1981); and Gerald W. Patton, *The Black Officer in the American Military, 1915–1941* (1981), a helpful survey. Daniel Yergin's *The Prize* (1991) is a prize-winning account of the key role of oil.

Recent work on the peace settlement includes William C. Widenor, "The United States and the Versailles Peace Settlement," in *Modern American Diplomacy*, ed. John M. Carroll and George C. Herring (1986); Edwin A. Weinstein, *Woodrow Wilson: A Medical and Psychological Biography* (1981), a provocative analysis; the relevant chapters on post-1917 affairs in *Woodrow Wilson and a Revolutionary World, 1913–1921*, ed. Arthur S. Link (1982); and Arthur Link, *The Public Papers of Woodrow Wilson* (1966–), especially volume 55 on early 1919 (1987). The critical question of Germany is discussed in A. Lentin, *Lloyd George, Woodrow Wilson, and the Guilt of Germany* (1985), provocative; Klaus Schwabe, *Woodrow Wilson, Revolutionary Germany and Peacemaking, 1918–1919* (1985), provocative and exhaustive; Manfred Jonas, *The United States and Germany: A Diplomatic History* (1984), a good overview with useful bibliography. For French relations, see Henry Blumenthal, *Illusion and Reality in Franco-American Diplomacy, 1914–1945* (1986). Thomas N. Guinsburg, *The Pursuit of Isolationism in the U.S. Senate from Versailles to Pearl Harbor* (1982), is an important work on the fight in Washington. The intervention into Russia is reinterpreted by a leading scholar of that affair, Betty Miller Unterberger, "Woodrow Wilson and the Bolsheviks: The 'Acid Test' of Soviet-American Relations," *Diplomatic History* 11 (Spring 1987); and important new sources are Benjamin D. Rhodes, "A Prophet in the Russian Wilderness: The Mission of Consul Felix Cole at Archangel, 1917–1919," *Review of Politics* 46 (July 1984), and Rhodes's *The Anglo-American Winter War with Russia, 1918–1919* (1988).

More recent, important contributions include John Milton Cooper, Jr., and Charles E. Neu, eds., *The Wilson Era: Essays in Honor of Arthur S. Link* (1991), especially the Levering, Cooper, Neu, and Knock essays on 1917–1921; Betty M. Unterberger, *The United States, Revolutionary Russia and the Rise of Czechoslovakia* (1989); Christine A. White, *British and American Commercial Relations with Russia, 1918–1924* (1992); Sevan G. Terzian, "Henry Cabot Lodge and the Armenian Mandate Question, 1918–20," *Armenian Review* 44 (Autumn 1991), 23–37; and the important overview, Akira Iriye, *The Globalizing of America, 1914–1945*, in *The Cambridge History of U.S. Foreign Relations*, ed. Warren Cohen (1993).

11

The Rise and Fall of the American Structure for World Order (1920–1933)

HARDING, HUGHES, AND HOOVER

A bitter, disillusioned young Wilsonian, Walter Lippmann, wrote in November 1920 that the election of Warren Gamaliel Harding to the presidency was "the final twitch" of America's "war mind." Harding won not because many admired this mediocre Republican senator from Ohio, but because, in Lippmann's view, the people's "public spirit was exhausted" after the war effort. "The Democrats are inconceivably unpopular."[1] The new president's intellectual abilities were not high. Journalist H. L. Mencken wrote that Harding's use of language (which Mencken called "Gamalielese") was "so bad that a certain grandeur creeps into it." Alice Roosevelt Longworth, TR's tart-tongued daughter, recalled that "Harding was not a bad man. He was just a slob."[2]

But the president understood two facts that made U.S. foreign policies between 1920 and 1933 most instructive to later Americans. First, he knew that although the country wanted to return to "normalcy" (he meant to say "normality," but Gamalielese got in the way), the pre-1914 "old order" could never be rebuilt. Nor should it be rebuilt, Harding told Congress in 1922, because "out of the old order came the war itself." A new international system, built by American hands and money, and based on American principles, now had to be erected on the bloody ruins of the old European order. Second, Harding recognized his own weaknesses and looked for smart cabinet members to run the new foreign policy.

He found one such person in Charles Evans Hughes, who became secretary of state. A superb legal mind, a former governor of New York, and the 1916 Republican nominee for president, Hughes believed that Americans must seek "to establish a *Pax Americana* maintained not by arms but by mutual respect and good will and the tranquilizing processes of reason."[3] His views were shared, and with even greater passion, by the new secretary of commerce, Herbert Hoover, who became the personal symbol for the Republican policies of 1920 to 1933.

Raised in Iowa and orphaned before the age of ten, Hoover graduated in Stanford University's first class. The impoverished young geologist soon worked for mineowners in Australia, China, Latin America, and Russia. By 1919, the forty-five-year-old Hoover enjoyed a fabulous international reputation and a multimillion-dollar fortune. Hav-

Charles Evans Hughes (1862–1948) was a professor of law who uncovered corrupt practices by "robber barons" in New York's utility and insurance industries, became the state's Republican governor, was defeated as the Republican nominee for the presidency in 1916, served as secretary of state (1921–1925), and then ruled as chief justice of the United States, where he opposed much of Franklin D. Roosevelt's New Deal legislation. This portrait, by H. C. Christy, captures the dignified but ruthless intelligence that put together the Washington conference treaties and the plan to rebuild Germany.

Herbert Hoover (1874–1964) was considered by many close observers as one of the ablest and most intelligent persons of his generation ("the damndest, smartest man I ever met," as one friend put it). Arising from poverty, he parlayed his engineering degree into a multimillion-dollar fortune, then became world-famous as a food administrator in World War I, secretary of commerce (1921–1929), president (1929–1933), and advocate of what he termed "American individualism." Known simply as "the Boss" to his close friends, Hoover's ideas shaped the 1920s—until he could not find the answers to deal with the economic depression and the 1931 Japanese invasion of Manchuria.

ing served brilliantly under Woodrow Wilson during the war and at the Versailles conference, Hoover broke with the president over Article 10 of the League of Nations charter. He insisted on complete U.S. freedom of action so that the nation could use its vast new power when and how it thought best. This did not mean following a policy of isolationism in world affairs. Instead, Hoover favored "independent internationalism," as historian Joan Hoff has called it[4]—that is, not retreating from the world (for that was impossible), but keeping American hands as free as possible to build a world order in which Americans could prosper.

Hoover believed that the ideas of "American individualism" had to govern world affairs as they had built the United States. In his view, state-controlled enterprise, whether it was of the conservatives in France or the radical Left in the Soviet Union, threatened the individual freedoms essential to happiness and peace. But to have "American individualism" in the new international arena, the United States had to realize that these freedoms were all intimately related: "I insisted that spiritual and intellectual freedom could not continue to exist without economic freedom," he wrote in his memoirs. "If one died all would die."[5]

Hoover finally accepted the cabinet post after Harding agreed that Hoover would be involved in key diplomatic decisions. The new secretary of commerce believed that individual freedom at home was closely linked with policy abroad: "I am thus making a plea for individualism in international economic life just as strongly as I would make a plea for individualism in the life of our own people," Hoover declared in 1921. But to assure such "individualism" abroad meant keeping the international arena open for individual enterprise. "Special privileges" (such as the European colonial empires in Asia and the Middle East) were not to be allowed. Hoover believed that, indeed, everything was at stake in foreign policy: "This system [of individualism] can not be preserved in domestic life if it must be abandoned in international life."[6] Most of all, he feared the effect of revolution, which, he noted, "is a tornado leaving in its path the destroyed homes of millions with their dead women and children." Historian Warren Cohen has noted the result: the old search for order at home, "so pronounced in the Progressive era, had become a search for world order."[7]

Rather than retreating from the world, Hoover and Hughes believed that they had to go out and restart the international economy so that freedom could be protected. It proved to be a heavier burden than they, or the American people, could carry. But Hoover was correct in his main point, for when the global system did collapse between 1929 and 1933 (as Hoover himself occupied the White House), individual freedom in the United States and elsewhere became gravely endangered.

NEW RULES FOR AN OLD GAME:
THE WASHINGTON TREATY SYSTEM (1921–1922)

Hoover and Hughes knew that their first step had to be stopping the growing military competition. As the United States, Japan, and the western Europeans raced to build great navies, it seemed that the world was crazily returning to the competition that had helped trigger the world war. Moreover, military budgets sucked up money that would have been better used to develop world resources and build societies before some of them fell victim to radical revolution. Senators, led by Progressive Republican William Borah (Idaho), demanded meetings with Great Britain and Japan to discuss cutting military budgets. Hughes seized the initiative by inviting nine leading powers to Washington in late 1921 to discuss the arms race and such related problems as the smoking revolutionary cauldron of the Far East. He, pointedly, did not invite the Soviet Union or even extend it diplomatic recognition.

Hughes and his State Department advisers hoped to combine the disarmament problem with a more immediate danger that needed discussion: growing Japanese power in Asia. In historian Charles Neu's words, the 1919 peace conference had "left an ugly heritage in Japanese-American relations."[8] U.S. fears rose as Japan built the region's most powerful military machine. It did so, moreover, just as China, Russia, and smaller Asian countries spun into revolution. Popular books appeared in the United States with such subtitles as *The Rising Tide of Color* and *Must We Fight Japan?* Japan seemed to be the key diplomatic problem in Asia, and that problem worsened because Tokyo still enjoyed an alliance with Great Britain that had been made in 1902. If the United States and Japan did fight each other, Americans could find themselves fighting against the British fleet as well. Hughes demanded that the alliance be broken. When the British ambassador once made the mistake of referring to the 1902 treaty, he later remarked that he had "never heard anything like Mr. Hughes' excited tirade outside of a madhouse."[9]

Hughes not only intended to force naval disarmament and break up the Anglo-Japanese alliance, but he had a third objective, too: to make Japan dependent on the New York City money market. Especially after a severe postwar economic downturn hit them, the Japanese needed capital for both their military and their economic development of Manchuria and Korea. During May 1920, in a deal that perfectly demonstrated how the new U.S. economic power could work, New York banker Thomas Lamont agreed to open the city's vast resources to the Japanese. But, in return, they had to agree to honor open-door principles in China (except in southern Manchuria, which Japan had controlled since 1905). Thus, in return for New York dollars and rights in Manchuria, the Japanese promised to treat U.S. trade and investment fairly in most of China. As historian Carl Parrini observes, "Hughes had no intention of relying upon good faith alone." The secretary of state intended to use dollars to pressure Japan "to abide by the open door pledge."[10] He also intended to use the "Black Chambers," a secret U.S. code-breaking operation that allowed him to read the most sensitive instructions from Tokyo to the Japanese delegation in Washington. Hughes was ready for his master stroke.

He opened the Washington Conference with one of the most stun-

Secretary of State Charles Evans Hughes talked with French leader Aristide Briand at the historic Washington conference of 1921. Other foreign ministers included (from left), Prince Tekugawa of Japan, Arthur Balfour of Great Britain, and, at front right, H. E. Carlo Sanchez of Italy. The smiles no doubt belied the leaders' shock at Hughes's astonishing proposals at the conference.

ning speeches in diplomatic history. Hughes proposed to achieve real disarmament by offering to scrap thirty major U.S. ships, totaling 846,000 tons. He then turned to a shocked British delegation and told them that they should do away with 583,000 tons of their large warships. Hughes next instructed the surprised Japanese that they should destroy 450,000 tons of their capital ships. He asked for a final limit of 500,000 tons for the British and Americans, 300,000 for the Japanese, and 175,000 tons each for France and Italy. These limits were agreed to in the Five-Power Treaty.

Hughes set these numbers despite strong opposition from the U.S. War and Navy departments. The military warned that the figures gave Japan superiority in Asia. The secretary of state did not mind. Given Lamont's deal with Tokyo bankers, the Japanese had become a more trusted—and more controllable—ally in Asia.

To put a double lock on Japan, Hughes signed two other treaties at the Washington Conference. The Four-Power Treaty ended the Anglo-Japanese Alliance of 1902 and provided instead that in the event of an Asian crisis, the four powers (the United States, Japan, Great Britain, and France) would consult. They would not, in other words, necessarily act. The Nine-Power Treaty (signed by the four powers plus Italy, China, Belgium, the Netherlands, and Portugal) finally put the open-door principles into international law. The pact thus fulfilled a dream of U.S. officials since John Hay, if not John Quincy Adams. Japan signed the Nine-Power Treaty, however, only after adding a "security clause" that recognized Tokyo's influence in Manchuria. The Japanese, moreover, agreed with the crucial Five-Power agreement only after Great Britain pledged not to extend its fortifications at Hong Kong and the United States promised not to fortify bases in the Philippines, Guam, and Alaska any further. U.S. military officials again protested, and Hughes again turned them down. Any belief that Guam, for example, could become a key naval base was, he remarked, "nothing but a picture of the imagination."[11]

Despite the Japanese reservations, the Washington Conference was a success. Historian Thomas Buckley summarized Hughes's accomplishment: the United States "achieved a better position in relation to its competitors in the Pacific by a limitation of arms than it might have gained by arming; therein lay the wisdom of the American proposal."[12]

Many joined the U.S. military in criticizing the three Washington Conference treaties. Fearing a revived Germany, France angrily fought restrictions on its own naval power. China was bitter that the powers had given Japan control over much of Manchuria. Great Britain worried that with Tokyo's naval superiority in the region, the British fleet was no longer the determining military power along the Pacific rim. Even the Japanese military complained that they needed a 10:10:7 ratio (not 5:5:3) to protect their expanding empire. For the next decade they continually demanded more ships. But Harding, Hughes, and Hoover were delighted. The Americans considered China an inferior power that was cuddling too closely with the Soviet Union. As one U.S. delegate to the conference believed, China had not yet become "a full-fledged member of the family of nations." Besides, Americans had done their part by protecting China with the open-door principles. With Japan dependent on the U.S. money market and with the Nine-Power pledge in his pocket, Hughes believed that he had built the necessary base for a joint U.S.-Japanese effort to develop China and other profitable portions of Asia. Japan soon showed its good faith by agreeing to return the Shantung Peninsula to China and—finally—by pulling its last troops out of Siberia.

For its part, the United States did nothing at the conference that tied its hands or "endanger[ed] our freedom of action," as Harding privately observed.[13] Moreover, the building of smaller ships (submarines and destroyers) was not limited. Historian Akira Iriye correctly notes that the Washington treaties "did not mean that imperialism as such was gone,"[14] only that in China the century-long presence of Great Britain and Russia had been reduced while Japan and the United States had become the dominant powers. If only the Chinese would stand still and not get caught up in their own revolution. And if only the New York money market remained flush and open.

"Capital . . . and state craft . . . go hand in hand": The Republicans' System

With the arms race under control, the Harding administration turned to rebuilding the war-devastated global system. U.S. officials had no doubt about their role. They would take the lead, and they knew just how they would rebuild: they would use their new economic wealth (not political or military power) to create a new, prosperous world that would be safe from the rivalries that had nearly destroyed everything in 1914. "Our international problems tend to become mainly economic problems," Hughes declared in 1922.[15] But the nation certainly had the resources to solve those problems. Americans had owed the world $3 billion when World War I started, but the world owed them more than $3 billion when the war ended. Gold and other international capital piled up in New York City. These riches meant, however, that somehow that money had to be recycled back to the poorer nations. Otherwise they could not buy U.S. goods.

This recycling, Washington officials agreed, had to be done by private bankers. The government should not become involved in the private marketplace. Too much government involvement led, as Hoover and other leaders constantly preached, to either socialism or fascism. But, these leaders quickly added, there did have to be close cooperation between bankers and government. Each needed the other: the bankers could carry out policies that benefited the entire country, while the government could quietly aid and protect the bankers overseas.

As Washington politicians and New York bankers worked together, critics cried that "Wall Street" was running the government. A top State Department official, Huntington Wilson, responded by explaining the new facts of international life. Critics have, "in the debauchery of their muck raking, been silly enough to insinuate that the Department of State was run by Wall Street," he observed. "Any student of modern diplomacy knows that in these days of competition, capital, trade, agriculture, labor and state craft all go hand in hand if a country is to profit."[16]

The Rules for the New Republican System

Hoover and Hughes set the ground rules for this cooperation. In 1921, they informed the bankers that money must not go to the Soviet Union or certain projects in China. These talks led to the greatest figure on Wall Street, J. P. Morgan, Jr., agreeing to keep Hughes "fully informed of any and all negotiations for loans to foreign governments."[17] Hoover tried to claim that this meant that the bankers would have to submit loan projects to him and Hughes for quiet, informal approval or disapproval. Thus, the money would go where the government wanted, but the government would not be directly responsible if anything went wrong with the loan.

The Hughes-Hoover policy on loans was perfectly in tune with the U.S. policy on war debts. Washington officials insisted that the war-scarred Europeans must repay the multibillion-dollar debt not only on grounds of principle ("They hired the money, didn't they?" President Calvin Coolidge growled), but because the debt was a weapon for U.S. officials. Hughes and Hoover could use the debt like a carrot and stick to force Europeans to behave. If the Europeans cooperated, the war debt might be discussed. But if, as they usually did, Europeans objected to U.S. policies, they could be threatened with quick collection of the debt.

Thus, Hoover and Hughes could use the debts and the loan-approval policy as sharp tools. When the British government tried to drive up the world price of rubber by controlling the British Empire's production, Hoover declared economic war. He was determined not to have the new, already rich American automobile industry held hostage by London. By using U.S. power over loans and war debts to threaten the British, and by encouraging such American producers as Firestone to enlarge their rubber plantations in Liberia and Southeast Asia, Hoover drove down the price from $1.21 a pound in March 1926 to 40 cents in just three months. He did much the same thing when Brazil tried to raise coffee prices and Germany attempted to corner the market on such vital raw materials as potash.[18] Hoover and Hughes were certainly not "isolationists." But, to use a later term, they delighted in playing "hard ball" diplomacy. They especially insisted that dollars not be spent on U.S. enemies (such as the Soviet Union) or on nonproductive enterprises (as war industry), but on friends and peaceful businesses—especially those who would buy American goods.

By the mid-1920s, however, the policy was no longer working. The bankers increasingly wanted to go their own way, even if it meant investing in the Soviet Union or in quick-profit schemes rather than in productive enterprises. For example, Hoover urged them to provide credit for U.S. exporters who were trying to conquer new foreign markets against stiff European and Japanese competition. The bankers, however, preferred to invest in more fly-by-night businesses abroad that promised a quick payoff. U.S. manufacturers, who needed credit, grew bitter. So did Hoover. But when he tried to tighten controls over the bankers, he ran into opposition from Secretary of the Treasury Andrew Mellon and President Calvin Coolidge (who entered the White House after Harding's sudden death in 1923). Mellon and Coolidge felt that government should not be so involved. The new president deeply disliked Hoover's activism. Whereas Harding had once called Hoover "the damndest smartest man I have ever met," Coolidge later groused that "that man [Hoover] has offered me unsolicited advice for six years, all of it bad."[19] While Hoover raced around Washington and seemed to be involved in everything, Coolidge liked to sleep eleven hours a day. (When writer Dorothy Parker was told in 1933 that Coolidge had died, she replied, "How can they tell?")

As these Washington officials fought each other, the bankers spun out of control—as did the economy. The history of the tariff during the 1920s became a classic example of how Americans tried to have everything and ended up with almost nothing. In 1922, the Fordney-McCumber Act raised tariff walls around American producers, who loudly demanded protection from cheap foreign goods. This act made little sense. Europeans could not repay their debts if they could not sell their goods in the rich U.S. market.[20] By 1928, the Hoover-Hughes policy of gently guiding the world into a happy, freer-market economy was in shambles. The two men had been unable to control Coolidge, Mellon, or the bankers.

Most Americans—as usual—paid no attention to these ominous storm clouds. People had never been wealthier or the nation more powerful. American holdings of the world's gold had doubled, and the United States was dominating the global economy. Europeans warned of the "Americanizing of the world" not only through the power of the almighty dollar, but through the new Hollywood motion pictures that spread U.S. culture across the world and whipped up a demand for the products shown in the films. A Belgian paper cried that Europe was threatened with more barbarism from the United States than from the Soviet Union. Famous British author George Bernard Shaw surveyed the source of this supposed barbarism and announced that "an asylum for the sane would be empty in America."[21]

But most Americans cared little about Shaw's comments. They instead tended to admire the new Italian leader, Benito Mussolini, whose loud approval of masculinity, athletics, efficiency, and activism seemed to be borrowed from American virtues. As historian David F. Schmitz notes, moreover, U.S. officials' desire for stability and a non-Bolshevist Europe led them to welcome Mussolini's seizure of power in 1922 and "to support Fascism in Italy" through the 1920s and 1930s "in direct contradiction with purported U.S. ideals."[22]

A CASE STUDY: EUROPE AND THE NEW RULES OF THE GAME

U.S. officials understood that European recovery was especially important. Secretary of State Hughes told the Brown University graduating class in 1921 that "the prosperity of the United States largely depends upon the economic settlements which may be made in Europe, and the key to the future is with those who make those settlements." Hughes knew that Americans held that key. Within Europe itself, Germany was the critical problem. Before 1914, it had been the dominant power on the Continent. As Hughes declared, "There can be no economic recuperation in Europe unless Germany recuperates."[23] Moreover, U.S. officials feared that if Germany were not well treated, it would turn to the Russian Bolsheviks for trade and sympathy.

The Germans, however, had been socked with a $33-billion bill for war reparations by the 1919 peace conference. The French were delighted. They believed that it would be generations before the debt-bound Germans could again threaten neighbors. But the reparations not merely weakened Germany, they almost suffocated it. In 1923, the country could no longer pay. The French struck back by sending troops into the strategic Ruhr Valley that they had long wanted. Germans responded by going on strike. European financial exchanges went haywire. Quietly, but decisively, Hughes moved.

The secretary of state put tremendous pressure on France by demanding payment of the debt that the French owed the United States. As the French franc sank in value, Paris officials had to come to New York and beg for $100 million in credit from J. P. Morgan & Company. With western Europe at his mercy, Hughes agreed to sponsor a meeting in 1924 to solve the crisis. The meeting was to be run, however, not by U.S. officials, but by private American bankers and businessmen. Thus, the government officials would not be directly responsible for the results, and—of special importance—Congress would not have to be consulted formally about the results of the meeting.

The major result was the Dawes Plan (named after Chicago banker and, later, vice-president of the United States, Charles G. Dawes, who pieced the deal together). Germany's reparations payments were sharply reduced to $250 million annually. They were to rise slowly over five years as the economy improved. To trigger that improvement, the Dawes Plan provided for an immediate $200-million loan to pump life into German production. U.S. private bankers were to provide half the amount, with the rest coming from foreign banks.

Suddenly, a snag appeared. J. P. Morgan, Jr., rightly feared that placing the Germans under new debt might make them angry about "the extent to which what was once a first-class power has been subjected to foreign control."[24] But after receiving more guarantees that secured the loan, Morgan went along. When Morgan floated the loan on the public U.S. market, it succeeded beyond anyone's wildest dreams. In a few days, over $1 billion was subscribed, or ten times the amount needed. Americans liked the idea of putting their dollars into German securities. By 1927–1928, money flooded into Germany faster than safe investments could be found for it. But the Dawes Plan had scored a stunning success. As one U.S. official in Europe reported home, "That America is the creditor nation and is trusted in all Europe even where she is despised . . . gives us a potential power to straighten out affairs over here."[25]

The Dawes Plan assumed that the $200 million would restart German industry so that the Germans could repay their debts. But it never worked out that way. Germany—and U.S. investors—became addicted to the loans. As historian Frank Costigliola explains, the Americans failed to see that their hope for a "limited, initial commitment" to ignite the German economy "would quickly and uncontrollably mushroom into a massive and ongoing obligation to keep the system working."[26] The Americans had to keep pouring new money in to support their old money. They had to run ever-faster to stay in the same place. Almost as bad, they entered into cutthroat competition with powerful British banks to see who could control German trade, Austrian and other European money markets, and, indeed, half the world's daily export trade, which London had financed and grown rich from before 1914.

As U.S. relations with Germany and France improved, U.S.-British ties became so bad that by 1927 a British diplomatic official privately warned that Americans had been treated "too much as blood relations, [and] not sufficiently as a foreign country."[27]

That very year, 1927, relations worsened when U.S., British, and Japanese officials met at Geneva, Switzerland, to try to limit the building of smaller warships (such as cruisers) that had not been dealt with at the Washington Conference. France and Italy refused to attend. The British and U.S. delegates so insulted each other that the *New York Times* reporter in Geneva was finally asked by his editor whether he was reporting from a disarmament conference or a battlefield. American arms manufacturers paid expensive lobbyists to ensure that the Geneva talks would fail.[28] But the problem went deeper than that. A declining Great Britain was desperately trying to protect its empire against upstart Americans whom it mistrusted and feared. Chancellor of the Exchequer Winston Churchill secretly told the British cabinet in 1927 that war with the United States was not "unthinkable."[29]

In one key region, however, Americans and British finally worked together. Before World War I, Great Britain dominated the Middle East's oil reserves. The riches had only been glimpsed (the incredible Saudi Arabian wells, for example, had not yet been discovered), but by 1921–1922, Western automobiles, industry, and battleships drank more and more barrels of petroleum. As a French leader put it, "Oil is as necessary as blood." U.S. oil companies appeared in the region of the former Ottoman Empire only after the war. Before that, they had produced their oil mostly in the Western Hemisphere. Now, led by John D. Rockefeller's Standard Oil, they fought for control of Middle East production as well.

The British and French at first tried to exclude U.S. companies. The Americans, joined by the State Department, loudly demanded an "open door" to the region's riches. After years of fighting and talking, five American companies (Gulf, Texaco, Mobil, Standard Oil of New York, all of which were led by Standard Oil of New Jersey) cut a deal with their competitors. They all sat down in 1928 and drew a red line around the area whose oil production they agreed to divide among themselves. This Red Line Agreement marked out the boundary for the world's greatest oil-producing regions, and it aimed to keep all other companies on the outside while "the open door," in historian Anthony Sampson's words, "proved to be a mysterious portal, with the habit of swinging shut again, just as the Americans had got inside." Or, as one of the 1928 participants declared, "Oilmen are like cats; you can never tell from the sound of them whether they are fighting or making love."[30] The Red Line Agreement proved so satisfying that the oilmen maintained this love affair until after World War II.

The Europeans tried to follow these economic settlements with political agreements. At Locarno, Switzerland, in 1925, Germany, France, and Belgium guaranteed each other's boundaries. Great Britain and Italy signed as guarantors. The "Spirit of Locarno" proved to be the peak of European diplomacy in the 1920s. The French, however, wanted more. Worried over possible German military revival, they asked the United States in early 1927 not for an alliance (which they knew Washington would refuse), but for a pact outlawing war between the two nations. It was a clever move. French premier Aristide Briand believed that such a pact would help France by preventing a repeat of 1914–1917, when Americans threatened to break with the French (and British) over neutral U.S. trading rights during wartime. American church groups quickly supported Briand's initiative. These groups had long unsuccessfully urged the Coolidge administration to join international organizations. (They had even held a "World Court Sunday.")

But Coolidge and his new secretary of state, Frank Kellogg, wanted nothing to do with Briand's idea. They feared that it would restrict American freedom of action and tie U.S. interests too closely to France. Kellogg instead made a counterproposal: a statement outlawing war that any nation could sign. Briand, bitterly disappointed, nevertheless could hardly object publicly to a statement opposing war, meaningless though it was. The Kellogg-Briand Pact of 1928, signed by most nations in the world, condemned war and pledged the signatories to settle disputes peacefully. (Within weeks, the U.S. Congress appropriated $250 million to build new warships.) The peace pact soon became known as a mere "international kiss." Dollars and the Washington treaty system of 1921–1922 remained the real weapons of U.S. foreign policy.

THE OUTCAST—SOVIET RUSSIA— AND THE RULES OF THE GAME

The weapons seemed ever more effective, even in handling the great outcast, the Soviet Union. In 1920, the United States had refused to recognize the Soviets officially. During the next two years, however, U.S. officials were shocked into rethinking their position. Great Britain opened relations with Lenin's government in 1921. The next year, the two pariahs—Germany and the Soviet Union—stunned the world by signing a pact at Rapallo, Italy, that publicly recognized each other's interests. That pact also secretly cleared the way for the two nations to cooperate militarily.

Meanwhile, Lenin had announced his New Economic Policy (NEP) that invited capitalists to help develop Soviet resources. Western officials believed that he had seen the light and was turning the Soviet Union away from communism. Lenin was actually trying to develop the Communist economy as rapidly as possible, make westerners less interested in military interventions, and pit capitalist against capitalist for the profit of the Soviets. Secretary of Commerce Hoover declared the Soviet Union to be an "economic vacuum." U.S. business pushed forward to fill the vacuum with its goods. Relations further grew in 1921–1922, when Americans responded to a severe famine by setting up 18,000 feeding stations, sending $60 million in aid, and saving an estimated 11 million Soviet lives.

These openings, however, were not enough to warm Soviet-American political relations. The American Legion, the Roman Catholic church, and the American Federation of Labor (AFL) especially opposed any ties. AFL leader Samuel Gompers charged that even as the Bolsheviks were trying to undermine the U.S. government, short-sighted, greedy American bankers wanted to help Lenin for their own profit. Hoover and Hughes tried to ensure that the loans would not benefit the Soviet Union. But they fought a losing battle. Large corporations, led by General Electric, General Motors, and even Henry Ford's company, moved into the fertile Soviet market. W. Averell Harriman, the young, handsome heir to a huge railroad empire, opened extensive contacts and negotiated the rights to mineral resources estimated at $1 billion. The deal finally collapsed, but Harriman left the Soviet Union on friendly terms (and returned during World War II as the U.S. ambassador). In 1924, the Soviets set up Amtorg, a trading company located in New York City, to handle their business. By 1925, U.S.-Soviet trade reached $37 million but in the next five years jumped to $95 million, or twice the pre-1914 total of U.S.-Russian trade. Germany continued to be the Soviets' leading trading partner. The Americans, however, were closing ground—and doing so without the U.S. government even recognizing that the Soviet Union officially existed.[31]

Dollars seemed to be creating the new and better world everywhere. When the German economy slowed in 1928, U.S. officials again stepped in. During 1929, the Young Plan (named after Owen D. Young, head of General Electric, who negotiated the deal) further reduced German reparations. The $33 billion of 1921 shrank to $8 billion payable over fifty-eight years. Meanwhile, since 1925, U.S. banks had pumped nearly $1.25 billion of loans into Germany and had granted billions more in short-term credits. Americans directly invested $200 million into German plants.[32] Almost single-handedly, the United States had rebuilt Germany and much more of Europe besides.

"God, J. P. Morgan and the Republican Party" Are Not Enough: The Collapse of the System (1929)

By early 1929, newly elected President Herbert Hoover believed that continued prosperity was built into the nation's system. Even the usually critical journalist, Lincoln Steffens, agreed: "Big Business in America is producing what the Socialists held up as their goal: food, shelter, and clothing for all."[33] Naturally, Wall Street was optimistic. In 1927, a bull market made investors instant millionaires by shooting stock prices skyward. "There was a spirit of tremendous euphoria," one stockbroker recalled years later. "God, J. P. Morgan and the Republican party were going to keep everything going forever."[34] But the Great Bull Market was built on weakly supported loans as well as on a short-sighted and corrupt banking system.

In September 1929, investors found that they could not pay their loans and so began selling stocks. By October, the selling became a torrent. The money exchanges went crazy as prices dropped. Hoover, the bankers, and Harvard and Yale economists denounced the panic. They solemnly announced that the economy was sound. By the end of the year, however, stock prices had been chopped 50 percent. In March 1930, Hoover declared, "The crisis will be over in sixty days." John D. Rockefeller announced that such a bright future lay ahead that he and his sons were buying stocks. ("Sure," answered one observer, "who else [has] any money left?")[35] By the end of 1930, the economy slid downhill ever more rapidly. It had produced a gross national product (or the sum of all production and services in the economy) of $104 billion in 1929, but by 1933 it amounted to only $56 billion. In 1930 alone, 800 banks declared bankruptcy and ruined small savers who had trusted them. Unemployment was 3 percent, about 1.5 million people, in 1929, but 25 percent, or 12.6 million people, in 1933. And not only the average person suffered. A founder of General Motors, William C. Durant, lost his fortune and wound up operating a bowling alley in Flint, Michigan.

Few understood what was happening. Former President Coolidge exemplified the confusion: "The future may be better or worse," he actually told the nation. Coolidge added: "The final solution for unemployment is work."[36] But several problems became clear. First, the U.S. economy had tried to act as the foundation for the rebuilding of the world economy when, in reality, parts of that foundation were crumbling. The farm sector, for three hundred years the most important producer and buyer, was depressed throughout the 1920s. Textiles and mining were sick industries. Americans who made great profits in the decade did not use them to cure these trouble spots, but instead tried to make a quick killing in the stock market. Nor did the government help correct the foolishness. By the late 1920s, even the Hoover-Hughes attempt to police foreign loans had collapsed. Bankers went their merry way investing money wherever they saw a glimmer of profit. As Germany was flooded with too many dollars, the banks turned elsewhere and, if necessary, created markets: National City Bank of New York forced $90 million in loans on Peru in 1927–1928 by giving a $450,000 bribe to the son of Peru's president. In 1931, Peru defaulted on all the loans.

Even those kinds of opportunities began to dry up in 1928–1929, and so bankers put their funds in the stock market. Dollars had been the blood in the arteries of world commerce. As the dollars stopped flowing overseas by 1929, the economies of Canada, Japan, western Europe, and Latin America became severely ill. Nor could these countries easily buy Americans' cotton, wheat, and autos any longer. U.S. private lenders had supplied $355 million to foreigners in 1927 but only $191 million in 1933, and world trade dropped a full 40 percent in value. Congress responded by passing the Smoot-Hawley Tariff in 1931. It raised the average tariff on protected goods to 59 percent, the highest level in twentieth-century American history. Other nations had been repaying their debts to the United States or selling goods to Americans. Now the U.S. market was largely closed to the goods after the Smoot-Hawley Tariff passed. One expert reported that "in France our tariff was compared to a declaration of war, an economic blockade."[37]

By early 1931, President Hoover understood that he was in a world crisis and that it had to be handled in the global arena. He watched with horror as the Bank of England, the great financial backbone of the British Empire, lost $200 million in just two weeks. Great Britain finally went off the gold standard in September 1931. That standard had been pushed on London by the Americans in 1926 because they owned much of the world's gold and wanted to make the British dependent on it. Now Great Britain was freeing itself so that it could manipulate its own currency and declare economic war on the United States. Even worse threatened in Germany. Both the Communists and Adolf Hitler's National Socialists gained strength. The U.S. ambassador to Germany told Hoover that unless quick action were taken, revolution would overthrow Germany's democratic Weimar Republic.

Hoover responded with a proposal. In mid-1931, he declared that the United States would place a "moratorium" (temporary stop) on war debts owed to it by other nations such as France and Great Britain if, in turn, those nations quit taking war reparations out of Germany. Hoover hoped that this would give everyone time to come to their senses. But the French disagreed. They did not want Germany to escape the controls imposed by the reparations.

Other nations went off on their own. In 1932, the British met at Ottawa, Canada, with their Commonwealth members. They agreed to create an Imperial Preference System that gave each other's products preferred treatment (and pointedly discriminated against U.S. goods). Because many of the Commonwealth members, especially Canada and Australia, had been leading customers for Americans, U.S. officials were furious about the Ottawa deal. For the next fifteen years, these officials worked hard to destroy such economic blocs. Meanwhile, the Europeans met in 1932 to demand relief from paying their debts to New York. Nearly all had defaulted. The one that did not, Finland, forever held a special place in American hearts. In January 1933, Adolf Hitler came to power in Germany and repudiated the country's war debts and liberal trade policies. As historian Frederick C. Adams summarizes the situation at that point: "America found itself confronted by increased trade barriers and a united front of debtor nations."[38]

Hoover tried one other tactic to ease the crisis. As a Quaker and as an engineer who hated wasting resources on nonproductive goods, he had worked for disarmament. In Melvyn Leffler's words, "Hoover hoped that limiting armaments would reduce the burden of taxation and curtail the waste of human and capital resources without jeopardizing the nation's security."[39] In 1929, the president tried to lessen tension with the British by inviting Prime Minister Ramsay MacDonald to a fishing expedition (one of Hoover's greatest loves) at the president's hideaway in Virginia. The two leaders agreed to new ratios for warships and called for a major naval conference in 1930. The conference did agree on new figures and even gave Japan a higher ratio (10:10:7 instead of the old 10:10:6) on cruisers, but not on battleships. The economic crisis had now hit with full force. The Japanese demanded even more ships. The French and Italians also wanted more. These three nations prepared to quit the Five-Power Treaty of 1922.

The president had only one idea left. In 1932, he proposed a kind of diplomatic grand slam: a conference that would deal simultaneously with war debts, reparations, the economic crisis, and disarmament. He was correct in believing that these were linked. Nations were not willing to disarm until their economic security was assured. But their economies also needed relief from rising military budgets. The 1932 elections in the United States intervened, however, and Hoover went down to a humiliating defeat. The new president, Franklin D. Roosevelt, the former Democratic governor of New York, refused to tie his hands by accepting Hoover's proposal.

The disarmament issue soon became irrelevant. In 1933–1934, as Hitler consolidated his power, he tore off the restraints imposed in 1919–1920 on German rearmament. The Japanese had begun their march of armed conquest two years earlier.

COLLAPSE OF THE WASHINGTON
TREATY STRUCTURE: ASIA AND WAR

War erupted when Japan invaded northern China in September 1931. U.S. officials were confused. They thought Japan had been brought under control by the Washington treaties and Tokyo's dependence on American dollars. By 1926, Japan had borrowed $200 million. Nearly 40 percent of its foreign loans rested in U.S. hands. It also bought more goods from Americans than from other people. In turn, Americans bought more than 40 percent of Japan's exports in the 1920s.[40]

Hoover was delighted with these figures. He was also happy, however, with the 1924 Immigration Law. The U.S. Congress decided to shut off the inflow of those it considered undesirable, both from eastern Europe and Asia, by sharply reducing immigration quotas. In part because of pressure from California, where anti-Japanese feeling was rampant, the law completely excluded Asians. Hoover privately agreed: "The biological fact makes mixture of bloods disadvantageous to Japan if it occurred there and to us if it occurs here." As he concluded, "We have set up a nation which must . . . be of a character that can evolve a consolidated race."[41] The humiliated Japanese bitterly protested. Dollars, however, helped in steadying relations—until 1929, when the dollars stopped. Japanese militants then used anti-U.S. feeling to gain support for their attacks on American interests.

Meanwhile, during the 1920s, the Republicans' dollar diplomacy also seemed to be working in China. Some $50 million of U.S.-Chinese trade in 1914 nearly quadrupled to $190 million by 1930. Those exchanges represented only 3 percent of total U.S. trade (and some $155 million of U.S. investment amounted to less than 5 percent of total U.S. foreign investment in 1930), but future profits seemed limitless. As a popular book title suggested, the Chinese had to be seen as *Four Hundred Million Customers.* Cigarette sales, for example, had grown from one each year per Chinese in 1900 to 19 per person in 1920. One of Hoover's top aides liked to observe: "Add one inch to the shirt tail of every Chinese and you will keep the cotton mills of the world busy for a year supplying the increased demand."[42]

Saving souls also seemed to be a growth industry. Some 1,000 Christian missionaries in 1900 had become nearly 3,000 by 1920. Since they had converted only 800,000 Chinese (out of a total population of 400 million), obviously much remained to be done. In 1926, Hoover's Commerce Department estimated that U.S. missionary and philanthropic groups had invested $69.3 million in China. It noted that the importance of the Rockefeller Foundation, which had given $34 million to establish a medical school in Beijing (Peking) and other funds for other Western-style colleges, "is not to be underestimated."[43]

The great question, however, was whether the Chinese wanted to be Westernized. On May 4, 1919, the flames of the revolution that had been lit eight years earlier suddenly blazed again when Beijing (Peking) students massively protested against the humiliations piled on China at the Paris peace conference. The May Fourth Movement was also fueled by foreign control of the nation's tariff collection and by British and Standard Oil monopoly of the kerosene trade used to light China's lamps. Sun Yat-sen, who had helped to overthrow the Manchu dynasty in 1911, again led the revolution. His Nationalist movement worked closely with the one nation willing to help revolutionaries—the Soviet Union. Indeed, the 1924 China-USSR agreement so stunned the Japanese that they quickly established relations with the Soviet Union in 1925. Now Americans were stunned. An Asiatic phalanx seemed to be rising. "That there is a menace to the entire West in such a combination seems self-evident," a U.S. diplomat warned.[44]

And as Chinese nationalism surged, Americans found it difficult to pose as protectors because the Chinese no longer wanted protection. Even worse threatened when the Chinese Communist party was officially founded in 1921. But Sun held real power, and by 1925 he had succeeded in achieving his two objectives: conquering various local "war lords" whose private armies controlled key regions, and destroying foreigners' special privileges. That year, Sun suddenly died. His power was seized by a young aide, Chiang Kai-shek, whose training by the Soviets and talent for intrigue were quickly mistrusted in Washington. After a series of military victories in 1926, however, Chiang was afraid that the Soviets and Communists were ready to eliminate him. In 1927, he beat them to the punch. He threw out the Soviet advisers and, with the help of gangster friends from the Chinese underworld, killed thousands of Communists and forced the rest into hiding.[45]

U.S. officials should have been pleased, but they were not. In 1925–1926, Chiang's success had intensified China's antiforeignism. That hatred of foreigners increased when British-led police and British and French troops killed sixty-five Chinese protesters. Foreigners, including missionaries, were sought out for revenge. By 1927, nearly 70 percent of the Protestant missionaries had left China. U.S. troops landed to help restore order in 1928 at Tianjin (Tientsin), 70 miles from the capital of Beijing (Peking). Soon, dance halls, bowling alleys, bars, gambling, and prostitutes (mostly Russian women in exile) were in evidence. A year later, the U.S. Marines were gone, but the memories—and unpaid bar bills signed by "Herbert Hoover" and "George Washington"—remained in Chinese minds.[46] Chiang's regime now demanded respect: "The time has come to speak to foreign imperialism in the language it understands," the Chinese foreign minister declared.[47] The foreign powers did restore tariff autonomy to China in 1928 but refused to give up other legal or military power they had exercised in a different China. Chiang and his Kuomintang (KMT) movement were feared as revolutionary and antiforeign.

This background must be understood if one hopes to grasp why the United States did nothing when Japan invaded Manchuria in 1931 and, in reality, tore up the Washington treaties before astonished American eyes. The invasion surprised Hoover and his secretary of state, Henry Stimson. Stimson was a wealthy New York lawyer who appreciated the Tokyo–New York dollar link. He (like his hero, Theodore Roosevelt) believed that Japan supported U.S. interests in Asia. As a conservative former governor general of the Philippines, Stimson viewed many Asians as inefficient and inferior, but he especially feared and disliked revolutionary Asians.

Stimson had agreed with Hoover's belief in September 1929 that "there is the most profound outlook for peace today that we have had

The life of Henry Stimson (1867–1950) in many ways was a history of American foreign policy between his service as secretary of war to President Taft (1911–1913) and to President Truman in 1945. In between, Stimson fought on the western front in World War I, acted as U.S. governor general of the Philippines in 1927–1929, became Hoover's secretary of state (1929–1933), then—after vigorously opposing German and Japanese expansion while growing wealthy from his law practice—received Franklin D. Roosevelt's appointment as secretary of war in 1940. As a godfather of the "American establishment," he strongly influenced many of the younger men who shaped U.S. economic and foreign policy after the 1930s. A Republican, Stimson exemplified the conservative, internationalist policies of U.S. diplomacy.

at any time in the last half century."[48] A month later the New York stock market collapsed. The Japanese, who had bet their economy and foreign policy on the dollar, now began to search for other alternatives. A liberal, pro-Western cabinet in Tokyo gave way to moderate groups and finally to a government in which militarists had a strong voice. The Chinese Revolution, moreover, directly threatened vast Japanese holdings in Manchuria and China proper. U.S. officials sympathized with Tokyo's predicament. They allowed Japan to increase its naval power at the 1930 naval conference. Hoover agreed with a journalist friend who wrote: "I think the Japs are our first line of defense in the Far East; and I am certainly glad they are well armed."[49]

On September 18, 1931, Japanese troops apparently set off an explosion on the South Manchurian Railroad that Japan had controlled since 1905. They then used the incident as an excuse to seize Manchuria once and for all. Hoover's mind was elsewhere. Americans were starving. Western Europe seemed on the edge of chaos. At first, Stimson

This cartoon by Cesare in Outlook *depicts how Japanese aggression in Manchuria in 1931–1932 destroyed the Kellogg Pact, ended a close U.S.-Japanese relationship, and violently shut a long chapter of the American open-door policy in Asia.*

thought the rail incident only a local crisis. Believing that because of his experience in running the Philippines he "knew something" about the "Oriental mind," the secretary of state decided not to pressure Japan and not to defend Chinese revolutionaries. As the U.S. ambassador to London told the Japanese, "The Chinese are altogether too cocky. What you people need to do is to give them a thoroughly good licking to teach them their place and then they will be willing to talk sense."[50] Japan agreed. By January 2, 1932, its army had seized key ports some 1,700 miles from where the war had started.

Stimson was now aware that he had misread the "Oriental mind" and desperately turned to a series of responses. He tried to wield the Kellogg-Briand Pact of 1928, but Japan paid no attention to its supposed moral force. Stimson hoped that the Japanese economy would crumble under war demands, but instead it improved. He hoped the League of Nations would stand up to Tokyo, but the League merely condemned the invasion. As for economic retaliation, Hoover bluntly refused. He feared that if the economic sanctions did not work, military involvement would have to follow, and he wanted none of that. Moreover, such sanctions would be the knockout blow to U.S.-Japan economic relations. "The result," in historian Gary Ostrower's words, "was confusion because Stimson wanted both to stop Japan militarily and expand relations with Japan economically."[51] (For its part, Japan quit the League in early 1933.)

On January 7, 1932, Stimson declared in the so-called "Hoover-

Stimson Doctrine" that the United States would not recognize Japan's control over Manchuria (or "Manchukuo," as Tokyo had renamed it). The Japanese militarists cared little. Eleven days later, their troops seized the great port city of Shanghai. On February 24, Stimson played his highest card. He sent an open letter to Senator Borah, who had strongly opposed Japan's actions. Stimson warned that unless Tokyo upheld the Nine-Power Treaty promise to observe the open door in China, Washington would not uphold the Five-Power Treaty limiting the building of warships. Thus, the United States threatened Japan with a war fleet in the Pacific—at least sometime in the future after the fleet was built. But this threat also had little effect. Stimson was now ready to get tougher with Japan. But Hoover flatly refused. Stimson fretted privately that the president was a good engineer who thought that foreign policy could be carefully calculated—"like building a bridge." Actually, the secretary of state told Hoover, "You . . . make your plans only for a certain distance," and the best rule is that "in case of doubt . . . march toward the guns."[52]

Hoover refused to march. He was afraid that a break with Japan could destroy all order in Asia. After all, he told his cabinet, Tokyo faced danger from "a Bolshevist Russia to the north and a possible Bolshevist China" on the flank. The president also told an aide that "just between ourselves, it would not be a bad thing if Mr. Jap should go into Manchuria, for with two thorns in his side—China and the Bolsheviks—he would have enough to keep him busy for awhile."[53] But the Soviets themselves were playing a two-faced game. They asked Japan for a friendship treaty, then secretly approached the United States to join them in "breaking [Japan] as between the two arms of a nutcracker."[54] Hoover, however, could never diplomatically recognize a Soviet Union that, as Stimson complained, was always "violating the fundamental tenets of international intercourse."[55] The United States thus stood paralyzed amid the ruins of its economy and, therefore, the ruins of its entire postwar foreign policy.

GETTING "BLUE" OVER LATIN AMERICA

The 1922 treaty system implied that the military forces of certain powers would maintain order in their regions—for example, Japan in Asia and the United States in Latin America. The U.S. military was accompanied by bankers and traders seeking profit. They found it. Between 1924 and 1929, U.S. investments in Latin America more than doubled from $1.5 billion to over $3.5 billion, twice as much as Americans invested in any other geographical area. Much of the money was used to take over vital mineral resources such as Chile's copper and Venezuela's oil. Before 1914, most U.S. investors worked in the Central American–Caribbean region. But now they moved throughout the larger nations to the south. They were replacing the British, who had bankrolled South American development for a century. Washington officials believed that the dollars only produced happiness and order. "The number of rebellions per capita is highest in those republics where the per capita mileage of . . . highways is lowest," one wrote. "Romance may have been driven out by the cement mixer, but the mixer has paved the way for law and order."[56]

President Coolidge was not so sure. The more Americans invested, the more they seemed to be attacked by angry Latin Americans. Coolidge finally warned in 1925 that because "the person and property of a citizen are a part of the general domain of the nation, even when abroad," he had the right to send troops to protect that "domain."[57] Thus, U.S. Marines controlled Nicaragua, the Dominican Republic, Haiti, and Panama, and overshadowed many other nations. The easy excuse for sending in troops was the Monroe Doctrine. The founder of Christian Science, Mary Baker Eddy, spoke for millions of North Americans when she said in 1923, "I believe strictly in the Monroe Doctrine, in our Constitution, and in the laws of God."[58] Another motive was racism. U.S. officials running Haiti once had a Marine-trained band honor the Haitian president by playing "Bye, Bye Blackbird." Many of these officials were from the U.S. South and were sent to the Caribbean nations because they supposedly knew how best to handle black people.

By the late 1920s, Latin Americans were fighting such policies. They happily joined the League of Nations and were cool toward the idea of Pan-Americanism precisely because North Americans were not in the former and tried to dominate the latter. A leading Chilean newspaper warned in 1930 that the United States "Colossus" had "financial might" without "equal in history," and that its aim was "Americas for the Americans—of the North."[59] An earlier survey showed that of the twenty Latin American nations, all but six were controlled or heavily influenced by U.S. Marines, U.S. bankers, or both. In 1928, at the Havana Inter-American Conference, a resolution stated that "no state has a right to intervene in the internal affairs of another." When former Secretary of State Hughes tried to kill the resolution, he found only four

Latin American supporters—three of whose nations were run by U.S. military forces.

The State Department finally tried to deal with the growing condemnation in 1929–1930 by issuing a memorandum written by Undersecretary of State Reuben Clark. The Clark Memorandum declared that the Monroe Doctrine—or, more accurately, the Roosevelt Corollary to the doctrine (see p. 247)—should not be used to justify U.S. intervention. (Clark argued, however, that North Americans had other legal rights to protect themselves and their property abroad.) President Hoover scored a major success by announcing that he planned to withdraw the marines from the Caribbean and take a triumphant tour of South America.

But the turnaround came too late. Wall Street's collapse in 1929 meant in Latin America, as elsewhere, the collapse of what Hughes had called *Pax Americana.* Between 1929 and 1931, revolution struck seven hemispheric nations. By 1933, only Colombia, Uruguay, and Venezuela had escaped revolution. The United States, joined enthusiastically by the sitting governments, had refused in 1923 to recognize regimes that rose to power by force. In 1931, Stimson had to reverse that policy simply because the southern continent was in continual upheaval. The cement-mixer approach had not worked. "I am getting quite blue over the bad way in which all Latin America is showing up," Stimson wrote in his diary in 1932. They do not help themselves. "Yet if we try to take the lead for them . . . there is a cry against domination and imperialism."[60]

THOSE "BOLSHEVISTS" IN MEXICO AND NICARAGUA

Such a cry had been going up for years in two key nations, Mexico and Nicaragua. In Mexico, the long-festering dispute between U.S. officials and the revolutionary government finally stopped in 1923. An agreement was reached giving North Americans an indemnity for their lands seized by Mexico for redistribution to peasants. U.S. oil companies also received protection for their holdings. But these deals were never ratified by the U.S. Senate. In 1925, President Plutarco Calles bowed to rising protests in Mexico by trying again to tighten control over his country's rich oil reserves. Another crisis threatened U.S.-Mexican relations. This time, however, both sides quickly tried to find a compromise.

Coolidge and Secretary of State Kellogg hated what they saw as "Bolshevist" influences in the Mexican Revolution. They nevertheless listened to oil companies that wanted to make a deal. Coolidge consequently sent Dwight Morrow to negotiate a settlement in 1927. As a Wall Street lawyer, Morrow was acceptable to North Americans. As a smart, broad-minded negotiator who ordered a good-will visit to Mexico by his future son-in-law Charles Lindbergh (perhaps the world's most famous celebrity because he had been the first to fly across the Atlantic Ocean alone in 1927), Morrow became well liked in Mexico. The Calles government agreed to validate in perpetuity all titles to oil lands obtained before May 1917. The president's retreat soon paid off. When a revolt against Calles erupted in 1929, Hoover sent him arms and refused to deal with the rebels, who soon surrendered.

The Nicaraguan story did not have such a happy ending. U.S. troops had controlled the country since 1911–1912. In 1925, however, Coolidge concluded that order and the strength of pro-U.S. groups were sufficient to bring the boys back home. Within weeks, fighting again erupted. After a U.S. admiral tried to mediate aboard his warship, Adolfo Díaz emerged as a president acceptable to Coolidge. But again fighting broke out, with Mexico on the side of the anti-Díaz rebels. Crying that Russian bolshevism threatened Nicaragua, in 1926 Coolidge again landed the marines. Norman Davis, a leading Democrat and an experienced diplomat, blasted the decision: "By basing our policy with Latin America upon a fear of Bolshevism, we not only destroy our influence and prestige with Latin America, but we give great encouragement to the Bolshevists."[61] Coolidge nevertheless sent Henry Stimson in with the troops to work out an acceptable deal. Stimson talked both sides into laying down arms and cooperating with an election in 1928 held under U.S. supervision.

But one leader rejected Stimson's settlement. Augusto Sandino replied: "The sovereignty and liberty of a people are not to be discussed but rather defended with weapons in hand."[62] He organized a small guerrilla band to resist the marines. Sandino's well-to-do father, who gave his son a good education, had lost his political power when the marines appeared in 1911–1912. The son became further angered at the United States when he saw firsthand Woodrow Wilson's landing of U.S. troops in Mexico during 1914. By 1927, Sandino was less a revolutionary (he rejected the Marxism-Leninism of other Central American revolutionaries) than an anticolonialist. He simply wanted the United States out of his country.

His small army attacked U.S. troop camps. In 1927, the marine com-

Augusto Sandino (1893–1934) is pictured here (in the center, wearing a checked shirt) with his aides in Nicaragua. Sandino led the resistance to the U.S. occupation of 1927–1933 and—as it turned out by the 1970s and 1980s—both opened a new chapter in U.S.–Central American relations and gave a bloody preview of the problems that Washington officials would have in dealing with Third World nationalist revolts.

mander responded to a Sandino attack on Ocotal by calling in five aircraft. In the first organized dive-bombing attack in the hemisphere's history, the planes bombed and machine-gunned the rebels with bloody results. Over one hundred Sandinistas were killed or wounded in minutes. But their leader survived. He found strong support in the mountains from peasants who had gained nothing from the long U.S. occupation. Sandino ruthlessly destroyed American property and often dealt with disloyal Nicaraguans by giving them a "gourd cut"—slicing off a part of the skull, exposing the victim's brain, and causing hours of convulsions and suffering before dying. "Liberty is not conquered with flowers," Sandino believed.[63]

By 1929, 5,500 marines were unable to capture the "bandits," as Stimson called the Sandinistas. But the troops were taking casualties and costing U.S. taxpayers millions of dollars. High-school debaters soon discussed the national debate topic of whether the marines should leave Nicaragua. Republican senator Burton K. Wheeler from Montana acidly declared that if the marines were really supposed to fight "bandits," they could best do it in Chicago. Another critic wrote that if the U.S. government actually thought it could impose democratic elections, it might try to begin in Philadelphia. A businessman warned that U.S. policy "has proved a calamity for the American coffee planters. . . . Today we are hated and despised" because the marines were sent "to hunt down and kill Nicaraguans in their own country."[64] Stimson was especially embarrassed to have to defend the marines in Nicaragua while he condemned the Japanese invasion of China.

He and Hoover decided to pull out the troops. But they left behind a U.S.-trained National Guard to maintain order. The guard's commander was Anastasio Somoza, a Philadelphia-educated Nicaraguan whose love of baseball and talent for cussing in English helped win Stimson's trust. As Sandino had promised, once the marines left in 1933, he laid down his arms. With a grant of amnesty, he began talks with the Nicaraguan government. After one session in February 1934, Somoza's henchmen seized Sandino and two of his closest aides, took them to a government airfield, and executed them. By 1936, Somoza had used the guard to claim dictatorial power. Elected civilians in Managua appealed to Washington for help. The State Department replied, apparently with a straight face, that it was contrary to U.S. policy to interfere in Nicaraguan affairs.[65]

But the story was not over. Sandino had presented a new challenge to the United States: a guerrilla leader who had strong mass support, an anticolonial ideology, and the military capacity to defy U.S. power. Some 136 marines lost their lives (including twelve who committed suicide in Nicaragua), but Sandino's success went far beyond battle casualties. He anticipated the problems that North Americans were to encounter later in China, Cuba, Vietnam, and, finally, Nicaragua itself after 1979, when the self-styled "Sandinista" revolutionaries would overthrow the Somoza dynasty and once again defy the United States.

CONCLUSION

North Americans did not retreat from the world in the 1920s. They, instead, tried nothing less than to restructure its affairs. The foundation of the new structure was the dollar, and atop it were piled the treaty systems of Washington, Locarno, Geneva, and Kellogg-Briand. The blueprint for the structure was based on the needs of Americans. They had become a great world power—indeed, the greatest economically. Hoover wanted them, however, to maintain their "American individualism" (to use the title of his widely read essay) as they circled a globe now shaped by new technology, industry, and national hatreds. World War I itself could never be repeated, the argument ran, because the world was going to be too integrated, too open, too Americanized for another such bloodletting. "We believed . . . that such a change [for peace] could now be predicated upon definite economic and evolutionary facts," Stimson wrote in 1933.[66]

By then, of course, the dollar had collapsed. The delicate treaty structure fell on top of it. In historian John M. Carroll's words, "The foundations of economic and political stability" laid during the 1920s were simply "swept away during the economic crisis of the 1930s."[67] Hitler, Japanese militarists, and the Somozas of the less-industrialized nations—not "American individualism"—threatened to restructure the world. Washington's response now came from the newly elected president, fifty-one-year-old Franklin D. Roosevelt, who searched through the wreckage of the 1920s for a new, workable blueprint. He never found it during peacetime.

NOTES

1. John Morton Blum, *Public Philosopher: Selected Letters of Walter Lippmann* (New York, 1985), pp. 136–137.
2. Paul F. Boller, Jr., *Presidential Anecdotes* (New York, 1981), pp. 229–230.
3. Charles Evans Hughes, *The Pathway of Peace* (New York, 1925), p. 159.
4. Joan Hoff Wilson, *Herbert Hoover: Forgotten Progressive* (Boston, 1975), pp. 168, 179.
5. Herbert C. Hoover, *Memoirs*, 3 vols. (New York, 1951–1952), II, p. 28.
6. David Green, *Shaping Political Consciousness: The Language of Politics in America from McKinley to Reagan* (Ithaca, N.Y., 1988), ch. 3.
7. Warren I. Cohen, *Empire without Tears: America's Foreign Relations, 1921–1933* (New York, 1987), p. 13; Herbert Hoover, *American Individualism* (Washington, D.C., 1922), p. 31.
8. Charles E. Neu, *The Troubled Encounter: The United States and Japan* (New York, 1975), pp. 100, 103.
9. Ira Klein, "Whitehall, Washington, and the Anglo-Japanese Alliance, 1919–1921," *Pacific Historical Review* 46, no. 2 (1968): 468–469; Lloyd C. Gardner, *Safe for Democracy* (New York, 1984), pp. 307–319, has a fine discussion.
10. Carl P. Parrini, *Heir to Empire: United States Economic Diplomacy, 1916–1923* (Pittsburgh, 1969), pp. 202–203.
11. The Washington treaties and Harding's rationale for them can be conveniently found in *The Record of American Diplomacy*, ed. Ruhl J. Bartlett, 4th ed. (New York, 1964),

pp. 486–497; the quote is from Lloyd Gardner, Walter LaFeber, and Thomas McCormick, *The Creation of the American Empire* (Chicago, 1973), p. 357.

12. Thomas Buckley, *The United States and the Washington Conference, 1921–1922* (Knoxville, Tenn., 1970), p. 187.

13. Andrew Sinclair, *The Available Man: The Life behind the Masks of Warren Gamaliel Harding* (New York, 1965), p. 244.

14. Akira Iriye, *After Imperialism: The Search for a New Order in the Far East* (New York, 1969), p. 20.

15. Charles Evans Hughes, "Some Aspects of the Work of the Department of State," *American Journal of International Law* 16 (May 1922): 358–359; a fine brief analysis is Justus D. Doenecke, "The Most-Favored-Nation Principle," in *Encyclopedia of American Foreign Policy*, ed. Alexander DeConde, 3 vols. (New York, 1978), II, p. 608.

16. Brenda Gayle Plummer, "Epilogue," in "Black and White in the Caribbean: Haitian-American Relations, 1902–1934" (Ph.D. diss., Cornell University, 1981).

17. Parrini, pp. 186–187.

18. Hoover, *Memoirs*, II, pp. 81–82.

19. Rexford G. Tugwell, *The Democratic Roosevelt* (Garden City, N.Y., 1957), p. 132.

20. Melvyn P. Leffler, *The Elusive Quest: America's Pursuit of European Stability and French Security, 1919–1933* (Chapel Hill, N.C., 1979), pp. 48, 170.

21. Ivy Lee, "The Black Legend: Europe Indicts America," *Atlantic Monthly* 143 (May 1929): 577–588.

22. David F. Schmitz, *The United States and Fascist Italy, 1922–1940* (Chapel Hill, N.C., 1988), pp. 1, 42; John P. Diggins, *Mussolini and Fascism: The View from America* (Princeton, 1972), tells this fascinating story.

23. Frederick C. Adams, *Economic Diplomacy: The Export-Import Bank and American Foreign Policy, 1934–1939* (Columbia, Mo., 1976), ch I, contains the quotes and a useful context.

24. Herbert Feis, *The Diplomacy of the Dollar, 1919–1923* (New York, 1950), pp. 40–42.

25. Leffler, p. 100.

26. Frank Costigliola, "The United States and the Reconstruction of Germany in the 1920s," *Business History Review* 50 (Winter 1976): 477–502, esp. 488.

27. D. Cameron Watt, *Succeeding John Bull: America in Britain's Place, 1900–1975* (Cambridge, 1984), p. 50.

28. *Ibid.*, p. 58–59.

29. *Ibid.*, p. 59. A similar U.S. view of Great Britain is nicely analyzed in Raymond G. O'Connor, *Perilous Equilibrium: The United States and the London Disarmament Conference of 1930* (Lawrence, Kans., 1962, 1969), pp. 13–14.

30. Anthony Sampson, *The Seven Sisters* (New York, 1975), pp. 58, 65; William Stivers, "A Note on the Red Line Agreement," *Diplomatic History* 7 (Winter 1983): 23, 30, 34.

31. William Appleman Williams, *American-Russian Relations, 1781–1947* (New York, 1952), pp. 193–201, 211–214; Joan Hoff Wilson, *American Business and Foreign Policy, 1920–1933* (Lexington, Ky., 1971), p. 105.

32. Manfred Jonas, *The United States and Germany, a Diplomatic History* (Ithaca, N.Y., 1984), pp. 182–183.

33. Arthur Schlesinger, Jr., *The Crisis of the Old Order, 1919–1933* (Boston, 1957), pp. 142–143.

34. *New York Times*, 23 September 1979, p. F8.

35. *Ibid.*

36. Boller, pp. 234–235.

37. Leffler, p. 198. The loan figures are in the U.S. Department of Commerce, *Historical Statistics of the United States, Colonial Times to 1957* (Washington, D.C., 1961), p. 564.

38. Adams, ch. II.

39. Leffler, p. 219.

40. Grosvenor Jones, Bureau of Foreign and Domestic Commerce, to Herbert Hoover, 7 August 1926, Commerce, Official Files, Box 130, Herbert Hoover Library, West Branch, Iowa; Iriye, p. 26.

41. "Draft" verbally stated to the president, 21 April 1924, Commerce, Official Files, Box 234, Hoover Library; Herbert Hoover to Mark L. Requa, 21 April 1924, Commerce, Official Files, Box 170, Hoover Library.

42. William L. Neumann, "Ambiguity and Ambivalence in Ideas of National Interest in Asia," in *Isolation and Security*, ed. Alexander DeConde (Durham, N.C., 1957), p. 136; William L. Neumann, "Determinism, Destiny, and Myth in the American Image of China," in *Issues and Conflicts: Studies in Twentieth Century American Diplomacy*, ed. George L. Anderson (Lawrence, Kans., 1959), pp. 11–12; C. F. Remer, *Foreign Investment in China* (New York, 1933), p. 274.

43. Grosvenor Jones, Bureau of Foreign and Domestic Commerce, to Herbert Hoover, 7 August 1926, Commerce, Official Files, Box 130, Hoover Library.

44. Pauline Tompkins, *American-Russian Relations in the Far East* (New York, 1949), p. 212.

45. John King Fairbank, *The Great Chinese Revolution: 1800–1985* (New York, 1986), pp. 182–183, 204–216.

46. *New York Times*, 12 July 1973, p. 14.

47. Foster Rhea Dulles, *China and America: The Story of Their Relations since 1784* (Princeton, 1946), pp. 166–167.

48. Robert H. Ferrell, *American Diplomacy in the Great Depression* (New Haven, 1957), p. 19.

49. O'Connor, p. 160n.

50. Ferrell, p. 146; Elting E. Morison, *Turmoil and Tradition: The Life and Times of Henry L. Stimson* (Boston, 1960), pp. 373–374.

51. Gary B. Ostrower, *Collective Insecurity: The U.S. and the League of Nations during the Early Thirties* (Lewisburg, Pa., 1979), p. 203; Armin Rappaport, *Henry L. Stimson and Japan, 1931–1933* (Chicago, 1963), pp. 148–149.

52. Morison, p. 313; Lloyd C. Gardner, *Economic Aspects of New Deal Diplomacy* (Madison, Wis., 1964), pp. 80, 111. There is also an important analysis in *The Diplomacy of Frustration: The Manchurian Crisis of 1931–1933 as Revealed in the Papers of Stanley K. Hornbeck*, ed. Justus D. Doenecke (Stanford, 1981), p. xii.

53. Richard N. Current, *Secretary Stimson: A Study in Statecraft* (New Brunswick, N.J., 1954), pp. 79, 87; Doenecke, ed., *The Diplomacy of Frustration*, p. 13.

54. Tompkins, ch. XII.

55. Morison, p. 312.

56. Julius Klein, *Frontiers of Trade* (New York, 1929), p. 39. Klein's view is well analyzed in Robert N. Seidel, *Progressive Pan Americanism*, Cornell University Latin American Studies Program Dissertation Series (Ithaca, N.Y., 1973), pp. 136–186.

57. Feis, p. 29.

58. Gaddis Smith, "The Legacy of the Monroe Doctrine," *New York Times Magazine*, 9 September 1984, p. 125.

59. Donald M. Dozer, *Are We Good Neighbors?: Three Decades of Inter-American Relations, 1930–1960* (Gainesville, Fla., 1959), pp. 4–7.

60. Gardner, *Economic Aspects of New Deal Diplomacy*, pp. 35–36.

61. Norman Davis to Claude A. Swanson, 14 January 1927, Box 53, Papers of Norman Davis, Library of Congress, Washington, D.C. Robert Freeman Smith found a poem written by Senator George Norris that satirized Coolidge's fear of Bolsheviks in the southern nations. (The form parodies a popular poem by James Whitcomb Riley.)

> "Once't there was a Bolshevik who wouldn't say his prayers, So Kellogg sent him off to bed, away upstairs; An' Kellogg heered him holler, and Coolidge heered him bawl, But when they turn't the kivers down he wasn't there at all. They seeked him down in Mexico, they cussed him in the press, They seeked him round the Capitol, an' evey'where I guess. But all they ever found of him was whiskers, hair and clout; An' the Bolsheviks 'ill get you ef you don't watch out."

(Robert Freeman Smith, "Republican Policy and the Pax Americana, 1921–1932," in *From Colony to Empire: Essays in the History of American Foreign Relations*, ed. William A. Williams [New York, 1972], pp. 256–257.)

62. Thomas W. Walker, *Nicaragua: The Land of Sandino* (Boulder, Col., 1981), p. 22.

63. Neill Macaulay, *The Sandino Affair* (Chicago, 1967), pp. 211–212.

64. Dozer, pp. 11–12.

65. Juan Sacasa, Emiliano Chamorro, Adolfo Díaz to Cordell Hull, 30 November 1936, in U.S. Department of State, *Foreign Relations of the United States, 1936*, 5 vols. (Washington, D.C., 1954), V, pp. 844–846.

66. Henry L. Stimson, "Bases of American Foreign Policy during the Past Four Years," *Foreign Affairs* 11 (April 1933): 383.

67. John M. Carroll, "Owen D. Young and German Reparations," in *U.S. Diplomats in Europe, 1919–1941*, ed. Kenneth Paul Jones (Santa Barbara, Calif., 1981), p. 60. The essays in this volume on the 1920s by Hogan, Jones, Costigliola, and Swerczek are also valuable.

FOR FURTHER READING

Check also the notes to this chapter and the General Bibliography at the end of this book; most of those references are not repeated here. But begin with *Guide to American Foreign Relations since 1700*, ed. Richard Dean Burns (1983), which is incomparable for helping those who wish to research specific topics. Because of Burns's work, the following references are almost entirely post-1981 publications.

The most helpful overviews on 1921–1933 are Warren I. Cohen, *Empire without Tears: America's Foreign Relations, 1921–1933* (1987), with lively writing and an excellent bibliography; Martin Sklar's pioneering, *The United States as a Developing Country* (1992);

Frank Costigliola, *Awkward Dominion: American Political, Economic, and Cultural Relations with Europe, 1919–1933* (1985), superb on Europe and especially cultural relations; Akíra Iriye, *The Globalizing of America, 1914–1945*, in *The Cambridge History of U.S. Foreign Relations*, ed. Warren Cohen (1993); John M. Carroll, "American Diplomacy in the 1920s," in *Modern American Diplomacy*, ed. John M. Carroll and George C. Herring (1986), a useful brief analysis; and two most important overviews by John Braeman: "Power and Diplomacy: The 1920s Reappraised," *Review of Politics* 44 (July 1982), and "The New Left and American Foreign Policy during the Age of Normalcy: A Re-examination," *Business History Review* 57 (Spring 1983). Cultural and economic expansion is nicely woven together in Emily S. Rosenberg's important *Spreading the American Dream* (1982), which covers 1890 to 1945 but is especially good on the "cooperative" state of the 1920s. On the peace movement, important accounts include Harold Josephson, "Outlawing War: Internationalism and the Pact of Paris," *Diplomatic History* 3 (1979), and George Peter Marabell, *Frederick Libby and the American Peace Movement* (1982).

Patrick Hearden, "Herbert C. Hoover and the Dream of Capitalism in One Country," in *Redefining the Past: Essays in Diplomatic History in Honor of William Appleman Williams*, ed. Lloyd C. Gardner (1986), is inclusive and gives additional sources; and the same can be said for Betty Glad, "Charles Evans Hughes, Rationalism and Foreign Affairs," in *Studies in American Diplomacy, 1865–1945*, ed. Norman Graebner (1985). An elite group whose origins tell much about 1920s policies is analyzed in Robert D. Schulzinger, *The Wise Men of Foreign Affairs: The History of the Council on Foreign Relations* (1984).

On Europe, the following are important (along with Costigliola, noted above): B.J.C. McKercher, *Anglo-American Relations in the 1920s* (1990); Michael Hogan, "Thomas W. Lamont and European Recovery," in *U.S. Diplomats in Europe, 1919–1941*, ed. Kenneth Paul Jones (1981), a book whose essays are most helpful for the entire interwar era; Peter H. Buckingham, *International Normalcy: The Open Door Peace with the Former Central Powers, 1921–1929* (1983); Henry Blumenthal, *Illusion and Reality in Franco-American Diplomacy, 1914–1945* (1986); Neal Pease, *Poland, the United States and the Stabilization of Europe, 1919–1933* (1986). Two crucial books on Middle East and oil policies are William Stivers, *Supremacy and Oil: Iraq, Turkey, and the Anglo-American World Order, 1918–1930* (1982), and Stephen J. Randall, *U.S. Foreign Oil Policy, 1919–1948* (1985), which stresses an "associational state" approach.

On the Far East, Roger Dingman, *Power in the Pacific: The Origins of Naval Arms Limitations, 1914–1922* (1976), is standard; Sandra C. Taylor, *Advocate of Understanding: Sidney Gulick and the Search for Peace with Japan* (1984), is important for far more than its excellent biography; Bernard D. Cole, *Gunboats and Marines: The U.S. Navy in China, 1925–1928* (1983), revealing for its analysis of divisions among U.S. officials; *The Diplomacy of Frustration: The Manchurian Crisis of 1931–1933 as Revealed in the Papers of Stanley K. Hornbeck*, ed. Justus D. Doenecke (1981), a pivotal source on a pivotal figure; William F. Wu, *The Yellow Peril: Chinese Americans in American Fiction, 1850–1940* (1982), interesting as cultural and diplomatic history.

On Latin America, see Robert Freeman Smith, "Thomas W. Lamont," in T. McCormick and W. LaFeber, eds., *Behind the Throne* (1993), essays in honor of Fred Harvey Harrington; Kenneth J. Grieb, *The Latin American Policy of Warren G. Harding* (1977), an important starting point; John H. Findling, *Close Neighbors, Distant Friends: United States–Central American Relations* (1987), very useful, inclusive, and with good sources for further research; Stephen G. Rabe, *The Road to OPEC: U.S. Relations with Venezuela, 1919–1976* (1982), superb on oil as well as Latin American policies; John A. Britton, *Carleton Beals: A Radical Journalist in Latin America* (1987), a much-needed biography of an outspoken critic; Kenneth A. Jennings, "Sandino against the Marines: The Development of Air Power for Conducting Counterinsurgency Operations in Central America," *Air University Review* 37 (July–August, 1986), a different perspective; and Michael Krenn's important *U.S. Policy Toward Economic Nationalism in Latin America, 1917–1929* (1990).

12

FDR and the Entry into World War II (1933–1941)

The Second Roosevelt

Franklin D. Roosevelt entered the White House in March 1933 as Americans reeled in shock from the economic crisis. The banking system lay in shambles, one of four workers had no job, formerly comfortable businessmen sold apples for 5 cents each on street corners, and dust storms choked those farmers not already driven off their land by bankruptcy. Hitler and Japanese expansionists began to shape world politics, while the League of Nations, mortally wounded by the U.S. and British refusal to support its call to action against Japan in 1932, stumbled slowly to its death.

No one could predict how Roosevelt might react to these crises. Born into a wealthy New York family, distantly related to Theodore Roosevelt, educated at an elite prep school and at Harvard (where his C average indicated that he spent most of his time editing the school newspaper), Roosevelt knew little about grass-roots America. But he moved successfully into New York state politics, then became assistant secretary of the navy under Woodrow Wilson. In 1920, the thirty-eight-year-old ran as vice-president on the Democratic party ticket that promised to support Wilson's League of Nations. The Democrats lost, but Roosevelt's future looked limitless—until he was struck down with polio in 1921. His legs were paralyzed for life, his political career apparently ruined. But, with the help of his wife Eleanor and close political friends, FDR fought back. He later said that global crises should be put in perspective: "If you had spent two years in bed trying to wiggle your big toe, after that anything else would seem easy."[1] In 1928, he won the governorship of New York and, four years later, defeated the hapless Herbert Hoover for the presidency. Roosevelt had gained the Democratic nomination, however, only after pleasing the party's isolationists by separating himself from the League and by delighting conservatives with his promises of a balanced budget.

FDR's consuming problem was how to lift the depression off American backs. His priority at first seemed clear: "I shall spare no effort to restore world trade by international economic readjustment," he declared in his inaugural address, "but the emergency at home cannot wait on that accomplishment." Foreign-policy aims were limited to a single paragraph of the speech. He only promised "the policy of the good neighbor—the neighbor who resolutely respects himself and, because he does so, respects the rights of others." During his first months in office, Roosevelt consequently searched for domestic solutions to the depression and downplayed foreign relations. Seeking relief at home, the president wanted no obligations overseas that might prevent him from doing whatever he thought necessary to ease the economic pressures in the United States.

A first target was the international gold standard. Often thought of as mysterious, magical, and impossible to understand (except by a chosen few in Washington or Wall Street), the gold standard actually worked quite simply. During the McKinley administration thirty-five years before, the United States had tied itself to the standard. Great Britain and other industrial powers also were linked to it. By doing so, these nations pledged to tie their national currencies (such as dollars or pounds) to their supply of gold. Because the gold supply was limited, the nations could not pay their debts merely by printing large amounts of money. The gold standard thus prevented inflation by preventing the printing of too much money. It also forced nations to curb their expenditures and balance their budgets. The gold standard supposedly kept expensive and dangerous military budgets from building up. Those nations that were creditors (and, thus, did not want to be repaid in cheaper, inflated dollars) and that had large supplies of gold were— not surprisingly—deeply in love with the gold standard.

Now it happened that the United States had become the world's great creditor in 1914–1917. In the 1920s it steadily added to an already large supply of gold. So Americans were especially charmed by the

In only the second photo he ever allowed taken of a White House press confer-ence, FDR demonstrated how he informally and charmingly—but steadily and successfully—handled reporters and got his message to the American people. Here he tells the reporters, on August 25, 1939, that world war can still be avoided.

gold standard. By 1933, however, the standard was under attack. In order to raise their prices (that is, print more money) and take control of their economy away from the United States, the British, French, and many others broke with gold. In mid-1933, FDR decided he could no longer stick with it either. He wanted to be able to raise U.S. prices or to go into debt—that is, have an unbalanced government budget—to build large public projects such as dams and roads that would give people work. His budget director, Lewis Douglas, and the young undersecretary of the Treasury, Dean Acheson, resigned in protest. Douglas even declared that breaking with the gold standard was "the end of western civilization."[2] He feared that the United States had cut itself off from the rest of civilization and that hordes of selfish Ameri-cans would descend on Washington to demand the printing of paper money to pay for their own pet projects.

LONDON, FAILURE, AND HULL

The meaning of FDR's act for foreign policy was immediate. In 1932, Hoover had arranged a London Economic Conference to discuss cooperative efforts for increasing trade and reducing arms. As he left office, Hoover warned that only such international cooperation could maintain American individualism *and* world peace. For, he continued, if FDR tried instead to save the U.S. economy by increasing government's role in the society, the country would soon be on the road to socialism or fascism. The early New Deal confirmed some of Hoover's fears. Roosevelt did send a U.S. group to the London Economic Conference in the spring of 1933, but without instructions. When he learned that the conference wanted to tie the dollar and other currencies to a new international standard, FDR sent a telegram rejecting the deal. As the newspaper headlines proclaimed, he "torpedoed the conference." Roosevelt was determined to maintain control over the dollar—damn the foreign relations.

By late 1933, however, his domestic experiments had not worked. The depression continued to suffocate the economy. FDR knew that the nation stood at a historic turn. Something was fundamentally wrong with the system. In a 1932 campaign speech in San Francisco, he had used Frederick Jackson Turner's "frontier thesis" (see p. 185) to explain the crisis: "As long as we had free land . . . as long as our industrial plants were insufficient to supply our own needs, society chose to give the ambitious man free play and unlimited reward."[3] Now, the free land had mostly disappeared. The plants and farms produced great gluts of goods. His analysis implied that a radical solution was needed. But FDR was no radical. When his New Deal proposals failed to do the job quickly in 1933, he reversed himself and went back to the traditional American tactic of searching for markets abroad. "The plain truth is," wrote a journalist who knew him well, "that Roosevelt was perfectly ready to follow a political course that would have broken a snake's back."[4]

He already had a most traditional secretary of state in Cordell Hull. FDR had appointed him because Hull's long service in Congress helped ensure support from friends on Capitol Hill for whatever foreign policy the president wanted. But Hull was a tough sixty-two-year-old Tennessee mountaineer who uttered profanity with great skill gained from frequent use. He also knew his own mind, a mind shaped by his idol, Woodrow Wilson. Hull fervently believed that "unhampered trade

Cordell Hull of Tennessee (1871–1955) served as secretary of state longer than anyone else (1933–1944). President Roosevelt often ignored the former congressman's single-minded determination to create a freer-trade world that had no spheres of influence. But the stubborn, shrewd secretary of state nevertheless greatly shaped policy in the 1930s and the early cold war of the 1940s. He placed special emphasis on closer relations with Latin America.

dovetailed with peace; high tariffs, trade barriers, and unfair economic competition [dovetailed] with war." "A freer flow of goods," he emphasized, raised everyone's living standard, "thereby eliminating the economic dissatisfaction that breeds war." Widely read newspaper columnist Dorothy Thompson captured Hull: he was "a backwoods Tennessean, who looks very much like a gentle and long suffering saint. . . . Yet this quiet man is a person of considerable force; this restrained man is capable of complete and almost fanatical devotion to an idea [of the freest possible international trade] he believes in."[5]

Hull, therefore, thought FDR's attempt to make the country self-sufficient not only foolish, but dangerous. Self-contained economic blocs, Hull believed, meant international disagreement (as at the London conference) instead of cooperation, and such disagreement could lead to war. Hull served longer (1933–1944) than any other secretary of state in American history. He stuck so firmly to his Wilsonian course during those years that his policies are crucial if we are to understand the New Deal's foreign policy in the 1930s and the roots of the cold war in 1943–1945. FDR usually tried to avoid dealing with Hull and, instead, to keep foreign policy in his own hands. But after flitting around so that he could have "broken a snake's back," the president often ended by agreeing with Hull.

And so it was in 1934. FDR would not go back to the gold standard, but he had so cheapened the dollar (it was now at about half of its 1932 value) that the dollar was more competitive abroad. (In other words, foreigners could now buy many more dollars with their own currencies than they could have bought two years earlier and could use those dollars to buy more U.S. goods.) To push the glut of U.S. goods into foreign markets, Roosevelt and Hull devised two weapons that still remain in the U.S. economic arsenal: the Export-Import Bank (Ex-Im Bank) and the Reciprocal Trade Act (RTA).

The New Deal devised the first Ex-Im Bank to finance trade with Cuba and the Soviet Union. Before this time, private bankers had performed this job, but they had self-destructed between 1929 and 1933. Only the government had the resources to help U.S. merchants finance their overseas sales. But the bank's help was limited in 1934, when an angry Congress passed the Johnson Act forbidding private or public loans to the many governments that had defaulted on their debts to the United States. (The act passed despite strong European protests. As historian Benjamin Rhodes recounts, the British ambassador to Washington even recited the "forgive our debts" phrase from the Lord's Prayer to FDR's advisers, but to no avail.)[6] The bank, however, did obtain special permission to deal with the Soviet Union, and the Johnson Act did not affect foreign *individuals* who needed credit to buy U.S. goods.

In 1934, the Ex-Im Bank expanded so that it could help Americans trade with anyone. It especially scored successes in Latin America. Working through the bank, Roosevelt and Hull could control the flow of capital. If another nation needed dollars, it had to promise to buy U.S. goods and reduce its own barriers to North American investors and traders. Frederick Adams, the best historian of the bank, notes that such conditions increased trade, but "produced additional American interference in the internal affairs of neighboring states," and thus became a sophisticated version of the old "dollar diplomacy."[7]

The Reciprocal Trade Act of June 1934, one of Hull's pet projects, gave the president new powers to bargain for foreign markets. He could make a three-year treaty reducing the U.S. tariff by as much as 50 percent for another nation's goods, if that nation reciprocated by giving similar preferences to U.S. goods in its market. This approach became known as "unconditional-most-favored-nation," for Roosevelt could automatically extend tariff preferences unconditionally to all nations that cooperated. The act gave the chief executive vast new powers in foreign economic policy.

RTA was thus supposed to resemble a great wrecking ball knocking down tariff walls. When the president gave special breaks to one nation that had promised to reduce its tariff to Americans, those breaks automatically went to all other nations that also lowered their walls. The RTA also gave the president new powers to make the treaties without congressional assent. Those powers led one angry Republican senator to fume that RTA was "fascist" and "economic dictatorship come to America." But the Republicans had nothing better to offer.[8]

Again, RTA was especially effective in Latin America, where it helped integrate much of the Western Hemisphere's trade under Washington's control by exchanging the north's industrial goods for the south's minerals. In 1932, the United States accounted for one-third of Latin America's trade, but by 1938 it was involved in nearly half that trade. Globally, between 1934 and 1945, twenty-nine RTA treaties were made that reduced the U.S. tariff by nearly three-quarters. In the five years after the first act in 1934, U.S. exports rose more than $1.0 billion, and the nation's favorable trade balance (that is, more sales than purchases overseas) soared from $0.5 billion to nearly twice that amount.[9] A variation of RTA was passed in 1934 when, under the Tydings-McDuffie Act, Congress promised independence to the Philippines in ten years. (World War II delayed it until 1946.) American economic interests in the islands, especially the sugar growers, were protected by using reciprocity arrangements to tie the Philippine and U.S. markets closely together.

Improving the Neighborhood

As the Ex-Im Bank and RTA illustrated, Roosevelt and Hull lavished special attention on Latin America. That region contained oil, sugar, coffee, and raw materials prized by North Americans, especially those who had $4 billion in investments in the region. Moreover, this "back yard" had been watched over since the 1823 Monroe Doctrine. When Roosevelt referred to the "good neighbor," he revived a phrase first applied by Henry Clay to Latin America in the 1820s, by the treaty of 1848 (even as that treaty seized one-third of Mexico from the Mexicans), and, more recently, by Hoover.

But FDR gave "neighbor" a special meaning by pulling the marines out of Haiti, ending the Platt Amendment that gave presidents the right to intervene in Cuba, opening new economic relations, and signing treaties with Panama in 1936 that finally recognized that nation's right to help operate and protect the great canal that cut the country in half. Not that everything went well. U.S. economic control in Haiti actually tightened to protect foreign investors and, in the later words of a top State Department official, "was an excessive drain on a country as poor as Haiti."[10] But Roosevelt shrewdly removed the U.S. political and military policies that had deeply angered Latin America since the 1890s. In the new atmosphere, he was able to increase U.S. economic influence. That influence accelerated after 1937, when Nazi Germany tried to infiltrate Latin America with trade deals and with such attractive services as those offered by its Lufthansa German Airlines. Washington responded by giving special help to Pan American Airlines and also by ordering the famous "G-men" of the Federal Bureau of Investigation (FBI) to expose Nazis and Communists alike in the region. A new State Department bureau appeared under the leadership of the young and ambitious Nelson Rockefeller (John D. Rockefeller's grandson) to expedite trade deals with Latin America. Rockefeller focused on the pivotal nation of Brazil, where he used the Ex-Im Bank to finance the vast $70-million Volta Redonda Steel plant project. He thus undercut growing German influence in Brazil.

The new economic ties were strengthened by historic political agreements. At the 1933 Pan-American Conference at Montevideo, Uruguay, Hull led the U.S. delegation that finally (if reluctantly) accepted the principle that no nation "has the right to intervene in the internal or external affairs of another." The U.S. Senate unanimously ratified the Montevideo pledge. In 1936 at Buenos Aires, Argentina, the inter-American conference tightened the pledge by declaring "inadmissible the intervention of any of [the Parties], directly or indirectly, and for whatever reason, in the internal or external affairs of any other of the Parties." The 1936 conference also provided for joint consultation in case of trouble.

When the American governments met next at Lima, Peru, in 1938, Hitler's shadow haunted the talks. The Lima Pact created machinery so that the region's foreign ministers could quickly consult in an emergency. After World War II began, the foreign ministers met with Hull in Panama during October 1939 and pledged to stand together to protect their neutral rights. A year later, they issued the Havana Declaration, announcing that they would defend any of the hemisphere's territories owned by non-Americans (for instance, Great Britain or France) so that other nations (such as Germany) could not seize them. In 1941, when the United States went to war, nearly all Latin Americans went with it (Argentina was the major exception). Hull later bragged with good reason that "the political line-up followed the economic line-up."[11]

Not all the good-neighbor policies turned out happily. Unappetizing dictators seized power in many Latin American nations and then held on to it with corruption and brutality. Anastasio Somoza of Nicaragua exemplified this type of leader, growing like a fungus on the debris of the depression. The Nicaraguan cracked down on the free press, broke up labor unions, and attacked the Roman Catholic church—that is, he tried to destroy anyone who threatened his personal power. But, in historian Lester Langley's words, at the same time he "kowtowed to the United States."[12] Somoza, who soon owned 15 percent of the country's land, declared that "Nicaragua is my farm." He nevertheless rode several blocks to work each day in a huge blue Cadillac protected by troops and aircraft. When Roosevelt welcomed the dictator on a state visit to Washington in 1939, a Mexico City newspaper charged that the good neighbor was becoming a "guarantee" for "the slavery of Latin American peoples."[13] But FDR, who with war on the horizon cared more about cooperation than guaranteeing democracy in Central America, privately dismissed such criticism with the alleged remark that Somoza "may be a son-of-a-bitch, but he's our son-of-a-bitch."

Other journals were friendlier. A Colombian newspaper wrote in 1938 that "from the 'Big Stick' to the 'Good Neighbor' was not only an evolution but a revolution." The "second Roosevelt," the editors thought, "has really been a good neighbor to Latin Americans."[14] One conclusion is certain: FDR and Hull changed the hemisphere's general mistrust of Washington in 1933 to general cooperation as they went to war in 1941. "That is a new approach I am talking about to these South American things," the president privately declared in 1940. "Give them a share. They think they are just as good as we are and many of them are."[15]

THE IMMEDIATE NEIGHBORHOOD: CUBA AND MEXICO

He followed this principle in dealing with pressing problems in Cuba and Mexico. Under U.S. control (although supposedly self-governing) since 1901, the Cubans were integrated into the North American economy by 1929. The small country was the fourth best U.S. customer, purchasing $200 million of goods and selling to the mainland all of its one-crop economy, sugar (owned mostly by North Americans). By 1933, however, Cuba's purchases had dropped 80 percent. Its sugar sales fell in half despite the price sliding to one-tenth of a cent per pound.[16]

By August 1933, internal discontent grew so rapidly that Hull sent his undersecretary of state, Sumner Welles (who had long been a close friend of FDR's), to help ease out the Cuban dictator Gerardo Machado. To Welles's dismay, however, Ramón Grau San Martín assumed power. Welles branded him "frankly communistic," and asked for U.S. military intervention. Hull rejected the request. He was supported strongly by Josephus Daniels, a North Carolina newspaperman under whom Roosevelt had served in the Navy Department and who now was the U.S. ambassador to Mexico. Daniels agreed with the secretary of state that "if we have to go in there again we will never be able to come out." Hull preferred to "walk from here to the South Pole than to have to intervene."[17]

U.S. diplomats began to pressure a young army sergeant, Fulgencio Batista, who with other officers had placed Grau San Martín in power. Welles held out the bait of economic aid to Batista, who soon placed Colonel Carlos Mendieta in power. A new commercial treaty and the Export-Import Bank helped shower economic benefits on the new regime. North Americans, meanwhile, increased their exports to Cuba by some 300 percent between 1934 and 1937. None of this exactly complied with the U.S. pledge at Montevideo in 1933 not to interfere in the affairs of other Latin American nations, but Roosevelt nicely deflected any criticism by abrogating the 1901 Platt Amendment that gave the United States the right to intervene in Cuba. He had just proven that the Platt Amendment was no longer necessary anyway: private political pressure and U.S. economic leverage seemed to be enough to make Cubans behave. Or so it appeared in 1934.

Mexican leaders, in Washington's view, had not behaved well since that nation's revolution began in 1911. A major problem was that the revolution had never been completed—that is, it never produced the equality, either political or economic, promised by its early champions. In 1934, a new president, Lázaro Cárdenas, pledged "Mexico for the Mexicans" and promptly strengthened labor unions so that they could strike against foreign corporations. In 1937, workers struck U.S. oil companies and demanded wage increases as high as 33 percent. The companies ignored court rulings upholding the unions. Cárdenas then retaliated by nationalizing the properties of the stunned foreign oil firms. He was also perhaps testing FDR to see whether the American president meant it when he accepted the nonintervention principle of the 1936 Buenos Aires meeting. Roosevelt apparently did, but Hull weakened.

Fearing that the seizure could trigger a chain reaction that would nationalize North American properties throughout the hemisphere, Hull sided with the oil companies, who demanded $262 million in compensation. Mexico insisted that $10 million was enough. Hull urged tough economic retaliation since "I have to deal with those Communists down there." But he was blocked by FDR, Ambassador Daniels, and Secretary of the Treasury Henry Morgenthau, who warned that if Cárdenas was driven to the wall, "we're just going to wake up and find that inside a year that Italy, Germany, and Japan have taken over Mexico."[18]

Morgenthau's fears were justified. When U.S. companies and banks tried to hurt Mexico, the Mexicans, in turn, boycotted U.S. goods and turned to Japan and Germany for products. Cárdenas leaked the news that Mexican oil might be sold to Hitler. After FDR tried several compromises that failed, in 1940 Sinclair Oil broke the solid front of U.S. companies and made a settlement. In November 1941, Washington and Mexico City finally agreed on $40 million in compensation for foreign-owned farmlands that had been seized and $29 million for the oil lands. Mexico's own national oil company, PEMEX, took over the fields. Nevertheless, U.S. influence steadily grew. Through a 1942 reciprocity treaty, Export-Import Bank activities, and U.S. purchases of silver (on which the value of the Mexican currency rested), Mexico's economy became quite dependent on North Americans. U.S. oil companies even continued to manage and market Mexican oil. Historian Clayton Koppes suggests that if the use of this economic power is seen together with U.S. support for client military figures in Nicaragua, the Dominican Republic, Cuba, and El Salvador (among other places), there appears "a combination of military, economic, and diplomatic levers" that demonstrated how "the Good Neighbor policy was United States hemispheric hegemony pursued by other means."[19]

GERMANS, JAPANESE, AND A ONE-ARMED NUTCRACKER

From his first moments in office, FDR was preoccupied with these German and Japanese threats. By May 1933, he personally warned Nazi officials about their violence against Jews. By 1934, German state control of trade clashed with Hull's reciprocal trade plans to open commercial channels. Hitler quit the League and all disarmament conferences while he built up an internal police (the future Gestapo) and a new army. The Americans watched with apprehension but did little. They believed that the British and French were responsible for maintaining peace in Europe. Growing U.S. public concern about European involvements (especially to help those cheaters who had refused

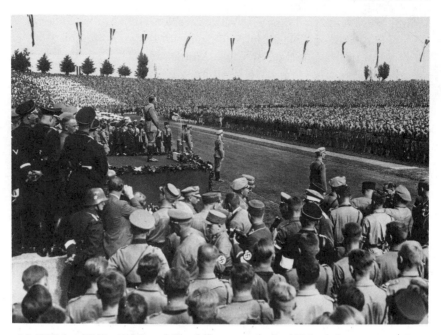

Adolf Hitler (1889–1945) mobilized Germany in the 1930s with a sweep and brutality that most Americans could not comprehend. Here he addresses thousands of Hitler youth at Nuremberg Stadium.

to pay their debts) also made FDR reluctant to become further involved.

Japan was a different story. Along with many other Americans, Roosevelt believed that the United States had rights in Asia that dated back a century. During his first year in office, FDR tried to cut off European loans to Japan. Then he obtained a $50 million credit from Congress so that besieged China could buy cotton, wheat, and airplane parts. He also spent $238 million as "public works" to begin building thirty-two warships, including two aircraft carriers. In April 1934, Japan struck back by issuing the so-called Amau statement: because Tokyo had the right to act alone to preserve Asian "peace and order," any outside interference, such as military aid to China, was unfriendly to Japan. Hull refused publicly to accept the Amau statement, but the United States did nothing else. Sino-Japanese battles quieted as Japan digested its conquests of the past three years.

One other bright signal flashed across the international skies in 1933–1934, but few could tell exactly what it meant. In November 1933, Roosevelt formally recognized the Soviet Union. He did so over vigorous objections from the American Legion, the American Federation of

Labor, the Daughters of the American Revolution, and—most significantly—his own State Department. In historian Thomas R. Maddux's words, the State Department was afraid that Moscow would "not live up to the standards of civilized society." Hull, of course, despised the state-run Soviet economy. He received ardent support from Robert Kelley, a long-time scholar of Russia who, as the ambitious son of a working-class Boston Irish family, had studied among the violently anti-Bolshevist Russian exiles living in Paris. By 1924, Kelley had convinced the State Department to train young experts so that they could deal with the Soviet danger. As head of the department's Eastern European Affairs desk, Kelley directed the education of the famous first class of experts, including George F. Kennan, Charles Bohlen, and others who were to shape post-1945 policy. "Without exception," historian Frederic L. Propas notes, these men "all emerged as hostile observers of the Soviet Union" in 1933.[20] Kelley warned his superiors that if recognized, the Soviets would never keep agreements, but instead foment revolution—as, he argued, they were then doing in Cuba.

FDR, however, apparently thought it strange that the United States did not recognize the existence of the world's largest nation. He received support from William C. Bullitt, still full of hatred for Wilson's supposed betrayal of Soviet-American relations at the Paris peace conference (see p. 319) and now an adviser to FDR. There were also strong economic reasons for recognition. Despite lack of diplomatic ties, U.S.-Soviet trade steadily rose in the 1920s but dropped sharply after 1931. A major reason was the Soviet five-year plans begun in 1928 by dictator Joseph Stalin to make the Soviet Union self-sufficient. But U.S. business noted that Germany, which did recognize the USSR and provided long-term credits, continued to profit from the trade. The Soviets, moreover, seemed to be enduring the depression better than the capitalists. The Soviets were paying a price, however. Stalin ordered the collectivization of agriculture. When peasants fought to hold their private plots, Stalin seized their grain, causing mass starvation. At least 10 million to 14 million Soviets died between 1929 and 1934. Roosevelt apparently knew little of the magnitude of these events. He might, however, have agreed with one U.S. economist who said that trade relations were needed because "the Russians are more dependable financially than Wall Street."[21]

Roosevelt also understood that a new U.S.-Soviet relationship could threaten to box in Japan—to put Tokyo between the arms of that "nutcracker" a Soviet official had asked for in 1931. Certainly, the Soviets responded quickly to FDR's opening because they hoped, above all, to contain Japan.[22] But the president, and especially the State Department, had no such commitment in mind. As FDR opened talks with Soviet foreign minister Maxim Litvinov, the State Department set about " 'reassuring' the Japanese," as one top official termed it.[23] Bullitt thus went to Moscow as the first U.S. ambassador to the Soviet Union with no aid for Stalin, but with great hopes. "A striking man: young, handsome, urbane, full of charm and enthusiasm, a product of Philadelphia society and Yale . . . , and with a flamboyance of personality that is right out of F. Scott Fitzgerald," George Kennan described his new boss. Bullitt was "confident in himself, confident of the President's support, confident that he will have no difficulty in cracking the nut of Communist suspicion and hostility which awaits him in Moscow," Kennan continued.[24]

But this nut was not cracked either. When Litvinov discovered that the United States refused to help contain Japan, his own ruler, Stalin, lost interest in Bullitt. Stalin instead tried to protect his flanks by working with France against Germany. The Soviets refused to pay the $150 million debt that they owed Washington. If they did pay, they would have to pay vastly larger amounts owed to the British and French. Bullitt became angry. The anger turned to fury in 1935, when U.S. Communist party leaders appeared in Moscow at the Seventh Party Congress to denounce the United States. Bullitt and Hull considered this a direct violation of the Soviets' promise in 1933 not to spread anti-U.S. propaganda. Bullitt left the Soviet Union in 1936 and forever after worked tirelessly against the Soviets.

"Isolationists" versus "Internationalists"

In 1935, Mussolini's Italy invaded Ethiopia in the hope of realizing that dictator's crazy dream of resurrecting the Roman Empire of two thousand years earlier. The League of Nations responded by asking members to stop trading with Italy. The League, however, did not ask the members to stop trading in the most important item, oil. And besides, Great Britain, France, and the United States refused to get tough with Mussolini. In 1936, Hitler tore up the Versailles peace treaty and the Locarno agreement by seizing the Rhineland.

Americans were sharply divided over how they should deal with this inflamed world. One group, the "isolationists," believed that the nation should maintain complete freedom of action. In the words of historian Wayne Cole, "Unilateralism and non-interventionism were central themes in the thinking of most of them."[25] This group, however, did not want the United States to be entirely isolated. One of its leaders, Senator Borah, was willing to consider working with the Soviets in order to stop Japan. Indeed, many isolationists wanted to help China. They just opposed military involvements in Europe. They received support for their anti-European views in 1934–1935 when a congressional committee under Republican Senator Gerald P. Nye from North Dakota investigated the causes of American involvement in World War I. The Nye committee concluded that bankers and arms exporters (the "Merchants of Death") had, for their own profit, pushed the country into the conflict. In truth, the explanation for that involvement was much more complicated. (Nye himself, for example, thought that the entire American system, not just a few "Merchants of Death," was at fault.) But the public liked to label J. P. Morgan and the arms traders as the villains. Americans vowed never again to allow the profiteers to take them into world war. Pacifist groups also determined not to be misled again as they felt they had been by Wilsonian ideals ("make the world safe for democracy") in 1914–1917.[26]

"Internationalists," on the other hand, assumed that new technology (such as the airplane, now flying regularly across the Atlantic and Pacific) had drawn the world together and that U.S. prosperity depended on orderly world markets. Americans consequently bore responsibility for cooperating in the maintenance of a stable world that was in their own selfish interest. Historian Robert Divine notes that most internationalists were old-stock Protestants, felt close to Great Britain, and believed that America had replaced Britain as the world's great power. They cared about Europe while "they took Latin America for granted and neglected the Orient."[27] This group included executives of the great multinational, capital-intensive corporations—IBM, General Electric, Eastman Kodak, Standard Oil. They wanted an open world and low tariffs. Some firms, led by du Pont, Standard Oil, General Motors, and Union Carbide, even worked closely—sometimes secretly and illegally—with Nazi German firms until the late 1930s, or in some cases, even to 1941. At one point, Ford and General Motors subsidiaries actually produced half of Hitler's tanks in the 1930s.[28]

But the internationalists won few victories in the mid-1930s. U.S. officials, led by Hull, were frightened of the isolationists' strength in Congress. Roosevelt was also wary. In 1935, he had bowed to State Department and internationalist demands that the United States join the League's World Court. The president sent the appropriate agreement to the Senate for ratification. He quickly ran into a buzz saw of

"COME ON IN. I'LL TREAT YOU RIGHT. I USED TO KNOW YOUR DADDY."

BATCHELOR, NEW YORK *DAILY NEWS*

As this 1936 cartoon indicates, Americans had vivid memories of 1914 through 1920 and were determined never again to follow in Europe's bloody footsteps. The cartoon shows an American view of Europe's morality, as well as its foreign policy, being corrupted once more.

opposition, led by publisher William Randolph Hearst and several Roosevelt-hating demagogues of the day: Father Charles E. Coughlin (the "radio priest") and Senator Huey ("the Kingfish") Long of Louisiana. Roosevelt refused to wage what he saw as a losing fight, and the agreement went down to a humiliating defeat.[29]

Worse lay ahead for FDR. The isolationists next whipped the 1935 Neutrality Act through Congress. According to the act, if the president declared that a war existed in the world, Americans could not ship arms or other weapons to any belligerent nation; U.S. ships could not deal in such arms traffic; and American travelers were warned that they sailed on belligerent ships at their own risk. The crises of 1914–1917 were not to be repeated. The 1936 Neutrality Act further restricted FDR's power. Professor Richard Harrison believes that "it was the most serious defeat Roosevelt ever suffered" in foreign policy.[30] The measure reaffirmed the earlier act and tightened it by prohibiting loans.

That act took effect as FDR prepared to run for his second term and as General Francisco Franco moved to overthrow the republic in Spain during 1936 to establish a fascistic regime. The United States government shed few tears for the Spanish people. Since 1931, Americans, especially such giant U.S. multinationals as International Telephone

& Telegraph, had fought the new Spanish republic's attempt to regulate them. Washington, therefore, believed (wrongly) that the republic was deeply infected by communism. In the best account of the relationship, historian Douglas Little concludes that because these economic and political conflicts had, "like a cancer, rotted Spanish relations" with the Americans and the British, Washington and London officials were willing to let the republic die "before the infection had a chance to spread."[31] FDR knew, moreover, that the republic's anticlericalism deeply angered the U.S. Roman Catholic hierarchy and the Vatican. Amid the election, he was content to follow British and French policies on Spain. These policies amounted to doing nothing to stop Franco. Three thousand Americans volunteered to fight for the republic (the Abraham Lincoln Battalion became the most famous American group), but they were not enough to stop the final fascist triumph in 1939. Meanwhile, Congress extended the 1936 Neutrality Act so the nation would not become involved in such civil wars as Spain's.

The 1937 Neutrality Act had a new wrinkle. Congress kept the main provisions of the earlier acts but, at the suggestion of financier Bernard Baruch, added a "cash and carry" clause. Belligerents could now purchase certain war materials from the United States if they paid for them promptly and carried them away in their own ships. As Robert Divine summarizes: cash and carry was "an ingenious method of preserving the profits of neutral trade while minimizing the risk of involvement in a major war."[32] It was, after all, tough for Americans to deny themselves overseas markets while they suffered from a crushing economic depression. Needs at home dictated policies abroad.

These needs worsened in 1937–1938, when Roosevelt reduced government spending to balance the budget and promptly threw the nation into the most severe economic tailspin in its history. Profits dropped 78 percent in nine months. With no new ideas, FDR tried to pump life into the system by sending Congress a $3 billion spending program in 1938. Part of the money was to build battleships. A leading New Dealer, Maury Maverick of Texas, explained that "the reason for all this battleship and war frenzy is coming out. . . . The Democratic administration is getting down to the condition that Mr. Hoover found himself. We have pulled all the rabbits out of the hat and there are no more rabbits."[33] In this gut-wrenching moment, FDR had to make three historic foreign-policy decisions during 1937–1938: how to deal with the Nazis' policy toward Jews, the Japanese invasion of China, and the Munich crisis.

AMERICANS AND THE HOLOCAUST

Hitler's hatred of Jews was well known in the United States by 1938. Vowing to "purify" Germany of its half a million Jews, he struck against them immediately after assuming power. By 1935, his Nuremberg Laws stripped them of citizenship. Teachers, doctors, and other professionals could not practice their craft, and half of all German Jews were unemployed. In early 1938, Hitler burned Munich's Great Synagogue, then sent 15,000 Jews to Buchenwald, the concentration camp whose name was soon to become synonymous with the most horrible crime that the Nazis committed.

Roosevelt responded by calling a conference of thirty-two nations in 1938 at Évian-les-Bains, France, to discuss which countries could accept Jews as émigrés. He believed that the United States could accept few: the depression and Americans' fear of allowing in more immigrants of any kind prohibited an open door, he concluded. None of the other larger, less-populated nations such as Brazil or Australia would accept many either. Only Holland, already densely populated, willingly took in large numbers. (Germany invaded Holland in 1940 and exterminated 75 percent of the Jews there.) Noting the world's reluctance to accept his "problem" and using as an excuse the assassination of a Nazi official in Paris by a Jew, in 1938 Hitler launched *Kristallnacht* (or "Crystal Night," so named for the shattered glass that littered the sidewalks after the destruction of Jewish businesses and homes). He sent 20,000 to 30,000 Jews to concentration camps. FDR expressed his shock, recalled the U.S. ambassador to Germany, and allowed 15,000 refugees on visitor permits to remain longer in the United States. But he would not do more—such as breaking trade relations with Hitler.[34]

The Nazis launched their "final solution" to the "problem" after they drove into the Soviet Union in 1941. Much of the Jewish population of eastern Europe (especially Poland) and the Soviet Union were packed into railroad freight cars and dumped at such camps as Buchenwald and Dachau to conclude, as Hitler called it, "the complete annihilation of the Jews." Certain names became engraved in memory as Russian Jews were slaughtered at Babi Yar in 1941 and during Purim in 1942 (small children were thrown into pits and Hitler's SS officers pitched candy to them as the victims were buried alive). The Germans tried to keep much of the brutality secret, but as early as autumn 1942, U.S. newspapers published reports of the horror. By late 1942, Rabbi Stephen S. Wise, chairman of the World Jewish Congress, declared that 2 million Jews had been slaughtered. The Roosevelt administration confirmed that figure. U.S. newspapers, however, placed the revelation on the inside pages. The *Atlanta Constitution* pushed it back to page 20, next to the want ads.[35] For the remainder of the war, the Allies did little, either to bomb the railways running to the concentration camps' gas ovens or to lower immigration bars so that Jews could find new homes.

There are many reasons why U.S. officials stood by as one of history's greatest atrocities unfolded. First, Americans simply desired no new immigrants of any type during economic bad times. Anti-Semitism reinforced that desire. Well-known German and Austrian Jews did enter the country (Albert Einstein, composer Kurt Weill, architect Walter Gropius, physicists Hans Bethe and Edward Teller among them). But an annual average of only 8,500 Jews were allowed into the country between 1933 and 1941. Between 1941 and 1945, the U.S. War Refugee Board rescued 200,000 Jews, but only 20,000 were allowed into the United States. Even then, the American record was better than the British or Soviet.

Second, the stories of the death camps seemed too terrible to be true. Americans remembered that World War I tales of torture had turned out to be propaganda. They swore that they would not be taken in a second time by "foreigners." When eyewitness stories reported millions being murdered in the death camps, one U.S. journalist responded, "We are from Missouri. We have to be shown."[36]

Third, top U.S. officials refused to deal with the issue. Some, such as the State Department's Breckinridge Long, who was responsible for handling immigration problems, were anti-Semitic and more concerned with diplomatic dealings with Hitler than dramatizing the plight of his victims. In 1933–1936, when Jewish and other groups demanded U.S. trade boycotts against Hitler, Hull refused to go against his belief that only good trade could lead to good political relations. During the war, officials refused to divert resources to liberate the death camps. Throughout the 1933–1944 period, U.S. and British officials especially feared that Germany would simply dump millions of Jews on them— or on Palestine—and they did not want to face such a dilemma. Top officials who were Jews, such as Secretary of the Treasury Henry Morgenthau and FDR's speechwriter, Samuel Rosenman, moved slowly, fearful of being branded "too Jewish." The *New York Times*, owned by a Jewish family, downplayed death-camp stories for the same reason. Nor did Congress want to help the refugees. When Democratic senator Robert Wagner of New York proposed bringing 20,000 more German

Jewish children into the United States, the Senate flatly refused to act on the Wagner bill.

Fourth, the Jewish community was itself divided. Zionists, dedicated to creating a Jewish state in Palestine, emphasized their cause rather than giving first priority to the rescue of east Europeans. Even leaders such as Rabbi Wise decided to move slowly rather than possibly further alienate the State Department, anti-Semitic Americans, and cautious Jews. Finally, as for Roosevelt himself, a distinguished historian concluded that FDR's "indifference to . . . the systematic annihilation of European Jewry emerges as the worst failure of his presidency."[37] By mid-1945, 6.5 million Jews had died in the Holocaust.

THE DILEMMA OF "QUARANTINING" JAPAN (1937–1939)

Throughout the years 1933–1939, U.S. officials followed a century-old tradition by devoting more attention to Asia than to Europe. That attention riveted on the region in July 1937, when Japan reignited its war to conquer China. Tokyo was determined to create buffer states to protect its holdings in Manchukuo, to stop Chinese discrimination against Japanese goods, and—perhaps most importantly—to guarantee Japan's self-sufficiency by conquering mainland markets and raw materials. China, romanticized in the 1937 movie of Pearl Buck's best-selling novel, *The Good Earth*, had never been more popular among Americans. But U.S. officials, already dizzied by the recent economic downturn, were nearly paralyzed. As a top State Department figure had said in 1936, the United States had "no intention of using force for the preservation of the 'open door.' "[38] On the other hand, Japan's aggression and the closing off of Asian markets posed a deadly challenge to Hull's and FDR's hope for a more open world and set a dangerous precedent for other aggressors. But the Americans could not get tough: their military capabilities remained small, and Japan remained the third-best customer of U.S. goods.

FDR responded by refusing to issue the state-of-war declaration needed to trigger the application of the 1937 Neutrality Act. Applying the act would have favored Japan's stronger navy, which could "cash and carry" U.S. goods. The president next delivered a tough speech on October 5, 1937, in Chicago (virtually in the shadow of the Chicago Tribune Building, home of the nation's leading isolationist newspaper). He asked other nations to join in a "quarantine" to protect the world against the spreading "epidemic of world lawlessness."[39] A public uproar ensued, and, in a press conference, FDR—after being pressured by Hull, who feared isolationist feeling in Congress—blandly denied that the "quarantine speech" threatened anyone. Hull and FDR probably misread public opinion. Americans were more shocked and angry at Japan than ever before.[40]

Even the dying League of Nations aroused itself to seize upon FDR's speech and call a conference in Brussels, Belgium, to discuss how to stop Japan. After much anguish, the president sent a delegation to Brussels. The Japanese, not surprisingly, refused to attend a meeting called to condemn them. But the Soviets did appear and promptly asked the United States to cooperate against both Japan and Germany. The Americans coldly rejected the deal. Having refused the courtship of possible allies, the United States, in the words of historian Stephen Pelz, now faced a bitter choice: either to "run a hard-paced naval race with Japan" or "foresake its commitments in Asia."[41]

The corpse of the Brussels Conference was barely rigid before Japanese planes attacked a U.S. gunboat, the *Panay*, in China's Yangtze River on December 12, 1937. Two sailors died. Tokyo officials quickly condemned the attack as an error and apologized. But the next day Representative Louis Ludlow of Indiana seized the moment to push a constitutional amendment that would require a national referendum before the country could go to war. Fearing that the Ludlow Amendment could paralyze U.S. diplomacy, FDR pulled out all stops to defeat it.[42] Roosevelt then proposed a spending bill of $1.0 billion to increase the navy by 20 percent. He also prepared to fortify Guam and other Pacific bases. Undeterred, in November 1938, Japan proclaimed a Greater East Asia Co-Prosperity Sphere that was aimed against "bolshevism." More accurately, it announced Japanese determination to dominate Asia's resources. In April 1939, FDR sent fresh requests to Congress, including a $0.5 billion measure to create a 5,500-plane air force. The two close friends of the 1920s were now on a collision course.

CONJURING UP THE GHOST OF MUNICH (1937–1939)

The United States was also on a collision course with another close friend of the 1920s. Germany seized Austria in March 1938. In September, Hitler demanded that Czechoslovakia surrender the German-populated Sudetenland that the Paris peace conference gave to the Czechs in 1919. U.S. newspapers condemned the dictator's act, but Washington officials were restrained. One key adviser, Adolf Berle, reminded FDR that many thought that the breakup of the Austro-Hungarian Empire in 1919 simply for the sake of self-determination had been a "mistake." William Bullitt added that French officials now called the Versailles Treaty of 1919 "one of the stupidest documents ever penned by the hand of man."[43]

U.S. policy was also shaped by growing mistrust of Great Britain, the nation that FDR and Hull believed should take the lead in European affairs. As Anglo-U.S. trade talks broke down in 1938, Hull considered telling the British "to go to hell," while London officials complained of the "bitterness and exasperation" of having to deal with the Americans.[44] Conservative prime minister Neville Chamberlain especially mistrusted what he believed to be Roosevelt's shallowness and bizarre economic and foreign policies. Chamberlain preferred striking a deal that would satisfy the Japanese and keep them away from the British imperial holdings of Hong Kong, Singapore, and India. Meanwhile, he planned to carry out a policy of appeasement—that is, allowing Hitler to rectify the 1919 treaty provisions—that would give the British military time to catch up with Germany's rising military power.

Roosevelt feared Chamberlain's policy in Asia. He believed that the weakened British hoped to push off on Americans the dirty job of containing Japan and—of special concern—protecting the British Empire. These mutual mistrusts and divergent interests explain why the two nations never cooperated to resist the Japanese between 1931 and 1941. In Europe, however, FDR supported Chamberlain's appeasement of Hitler. As the Czech crisis threw a dark shadow of war over Europe in September 1938, the president publicly asked Hitler for a peaceful settlement. Roosevelt especially hoped to use the Italian Fascist dictator, Benito Mussolini, as an honest broker to appease Hitler and prevent war. FDR privately told the British and French, who had guaranteed Czech borders, that he could not help them if conflict erupted.

Stalin, desperate to protect his dictatorship, signaled that if the French and British defended the Czechs, he would help them. Chamberlain and the French wanted no part of such a deal. The British prime minister feared communism, did not want Soviet armies marching through eastern Europe to reach the Czechs, and believed that the Soviet military was too weak to resist Hitler effectively. Instead, Chamberlain flew to Munich with French officials and surrendered the Sudetenland to Hitler—without Czechoslovakia's consent. Adolf Berle quietly breathed, "Thank God." FDR sent a two-word cable to Chamberlain: "Good man." But within days, Roosevelt realized the tragedy that had occurred. Hitler quickly launched "Crystal Night" against German Jews and then demanded the remainder of a now defenseless Czechoslovakia. Mussolini, whom FDR believed could be used to reason with Hitler, conquered Albania in March 1939. Increasing numbers of Americans condemned Chamberlain's appeasement policy. As columnist Dorothy Thompson acidly phrased it, he had somehow managed to go to Munich "on his knees at 200 miles an hour."[45]

But others believed that the Munich deal produced one good result. By giving Hitler what he wanted in the west, he could now turn and confront the Soviet Union, which seemed too weak to resist.[46] Stalin had ruthlessly carried out a bloody purge between 1934 and 1938 that not only killed millions of his real or imagined political opponents, but executed or imprisoned one-third of the Red Army officers and three of his top five marshals. Convinced that the British and French were trying to turn Hitler against him, Stalin secretly approached Berlin for a deal. He began by replacing his foreign minister, Maxim Litvinov, a Jew, with Vyacheslav Molotov, a gentile totally subservient to Stalin.

Western leaders ignored Stalin's signal. Chamberlain stuck to his appeasement policy. Roosevelt asked in April 1939 for a conference to deal with disarmament and equal access to world markets. Hitler's close adviser, Field Marshal Hermann Göring, told Mussolini that FDR's proposal must be evidence of "an incipient brain disease."[47] Hitler publicly humiliated the president by violently denouncing the idea. More pointedly, throughout the summer of 1939, the United States did not even bother to keep an ambassador in Moscow.

On August 23, 1939, Stalin and Hitler suddenly announced that they had signed a nonaggression pact. A stunned world at first refused to believe it. Fascists and Communists supposedly mixed no better than oil and water. But both men now needed time—Hitler to absorb western Poland and prepare an attack westward, Stalin to absorb eastern Poland and avoid a conflict with the superior Nazi armies. With the European harvest largely taken in, Hitler attacked Poland on September 1. The British and French, who had guaranteed Polish borders, had no choice but to declare war. Stalin followed through on his secret deal with Hitler by seizing eastern Poland and the three Baltic States of Latvia, Estonia, and Lithuania, which the Russian Empire had once ruled.

Forever after, "Munich" held powerful, but quite different meanings for Americans and Russians. To Americans, "Munich" meant the utter failure of appeasement, the uselessness of trying to stop aggressors with talk instead of force. To Russians, however, it meant—as Soviet leader Mikhail Gorbachev declared in 1985—"the ultimate political irresponsibility when the leading groupings of monopoly capital tried to manipulate the expansion of German fascism, directing it to the East." That policy, Gorbachev concluded, "brought a terrible tragedy to all the peoples of Europe."[48] The many-faced ghost of Munich would long haunt world affairs, but its first and worst shadow fell over the globe in September 1939.

AMERICA'S PHONY WAR OF 1939–1941

Hitler did not intend to repeat Germany's error of 1914–1917. Determined to keep the United States out of this war, he ordered his submarines not to attack passenger liners or U.S. ships. Roosevelt finally obtained repeal of the Neutrality Acts' arms embargo so that England and France could purchase weapons and ammunition from the United States.[49] Over the next two years, the president never resolved the key contradiction in his policy: the wish for no direct U.S. involvement in the war, but the belief that Germany and Japan had to be stopped before they stood astride Europe and Asia.

This contradiction sharpened in December 1939, when Stalin, determined to protect his northern cities, demanded a strategic buffer area from neighboring Finland. The Finns refused, and the Red Army invaded. FDR quickly condemned "this dreadful rape of Finland," but the Finns surprisingly battled the Soviets to a standstill in the Winter War of 1939–1940. Americans, led by Herbert Hoover, moved to help "brave little Finland," which had won their hearts by paying its debt to the United States after other debtors had stopped. But only about $10 million in aid went to the Finns. Roosevelt did place a "moral embargo" on airplanes, gasoline, and metals to the Soviet Union, but trade figures were telling: U.S. exports to the Soviet Union doubled to $29 million between November 1939 and January 1940. In March 1940, the Finns finally agreed to the border revision. The war ended, and Finland began moving closer to Hitler.

Meanwhile Germany absorbed Poland but did little else during the winter. The French, supposedly secure behind their heavily fortified Maginot line, and Chamberlain began to believe that it was all a "phony war." In April–May 1940, Hitler struck. His divisions knifed through Holland and Belgium to destroy the Maginot line from the rear. (The phrase "Maginot line mentality" afterward applied to a person or nation too rigid to respond to new challenges.) Chamberlain resigned in disgrace and was replaced by sixty-six-year-old Winston Churchill, who had long condemned appeasement. Hitler then tried to soften Great Britain with a blitz by his air force, which, during daylight and then nightly, bombed London and other major cities during the 1940–1941 winter. The Royal Air Force, however, made the Germans pay heavily for the raids. Unable to control the air, Hitler decided to delay a planned invasion of Great Britain.

Many Americans gave up on the British. "Saw Joe Kennedy [the U.S. ambassador to Great Britain and the father of John F. Kennedy]," Chamberlain told his diary in January 1940, "who says everyone in U.S.A. thinks we shall be beaten before the end of the month."[50] But other Americans vigorously disagreed. On May 15, 1940, journalist William Allen White helped found the Committee to Defend America by Aiding the Allies. The new group released studies showing the terrible impact on the U.S. economy of a Hitler victory, and it lobbied for a stronger defense and sending massive aid to the British. After Paris fell to the Nazis in June 1940, FDR, in a speech at the University of Virginia, pledged to help "opponents of force" with U.S. supplies. But he continued to downplay the idea that the United States might become militarily involved.[51] White's and FDR's actions helped produce one important result in mid-1940. Congress passed the first peacetime draft of young Americans in U.S. history and began the process that brought 15 million men and women into the armed services over the next five years.

As historians J. Garry Clifford and Samuel Spencer, Jr., show, the Selective Service Act climaxed a bitter three-month public debate that shattered much of the isolationists' strength.[52] The isolationists had come together in a group called "America First." Begun by Princeton students, supported by leading midwestern politicians, and bankrolled by executives of Quaker Oats, Montgomery Ward, Hormel meat packing, and Inland Steel, America First launched massive protest rallies. Lobbying efforts were led by Charles A. Lindbergh, the "Lone Eagle," who in 1927 first flew the Atlantic alone and became perhaps the nation's greatest hero. Lindbergh had personally analyzed Hitler's air force and, overrating its strength by a factor of ten, warned Americans not to get involved in Europe's quarrels. Great Britain's brave resistance and Lindbergh's remarks in 1941 that were widely viewed as anti-Semitic hurt the isolationists' cause. The isolationists were strongest in the farming areas of the Midwest and West, and also in Roman Catholic and Lutheran churches, where Irish-Americans, Italian-Americans, and German-Americans worshiped. But the farmers were also sensitive to chaos in international markets, and many Americans began to realize that two oceans might no longer protect them.[53]

These Americans were shocked by the new air power whose bombs lit the skies each night over Great Britain. The United States was no longer a fortress defended by ocean moats, but an island that could someday be attacked by planes flying over the arctic routes from northern Europe. When the globe was viewed from the poles, Americans were closer to Europe than to much of South America. New strategists, led by Sir Halford Mackinder and Nicholas Spykman, detailed the obvious military and political consequences of such a perspective.[54] By late 1940, growing U.S. fears were intensified by the media. Edward R. Murrow pioneered radio news when he broadcast the horrors and sounds directly into American homes from bombed London streets on the CBS network. Even children's programs joined in. On "Captain Midnight," a popular radio show, many segments were spent (between Ovaltine commercials) tracking and capturing the treacherous "Ivan Shark," who somehow seemed to be both Japanese and Communist.[55]

The isolationists were not able to kill a single major foreign-policy proposal of Roosevelt's in 1940–1941, although they did come close (for instance, on the Selective Service Act, which was renewed by a lone vote in 1941). Public-opinion polls showed that after the fall of France in June 1940, nearly 75 percent of Americans surveyed wanted to do more to help Great Britain. By early 1941, one poll revealed that two-thirds of those surveyed preferred to help the British than to stay out of the war. Roosevelt, who read highly detailed public-opinion analyses, knew of this growing internationalist sentiment, but he believed that Congress remained isolationist. When the British ambassador begged him to help in early 1940, FDR admitted that 40 percent of the people might support such help, but that he "could not get 25 percent of Congress."[56]

The president, moreover, had decided to break a tradition going back to George Washington and run for a hotly disputed third presidential term. He wanted as little public debate as possible over his foreign policy. Thus, when Churchill begged for some ships to protect the British Isles, FDR did not respond for six weeks. He finally (and ingeniously) worked out a deal that offered fifty aged U.S. destroyers to Great Britain in return for long-term leases to military bases located on British possessions between Newfoundland and Trinidad. Even then, Roosevelt made the deal only after he had received the pledge of his Republican opponent (Wendell Willkie of Indiana) not to make the swap a political issue. Roosevelt also moved only after his attorney general had made a questionable legal interpretation that justified the deal without forcing the president to ask Congress for permission. In September 1940, Japan moved to capture vital raw materials by entering the northern part of French Indochina. The Japanese, as historian Akira Iriye observes, assumed that U.S.-Japan relations would remain peaceful, and they had little "sense that the two nations were on a fatal march toward collision."[57] But FDR stunned Tokyo by cutting off iron and steel exports, a decision that was certain to drive the Japanese farther into Asia in quest of these resources. Nevertheless, in October 1940, FDR told a roaring Boston campaign audience, "I shall say it again and again: Your boys are not going to be sent into any foreign wars." Willkie was furious: "That hypocritical son of a bitch! This is going to beat me." Roosevelt overwhelmed Willkie 449 to 82 in the electoral college, 27 million to 22 million in the popular vote.[58] FDR now prepared to be bolder. "We must be," he told the nation in December 1940, "the great arsenal of democracy."

In September 1940, Germany, Italy, and Japan had signed the Tripartite Pact that formed the Axis bloc. Hitler clearly wanted to use Japan to keep the Americans busy in the Pacific. Churchill again begged from London's bombed rubble for massive U.S. aid. Vowing he wanted to "keep war away from our country and our people," Roosevelt proposed "lend-lease" to Congress: the United States would lend or lease goods to the British, who were then somehow to return the goods after the war. This, FDR declared, would avoid hard feelings about war debts by "leaving out the dollar mark." The plan resembled merely a "garden hose" lent to a neighbor whose house is on fire and to whom you say, "I don't want $15—I want my garden hose back after the fire is over." Or so the president argued. His supporters shrewdly had the plan proposed as House Resolution 1776, and Roosevelt lobbied hard for it. The $7 billion program survived violent attacks to pass by 100 votes in the House and by a 2-to-1 margin in the Senate on March 11, 1941. As the *New York Times* understood it, "the Battle of the Atlantic is on."[59] For FDR now had to ensure that the lend-lease goods survived the North Atlantic waters, where Hitler's U-boats were destroying 500,000 tons of British shipping each month.

THE REAL WAR (1941)

In taking this step, Roosevelt set precedents and created a long and bitter debate. The president believed, as he told advisers, that "public

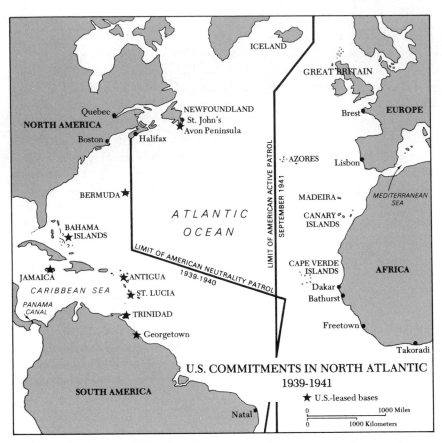

ICELAND

GREAT BRITAIN

NEWFOUNDLAND

Quebec

NORTH AMERICA

St. John's

Avon Peninsula

Boston

Halifax

Brest EUROPE

AZORES Lisbon

BERMUDA

ATLANTIC

OCEAN

MADEIRA

CANARY
ISLANDS

MEDITERRANEAN
SEA

LIMIT OF AMERICAN ACTIVE PATROL
SEPTEMBER 1941

BAHAMA
ISLANDS

LIMIT OF AMERICAN NEUTRALITY PATROL
1939-1940

JAMAICA

CARIBBEAN SEA

ANTIGUA

ST. LUCIA

PANAMA
CANAL

TRINIDAD

Georgetown

CAPE VERDE
ISLANDS

Dakar

Bathurst

AFRICA

Freetown

Takoradi

U.S. COMMITMENTS IN NORTH ATLANTIC
1939-1941

SOUTH AMERICA

★ U.S.-leased bases

Natal

| 0 | 1000 Miles |
| 0 | 1000 Kilometers |

*Between 1939 and 1941, FDR pushed U.S. naval power ever farther into the
Atlantic to protect British ships and American exports from German submarine
attacks.*

opinion was not yet ready for the United States to convoy ships." He,
therefore, decided to use his commander-in-chief powers, granted by
the Constitution, to deploy U.S. warships without telling either Congress or the American people what he was doing.

As early as January 1941, U.S. and British military chiefs had secretly
worked out joint plans to defeat the Axis. Canada, at war against Hitler, and the United States also set up a joint committee to coordinate
war production. FDR, moreover, agreed to allow U.S. ships to patrol
for German submarines 300 miles into the Atlantic. After subs sank
nearly half of a twenty-two-ship British convoy during a single April
night, Roosevelt instructed the U.S. fleet to patrol halfway across the
Atlantic and report any subs to British ships (although he publicly said

that the ships would report to Americans and warned journalists not to speculate about his policies). In April, he cast a U.S. protectorate over Greenland and the Azores. In July, he landed troops in Iceland to ensure the passage of Allied goods through these strategic areas. Secretary of War Henry Stimson asked FDR to tell Americans what he was doing, but the president refused. By November 1941, the United States had already spent billions in lend-lease goods for the British, Soviets, and Chinese, and had not even declared war yet. When isolationists questioned these actions, FDR secretly ordered the FBI to gather evidence that Lindbergh was a Nazi sympathizer (no such evidence was ever found), called Senator Nye a "boob," and complained that many critics were simply "wild Irish" who hated the British. Hull, meanwhile, became so saddened by the United States' inability to respond more fully that in cabinet meetings he kept muttering, "Everything [is] going hellward."[60]

But Hull's concern radically changed on June 22, 1941, when Germany invaded the Soviet Union in the largest land operation in history. Hitler and Stalin had squabbled over many issues, most notably who was to be dominant in the Balkans and the Black Sea region. Stalled in his plans to invade Great Britain, Hitler turned to the vast Eurasian landmass. Stalin, meanwhile, had gained maneuvering room on April 13, 1941, when he and the Japanese stunned the world—not the least Hitler—by signing a nonaggression pact. Both sides benefited. The Soviets no longer worried about their eastern border with Manchukuo, where shooting incidents between the Red Army and Japanese troops had occurred since 1934. Japan was free to strike south against British and U.S. holdings.

Stalin was, nevertheless, surprised by the Nazi invasion. "What have we done to deserve this?" Molotov innocently asked German officials. The dictator disappeared from sight for ten days and apparently almost suffered a nervous breakdown. Most Americans were equally puzzled. The State Department was unable to issue a statement for twenty-four hours, then published an announcement that blasted Soviet violations of human rights, but concluded that Washington supported any "forces opposing Hitlerism." Politicians were more direct. Senator Burton K. Wheeler declared, "Just let Joe Stalin and the other dictators fight it out." Democratic Senator Harry Truman from Missouri agreed: if Germany was winning, "we should help Russia and if Russia is winning we ought to help Germany . . . although I don't want to see Hitler victorious under any circumstances." The Soviets were equally suspicious of their new partners in the West. When a British official told a

Soviet leader how wonderful it was to be united in the common cause, the Soviet replied, "Perhaps."[61]

Hitler's divisions quickly advanced nearly to the gates of Moscow and Leningrad. U.S. Secretary of War Stimson and his military advisers concluded that the Soviets would last no longer than three months. But Churchill, who had long hated and fought bolshevism, now saw that the Red Army could prevent a Nazi invasion of Great Britain and demanded all-out support for the Soviet Union. FDR agreed. Overruling aides who thought that sending lend-lease supplies to the retreating Soviet troops was like pouring millions of dollars down a rat hole, the president demanded "a burr under the saddle" to "get things moving."[62] The first of some $12 billion in aid for the Soviet Union over the next four years left U.S. ports. The Red Army and its close ally, winter, finally stalled the Nazi armies in 1941–1942. The costs were enormous. Some 600,000 died in the Leningrad siege alone, many of starvation. Hitler had lost over 700,000 troops by late 1941, but he could not conquer Leningrad or Moscow.

FDR knew that a turning point had been reached. Rushing supplies to Churchill and Stalin could quickly lead to "shooting," he told the British ambassador in July 1941. The president was now "more hopeful" than he had been earlier.[63] In July, the Japanese turned south to seize the remainder of the French Empire in Indochina. Japanese politics, even the relatively moderate rule of Prince Fumimaro Konoye's faction, depended on foreign conquests rather than internal reforms. Roosevelt shocked Japan by freezing all Japanese assets in the United States (thus making it impossible, for example, for Japan to use its bank accounts in New York to buy U.S. goods) and persuaded Churchill to do the same in Great Britain. The president meant to place only a partial embargo on oil shipments to Japan. He did not want to push Konoye toward more conquest to obtain the vital resource. But a bureaucratic mix-up in Washington totally stopped oil shipments, and Roosevelt did not think that he could reverse the error without appearing to be retreating before Japanese aggression. Meanwhile, FDR accelerated military aid to Chinese forces fighting Japan.

Konoye, indeed, found his nation in a corner, stripped of oil and other goods that it depended on Americans to supply, and sucked into an endless war in China. In September, he proposed a summit meeting with FDR to discuss the crisis. The president was agreeable, but Hull insisted on prior Japanese concessions. Roosevelt finally declared that a summit could be held only if Japan agreed beforehand to pull back from China and Indochina, and pledge an open door in Asia. No Japanese government could accept such terms. The summit was never held.

SERGEANT YORK AND THE ANNOUNCEMENT OF THE AMERICAN CENTURY

By mid-summer 1941, leading Americans believed that the United States was actually in the war, although the country had not formally declared it. Hollywood seemed to be leading the way, despite bitter opposition from other media (especially some newspapers and radio commentators) to U.S. intervention in the conflict. The breakthrough for Hollywood was the midsummer 1941 film, *Sergeant York*, starring Gary Cooper. The story glorified the actual life of a former backwoods pacifist, Alvin York, who became a hero in World War I by single-handedly killing 20 German soldiers and capturing 132 others. As historians Clayton R. Koppes and Gregory D. Black observe, young male viewers "got the message that they, like York, should go off and fight for democracy. . . . *Sergeant York* capped an evolution in American motion pictures that took them from being fearful of political subjects to being aggressively interventionist."[64]

It was time to decide what Americans should fight for. This fascinating debate was led by Henry Luce, the powerful publisher of *Life*, *Time*, and *Fortune* magazines (which, not accidentally, had also widely publicized *Sergeant York*.) In a series of editorials published during the summer (and later collected in a small book, *The American Century*), Luce assumed that not only was the United States already involved in war, but that "only America can effectively state the aims of this war." Those aims had to include creating, under U.S. leadership, "a vital international economy" and "an international moral order." These were needed, Luce declared, because "Franklin Roosevelt failed to make American democracy work successfully on a narrow, materialistic, and nationalistic basis" between 1933 and 1939. Americans had to use their new power to create an international capitalist marketplace open to all, and which embodied the U.S. ideals of freedom, justice, and opportunity. Only then, Luce concluded, could American democracy itself survive. Thus, every American was called, he announced, "each in the widest horizon of his own vision, to create the first great American century."[65]

Luce spoke for a growing U.S. consensus, but a few strongly disagreed. Raymond Moley, a former FDR adviser but now angry with the

The real Sergeant Alvin York, one of World War I's heroes for single-handedly capturing 132 German soldiers, looks at the handsome Hollywood leading man, Gary Cooper, who played the lead in the 1941 film. Sergeant York *strayed rather far from the facts of York's Tennessee upbringing and battlefield exploits, but it was wildly popular, won Cooper an Academy Award for best actor, and played a part in the 1941 debates over U.S. neutrality policies.*

New Deal, warned that Americans had to resist this "temptation to drift into empire," because "an empire on which the sun would never set is one in which the rulers never sleep." Talk of "our century" was "childish" and could lead to "pure tragedy." One of Luce's own editors, John Chamberlain, questioned how Americans were sliding into war, then warned that "Luce's program requires a faith that can be sustained for short periods, when people are in the heroic mood." When those "short periods" end, Chamberlain believed, "Uncle Sam would . . . desert his trusting friends" abroad to take care of problems at home— and the American-century ideal could indeed become a tragedy.[66]

Roosevelt seemed to agree with Luce. On August 8, 1941, he secretly traveled to Newfoundland for his first meeting with Churchill. The president wanted nothing less than a joint declaration of war aims (although it was to be another four months before Americans formally declared war). After hard negotiating, FDR obtained a statement from the British that went far to meet the ideals of Hull, Luce, and himself. The Atlantic Charter told the world that the war was to be fought to protect self-government by all, freedom of the seas, a postwar "general security" system, freedom from fear and want, and a fair economic system that guaranteed equal access to world wealth to "all States, great or small, victor or vanquished." But Churchill bristled at the last point. He rightly understood that it was Roosevelt's and Hull's attempt to knock down the trade barriers around the British Empire, barriers that Churchill believed had to be reinforced against the U.S. power-house if a devastated Great Britain was to maintain its independence after the war. He insisted that a phrase be added: equal access would be guaranteed only "with due respect for . . . existing obligations." Thus, he tried to preserve Britain's colonial arrangements, such as the Imperial Preference System (see p. 351), already in place. FDR reluctantly agreed to this phrase.

Churchill, moreover, had his own ideas for the conference. He wanted the United States to enter the war immediately. Roosevelt was apparently amazingly candid, according to Churchill's account of the talks: "The President . . . said he would wage war, but not declare it" because of isolationist opposition in Congress, "and that he would become more and more provocative. If the Germans did not like it, they could attack American forces." FDR continued: "Everything was to be done to force an 'incident' that could lead to war."[67] None of these words of Roose-

President Franklin D. Roosevelt and Prime Minister Winston Churchill (seated at the center left of the picture) met off Newfoundland in August 1941 to plan how to coordinate the fighting of World War II—although the United States was not yet formally in the war. In this photograph, the two leaders, their aides, and the crew of the British warship Prince of Wales *are singing a hymn at a church service.*

velt's were made public until more than thirty years later. Meanwhile, in August 1941, as historian Theodore Wilson notes, "the American people continued to hang in midair between the precipice of all-out aid to England and Russia and the rocks of war which lay below."[68]

But the rocks seemed to be getting rapidly closer. In early September, a U.S. destroyer, the *Greer*, tracked a German U-boat for three hours and signaled its location to British forces before the sub turned and attacked. The *Greer* escaped unharmed, but FDR used the incident to denounce Germany for an unprovoked attack. He never told Americans how the ship actually provoked the submarine. On September 11, 1941, he termed U-boats "the rattlesnakes of the Atlantic" and implied that, like such snakes, the subs were to be destroyed before they could attack. In October, three U.S. warships were torpedoed (one sank) while on convoy duty in the North Atlantic, and 172 men were lost. Roosevelt used the sinking to persuade Congress to repeal what remained of the Neutrality Acts' restraint upon his power to act as he saw fit.

PEARL HARBOR AND A "FEELING . . . OF RELIEF"

It seemed only a matter of time before war would erupt full-scale in the Atlantic. But when war came for Americans, it occurred 6,000 miles in another direction. Throughout October and November 1941, Hull negotiated with Japanese ambassador Kichisaburo Nomura to find a settlement for Asia. Actually, both sides were also preparing for war. After Prince Konoye rejected the U.S. conditions for a summit meeting, he lost power to an ardent militarist, General Hideki Tojo. Japan organized a secret attack to destroy U.S. bases in the Pacific. Talks in Washington did continue on three issues: Japan's possible repudiation of its Axis pact with Hitler; Japanese withdrawal from Indochina in return for American reopening of trade in oil and metals; and Hull's demand that Tokyo retreat from China and pledge the open door. Agreement was close on the first two issues. Japan, however, could not give up the fruits of its ten-year war in China. Thus, in historian Jonathan Utley's words, "Hull's insistence on total Japanese withdrawal from China would result in war."[69] By November 26, Tojo's government had given up on the talks and ordered the navy to launch the attack.

Hull and FDR knew about the Japanese decisions. U.S. intelligence had cracked the top-secret Purple Code in which the Japanese com-

This is the view of Japanese airmen as they swooped over Pearl Harbor naval base on December 7, 1941, to destroy much of the U.S. Pacific Fleet. The ships appear to be lined up as if in a shooting gallery, but the important aircraft carriers had been sent to open sea days before and escaped the destruction.

municated their most sensitive messages. Hull, indeed, had used these so-called MAGIC intercepts to read the secret messages sent to Nomura before the ambassador even came in to negotiate. Roosevelt and Hull, however, did not know where Japan planned to attack. They assumed that the strike would occur in Southeast Asia and on the large U.S. base in the Philippines. The American military knew that it was not ready for an attack. As late as November 5, FDR's top military advisers begged him to fight only Hitler and not become involved in a two-front war—at least not until mid-1942, when U.S. defenses could be strengthened in the Pacific. But by late November, these military leaders knew that time had run out. On November 27, they told the U.S. commanders at Pearl Harbor naval base in Hawaii that Japan would probably attack in the next few days, but no one knew where.

Pearl Harbor seemed to be a logical target because much of the U.S. Pacific Fleet anchored there. In 1941, however, most Washington officials doubted that Japan had the power to strike the base. Incredibly, in early December they lost track of the Japanese fleet and knew only that it was somewhere in the west-central Pacific. U.S. aircraft carriers in Hawaii were ordered out to sea; but otherwise, Pearl Harbor, with five major battleships riding at anchor, was in a state of low alert on

FDR's draft of his historic speech asking Congress to declare war against Japan. Note how most of his changes made the message simpler, more direct, and forceful.

the morning of December 7, 1941. About one and one-half hours before the Japanese planes struck, Washington officials intercepted coded messages from Tokyo that war was imminent. But even this vague signal was relayed to Pearl Harbor by slow commercial telegraph and arrived after much of the base, including three battleships, had been destroyed. A failure to collect sufficient intelligence left Pearl Harbor a sitting target. This failure was in large part due to top U.S. military officers who were jealous of other branches that grew with new technology (such as intelligence) and so had refused to give these branches funds to develop better intelligence collecting.[70]

Some of the U.S. military were humiliated, but top civilians reacted quite differently. "My first feeling," Secretary of War Stimson wrote in his diary on December 7, "was of relief that the indecision was over and that a crisis had come in a way which would unite all our people."[71] The next day, Roosevelt appeared before a joint session of Congress, declared December 7, 1941, "a date which will live in infamy," asked for a declaration of war against Japan, and swore to fight until total victory was won. The Senate approved the war resolution 89 to 0, the House 388 to 1. The lone dissenter was Jeanette Rankin of Montana, a pacifist and suffragist who, as a member of Congress, had also opposed war in 1917.

A great irony then became apparent. For nearly two years, FDR had prepared to fight Germany, but now he had to ask for war only against Japan. Roosevelt was not certain that a declaration of war against Germany was possible. On December 11, however, Hitler solved the dilemma by declaring war on the United States. He evidently did so because of his treaty ties to Japan; but more important were his beliefs that the Japanese had perhaps mortally wounded the Americans and that FDR's growing aid to the British and Soviets had to be stopped by force. Tokyo officials appreciated Hitler's support. They had few illusions and realized that they had no chance for victory if the war dragged on and the incredible U.S. industrial powerhouse had time to gear up to full blast.

THE LESSONS OF THE 1930s

The two major historical lessons of the era went far beyond the Pearl Harbor attack. The first was that, in the end, the United States admitted that its decades-long hope that Japan could be depended on to protect the open door in Asia had been a pipe dream. As diplomat John Paton Davies later wrote, in the U.S.-Japan-China triangle before 1941, "Japan was . . . the actor, China the acted upon. And the United States was the self-appointed referee who judged by subjective rules and called fouls without penalties, until just before the end of the contest. This provoked the actor into a suicidal attempt to kill the referee." The long, historical background that climaxed with this "suicidal attempt" has been well summarized by historian Michael Barnhart: "The Pacific War was, in essence, a conflict between two visions for East Asia. Each vision had a strong economic element. Japan's fundamental war aim was to establish the Greater East Asian Coprosperity Sphere as a self-sufficient and powerful unit with the Japanese Empire at its core. The United States," Barnhart notes, "sought, first, to thwart Japan's attempt and, second, to 'restore' the principles of . . . the Open Door." These two visions climaxed in the Pacific War.[72]

A second major lesson was that the Constitution's provisions that outlined how Americans were to go to war in an open, accountable process had broken down. Roosevelt secretly placed U.S. ships in areas where incidents could force Americans into war. He then misled the

American people about his actions. FDR also allowed the FBI to break the law by wire-tapping phones and opening mail of suspected Axis sympathizers; he also let the FBI spy on congressmen who merely criticized him. The president believed that Hitler posed a mortal threat to the United States. He also feared that openness would result in a violent isolationist backlash against his policies. Both those fears were valid, but the central question remains: whether those fears justified the damage to the constitutional restraints carefully placed by the Founders upon presidential power. Historian Robert Dallek notes how ironic it was that in his determination "to save democracy from Nazism, Roosevelt contributed to the rise of some undemocratic practices in the United States." Dallek adds, however, that the isolationists' failure to understand the Nazi menace might have pushed FDR into abuses of power that later presidents would repeat for less-exalted reasons. Amid the horrors of the Vietnam War a generation later, Democratic Senator J. William Fulbright of Arkansas made the link directly: "FDR's deviousness in a good cause made it much easier for [President Lyndon Johnson] to practice the same kind of deviousness in a bad cause."[73]

Americans felt the full impact of these two historical lessons much later. In 1941, Roosevelt had been purposely "vague" and had tried to "stifle national debate," as historian Richard Steele concludes. "The result was that when war did come, a great many Americans remained uncertain of the circumstances (beyond the Japanese attack on Pearl Harbor) that led them into global conflict."[74] They only knew that a history they did not understand must never be repeated—especially since before them, a glorious American century dawned over the limitless horrors of World War II. Or as Sidney Greenstreet explained to Humphrey Bogart in the classic film *Casablanca*, "Isolationism is no longer a practicable policy."

NOTES

1. Paul F. Boller, Jr., *Presidential Anecdotes* (New York, 1981), p. 266.
2. Frank Costigliola, *Awkward Dominion: American Political, Economic, and Cultural Relations with Europe, 1919–1933* (Ithaca, N.Y., 1985), ch. I; Arthur Schlesinger, Jr., *The Age of Roosevelt: The Coming of the New Deal* (Boston, 1959), pp. 199–201.
3. Lloyd C. Gardner, *Economic Aspects of New Deal Diplomacy* (Madison, Wis., 1964), p. 5, has the quote with a good analysis.

4. Joseph Alsop, *FDR, 1882–1945: A Centenary Remembrance* (New York, 1982), p. 112.

5. Cordell Hull, *The Memoirs of Cordell Hull*, 2 vols. (New York, 1948), I, pp. 81–82; "Pall-Mall Broadcast," 31 December, 1937, Papers of Cordell Hull, Library of Congress, Washington, D.C.

6. Benjamin D. Rhodes, "Sir Ronald Lindsay and the British View from Washington, 1930–1939," in *Essays in Twentieth Century American Diplomatic History Dedicated to Professor Daniel M. Smith*, ed. Clifford L. Egan and Alexander W. Knott (Washington, D.C., 1982), p. 72.

7. Frederick C. Adams, *Economic Diplomacy: The Export-Import Bank and American Foreign Policy, 1934–1939* (Columbia, Mo., 1976), pp. 224–225.

8. Schlesinger, pp. 253–255.

9. A useful discussion of the treaties' effect is in Dick Steward, *Trade and Hemisphere: The Good Neighbor Policy and Reciprocal Trade* (Columbia, Mo., 1975), pp. 208–220.

10. Laurence Duggan, *The Americas: The Search for Hemisphere Security* (New York, 1949), pp. 65–66.

11. Hull, I, p. 365. The 1930s agreements are excerpted in *The Record of American Diplomacy*, ed. Ruhl F. Bartlett, 4th ed. (New York, 1964), pp. 551–558.

12. Lester D. Langley, *The United States and the Caribbean, 1900–1970* (Athens, Ga., 1980), p. 203.

13. Donald M. Dozer, *Are We Good Neighbors?: Three Decades of Inter-American Relations, 1930–1960* (Gainesville, Fla., 1959), pp. 5–51.

14. *Ibid.*, pp. 35–37.

15. Gardner, p. 32.

16. *New York Times*, 19 November 1933, sec. 8, p. 3.

17. U.S. Department of State, *Foreign Relations of the United States, 1933*, 5 vols (Washington, D.C., 1952), V, pp. 389–414.

18. Gardner, p. 51.

19. Clayton R. Koppes, "The Good Neighbor Policy and the Nationalization of Mexican Oil: A Reinterpretation," *Journal of American History* 79 (June 1982): 80–81.

20. Thomas R. Maddux, *Years of Estrangement: American Relations with the Soviet Union, 1933–1941* (Tallahasee, 1980), p. 17; Frederic L. Propas, "Creating a Hard Line toward Russia: The Training of State Department Soviet Experts, 1927–1937," *Diplomatic History* 8 (Summer 1984): 222.

21. Richard W. Stevenson, *The Rise and Fall of Detente* (Urbana, Ill., 1985), p. 19.

22. "Summary of the Morning Newspapers, Tuesday, Nov. 7, 1933," Box 18, Papers of R. Walton Moore, Library of Congress, Washington, D.C. A good, brief analysis of the 1933 talks, especially in regard to USSR motives, is in U.S. Congress, House Committee on Foreign Affairs, *Soviet Diplomacy and Negotiating Behavior: Emerging New Context for U.S. Diplomacy*, House Document no. 96-239, 96th Cong., 1st sess. [prepared by Joseph G. Whelan], (Washington, D.C., 1979), pp. 65–83.

23. Stanley Hornbeck to Cordell Hull, 28 October 1933, and Stanley Hornbeck to William Phillips, 31 October 1933, which Phillips sent to Hull on 3 November, 711.61/333, RG 59, National Archives, Washington, D.C.

24. George Kennan, "Reflections: Flashbacks," *New Yorker*, 25 February 1985, p. 57.

25. Wayne S. Cole, "Senator Key Pittman and American Neutrality Policies, 1933–1940," *Mississippi Valley Historical Review* 46 (March 1960): 644n.; for background, see

Manfred Jonas, "Isolationism," in *Encyclopedia of American Foreign Policy*, ed. Alexander DeConde, 3 vols. (New York, 1978), II, p. 496.

26. Wayne S. Cole, *Senator Gerald P. Nye and American Foreign Relations* (Minneapolis, 1962), pp. 95–96. A new, most useful analysis of Nye's midwestern region is in Warren F. Kuehl, "Midwestern Newspapers and Isolationist Sentiment," *Diplomatic History* 3 (Summer 1979): 283–306. Kuehl believes that the region was more internationalist than most historians have believed.

27. Robert A. Divine, *Second Chance: The Triumph of Internationalism in America during World War II* (New York, 1967), pp. 21–23.

28. Manfred Jonas, *The United States and Germany, a Diplomatic History* (Ithaca, N.Y., 1984), p. 222. The thesis on labor-intensive versus capital-intensive firms that battled inside the New Deal is given in Thomas Ferguson, "From Normalcy to New Deal . . . ," *International Organization* 38 (Winter 1984): 41–94.

29. Gilbert N. Kahn, "Presidential Passivity on a Nonsalient Issue: President Franklin D. Roosevelt and the 1935 World Court Fight," *Diplomatic History* 4 (Spring 1980): 137–159.

30. Richard A. Harrison, "A Presidential Démarche: FDR's Personal Diplomacy and Great Britain, 1936–1937," *Diplomatic History* 5 (Summer 1981): 249.

31. Douglas Little, *Malevolent Neutrality: The United States, Great Britain and the Origins of the Spanish Civil War* (Ithaca, N.Y., 1985), p. 265.

32. Robert A. Divine, *The Illusion of Neutrality* (Chicago, 1962), pp. 165–166.

33. David Green, *The Shaping of Political Consciousness* (Ithaca, N.Y., 1988), ch. V.

34. Robert Dallek, *Franklin D. Roosevelt and American Foreign Policy, 1932–1945* (New York, 1979), pp. 166–168.

35. The background is well presented in Arnold Offner, *American Appeasement: U.S. Foreign Policy and Germany, 1933–1938* (Cambridge, Mass., 1969), esp. pp. 69–91, and Peggy Mann, "When the World Passed By on the Other Side," *Guardian*, 7 May 1978, pp. 17–18.

36. This example and others are given in a superb context in Deborah Lipstadt, *Beyond Belief: The American Press and the Coming of the Holocaust, 1933–1945* (New York, 1986).

37. David S. Wyman, *The Abandonment of the Jews* (New York, 1984), pp. x–xi, 80, 180–198, 311–340, 345–347; Gordon Craig, "Schreibt un Farschreibt!" *New York Review of Books*, 10 April 1986, pp. 7–11; Geoffrey S. Smith, "Isolationism, the Devil, and the Advent of the Second World War . . . ," *International History Review* 4 (February 1982): 87–88.

38. William L. Neumann, "Ambiguity and Ambivalence in Ideas of National Interest in Asia," in *Isolation and Security*, ed. Alexander DeConde (Durham, N.C., 1957), pp. 147–148.

39. The text is in *The Record of American Diplomacy*, pp. 577–580.

40. The pioneering study of this episode is Dorothy Borg, *The United States and the Far Eastern Crisis of 1933–1938* (Cambridge, Mass., 1964), and a good analysis of public opinion is also in Michael Leigh, *Mobilizing Consent, 1937–1947* (Westview, Conn., 1976), pp. 32–40.

41. Stephen E. Pelz, *Race to Pearl Harbor* . . . (Cambridge, Mass., 1974), p. 67; "4th Meeting, Brussels Conf.," Box 5, Meetings, November 1937, Papers of Norman Davis, Library of Congress, Washington, D.C.; Gardner, pp. 95–96.

42. A good brief context is given in Smith, 63–64. Especially good on the *Panay* is Irvine

H. Anderson, Jr., *The Standard-Vacuum Oil Company and U.S. East Asian Policy, 1933–1941* (Princeton, 1975), pp. 107–110.

43. Arnold A. Offner, "Appeasement Revisited: The United States, Great Britain, and Germany, 1933–1940," *Journal of American History* 64 (September 1977): 381–382.

44. D. Cameron Watt, *Succeeding John Bull: America in Britain's Place, 1900–1975* (Cambridge, 1984), p. 85.

45. Christopher D. Morley, *History of an Autumn* (Philadelphia, 1938), p. 7.

46. Offner, *American Appeasement*, pp. 215–216.

47. Jonas, *United States and Germany*, p. 234.

48. Excerpts of speech in *New York Times*, 9 May 1985, p. 10.

49. Robert A. Divine, *Roosevelt and World War II* (Baltimore, 1969), ch. II.

50. Ian Macleod, *Neville Chamberlain* (New York, 1962), p. 279.

51. Jonas, *United States and Germany*, pp. 245–246.

52. J. Garry Clifford and Samuel R. Spencer, Jr., *The First Peacetime Draft* (Lawrence, Kans., 1986).

53. Wayne S. Cole, *Roosevelt and the Isolationists, 1932–1945* (Lincoln, Neb., 1983), superbly presents the background (esp. p. 8).

54. Alan K. Henrikson has done crucial work on this subject, especially in "The Map as an 'Idea': The Role of Cartographic Imagery during the Second World War," *American Cartographer*, 2 April 1973, pp. 19–53.

55. Jim Harmon, *The Great Radio Heroes* (Garden City, N.Y., 1967), p. 232.

56. Philip Henry Kerr Lord Lothian to Foreign Office, 7 February 1940, FO 371 C5072/ 285/18, British Public Record Office, Kew, Eng. A good analysis of FDR's use of public opinion (and how it did not always restrain him) is in Hadley Cantril, *The Human Dimension: Experience in Policy Research* (New Brunswick, N.J., 1967), esp. pp. 35–42.

57. Akira Iriye, "The Role of the U.S. Embassy in Tokyo," in *Pearl Harbor as History*, ed. Dorothy Borg and Shumpei Okamoto (New York, 1973), p. 121.

58. A good context is in Dallek, pp. 247–251; Wayne Cole, "The Role of the U.S. Congress and Political Parties," in *Pearl Harbor as History*, ed. Borg and Okamoto, pp. 303–307; and the Willkie quote is cited by Robert A. Divine, *Foreign Policy and U.S. Presidential Elections, 1940–1948* (New York, 1974), pp. 82–83.

59. The quote and a most useful analysis is in Waldo Henrichs, "President Franklin D. Roosevelt's Intervention in the Battle of the Atlantic," *Diplomatic History* 10 (Fall 1986): esp. 313–314; Dallek, p. 255.

60. The Diary of Henry L. Stimson (microfilm), 27 May, 1941, Yale University; J. Garry Clifford and Robert Griffiths, "Senator John A. Danaher and the Battle against Intervention in World War II," *Connecticut History* no. 25 (January 1984): 55.

61. Laurence A. Steinhardt to Cordell Hull, 24 June 1941, U.S. Department of State, *Foreign Relations of the United States, 1941*, 7 vols. (Washington, D.C., 1958), I, pp. 174–175; Truman's quote is in *New York Times*, 24 June 1941, p. 7; the State Department and Wheeler statements are noted in Foster Rhea Dulles, *The Road to Tehran: The Story of Russia and America, 1781–1943* (Princeton, 1944), pp. 231–232.

62. "Memorandum for Wayne Coy" from FDR, 2 August 1941, President's Secretary File, Box 18, Russia, Papers of Franklin D. Roosevelt, Franklin D. Roosevelt Library, Hyde Park, New York.

63. Edward Viscount Halifax to Foreign Office, 7 July 1941, FO 954/29, British Public

Record Office; I am greatly indebted to Professor Warren Kimball of Rutgers—Newark for a copy of this document.

64. Clayton R. Koppes and Gregory D. Black, *Hollywood Goes to War* (New York, 1987), pp. 37–41.

65. Henry Luce, *The American Century* (New York, 1941), pp. 5–40.

66. *Ibid.*, p. 68; Moley is quoted in Frank Annunziata, "Raymond Moley and New Deal Liberalism," manuscript in possession of author, pp. 40–41.

67. British War Cabinet Minutes, 19 August 1941, CAB65 84 (41), British Public Record Office; I am indebted to Professor Warren Kimball and Professor Lloyd Gardner, Rutgers—New Brunswick, who discovered this document. A superb brief analysis can be found in *Churchill and Roosevelt: The Complete Correspondence*, ed. Warren Kimball, 3 vols. (Princeton, 1984), I, pp. 227–231.

68. Theodore A. Wilson, *The First Summit* (Boston, 1969), p. 267.

69. Jonathan G. Utley, *Going to War with Japan, 1937–1941* (Knoxville, Tenn., 1985), p. 162, with a good summary on pp. 178–181.

70. David Kahn, "U.S. Views of Germany and Japan in 1941," in *Knowing One's Enemies: Intelligence Assessment before the Two World Wars*, ed. Ernest R. May (Princeton, 1984), pp. 496–501.

71. Diary of Henry Stimson, 7 December 1941; *Churchill and Roosevelt*, I, p. 281.

72. John Paton Davies, "America and East Asia," *Foreign Affairs* 55 (January 1977): 381. A useful overview of recent scholarship on this topic by Japanese and Americans is Richard Leopold, "Historiographical Reflections," in *Pearl Harbor as History*, ed. Borg and Okamoto, pp. 1–24; Michael Barnhart, *Japan Prepares for Total War* (Ithaca, N.Y., 1988), p. 272. Barnhart's analysis is of great importance for both U.S. and Japanese policies.

73. Dallek, pp. 312–313; Clifford and Griffiths, 54. A great scholar of constitutional law wrote in late 1941: "Contrary to a common, but quite mistaken impression, no President has a mandate from the Constitution to conduct our foreign relations according to his own sweet will. If his power in that respect is indefinite, so is Congress' Legislative power, and if he holds the 'sword,' so does Congress hold the 'purse strings.' Simply from constitutional necessity, therefore, the actual conduct of American foreign relations is a joint affair." Edward S. Corwin, "Some Aspects of the Presidency," *Annals* 218 (November 1941): 122–131.

74. Richard W. Steele, "The Great Debate: Roosevelt, the Media, and the Coming of the War, 1940–1941," *Journal of American History* 71 (June 1984): 69.

FOR FURTHER READING

Begin with the notes to this chapter and the General Bibliography at the end of the book; these sources are usually not repeated here. For pre-1981 materials, there is nothing to match the usefulness of the *Guide to American Foreign Relations since 1700*, ed. Richard Dean Burns (1983), for either exhaustiveness or accessibility. Therefore, what follows deals mostly with post-1981 work.

Important overviews and further references can be found in Akira Iriye, *The Global-*

izing of America, 1914–1945, in *The Cambridge History of U.S. Foreign Relations*, ed. Warren Cohen (1993); Richard Dean Burns, "Cordell Hull and American Interwar Internationalism," in *Studies in American Diplomacy, 1865–1945*, ed. Norman Graebner (1985); Jane Karoline Vieth, "The Diplomacy of the Depression," in *Modern American Diplomacy*, ed. John M. Carroll and George C. Herring (1986); Kenneth S. Davis, *FDR* (1986), a biography on the 1933–1937 years; Thomas McCormick, "Adolf Berle," in *Behind the Throne*, eds. T. McCormick and W. LaFeber (1993), essays in honor of Fred Harvey Harrington; and David Green's pioneering *Shaping Political Consciousness: The Language of Politics in America from McKinley to Reagan* (1988), with an emphasis on the 1930s. The peace movement is well presented in Lawrence S. Wittner, *Rebels against War* (1984), with a new epilogue for a 1969 book. A new and crucial primary source is Larry I. Bland *et al.*, *The Papers of General George C. Marshall* (1981–   ), available to 6 December 1941.

The domestic debate is exhaustively presented in Wayne S. Cole, *Roosevelt and the Isolationists, 1932–1945* (1983), the summation of a life's work, with the use of important British and FBI records; Ellen Nore, *Charles A. Beard* (1983), on an outspoken critic and great historian; Justus D. Doenecke, "The Literature of Isolationism, 1972–1983: A Bibliographical Guide," *Journal of Libertarian Studies* 7 (1983), the crucial place to find more sources; Richard W. Steel, *Propaganda in an Open Society* (1985), key on FDR, 1933–1941. Leo V. Kanawada, Jr., *Franklin D. Roosevelt's Diplomacy and American Catholics, Italians, and Jews* (1982), on three key ethnic groups; and a sad story on a central figure is Betty Glad's *Key Pittman: The Tragedy of a Senate Insider* (1986).

On European policy, start with Melvin Small and Otto Feinstein, eds., *Appeasing Fascism* (1991); David F. Schmitz and Richard D. Challener, eds., *Appeasement in Europe* (1990); William R. Rock, *Chamberlain and Roosevelt* (1988), focuses on 1937 to 1940; C. A. MacDonald, *The United States, Britain and Appeasement, 1936–1939* (1981), is good on trade policies; Malcolm H. Murfett, *Fool-Proof Relations* (1984), is important for the British side in U.S.-U.K. naval cooperation, 1937–1940; David Reynolds, *The Creation of the Anglo-American Alliance, 1937–1941* (1982), is a standard in the field; *Essays in Twentieth Century American Diplomatic History Dedicated to Professor Daniel M. Smith*, ed. Clifford L. Egan and Alexander W. Knott (1976), has two useful essays: Brooks Van Everen's "Franklin D. Roosevelt and the Problem of Nazi Germany" and Benjamin D. Rhodes's "Sir Ronald Lindsay and the British View from Washington, 1930–1939." Patrick J. Hearden, *Roosevelt Confronts Hitler: America's Entry into World War II* (1987), is important for moving far beyond the FDR-Hitler confrontation; Theodore A. Wilson, *The First Summit* (1991), is a revised account of the Atlantic conference; Holger H. Herwig, "Miscalculated Risks: The German Declaration of War against the United States, 1917 and 1941," *Naval War College Review* 39 (1986), is suggestive; Jesse H. Stiller, *George S. Messersmith, Diplomat of Democracy* (1987), is a well-researched work on a central U.S. diplomat in Europe. In addition to David Wyman's standard works, Martin Gilbert, *Auschwitz and the Allies* (1981), analyzes the Allied inaction while the Holocaust developed.

For U.S.-Asian (especially Japanese) relations, the following are good in bringing together the best scholarship and suggesting further sources for research: *Diplomats in Crisis: U.S.-Chinese-Japanese Relations, 1919–1941*, ed. Richard Dean Burns and Edward M. Bennett (1975), with essays on Nomura, Hornbeck, and Grew, among others; Michael A. Barnhart, *Japan Prepares for Total War* (1988), noted above in the footnotes; Daniel Yergin's prize-winning account of the key role of oil in *The Prize* (1991); Jonathan C.

Utley, *Going to War with Japan, 1937–1941* (1985), good on Hull and the State Department; and two books widely discussed because of their divergent views of the Pearl Harbor attack: Gordon W. Prange's *Pearl Harbor: The Verdict of History* (1986), and Edwin T. Layton, *"And I Was There": Pearl Harbor and Midway—Breaking the Secrets* (1986). All of this is put into historical perspective with superb new research in the essays edited by Warren I. Cohen, *New Frontiers in American–East Asian Relations: Essays Presented to Dorothy Borg* (1983); and Akira Iriye and Warren Cohen, eds., *American, Chinese, and Japanese Perspectives on Wartime Asia, 1931–1949* (1990).

On U.S.-Soviet relations, a fine overview is Edward M. Bennett, *Franklin D. Roosevelt and the Search for Security* (1985), covering 1933 through 1939; *A Question of Trust— The Origins of U.S.-Soviet Diplomatic Relations: The Memoirs of Loy W. Henderson*, ed. George W. Baer (1986), by a hard-liner who was a key State Department official, covers the 1933 to 1938 years; James W. Crowl, *Angels in Stalin's Paradise* (1982), a critical study of two influential American reporters who covered the Soviet Union—Louis Fischer and Walter Duranty; Douglas Little, "Antibolshevism and American Foreign Policy, 1919–1939," *American Quarterly* 35 (1983), which ranges far beyond the U.S.-USSR relationship; and, for the war with Finland, Travis Beal Jacobs, *America and the Winter War, 1939–1940* (1981). A key book on a key subject is Louis A. Pérez, Jr., *Cuba under the Platt Amendment, 1902–1934* (1986); and a key dissenting view on U.S. policy is given in John A. Britton, *Carleton Beals: A Radical Journalist in Latin America* (1987).

13

World War II: The Rise and Fall
of the Grand Alliance (1941–1945)

THE WASHINGTON CONFERENCE:
LAYING FOUNDATIONS IN THE GLOOM (1941–1942)

The most famous film of the early war years has become *Casablanca*,
with Humphrey Bogart playing Rick Blaine, the American exile who
owned a saloon in pro-Nazi French Morocco. The story takes place in
1941, just before the Pearl Harbor attack. U.S. audiences saw themselves when Rick is asked to help a leader of the anti-Nazi underground in Europe and snaps, "I stick my neck out for nobody."[1] It
turns out, however, that, being a good American, the worldly Rick had
already stuck his neck out: he had fought with the Ethiopians against
the Italian invaders in 1935 and with the Spanish republic against
Franco's fascists in 1936. And, in 1941, he finally agrees to save the
life of the anti-Hitler underground agent. Americans, once aroused
and fully committed, could not be distracted even by the beautiful Ingrid
Bergman from risking their neck to defeat the Axis.

Casablanca's message reassured viewers, but in reality Americans
seemed to have stuck out their neck too far by 1942–1943. They were
trying to fight a worldwide, multifront war while suddenly having to
deal with the most complex and far-reaching diplomatic decisions. No
more had the Big Three (that is, the United States, Great Britain, and
the Soviet Union) joined to fight the war, than they began to argue

bitterly over the postwar peace. They did so, moreover, during days made so dark by German and Japanese victories that it was not clear in early 1942 which side would win the war.

In the Atlantic, U.S. ships became easy targets for Hitler's U-boats. With only 40 submarines available at one time, Germany sank an average of 100 Allied ships per month. U.S. and British crews destroyed 21 U-boats, which Hitler's plants replaced with 123 subs built in 1942. The subs' success threatened to starve an already war-shocked British people. It also made difficult any large U.S.-British operation to relieve the blood-soaked Russian front, where Nazi armies pressed their sieges of Leningrad and Moscow.

In the Pacific, Japanese forces struck with surprising ease and seized Hong Kong, Singapore, and Malaya from the British Empire. Americans were stunned at the humiliating defeat of Allied forces in Burma and the inability of Chiang Kai-shek (the leader of China) to protect either Burma or his own country from Japan. Preoccupied with destroying Mao's Communist forces in northern China, Chiang preferred to let the United States fight Japan. The U.S. commander attached to Chiang's headquarters, the tough, salty General Joseph W. ("Vinegar Joe") Stilwell, bluntly declared that in Burma "We got a hell of a beating . . . and it is humiliating as hell." When a reporter asked how it happened, Stilwell flashed, "We are allied to an ignorant, illiterate peasant son-of-a-bitch called Chiang Kai-shek."[2] Clearly, U.S. relations with its most important Asian ally, China, could be improved.

In the Pacific, the Japanese quickly took U.S. bases at Guam and Wake Island, then pressed the rich Dutch East Indies and Australia. In the Philippines, General Douglas MacArthur failed to protect his small air force, which Japanese bombers destroyed on the ground on December 8, 1941. Allowing his immense ego to overrule military judgment, MacArthur tried to fight the invaders with inadequate forces, who were largely wiped out. Some brave Filipino and U.S. troops held out on the natural fortress of Corregidor Island until May, when the Japanese took the survivors on a tortuous "death march" to prison camps. Meanwhile, MacArthur escaped to Australia, promising "I shall return." Roosevelt hoped that MacArthur could somehow do so with the inadequate army and navy that was at the general's command. The president, believing that Germany's power most threatened Allied survival, infuriated MacArthur by giving military priority to the European theater. U.S. bombers under the command of General James Doolittle did use aircraft carriers to bomb Tokyo in 1942. The surprise attack bolstered sagging U.S. morale but did little to damage Tokyo and even less to reverse the disastrous tide of the war in the Pacific. (Again, Hollywood improved on reality in three popular films—*Bombardier, Purple Heart,* and *Thirty Seconds over Tokyo*—which overlooked how three of Doolittle's pilots were executed as war criminals by Japan after they crash-landed in China.)[3]

Amid the gloom, Winston Churchill secretly traveled to Washington in December 1941 to discuss strategy with Roosevelt. As far as the public was concerned, the climax came on New Year's Day 1942, when the United States, Great Britain, the Soviet Union, and twenty-three other nations grandly announced a "Declaration of the United Nations" to fight to victory and make no separate peace with the Axis powers of Germany, Japan, and Italy. Secretly, however, the British and Americans argued long and passionately. Churchill, realizing that British power could not match America's, wanted separate military commands or at least key strategic decision makers located in London. FDR, advised by his army chief of staff, George C. Marshall, overruled Churchill.

Marshall was a different type of U.S. military leader. A graduate of Virginia Military Institute (not West Point), he had attended the new post–World War I Officers' Training Schools and represented the best of the crop: thoroughly professional, systematic, low-keyed, brilliant in developing and using younger staff (such as a Kansan, Dwight D. Eisenhower, who quickly became a Marshall protégé). He insisted on "unity of command." Thus, the top British and U.S. officers formed a Combined Chiefs of Staff located in Washington (not London) to handle the vast supplying of armies around the globe and to make broad strategic decisions. The Soviets were not included because Stalin did not want to become involved in the war against Japan. Marshall was less successful in stopping Churchill's drive for an invasion of North Africa. The prime minister eyed that region because British troops and imperial interests were already heavily involved. Marshall wanted to strike first at France. FDR sided with Churchill in 1942. He feared the Allies lacked the power to attack the Nazis on the European mainland.

But on a pivotal postwar question, Churchill had to give in. As historian Gabriel Kolko notes, U.S. officials assumed that "the key to the attainment of American postwar objectives for the world economy was Great Britain," because before 1939 the British and Americans together "accounted for about one-half of the total world trade."[4] Secretary of State Cordell Hull was at his Tennessee-mountaineer's toughest in trying to destroy the British Imperial Preference trading system (see p. 351) and do away with the hated closed "spheres of influence." Hull's weapon was the Lend-Lease Act's Article VII, which demanded that the British

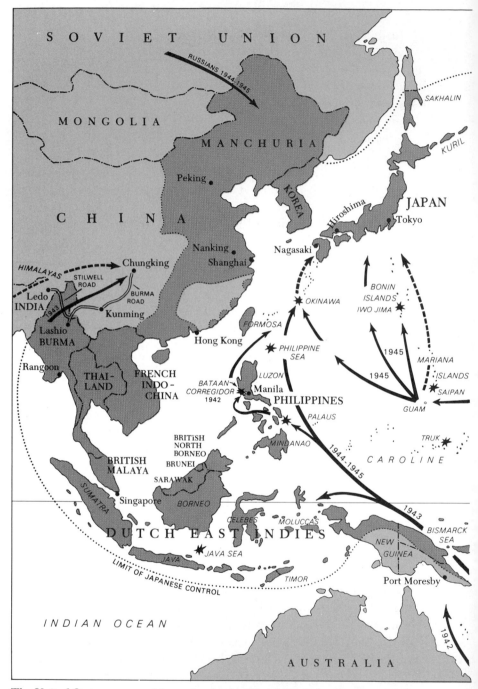

The United States recovered from the shock of Pearl Harbor to start an island-hopping campaign that was to climax with an invasion of Japan. Note how China is largely bypassed by U.S. war planners.

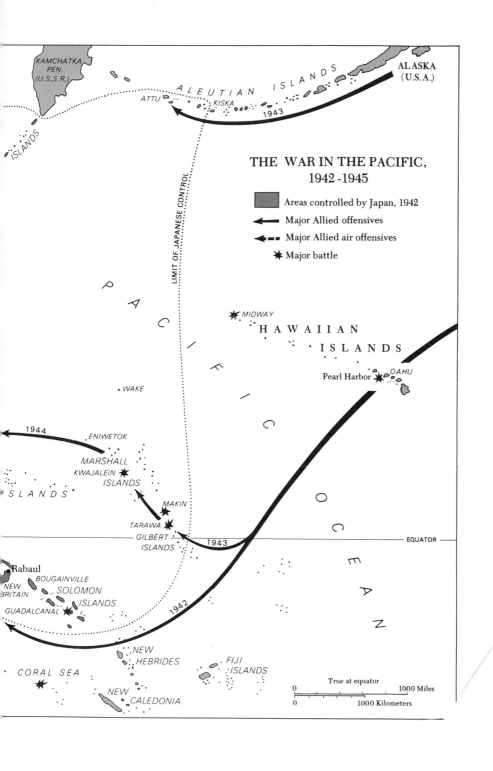

KAMCHATKA
PEN.
(U.S.S.R.)

ALEUTIAN ISLANDS

ALASKA
(U.S.A.)

ATTU

KISKA

1943

ISLANDS

LIMIT OF JAPANESE CONTROL

**THE WAR IN THE PACIFIC,
1942-1945**

Areas controlled by Japan, 1942

Major Allied offensives

Major Allied air offensives

✹ Major battle

P A C I F I C

✹ *MIDWAY*

H A W A I I A N

I S L A N D S

Pearl Harbor ✹ ○ *OAHU*

• *WAKE*

1944

ENIWETOK

MARSHALL

KWAJALEIN ✹

ISLANDS

S L A N D S

MAKIN

TARAWA ✹

GILBERT

ISLANDS

1943

EQUATOR

O C E A N

Rabaul

BOUGAINVILLE

NEW
BRITAIN

SOLOMON

GUADALCANAL ✹

ISLANDS

1942

*NEW
HEBRIDES*

*FIJI
ISLANDS*

• CORAL SEA

✹

*NEW
CALEDONIA*

True at equator

0 _____ 1000 Miles

0 _____ 1000 Kilometers

not create any more closed economic systems after the war. Fully real-izing that his nation would not be able to compete on equal economic terms with the United States, and fully understanding that FDR and Hull intended nothing less than to dismantle the British Empire, Churchill fought Article VII. In the end, however, he had to accept Hull's principle because British survival depended on U.S. help. The prime minister did try, however, to qualify his acceptance with reser-vations.

Churchill had more luck in handling Roosevelt's request that Great Britain give India immediate independence. The president was afraid that London's hold on the jewel of the empire would lead to revolution and instability throughout southern Asia. More immediately, he wanted Indians to fight Japan. The largest political group, Mohandas Gandhi's Congress party, refused to fight until Churchill guaranteed indepen-dence. Churchill bluntly rejected the demand, partly because he wanted to hold on to India, partly because he was afraid that independence would lead to civil war between the Hindu-dominated Congress party and the minority Moslem population that demanded its own nation. But FDR warned, in historian Kenton Clymer's words, that "if the West failed to support Indian nationalism, Japan would likely capture Asian nationalism generally and inspire a full-fledged anti-Western revolt."[5]

The president even sent special agents to push the British toward Indian independence. Churchill lashed back at one agent with "a string of cuss words . . . for two hours in the middle of the night," as a U.S. observer recorded. Proclaiming in November 1942 that "I have not become the King's First Minister to preside over the liquidation of the British Empire," Churchill threatened to resign. He finally was able to block independence until 1947.[6] But Hull could at least be pleased with London's acceptance of Article VII, for now, he believed, "the foundation was laid for all our . . . postwar planning in the economic" realm.[7]

AT WASHINGTON AND CASABLANCA: PREVIEWING THE COLD WAR (1942–1943)

Actually, only some of the "foundations" were laid. Hull himself pointed to the great obstacle to finishing the postwar structure when, shortly after Pearl Harbor, journalists asked him whether "Russia is to become our active ally, make peace with Germany and / or Japan, collapse, or what." Hull answered, " I wish I knew."[8] Certainly, he knew how Stalin had responded to the Atlantic Charter's call for self-determination and an open world marketplace. The dictator, even with his back to the wall before onrushing Nazi armies, had added a reservation that made his acceptance of the document meaningless.

Even worse occurred in late December, when British foreign minister Anthony Eden flew to Moscow. FDR and Hull were afraid that the British were trying to cut a secret deal with the Soviets. They warned Eden to make no postwar commitments. Stalin quickly asked Eden to guarantee the June 1941 boundaries—that is, to allow the Soviets to have the three Baltic States and a large slice of Poland. When Eden refused to agree, the dictator furiously declared that he thought the Atlantic Charter had been directed against Hitler, but it appeared now to be targeted against him. U.S.-British-Soviet relations were off to a bad start. They improved only slightly when Stalin's foreign minister, Vyacheslav Molotov, came to Washington to repeat Stalin's demands and ask, in addition, for an early invasion of western Europe so that pressure could be lifted from the Russian front. FDR and Hull held firm on postwar boundaries. Molotov finally dropped the territorial issue.

He apparently did so because the president did offer a second front "this year." Roosevelt further stroked Molotov by suggesting that after the war, "four policemen" (the Americans, British, Soviets, and Chinese) should walk the beat to keep order in their neighborhoods. This suggestion, however vague, was exactly what the Soviets wanted to hear because it could make them supreme in their neighborhoods of eastern Europe and northern Asia. When FDR asked whether the Soviets liked his idea, a delighted Soviet diplomat responded—apparently with a straight face—"anything for the common cause."[9] The president, however, soon had to break his promise for a second front because Churchill refused to agree and the West's military forces were too weak to mount a successful invasion. By mid-1942, the diplomatic outlook seemed nearly as bleak as the military situation.

Americans were so angry with Churchill's rejection of a second front in France that Marshall threatened to swing U.S. resources to the Pacific theater. In that region, on May 7, 1942, the Allies had stopped a possible Japanese invasion of Australia by destroying 100,000 tons of Tokyo's shipping at the Battle of the Coral Sea—the first naval battle waged largely by U.S. planes as well as ships. The U.S. Navy and Air Force, helped by brilliant intelligence work that intercepted messages and so could predict Japan's military plans, also won the Battle of the Midway Islands in June. Surprising victories stopped Japan's offensive and made possible U.S. landings on Guadalcanal (where seven Japanese troopships were sunk) and Tulagi. Costs were high. Ten thousand U.S. sailors died in the Solomon Islands actions alone. The Japanese lost 30,000 men. A counterattack put the last two U.S. aircraft carriers in the Pacific temporarily out of action, but the Japanese failed to stop the driving U.S. and Australian forces. MacArthur started an "island-hopping" campaign toward Tokyo.

Afraid that FDR might indeed divert resources to the Pacific, Churchill countered with a plan to send U.S. and British troops into action by invading North Africa.[10] Roosevelt finally agreed. Marshall and the U.S. military, however, bitterly protested. The general thought it a waste of resources. But later, he admitted that the military had "failed to see that the leader in a democracy has to keep the people entertained. That may sound like the wrong word, but it conveys the thought."[11] In other words, the president had to show Americans that U.S. soldiers were taking the offensive someplace in the European theater.

But FDR paid a high political price for invading North Africa. Vichy France controlled part of the region, while other points were held by Hitler's leading tank commander, Field Marshal Erwin Rommel, the famous "Desert Fox," who planned to conquer Egypt and the pivotal Suez Canal area. Roosevelt allowed the U.S. military commander, General Eisenhower, to try to save lives by making a secret deal with the Vichy French commander, Admiral Jean Darlan, so that the French would not resist the invaders. This attempt to work with fascist elements (FDR even called Darlan "my dear old friend") drew condemnation then and after the war. The British disliked Darlan for being pro-Nazi. Churchill, instead, wanted to deal with a tall, charismatic French general, Charles de Gaulle. A shrewd political operator who mystically believed that he personally embodied a thousand years of French history, de Gaulle had disavowed Vichy France and established Free French headquarters in London. Roosevelt, however, detested the vain, imperious de Gaulle, who correctly understood that FDR did not believe that the French people should play any major role (during or after the war), given their quick collapse in 1940 and their collaboration with Hitler. (Hull simply dismissed de Gaulle's Free French as "Polecats.")

The Americans again overruled Churchill and de Gaulle. FDR allowed Eisenhower to try to work with Darlan and invade North Africa in November 1942. Darlan then failed to keep up his part of the deal.

Eisenhower's forces met stiff resistance. French sailors blew up their ships rather than allow the Allies (or Germans) to take them. An assassin removed Darlan from the scene in December. The Americans' "Vichy gamble" became known as their "Vichy fumble." Hitler seized the rest of southern (Vichy) France. The only good news occurred in October 1942, when British and Australian forces stopped Rommel at the Battle of El-Alamein.

In January 1943, Roosevelt secretly traveled to Casablanca for summit talks with Churchill. The discussions focused on both military and diplomatic questions. Militarily, the Americans reluctantly agreed with the British that, contrary to their earlier assurances to Stalin, an invasion of France in 1943 would be too costly. They instead planned to invade Sicily and then Italy. On the diplomatic front, FDR again tried to destroy de Gaulle's Free French forces by combining them with the more pliable (and pro-U.S.) forces led by Henri Giraud. When de Gaulle refused to come when the President called, Roosevelt disgustedly wrote Hull: "We delivered our bridegroom, General Giraud, who was most cooperative on the impending marriage. . . . However . . . the temperamental lady DeGaulle . . . has got quite snooty . . . and is showing no intention of getting into bed with Giraud." When de Gaulle finally did appear, he was so mistrusted that Secret Service guards pointed tommy-guns at him from hidden curtains when he talked with the president. Historian Frank Costigliola has noted how Americans since 1919 (most notably FDR in 1943–1945) characterized France "in terms that connoted a flighty, not-so-capable female: excessively emotional, hypersensitive, . . . licentious, too concerned with food, drink, fashion, sex, and love." Americans meanwhile saw themselves "in a 'masculine' mode—rational, calm, pragmatic, efficient, and wise." Such irrational biases poisoned U.S.-French relations even before their leaders sat down to talk.[12] De Gaulle emerged from the talks as powerful as ever.

FDR believed he accomplished much more at Casablanca on another diplomatic front. He dramatically announced in a press conference that this time the Allies would settle for nothing less than the "unconditional surrender" of Germany and Japan. Critics quickly cried that such a policy ruled out a negotiated peace and would drive the Axis to fight to the last soldier. But Roosevelt and Churchill were desperately trying to show Stalin that the absence of a second front did not mean that they were going to make a deal with Hitler. They were rightly concerned that the Soviet ruler himself might make another Moscow-Berlin arrangement at the West's expense. They pledged to fight to end the Nazi Empire, and they hoped Stalin would, too.

TEHRAN: THE MOMENTS OF TRUTH (1943)

Stalin's power rose significantly in 1943. During February, his troops began to cut off Hitler's Sixth Army that had already besieged Leningrad for sixteen months. The Soviets captured 300,000 Germans, including 25 generals. Stalin's armies, for the first time, also drove back the Germans without the aid of winter weather. At Kursk, in history's greatest tank battle, the Soviets triumphed during the summer despite Hitler's throwing into the fray 2,000 tanks and planes. Two-thirds of the territory lost to the Nazis soon fell back into the Soviets' hands. The Soviets had taken on 80 percent of the Nazi striking force, had stopped it, and were now turning it back—all without the help of the second front that FDR had promised. The Americans and British, meanwhile, put off their planned invasion of Sicily. "I think it is an awful thing," Churchill wrote FDR's closest adviser, Harry Hopkins, "that in April, May, and June, not a single American or British soldier will be killing a single German or Italian soldier while the Soviets are chasing 185 divisions around."[13] When the Allies finally invaded Sicily in July, their armies survived a German armored attack only through incredible bravery on the part of the U.S. Eighty-second Airborne Division. General George S. Patton's daring offensive finally broke the defenders' back. Eisenhower next led his forces into Italy. The Italians surrendered on September 8, 1943, but 11 German divisions quickly appeared and stopped Eisenhower's 14 divisions south of Rome.

Allied officials were deeply concerned. On August 22, 1943, an intelligence report for the U.S. Joint Chiefs declared that American "fundamental aims" in the war were "(1) to destroy the German domination of Europe, and (2) to prevent the domination of Europe in the future by any single power (such as the Soviet Union), or by any group of powers in which we do not have a strong influence. If we do not achieve *both* these aims," the report warned, "we may consider that we have lost the war." The authors of the report urged a massive landing of Allied troops in western Europe as soon as possible for diplomatic as well as military purposes. The next day, August 23, U.S. and British military chiefs approved a plan, code-named RANKIN, to inject troops into Germany immediately if it appeared that the Germans might collapse before the Soviet blows. As late as November, while traveling to Tehran to meet Stalin for the first time, Roosevelt discussed RANKIN and warned his advisers that there "would definitely be a race" for Berlin. As historian Mark Stoler concludes, U.S. officials had early "realized that the . . . 'second front' across the Channel could be used to aid the Soviets militarily and block their expansion at the same time."[14]

But such action would only solve half the problem. The other half was the organization of Europe *after* the Soviets were blocked and the war ended. Ivan Maisky, the Soviet ambassador to Great Britain, told Foreign Secretary Eden that "there were two possible ways" to handle Europe. Stalin, Churchill, and FDR "could agree each have a sphere of interest," or each could "admit the right of the other to an interest in all parts of Europe."[15] Maisky said he preferred the latter plan, but his boss, Stalin, no doubt wanted the former. On the American side, Secretary of State Hull preferred the second approach, while his boss, like Stalin, seemed to be moving toward the former with his "policemen" idea.

In truth, the president and Prime Minister Churchill had already made their choice. As their armies liberated part of Italy in early autumn 1943, Stalin demanded that he be involved in deciding occupation policy. FDR and Churchill refused. The British, who wanted to reinstall the Italian monarchy, did not want the Soviets stirring up Italy's large number of Communists. Churchill said it directly to Roosevelt: "We cannot be put in a position where our two armies are doing all the fighting but Russians have a veto and must be consulted."[16] The Soviets were effectively kept out of Italy.

Despite the obvious U.S.-British "sphere of influence," Hull—who opposed all spheres—refused to give up his dream. In October 1943, he flew across the Atlantic (for the first time and despite a lifelong problem with claustrophobia that made him terrified of airplanes). At the Moscow Conference, the secretary of state convinced the Soviets, British, and Chinese to agree to a "declaration" pledging them to join in a postwar international organization in which all would work cooperatively. An overjoyed Hull returned to tell Congress that the Four-Nation Declaration meant that "there would no longer be need for spheres of influence, for alliances, for balance of power," or for other bad things from "the unhappy past." Hull was as wrong, however, as he was happy. In Moscow, he had asked Stalin to agree to a plan in which the Allies would only act together in deciding how liberated areas were to be governed. This meant that Americans could have a veto power over Soviet actions in eastern Europe, and the Soviets could have similar power in Italy and western Europe. Doubtless vividly remembering how he had just been shut out of Italy, Stalin refused to agree. Hull accepted the rejection without protest. The other and larger half of the problem was now in full view: Stalin intended to control

Generalissimo Chiang Kai-shek, FDR, Churchill, and Madame Chiang at Cairo in 1943. This meeting marked the high point of U.S.-Chinese relations, which rolled downhill rapidly in 1944–1945. Given Churchill's mistrust of Chiang, the prime minister is probably forcing himself to be sociable.

eastern Europe as his own sphere of influence. FDR and Churchill had actually set up such a sphere of their own already in Italy. But many Americans, including Hull and key members of Congress, intended to keep on pushing for an open, cooperative, democratic world without spheres—at least in eastern Europe. They knew full well that the bricks needed to build an open, liberal world order could not be made from the straw of Communist regimes.

This was the dilemma that Roosevelt faced when he sailed to meet Stalin and Churchill at Tehran in late 1943. (The president almost missed the conference. En route, a destroyer in his convoy accidentally released a torpedo that barely missed blowing up the president's ship.) FDR first stopped at Cairo, Egypt, to meet Chiang Kai-shek and Churchill. Roosevelt was determined to treat the Chinese as one of the "four policemen" despite Churchill's protests that the Chinese—especially Chiang—were corrupt, weak, and attractive to Americans only because they planned to replace the British as the dominant foreign power in China after the war. All of those charges were true. But they only strengthened Roosevelt's belief in his Far East policies. China had to be built up, he believed, so that it could be a worthy junior partner to the United States. To achieve this, the president pledged that he would supply 90 Chinese divisions so that they could launch a major offensive against Japan. Churchill growled that Chiang was no more than a "faggot-vote" that supported whatever Roosevelt wanted. Nevertheless, the president obtained a Cairo declaration that called for Japan's unconditional surrender and promised the return of strategic areas—most notably Formosa (or Taiwan)—from Japan to China. With good reason, Churchill feared that FDR's next step would be to encourage Chiang to push the British out of their imperial holdings at Hong Kong, Singapore, and even India after the war. U.S. military power in the Asian theater now surpassed Great Britain's. Roosevelt intended to use that power as well as America's great economic influence in China to create a postwar Asia that suited American, not British, interests.

Churchill and FDR then flew to Tehran to meet Stalin. For security reasons, Stalin insisted that the president stay in the Soviet Embassy. Roosevelt did so, but the rooms were no doubt bugged with listening devices. FDR had little to hide. He went out of his way to develop a warm relationship with the Soviet dictator and even teased Churchill in order to amuse Stalin. Quick agreement was reached on launching the second front in France during early 1944. The Big Three also concluded that they should dismember a defeated Germany. Roosevelt's one moment of indecision occurred when Stalin proposed that the postwar world be run by regional committees controlled by the "four policemen." The dictator was picking up Roosevelt's earlier idea, an idea that could give the Soviets domination in eastern Europe.

But Roosevelt now backed off. He faced the impossible job of squaring his "four policemen" approach with Hull's determination to have an open, international system. When Roosevelt could not reconcile the two U.S. policies, Stalin and Churchill agreed to put off discussion. The Soviet leader, however, noted Roosevelt's doubt that Congress would allow U.S. troops to be stationed in Europe after the war. The Tehran talks brought into the open the several key contradictions that haunted—even paralyzed—U.S. policy into the postwar years.

The most important decision at Tehran involved Poland. That unfortunate nation had spent most of the earlier three centuries suffering under Russian rule or, as between 1919 and 1939, clutching its independence while trying to fight off pressure from both Germans and Soviets. World War II nearly destroyed Poland. The United States lost 0.3 percent of its population (400,000 dead), the USSR 9 percent

*After the Tehran Conference of November 28–December 1, 1943, a jaunty FDR
flew to Sicily to inform a smiling Dwight Eisenhower (who had commanded
the Allied invasion of Sicily and Italy) that the general would lead the great
invasion of France planned for mid-1944.*

(15 million to 20 million), but Poland lost at least 14 percent of its
population (5 million). Many of these were Jews who disappeared in
the Holocaust.

After the Germans and Soviets invaded in 1939, two exile Polish
governments formed. The London Poles represented the most pro-
Western elements and were determined to regain their 1939 borders.
The second group, the Lublin Poles, were pro-Communist, under Stalin's thumb, and, thus, willing to give the dictator those parts of eastern
Poland he wanted. Stalin nevertheless kept his ties to the London group
until April 1943. Then the Germans discovered in the Katyn Forest the
bodies of 4,500 Polish military men who, Hitler claimed, had been
massacred by the Soviets when the latter controlled the region in 1939–
1940. Stalin naturally blamed the Germans for the slaughter. (But evidence, in 1943, and especially nearly a half-century later when Moscow finally released documents on the event, proved that Stalin had
ordered the brutal executions.) When the London Poles demanded an

investigation, Stalin seized the chance to break relations with them. Churchill asked the dictator to reconsider. Stalin refused, although he made a friendly gesture in mid-1943 by grandly disbanding the Comintern (the worldwide Soviet-run organization of Communist parties). He was attempting to assure westerners that he had no intention of subverting their governments. In reality, most Communist parties, including the American Communist party, continued to receive guidance from Moscow.

Churchill had little love for the London Poles, whom he found difficult, but he had a lifelong love for the British Empire. At Tehran, he was willing to make deals with Stalin. On the first night of the conference, Roosevelt went to bed after dinner, coffee, and cigars, but Churchill urged Stalin to stay up and discuss postwar affairs. The prime minister got straight to the point: using three matchsticks he showed how the Soviet Union could have part of eastern Poland and, in return, the Poles could move westward and take part of Germany. Stalin, to understate the case, was most pleased. When Roosevelt discovered what had occurred, he did not object. He only remarked that he could not then agree because of the possible political effect back home. Roosevelt was thinking of the large Polish–eastern European vote and his intention to run for a fourth term as president within eleven months.

Warren Kimball has assessed the Tehran talks by noting that they "avoided the hard questions" and performed "a kind of diplomatic papering over cracks in the wall." Nevertheless, they were "the most significant in the war" because the "postwar shape of Europe and East Asia was sketched out," a United Nations organization was agreed upon, and plans for the second front were finally launched.[17]

To Yalta: By Way of Omaha Beach (1944)

The course of the war would largely shape the final diplomatic settlement. Whoever killed the most Germans and Japanese and first reached the heart of Germany and Japan would hold high cards at the peace table. In early 1944, those high cards remained in the deck and were yet to be drawn. The Red Army drove west but encountered stiff resistance, including a fight to the death with Ukrainian nationalists who so hated both Nazi and Soviet leaders that they held out against the Soviets until 1947. In western Europe, massive Allied air raids tried to soften up Germany for the planned invasion. The Italian campaign

WAR IN EUROPE AND AFRICA, 1942-1945

Axis Powers at outbreak of war

Maximum extent of Axis military power

Allies

Neutral countries

← Allied offensives

--- Heaviest Allied aerial bombing

.... Inside limit of German U-boat operations

By late 1943, the German armies were in retreat from Soviet soil. In June 1944, the United States and British armies led the invasion that finally opened a second front on the shores of France. By early 1945, Hitler's Reich, which was to last a thousand years (so he claimed), was besieged from both east and west.

had bogged down, and the bomber pilots of the U.S. Air Force and the (British) Royal Air Force became heroes. Hollywood movies sang their praises. In *Desperate Journey* (1943), Ronald Reagan portrayed a captured U.S. flier who confused the Nazis by making up the names of airplane parts, such as "thermotrockles."[18] (Reagan, who spent the war in California portraying soldiers in films, later, as president of the United States, said that he had been "in uniform" between 1941 and 1945.) But Hollywood and the U.S. government told only part of the story. The U.S. Air Force lost over 40,000 crewmen and nearly 5,000 bombers in near-suicidal attacks against German industries. The Nazis lost only half as many airmen, yet their production continued to rise. Only by mid-1944, when new technology (such as radar-guided bombing) and long-range fighter planes were available, did the Allies gain full command of western Europe's skies.[19]

It occurred just in time. On June 6, 1944, 5,000 ships, 14,000 aircraft, and 100,000 troops launched the D-day invasion that centered on France's Normandy region. But the greatest amphibious invasion in history nearly failed. Dug-in German units, commanded by Field Marshal Rommel, inflicted 100,000 American casualties in the first month of fighting. The Allies were nearly driven back into the sea. Churchill's long-held fear that the English Channel would be "awash with corpses" came close to being realized. U.S. divisions, again with General Patton's Third Army tanks in the fore, worked with British troops to make a breakthrough. Paris was liberated on August 25, 1944. But then the Allies again bogged down as they overextended their supply lines and the Nazis fought ferociously. To add to the bad news, in mid-June 1944, Hitler's scientists began launching the V-1 and then the V-2 rockets on Great Britain. These pilotless missiles, which gave little warning before they exploded, struck fear into a British people already suffering from five years of war.

As he closely watched the invasion of Europe, Roosevelt also had to deal politically with the Allies. Free French leader Charles de Gaulle had destroyed all the rivals the president had sent to oppose him. Roosevelt wanted de Gaulle excluded from the invasion until Churchill noted that "it is very difficult to cut the French out of the invasion of France." The two leaders then instructed de Gaulle to broadcast their messages to the French people. The Frenchman refused to take orders. "He's a nut," FDR concluded. But de Gaulle got his way. He made the broadcast and told the French to follow his own orders. The tall general was beating Roosevelt in the high-stakes game of who was to control postwar France.[20]

To Yalta: By Way of Bretton Woods and Quebec (1944)

Nor was the president able to control Churchill, despite the awesome economic and military power of the Americans. Between 1940 and 1944, U.S. industrial production shot up 90 percent, agricultural output 20 percent, and the total gross national production of all goods and services 60 percent. Most other economies, including the British, were devastated by war. U.S. leaders agreed with Will Clayton, former corporate executive and now State Department official, who warned in late 1943 that isolationism was dead. The nation's growing production and political interests demanded an open, orderly world, Clayton declared, or Americans would have to become an "armed camp, police the seven seas, tighten our belts, and live by ration books for the next century or so." Another of FDR's economic experts, Henry Grady, put the problem bluntly: "The capitalistic system is essentially an international system. If it cannot function internationally, it will break down completely."[21]

Roosevelt joined in by announcing that "Dr. New Deal" (which had emphasized domestic solutions) had been replaced by "Dr. Win-the-War." *Time* magazine, edited by Henry Luce, who had long argued that the New Deal failed to fix the U.S. economy, ran a sarcastic note in its "Milestones" section on January 3, 1944:

> Death Revealed. The New Deal, 10, after long illness; of malnutrition and desuetude. Child of the 1932 election campaign, the New Deal had four healthy years, began to suffer from spots before the eyes in 1937, and never recovered from the shock of war. Last week its father, Franklin Roosevelt, pronounced it dead.

As Clayton observed, U.S. officials now had to come up with an international plan to replace the New Deal, a plan that could keep the nation's economy pumping away so that the war-shocked world could be rebuilt and the U.S. system saved from a possibly fatal shock of another 1930s-like depression.

To solve these problems, U.S. leaders called a conference of the world's non-Axis nations at Bretton Woods, New Hampshire, in mid-1944. The meeting established two new organizations to ensure an open, capitalist postwar world. The first was the International Bank for

Reconstruction and Development (or the World Bank) that had a $7.6 billion treasury—nearly all from the United States—to help rebuild war-torn Europe and develop the newly emerging countries in Africa, Asia, and Latin America. By promoting growth and providing capital, the World Bank was to make less necessary state-controlled, perhaps socialistic, measures for development.

The second organization was the International Monetary Fund (IMF). Its $7.3 billion aimed to help nations suffering from high trade deficits. The IMF funds were to be used to stabilize those nations' currencies that were under pressure because of internal economic problems. The IMF hoped to prevent the highly destructive trade and currency wars of the 1930s (see p. 371). Moreover, Americans insisted at Betton Woods that the postwar economic system rest on gold and the U.S. dollar. Such insistence was not surprising. The United States controlled two-thirds of the world's gold. Washington officials dominated both the World Bank and IMF. They planned to use that power to create an open, international marketplace that did not need excessive state inter-ference or high tariffs.[22]

Just as this economic structure was erected at Bretton Woods, the Allies also met at the Dumbarton Oaks estate in Washington, D.C., to build the political structure: the United Nations. The UN was to have a general assembly in which all the world's nations were represented. But the real power was to be in a twelve-member security council, with each of the five permanent members (the United States, the Soviet Union, Great Britain, France, and China) having a veto. The other seven seats on the council would rotate among all other members. Sta-lin agreed to join the UN but notably refused to join the World Bank and IMF.

Churchill and other British leaders had fought to redraw the U.S. plans at Bretton Woods. They knew that Roosevelt intended to use the new World Bank and IMF—as well as the all-powerful dollar—to force the British Empire to open up to American goods and investment. U.S. officials, however, simply steamrolled over London's objections. But an even worse clash occurred between Churchill and Roosevelt at a meeting in Quebec, Canada, in September 1944. The two bitterly argued over what to do with postwar Germany. At the Tehran Conference in late 1943, FDR had gone along with the idea of dividing Germany. At Quebec, however, Roosevelt was convinced by his secretary of the Treasury, Henry Morgenthau, not only to divide Germany, but rip all industry out of it (make it "pastoral") and heavily police it. The Mor-genthau Plan aimed at creating an economic wasteland where the industrial hub of Europe once existed. Churchill hated the idea; he did not believe that the British economy could survive without a healthy Europe. He reluctantly went along after Morgenthau offered the British a $6.5 billion postwar credit. Roosevelt and Morgenthau were ready to pay a high price to make sure Germany would never rise again.

But back in Washington, Secretary of State Hull and Secretary of War Stimson were shocked. Hull later declared that nothing "angered me as much" as the Morgenthau Plan. Stimson and Hull told Roosevelt that an open, economically workable world could not exist without a healthy Europe. And a healthy Europe required a functioning Germany.[23] Roosevelt thought it over, then admitted that he had "pulled a boner" at Quebec. The president disavowed the Morgenthau Plan. Churchill wondered if the Americans knew what they were doing.

He had good reason to wonder—and fear. As historian Fraser Harbutt observes, after the Tehran Conference, FDR and his advisers "began to think of the Soviet Union" (not the weakening British Empire) "as their main postwar partner."[24] At Quebec, Roosevelt had so rudely brushed aside British concerns that Churchill finally blurted out, "Do you want me to beg, like Fala [FDR's dog]?" Moreover, how could Churchill (or Stalin) be certain that FDR could cooperate with them after the war even if the president wanted to do so? In 1943–1944, powerful figures in the United States, led by Senator Robert Taft, journalist Walter Lippmann, and historians Charles and Mary Beard, all issued warnings against the United States undertaking to police the world after the war. The Beards even went further. In books that sold millions of copies and reached 40 million Americans when Henry Luce published parts of them in his *Life* magazine, they argued that FDR had violated the Constitution in conducting foreign policy and that Congress had to regain its power.[25] In European eyes, such a change would make U.S. policy even more unpredictable. FDR won a fourth term as president in 1944 with a relatively unknown running mate, Senator Harry Truman of Missouri. But many wondered whether, with his sinking health, the president could live another term.

To Yalta, with a Detour at Moscow

Thus, Churchill had good reasons to worry about U.S. postwar policy. He determined to protect vital British interests in Greece by making a private deal with Stalin. As German troops were pushed out of that nation, civil war erupted between monarchical groups, whom Churchill supported, and Greek leftists. In May 1944, the British prime minister made an arrangement with Stalin: the British would control Greece, and the Soviets would control Romania. Hull quickly objected, pointing out that the deal created unacceptable "spheres of interest." The British were bitter. "As if there was ever such a sphere of influence agreement as the Monroe Doctrine!" complained one London official. Churchill privately groused that U.S. complaints about the evils of "power politics" were pure hypocrisy: "Is having a Navy twice as strong as any other power 'power politics'? . . . Is having all the gold in the world buried in a cavern 'power politics'? If not, what is 'power politics'?"[26] The prime minister cared little about labels but much about getting things worked out with Stalin.

His concern increased in August–September 1944, when the Red Army drove to the gates of Warsaw. The city's underground resistance rose up to destroy the Nazis and take the city before the Soviets entered. But the Red Army stopped, then sat outside the Polish capital for nearly two months as German troops turned and smashed the resistance. Stalin pleaded that his army was unable to advance because of supply and other military reasons, but he also damned the resistance as "a handful of power-seeking criminals" and refused to help U.S. and British attempts to drop supplies to the anti-Nazi forces. It seemed that Stalin would not tolerate any rival for power in Poland.

Churchill observed the Warsaw uprising's fate and the confusion in U.S. policy, then flew to Moscow in October 1944 to talk—as Stalin liked to call it—"practical arithmetic." FDR was told of the meeting and sent the U.S. ambassador, W. Averell Harriman, to the Soviet Union as an observer. But Churchill and Stalin also met privately without Harriman and worked out a trade: the Soviets would have 90 percent influence in Romania and 75 percent influence in Bulgaria and Hungary; in return, the British would have 90 percent influence in Greece; Yugoslavia was to be split 50–50. The prime minister added that all this must be explained diplomatically and that "the phrase 'dividing into spheres' [must not be used], because the Americans might be shocked." Churchill later wrote that Stalin never uttered "one word of reproach" when the British moved to smash the Greek leftists.[27]

The two men also agreed that Germany had to be dismembered and its heavy industry destroyed. Otherwise, Stalin noted, "every 25 or 30 years there would be a new world war which would exterminate the young generation. . . . [Thus,] the harshest measures would prove to be the most humane." The two leaders then quickly agreed on moving the Polish-Soviet and Polish-German boundaries westward, as the Tehran talks provided. Churchill pleaded with Stalin to bring the London Poles into agreement with the pro-Communist Lublin group. The Soviet dictator said that he would try. Both men agreed that the Polish leaders were difficult. Churchill: "Where there were two Poles there was one quarrel." Stalin: "Where there was one Pole he would begin to quarrel with himself through sheer boredom."[28]

Roosevelt raised no objection to the Polish arrangement, but he was not fully told by Churchill about the percentages deal. Earlier in the war, went one story, FDR was moving through the White House hallway when Churchill, who was on a brief visit, suddenly stepped, stark naked, out of a door. Roosevelt was visibly embarrassed, but Churchill quickly declared: "The Prime Minister of Great Britain has nothing to conceal from the President of the United States." This was not, however, quite true.

To Yalta: FDR's Rocky Road

Despite his smashing re-election victory over Governor Thomas E. Dewey of New York, October 1944 through February 1945 was FDR's

Franklin D. Roosevelt (1882–1945) loved ships and sailing. He vacationed by boating at Campobello Island on the U.S.-Canadian border, and he frequently sailed on the presidential yacht. Here he is aboard the USS Quincy, *off Malta, just before the February 1945 summit conference at Yalta. He is joined by his top military advisers (clockwise from lower left): Admiral Ernest J. King, Admiral William D. Leahy, General George C. Marshall, and General L. S. Kuter (representative for Air Force Chief of Staff General Henry "Hap" Arnold).*

winter of discontent. No doubt thinking of Churchill's and Stalin's plans, the president told a press conference in December that the Atlantic Charter's grand principles were "slipping away from us."[29]

Nor did the military campaigns in western Europe give him an advantage. Hitler suddenly counterattacked with 250,000 troops during mid-December. In the ensuing Battle of the Bulge, only courageous, last-ditch Allied resistance and a dry German supply line prevented a massive defeat. The Americans lost 100,000 men (the Germans 120,000) and were driven back from the German border. Meanwhile, a Soviet force of 7 million resumed its drive and in February, on the eve of the Yalta Conference, was only 50 miles from Berlin. At Churchill's prodding, bombing attacks were increased—partly to break German morale, partly to impress the Red Army with Western air power. The most infamous bomber attack occurred on February 13, 1945, when the magnificent—and militarily unimportant—city of Dresden was destroyed and 35,000 German lives lost. The next day, U.S. Mustang fighters machine-gunned refugees trying to flee the still-burning city. "There was a sea of fire covering in my estimation some 40 square miles," a British pilot recalled.[30] The systematic bombing of civilians, which had sickened and angered the West when it had occurred in China or Spain during 1937, now, just eight years later, had become an accepted act of war.

Allied forces in the Pacific also faced a difficult time. Proclaiming "I have returned," General MacArthur was recorded by movie cameras wading through knee-deep water as 200,000 U.S. troops invaded the Philippines in October 1944. But bad weather and suicidal Japanese resistance bogged down the invasion and finally forced MacArthur to fight a battle for the capital of Manila that cost 100,000 Filipino civilian lives in a single month. It was, historian Carol Morris Petillo writes, "one of the most destructive, albeit well-intentioned, armies of 'liberation' the world had ever seen."[31] The Japanese left little alternative. At Iwo Jima in February through March 1945, and at Okinawa during April through June, the struggle to control the small islands proved to be among the war's most costly. On Okinawa, the Americans lost 12,000 men in order to kill 80,000 Japanese entrenched in caves and bunkers. Such numbers doubtless haunted Roosevelt when he pressed Stalin to enter the war against Japan as quickly as possible. (See map, p. 416.)

The Allied position in China was also endangered. During mid-1944, the Japanese attacked General Stilwell's forces and threatened the entire south China theater, including bomber bases that FDR had hoped to use against Japan. The president begged Chiang Kai-shek to throw his

U.S.-supplied troops into the battle. Fearful of the Chinese Communists to the north, Chiang refused. A furious Stilwell marched into Chiang's office and, in the general's words, "hit the little bugger right in the solar plexus" with the demand that Chiang move immediately. The Chinese leader instead demanded Stilwell's recall. A discouraged Roosevelt ordered Stilwell home. The president realized that Chiang would neither protect U.S. interests in Asia nor responsibly help Americans dismantle the discredited European colonies in Asia.[32]

FDR most notably found himself in a fix over the French colonies in Indochina (especially Vietnam). He might consider the Free French leader, Charles de Gaulle, a "nut" and despise him for being so "snooty," but the arrogant French general had become FDR's best hope for maintaining order in both France and Vietnam against the Communist-led opposition. At stake, after all, were French cooperation in Europe and an overseas empire twenty-two times larger than France itself. Moreover, as Ambassador Harriman warned Roosevelt from Moscow, the Soviets were threatening to "become a world bully wherever their interests are involved. This policy will reach into China and the Pacific as well." By March 1945, FDR agreed to look the other way while de Gaulle moved to re-establish French colonial control over Indochina.[33]

But Roosevelt would not challenge Stalin directly. The president believed that he needed Soviet help against Japan and knew that he needed it to build a peaceful postwar world. Nor could the Red Army be overlooked. Of Germany's 13.6 million casualties in the war, the Russian front claimed 10 million, often in unimaginably brutal fighting. Henry Luce's *Life* magazine called Lenin "perhaps the greatest man of modern times" and the Soviets "one hell of a people" who, "to a remarkable degree . . . look like Americans, dress like Americans, and think like Americans." Such movies as *Mission to Moscow* and *North Star* led one critic to observe that "war has put Hollywood's traditional conception of the Muscovites through the wringer and they have come out shaved, washed, sober . . . Rotarians, brother Elks."[34] Roosevelt did hear, however, from some dissenters, including Secretary of the Navy James Forrestal, who complained to a friend in autumn 1944 that whenever an American tries to protect U.S. security, "he is apt to be called a god-damned fascist or imperialist." But

> if Uncle Joe [Stalin] suggests he needs the Baltic Provinces, half of Poland, all of Bessarabia and access to the Mediterranean [through Turkey], all hands agree that he is a fine, frank, candid, and generally delightful fellow who is very easy to deal with because he is so explicit in what he wants.[35]

YALTA . . .

As Roosevelt sailed for the Soviet Black Sea resort city of Yalta and his final summit conference, he perhaps sympathized with Forrestal's frustration. But the president knew he could do little more. The reality was that Stalin and Churchill had already made their own deal to create spheres of influence in eastern Europe and the Mediterranean. FDR realized that he was not dealing with an irrational or a paranoid Soviet leader, but rather with Soviet leadership that, as Harriman explained, was totally preoccupied "with 'security' as Moscow sees it." Having been invaded at least four times since 1914 and having suffered the destruction of much of the western Soviet Union, he added, the Soviets wanted "puppet regimes in all contiguous countries" and a guaranteed "period of freedom from danger" to recover and industrialize.[36]

However, FDR also knew that Americans believed that they were fighting for self-determination and the Atlantic Charter principles. The State Department warned Roosevelt, moreover, that the Balkans and Poland had to have self-government, freedom for journalists, and "furtherance of legitimate economic rights, existing or potential." The Soviets would probably "exert predominant political influence" over eastern Europe, the State Department concluded, but the United States—for its own vital interests—had to have "trade . . . under the freest possible conditions." A conflict was brewing because "the United States is no longer so much a land of opportunity as a land looking for opportunity; and to an increasing extent Americans will seek it outside their own borders."[37]

How Roosevelt could ever maintain equal U.S. access to (for example) Romania while not undercutting Churchill's and Stalin's agreement of 90-percent Soviet control over that country, no one could say. Certainly, FDR's new secretary of state was of little help. Edward R. Stettinius had been a young corporation executive with slight experience in, and less talent for, international diplomacy. "A Secretary of State should be able to read and write and talk," a friend complained to Roosevelt. "He may not be able to do all of these, but Stettinius can't do any of them."[38] FDR, nevertheless, appointed him because Stettinius (unlike Hull) could be trusted to carry out orders without asking questions.

The Big Three efficiently settled certain problems at Yalta. With regard to the United Nations, Stalin dropped his demand for a veto over procedural questions in the Security Council and, in return, asked for two

The conference at the Russian resort of Yalta, February 1945. Stalin is seated at the right, Roosevelt is in the center, and, on the left, with the ever-present cigar, is Churchill. Eden, Stettinius, and Molotov stand behind the chairs.

or three Soviet republics to have votes in the General Assembly, where all the world's nations were to be represented. FDR accepted this on the condition that, if he thought it necessary to get the UN Charter through the Senate, the same number of U.S. states could have similar voting rights. (Roosevelt never had to invoke this agreement.) Other questions, however, raised tempers and fears on both sides.

Most telling was the discussion about Poland. Stalin again asked that eastern Poland be "returned" to the Soviets. He had made the point clear in late 1944 by recognizing his Lublin Poles as the country's legitimate regime. FDR and Churchill had earlier granted Stalin's boundary demands, but now they asked that the boundary be modified and the new government be "more broadly based" by including Poles from London. They also asked for "free and unfettered elections as soon as possible." Churchill said that British "honor" was involved. FDR, for his part, did not refer to the State Department's argument for the need of an open eastern Europe. Instead, he insisted that the concessions were needed to please the 6 million to 7 million

Polish voters at home. Stalin blew up. Reminding them that the Soviet Union had been attacked through Poland, he declared that "it was a question both of honor and security." The dictator finally agreed to the loose phrases ("broadly based" governments and "free . . . elections"), but it was understood that Stalin interpreted such words differently than the two Western leaders.[39]

Stalin had once said that communism fit Germany like a saddle fit a cow. He now moved to dismember the cow. In discussing Germany, Churchill and FDR had (again) agreed to certain principles at Tehran fourteen months earlier. They had agreed, for example, on dismemberment. But two other questions about Germany caused problems. The three men had earlier given German land to Poland, but Churchill now questioned whether the Poles could handle such an area. The prime minister was probably beginning to see that such a transfer of land could anger many Germans and make Poland dependent upon the Soviets for protection against an angry Germany. (This boundary problem was only settled in 1970, when the West German government recognized the Polish borders that included a slice of pre-1939 Germany.) The second question involved Stalin's demands for $20 billion in reparations from Germany, with half going to the Soviets. Such reparations were to make Germans help pay for the 70,000 destroyed Soviet villages and the nearly 25 million homeless that the war produced. It would, of course, also make Germany weak for a long time. But the British opposed the $20 billion sum. Stalin again became angry. Roosevelt restored some calm by merely agreeing "in principle" to figures. Details were to be worked out later. Finally, to Stalin and FDR's disgust, Churchill succeeded in making France one of the occupying powers in Germany.

Stalin doubtless intended from now on to take whatever reparations he wanted from the German areas controlled by his Red Army. The only possible alternative might have been a $6 billion credit that his foreign minister, Molotov, asked from the United States in January 1945. The Soviets made other requests for varying amounts of money over the coming months, but nothing could ever be worked out. The Americans demanded in return, to use Ambassador Harriman's words, proper Soviet "behavior in international matters."[40] This meant that the Soviets were to allow an open eastern Europe and join the World Bank and International Monetary Fund. Stalin, however, was unwilling to sell out Soviet security, as he defined it, for any amount of money, no matter how large. FDR, for reasons best known to himself, never raised the issue of a loan to the Soviets at Yalta.

A German woman shows shock at the ruins of Bensheim as U.S. troops move by her. Taken in March 1945, the photo shows what had happened to Hitler's Reich just twelve years after he had assumed power. It also indicates the rebuilding job that faced the United States when it moved to restore West Germany's economy.

But Roosevelt did push a pet State Department project by asking that all agree on the Declaration of Liberated Europe. This declaration repeated the Atlantic Charter's principles; it also pledged the signers "to act in concert" in governing newly liberated countries. Taken literally, this could mean a U.S. veto over Soviet actions in, say, Poland. It was an attempt to take back much of what had been lost to the Soviets at Tehran, Moscow, and Yalta. But Molotov quickly insisted that a line be added stating that only *mutual consultations* were needed before an occupying power governed liberated countries. Thus watered down, the declaration lost its force, and the Soviets signed it.[41]

Finally, FDR (with little concern for Churchill's views) worked out a deal on the Far East. Stalin promised to fight Japan within three months after the German surrender. In return, Roosevelt agreed that the Soviets could (1) regain the Kuril Islands and the southern part of Sakhalin from Japan, (2) formally obtain a sphere of influence in Outer Mongolia, (3) work with China in running the valuable South Manchurian Railroad, and (4) have special rights in the Chinese ports of

Port Arthur and Dairen. By the early 1950s, Yalta had become a dirty word in American politics because many (especially Republicans) believed that FDR had sold out China at Yalta. But the reality was more complex and interesting. Roosevelt insisted on Stalin's making a formal deal with Chiang Kai-shek about the agreements reached at Yalta. The president thus maneuvered Stalin into working directly with Chiang instead of possibly recognizing the Chinese Communists. Moreover, the Soviet Union had long-standing claims to some of the concessions, such as the Kurils and Sakhalin, and would probably have the Red Army in position to seize rights in the other areas at the end of the war.

The American humorist Josh Billings (i.e., Henry Wheeler Shaw) once observed that "the glory is not whether you won or lost, but how you played a bad hand." Given the military problems in western Europe and Chiang's weakness in Asia—not to mention the earlier Stalin-Churchill percentage deal—FDR had won some glory. As historian Diane Clemens writes in her study of the conference, "The decisions at Yalta involved compromise by each nation, probably more by the Soviets than by the Western nations."[42] Roosevelt lost little at Yalta that had not already been agreed on earlier or had been taken by the Red Army. He worked to create ties between Stalin and Chiang. Roosevelt returned home knowing that the Atlantic Charter principles had been violated. But he believed that a basis had been laid for a victorious war effort and postwar cooperation by the Big Three. As journalist Walter Lippmann later observed, FDR never thought that he could simply "charm Stalin into agreeing with him. Roosevelt was a cynical man. . . . What he thought he could do was outwit Stalin, which is quite a different thing."[43]

. . . AND AFTER

Stalin clearly felt that the Yalta talks had confirmed the deal with Churchill at Moscow in 1944. The dictator set about reconstructing eastern Europe. Romania had been recognized by Churchill as part of the Soviet sphere. Stalin's agent told the Romanian king that a pro-Soviet government must assume power, then underlined the point by slamming the door so hard as he left the room that the plaster cracked. The State Department tried to help the king by insisting that Romanians should be governed by the Declaration of Liberated Europe. The Soviets replied that FDR and Churchill had done as they pleased in Italy, so now Stalin would do as he pleased in Romania.[44]

In Moscow, no agreement could be reached over how the Polish government was to be reorganized. The arguments grew bitter. "The map shows Mexico is nearer to America while Poland is nearer to us," Soviet Foreign Minister Molotov lectured the Americans, "and what happens in Poland is more important to Russia than to you."[45]

Danger also flared in Switzerland. U.S. secret agents led by Allen Dulles opened surrender talks with Nazi generals. Stalin learned about the meetings and strongly complained to FDR and Churchill. He implied that Dulles was attempting to arrange a secret Munich-type surrender so that Nazi armies would be free to turn against the Soviet Union. FDR had to send several messages to reassure the dictator. Meanwhile, Red Army troops drove on Berlin. General Eisenhower's Western forces were pushing toward the capital as well, but he ordered them to swing south. It was one of the most controversial decisions in the war. Eisenhower justified allowing the Soviets to take Berlin because, first, the Big Three had already agreed to put Berlin in the Soviet occupation zone and, second, he feared that fighting the 200 miles to the capital would kill far too many of his troops to capture a city that he would have to leave anyway.

Churchill, dismayed by Stalin's actions and facing a difficult election campaign at home, began prodding FDR to get tough with the Soviets. The prime minister was trying to eat his cake and have it, too—that is, maintain his Moscow deal of 1944 that gave him a free hand in Greece, while pushing Roosevelt to demand that Stalin allow Romania and Poland to be more open. FDR responded slowly—in part because he was ill at his vacation retreat in Warm Springs, Georgia, and in part because he apparently doubted that Stalin was breaking the rubber-band-like Yalta agreements. The president, moreover, wanted the reluctant Soviets to attend a conference in San Francisco to establish the new United Nations. He had to move carefully. On April 6, he told Churchill that no one must think that "we are afraid. Our armies will in a very few days be in a position that will permit us to be 'tougher.' "[46] Exactly what these words meant will never be known. Six days later the president died from a massive stroke.

HARRY TRUMAN AT POTSDAM

The new president, Harry Truman, had been a senator from Missouri and a compromise nominee for the vice-presidency at the 1944 Democratic party convention. He knew little about foreign policy, and FDR

Churchill, Truman, and Stalin during one of the few light moments at the conference at Potsdam (just outside Berlin, Germany), July 17–August 2, 1945. Churchill was soon voted out of office. U.S. and Soviet leaders would not hold hands again for ten years.

did absolutely nothing to educate him. The British ambassador to Washington called the new president "an honest and diligent mediocrity" and noted the "Missouri County court-house calibre" of his personal friends.[47] Truman, however, did not listen to those Missourians, but to Ambassador Harriman and such poker-playing friends as Secretary of the Navy Forrestal, who believed that the time had arrived for a showdown with Stalin.

A cabinet meeting on April 23 was crucial. Truman listened to seventy-eight-year-old Secretary of War Henry Stimson, who warned that the Soviets had rights in Poland and were needed to defeat Japan. General George Marshall supported Stimson. But the president then followed Harriman's and Forrestal's tough advice. Clearly, the inexperienced leader did not want to be thought of as insecure. Moreover, Truman knew little as yet about the 1943–1945 deals that had been reached on eastern Europe. He summoned Foreign Minister Molotov to the White House and "in words of one syllable," as Truman later reported, told the Russian that unless Stalin began behaving better, Americans would turn anti-Soviet. Molotov supposedly protested that he had never been talked to like that in his life. Truman shot back that if Molotov carried out his agreements, he would not be talked to like that. The president later bragged to a friend that he had given Molotov "the straight one-two to the jaw." But the insecure Truman then asked his friend, "Did I do right?"[48]

Perhaps Truman had doubts because Stalin had refused to budge. The dictator responded with a "one-two" of his own. He reminded Truman that "Poland has the same meaning for the security of the Soviet Union as . . . Belgium and Greece [has]" for British security. Privately, the dictator prophesied that the Germans would be "on their feet" in fifteen years, "and then we'll have another go at it." Next time, he would not be caught unprepared: "Everyone imposes his own system as far as his army can reach. It cannot be otherwise."[49]

Truman backed off to reassess the situation. Germany surrendered on May 7, 1945. Hitler and his mistress, Eva Braun, committed suicide several days earlier as Soviet troops swept over Berlin. But Truman still needed Stalin's help against Japan. The president agreed to meet in a summit conference at Potsdam (Germany) in July 1945. Churchill looked forward to the talks, only to have Clement Attlee's Labour party stun the British leader in a national election. Attlee replaced Churchill as prime minister midway through the Potsdam Conference.

In preparing for the conference, Truman did not give up hope of blocking the Soviets in eastern Europe. Indeed, he believed it to be essential. As he told advisers, all of Europe must be united because the eastern sections grew cattle and wheat while the west's "big industries" produced iron and steel. Each had to have the other for an orderly, prosperous Europe. Truman believed as well that Germany had to be unified and Poland at least open to U.S. "trade, investments and access to sources of information," as the State Department put it.[50]

The Big Three talks at Potsdam revolved around the endless problem of Germany. Truman and the State Department now concluded that the dismemberment plan accepted at Tehran and Yalta was wrong. Germans would never accept it, except through force, and Germany could, thus, "keep the world in lasting perturbation."[51] Moreover, a prosperous, orderly Europe required a prosperous, orderly Germany at its center, much as an apple could not be good if its core were rotten. Truman now even flatly opposed giving German territory as compensation to Poland. Stalin bitterly complained, but his policy actually put Truman in a corner. The president could either have a united Germany under the control of occupying powers or a divided Germany with Soviet influence limited to just one zone. Because the first alternative threatened to spread Stalin's power throughout much of central Europe, Truman finally chose the second alternative. He signaled this choice by changing the U.S. position on reparations. The president backed away from the $20 billion figure that had been discussed at Yalta. He instead insisted on a percentage arrangement that mentioned no specific figures. In reality, Truman's new policy prevented the Soviets from taking reparations out of the U.S., British, and French occupation zones. After all, a percentage of nothing was nothing. Potsdam, in truth (but not through mutual agreement), settled three key German problems: dismemberment went forward; reparations from the western zones to the Soviet Union were soon stopped; and, over Truman's and Attlee's objections, Stalin insisted that the new Poland have German territory.

A DIFFERENT WORLD:
THE ATOMIC BOMB AND JAPAN'S SURRENDER

On July 18 at Potsdam, Truman casually told Stalin that a new weapon had been exploded at a test site in New Mexico two days before. The program that climaxed with the explosion of an atomic bomb had begun in 1939, when two scientists, Albert Einstein and Leo Szilard—both refugees in America from Hitler's genocidal campaign against Jews— told Roosevelt that it was "conceivable" that a "new type" of an "extremely powerful" bomb could be released from the atom of uranium ore.[52] By the time of the Pearl Harbor incident, Americans worked with British and Canadian scientists to develop the weapon. In early 1942, FDR tried to cut the other two nations from the project. Churchill fought back and regained British access to the work, but the British rightly suspected the Americans of wanting to keep the secret to themselves. "The salad is heaped in a bowl permanently smeared with the garlic of suspicion," one London official observed in early 1945.[53] Roosevelt never seriously considered bringing Stalin into the project. As historian Barton Bernstein concludes, FDR followed "the strategy of excluding the Soviets from knowledge of the bomb and of reserving the options of using it in the future as a bargaining lever, threat, military counterweight, or even a weapon against the Soviets."[54]

Truman continued this policy. His secret "Interim Committee" of scientists and government officials, chaired by Secretary of War Stimson, discussed how to use the new bomb to make "Russia more manageable in Europe." Throughout the Manhattan Project at Los Alamos, New Mexico, where the bomb was made, top officials assumed that the bomb had to be built (especially because they knew that Hitler's scientists were working on one, too). They also assumed that it was being built at a cost of $2 billion to be used. Truman wondered aloud to Stimson how the weapon might help settle the Polish, Romanian, Yugoslav, and Manchurian problems on his terms. There is evidence that the president scheduled the Potsdam Conference on dates he believed the bomb was to be tested so that he would be able to use it as a diplomatic lever against Stalin. When the president learned at Potsdam that the weapon indeed worked, he "was tremendously pepped up," Stimson recorded. Churchill noted that Truman was "a changed man" as he suddenly got tougher with Stalin.

The president had set his sights high. He had earlier declared that he might not get "100 percent" of what he wanted from Stalin, but he would get "85 percent." He could never figure out, however, how to use the new bomb to obtain even that figure. This first attempt at "atomic diplomacy"—that is, waving the bomb without making overt threats and hoping that the Soviets would give in—never worked. Even when Truman mentioned the new bomb to Stalin at Potsdam, the Soviet dictator was, to the president's surprise, unmoved. And with good reason. Documents found in Moscow after the Soviet Union's collapse in 1991 revealed that Stalin's spies had penetrated the Manhattan Project, which was developing the U.S. bomb, and had been feeding information back to the Kremlin since late 1941. One analysis even suggests that "Stalin could well have been better informed about the making of the U.S. atom bomb than Truman himself." In any case, the dictator only reacted by secretly instructing Soviet scientists to speed up their own work.[55]

The director of the scientists at Los Alamos, J. Robert Oppenheimer, watched the giant mushroomlike cloud rise over the New Mexico desert and remembered a Hindu text: "Now I am become death, destroyer of worlds." Another scientist declared, "I am sure at the end of the world—in the last millisecond of the earth's existence—the last man will see what we saw."[56] Several scientists pushed U.S. officials to warn Japan with a demonstration of the weapon on a deserted Pacific island, not on a Japanese city. The suggestion was rejected—the weapon might not work properly, U.S. officials feared, and only two bombs were available to help end the war.

Truman later declared that he dropped the bombs on Japan to avoid "a half million" Americans dying in an invasion of the home islands. Others used the figure of 1 million possible casualties. In reality, at the time, Truman had reports that the U.S. losses would probably be 40,000 to 50,000.[57] U.S. planes using incendiary bombs were already burning entire cities. On March 9–10, a single such attack on Tokyo "scorched and boiled and baked to death" 84,000 people, as a U.S. Air Force officer described the results.[58] Japanese officials approached the Allies for surrender terms that would preserve the religious figure of the emperor. Truman rejected this offer because he wanted unconditional surrender. Stalin rejected it because he wanted to declare war and to claim Japanese territory.

Few had moral qualms about dropping atomic bombs on Japan's cities. World opinion had been horrified by Fascist and Japanese bombing of civilians in 1937–1938 but, by 1945, accepted the slaughter of 80,000 or more civilians on a single night without a murmur. The Japanese especially seemed fair game. As Truman liked to note, their attack on Pearl Harbor earned them any penalty that Americans could inflict. In a key work on the racial hatred between Americans and Japanese, historian John Dower quotes a 1946 remark of an American who believed his country hated Japan with "emotions forgotten since our most savage Indian wars." One of FDR's advisers publicly declared in April 1945 that he favored "the extermination of the Japanese in toto." Journalists who worked in both war theaters noted how Germans were hated but treated like human beings, while Japanese were treated as if they were jungle beasts. Popular motion pictures of the war defined Japanese as "monkey people," "ringtails," and "rats" usually prefixed by "yellow." Hollywood films sometimes (as in Alfred Hitchcock's classic *Lifeboat* of 1944) noted differences between bad Nazis and good Germans, but movies almost never showed a good Japanese. Such racial hatred and fears had allowed Roosevelt to incarcerate nearly 112,000 Japanese-Americans in concentration camps in early 1942. (They remained there even though their sons in a Japanese-American unit fighting in Italy were among the bravest and most honored of U.S. military forces.) Meanwhile, Tokyo officials stressed their nation's divine origin and racial purity while belittling other less-civilized Asians and, especially, the multiracial, "liberal," "barbarian," and "soft" Americans.[59]

In addition to U.S. moral views about using the atomic bomb, Truman felt that, because of the weapon, he did not need (or want) the Soviets to invade Manchuria and Japan. Or, as Stimson put it, "I hope to hell [Stalin] doesn't come in."[60] A U.S. B-29 bomber, the *Enola*

*The beginning of a new era in human history and the end of World War II:
Hiroshima at Ground Zero in August 1945 after the United States dropped the
first atomic bomb.*

Gay, dropped the world's first atomic bomb on Hiroshima at 8:15 A.M.
on a hot, humid August 6, 1945. Within a second, a 650-foot fireball
seared everything in its path; every brick building within a mile disappeared; every wooden structure within 1.2 miles blew apart; and,
within thirty minutes, a firestorm was triggered whirled by a 40-mile-
an-hour wind and accompanied by black, radioactive rain. By 4:00 P.M.,
80,000 had died; 120,000 more suffered from burns and other effects
of radiation. A physician recalled that patients "had no faces! Their
eyes, noses, and mouths had been burned away, and it looked like their
ears had melted off. It was hard to tell front from back."[61]

On August 8, almost three months to the day after Germany's surrender, Stalin declared war on Japan. On August 9, the United States
dropped the second atomic bomb; this fell on Nagasaki. Another 65,000
Japanese immediately died. Truman now wanted Japan to surrender
quickly, especially before Soviet troops approached the Japanese home
islands. But for the next four days the president's advisers argued heatedly over whether to allow even a greatly limited Japanese emperor to
remain in power. Stimson wanted to compromise and end the conflict

immediately. Secretary of State Byrnes, however, hoped to appease American hatred for Japan by further restricting the emperor's powers. The result was a vague U.S. response to Tokyo's peace feelers that made some Japanese militarists decide to fight to the end. Between August 10 and 14, wave after wave of U.S. planes destroyed Japan's cities and killed thousands of civilians. A third atomic bomb was to be readied by August 19, but Truman never had to make the decision to use it. On August 14–15, the emperor, fearing that his nation would be "annihilated," overruled the militarists and accepted a U.S. position that implied the continuation of his imperial institution, but in greatly reduced form. Truman now approved the condition. If he had so accepted the emperor's continued role earlier, much death and destruction might have been avoided. Historian Martin Sherwin concludes that "*neither* bomb may have been necessary; and certainly . . . the second one was not."[62]

CONCLUSION

On September 2, 1945, General MacArthur sailed into Tokyo Bay on the USS *Missouri*. He watched as Japanese officials signed the papers of surrender. World War II was over. Another war, however, had already begun in a world remade by fourteen years of global destruction and two atomic bombs.

This different world demanded new thoughts. One view was formulated by David Lilienthal, a close adviser of Truman: "The fences are gone. And it was we, the civilized, who have pushed standardless conduct to its ultimate." A quite different view was much later expressed by Phyllis Schlafly, a leader of conservative Republicans: "The atomic bomb is a marvelous gift that was given to our country by a wise God."[63] In the new war and the different world, Americans would have to choose between foreign policies those two statements suggested.

It was already clear, however, that the gigantic U.S. power, even the atomic bomb, could not resolve the problems and contradictions that had developed in foreign policy. On the one hand, FDR and Truman had hoped to construct an open, liberal world along the lines of the Atlantic Charter principles. On the other hand, they had to recognize Stalin's determination to control eastern and perhaps central Europe, especially because the Red Army had the power to support such determination. Because both superpowers hoped to be dominant over a united (but weak) Germany, neither power could take the chance that the other might actually end up controlling this hub of Europe. As historian Frank Ninkovich phrases it, "The immense force of the global superpower confrontation had, like the collision of two geological plates, created a new mountain barrier whose most formidable massif was a divided Germany."[64] Nor could the Americans reconcile their commitment to self-government with their standing by as the British and French moved back into their Asian and African colonies. Truman faced a dangerous, incredibly complex world, even while he believed that he held the power in his hands to obtain at least "85 percent" of what he and most Americans wanted.

NOTES

1. Bernard F. Dick, *The Star-Spangled Screen* (Lexington, Ky., 1985), pp. 21–22, 167–171.
2. E. J. Kahn, Jr., "Profile," *New Yorker*, 8 April 1972, p. 64; Allan R. Millett and Peter Maslowski, *For the Common Defense: A Military History of the United States of America* (New York, 1984), pp. 401, 415.
3. Important on the MacArthur-Philippine connection is Carol Morris Petillo, *Douglas MacArthur, the Philippine Years* (Bloomington, Ind., 1981), esp. pp. 201–205; also see Dick, p. 132.
4. Gabriel Kolko, *The Politics of War: The World and U.S. Foreign Policy, 1943–1945* (New York, 1968), p. 280.
5. Kenton J. Clymer, "The U.S. and the Decolonisation of Empire in Asia," in *American Studies in Malaysia*, ed. K. S. Nathan (Kuala Lumpur, Malaysia, 1986), p. 14.
6. *Churchill and Roosevelt: The Complete Correspondence*, ed. Warren Kimball, 3 vols. (Princeton, 1984), I, pp. 446–447, quotes the American observer (Harry Hopkins); D. Cameron Watt, *Succeeding John Bull: America in Britain's Place, 1900–1975* (Cambridge, 1984), p. 234.
7. Cordell Hull, *The Memoirs of Cordell Hull*, 2 vols. (New York, 1948), II, p. 1153.
8. "Private Memorandum" of conversation with Cordell Hull, 11 December 1941, Black Book #I, Papers of Arthur Krock, Princeton University.
9. Robert A. Divine, *Roosevelt and World War II* (Baltimore, 1969), pp. 59–61.
10. Joseph L. Strange, "The British Rejection of Operation Sledgehammer: An Alternative Motive," *Military Affairs* 46 (February 1982): 6–14.
11. Eric Larrabee, *Commander in Chief: Franklin Delano Roosevelt, His Lieutenants, and Their War* (New York, 1987), p. 9.
12. Frank Costigliola, "The Image of France in the United States," unpublished manuscript in author's possession, pp. 1–6.
13. *Churchill and Roosevelt*, II, p. 148.
14. "Joint Chiefs of Staff Memorandum for Information No. 121," 22 August 1943, in *Records of the Joint Chiefs of Staff*, Soviet Union, Pt. I, 1942–1945, p. 11. I am indebted

to Richard Mandel for a copy of this memorandum; Mark A. Stoler, "The 'Second Front' and American Fear of Soviet Expansion, 1941–1943," *Military Affairs* 39 (October 1975): 136–140.

15. Vojtech Mastny, *Russia's Road to the Cold War* (New York, 1979), pp. 107–108.

16. *Churchill and Roosevelt*, II, pp. 487–488; Kolko, pp. 37–39.

17. *Churchill and Roosevelt*, II, p. 612.

18. Dick, p. 201.

19. Millett and Maslowski, pp. 438–440.

20. This section draws from Frank Costigliola's important and highly readable analysis, *France and the United States* (New York, 1992), Ch. I; and from Walter LaFeber, "Roosevelt, Churchill, and Indochina, 1942–1945," *American Historical Review* 80 (December 1975): 1277–1295.

21. Lloyd C. Gardner, *Economic Aspects of New Deal Diplomacy* (Madison, Wis., 1964), p. 308, has the Clayton quote; also note p. 344.

22. A good, succinct overview is in David Baldwin, "The International Bank in Political Perspective," *World Politics* 18 (October 1965): 68–81.

23. Hull, II, pp. 1614–1615.

24. Fraser Harbutt, "Churchill, Hopkins, and the 'Other' Americans . . . ," *International History Review* 8 (May 1986): 261.

25. "Beard's Republic," *Life*, 20 March 1944, p. 36.

26. Christopher Thorne, *Allies of a Kind: The U.S., Britain and the War against Japan, 1941–1945* (New York, 1978), p. 515; Daniel Yergin, *Shattered Peace: The Origins of the Cold War and the National Security State* (Boston, 1977), p. 64.

27. Winston S. Churchill, *The Second World War*, 6 vols. (Boston, 1948–1953), VI, p. 293; "Record of Meeting at the Kremlin," 9 October 1944, PREM 3 / 4347, British Public Record Office, Kew, Eng. I am indebted to Professor Warren Kimball for a copy of this document.

28. "Record of Meeting at the Kremlin," 9 October 1944, PREM 3 / 4347, British Public Record Office; the context is well analyzed in Warren F. Kimball, "Naked Reverse Right . . . ," *Diplomatic History* 9 (Winter 1985): 1–7.

29. *Washington Post*, 23 December 1944, p. 17.

30. A good analysis of how the military background shaped the Yalta discussions is in Diane Shaver Clemens, *Yalta* (New York, 1970), pp. 82–95; for a retrospective on the Dresden bombing, see the *New York Times*, 30 January 1985, p. 2.

31. Petillo, pp. 221–228, esp. quote on p. 224.

32. Larabee, pp. 509–578; see also Jonathan Spence, who puts Stilwell's experience in the context of three hundred years of China's experience in *To Change China* (New York, 1980), pp. 263–264.

33. U.S. Department of Defense, "U.S. Policy, 1940–1950: Summary," in *United States–Vietnam Relations, 1945–1967*, 12 vols. (Washington, D.C., 1971), I, pp. IA1–A4. These are the original "Pentagon Papers." W. Averell Harriman to Harry Hopkins, 10 September 1944, Harriman File, Box 96, Papers of Harry Hopkins, Franklin D. Roosevelt Library, Hyde Park, New York.

34. Clayton R. Koppes and Gregory D. Black, "What to Show the World: The Office of War Information and Hollywood, 1942–1945," *Journal of American History* 64 (June 1977): 98–99; *Churchill and Roosevelt*, I, p. 421.

35. Gaddis Smith, *American Diplomacy during the Second World War, 1941–1945* (New York, 1965), p. 128.

36. U.S. Department of State, *Foreign Relations of the United States: The Conference at Malta and Yalta, 1945* (Washington, D.C., 1955), pp. 450–451.
37. *Ibid.*, pp. 234–235, 237.
38. Martin Weil, *A Pretty Good Club: The Founding Fathers of the U.S. Foreign Service* (New York, 1978), p. 183.
39. U.S. Department of State, *Malta and Yalta*, pp. 668–669, 677–678, 898; Smith, pp. 138–139, 148–149.
40. Herbert Feis, *Churchill, Roosevelt, Stalin: The War They Waged and the Peace They Sought* (Princeton, 1957), pp. 645–646. A good summary of the discussion over Germany is in Clemens, pp. 275–282.
41. U.S. Department of State, *Malta and Yalta*, pp. 977–978.
42. Clemens, p. 290.
43. Oral History of Walter Lippmann, Columbia University, p. 217.
44. "Daily Staff Summary," 19 March 1945, Lot File, RG 59, National Archives, Washington, D.C.; Mastny, pp. 250–258.
45. "Daily Staff Summary," 6 April 1945, Lot File, RG 59, National Archives.
46. A good analysis is Kimball, "Naked Reverse Right," 14–24; the documents and editorial comment are in Kimball, *Churchill and Roosevelt*, III, p. 617; and *Roosevelt and Churchill*, ed. Francis L. Loewenheim, Harold D. Langley, and Manfred Jonas (New York, 1975), pp. 704–709.
47. Watt, p. 105.
48. Martin Sherwin, *A World Destroyed* (New York, 1975), p. 172; Harry S. Truman, *Memoirs*, 2 vols. (Garden City, N.Y., 1955–1956), I, p. 80; Henry L. Stimson and McGeorge Bundy, *On Active Service in Peace and War* (New York, 1949), p. 609.
49. Milovan Djilas, *Conversations with Stalin* (New York, 1962), p. 114.
50. U.S. Department of State, *Foreign Relations of the United States: The Conference of Berlin (The Potsdam Conference), 1945*, 2 vols. (Washington, D.C., 1960), I, p. 715. For Truman's view of how Europe had to be united, there is an important analysis in Lloyd C. Gardner, *Architects of Illusion: Men and Ideas in American Foreign Policy, 1941–1949* (Chicago, 1970), pp. 78–81.
51. U.S. Department of State, *The Conference of Berlin*, I, pp. 456–461.
52. The standard account is Sherwin, esp. pp. 14–21.
53. Watt, p. 97.
54. Barton J. Bernstein, "Roosevelt, Truman, and the Atomic Bomb: A Reinterpretation," *Political Science Quarterly* 90 (Spring 1975): 31.
55. Sherwin, pp. 220–228; *Washington Post*, October 4, 1992, p. A1.
56. George Kistiakowsky, quoted in the *New York Times*, 12 December 1983, p. E18.
57. Barton J. Bernstein, "A Postwar Myth: 500,000 U.S. Lives Saved," *Bulletin of Atomic Scientists* 42 (June/July 1986): 38–40.
58. John Dower, *War without Mercy* (New York, 1986), pp. 40–41.
59. *Ibid.*, pp. 33, 54–55, 240–259; Clayton R. Koppes and Gregory D. Black, *Hollywood Goes to War* (New York, 1987), pp. 277–315. Dick, p. 230; Geoffrey S. Smith, "Doing Justice: Relocation and Equity in Public Policy," *Public Historian* 6 (Summer 1984): 83–97, a good brief analysis of the Japanese-American experience.
60. Bernstein, "Roosevelt, Truman, and the Atomic Bomb," 44n.
61. Robert Karl Manoff, "American Victims of Hiroshima," *New York Times Magazine*, 2 December 1984, p. 118.
62. Sherwin, p. 237; a most important analysis is Barton J. Bernstein, "The Perils and

Politics of Surrender: Ending the War with Japan and Avoiding the Third Atomic Bomb," *Pacific Historical Review* 46 (February 1977), pp. 1–27.

63. Paul Boyer, "The Fences Are Gone," *Reviews in American History* 10 (September 1982): 453; *The Progressive, No Comment* (Madison, Wis., 1983), p. 35.

64. Frank A. Ninkovich, *Germany and the United States* (Boston, 1988), p. 73.

FOR FURTHER READING

References for specific topics can also be found in this chapter's notes and in the General Bibliography at the end of this book; these references usually are not repeated below. The following focuses on post-1981 works because the pre-1981 accounts are presented in full, with helpful comments, in the *Guide to American Foreign Relations since 1700*, ed. Richard Dean Burns (1983).

For the overall war effort, Robert Leckie, *The Wars of America*, rev. and updated ed. (1981), is readable and useful; Eric Larrabee, *Commander in Chief: Franklin Delano Roosevelt, His Lieutenants, and Their War* (1987), is exhaustive and beautifully researched; *America Unbound*, ed. Warren F. Kimball (1992); and Warren F. Kimball, *The Juggler* (1991), on FDR's wartime planning, provide details and new perspectives on the war's diplomacy; Michael S. Sherry, *The Rise of American Air Power* (1987), is important because it ranges far beyond the strategic-bombing campaign itself into the American psyche. The domestic side of foreign policy is delineated in H. Schuyler Foster, *Activism Replaces Isolationism: U.S. Public Attitudes, 1940–1975* (1983), by a former State Department official who supervised the public-opinion polling; Susan M. Hartmann, *The Home Front and Beyond: American Women in the 1940s* (1982); Deborah Gesensway and Mindy Roseman, *Beyond Words: Images from America's Concentration Camps* (1987), a powerfully presented account; John J. Bukowczyk, *And My Children Did Not Know Me: A History of the Polish-Americans* (1987); Clayton R. Koppes and Gregory D. Black, *Hollywood Goes to War* (1987), is superb on the war's movies.

For new approaches to U.S.-Asian relations (in addition to John Dower's prize-winning *War without Mercy*, cited in the notes), important accounts include Arne Westad, *Cold War and Revolution: Soviet-American Rivalry and the Origins of the Chinese Civil War, 1944–1946* (1993), with superb use of Chinese sources; Akira Iriye, *Power and Culture: The Japanese-American War, 1941–1945* (1981); John J. Sbrega, *Anglo-American Relations and Colonialism in East Asia, 1941–1945* (1983); Dennis Merrill, *Bread and the Ballot: The U.S. and India's Economic Development, 1947–1963* (1990), a major account; Kenneth Chern, *Dilemma in China, 1945* (1980), good on the U.S. debate; Gary R. Hess, *The United States Emergence as a Southeast Asian Power, 1940–1950* (1986), a fine overview; *Child of Conflict: The Korean-American Relationship, 1943–1953*, ed. Bruce Cumings (1983), a collection of superb essays; Marc S. Gallichio, *The Cold War Begins in Asia* (1988).

Scholars of U.S.-European relations have recently produced valuable work, especially on U.S.-British ties and how those ties related to the outbreak of the cold war. Warren Kimball's three volumes of Churchill-Roosevelt correspondence, cited in the notes, are the place to begin, and his work can be well supplemented with Randall B. Woods, *A*

Changing of the Guard . . . 1941–1946 (1991); Terry H. Anderson, *The United States, Great Britain and the Cold War, 1944–1947* (1981), which sees FDR as being highly aggressive at the end of his life; Robert M. Hathaway, *Ambiguous Partnership: Britain and America, 1944–1947* (1981), which argues that there never was a real partnership; Alan P. Dobson, *U.S. Wartime Aid to Britain, 1940–1946* (1986), highly detailed on the nature of the aid; Henry B. Ryan, *The Vision of Anglo-America* (1987), which explores 1943 through 1946 to outline the ideal as well as the real world of each nation; and, of special importance, Lawrence Wittner's analysis of how Americans finally joined the British in a crucial region, *American Intervention in Greece, 1943–1949* (1982). For France, Raoul Aglion, an associate of de Gaulle's, provides one view in *Roosevelt and de Gaulle: A Personal Memoir of Allies in Conflict* (1988); and a good overview is Henry Blumenthal, *Illusion and Reality in Franco-American Diplomacy, 1914–1945* (1986). U.S.-Italian relations are well analyzed in James Edward Miller, *The United States and Italy, 1940–1950* (1986). In addition to David Wyman's standard work on the Holocaust (see Chapter 12, above), important for the wartime years is Leonard Dinnerstein, *America and the Survivors of the Holocaust* (1982).

Other works that focus on East-West (i.e., Soviet-U.S.) relations and the wartime origins of the cold war include Edward M. Bennett, *Franklin D. Roosevelt and the Search for Victory: American-Soviet Relations, 1939–1945* (1990); Robert L. Messer, "World War II and the Coming of the Cold War," in *Modern American Diplomacy*, ed. John M. Carroll and George C. Herring (1986), a most useful overview; Robert A. Pollard, *Economic Security and the Origins of the Cold War* (1986), a detailed account; Michael T. Ruddy, *The Cautious Diplomat: Charles E. Bohlen and the Soviet Union* (1986), readable and important on a key State Department expert; *Witnesses to the Origins of the Cold War*, ed. Thomas T. Hammond (1987), interviews with U.S. diplomats who were in eastern Europe; Hugh DeSantis, *The Diplomacy of Silence* (1980), on Foreign Service officers involved with Soviet policy between 1933 and 1947; Keith Sainsbury, *The Turning Point* (1985), now a standard study on the 1943 summit conference, with superb use of British sources; Paul D. Mayle, *Eureka Summit* (1987), which, like Sainsbury, uses British materials well and sees the Tehran Conference as the war's diplomatic turning point; Russell D. Buhite, *Decision at Yalta* (1986), a critical view of FDR's diplomacy; P. G. H. Holdich, "A Policy of Percentages?: British Policy and the Balkans after the Moscow Conference of October 1944," *International History Review* 9 (Feb., 1987), on the pivotal 1944 Churchill-Stalin deal. For the Soviet side, William Taubman, *Stalin's American Policy* (1982), is a useful introduction; Joseph G. Whelen, *Soviet Diplomacy and Negotiating Behavior* (1982), is a mind-boggling, detailed, and irreplaceable analysis; *History of Soviet Foreign Policy, 1917–1945*, ed. B. Ponomaryov, A. Gromyko, and V. Khvostov (1974), remains perhaps the best Soviet view; while *The Impact of World War II on the Soviet Union*, ed. Susan J. Linz (1985), provides an important context.

Five superb books have recently been published on U.S.–Middle East relations and oil policies: Irvine Anderson, *ARAMCO, the U.S., and Saudi Arabia* (1981), which covers the 1933-to-1950 origins of the relationship; David S. Painter, *Oil and the American Century: The Political Economy of U.S. Foreign Oil Policy, 1941–1954* (1986), now a standard overall study; Aaron David Miller, *Search for Security* (1980), a pioneering analysis on U.S.-Saudi relations between 1939 and 1949; and Michael Stoff, *Oil, War, and American Security* (1980), especially important on the attempt to bring the U.S. government into the oil marketplace; and Daniel Yengin, *The Prize* (1991).

On Latin America, the place to begin is David Green's *Containment of Latin America*

(1971); and a new, useful work is Leslie B. Rout, Jr. and John F. Bratzel, *The Shadow War* (1986), which analyzes how five hundred German spies in Latin America brought unilateral U.S. responses, especially through the FBI. A fine overview is Randall Bennett Woods, *The Roosevelt Foreign Policy Establishment and the Good Neighbor* (1979), on the United States and Argentina.

Some of the effects of technology on diplomacy are examined in Alexander S. Cochran, Jr., " 'Magic,' 'Ultra,' and the Second World War," *Military Affairs* 46 (April 1982), a good overview of publications on intelligence operations; the ultimate technology is examined in a blockbuster of a book, Richard Rhodes, *The Making of the Atomic Bomb* (1987); and see John S. Gilkeson, Jr., *Gathering Rare Ores: The Diplomacy of Uranium Acquisition, 1943–1954* (1987).

Robert C. Hilderbrand, *Dumbarton Oaks* (1990), is now the standard volume on the origins of the United Nations.

14

The Cold War, or the Renewal of U.S.-Russian Rivalry (1945–1949)

TRUMAN AND A NEW WORLD

For President Harry Truman, events in 1945–1946 resembled a space-ship that rocketed him from a known world to a quite different universe. The end of the war in August 1945 brought wild celebration throughout the Allied camp. To most observers, the Big Three relationship of the United States, Great Britain, and the Soviet Union seemed so solid that many agreed with Eric Johnston, president of the U.S. Chamber of Commerce, who prophesied: "Russia will be, if not our biggest, at least our most eager consumer."[1] Truman privately (and colorfully) doubted it: "Our agreements with the Soviet Union have been a one-way street," the president complained, and the Soviets "could go to hell."[2] But the Soviets only remained in central and eastern Europe. They refused to cooperate economically, as Johnston and Truman had once hoped. In 1945, one set of U.S. policies, devised during the war by Franklin D. Roosevelt and Cordell Hull to create an open, cooperative, unified world, rapidly dissolved in the acidic aftermath of the Yalta and Potsdam disagreements.[3] No new policies were yet available.

At home, Truman had to spend much of 1945–1946 replacing FDR's advisers with officials whom he knew and trusted. Meanwhile, the nation's incredibly productive factories and farms, turning out an unbelievable 50 percent of the world's goods and services, required new markets. With their huge wartime savings, Americans also demanded new and more goods. The question became whether Truman, as head of the most powerful nation in recorded history, could navigate the spaceship so that everyone could reach the new postwar world safely.

THE VICTOR IN A HOSTILE WORLD: EUROPE

No one doubted the amazing extent of U.S. power. Americans dominated world trade, alone held the secret of the atomic bomb, and controlled the oceans with their fleets, while much of the rest of the world, including the Soviet Union, shoveled away the rubble that had once been towns and cities. The war, however, also destroyed a large portion of Germany and Japan, which for decades had been the industrial and military hubs around which their regions of the world revolved. Those two nations, moreover, had been the walls to stop any expansion of Soviet influence.

Another problem also arose from the destruction. Western Europe and Great Britain, as well as eastern Europe, turned sharply left in an effort to find the resources needed for massive rebuilding. Communists flourished, but so did Socialists. Thus, in mid-1945, the British Labour party replaced Churchill's Conservatives, who were in power. Some European right-wing leaders had collaborated with the Nazis and were totally discredited. The most important partners of the United States, in other words, were moving left and away from capitalist models just as Americans wanted more open markets and less government involvement.[4]

Great Britain dramatized the problem. For centuries it had been dependent on imports (even of meat and butter) but now found overseas markets as well as British factories devastated by war. U.S. leaders had long realized that they were going to replace the British as the great world power. But there was a price to be paid. As one Washington official observed in 1944, in every alliance one partner wears boots and spurs while the other wears a saddle. "We are obviously wearing the boots," he noted; but "if we want to stay in this fortunate position, we have to find some way to feed the horse."[5] The way was temporarily found in late 1945, when the United States forgave much of London's lend-lease debt. Then Washington gave Britain a $3.75 billion credit with low interest, but in return cold-bloodedly required the British to spend the money in the United States and open the British Empire to American competition.[6]

Awesome U.S. power at the end of World War II. On Navy Day, October 27, 1945, millions of New Yorkers joined the president to hail the return of the fleet. The climax of the celebration was a review of a seven-mile line of men o'war anchored in the Hudson River as 1,200 navy planes roared overhead.

The next question was whether the other member of the Big Three would play by such rules, voluntarily or otherwise. Observers could point out that Stalin's European empire did not equal in size the empire of Tsar Alexander I at the end of the Napoleonic Wars in 1815. The United States, moreover, enjoyed overwhelming naval and air superiority. With its gigantic fleet of 70,000 vessels (equal to the rest of the world's navies combined) and 100,000 planes, and its monopoly on the atomic bomb, Americans felt justified in demanding that their soldiers be returned home. Truman, however, had dropped his only two available atomic bombs on Japan in 1945; and, in Europe, Stalin—although he quickly discharged 9 million Russians so that they could help rebuild the economy—poised 30 divisions against 10 U.S., British, and French divisions in central Europe. If the United States launched an atomic attack, Stalin was apparently prepared to overrun and hold hostage much of Europe.[7]

Truman simply could not figure out how to transform his atomic monopoly and economic superiority into a foreign policy that could push Stalin back and reunite Europe. His secretary of war, Henry Stimson, who was about to retire after nearly forty years of public service, had once thought that the A-bomb could be used to break down "Russia's secret police state." By September 1945, however, Stimson had second thoughts. He believed that the bomb could not be used as "a direct lever to produce the change" and urged Truman to negotiate the best settlement possible with Stalin. If we, instead, only wear "this weapon rather ostentatiously on our hip," Stimson warned, "suspicions" and "distrust" would mount. But the president was not willing to settle for Stimson's approach.[8]

As for U.S. economic power, the Soviets refused to cooperate with the U.S.-controlled international economic institutions constructed at Bretton Woods (see p. 431). "At first sight," a top Soviet official remarked, the U.S. plans at Bretton Woods "looked like a tasty mushroom, but on examination they turned out to be a poisonous toadstool."[9] Americans might think the "open door" and "equal opportunity" for their dollars and trade the best principles for an international system, Soviet foreign minister Molotov declared in 1946. But, he continued, the United States was so strong that if these principles prevailed, American dollars would take over most European businesses. The radio in these countries would then broadcast not native languages, but "one American gramophone record after another." "Was this what we fought for when we battled the fascist invaders?" Molotov asked.[10]

U.S. officials thus failed when they tried to use dollar loans as a lever to push back Soviet influence in Poland—or even in Czechoslovakia, where an independent government held on despite increasing Soviet pressure. Truman also failed when he demanded new elections in Romania and Bulgaria. Stalin, however, moved cautiously in eastern Europe through much of 1945–1946. He allowed pro-Western factions to share power in parts of the region. The dictator wanted to do nothing that would force Truman to take retaliatory measures. But by late 1946, Soviet stubbornness drove even the British Labour party's foreign minister, Ernest Bevin, over the brink during one conference. A smart, tough, husky former dock worker, Bevin, tired of hearing Molotov defend Soviet policies and attack British proposals, rose to his feet, clenched his fists, and lurched toward the Soviet foreign minister, shouting, "I've had enough of this, I'ave," before security guards moved in.[11]

Although frustrated in eastern Europe, Truman enjoyed tremen-

DENMARK SWEDEN U.S.S.R.

NORTH
SEA

BALTIC SEA

Danzig TO U.S.S.R.

EAST PRUSSIA TO POLAND

Hamburg

Bremen

EAST
Berlin ANNEXED BY POLAND

ACCESS CORRIDOR
JOINT OCCUPATION BY FOUR POWERS

Oder R.

Warsaw

POLAND

Lublin

Neisse R.

GERMANY

WEST

Bonn

BEL.

LUX.

Frankfurt

SAAR GERMANY

CZECHOSLOVAKIA

IRON CURTAIN

FRANCE

Munich

Vienna

AUSTRIA

HUNGARY

SWITZERLAND

0 100 Miles
0 100 Kilometers

ITALY YUGOSLAVIA

NETHERLANDS

OCCUPATION OF GERMANY AND AUSTRIA, 1946-1949

French zone   British zone   U.S. zone   Soviet zone

Divided Europe, 1946–1949. Note the vulnerable positions of Berlin and Czechoslovakia.

dous power in western Europe. He could treat the U.S. occupation zone in Germany as he pleased. By early 1946, the few German reparations that had gone to the Soviets were stopped. JCS 1067 (Joint Chiefs of Staff Directive 1067) of April 1945 had instructed the U.S. military governor, General Lucius Clay, to limit Germany's industry severely as well as to destroy all hints of Nazism. By mid-1945, however, U.S. officials concluded that the plan must have been made "by economic idiots." Clay ditched JCS 1067 and allowed industry to rebuild so that American taxpayers would not have to feed and clothe Germans. He also urged that the four occupation zones merge into a single unit. Neither the French, who turned livid whenever German recovery was mentioned, nor the Soviets agreed with Clay, but the general's plans moved ahead anyway.

Secretary of State James Byrnes, in a speech given in Stuttgart, Germany, in September 1946, emphatically stated U.S. determination to retain control over at least western Germany's affairs. Byrnes had grown frustrated after endless wrangling with Molotov ("Old Iron Pants"), especially when the Soviets played to German opinion by urging that a unified Germany be created. Molotov wanted Soviet access to the industrially rich western regions of such a united Germany. Byrnes's speech undercut Molotov by declaring that the German-Polish boundary remained an open question (a remark that surprised and pleased the Germans, who hated giving their land to Poland). The secretary of state then announced that Germany could only be unified through democratic elections and a "national council" (in which the three Western powers could outvote the Soviets 3 to 1). Byrnes emphasized U.S. intentions to stay in central Europe. Not surprisingly, Stalin turned aside Byrnes's proposals. Germany remained divided as Americans and Soviets remained in Germany.[12]

Meanwhile, Soviet and U.S. agents were secretly wooing German scientists to the Soviet Union or America to work on supersensitive missile and bomb projects. Truman gave the order that no active supporters of "Nazism or militarism" be employed on these projects. But under Project Paperclip, about 765 German scientists entered the United States between 1945 and 1955. Some of them were later charged with having experimented on humans during the war and for using slave labor in Nazi Germany.[13] At this point, however, the growing cold war led Soviets and Americans to hire, not imprison, former Nazis.

THE VICTOR IN A HOSTILE WORLD: ASIA

Truman had better luck rebuilding Japan. He simply froze out all other powers (especially the British and Soviets) and installed General Douglas MacArthur to run the country as U.S. interests dictated. MacArthur immediately established his authority. With Japanese cities still burning, he landed, unarmed, at Yokohama airport (the bravest of "all the amazing feats in the war," Churchill declared) and drove into the city. Some 30,000 Japanese troops with fixed bayonets lined his route, but they had their backs to him—the same position they assumed when their emperor passed. MacArthur imprisoned or hanged military war criminals, planted democratic political processes in a new constitution, placed severe limits on industrial recovery of the old (and huge) corporate combines called *zaibatsu*, and started a successful land-reform program.

China did not present as happy a picture. Chiang Kai-shek's Kuomintang (KMT or Nationalist) party was engaged in a battle to the death with Mao Zedong's (Mao Tse-tung's) Communists. U.S. officials had sided with Chiang. But such experienced Foreign Service Officers (FSOs) as John Stuart Service, John Carter Vincent, and John Paton Davies (the "three Johns," as their critics soon called them) pushed hard to work with Mao for two reasons: their belief that he might win the long civil war, and their fervent hope that U.S. aid and friendship could separate Mao from any close ties with the Soviet Union, which they hated and feared. While on the so-called "Dixie Mission" of 1944, some of the FSOs had come to know the Communists well. They watched Mao's troops consolidate their power with the peasants in the north and enjoyed playing softball with the Communists.

The advice of the FSOs was countered, however, by General Patrick J. Hurley, FDR's personal representative to Chiang. Hurley knew little about China (when he landed in China, the native Oklahoman greeted his startled hosts with a Cherokee war cry) and cared little about learning. One expert sent to brief Hurley on China instead had to listen to a 45-minute monologue not "connected by any readily discernible pattern of thought," as the expert recalled.[14] But Hurley knew what he wanted: to eject British interests from China, to keep the Soviets out, and to ensure that Chiang triumphed over Mao. Roosevelt backed Hurley, and the president even rejected feelers from Mao for a top-level Chinese Communist visit to Washington.

By November 1945, however, Chiang's power was being threatened by Mao's successes. Meanwhile, the Soviets were moving into Manchuria to disarm Japanese troops and to seize industrial plants for use in the Soviet Union. Truman made a series of decisions. First, he ordered some of the 1 million Japanese troops in Manchuria and northern China to remain until they could be replaced by Chiang's or U.S. forces. Next, he sent his own troops into the region. By late 1946, 110,000 U.S. soldiers tried to police parts of northern China. Finally, he overruled Hurley and decided to send a mission to work out a deal between Chiang and Mao. Hurley dramatically resigned on November 27, 1945. He blamed the FSOs for siding with the Communists. The FSOs, however, had a more realistic policy than Hurley believed.

Truman sent his own hero, General George Marshall, to work out a military truce and political settlement. The president backed Marshall with the 110,000 U.S. troops and a pledge of $800 million in aid to buy Chiang's cooperation. Truman clearly assumed that Chiang, not Mao, was to be the undisputed leader of China. The Marshall mission quickly gained the trust of both sides and worked out a military truce and a political settlement that recognized the Communists' grass-roots strength. A plan to integrate the KMT and Communist armies reflected Chiang's 3-to-1 superiority in manpower. Nevertheless, the armies continued to fight over Manchurian positions. After one struggle around Changchun in February 1946, Chiang declared that the Communists had broken the truce. He launched a full-scale military campaign. Marshall warned Chiang not to do so. Despite the KMT's over-whelming superiority in men and firepower, Marshall knew that Chiang's forces were overextended and badly led.

By mid-1947, Mao's armies were cutting off and chopping up chunks of the KMT's best forces. Chiang assumed that he could ignore Mar-shall's advice, as he had Stilwell's in 1944, because the United States had no choice but to support him. Chiang's confidence increased when Henry Luce's powerful *Life* magazine began attacking Marshall's pol-icies. But Chiang had made a fatal error. Marshall could only stand by and watch while both the KMT forces and the Chinese economy dis-solved. Under the KMT's corrupt leadership, inflation skyrocketed until prices in mid-1948 were 3 million times those of late 1945. In January 1947, Truman and Marshall decided to terminate the general's mis-sion. They blamed both sides for the failure but singled out Chiang for not cooperating and for using bad military judgment.[15]

Under pressure from pro-Chiang supporters in the U.S. Congress, Marshall (now secretary of state) sent General Albert C. Wedemeyer to investigate the situation in mid-1947. Wedemeyer's report recom-mended massive U.S. economic aid and as many as 10,000 American advisers to work with KMT troops. Knowing firsthand that such help would not be enough, Marshall rejected Wedemeyer's report. But he also unfortunately kept it secret and so gave new ammunition to those who later claimed that he and Truman had "lost" China (as if it were theirs to lose) and then tried to hide their sin. By this time, moreover, the Soviets had withdrawn from Manchuria and posed no direct threat to China. In all, as historian Steven Levine concludes, Marshall "had no intention of pulling [Chiang's] chestnuts from the fire."[16]

Truman came under harsh attack for retreating from China. Gen-eral MacArthur had long argued that Asia had to be seen as the new American West, an extension of the four-hundred-year-old frontier: "Europe is a dying system," he had declared in 1944. "The lands touching the Pacific with their billions of inhabitants will determine the course of history in the next ten thousand years." In 1948, Mac-Arthur announced that "to our western horizon we must look for . . .

yet untapped opportunities for trade and commerce."[17] The general spoke for many who wanted to carry on the long U.S. tradition embodied in John Hay's open-door notes and Henry Luce's "American Century" vision.

DEAN ACHESON'S AMERICAN CENTURY

But that tradition carried little weight with the most influential diplomat of the Truman presidential years and, in Secretary of State Henry Kissinger's words of 1976, "the greatest Secretary of State of the 20th-century."[18] Dean Acheson rightly entitled his memoir of 1941 through 1953 *Present at the Creation*. His outlook and policies, as much as any others, shaped U.S. diplomacy during these critical cold-war years.

Dean Acheson (1893–1971) was, as this photograph suggests, an elegant and thoughtful man who was perhaps the most important secretary of state in the twentieth century. He was a leader in creating the Bretton Woods institutions, the Truman Doctrine, the Marshall Plan, NATO, NSC-68, the hydrogen-bomb project, and pivotal policies toward Vietnam and the People's Republic of China. By the end of his term as secretary of state (1949–1953), he was highly unpopular—in part because of his personal elegance, which, in the eyes of some congressmen, made him more British than American, and in part because he was viewed as not sufficiently tough on communism, especially in Asia.

He was born in 1893. His Canadian mother's family derived its wealth from banking and whiskey interests; his father was an Episcopal rector. Acheson's perception of what was "decent and civilized" came from "an image of upper middle class life in England, Canada, and the eastern United States in the late Victorian era—and he measured other men and nations by that perception," in the words of biographer Gaddis Smith.[19] That perception was reinforced by education at exclusive private schools, Yale, and Harvard Law School. He closely studied British history and admired London's use of its financial and military power to create the long post-1815 era of peace. As assistant secretary of state specializing in Anglo-American economic relations between 1941 and 1945, Acheson saw firsthand how the British were going bankrupt. He assumed that the United States would take top place in the world.[20] He also assumed, as he rose to undersecretary of state (1945–1947), that the alliance with the Soviet Union could continue into peacetime, but only if the Soviets accepted the guidelines he had helped write at the Bretton Woods Conference of 1944. Acheson's attitude toward the Soviets grew very tough in 1946 as the two nations clashed over German, Japanese, Iranian, Turkish, and atomic-energy questions.

But throughout all these years he held tightly to beliefs that guided his foreign policy. Seeing himself as a realist, he thought that "there are moral problems and real problems." Foreign policy's real problems, Acheson once observed, were not "a lot of abstract notions," but involved "what you do—these business transactions, credit through central banks, food things . . .—all this makes foreign policy." He wrote that "industrial productivity" formed the most important source of national power.[21] He constantly warned in 1944–1945 that Americans either had to find open markets and liberal international trade or they would find themselves again facing the economic horrors of the 1930s. Since the Soviets refused to open their empire or join the Bretton Woods system, Acheson turned to a reliance on military power. He concluded that Stalin could only be dealt with from "positions of strength," to use one of Acheson's more famous phrases. His understanding of history shaped his view of the present. Among other lessons that history taught, Acheson concluded, was that American survival could not be entrusted to merely the rule of law. "Law," he once declared, "simply does not deal with such questions of ultimate power." Or again: "The survival of states is not a matter of law," but of power.[22]

As Acheson tried to teach Americans the importance of economics and power, he also told them where they could find protection. Certainly, they should not look to the United Nations, which was a mere

*Eleanor Roosevelt (1884–1962) became a powerful voice for international coop-
eration, human rights, and critics who believed that the Truman-Acheson policies toward the Soviet bloc were too dependent on military confrontation. In the
late 1940s and early 1950s, she was an influential member of the U.S. delegation to the United Nations—an organization she devoutly believed in, as did
Warren Austin (center), the first U.S. ambassador to the United Nations, but for
which Secretary of State Dean Acheson (seated at right) sometimes had an ill-
concealed contempt.*

"forum." Speeches in the UN counted for little: "In the Arab proverb,
the ass that went to Mecca remained an ass, and a policy has little
added to it by its place of utterance." Nor did he have much hope for
the U.S. Congress. A senator, Acheson complained, too easily gets
excited, and his mind does not work "in a normal way. . . . He is a
violent partisan" and ignorantly "goes in swinging." Acheson lamented
that Congress listened to a usually uninformed public opinion. Americans had become "a somewhat hypochrondiac type" and "ascertain
our state of health by this mass temperature taking of public opinion
polls," he complained in 1946.[23] For its part, Congress mistrusted the
brilliant Acheson. One senator had to admit that Acheson was "the
kind of lawyer I'd like if I were guilty as hell." But another senator
complained that Acheson talked to him arrogantly, "as if a bit of fish
had got stuck in his mustache." Yet another referred to the elegantly
dressed official as "that goddam floorwalker."[24] Even friends admitted
that he handled Congress and the press badly because "he sometimes

talks over their heads. . . . He knows so much more than they do that it embarrasses them and they don't like it."

As undersecretary of state (1945–1947) and then secretary of state (1949–1953), Acheson enjoyed Truman's total support. They were an odd couple, this down-home president from a Missouri political machine and the highly polished member of elite eastern schools and law firms. But they admired and worked closely with each other. Acheson could lose patience on those rare occasions when the president failed to take his advice. ("Truman is like a boy you tell not to stick peanuts up his nose," Acheson complained to a friend, and "the minute you turn around, there he is sticking peanuts up his nose.")[25] But Acheson knew that his own power totally rested on his "constituency of one"—the president. He respected Truman's political talents, his hard work, his decisiveness, and especially his willingness to take Acheson's advice. In return, the State Department official was completely loyal as well as ruthless in carrying out Truman's policies. When once asked the trait a secretary of state most needed, Acheson replied, "The killer instinct."[26]

The Awful Year of 1946: Europe and the Middle East

Acheson's changed attitude toward the Soviets in 1946 reflected the more general change of U.S. foreign policy. He focused on events in the European region because he and most U.S. officials believed that the American future depended not on vague Asian frontiers—conjured up by General MacArthur's word magic—but on Europe. For in that region, Americans had historically looked first for their trade, culture, and—as two world wars in twenty-four years bloodily demonstrated— most vital security interests. Moreover, not only were the Red Army's divisions concentrated in eastern Europe, but large Communist parties in war-devastated France and Italy were poised to seize power. Byrnes and Molotov fought bitterly at foreign ministers' meetings until they finally agreed on peace treaties for Finland and Italy that Americans liked, and for Romania, Hungary, and Bulgaria that the Soviets could accept.

Europe was the site of continual diplomatic talks in 1946, but the Mediterranean–Middle East region threatened to become an actual U.S.-Soviet battleground. Iran posed the first danger. That country was occupied by the British, Soviets, and Americans during the war to ensure a route for lend-lease goods to the Soviets. After 1941, the three powers scrambled for postwar rail and, especially, oil concessions until a truce was declared in 1944. The Tehran Conference Declaration of 1943 agreed that the three powers would withdraw within six months after the war's end. The Americans pulled out in January 1946 and the British on March 2. But Red Army troops remained. Moscow demanded oil rights as well as a pro-Communist regime in the Azerbaijan Republic that bordered the Soviet Union. Stalin perhaps again thought that he was only collecting earlier tsarist claims. A 1907 treaty had recognized dominant Soviet interests in northern Iran, and this recognition had been confirmed by post-1917 pacts.

The British, however, had long fought to block any Soviet penetration into the Middle East. Truman picked up that British commitment. As reports reached Byrnes of Soviet tanks moving toward the Iranian border in early March 1946, he sent warnings to Moscow. The secretary of state then went to the United Nations and, in the new organization's first major crisis, focused world attention on the Soviet move. It was not a good start for the UN. Most importantly, a shrewd Iranian government delegation met with Stalin to work out a deal: the Communist Tudeh party would have certain rights in Azerbaijan, and the Soviets could have oil concessions—subject, however, to the withdrawal of the Red Army from Iran and to the approval of the Iranian legislature. Stalin withdrew his troops; the Iranians then seized and executed a number of Tudeh party leaders; the legislature refused to ratify the agreement—and Iran, under a new, young shah, seemed firmly in the Western camp.[27]

In Iran, as well as most other places, FDR's "four policemen" were now down to one. The U.S. policeman next moved his beat into the highly sensitive and strategic Straits, which linked the Mediterranean Sea to the Black Sea and to the Soviet Union itself. The Montreux Convention of 1936 had given Turkey control of The Straits. But for centuries the Russians had sought access through the Black Sea to the warm-water Mediterranean. At Tehran in 1943 and again at Moscow in 1944, Churchill promised Stalin such access. A month after the Yalta Conference in 1945, Stalin tried to cash Churchill's blank check by denouncing Turkey (which had worked with Hitler) and demanding some control over The Straits. But when Stalin next presented the blank check at the Potsdam Conference in July 1945, he discovered that the new cashier, Harry Truman, had other plans. The president cleverly asked that all "inland waterways" bounded by more than two states be placed under international control. With this simple move, Truman blocked Soviet control of The Straits and threatened to open much of eastern Europe by putting the Danube under multinational (instead of Red Army) control, but neatly protected Turkey's domination of The Straits, the U.S. hold on the Panama Canal, and the British authority over the Suez Canal because only a single country bordered those waterways.

Protesting that the new cashier was changing the rules in the middle of the deal, Stalin tried other tactics. In early 1946, he made demands directly on Turkey. Truman thought of sending an aircraft carrier to the region, but tension eased. Then on August 7, 1946, Stalin demanded from the Turks joint control of The Straits. Acheson warned Truman that the Soviets aimed to dominate Turkey; then Greece, the Middle East's oil, and "India and China" could fall next. Only "force of arms" could stop Stalin. Truman agreed with this early version of the so-called "domino theory." The president replied, "We might as well find out whether the Russians [are] bent on world conquest now as in five or ten years."[28] With tough U.S. backing, Turkey turned down Stalin's demand. A month later, the U.S. Navy announced that its newly dispatched fleet, led by the giant aircraft carrier *Franklin D. Roosevelt*, was to remain permanently in the eastern Mediterranean.[29]

The Awful Year of 1946: Atomic Energy and Henry Wallace

The American people knew of these crises but realized neither the extent nor danger for the Big Three relationship. In 1946, Truman did not use the crises to damn the Soviets publicly. Nor did he try to mobilize the American people to fight a cold war. He instead tried to come to terms with major changes in his own foreign and domestic affairs.

In foreign policy, Stalin challenged the fundamentals of U.S. plans in a speech of February 9, 1946. The dictator announced that the Soviet Union planned to turn inward and rebuild itself with more five-year plans that demanded sacrifice from his people. Stalin thus rejected once and for all any possibility of entering the Bretton Woods economic arrangements. Apparently for that reason, U.S. Supreme Court Justice William O. Douglas called Stalin's speech "the Declaration of World War III."[30] A month later, former Prime Minister Winston Churchill declared at Westminster College in Fulton, Missouri, that "an iron curtain has descended" to cut off the world from the "police governments" in eastern Europe. With Truman looking on, Churchill thanked God for entrusting the atomic bomb to the Anglo-Saxon people and demanded an alliance of the English-speaking nations for the coming "trial of strength." Truman had no intention of weakening his nation's policies by tying them to Britain's rapidly declining power. But the president agreed with Churchill's view of the Soviet threat. In Moscow, Stalin angrily responded that Churchill was with the "war-mongers" who followed the "racial theory" that only those speaking English could "decide the destinies of the entire world."[31]

Against this grim backdrop, Truman had to deal with a U.S.-Soviet agreement of December 1945 to discuss possible international control of atomic energy. The deal had been made by Secretary of State Byrnes with Stalin. Truman knew little of Byrnes's bargaining in Moscow until the secretary of state returned. The president then blew up. He ordered Byrnes to meet him on the presidential yacht in Chesapeake Bay even "if he [had] to swim," as one aide phrased the order, and then gave Byrnes "the trimming of his life." Within eleven months, Byrnes was replaced by Marshall. But Truman still had to deal with the atomic-energy agreement negotiated by Byrnes.

He appointed a committee headed by Dean Acheson and David Lilienthal (the respected administrator of the Tennessee Valley Authority) to draft a policy. The Acheson-Lilienthal Plan provided for an international body to control the raw materials and the production facilities used for atomic energy. It assumed that the United States was far ahead in the field and could build bombs quickly, so the authors worried little about what might occur if the Soviet Union violated the agreement and began to build its own atomic weapons.

Truman then asked Bernard Baruch to present the plan at the United Nations. That was a mistake. A seventy-six-year-old multimillionaire, Baruch's fame rested not only on real administrative talents, but also on hired public-relations agents and his large contributions to as many as sixty members of Congress. He knew nothing about atomic-energy policy. Nevertheless, Baruch changed the Acheson-Lilienthal Plan by inserting a voting procedure that would give the United States control over every step—even the establishment of atomic power for peaceful purposes *within* the Soviet Union. Not surprisingly, when he presented this "Baruch Plan" in June 1946 at a dramatic UN session, the Soviets soon rejected it. Suddenly aware that a historic chance to control atomic power had been ruined, leading U.S. journalists blasted Baruch for "inflexible diplomacy." Truman, now besieged by crises abroad and at home, admitted privately that appointing Baruch was "the worst blunder I ever made. . . . But we can't fire him now, not with all the other trouble." Before the end of 1946, however, Baruch had resigned. Con-

*Henry Wallace (1888–1965) had been FDR's popular secretary of agriculture
(1933–1940), then vice-president (1941–1945), and secretary of commerce
(1945–1946) until President Truman fired him in mid-1946 after Wallace criticized the growing U.S. and British confrontation with the Soviets. Running as a
Progressive against Truman in 1948, Wallace was not only defeated badly, but
his loss helped discredit left-liberal analyses of the growing cold war and led to
the American consensus on how to fight that war. A native of Iowa, Wallace
retired after 1948 to become a gentleman farmer.*

gress passed the Atomic Energy Act, which essentially outlawed any
exchange of atomic-energy information. The world remained embarked
on an uncontrolled atomic-arms race.[32]

One U.S. official publicly objected. Henry A. Wallace had been FDR's
vice-president from 1941 to 1945 (until he was replaced, at Roosevelt's
request, by Truman) and was widely admired as an ardent New Dealer.
As secretary of commerce, Wallace gave a speech at New York's Madison Square Garden in September, 1946, in which he condemned the
arms race and blamed U.S. as well as Soviet policy. Wallace urged a
return to economic cooperation between the two powers. He hoped
that Stalin would open eastern Europe to U.S. trade and investment.
Byrnes and Republican Senator Arthur Vandenberg from Michigan,
who were at the time suffering through negotiations with the Soviets
in Europe, immediately demanded that Truman fire Wallace. The

president was trapped. He badly needed Wallace's wide political support. But amid the uproar, he also privately blasted his secretary of commerce as one of "the Reds, phonies, and the 'parlor pinks' [who] . . . are becoming a national danger."[33] He removed Wallace, who now prepared to challenge Truman for the presidency in 1948.

Truman endured a bad year in 1946. In addition to problems with Byrnes and Wallace at home, even leading scientists came out against the president's policies. In late 1945, they began publishing the *Bulletin of Atomic Scientists* each month "to preserve our civilization," as one scholar said, "by scaring men into rationality."[34] But for Truman, the worst blow came in November 1946, when congressional elections gave Republicans a majority of 6 members in the Senate and a stunning 127 in the House. The president's public-approval rating that had stood at 87 percent in mid-1945 now sank like a stone to a historic low of 32 percent.

Then, in early 1947, Truman and Acheson used foreign policy to pull off a political miracle. They were so successful, moreover, that other presidents have tried to repeat the original miracle ever since.

CREATING THE POSTWAR WORLD:
KENNAN AND THE LONG TELEGRAM

The miracle actually began in February 1946, when the longest telegram in State Department history began to clatter over the department's Telex machines. It was sent from Moscow by forty-two-year-old George Frost Kennan, the chargé d'affaires in the U.S. Embassy. The cable was the result of an urgent State Department request for an explanation of Stalin's "election speech."

Kennan had long waited for the opportunity to educate U.S. officials. A native of Milwaukee and educated at Princeton, the quiet, bookish Kennan joined the Foreign Service in the 1920s. Fluent in Russian and German, and an authority on classic nineteenth-century Russian literature as well as twentieth-century politics, he trained as a member of the initial group of U.S. experts on the Soviet Union in the American listening post of Riga, Latvia. In 1933, he helped William Bullitt open the first U.S. Embassy in the Soviet Union. For much of the next twelve years, Kennan lived in the Soviet Union and eastern Europe. He loved the Russian people and many of their pre-1917 traditions. But Kennan strongly disliked the Bolshevist Revolution. As he witnessed Stalin's bloody purges of the 1930s, the ever-growing police state, and the ris-

George Frost Kennan (1904–   ) became the nation's best-known expert on Soviet affairs and was the famous "X" who wrote the containment policy in 1946–1947. A reserved, conservative graduate of Princeton, Kennan loved traditional, nineteenth-century Russian literature and society but feared Stalinist Russia. Highly mistrustful of public opinion, he wanted diplomacy controlled by professional diplomats (like himself)—until after 1949, when U.S. diplomacy became, in his view, overmilitarized. He then left the State Department to become a prize-winning historian who appealed to public opinion to support détente with the Soviets and a mutual withdrawal of the two superpowers from central Europe.

ing disputes with the United States, he became a bitter critic of Soviet policies. By 1945, the young Foreign Service officer believed that Roosevelt's hopes of cooperation with Stalin were hopelessly naïve. Kennan, however, did not want to go to the other extreme and declare war on the Soviets to free eastern Europe. Believing that the Soviets were unable to conquer—and, at present, uninterested in conquering—what Kennan considered to be the great power bases in the world (western Europe, Japan, and the United States), he urged U.S. officials to remain cool and prepare for a long political struggle.

He detailed his argument about "containing" the Soviets in the long, secret telegram of February 22, 1946. In July 1947, he published a public version, "The Sources of Soviet Conduct," under the name of "X"—a disguise that fooled no one.[35] Why was Stalin so uncooperative? Because, Kennan answered, the dictator needed to portray the West as evil in order to justify his own control over the Russian people. Kennan said nothing about the U.S. and Allied military invasions of Russia in 1918–1920 nor about Washington's refusal to deal diplomatically with the Soviets until 1933. He instead stressed that because of the Soviet leadership's internal needs, the Soviet Union viewed the West as an enemy and would exert constant pressure to reduce Western power. He believed, however, that the Communists, unlike Hitler, were in no hurry and had no timetable. The Soviets would have to "be contained by the adroit and vigilant application of counterforce at a series of constantly shifting geographical and political points." If Americans could be patient and work to ensure the long-run prosperity and stability of their own system, then Marxism would be disproved and "containment" end in a great climax: "either the break-up or the gradual mellowing of Soviet power." (A self-described "conservative," Kennan doubted whether Americans could create and stay with such a long-term policy. But he kept these doubts mostly to himself in the 1940s.)

The Long Telegram of 1946 and the "X" article a year later caused a sensation. Kennan was recalled from Moscow and became a powerful voice in Washington. "Containment" became the magic term of U.S. foreign policy. Then and later, Kennan puzzled over why he and his ideas suddenly became so famous. Other State Department officials were also analyzing Soviet actions and coming up with explanations different from Kennan's. One policy paper, for example, claimed that because U.S. power was so much greater than the Soviet power, Truman could safely try to work out a long-term settlement with Stalin—including the possible sharing of atomic secrets.[36] But such views were discarded. Kennan's analysis was accepted for a number of reasons.

First, Kennan's timing was perfect. Stalin had just stunned Washington with his "election speech" and his policies in Iran, Turkey, and Germany. Kennan immediately provided a detailed explanation for the dictator's actions. Second, Kennan's explanation was attractive because it entirely blamed the Soviet Union for the growing cold war. The alternative views suggested that the United States had also made some errors, but Washington officials did not want to hear about what they had been doing wrong since 1917. Third, "X's" suggestion that the Soviet Union be contained, and no longer negotiated or compromised with, perfectly fit Truman's and Acheson's view of Soviet issues. Of course, diplomatic talks did not end between the two superpowers in

1946–1947. But at that point, U.S. officials depended more on economic and military power than on diplomacy to deal with the Soviets, and Kennan's containment theory justified the use of such power.

That turn was nicely marked in September 1946, when Truman's special counsel in the White House, Clark M. Clifford, wrote a long policy paper for the president. Using the Long Telegram as his starting point and after talking with top officials throughout the government, Clifford concluded that the Soviets believed that a war with the capitalists was going to occur. "The language of military power is the only language" Moscow understands, he told Truman. "The main deterrent to Soviet attack on the United States, or to attack on areas of the world which are vital to our security," will not be negotiations, but "the military power of this country."[37] Truman, tired of dealing with Stalin abroad and Henry Wallace at home, was ready to act on the Kennan-Clifford advice.

CREATING THE POSTWAR WORLD: THE TRUMAN DOCTRINE

His chance came on a wintery morning in late February 1947, when a British official drove to the new State Department building in the Foggy Bottom section of Washington. The official told Acheson that Great Britain had to pull out of Greece and Turkey. The bankrupt British admitted that they could no longer aid the conservative Greek government that had been fighting left-wing forces since 1944–1945. Nor could the British any longer help Turkey's military forces, which had come under Soviet pressure.

Acheson knew about the Greek problem. Since the Nazis had withdrawn from Greece in 1944, the British had tried to restore a monarchy. But leftist forces, headed by Communists, had fought back and had gained much support—in part because they had led the courageous underground resistance against the Nazis. By early 1947, the United States had contributed $200 million and many advisers to help the British. The leftists, however, gained strength with the help of a Communist neighbor, Marshal Tito (Josip Broz), the leader of Yugoslavia. In return, Tito hoped to include parts of Greece in a Balkan federation under his rule. Stalin had been very cool to Tito's plans. The Soviet dictator disliked Tito's personal imperialistic ambitions. Stalin wanted to run the Communist camp himself. Moreover, he had promised Churchill in 1944 to stay out of Greek affairs and had kept the promise, as even Churchill admitted.

Stalin's hands-off policy made things difficult for Truman and Acheson. They could not publicly accuse the dictator of interference in Greece because it was not true. But if they warned of Tito's interference, few Americans would care. They also faced a second problem. To prop up the Greek and Turkish governments could cost hundreds of millions of dollars. The new Republican Congress, however, intended to cut taxes for the folks back home, not increase taxes to spend dollars in countries most Americans cared little about. Congress was especially suspicious about spending large amounts for the apparent rescue of the British Empire. Americans had mistrusted that empire since 1776. And, finally, Truman had become unpopular throughout the country.

Acheson solved all these problems in a few minutes in late February. He and Truman had concluded that the British retreat opened a historic opportunity to launch an offensive against the Soviet Union. They could have solved the problem, after all, by sending Greece leftover military equipment from U.S. stockpiles from World War II. Or they could have turned the Greek problem over to the United Nations. Instead, they decided to go for broke. Acheson explained why to suspicious congressional leaders that late February afternoon. The crisis, he argued, had little to do with the British Empire but everything to do with whether Americans would contain communism. If the United States backed away, he warned, then, "like apples in a barrel infected by one rotten one, the corruption of Greece would infect Iran and all to the east." The "infection" could communize Africa, then Europe, until the United States virtually stood alone. "The Soviet Union was playing one of the greatest gambles in history at minimal cost," Acheson told his listeners. "We and we alone" could "break up the play." A stunned silence followed until the Republican foreign-policy leader, Senator Vandenberg, told Truman that if the president said that to Congress, "he would be supported."[38]

Another version had Vandenberg telling Truman that he should "scare hell out of the American people." Acheson tried to do that when writing Truman's speech that the president gave before Congress on March 12, 1947. In a brilliant move, the speech simply divided the world between "free peoples" and governments that relied upon "terror and oppression . . . the suppression of personal freedoms." Which side, Truman asked Congress in so many words, are you on? No third choice was given. Nor did the speech note that the Greek regime and the Turkish government were known for corruption and brutal oppression.

"No government is perfect," Truman admitted. He, nevertheless, demanded that Americans now choose between two "ways of life."

The president never mentioned the Soviet Union by name in the speech. Instead, he asked Congress to oppose a certain ideology wherever it appeared in the world. The commitment could be open-ended, and that deeply worried some officials. Secretary of State George Marshall and his closest adviser on Soviet affairs, Charles Bohlen, objected to Acheson's draft of the speech because it contained "a little too much flamboyant anti-communism." Even Kennan disliked such sweeping language. He especially opposed sending military aid to Turkey, which bordered the Soviet Union. Stalin might react to that aid as Truman would if Soviet military supplies suddenly appeared in Mexico. But most importantly, Kennan attacked Acheson's key assumption: the "rotten apple" theory (a version of the later "domino" theory). Kennan believed that Communist "infection" could not spread through the Middle East, for example, where devout Moslems hated the Soviets and godless communism. Nor was communism attractive enough or the Red Army strong enough to infect regions beyond.

Truman and Acheson overruled these objections. They wanted a broad call to action, not a precise analysis of the world situation. The Republicans, one delighted Democrat declared, were now to be "smoked out," for they would either have to quit posing as anti-Communists or else hand Truman the money he requested. Within weeks, the president received the $400 million he had asked for, $250 million for Greece and $150 million for Turkey. U.S. aid poured into Greece, as did 350 U.S. advisers. But the well-led leftists actually increased their strength. By late 1947, the crisis had grown until Washington officials debated whether to send in several divisions of U.S. troops. That decision could have involved the Americans in a morass resembling their later involvement in Vietnam. But that ultimate decision never had to be made. In June 1948, Tito and Stalin publicly and violently split apart. Tito fought off Soviet attempts to overthrow him, but the Yugoslav had no time to continue helping the Greek Left. By 1950, the civil war was over. In historian Lawrence Wittner's words, however, U.S. policies had helped fasten "right-wing governments and policies" on Greece.[39]

Americans also long felt the aftereffects of Truman's speech. The president's success made him increasingly popular and put him on the road to his surprising re-election in 1948. In late March 1947, he ordered a federal loyalty program—the first such program in U.S. peacetime history—to uncover possible Communists in government. The attorney general, moreover, for the first time published lists of suspected subversive organizations. Truman's order increased his power by pushing Congress to follow his lead in fighting communism. A "Red Scare" developed, a scare that Truman soon lost control of to less responsible politicians.

And there were other aftereffects. Americans, who before the speech were concerned about economic problems at home, now became excited about foreign-policy issues.[40] They were more willing to support strong anti-Communist action by the president. U.S. military and economic influence in Greece, Turkey, and the rich oil-producing areas of the Middle East also grew by leaps and bounds. The idea developed, moreover, that if Americans could win such a victory in Greece, they could win anywhere—say, in Vietnam or Korea, two areas where U.S. officials became more active in late 1947. From Truman to Ronald Reagan, presidents repeatedly revived the Truman Doctrine's specific words to justify their policies in such places as Lebanon, Southeast Asia, and Central America. As Senator J. William Fulbright wrote in the 1970s, "More by far than any other factor the anti-communism of the Truman Doctrine has been the guiding spirit of American foreign policy since World War II."[41]

CREATING THE POSTWAR WORLD: THE MARSHALL PLAN

The most spectacular spinoff of the early 1947 crisis was the Marshall Plan, a $13 billion program that rebuilt war-devastated western Europe between 1948 and 1952. In doing so, it helped integrate that key region into a U.S.-controlled alliance against the Soviets. The roots of the Marshall Plan went back to World War II. In 1944–1945, leading U.S. business groups warned that if Americans hoped to avoid a terrible postwar depression, they had to double their merchandise exports to the then-unbelievable figure of $10 billion. To do that, however, Europeans—virtually bankrupted by war—would have to receive loans from the United States so that they could buy American exports. In 1946, a young State Department official, Paul Nitze, estimated that the Europeans quickly needed as much as $8 billion. The most dangerous problem, as Nitze (a former Wall Street investment broker) and business leaders saw it, was not the threat of Soviet invasion, but a European economic collapse that could turn the pivotal region toward socialism, paralyze the U.S. economy, and threaten the entire capitalist system.[42]

The State Department began developing a rescue plan at the same time (February–March 1947) that it formulated the Truman Doctrine.

Indeed, just six days before he announced his doctrine, Truman gave a speech at Baylor University that outlined the economic crisis. Not only their trade, but their very freedom was at stake, Truman told his listeners. "For, throughout history, freedom of worship and freedom of speech have been most frequently enjoyed in those societies that have . . . a considerable measure of freedom of individual enterprise." All those freedoms were, indeed, "indivisible." Nations had to cooperate to keep trade open—and not allow trade to be controlled by government interference (as in Socialist or Communist states) or tariff wars: "We must not go through the [nineteen] thirties again."[43]

The State Department's Policy Planning Staff, directed by Kennan, drew up a plan that was publicly revealed by Secretary of State George Marshall at Harvard University on June 5, 1947. Marshall warned that American prosperity depended on European recovery. That recovery, in turn, depended on a long-term program whose "initiative, I think, must come from Europe" itself. He pointedly did not exclude Soviet participation.[44] Privately, Kennan had urged Marshall to "play it straight" with the Soviet Union and exclude no one—that is, no one who would participate on certain U.S. conditions. Western Europeans and a large Soviet delegation traveled to Paris in mid-1947 to discuss the plan. Within days, however, the Soviets angrily left. Stalin had refused to agree to two particular U.S. conditions: a pooling of resources (that might, for example, use Soviet resources to help rebuild parts of western and central Europe) and open accounting so that Americans could see where their money was being spent.

Seventeen western European nations did agree to the conditions and estimated that they needed $27 billion. Truman and the U.S. Congress reduced that to $17 billion, and the final amount spent was nearly $13 billion—enough, as Marshall Plan administrator Paul Hoffman said, to "get Europe on her feet and off our backs."[45] The $13 billion was a huge amount. If Americans had wanted to repeat the plan in the late 1980s, the equivalent, relative to their gross national product, would have cost them $180 billion.

The largest amounts went to Great Britain, France, and Germany. In other words, most dollars went not to the nation with the largest Communist party (Italy), but to the key industrial nations whose recovery could lift living standards throughout the region. The effect on Communist parties was nevertheless quickly felt. The French, understanding U.S. feelings and needing dollars, kicked the Communist members out of the ruling ministry. Another result also soon appeared: the Soviets feared the sudden U.S. involvement in European recovery,

President Harry Truman (1884–1972), at right, believed General George Marshall (1880–1959) to be second only to George Washington as the greatest American. As Truman's secretary of state (1947–1949), Marshall (at left) helped fashion the Marshall Plan for rebuilding western Europe and, as secretary of defense (1950–1951), directed the U.S. effort in the Korean War. He won the Nobel Peace Prize in 1953 for the Marshall Plan. But Marshall's many accomplishments did not mean that Truman took the general's advice on such issues as the Truman Doctrine's wording or the recognition of Israel.

especially the rebuilding of a powerful West Germany. In the 1990s, a U.S. scholar, Scott D. Parrish, examined the newly opened Soviet archives to discover how Stalin and his advisers saw the Marshall Plan. Parrish concluded: "Conceived by American policymakers primarily as a defensive measure to stave off economic collapse in Western Europe," the Marshall Plan "proved indistinguishable to the Soviet leadership from an offensive attempt to subvert the security interests of the Soviet Union. The upshot was the Cold War."[46] Stalin ordered a retreat behind the iron curtain and, through Soviet-controlled trade pacts, set up a Molotov Plan to try to tie together the Communist bloc. Red Army troops cracked down on anti-Communists in Hungary. A massive ideological campaign led by Andrei Zhdanov forced a brutal conformity on eastern Europe. When Poland and Czechoslovakia hinted that they were interested in joining the Marshall Plan, Stalin ordered their leaders to forget it. In March 1948, a Red Army–supported coup overthrew what remained of Czech democracy and independence. The coup stunned the West. Truman immediately seized the opportunity to appear before Congress on March 17, 1948, and demand the passage of money bills required for the Marshall Plan. An anxious Congress soon granted his wish.

The Marshall Plan was nevertheless perhaps the greatest postwar success of U.S. diplomacy. Through it, as historian Michael J. Hogan writes, "American leaders sought to recast Europe in the image of American neocapitalism"—that is, a capitalism that combined freer trade (rather than government controls) and open-market forces. But it also demanded close cooperation between labor, owners, and government. Hogan calls this approach "corporatism." As he concludes, the Marshall Plan created "an integrated European market—one that could absorb German power, boost productivity, raise living standards, lower prices, and thus set the stage for security and recovery on the Continent."[47]

In 1947–1948, U.S. officials quickly moved to ensure that trade would remain as open and free as possible. They worked with twenty-two other nations to create the General Agreement on Tariffs and Trade (GATT). The twenty-three creators promised to abide by the most-favored-nation trade principle. That principle forced any lower tariff or trade favor given by one nation to another to be given automatically to all the other nations in GATT. The principle thus acted like a sledge hammer to knock down tariff walls and government restraints on trade. Within fifteen years, sixty-three nations controlling 80 percent of world trade belonged to GATT.[48] Using the Marshall Plan and GATT as tools, U.S. officials created a new, vast marketplace.

Truman had not been able to rip through Stalin's iron curtain and turn the entire globe into an open, capitalist trading system. But the president certainly was doing well on his side of the curtain. The Marshall Plan proved so successful that long afterward, experts preached the need for "another Marshall Plan" to solve problems in the Middle East or Vietnam or Central America. Marshall's approach, however, could only work in western Europe. Only there did a skilled labor force, a great potential industrial economy, and largely stable political societies exist. But there was a price to be paid even for this success, for the Marshall and Molotov plans sealed the division of Europe. The "two worlds" that James Monroe and other Americans had discussed during the previous 180 years now starkly appeared. Those worlds, however, were not Monroe's New and Old, but Truman's "free" and "totalitarian." Republican Senate leader Robert Taft of Ohio noted the result in 1947: "We apparently confront the Moscow challenge on every front and on every issue. It is a total 'war of nerves' at least."[49]

CREATING THE POSTWAR WORLD: LIPPMANN'S LAMENTS, TRUMAN'S TRIUMPHS

As cold-war tensions rose, so, too, did Truman's popularity and power. In 1947, he proposed, and Congress passed, a national-security act that greatly enlarged and centralized presidential power. The former War Department and Navy Department were combined into a powerful Defense Department. The first secretary of defense was James Forrestal, a hard-line anti-Soviet official who championed Kennan and Kennan's containment theory.

The 1947 act also created the Central Intelligence Agency (the CIA) to coordinate the government's intelligence operations and give the president quick, clear information. In 1948, after the fall of Czechoslovakia to communism, Truman gave the CIA authority to conduct covert political operations—or what State Department official Dean Rusk later called the "back alley war" against communism. The secret order authorizing covert "sabotage" and "subversion" also allowed for lying, if necessary. Operations were to be "so planned and executed that . . . if uncovered the U.S. Government [can] plausibly disclaim any responsibility for them." In 1948, the CIA ran its first secret operation by intervening with money and men in Italy's elections to ensure a Christian Democratic victory over a Communist challenge. The CIA's involvement was soon discovered and condemned, especially by Italians. The irony was that the Communists would doubtless have lost even if the CIA had not intervened.[50]

The 1947 act also established the National Security Council (NSC) in the White House. Its director was to coordinate foreign-policy information and decisions for the president. At first, the NSC was a paper-shuffling agency. By the 1960s, it had become a separate and, in some ways, more powerful State Department that developed and carried out policy secretly and at the president's pleasure.

Truman was scoring victories but also coming under heavy political fire. Republican senator Robert Taft and New Deal liberal Henry Wallace became well-known critics. Taft objected that "if we assume a special position in Greece and Turkey, we can hardly . . . object to the Russians continuing their domination" in eastern Europe.[51] But the most interesting attack came from Walter Lippmann, once Woodrow Wilson's young adviser and now a conservative and the most respected of American journalists.

In a series of newspaper columns, later published in book form as

The Cold War, Lippmann tore apart Kennan's containment theory and the Truman Doctrine. Any attempt to contain communism worldwide, Lippmann warned, would wreck the Constitution by necessarily creating an all-powerful president as commander in chief. It would also hurt the U.S. market economy by regimenting it to fight the Soviets. Containment, moreover, threatened whatever good the United Nations might do, for the world organization would either have to be "cast aside like the League of Nations" or "transformed into an anti-Soviet coalition. In either event the U.N. will have been destroyed." Most importantly, he feared that Kennan's theory would militarize U.S. foreign policy instead of seeking peaceful settlements. Indeed, it would militarily link Americans to their "puppets" and "clients" on Soviet borders, whom U.S. officials would neither understand nor control. Lippmann, on the other hand, strongly approved of the Marshall Plan.[52] It aimed at economic cooperation with America's natural and traditional allies in Europe. And it did so (unlike "X's" plan) with a limited, well-planned approach.

Lippmann's attack on containment was prophetic. But within a year, his hope that the Marshall Plan could mean a revived Europe was nearly destroyed. For reviving western Europe required reviving Germany—or at least West Germany, which had been the economic generator of the region. And reviving West Germany revived the Soviet fear that a third war with a new German state could lie ahead. Truman refused to change course. Given his view of U.S. economic and security needs, he had no choice. The western zones of Germany occupied by U.S., British, and French troops were in sad shape. Their economy, indeed, rested on Lucky Strikes; the popular cigarettes were used in trade because dollars were not available and the German currency was worthless. One journalist asked sarcastically if Truman intended to revive the country by lending 50-million cartons of Lucky Strikes.[53] In June 1948, the United States suddenly introduced a new and stronger German currency that was clearly designed to undergird a unified, perhaps independent West German state.

On June 24, the Soviets cut rail and other surface traffic that linked western Germany to the western-controlled zones of Berlin, the old capital city now located deep within Communist-dominated eastern Germany. "How long do you plan to keep it up?" a top U.S. official asked a Soviet general. "Until you drop your plans for a West German Government," the Soviet replied. In March, the U.S. military governor, General Lucius Clay, had sent a secret cable that rocked Washington by warning that war "may come with dramatic suddenness."

*The massive airlift of supplies into crowded and besieged West Berlin in 1948–
1949 was a political risk and logistical challenge that Truman and the air-force
fliers braved and won. In more than 200,000 flights the pilots landed 1.5 million
tons of supplies.*

Clay had sent the telegram, it turned out, not because he was afraid of
a Soviet attack, but merely because he had hoped to help his superiors
scare Congress into appropriating more money for the military—especially for the aircraft industry, which, led by Lockheed, was pushing
hard for military contracts. Secretary of Defense Forrestal, who was
attracted to the idea of conspiracies like metal filings were attracted to
a magnet, and who believed that the U.S. government moved only when
pushed by a crisis, seized the opportunity. He helped turn Clay's telegram into a sudden war scare. Within two months Forrestal's budget
for spending on military airplanes shot up 57 percent, and the Pentagon budget rose 30 percent. "No President before or since—not even
Ronald Reagan at his most influential [in the 1980s]," writes historian
Frank Kofsky, "has ever come close to expanding military expenditures so dramatically."[54]

The fake crisis in March quickly passed after the Pentagon budget
ballooned, but the June crisis in Germany turned out to be real. If the
United States retreated from Berlin, Secretary of State Marshall told
Truman, it meant the "failure of the rest of our European policy."[55]

The president declared that he was determined to remain in Berlin, but he would not do so by fighting the Red Army. Instead, he ordered an airlift to fly over that army and feed the 2.2 million West Berliners. Truman, however, did dispatch sixty B-29 planes, which could carry atomic bombs, to British bases as a signal to Stalin. (Probably unknown to the Soviet dictator, Truman had only five operational bombs and never sent any of them to Great Britain.) Against tremendous odds and despite crashes and horrible winter conditions, Western pilots landed almost minute by minute in the tiny West Berlin airfield to deliver 1.6 million tons of food and fuel over the next 320 days. In May 1949, Stalin lifted the blockade.

Presidential counsel Clark Clifford had earlier told Truman that there was "considerable political advantage" in fighting the Kremlin. "In times of crisis," Clifford noted, "the American citizen tends to back up his President."[56] Sure enough, the public's approval of Truman's foreign policy rose amid the Berlin crisis and as the 1948 presidential election approached. Truman made certain that he kept the support of one key Democratic party group—the American Jewish community— by recognizing the new state of Israel on May 14, 1948, just fifteen minutes after the state declared itself to be in existence. The recognition was astonishing because Arab nations, which were good friends of the United States and whose oil was important to the West's ability to conduct the cold war, violently opposed Israel's existence. Within hours after the new state appeared, Arab armies launched a full-scale offensive to end the state's life. (The Israelis stopped the offensive during bloody fighting over the next six months until a UN-sponsored truce was called.)

Truman's recognition of Israel was even more remarkable because he ignored bitter opposition from Secretary of State Marshall (whom the president revered) and Defense Secretary Forrestal. These officials were afraid that recognition could turn the Arab oil producers against the United States. They also believed that close Soviet-Israeli ties might turn the new nation into a pro-Communist outpost in the Middle East. Marshall, instead, favored a UN-supervised trusteeship over Palestine that would have Jews and Arabs within one country, not a partitioned region with an independent Israel. State Department officials even warned Truman that Soviet Jewish agents were being infiltrated into Israel.

The president, however, listened to Clark Clifford and others who urged recognition of a separate Jewish state. Truman had long respected pro-Israeli Jews in the United States. In addition to his hope of offsetting Soviet influence, the president doubted whether Arabs and Jews could live under a trusteeship. Warren Austin, the U.S. ambassador to the UN, innocently pleaded for Jews and Arabs to act as brothers and settle their differences "in a true Christian spirit." But only worse warfare flared. Jewish voters, moreover, were crucial in New York, Ohio, Illinois, and California, and Truman certainly understood the politics. "In all of my political experience," he told a friend in 1948, "I don't ever recall the Arab vote swinging a close election."[57] The president ended up with the best of both worlds, for while he recognized Israel, the State Department and U.S. oil companies redoubled efforts to cement their ties with Arab oil producers.

As the 1948 presidential campaign accelerated, the Republican candidate, Governor Thomas E. Dewey of New York, was heavily favored over Truman—so heavily, indeed, that Dewey decided to wage only a light campaign that said little about foreign policy. Dewey believed that by avoiding a partisan position, he would be able to develop a bipartisan foreign policy with Democrats after he replaced Truman in the White House, a replacement that seemed as certain in 1948 as the New York Yankees winning the pennant.

But Truman put on a dazzling political display. He accelerated containment policies in both Europe and Asia, while telling voters that he was the one who could assure peace but that his opponent, Dewey, was a Neanderthal "isolationist" of the 1930s who could not be trusted to fight communism. As for his opponent on the Left, Henry Wallace of the new Progressive party, Truman compared him to traitors who have sold out their country. As historian Robert Divine notes, Truman used his control over foreign policy to stand firm in the Berlin crisis and make "shrewd use of the peace issue," while exploiting his recognition of Israel. The president won the most stunning political upset in twentieth-century American politics by carrying twenty-eight of the forty-eight states. He destroyed the Progressives (who won not a single electoral vote) by linking Wallace with Stalin and Molotov.[58] And Cleveland upset New York to win baseball's American League pennant.

CREATING THE POSTWAR WORLD: ALLIANCES WITH LATIN AMERICA

Truman rounded out his containment policy with two military alliances. The first, involving Latin America, did not mark a historic break in U.S. foreign policy. The second, involving western Europe, did.

U.S.-Latin American relations were never closer than during World War II, nor were they ever more one-sided. Washington gave the southern nations $450 million in lend-lease aid, but 80 percent went to Brazil—long the closest U.S. partner in the region. For their part, Latin Americans sent 50 percent of their exports to North America to help the war effort. But they received low, controlled prices for those exports. Moreover, the income turned out to be worth less after the war as inflation drove up the prices of the U.S. goods that the Latin Americans wanted to buy. Sending their goods to Europe and Asia during and after the war, North Americans simply ignored Latin America. As early as 1942, Chile's president warned that by exporting valuable copper and iron to U.S. factories but getting nothing in return, Chile was "like the 'work horse' who carries an abundance of fresh hay but is not allowed to eat it." After the conflict, Bolivia's foreign minister was asked what North American businessmen had left behind from the war effort. He replied, "empty tin cans, . . . broken-down Frigidaires, rural air strips from which their airplanes took off with their household goods, their office employees, and their blondes. In the tin and wolfram mines, cavities in the ground and cavities among the democratic workers who left their lungs behind in the tunnels in order to save democracy."[59]

One nation rebelled. Argentina, long suspicious of both U.S. and Brazilian policies, remained neutral in the war until 1944. In early 1945, Washington's pressure finally forced the Argentines to break with Germany (otherwise they would be kept out of the UN). But the nation's leader, Colonel Juan Perón, continued to defy the United States. Perón and his charismatic wife, Evita, were very popular, especially with the labor unions. The State Department believed that the Peróns were fascists. In 1946, the U.S. ambassador to Buenos Aires, Spruille Braden, made the mistake of openly opposing Perón's candidacy in the presidential elections. Perón told Argentines that they had to choose between "the pig Braden or the patriot Perón" and won a landslide victory that humiliated the State Department. But that setback was an exception. With no other real political or economic alternative in the growing cold war, most Latin Americans marched to Washington's orders. Those orders were nicely exemplified during the UN conference of 1945, when a U.S. senator grew angry after several Latin American nations defied Washington's wishes. "Your God-damned peanut nations aren't voting right," the senator told a State Department official. "Go line them up."[60] They lined up.

By using such pressure, the United States controlled a sphere of influence in Latin America as surely as the Soviets controlled their sphere in eastern and central Europe, but by quite different means. Henry Stimson worried in 1945 about U.S. officials who were "anxious to hang on to exaggerated views of the Monroe Doctrine and at the same time butt into every question that comes up in Central Europe." But not even Stimson was willing to give up either U.S. rights under the Monroe Doctrine or the U.S. belief that it had the right to intervene in central Europe.[61]

To consolidate U.S. power in the hemisphere (and to show that they were paying some attention to the region), U.S. officials, led by Secretary of State Marshall, traveled to Brazil in 1947 and signed the Rio military pact. This alliance continued the process begun in the 1930s to make the enforcement of the Monroe Doctrine a more collective, multilateral effort instead of a U.S. solo. The signatories agreed that "an armed attack by any state against an American state shall be considered an attack against all the American states." Each state would "assist in meeting the attack" whenever two-thirds of the nations voted to do so, although no one had to respond militarily unless it wished. The pact also tightened relations between U.S. and Latin American military forces. In historian David Green's words, it helped establish "Latin American dependence upon the United States" by creating "a militarily closed hemisphere under United States domination."[62]

The Rio Treaty did not satisfy Latin Americans. They wanted a new economic deal with the United States so that they could enjoy better access to U.S. markets. Washington officials flatly refused. They argued that their resources must go to Europe and that if the Marshall Plan worked, the Latin Americans would benefit by having new European markets. As the U.S. ambassador to Brazil declared, Europe suffered from "a case of smallpox," while Latin America only had "a common cold." A compromise was finally reached. At a meeting of American states at Bogotá, Colombia, in the spring of 1948, Secretary of State Marshall offered $500 million of Export-Import Bank help. It was far less than the southern nations wanted. But the parties also signed the historic charter of the Organization of American States (OAS) that created a new institution to handle hemispheric relations. Most important was the charter's Article 15, which the Latin Americans inserted over U.S. objections: "No State or group of States has the right to intervene, directly or indirectly, for any reason whatever, in the internal or external affairs of any other State." As the OAS charter was signed, massive rioting—caused in part by food shortages and aimed at the United States—erupted in Bogotá. Public buildings were destroyed, over a thousand people were killed, and the U.S. delegates were at times unable

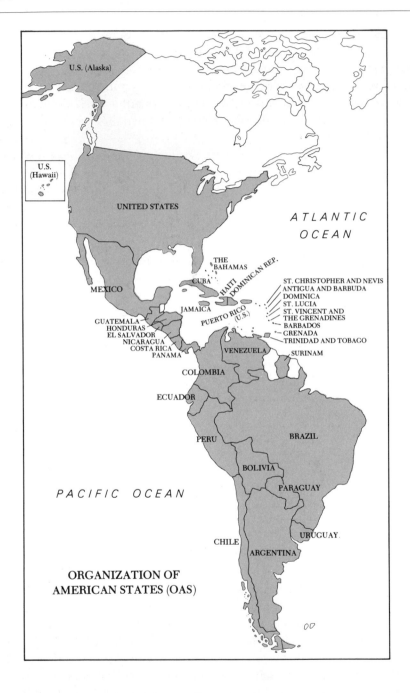

U.S. (Alaska)

U.S.
(Hawaii)

UNITED STATES

ATLANTIC
OCEAN

THE
BAHAMAS
CUBA
HAITI
DOMINICAN REP.
MEXICO

JAMAICA

PUERTO RICO
(U.S.)

ST. CHRISTOPHER AND NEVIS
ANTIGUA AND BARBUDA
DOMINICA
ST. LUCIA
ST. VINCENT AND
THE GRENADINES
BARBADOS
GRENADA
TRINIDAD AND TOBAGO

GUATEMALA
HONDURAS
EL SALVADOR
NICARAGUA
COSTA RICA
PANAMA

VENEZUELA

SURINAM

COLOMBIA

ECUADOR

PERU

BRAZIL

BOLIVIA

PACIFIC OCEAN

PARAGUAY

URUGUAY

CHILE

ARGENTINA

**ORGANIZATION OF
AMERICAN STATES (OAS)**

to leave their embassy.[63] Unfortunately, the riots, not Article 15, better previewed the next forty years of U.S.–Latin American relations.

CREATING THE POSTWAR WORLD: NATO

As historian Roger Trask notes, the Rio Treaty and the OAS were models "for a host of later Cold War collective defense treaties and regional organizations. They were among the earliest examples of [Truman's] implementation of the containment policy."[64] None of the treaties turned out to be more important than the one that created the North Atlantic Treaty Organization (NATO) of 1949. It was the first U.S. military alliance with Europe in 171 years.

But the 1949 pact differed from that first one made with France in 1778. Earlier, the United States was a very junior partner at the mercy of a great world power. In 1949, the United States was the greatest of all world powers. It could now dominate an alliance by using its partners to carry out U.S. foreign-policy aims. By 1948–1949, these aims in Europe were to contain the Soviet Union and to restore West German independence and economic power. The two objectives were closely related (a restored West Germany could best help contain the Soviet Union), but other western Europeans greatly feared German recovery. They not only agreed with Moscow that Germany should remain divided ("I love Germany so," a Frenchman wrote sarcastically. "Every day I thank God that there are two of them").[65] They also feared that U.S. policy was creating a powerful, armed West Germany.

Europeans moved to protect themselves. In March 1947, France and Great Britain signed the Treaty of Dunkirk to provide for their mutual defense. A year later, after the Communist takeover of Czechoslovakia and U.S. moves to build up West Germany, five European nations— Great Britain, France, the Netherlands, Belgium, and Luxembourg— signed the Brussels Pact to extend their mutual defense. U.S. officials now actively encouraged such cooperation. They saw it as the military side of the Marshall Plan. They also knew that it provided the reassurance needed as Germany recovered. In 1948, the Senate passed Senator Vandenberg's resolution that the United States become involved on the Continent, but within the broad framework of the UN Charter so that there would be no direct defiance of the world organization.

In April 1949, the NATO Treaty was signed by twelve nations—the United States, Canada, Great Britain, France, Italy, Denmark, Portugal, Norway, Iceland, Belgium, the Netherlands, and Luxembourg.

Truman's new secretary of state, Dean Acheson, signed for the United States. It was appropriate, for the pact created tight North Atlantic ties and a new military "position of strength," both of which Acheson believed to be fundamental. The partners pledged close political and economic collaboration, and "to develop their individual and collective capacity to resist armed attack." Most importantly, they agreed in Article 5 "that an armed attack against one or more of them . . . shall be considered an attack against them all." Each party would then "individually and in concert with the other Parties [take] such action as it deems necessary, including the use of armed force." The United States thus pledged to become involved in future European wars. In ratifying the treaty by an 82-to-13 vote in July, however, Vandenberg and the Senate carefully protected their own freedom of action—and tried to restrict the president's—by declaring that the constitutional "relationship" between the two branches of government remained the same. That is, Congress assumed it would continue to have the power to declare war.[66]

NATO nicely served the interests of all its members. It "kept the Russians out, the Americans in, and the Germans down," as one analysis phrases it. The French had finally succeeded in bringing Americans onto the Continent to help guarantee European security. But the United States gained the most. North Americans received valuable military bases in Europe. U.S. officials suddenly had a key role in deciding such internal European questions as "the length of military service required of each nation's troops" and even "recommendations of how much of a nation's gross national product should be dedicated to the alliance," in historian Lawrence Kaplan's words. U.S. military personnel flooded into Europe. In Norway, the sixty North Americans working with NATO were more numerous than the entire Norwegian Foreign Office.[67]

WINNING THE COLD WAR

By mid-1949, Truman and Acheson basked in the successes of their foreign policy as well as the warmth of a Washington summer. After a treacherous, unsure start in 1945–1946, Truman's doctrine, Marshall's plan, Kennan's containment theory, and Acheson's rotten-apple argument set U.S. policy on a straight course. U.S. officials did not think small. In historian Melvyn Leffler's words, they aimed for nothing less than "a strategic sphere of influence within the Western Hem-

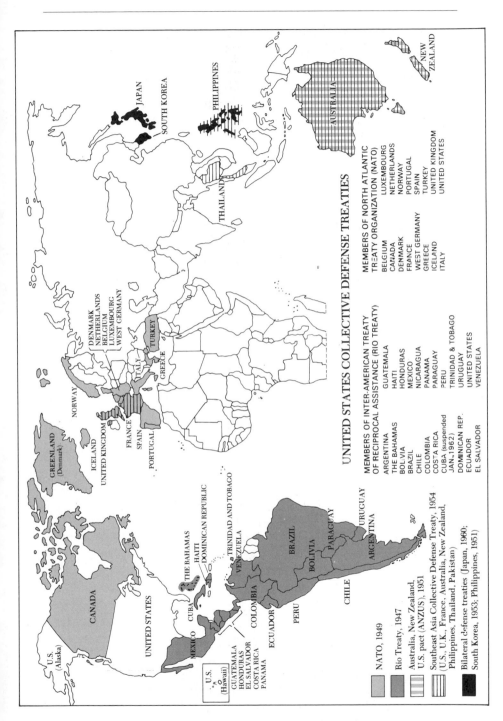

MEMBERS OF INTER-AMERICAN TREATY
OF RECIPROCAL ASSISTANCE (RIO TREATY)

ARGENTINA	GUATEMALA
THE BAHAMAS	HAITI
BOLIVIA	HONDURAS
BRAZIL	MEXICO
CHILE	NICARAGUA
COLOMBIA	PANAMA
COSTA RICA	PARAGUAY
CUBA (suspended	PERU
JAN.-1962)	TRINIDAD & TOBAGO
DOMINICAN REP.	URUGUAY
ECUADOR	UNITED STATES
EL SALVADOR	VENEZUELA

UNITED STATES COLLECTIVE DEFENSE TREATIES

MEMBERS OF NORTH ATLANTIC
TREATY ORGANIZATION (NATO)

BELGIUM	LUXEMBOURG
CANADA	NETHERLANDS
DENMARK	NORWAY
FRANCE	PORTUGAL
WEST GERMANY	SPAIN
GREECE	TURKEY
ICELAND	UNITED KINGDOM
ITALY	UNITED STATES

NATO, 1949

Rio Treaty, 1947

Australia, New Zealand,
U.S. pact (ANZUS), 1951

Southeast Asia Collective Defense Treaty, 1954
(U.S., U.K., France, Australia, New Zealand,
Philippines, Thailand, Pakistan)

Bilateral defense treaties (Japan, 1960;
South Korea, 1953; Philippines, 1951)

The U.S. global military web during the Cold War.

isphere, domination of the Atlantic and Pacific oceans, an extensive system of outlying bases to . . . project American power . . . , access to the resources and markets of most of Eurasia, denial of those resources to a prospective enemy, and the maintenance of nuclear superiority."[68] And they had hit all these targets by 1948. Truman's 1948 election triumph seemed both a sweet approval of past policies and a guarantee of future success.

The two cornerstones of postwar U.S. policy—a recovered West Germany and a resurrected Japan—seemed firmly in place even though both had been mortal and hated enemies of North Americans just several years earlier. Shortly after NATO came into being, the independent Federal Republic of Germany appeared. Some were afraid that Acheson's next step would be to flesh out NATO's small ground forces with West German troops. He strongly denied any such intention. Anyway, as Charles Bohlen privately told Acheson, the Soviets had already been "forced . . . from the offensive in Germany to an almost terrified defense of their control in the Eastern zone."[69]

Asia also seemed to be brightening. China might be falling to communism, but Truman could do nothing about that. In any event, the Communists would probably require decades to consolidate their power. Japan, not China, had long been the hub of Asia, and Japan was firmly in U.S. hands. That nation was again industrializing (although much too slowly), moving toward political independence, cracking down on Communist labor unions, and allowing the rebuilding of the giant Japanese corporations that could make the nation self-sufficient and a worthy friend of Washington's.

All seemed well in that summer of 1949. Truman was emerging as the winner in the cold war. Then, suddenly, in September, North Americans found themselves in new and possibly greater danger than ever before. Communists had completed their conquest of China in weeks, not decades. Much worse, the Soviets exploded their own atomic bomb. A new era had begun.

NOTES

1. Walter Z. Laqueur, "Brezhnev," *New York Times Magazine*, 17 June 1973, p. 52.
2. Diane Shaver Clemens, *Yalta* (New York, 1970), pp. 269–270.
3. Melvyn P. Leffler, "Adherence to Agreements: Yalta and the Experiences of the

Early Cold War," *International Security* 11 (Summer 1986): 88–123, a most important recent work on the disagreements, lays heavy responsibility on the United States.

4. David Reynolds, "The Origins of the Cold War: The European Dimension, 1944–1951," *Historical Journal* 28, no. 2 (1985): 500.

5. Robert M. Hathaway, *Ambiguous Partnership: Britain and America, 1944–1947* (New York, 1981), pp. 316–317.

6. Lloyd C. Gardner, *Architects of Illusion: Men and Ideas in American Foreign Policy, 1941–1949* (Chicago, 1970), ch. 5.

7. Thomas Wolfe, *Soviet Power and Europe, 1945–1970* (Baltimore, 1970), p. 33.

8. Henry L. Stimson and McGeorge Bundy, *On Active Service in Peace and War* (New York, 1949), pp. 638–650.

9. Frank Roberts to C. F. A. Warner, 19 September 1946, FO 371 N12380/97/38, Public Record Office, Kew, England.

10. V. M. Molotov, *Problems of Foreign Policy: Speeches and Statements, April 1945–November 1948* (Moscow, 1949), pp. 210–216.

11. Charles E. Bohlen, *Witness to History, 1929–1969* (New York, 1973), p. 255.

12. John Gimbel, *The American Occupation of Germany: Politics and the Military, 1945–1949* (Stanford, 1968), pp. 15–16; also see Gardner, pp. 250–256, for a good, brief discussion.

13. *Boston Globe*, 2 March 1985, p. 4; Clarence G. Lasby, *Project Paperclip: German Scientists and the Cold War* (New York, 1971), is a standard account; a new interpretation is John Gimbel, "U.S. Policy and German Scientists: The Early Cold War," *Political Science Quarterly* 101, no. 3 (1986): 433–451.

14. E. J. Kahn, Jr., "Profile," *New Yorker*, 8 April 1972, p. 61; for superb brief analyses of the FSO-Hurley fight, see Gary May, *China Scapegoat: The Diplomatic Ordeal of John Carter Vincent* (Washington, D.C., 1979), pp. 109–155; Akira Iriye, *The Cold War in Asia* (Englewood Cliffs, N.J., 1974), esp. pp. 82–83.

15. Harry S. Truman, *Memoirs*, 2 vols. (Garden City, N.Y., 1955–1956), II, pp. 90–92; the most recent authoritative account is Forrest Pogue, *George C. Marshall: Statesman, 1945–1959* (New York, 1987), pp. 54–143.

16. Steven I. Levine, "A New Look at American Mediation in the Chinese Civil War: The Marshall Mission and Manchuria," *Diplomatic History* 3 (Fall 1979): 374.

17. Tang Tsou, *America's Failure in China, 1941–1950*, 2 vols. (Chicago, 1963), II, p. 469.

18. *New York Times*, 27 October 1976, p. 44.

19. Gaddis Smith, *Dean Acheson*, vol. XVI of *The American Secretaries of State and Their Diplomacy*, ed. Samuel Flagg Bemis and Robert H. Ferrell (New York, 1972), p. 3.

20. This is discussed in David S. McClellan, *Dean Acheson: The State Department Years* (New York, 1976), pp. 30–31.

21. Dean Acheson, *Power and Diplomacy* (Cambridge, Mass., 1958), p. 29; Oral History Interview of Dean G. Acheson, 18 February 1955, Harry S. Truman Post-Presidential Papers, Truman Library, Independence, Mo.; Thomas L. Hughes, "Foreign Policy: Men or Measures?" *Atlantic* 234 (October 1974): 53.

22. Richard J. Barnet, *Roots of War* (New York, 1972), p. 121.

23. *The Pattern of Responsibility*, ed. McGeorge Bundy (Boston, 1952), p. 17; Princeton Seminar transcripts, 22–23 July 1953, Papers of Dean G. Acheson, Truman Library.

24. *Harper's Magazine* 211 (November 1955): 20; Gregg Herken, *The Winning Weapon: The Atomic Bomb in the Cold War, 1945–1950* (New York, 1980), p. 356.

25. Martin Weil, *A Pretty Good Club: The Founding Fathers of the U.S. Foreign Service* (New York, 1978), p. 258.

26. Roger Hilsman, *The Politics of Policymaking in Defense and Foreign Affairs* (New York, 1971), p. 168.

27. An original, comprehensive analysis is Mark H. Lytle, *The Origins of the Iranian-American Alliance, 1941–1953* (New York, 1987), esp. pp. xiii–xix, 156–170. Also, a key essay is Richard Pfau, "Containment in Iran, 1946: The Shift to an Active Policy," *Diplomatic History* 1 (Fall 1977): 359–372.

28. Thomas G. Paterson, *Soviet-American Confrontation: Postwar Reconstruction and the Origins of the Cold War* (Baltimore, 1973), pp. 192–193; James Forrestal, *The Forrestal Diaries*, ed. Walter Millis (New York, 1951), p. 192.

29. Dean Acheson, *Present at the Creation: My Years in the State Department* (New York, 1969, 1987), pp. 195–196.

30. Arnold A. Rogow, *James Forrestal* (New York, 1963), p. 204n.

31. William H. McNeill, *America, Britain and Russia: Their Cooperation and Conflict, 1941–1946* (New York, 1953), p. 658; Walter Bedell Smith, *My Three Years in Moscow* (Philadelphia, 1950), pp. 52–53.

32. Important analyses are Jordan A. Schwarz, *The Speculator: Bernard M. Baruch in Washington, 1917–1965* (Chapel Hill, N.C., 1981), pp. 495–505; Herken, pp. 160–190; and also David Lilienthal to Bernard Baruch, 14 April 1948, David F. Lilienthal File, Atomic Energy, Papers of Bernard Baruch, Princeton University, Princeton, N.J.

33. Allen L. Yarnell, *Democrats and Progressives: The 1948 Presidential Election as a Test of Postwar Liberalism* (Berkeley, 1974), p. 17; Henry A. Wallace, *The Price of Vision: The Diary of Henry A. Wallace, 1942–1946* ed. John M. Blum (Boston, 1973), pp. 589–601; Forrestal, pp. 206–209.

34. Urs Schwarz, *American Strategy: A New Perspective* (Garden City, N.Y., 1966), pp. 68–69; the standard account is Alice Kimball Smith, *A Peril and a Hope: The Scientists' Movement in America, 1945–47* (Chicago, 1965).

35. "X," "The Sources of Soviet Conduct," *Foreign Affairs* 25 (July 1947): 566–582; "Long Telegram" excerpts are in George Kennan, *Memoirs, 1925–1950* (Boston, 1967), pp. 547–559.

36. "The Bohlen-Robinson Report," *Diplomatic History* 1 (Fall 1977): esp. 397; a good analysis is in Robert L. Messer, "Paths Not Taken: The U.S. Department of State and Alternatives to Containment, 1945–1949," *Diplomatic History* 1 (Fall 1977): 297–319.

37. The Clifford Report can be found in Arthur Krock, *Memoirs* (New York, 1968), pp. 419–482.

38. Acheson, *Present at the Creation*, pp. 218–219.

39. Lawrence Wittner, *American Intervention in Greece, 1943–1949* (New York, 1982), p. 312. The Truman speech is in *The Record of American Diplomacy*, ed. Ruhl J. Bartlett, 4th ed. (New York, 1964), pp. 723–727; it is also given, with a commentary, in Walter LaFeber, "The Truman Doctrine," in *The Course of U.S. History*, ed. David Nasaw (Homewood, Ill., 1986), from which much of this section is drawn.

40. *Public Opinion Quarterly* 11 (Winter 1947–1948): 658.

41. J. William Fulbright, *The Crippled Giant* (New York, 1972), pp. 6–24.

42. U.S. Congress, House, 80th Cong., 1st and 2d sess., *United States Foreign Policy for a Post-War Recovery Program*, 2 vols. (Washington, D.C., 1948), I, pp. 68–81; Rich-

ard Freeland, *The Truman Doctrine and the Origins of McCarthyism* (New York, 1972), esp. chs. I and II, is a pioneering account; David W. Eakins, "Business Planners and America's Postwar Expansion," in *Corporations and the Cold War*, ed. David Horowitz (New York, 1969), pp. 143–168.

43. U.S. Government, *Public Papers of the Presidents of the United States: Harry S. Truman, 1947* (Washington, D.C., 1963), pp. 167–172.

44. The speech and an important contemporary analysis are in Joseph M. Jones, *The Fifteen Weeks* (New York, 1955), esp. appendix; also Pogue, pp. 197–217, 525–528.

45. Reynolds, 512.

46. *Los Angeles Times*, January 25, 1993, p. A4; I am indebted to Milton Leitenberg for this reference.

47. Michael J. Hogan, "American Marshall Planners and the Search for a European Neocapitalism," *American Historical Review* 90 (February 1985): 44–72, esp. 45.

48. Justus D. Doenecke, "The Most-Favored-Nation Principle," in *Encyclopedia of American Foreign Policy*, ed. Alexander DeConde, 3 vols. (New York, 1978), II, p. 608.

49. Arthur Vandenberg, *The Private Papers of Senator Vandenberg*, ed. Arthur H. Vandenberg, Jr. (Boston, 1952), p. 374.

50. Gregory F. Treverton, "Covert Action and Open Society," *Foreign Affairs* 65 (Summer 1987): 996–997, has the quote; Rusk's quote is in Lyman B. Kirkpatrick, Jr., "Intelligence and Counterintelligence," in *Encyclopedia of American Foreign Policy*, ed. Alexander DeConde, 3 vols. (New York, 1978), II, pp. 422–423. The standard account on CIA intervention in the Italian election is now James Edward Miller, *The United States and Italy, 1940–1950* (Chapel Hill, N.C., 1986), esp. pp. 248–252; an important detailed analysis is Eric Edelman, "Incremental Involvement: Italy and U.S. Foreign Policy, 1943–1948" (Ph.D. diss., Yale, 1981).

51. Lawrence S. Kaplan, *The United States and NATO: The Formative Years* (Lexington, Ky., 1984), p. 35.

52. Walter Lippmann, *The Cold War* (New York, 1947), esp., pp. 15–29, 52–59; a classic biography is Ronald Steel, *Walter Lippmann and the American Century* (New York, 1980), esp. ch. XXXIV–XXXV.

53. Richard J. Barnet, *The Alliance: America-Europe-Japan, Makers of the Postwar World* (New York, 1983), p. 40.

54. Frank Kofsky, *Harry Truman and the War Scare of 1948* (New York, 1993), ch. I; Forrestal, pp. 387, 395; Barnet, p. 46; Michael Howard, "Governor-General of Germany," *Times Literary Supplement*, 29 August 1975, pp. 969–970.

55. Forrestal, pp. 454–455, 459.

56. Yarnell, p. 37.

57. Francis O. Wilcox, *Congress, the Executive and Foreign Policy* (New York, 1971), p. 138; the Austin quote is in George T. Mazuzan, *Warren R. Austin at the U.N, 1946–1953* (Kent, Ohio, 1977), p. 99; for Marshall's opposition, see Pogue, pp. 337–375.

58. The best analysis of the foreign-policy issues is Robert A. Divine, *Foreign Policy and U.S. Presidential Elections, 1940–1948* (New York, 1974), pp. 167–276, esp. pp. 173, 262; also Yarnell, pp. 77–78.

59. Donald M. Dozer, *Are We Good Neighbors?: Three Decades of Inter-American Relations, 1930–1960* (Gainesville, Fla., 1959), ch. IV, pp. 200–201; an important analysis of the economic dimension by a top official is Laurence Duggan, *The Americas* (New York, 1949), esp. pp. 123–126.

60. Dozer, p. 200.

61. "A sphere of influence is an area into which is projected power and influence of a country primarily for political, military-strategic, or economic purposes, but sometimes cultural purposes may be added. States within the area are usually nominally independent, but the degree of influence may be so great as to leave little independence; or it may be so indirect and restrained as to permit considerable independence." John P. Vloyantes, *Spheres of Influence* (Tucson, Ariz., 1970), p. 2; Paul Keal, *Unspoken Rules and Superpower Dominance* (New York, 1983), p. 15.

62. David Green, *The Containment of Latin America* (Chicago, 1971), p. 260; the treaty's context and terms are outlined in Graham H. Stuart and James L. Tigner, *Latin America and the United States*, 6th ed. (Englewood Cliffs, N.J., 1975), esp. pp. 70, 80–85, 138.

63. Pogue, pp. 386–393.

64. Roger R. Trask, "The Impact of the Cold War on United States–Latin American Relations, 1945–1949," *Diplomatic History* 1 (Summer 1977): 284.

65. Barnet, p. 248.

66. The treaty and the Senate's declaration are in *The Record of American Diplomacy* pp. 733–736; especially important is Kaplan, chs. I and VI.

67. Lawrence S. Kaplan, "The Treaties of Paris and Washington, 1778 and 1949," in *Diplomacy and Revolution*, ed. Ronald Hoffman and Peter J. Albert (Charlottesville, Va., 1981), p. 182; the analysis quoted is by Allan R. Millett and Peter Maslowski, *For the Common Defense: A Military History of the United States of America* (New York, 1984), p. 483.

68. Melvyn P. Leffler, "The American Conception of National Security and the Beginnings of the Cold War, 1945–48," *American Historical Review* 89 (April 1984): 379, a most important essay.

69. Charles E. Bohlen to Dean G. Acheson, 9 June 1949, Bohlen Records, Box 1, Lot File, RG 59, U.S. Archives, Washington, D.C.

FOR FURTHER READING

References to specific topics can be found in the notes to this chapter and in the General Bibliography at the end of this book; most of these references are not repeated below. Three other bibliographies are important. Most detailed is the *Guide to American Foreign Relations since 1700*, ed. Richard Dean Burns (1983). J. L. Black, *Origins, Evolution, and Nature of the Cold War: An Annotated Bibliography* (1985), is exhaustive. Justus D. Doenecke, *Anti-Intervention: A Bibliographical Introduction to Isolationism and Pacifism from World War I to the Early Cold War* (1987), is indispensable, especially for references to dissenters of cold-war policy such as Senator Robert Taft.

Two new overviews are of significance, for their bibliographies as well as interpretations: Melvyn P. Leffler, *A Preponderance of Power* (1992), now the standard account for 1945–1952; and Warren Cohen, *America in the Age of Soviet Power, 1945–1991*, in *The Cambridge History of American Foreign Relations*, ed. Warren Cohen (1993). Especially helpful is Edward Crapol, "Some Reflections on the Historiography of the Cold War," *The History Teacher* 29 (1986–1987). Important biographies that cover these years include

Townsend Hoopes and Douglas Brinkley, *Driven Patriot: The Life and Times of James Forrestal* (1992); Kai Bird, *The Chairman: John J. McCloy* (1992); Thomas Alan Schwartz, *America's Germany* (1991), a fine examination of U.S. policy through an analysis of McCloy; Jean Edward Smith, *Lucius D. Clay* (1990), key on Germany but also on Clay's criticism of Kennan; H. W. Brands, *Inside the Cold War: Loy Henderson. . . .* (1991), an interesting perspective; Deborah Welch Larson, *Origins of Containment: A Psychological Explanation* (1985), for its biographical examinations; *Without Precedent: The Life and Career of Eleanor Roosevelt*, ed. Joan Hoff-Wilson and Marjorie Lightman (1984); Ronald Pruessen's standard biography, *John Foster Dulles* (1982), taking Dulles to 1952; Mark G. Toulouse, *The Transformation of John Foster Dulles* (1985), especially for the religious influences, 1947–1952; the key biographical studies of Kennan, Acheson, Lovett, McCloy, and others in Walter Isaacson and Evan Thomas, *The Wise Men: Six Friends and the World They Made* (1986); and David McCullough's popular *Truman* (1992).

On the outbreak of the cold war, key studies include U.S. Institute of Peace, *Origins of the Cold War: The Novikov, Kennan, and Roberts "Long Telegrams" of 1946* (1991), which contains important documents; James L. Gormley's succinct *The Collapse of the Grand Alliance, 1945–1948* (1987); Robert L. Messer, *The End of an Alliance* (1982), pivotal on the Truman-Byrnes relationship, as is Patricia Dawson Ward's important *The Threat of Peace* (1979); John Lewis Gaddis, *Strategies of Containment* (1982), with a suggestive overview; U.S. Department of State, *The State Department Policy Planning Staff Papers, 1947–1949*, with valuable introductions by Anna Kasten Nelson, 3 vols. (1983); Steven L. Rearden, *History of the Office of the Secretary of Defense*, Vol. I: *The Formative Years, 1947–1950* (1984), beautifully researched; Robert Conquest, *Stalin* (1991), the most recent one-volume biography; Michael M. Boll, *Cold War in the Balkans* (1984), important for its case study of Bulgaria; Robert A. Gason, "American Foreign Policy and the Limits of Power: Eastern Europe, 1946–1950," *Journal of Contemporary History* 21 (July 1986), a good overview; Edward J. Sheehy, *The U.S. Navy, the Mediterranean and the Cold War, 1945–1947* (1992), on the naval build-up; Scott L. Bills, *Empire and Cold War: The Roots of U.S.–Third World Antagonism, 1945–1947* (1990), on the Eurocentric U.S. view toward the third world between 1945 and 1947; and Chester J. Pach, Jr., *Arming the Free World* (1991), crucial for origins of military aid program, 1945–1950. The U.S. side of the nuclear-arms race is covered in Gregg Herken, *The Winning Weapon: The Atomic Bomb in the Cold War, 1945–1950* (1980), while the Soviet build-up is best traced by David Holloway's 2nd edition of *The Soviet Union and the Arms Race* (1984). Excellent biographies of Kennan provide important insights into the cold war's origins: Anders Stephanson, *Kennan and the Art of Foreign Policy* (1989); Walter L. Hixon, *George Kennan: Cold War Iconoclast* (1989); David Mayers, *George Kennan and the Dilemmas of U.S. Foreign Policy* (1989); Barton Gellmann, *Contending with Kennan* (1984); and Wilson D. Miscamble, *George F. Kennan and the Making of American Foreign Policy, 1947–1950* (1992).

On domestic issues, no one has better analyzed the impact of public opinion during these years than Thomas G. Paterson, "Presidential Foreign Policy, Public Opinion, and Congress: The Truman Years," *Diplomatic History* 3 (Winter 1979); Michael J. Heale's *American Anti-Communism* (1990) is a 140-year overview; Stephen J. Whitfield's *The Culture of the Cold War* (1990) is especially good on the late 1940s; Fred Inglis, *The Cruel Peace: Everyday Life and the Cold War* (1992); Thomas Hill Schaub, *American Fiction in the Cold War* (1991), especially on "liberal narratives" of the 1940s–1950s; Frank Ninkovich, *The Diplomacy of Ideas: U.S. Foreign Policy and Cultural Relations,*

1938–1950 (1981); and *For Better or Worse: The American Influence in the World,* ed. Allen F. Davis (1981). The last two references analyze how Americans exported their beliefs.

For U.S.-European relations, Frank Costigliola, *France and the United States: The Cold Alliance since World War II* (1992), is important and a delight to read, as is Frank Ninkovich, *Germany and the United States* (1988); *Power in Europe: Great Britain, France, Italy and Germany in a Postwar World, 1945–1950,* ed. Josef Becker and Franz Knipping (1986), is seminal for its European viewpoint and sources; *The Special Relationship: Anglo-American Relations since 1945,* ed. William Roger Louis and Hedley Bull (1986), is a distinguished overview; John W. Young, *Britain, France, and the Unity of Europe, 1945–1951* (1984), is a pivotal study on the subject; C. J. Bartlett, *The Special Relationship* (1992), is a political analysis of post-1945 Anglo-American relations; Richard A. Best, Jr., *"Co-operation with Like-minded Peoples": British Influences on American Security Policy, 1945–1949* (1986); Terry H. Anderson, *The United States, Great Britain and the Cold War, 1944–1947* (1981), stresses continuity from Roosevelt to Truman.

Many of the above citations are important for the Truman Doctrine and the Mediterranean. Lawrence S. Wittner, *American Intervention in Greece, 1943–1949* (1982), is indispensable and superb on these subjects. Other important studies include Howard Jones, *A New Kind of War: America's Global Strategy and the Truman Doctrine in Greece* (1989), placing Greece in U.S. global strategy; Theodore A. Couloumbis, *The United States, Greece and Turkey* (1983), good for the entire postwar era; and G. M. Alexander, *The Prelude to the Truman Doctrine: British Policy in Greece, 1944–1947* (1984), which gives the British side well.

On the Marshall Plan, reconstruction, Germany, and NATO, the starting place is Michael Hogan's *The Marshall Plan: America, Britain, and the Reconstruction of Western Europe, 1947–1952* (1987); other important works include Alan S. Milward, *The Reconstruction of Western Europe, 1945–1951* (1984); Sallie Pisani, *The CIA and the Marshall Plan* (1992); Carolyn Eisenberg, "U.S. Policy in Post-War Germany: The Conservative Restoration," *Science and Society* 46 (Spring 1982), a most important overview; John H. Backer, *Winds of History: The German Years of Lucius DuBignon Clay* (1984), to be used with the superb Smith and Schwartz biographies noted above; Daniel F. Harrington, "The Berlin Blockade Revisited," *International History Review* 6 (February 1984), a useful analysis and bibliography; Lawrence Kaplan, *The United States and NATO* (1984), by the leading U.S. scholar on the alliance; Jeffrey Diefendorft, *et al.,* eds., *American Policy and the Reconstruction of West Germany, 1945–1955* (1993). Along with the Edelman and Miller studies listed in the notes, a good volume on U.S.-Italian economic relations is John Lamberton Harper, *Reconstruction of Italy, 1945–1948* (1986). Extremely important is material on Truman and the CIA covered in Rhodri Jeffreys-Jones and Andrew Lownie, eds., *North American Spies* (1991).

On Asia, begin with the important essays in *Uncertain Years: Chinese-American Relations, 1947–1950,* ed. Dorothy Borg and Waldo Heinrichs (1980); Gordon H. Chang, *Friends and Enemies* (1990), on post-1948 U.S.-Chinese relations; Russell D. Buhite, *Soviet-American Relations in Asia, 1945–1954* (1981), one of the few attempts to set this in the larger context. American occupation policy in Japan is well traced in Michael Schaller, *The American Occupation of Japan* (1985); Kyoko Inoue, *MacArthur's Japanese Constitution* (1991), is a fascinating study of the language; Richard B. Finn, *Winners in Peace* (1992), is on MacArthur and Yoshida as key players; Toshio Nishi, *Unconditional Democracy: Education and Politics in Occupied Japan, 1945–1952* (1982), is a critical

Japanese view. A series of well-written and well-researched books give excellent overviews: Michael Schaller's *MacArthur* (1989); Howard Schonberger, *Aftermath of War* (1989), which is on Japan; Patricia Neils, *China Images in the Life and Times of Henry Luce* (1990); Marc S. Gallicchio's important *The Cold War Begins in Asia* (1988), especially on Vincent and the China Hands; Paul G. Lauren, ed., *The China Hands' Legacy* (1987); June M. Grasso, *Harry Truman's Two-China Policy, 1948–1950* (1987), to be used with Nancy Bernkopf Tucker's definitive *Patterns in the Dust* (1983); and Gary May, *China Scapegoat* (1982), another good analysis of Vincent. A superb study is Dennis Merrill, *Bread and the Ballot* (1990), on U.S.-Indian relations after 1947.

Hemispheric, Middle East, and African relations are discussed in the following works. A key Canadian official's view is John W. Holmes, *The Shaping of Peace* (1982), on Canada and the world, 1943–1957, especially Canada's relations with the United States; Thomas M. Leonard, *The United States and Central America, 1944–1949* (1984); Joseph Tulchin's important *Argentina and the United States* (1990), especially for the Perón showdown; and Lester Langley, *The United States and Mexico* (1991). A pathbreaking account is Thomas Borstelmann, *Apartheid's Reluctant Uncle* (1993), on U.S.–South African relations, 1945–1952, while the context is well presented in Thomas J. Noer, *Cold War and Black Liberation: The United States and White Rule in Africa, 1948–1968* (1985). For the Middle East, David S. Painter, *Oil and the American Century: The Political Economy of U.S. Foreign Oil Policy, 1941–1954* (1986), is good on the 1941–1954 years; Steven L. Spiegel, *The Other Arab-Israeli Conflict: America's Middle East Policy from Truman to Reagan* (1985), is important on domestic politics; Cheryl Rubenberg, *Israel and the American National Interest* (1986), is a critical analysis; Michael J. Cohen, *Truman and Israel* (1990), is very good, especially on the defeat of the Arabists in the State Department; and David Schoenbaum's *The United States and the State of Israel* (1993), is an important overview.

15

The Big Turn: The Era of the Korean War (1949–1952)

TWO SHOCKS AND A NEW WORLD

In early summer 1949, Americans could believe that victory in the cold war was within their grasp. They like their wars, hot or cold, the same way they like their baseball: easily understood, brief, and with a definite score at the end so that it is clear who won. By the end of 1949, however, two events—the conquest of China by Communist forces and the explosion of the first Soviet atomic bomb—so shocked Americans that they were still dealing with the results decades later.

Truman and Acheson had long known that China was lost. "We picked a bad horse," the president wrote privately in 1949. Chiang Kai-shek's (Jiang Jieshi's) Nationalist (Kuomintang or KMT) government "was one of the most corrupt and inefficient that ever made an attempt to govern a country."[1] Acheson and the president tried to prove that point by publishing a State Department white paper with vast numbers of diplomatic documents from 1844 to 1949. The white paper argued that the KMT was rotten and—more importantly—that nothing more the United States might have done could have saved Chiang. Republicans attacked Acheson for letting Chiang be driven back to the island of Taiwan by Mao Zedong's (Mao Tse-tung's) Communist armies. No serious critic, however, ever urged the only policy that might have saved the KMT: dispatching a mammoth U.S. force to China.

Giving up on Chiang as he fled to Taiwan did not mean embracing

Mao. The Soviets had played no important role in the Communist victory, but in June 1949 Mao declared that the Chinese would now "lean" toward the Soviets. At the same moment, U.S. and Chinese Communist diplomats cautiously sounded each other out about possible contacts. State Department officials encouraged further exchanges, but Truman killed the idea. The president apparently was furious with Mao's public statements, mistrusted the Communists, and feared political uproar in Washington from the Republicans. Nevertheless, as historian Nancy Bernkopf Tucker persuasively argues, Truman and Acheson carefully kept open the possibility of recognizing Mao's new government.[2] U.S. trade with the Chinese even continued well into 1950. But closer relations would require time and the capture of Taiwan by the Communists so that Chiang's embarrassing presence would finally disappear. U.S. officials believed that Communist conquest of Taiwan would occur within a year.

The possibility thus existed in 1949–1950 for the United States and the new China to recognize each other diplomatically. If it had occurred, some of the most humiliating and bloody pages in U.S. (and Chinese) history could have been prevented. But neither side moved. Mao bitterly mistrusted the country that had backed Chiang. Top Communist officials told historian Warren Cohen many years later that the last real chance of working out a deal with the Americans had occurred in 1945. When, however, both President Roosevelt and President Truman decided to stick with Chiang, the chance for friendship disappeared. By 1949, in Cohen's words, Mao was not interested in "reaching out to the United States."[3] The Chinese leader had to consolidate his control over the nation's vast expanse. He also had to get along with his giant next-door neighbor, the Soviet Union.

In Washington, Truman's anticommunism and mistrust of Mao were reinforced by those in Congress who demanded support for Chiang. One hope for friendly relations disappeared in November 1948, when the Chinese arrested and put on public trial the U.S. consul, Angus Ward, for alleged espionage activities. In January 1950, despite Acheson's direct warning, the Communists seized U.S. diplomatic buildings in the capital of Beijing (Peking). And in February 1950 came the great blow: Mao traveled to Moscow and signed an alliance with Stalin. The treaty emerged only after weeks of bitter talks (especially over Stalin's demands for territory that the Chinese considered theirs). But the West was stunned as these two powerful land masses were locked together by a joining of Communist hands.

Not even that historic event, however, proved to be as shocking as

Truman's announcement, in September 1949, that the Soviets had exploded an atomic weapon. U.S. airplanes had picked up radioactive evidence of the explosion in August. U.S. officials spent days planning how to break the news to the country. After all, many experts had predicted that Soviet scientists were not good enough to come up with such a bomb for years. Only a few U.S. scientists, led by Hans Bethe and Frederick Seitz, warned that such a secret could not be kept hidden and that Stalin could have a bomb by 1950. The Soviets were well on their way to building their own bomb, but Soviet scientists admitted in 1993 that U.S. secrets given them by a British spy, Klaus Fuchs (see below, p. 509), helped them develop a bomb two years earlier than they expected.[4] Truman broke the news in a quiet, understated announcement. But the real meanings could not be quieted: Americans and their allies were now as open to mass destruction as the Soviets had been. It "changed everything," Acheson later observed. And Truman "realized it ten seconds after it had happened, and within a month he had put the machinery of government into operation to work things out."[5]

NSC-68: WHY AND HOW THE U.S. WILL FIGHT THE COLD WAR

The U.S. response was NSC-68 (National Security Council paper 68). "This is the fundamental paper that still governs" American policy, Acheson said in 1955, and it continued to provide the United States with a plan for fighting the cold war for years to come. Many of its ideas became firmly fixed in the American mind and U.S. policy, even though it was classified top secret until 1975.

The paper was written as a result of Acheson's painful realization, in late 1949, that the cold war had entered a new stage. Fresh tactics had to be found to fight the Soviets. And fresh ideas had to be found as well to mobilize Americans so that they would wage—and pay for— that fight. Since 1947, Truman had enjoyed good relations (so-called "bipartisanship") with Congress in foreign policy. "Politics," the happy phrase went, "stopped at the water's edge." But Truman's smashing victory in 1948, Republican mistrust and dislike of Acheson, and the loss of China had made bipartisanship a dirty word to many Republicans. Acheson even had problems within his own inner circle. George Kennan wrote an anguished private letter asking that the secretary of state not allow the nation to respond to the Soviet explosion with a massive arms race, one that might include the building of a new,

Artist David Levine catches the jaunty, combative Harry Truman, complete with sharp teeth and boxing gloves. This is the Truman who was ready to tell the Russians "to go to hell" in 1945, who became the "Give-'em-Hell Harry" in the 1948 presidential campaign, and who surprised the world with his aggressive reaction in Korea throughout 1950.

incredibly destructive "super" hydrogen bomb. Kennan, the director of the State Department's Policy Planning Staff, asked instead for a full review of U.S. policy to search for other alternatives. For some time, Acheson had been worried that Kennan was losing his appetite for standing up to the Soviets. Kennan seemed to prefer negotiations, patient talks, and turning away from an arms race. Acheson preferred "positions of strength." Kennan resigned. Acheson named Paul Nitze, a veteran hard-liner, to replace Kennan and supervise the writing of NSC-68. There was to be a fundamental review of U.S. policy, but its conclusions would be quite different from those reached by Kennan.

The final draft, which Truman initialed in April 1950, began with a series of assumptions. If you accepted these assumptions, you had little choice but to accept the policy recommendations that followed. First, NSC-68 assumed that with the destruction of German and Japanese power, and the decline of Great Britain and France, world power was being contested for only by the United States and the Soviet Union. Second, the Soviets' top priority was establishing "absolute power" over their homeland and eastern Europe, but they were being driven by communism, "a new fanatic faith" that "seeks to impose its absolute authority over the rest of the world." Third, "conflict" between the two superpowers was thus "endemic." With growing numbers of "terrifying weapons of mass destruction, every individual faces the ever-present possibility of annihilation." Fourth, the "inescapably militant" dictatorship could nevertheless be checked. Because the Soviets depended on military power to carry out their "fundamental design" in the world, they could be stopped, in turn, by U.S. military power. Finally, if this military pressure worked, there was hope, because the Kremlin's weakest link was its "relations with the Soviet people." The mass of those people supported the Kremlin leaders only out of fear. Once the United States showed that it could contain and drive back Communist power, it would also "foster the seeds of destruction within the Soviet system." NSC-68 thus aimed not just at containing the Soviet system, but destroying it.

The paper then discussed tactics. It briefly considered several options (a U.S. retreat to the Western Hemisphere or, at the other extreme, the quick launching of war on the Soviet Union) and rejected them in favor of a rapid, massive military build-up. Most importantly, Americans had to create a large and expensive conventional force of troops and weapons so that they could stop a Soviet invasion in a limited war instead of having to fight a nuclear war of "annihiliation." As part of this effort, vast alliance systems were to be established. Moreover, not only were more "atomic weapons . . . necessary," but a new "thermonuclear" bomb of much greater explosive power had to be built—especially to "bring increased pressure on the U.S.S.R." Such a plan required huge sums of money, but Acheson and Nitze believed that Americans could increase their military spending by four times (from $13 billion to about $50 billion). Massive spending, unheard of in peacetime, could actually help the U.S. economy, they argued, because that economy was slowing and might face a depression unless it was spurred on by much larger military budgets. As historian Melvyn Leffler concludes, "What was new about NSC-68 was that Nitze simply called for more, more, and more money . . . to achieve the goals already set out. He envisioned higher taxes, and he thought that domestic social and welfare programs might have to be curtailed."[6]

Until this vast rearming occurred, no diplomatic talks with Stalin could be useful. He only understood power. However, if the Soviets were so militant that the United States had to conduct a long build-up before negotiating, there might not be any talks for years or decades. There was also the danger that such a build-up to fight a militarized cold war could undermine the U.S. constitutional system. Conservative journalist Walter Lippmann had made such an argument two years earlier (see p. 484). But that danger did not bother Nitze and Acheson. To the contrary, NSC-68 declared that anything goes: "The integrity of our system will not be jeopardized by any measures, covert or overt, violent or nonviolent, which serve the purposes of frustrating the Kremlin design." That optimism was to be severely tested.

In secret discussions, some U.S. officials strongly attacked these policies. Secretary of Defense Louis Johnson, for example, questioned whether the nation could (or should) spend such money to fight a global conflict. Thus, it was Acheson's State Department, not the military, that led the drive in 1949–1950 to militarize U.S. foreign policy. Even within the State Department, however, George Kennan and Charles Bohlen attacked NSC-68. These two top experts on the Soviets not only felt that Stalin had little intention of conquering the world, but had no capability of doing so. Stalin had far too many problems at home and in eastern Europe. Kennan especially feared that the militarization of U.S. foreign policy would destroy possible diplomatic solutions and, instead, lock the world into a horror-filled, decades-long cold war. Acheson overruled these and other objections. He obtained Truman's assent to the document in April 1950, but Truman wanted to know the exact cost of NSC-68 before he gave final approval.

THE DECISION TO BUILD THE "SUPER": ATOMIC POLICY (1945–1952)

In January 1950, however, Truman had already accepted one key conclusion of the paper. A thermonuclear, or hydrogen, bomb had to be built. He made the decision after long, intense wrangling among his advisers, but he believed that he had no other option. Because the Soviets might build one, the United States had to build one first.

Since 1945, moreover, U.S. military plans had assumed that such weapons would be used to resist any Soviet aggression. Of course, some embarrassing problems appeared in these early years. Secret U.S. war plans of 1946–1947 assumed that in a war, the United States would win by destroying seventeen key Soviet cities with atomic bombs. The problem was that the U.S. Air Force had no more than a dozen bombs. Moreover, these were disassembled weapons that were stored in New Mexico and that required nearly forty men over two weeks to put together. As late as mid-1947, Truman and his closest advisers did not know officially how many such weapons they had.[7]

These weird policies began to change with the Berlin crisis of 1948. Truman then had to think seriously about responding with atomic bombs. Tests earlier that year, moreover, had produced a technological breakthrough that allowed cheaper construction of more—and more efficient—bombs. The president also locked himself into dependence on the weapons when he insisted that the military budget be tightly controlled. Running for election in 1948, he wanted to give voters a balanced budget. But the decision forced him to move away from more expensive conventional forces and rely on the bomb. Late in 1948, the administration finally prepared a top-secret paper on the use of such weapons. In the event of war, the paper concluded, the bombs must be ready for quick deployment, and only the president should decide when and where to use them. Congress and the American people might consider this "annihilation without representation," but no alternative existed. In 1949 Truman told his advisers, "Since we can't obtain international control we must be strongest in atomic weapons."[8]

He thus ordered more atomic bombs to be built. Experts, however, concluded that in the foreseeable future the president would never have enough to bomb the Soviets into submission. At this point, scientists, led by Edward Teller, tried to convince Truman that an even more destructive weapon could be built. The atomic bomb worked on the principle of fission, in which a nuclear explosion is created by splitting atoms. The new bomb was to work on the principle of fusion, in which a fission explosion served only as the trigger to force light atoms to fuse together to form heavier atoms and thus set off a thermonuclear blast, which resembles the process that creates heat from the sun. Energy in atomic bombs was measured in kilotons, or a force equal to thousands of tons of TNT. But the energy in the superbomb was to be measured in megatons, or millions of tons of TNT.

Teller quickly met strong opposition from scientists led by J. Robert Oppenheimer, who had directed the U.S. effort to build the atomic bomb in 1942–1945. The opponents did not believe such a superbomb could be built. Even if it could be constructed, they argued, it would lead to an endless arms race. Scientific advice was so united in opposing the "super" that, as scientist Hans Bethe recalls, "we were really shocked when President Truman decided in favor of a crash program."[9] Teller's determination, Truman's growing dependence on such weapons, and the arguments appearing in the NSC-68 drafts shaped the president's January 1950 decision. The opponents next begged Truman in 1952 not to test the new weapon. They argued that since testing was necessary to produce a usable bomb, if neither the Americans nor the Soviets tested, an all-out arms race could be stopped. Nevertheless, the United States tested the "super" in 1952. The Soviets set theirs off a year later. And within twenty-five years, at least five more countries had tested such a weapon.

McCarthy, Acheson, and the Call to Action

As NSC-68 and the hydrogen bomb were being born, Acheson decided to deliver a series of speeches in early 1950 to warn Americans of the new dangers—indeed, to scare them into supporting new, more active policies. Too long, he noted later in the 1950s, U.S. officials were merely "trying to guess where each play [of the Soviets] would come through the line." But "no team can win a pennant this way. No team can win a pennant unless the hometown rooters give it every possible financial and moral support."[10]

But Acheson suddenly discovered "the hometown rooters" giving cheers he disliked. In January 1950, headlines announced that Alger Hiss had been convicted of perjury. Hiss was a symbol of the "Eastern Establishment"—an elegant, Ivy League–educated State Department official who had been with Roosevelt at Yalta in 1945. Journalist Whittaker Chambers claimed that in the 1930s Hiss had been a fellow Communist party member who passed secret government documents to him. Hiss denied it, but a young California Republican congressman, Richard Nixon, pursued him until documents hidden in a hollowed-out pumpkin on Chambers's farm convinced a jury that Hiss had lied when he denied that he had been a Communist. Nixon, overnight a national hero, declared that a "conspiracy" existed to keep Americans from "knowing the facts."[11] He hinted that communism had scored recent successes because of traitors within the U.S. government. Acheson, who barely knew Hiss, nevertheless loyally declared out of friendship for Hiss's family that "I do not intend to turn my back on Alger Hiss" and was promptly damned by congressional and newspaper critics. That same month (January 1950), a spy ring was discovered. It included Klaus Fuchs, a British scientist who had helped develop the atomic bomb and who had passed secrets to Soviet agents. (Fuchs was arrested in England, sentenced to a fourteen-year prison term, and died in East Germany in 1988.)

That same month, a virtually unknown Republican senator from Wisconsin, Joseph McCarthy, searched anxiously for an issue to win re-election in 1952. After discarding several possibilities, he seized on the issue in the headlines. At Wheeling, West Virginia, McCarthy charged that 205 Communists had infested the State Department. He had no evidence and, when pushed for proof, quickly changed the numbers to 81, 57, and, finally, "a lot." A Senate investigation con-

*Joseph McCarthy (1908–1957), the junior senator from Wisconsin (1946–1957),
gave his name to an era ("McCarthyism") by conducting a search for Communists within the U.S. government that uncovered no security risks, but nearly
destroyed the spirit of the Foreign Service, especially among experts on Asia.
The senator succeeded in driving out the critics of U.S.–Far Eastern policies—
including those officials who wanted to work more closely with Communist
China in order to split it from the Soviets. As this photo shows, McCarthy often
used charts and documents to bolster his arguments. But on close examination,
the visual aids usually proved far less than he claimed.*

cluded that McCarthy's accusations were empty, but a phenomenon
had been launched. "McCarthyism" became a name for the 1950–
1955 era. The term meant a ruthless search for Communists, a search
usually conducted without evidence but publicly and in a manner that
destroyed the reputations of its targets. Those targets ranged from government officials to college teachers to Hollywood actors and script
writers. Highly partisan (he dubbed the Democrats the "Commicrat
Party"), McCarthy actually had little interest in policy, only in headlines. As journalist Richard Rovere observes, "He was an essentially
destructive force, a revolutionist without any revolutionary vision." In
waging his fight, McCarthy used what Rovere calls the "multiple lie"—
that is, lies of so many parts and made so rapidly that no one could
keep track of the charges.[12]

The time was perfect for McCarthy's tactics in early 1950. Even
Acheson was traveling around the country to warn the populace about
communism. After the secretary of state spoke at a U.S. governors'

conference, one listener reported that Acheson "scared the hell out of us" as he discussed the international scene. McCarthy, however, saw Communists within the government, while Acheson feared them outside the country. Even then, however, Acheson tried to educate Americans about both the reality of the danger and the limits of U.S. power. In a soon-to-be-famous speech at the National Press Club in January 1950, the secretary of state stressed two points. First, he declared that the United States intended to defend Japan. The U.S. "defensive perimeter runs along the Aleutians to Japan," he said, and then "to the Philippine Islands." Beyond that "perimeter" (for example, in Korea), Americans could make no guarantees, although they would work "under the Charter of the United Nations" to help resist any other "armed attack." Second, Acheson urged that faith be placed in Asian nationalism, not communism. He believed that nationalism would someday turn China against the Soviet Union. He noted the historic territorial disputes between those two giants, then stated: "We must not deflect from the Russians to ourselves the righteous anger, and the wrath, and the hatred of the Chinese people which must develop."[13] On the other hand, Acheson had no intention of recognizing Mao's regime in the near future.

To Acheson's mind, the central problem was Soviet power. He made many speeches during the spring of 1950, he told a friend, to convince Americans that they were involved in "a cold war" that "is in fact a real war and that the Soviet Union has one purpose and that is world domination."[14] Public-opinion polls showed that Americans were responding slightly, but neither they nor their president were ready to spend additional billions of dollars as the secret NSC-68 paper demanded. The spy trials and economic problems at home reduced Truman's personal popularity dramatically. Affairs looked bleak to Acheson by June 24, 1950.

KOREA: THE UNEXPECTED WAR

That all changed during the next forty-eight hours. Late on June 24, Acheson received the message that North Korean troops had moved in force across the thirty-eighth parallel that separated Communist North Korea and U.S.-supported South Korea. By late June 25, Truman had committed the United States to stopping the invasion. A three-year war began, a war that took 33,000 American lives, twice that number of South Korean lives, and between 1 million and 2 million North Korean and Chinese lives. The bloodshed opened a new page in the cold war. "I think we can sum it up this way," Acheson observed in 1953, "that Korea moved a great many things from the realm of theory and brought them right into . . . the realm of urgency." The war "confirmed in our minds the correctness of the analysis of NSC 68." In addition, the war meant that "the USSR was willing to use forces in battle to achieve objectives."[15] Suddenly, a worldwide military confrontation with the Soviet Union loomed.

U.S. officials were stunned that the showdown seemed to start in Korea, of all places. In 1905, the rising Japanese Empire had seized that country because, as the saying went, Korea formed "a dagger pointed at the heart of Japan." At the Tehran Conference of 1943, the Big Three promised to create a united and free Korea after the war. In truth, however, U.S. Army officers (including a future secretary of state, Dean Rusk), concluded in 1944–1945 that to avoid conflict between U.S. and Soviet armies of occupation, the thirty-eighth parallel should serve as a temporary dividing line. During the next five years that line became the permanent boundary between the two Koreas.

From the moment of Japan's surrender in 1945, both Koreas were seething, anxious problems for U.S. officials. Left-wing groups, intent on creating a mass-based, independent government, started uprisings against the U.S. occupation in late 1945. Right-wing groups armed in opposition, usually with the help of American authorities. A virtual civil war raged, a war so intense that by 1950 it had claimed about 100,000 lives. But amid the fighting, two governments emerged. In the north, the Soviets helped establish Kim Il Sung's Communist regime and, in 1948, began to withdraw their troops. In the south, the United States demanded reunification through nationwide elections supervised by the United Nations. Kim and the Soviets would have none of that, so elections in the south during 1948 produced a right-wing regime led by Syngman Rhee. Since 1919, Rhee had been a leader in the Korean independence movement. By 1948, however, U.S. officials had grown to mistrust his corruption and dependence on Washington's support. The Americans, however, could find no better alternative.[16]

They could, nevertheless, reduce their relations with Rhee. Truman's military advisers told him in 1948–1949 that Korea "is of little strategic value to the United States and that commitment to United States use of military force in Korea would be ill-advised."[17] As Soviet and U.S. troops left in 1949, even General MacArthur believed that the defense of South Korea was beyond U.S. capability. Secretary of State Acheson repeated that belief in his Press Club speech of January

1950 but did so (as noted above) with careful reservations. The Soviets continued to train and supply North Korea's army. The United States did the same for Rhee's troops, but at a much slower pace.

Kim Il Sung, watching his own military build-up while Rhee suffered ever-larger political problems in the south, concluded that the moment was ripe for a strike. The North Korean Communist believed his armies could move so rapidly that U.S. forces could not arrive in time to save Rhee. Kim traveled to Moscow twice and finally persuaded Stalin to approve the attack. Documents released in Moscow more than forty years later, however, showed that Stalin was most reluctant to go along with Kim. The Korean War, contrary to Truman's and Acheson's (and most Americans') belief, was not triggered by a militarily aggressive Stalin who commanded a monolithic Communist Empire. Instead, the Communist bloc was already fragmented, and Stalin had begun to worry deeply about the challenge that Mao's China posed to Soviet interests. The Soviet dictator feared that if he did not go along with Kim's ambitious plans, the North Korean would turn to Mao for help, and the Soviets would lose the little leverage they had on the Koreans. Stalin also feared, with good reason, that Truman was pulling Japan into a U.S. military alliance that could threaten the eastern Soviet Union. A Communist Korea could help neutralize that threat. Stalin therefore went along with Kim, but with no enthusiasm—and carefully protected himself by telling Kim the Koreans were on their own. If they ran into trouble, Stalin was not going to bail them out.[18]

Truman was tending to family business in Missouri when the invasion began. On his plane ride back to Washington, the president determined to reverse years of U.S. policy in Korea. He would stand and fight. Acheson and most (but not all) of his top aides agreed for several reasons. First, as Truman declared publicly, the invasion "makes it plain beyond all doubt that communism has passed beyond the use of subversion to conquer independent nations and will now use armed invasion and war." Force had to be met with force. Second, not just Korea, but U.S. interests everywhere seemed to be at stake. For if Stalin and Kim won in Korea, Truman believed, the Soviets would next hit more pivotal U.S. interests, especially those in Japan and western Europe. The president reached these conclusions largely through his use (once again) of history. He and his top advisers believed that Soviet policy resembled Japan's attempt to take China piece by piece in the 1930s or Hitler's similar attempt to conquer Europe. If Stalin was "appeased," as Japan had been in 1931 and Hitler had been in 1936–1938, world peace would be threatened.[19]

Truman realized that the inexperienced 95,000-man South Korean force alone could not drive back the 135,000-man North Korean army. The president also felt that the entire world's security was at risk. He asked the United Nations to support his policies. On June 25, the Security Council passed a U.S. resolution condemning the invasion and calling for a cease-fire and the withdrawal of North Korea's armies to the thirty-eighth parallel. The resolution passed only because the Soviets had earlier walked out of the Security Council to protest the exclusion of Communist China from the UN. The speed of Truman's response had taken Stalin by surprise. Forty-eight hours later, the South Koreans were in headlong retreat while suffering 50 percent casualties in the early fighting. On June 27, the Security Council passed a new U.S.-written resolution that asked members to help South Korea "repel the armed attack and to restore international peace and security in the area."[20]

Truman had already ordered U.S. naval and air power into action. The president also appointed MacArthur to be the U.S. commander of the operations. The general then took control of the entire UN effort, although he always received his orders from Washington, not the United Nations. Nevertheless, the North Koreans rolled on. Truman finally ordered U.S. combat troops into action on June 30. They and the South Koreans, supported by unchallenged U.S. air and naval units, held on grimly to a small area (the Pusan Perimeter) and then, in July and August, actually began to move to the offensive. Meanwhile, Stalin, surprised by Truman's sharp response, showed how little stomach he had for the war by ordering Soviet ships, bound for North Korea with supplies, to turn around and come back home before they might encounter U.S. ships.

THE BIG TURN OF 1949–1950:
PRESIDENTIAL POWER AND THE UN

The events of 1949–1950 that included the Korean invasion transformed U.S. foreign policy. Presidential power, the United Nations, West Germany, Japan, even Vietnam—all were profoundly affected.

Truman vastly increased presidential power by sending U.S. troops to fight in Korea without following the Constitution's requirement that Congress declare war. Following Acheson's advice, the president justified his action by referring to his commander-in-chief powers (that is, his constitutional authority as the commander of U.S. military forces).

He also used the United Nations resolutions as justification for sending U.S. troops. Other presidents had used their commander-in-chief authority to deploy forces without consulting Congress, but none had involved Americans in such a long-term, costly war simply on the basis of this authority.

Truman and Acheson decided not to ask Congress to declare war because, they feared, such a declaration could easily lead to an all-out effort resembling World War II. They, instead, hoped to keep the conflict limited and short. The president accepted a reporter's suggestion that it was only a "police action," not a war. Truman also said that U.S. force merely had to defeat "a bandit raid." His confidence grew in early July 1950, when the Soviets defined the struggle as a civil war between the two Koreas. The great powers, Moscow urged, should stay out of it. Clearly, Stalin had no intention of becoming directly involved. But that raised a greater danger in Truman's mind: Korea was perhaps a trap to draw in U.S. forces while the Soviets struck in the most vital areas of Europe or the Middle East. "We are fighting the second team," Acheson warned, "whereas the real enemy is the Soviet Union."[21] Thus, he and the president wanted no congressional declaration of war on North Korea because the real war might soon erupt elsewhere. In that case, Truman told a reporter privately, the United States would abandon Korea because he wanted any showdown to come in western Europe, "where we can use the bomb."[22]

Meanwhile, Congress, at Truman's request, created ever-larger power for the president's use. During the summer of 1950, U.S. ground forces rose from 630,000 to 1 million. A volunteer army disappeared, and a military draft began to call up eighteen-year-olds. Congress did all this with remarkably little complaint. Only the Republican Senate leader, Robert Taft of Ohio, repeatedly declared that if Truman got away with sending troops to Korea without Congress's approval, the president "could send troops to Tibet . . . or to Indo-China or anywhere else in the world, without the slightest voice of Congress in the matter."[23] Until the war began to go bad in late 1950, however, most of Congress did not want to challenge the president's powers.

Taft also blasted Truman's use of the UN resolutions as a justification for sending Americans to faraway Korea. But the president and Acheson moved to increase the UN's authority. They knew that when the next crisis arose, the Soviets would probably be back in the Security Council to veto any attempt to stop a Communist invasion. The United States, therefore, proposed that if, in the future, the Security Council could not act, the General Assembly (where no veto power existed)

As the U.S. delegate to the United Nations General Assembly, Eleanor Roosevelt was world famous for her support of human rights and especially the rights of minorities everywhere in the world. Between 1950 and 1952, an alternate U.S. delegate was Judge Edith S. Sampson (1901–1979), shown at right with Mrs. Roosevelt. Judge Sampson was the first African-American woman elected to the Illinois court system. In the late 1940s and 1950s, as the cold war intensified, she was president of the "World Town Hall Seminar," which educated Americans about foreign-policy issues. She also traveled around the world (often at her own expense) to tell other peoples about the situation of African Americans and to answer the anti-American propaganda of Moscow radio.

could pass resolutions asking UN members to take collective action, including the use of force. This "Uniting for Peace" resolution passed in October 1950. It changed the UN. In the future, the organization could be mobilized by the United States regardless of the Soviet veto— if, that is, U.S. officials controlled a majority of the vote. They did enjoy such support in 1950. But what might occur if that majority turned neutral or even favored the Soviet case, the Americans apparently did not worry enough about in 1950.[24]

The world organization continued to be popular among Americans despite the Soviet veto. Much of this popularity was due to the work of Eleanor Roosevelt. During the 1930s and World War II, she had emerged first as a strong voice for the New Deal at home and then for cooperation abroad. After her husband's death in April 1945, Truman appointed Mrs. Roosevelt to the U.S. delegation to the United Nations. Her lectures, newspaper columns, and especially her work in drafting the UN's Declaration of Human Rights made Mrs. Roosevelt a major foreign-policy figure. She condemned the Truman Doctrine and other U.S. military acts that she believed undercut the UN's mission.[25] Rather than arguing with her (a dangerous venture for any Democratic politician), Truman used her popularity and the UN authority—but selectively, and when it was in his interest to do so.

THE BIG TURN OF 1949–1950: REMARRYING CHIANG ON TAIWAN

Truman built on decades of precedent when he multiplied his presidential powers. When making another crucial decision in June 1950, however, he broke sharply with the past. The decision involved Formosa (or Taiwan, as the Chinese preferred to call it), the large island off the China coast that Japan had controlled between 1905 and 1945. When the Korean War erupted, it was a last refuge for Chiang Kai-shek's failed forces. Some congressmen demanded that Truman protect Chiang. But the president was sick of the KMT leader; he agreed with Republican senator Arthur Vandenberg from Michigan, who said in August 1949 that sending aid to Chiang was "like sticking your finger in the lake and looking for the hole."[26] A group of U.S. military officers, led by MacArthur, also hoped to save the Nationalists. But when a senator asked in closed-door hearings whether Acheson thought it "inevitable" that the Communists would seize Taiwan, the secretary of state replied, "My own judgment is that it is."[27]

On January 5, 1950, Truman told a press conference that the United States did not want "Formosa or . . . any other Chinese territory," nor did he have any plans "at this time" to set up military bases on Taiwan. U.S. military and economic aid would not be sent to Chiang. The Korean War completely changed U.S. policy. On June 27, Truman announced that the United States opposed any Communist attempt to occupy Taiwan. He ordered the U.S. Seventh Fleet to seal off Formosa from Mao's troops. The new turn was forced by the Pentagon, which argued that the region around Taiwan formed a vital strategic area for the protection of U.S. forces in Korea. Acheson agreed for different reasons: he believed that communism must not be rewarded with new conquests, feared that if he opposed the decision he would be outgunned by the military, and understood that congressional "China-Firsters" were ready to attack him. By the end of 1950, U.S. military missions worked with Chiang's troops, and economic aid reopened.[28]

American allies, led by Great Britain, harshly criticized the new U.S.

commitment. They believed Chiang to be a lost cause and recalled the 1943 Cairo Declaration, signed by President Roosevelt, that recognized Taiwan as part of China. Acheson responded that Roosevelt never meant *this* China.

THE BIG TURN OF 1949–1950: JAPAN

With China's conquest by communism, the recently defeated Japanese became the key to U.S. policy in Asia. Acheson termed Japan "the workshop of Asia." By 1949–1950, U.S. policy makers saw it as the "stabilizer" of Asia. Historian Michael Schaller notes that Japan was to be the centerpiece of a "Great Crescent" of vital U.S. interests that stretched from the Alaskan boundary far along the vast Pacific rim to southern Asia.[29]

To make Japan the centerpiece of their policies, however, U.S. officials had to solve several problems. The first was a severe dollar shortage that threatened to paralyze the Japanese economy. The Korean War temporarily solved the problem by pouring billions of dollars into Japan, which served as the main base for UN forces. The nation's economy took off. Few booms in history match the Japanese economic expansion of 1950–1951.

Another problem was how to give Japan its independence but keep U.S. military bases on both the home islands and Okinawa, the strategic Japanese-populated island in the western Pacific. In early 1950, Acheson asked John Foster Dulles to find a solution to this dilemma. A leading Republican, Dulles helped restore some of the bipartisan spirit in Washington. An experienced diplomat and a famed international lawyer, Dulles had the necessary background. In early 1951, he solved the problem by convincing the government of Shigeru Yoshida—a shrewd and daring prime minister who was the key founding father of postwar Japan—to make a deal. The Japanese could have full independence if, in return, they agreed to create a small "self-defense" army and sign a ten-year treaty (that could be renewed) guaranteeing U.S. bases in Japan and Okinawa. Dulles pulled off the deal, moreover, while excluding the Soviets from any involvement.

Finally, when Yoshida indicated that he was thinking of opening trade relations with Japan's old economic partner, China, Dulles quickly stopped it. Any arrangement between Japan and the Communists could upset U.S. plans and anger Congress. In the so-called Yoshida Letter, the Japanese government indicated that it would work with Chiang and not with Mao. Yoshida signed the letter despite his belief that geography and economic need would soon force Japan and China to work together. As historian Howard Schonberger concludes, the deal brought Japan into "the American-sponsored economic and political blockade" of China but frustrated and angered the Japanese.[30]

In completing the peace treaty, Dulles encountered strong opposition from Australia and New Zealand, who, with fresh memories of Japanese invaders half a dozen years before, feared a revived Japan. The United States responded by creating the ANZUS (Australia, New Zealand, and the United States) Treaty in 1951. It provided for collective security in the region. The pact clearly signaled that Americans had replaced the British as the protector of Australia and New Zealand, both of whom were members of the British Commonwealth.

In all, Dulles and Acheson pulled off a most successful work of diplomacy. Ronald Pruessen, as Dulles's major biographer, writes that the Japanese peace treaty "is justifiably seen as a major landmark in the diplomatic history of the post–World War II era" and that Dulles was a "supervisor" of the pact's construction.[31] One more foundation stone was now required to complete the structure in the Pacific. It turned out to be one of the costliest pieces of work in U.S. history.

THE BIG TURN OF 1949–1950:
INDOCHINA AND SOUTHEAST ASIA

Long before the Korean War, U.S. officials concluded that if Japan were to recover, it needed Southeast Asia's markets and raw materials (including rich stores of tin, oil, natural rubber, and rice). Between 1931 and 1945, the Japanese had, indeed, tried to conquer that region. Now, as Dulles and others in Washington believed, if Southeast Asia were not open to their enterprise, the Japanese would turn to Communist China or would have to dump their goods on the U.S. market. But (as usual) there were problems. Much of Southeast Asia was underdeveloped and needed economic aid. In his so-called Point Four proposal of 1949, Truman suggested a "bold new program" to make U.S. science and technology available for such "underdeveloped areas" as Southeast Asia. However, Congress's reluctance to spend money, coupled with the Korean War's expenses, stunted Point Four's good idea from the start.

Most importantly, the region was in political turmoil. European colonial powers had controlled much of the area since the nineteenth century. Japan's occupation profoundly shook the colonial hold and encouraged nationalisms to emerge. In such nations as Malaya, Indochina, and Indonesia, that nationalism was often headed by leftists whom Americans feared. In Indonesia (Southeast Asia's largest country)—or the Dutch East Indies, as it had long been known—nationalists moved to overthrow the shell of Dutch colonialism. The United States mostly stood aside until 1947–1949, when it became clear that the Dutch could not maintain control and—of special importance—that further warfare could alienate the rising nationalists from the West's interests in the cold war. The United States then got tough. In historian Robert McMahon's words, Washington's pressure, "more than any other factor . . . compelled the Dutch to make key concessions."[32] The new sovereign nation of Indonesia appeared in 1949.

The story was less happy in Indochina. France's colonial hold on Vietnam, Laos, and Cambodia slipped under military blows struck by nationalists led by Ho Chi Minh. Because of those setbacks and U.S. pressure, the French promised autonomy to that country in early 1949, but the promise was empty because foreign policy and defense were to remain under France's control. Ho fought on. Paris officials then brought in an Indochinese, Bao Dai, to put a native face on the French-controlled government. But Bao Dai, who notably liked to spend his time on the French Riviera, could not compete with Ho's popularity and growing power.

The United States generally backed France despite at least eight requests from Ho to Washington for support of Vietnam's independence. None of these requests was answered. U.S. intelligence reported in late 1948 that Ho was not anti-American and that little evidence existed that he was under Moscow's control. That view changed, however, as China became Communist and Acheson became secretary of state. Ho must be an "outright Commie," Acheson cabled U.S. diplomats in Indochina in May 1949. The "question whether Ho [is] as much nationalist as Commie is irrelevant. All Stalinists in colonial areas are nationalists."[33] Acheson, moreover, needed France's help for his plans to build NATO and a revived West Germany. To obtain that help, the secretary of state actively supported the French war against Ho. U.S. involvement deepened in late 1949, when Acheson concluded that the victorious Chinese Communists might turn south in search of new lands to conquer.[34]

Japan's need for Southeast Asia sealed the U.S. commitment to France.[35] On March 10, 1950 (more than three months before the Korean War began), Truman sent the first major U.S. military aid to Indochina. Acheson knew that a chance was being taken, but he believed it necessary. The Korean outbreak led Truman to send much more help to the French. Ho was, after all, "a Moscow-trained Communist," and he already controlled in various degrees "more than two-thirds" of Vietnam. "Unavoidably, the United States is, together with France, committed in Indochina."[36] Or so the top U.S. policymakers believed.

Acheson saw no other way out. The situation was bad, but the stakes were great. As a joint State Department–Defense Department mission reported to him in December 1950: "America without Asia will have been reduced to the Western Hemisphere and a precarious foothold on the western fringe of the Eurasian continent. Success will vindicate [and] give added meaning to America and the American way of life."[37]

THE BIG TURN OF 1949–1950: REARMING WEST GERMANY

But Acheson also determined to hold and expand that "precarious foothold" on the "western fringe" of Eurasia. The new NATO military alliance was of little help. In early 1950, its badly equipped 12 divisions faced 27 ready Soviet divisions. Even before the Korean conflict, Acheson hinted to the new West German government that West Germany might have to rearm because only its people could provide the troops NATO needed. But Acheson could do little more. Although the Pentagon wanted West Germany to rearm, Acheson's State Department was badly split. Some officials feared the French, not to mention the Soviet, reaction if West Germans again held arms.

War in Korea forced a decision. If Communists used force in Asia, Acheson reasoned, they might well use it in central Europe. Moreover, the western Europeans were frightened of a possible Soviet move and they had to be reassured. Most importantly, however, the time was ripe to flesh out NATO. At a meeting with the French and British foreign ministers at the Waldorf-Astoria Hotel in New York City during September 1950, Acheson suddenly proposed West German rearmament. He urged that it be controlled, however, by placing the Germans within an integrated European army. No separate national German force would be created.

The stunned French foreign minister, Robert Schuman, had a habit of talking slowly (so slowly, one observer noted, that his voice sounded like a motor running out of gas). But on this occasion, Schuman rapidly made it clear that France wanted to kill the U.S. plan. Acheson, in turn, made it equally clear that West Germany would be rearmed. If the French did not wish to help set the controls on Germany, the Americans would go ahead on their own. In October 1950, the cornered French proposed the Pleven Plan: all forces, including West German, were to be integrated into the smallest possible unit of a European army, and the force was to be almost entirely controlled by Europeans (not by Americans, whom Paris officials suspected were dangerously pro-German). Thus, the argument took shape. It was to last four more years, but the West Germans were finally rearmed.[38]

Meanwhile, Truman acted alone to beef up NATO. In late 1950, he announced "substantial increases" in U.S. troop strength in Europe. Republicans, led by Senator Taft, exploded. They argued that the war was in Asia, not Europe, and that Truman was using Korea as an excuse to lock the United States into a declining Europe. They also condemned him for abusing his commander-in-chief powers again and ignoring Congress's wishes. A compromise was soon worked out: only four U.S. divisions were to be sent; Truman named General Dwight D. Eisenhower, hero of both Republicans and Democrats, to be NATO's supreme commander; and the president indicated that he would not again send troops without consulting Congress. He also agreed with Congress's and the Pentagon's wish that Greece and Turkey be brought into NATO, and that closer ties be established with Spain. Truman did not like the last part. He despised Spain's dictator, General Francisco Franco, who had cooperated with Hitler during the war. But containing the Soviets did demand a price, so as Truman swallowed hard, U.S.-Spanish relations grew warmer.

As for West Germany, its aged chancellor, Konrad Adenauer, especially profited from the U.S. proposals. Adenauer cleverly denied wanting his nation armed so soon after World War II. In truth, he was like a boy wanting to be coaxed to eat ice cream. As the top U.S. official in West Germany, John McCloy, pushed Adenauer to accept rearmament. Adenauer, in turn, demanded more independence, a navy, a German general staff, and equal rights in any European force. In one agreement alone, McCloy made 122 concessions to obtain the German leader's cooperation. The joke soon circulated that "Adenauer is the real McCloy."[39] In Paris, however, no Frenchman joked about the sharp turn taken by the United States toward Germany.

THE BIG TURN OF 1949–1950:
ROLLBACK AND THE START OF A TWENTY-YEAR
U.S.-CHINA CONFLICT

The new U.S. policies climaxed in late summer 1950, when Truman decided to cross the thirty-eighth parallel (which had separated North and South Korea since 1945), liberate North Korea, and drive to the very borders of China. The American policy of containment was to be replaced by a new idea of rollback. The Communists were to be removed, not merely contained, and Truman intended to roll them back to the borders of the two Communist giants themselves, the Soviet Union and China.

It was a historic gamble, but the odds seemed to favor the president. By mid-July 1950, General MacArthur's UN forces had stopped the North Korean invasion. Washington officials divided over the next step. Dean Rusk, assistant secretary of state for the Far East, and John Foster Dulles wanted to go on and take North Korea. They were joined by military officials from the Pentagon. Paul Nitze and George Kennan warned, however, that crossing the thirty-eighth parallel could anger European allies (who wanted no further Asian involvement) and cause the Chinese or Soviets to react. Truman and Acheson decided to go ahead with the new strategy as long as MacArthur did not meet heavy resistance, especially from Chinese troops.[40]

The president decided that he need not fear a Soviet response. Stalin had carefully distanced himself from the conflict. Nor did the president fear a massive Chinese move into Korea. Mao's troops, after all, had just emerged from a long, bitter civil war, and they had no air force to protect them against U.S. bombing. But Truman did fear attacks from Republicans and other critics at home. Senator Joseph McCarthy was again riding high by late summer. In July, Julius Rosenberg was arrested for passing atomic secrets to the Soviets. (He and his wife, Ethel, were later executed amid bitter dispute over their guilt.) Panic was setting in. When five people wrote "PEACE" on a wall in Brooklyn, a judge sent them to jail because he suspected that they were Communists.[41] By autumn, polls showed that nearly two-thirds of Americans wanted to drive the Communists out of all of Korea. On September 11, 1950, Truman approved instructions giving MacArthur permission to cross the thirty-eighth parallel.

Any doubts about the crossing disappeared four days later when

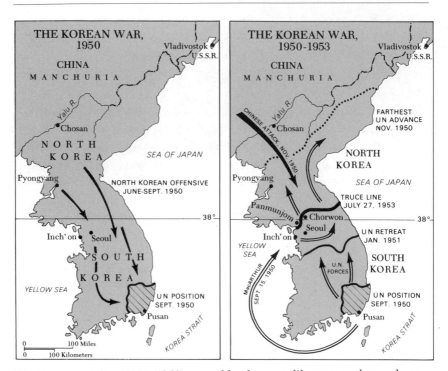

The Korean conflict (1950–1953) was a bloody yo-yo-like war, as the northern Communists nearly expelled the U.S.–South Korean forces and, in November, the UN forces nearly conquered all of North Korea only to have the Chinese human-wave attacks nearly seize all of Korea in early 1951. A two-year stalemate then ensued largely along the original dividing line between North and South Korea—the thirty-eighth parallel.

MacArthur surprised the North Korean force with a brilliant landing at Inch'on. He had cut them off, although main Communist forces slipped through and lived to fight again. The general triumphed despite warnings from Washington that the Inch'on operation was too dangerous and should not be attempted. His top field commander later wrote that MacArthur's reputation became so glorious after Inch'on that if, in another invasion, he had "suggested that one battalion walk on water to reach the port, there might have been someone ready to give it a try."[42] On October 7, the UN passed a U.S.-written resolution permitting MacArthur's army to push into North Korea. Such allies as the British, French, and Canadians had strong reservations, but Acheson overrode them and the allies reluctantly went along.

By mid-October, the UN force rapidly drove toward the Chinese-Korean border. To double-check the risks, Truman flew 6,000 miles to confer with MacArthur on Wake Island. The general assured the president that "we are no longer fearful of [Chinese] intervention." If Mao's troops did enter Korea, U.S. air power ensured that "there would be the greatest slaughter."[43] Throughout August to early October, Chinese officials warned UN forces against marching to the Yalu River that formed the China-Korea border. Truman and Acheson discounted the warnings. As the U.S. First Cavalry Division drove across North Korea, however, the first Chinese troops appeared on October 16. After a ten-day pause in which Mao was probably checking the U.S. reaction, MacArthur's attack continued. On October 26, the Chinese began to move in force. MacArthur marched on and, in defiance of Truman's orders, allowed U.S. and other non-Korean troops to approach China's borders. On November 24, the general announced an "end-the-war offensive." The boys, he declared, were to be home by Christmas.

The Chinese, however, had decided they would pay any price to prevent a permanent U.S. force on their northeast border of Manchuria. Fragmentary documents released by the Chinese in the early 1990s revealed that on October 13, 1950, Mao wrote Prime Minister Zhou Enlai (Chou En-lai): "If we do not send troops, allowing the enemy to press to the Yalu border and the arrogance of reactionaries [that is, Mao's political enemies] at home and abroad to grow, this will be disadvantageous to all sides. Above all it will be most disadvantageous to Manchuria; all of the South Manchurian electricity will be threatened." Mao concluded "we must enter the war" even if Truman ordered the bombing of Chinese cities. Otherwise, as the Chinese leader wrote on October 2, "Korean revolutionary power will suffer a fundamental defeat and the Americans will run more rampant. . . ." Mao's most frightening moment occurred, not because of Truman, however, but because of his supposed friend, Stalin. With a Chinese offensive scheduled for October 15, Stalin, at the last minute, refused to supply the air cover and supplies Mao believed he needed. The Soviets wanted no part of a confrontation with the United States. Perhaps Stalin also figured that if Mao's forces were crushed by MacArthur's, the main challenge to his own control of international communism would also be crushed. Mao quickly reassessed the situation and decided that the offensive nevertheless had to be ordered. It began on October 19, 1950, as 260,000 Chinese troops began to move into Korea.[44]

On November 26, hundreds of thousands of Chinese troops stormed UN positions in waves. Some 20,000 U.S. and South Korean soldiers were trapped at the Chosin Reservoir by 120,000 Chinese as a deadly winter began. The First Marine Division fought its way out over 78 miles of narrow road that was made a living hell by deep ravines, 2,500-foot cliffs, and 30-degrees-below-zero blizzards. A medic tending wounded soldiers dipped his fingers in blood to keep them warm. One company went into battle with 225 men, came out with 7, and lost 4 commanding officers in an hour.[45]

The marines finally got out, bringing their wounded with them, but with heavy losses. Throughout North Korea, Chinese "volunteers" (Mao's government carefully tried to maintain the fiction that its own troops were not directly involved) cut MacArthur's overextended supply lines and smashed UN forces. When the general demanded an air attack on China's home bases and the bridges across the Yalu, Truman allowed only the southern half of the bridges to be bombed. Nothing in China proper was to be attacked. The president feared that such strikes could bring the Sino-Soviet alliance into play and create all-out war between the two superpowers. Moreover, so much air power would be needed to bomb China effectively that U.S. forces in Europe would be denuded and leave that most vital of all regions open to Soviet attack.

The last days of 1950 were among the worst in American history. UN casualties in just two days rose to over 11,000. In a November 30 press conference, Truman mentioned that the use of the atomic bomb in Korea had always been under consideration. A stunned world response led the White House to downplay the remark. Behind the scenes, however, officials were, indeed, seriously debating whether to give China a warning to withdraw or else face the "prompt use of the atomic bomb."[46]

The British prime minister, Clement Attlee, quickly flew to Washington to stop any policy that was to end in an atomic fireball. Attlee was reassured about that possibility, but he failed to persuade Truman and Acheson that a political compromise had to be reached with China. Acheson strongly argued that Chinese military aggression must not be rewarded with political concessions (for example, China's entry into the United Nations). U.S. credibility in Europe, Acheson added, would be badly damaged if U.S. credibility in Korea were not defended. His comments meant that there would be more war. Attlee's remarks meant that the closest U.S. allies doubted the wisdom of Truman's policies. By late December, Chinese and North Korean troops drove back across the thirty-eighth parallel. UN forces finally stabilized the battlefront with a successful spring offensive in 1951, but costly fighting continued for another two years. And for the next twenty years, the United States and China were to be bitter enemies. A century of the open-door policy had somehow climaxed in a generation of hatred.

McCarthy and MacArthur

The Korean War gave new life to McCarthyism. Republicans won major congressional victories in the 1950 elections, and observers noted that key politicians who had opposed McCarthy went down to defeat. Of special interest was Helen Gahagan Douglas's loss to Richard Nixon in a no-holds-barred Senate contest in California. McCarthy's crusade soon spread to other causes. Book burners, for example, tried to ban the story of Robin Hood (which, after all, preached the Communist doctrine of taking from the rich and giving to the poor). Racists seized on McCarthyism to argue, in the words of one Washington state legislator, that "if someone insists there is discrimination against Negroes in this country . . . there is every reason to believe that person is a communist." In lighter moments, when college men began to leap into

President Truman and General MacArthur had little liking for each other (contrary to this picture). But Truman flew thousands of miles to meet with the general at Wake Island in October 1950, only to receive bad information and worse advice from MacArthur about possible Chinese intervention. As Truman privately described the meeting: "We arrived at dawn. Gen. MacArthur was at the airport with his shirt unbuttoned, wearing a greasy ham and eggs cap that evidently had been in use for twenty years. . . . The General assured the President that the victory was won in Korea . . . , and that the Chinese Communists would not attack." (Longhand Notes, 1950, PSF: Long Hand Notes, 1945–1952, Box 333, Harry S. Truman Papers, Harry S. Truman Library, Independence, Missouri.)

women's dormitory rooms to conduct panty raids, one observer declared that this was the only outlet for student energy because McCarthyism had imposed "a vast silence" on students and had made serious work impossible.[47] As McCarthy continued to flay Acheson for "losing" China, Truman defended his secretary of state by responding, "If communism were to prevail," Acheson "would be one of the first, if not the first, to be shot by the enemies of liberty and Christianity."[48] It was not one of the more profound debates in American history.

In this context of McCarthyism and war with China, the president raised a political fire storm by firing General MacArthur. Since mid-1950, the general had publicly disagreed with Truman's policies of fighting a limited war, not bombing China itself, and not allowing Chiang Kai-shek's Nationalist exiles on Taiwan to become involved in the fighting. MacArthur's miscalculations about a possible Chinese invasion shook the president's confidence in his commander.

In March 1951, Truman took steps to open truce talks with North Korea, but MacArthur undercut the president by declaring that North Korean and Chinese armies should surrender before they collapsed. Truman was furious but did little. During early April, Republican leader Joseph W. Martin, congressman from Massachusetts, released a letter from MacArthur. It declared that "we must win. There is no substitute for victory." Truman now had enough. He carefully consulted with his top military officers (the Joint Chiefs), who agreed that MacArthur should be recalled. They concluded he had undercut his civilian commander in chief and, of special importance, was losing the confidence of his own troops in Korea. As MacArthur's replacement, Truman named General Matthew Ridgway, a hero of World War II, the top field commander in Korea, a soldier who was totally loyal to his civilian superiors. As Truman nicely explained privately, "I was sorry to have to reach a parting of the way with the big man in Asia but he asked for it and I had to give it to him."[49]

The American people also "gave it to him" on his return—huge ticker-tape parades, rallies, pro-MacArthur hysteria in cities from San Francisco to Boston. But as is often the case when Americans respond wildly to a supposed hero, they cooled off after listening closely to what he said. In the public "MacArthur hearings" of spring 1951, Americans could listen to a congressional investigation of the war. The general eloquently described the terrible bloodshed that, in his view, demanded total victory. But tough questioning revealed that such a victory was impossible without all-out war with China. Moreover, he wanted power placed in military hands and taken from civilians. MacArthur dis-

A cartoonist critical of Truman's decision to fire MacArthur in April 1951 warns that public opinion will make the president suffer for his act. Note the duck-tailed figure resembling Acheson.

missed any possibility of Soviet intervention despite the Sino-Soviet alliance. He had not been in the United States for more than thirteen years, and his answers indicated that he was out of touch with American feelings.

In rebuttal, Acheson and top U.S. military officials blistered MacArthur's position by emphasizing that a costly all-out war with China had to be avoided. Such a conflict would lose the support of the European allies. The chairman of the Joint Chiefs, General Omar Bradley, condemned MacArthur's desire for total war in Asia as "the wrong war, at the wrong place, at the wrong time, and with the wrong enemy."[50]

On April 19, 1951, in an eloquent speech before a hushed joint session of Congress, MacArthur presented his case for winning. He then recalled an old West Point song that said, "Old soldiers never die, they just fade away." Much to Truman's relief—and MacArthur's surprise—the general did exactly that.

Conclusion: The Big Turn of 1949–1951

The twenty months between the announcement of the Soviet A-bomb explosion in September 1949 and the fading away of MacArthur in June 1951 marked a major turn in American diplomatic history. NSC-68 provided the guidelines for the next generation of U.S. policy. The document urged a quadrupling of defense expenditures. When Truman achieved that goal with a $50 billion figure in 1952, the modern defense budget was born. The nation made its first significant military commitments to both Vietnam and Taiwan. West Germany was put on the road to rearmament. Japan became independent and agreed to allow long-term U.S. military bases on its territory. Power in the United Nations began moving from the Security Council (where the Soviets could use their veto) to the General Assembly. Presidential power soared as Truman, without obtaining a congressional declaration of war, took Americans into a long war on the Asian mainland. Civilian control of the military was reaffirmed in the MacArthur-recall episode.

But Truman and Acheson also suffered telling setbacks. Americans were to pay dearly for extending containment to Vietnam and Taiwan. In the nearer term, Truman's exercise of presidential powers and his dismissal of MacArthur triggered a political reaction that made it impossible for him to seek re-election in 1952. The war, moreover, had unleashed McCarthyism. Hollywood films recorded the turn. The pro-Soviet *Song of Russia* of World War II was replaced by *The Red Menace* (1949) and *I Was a Communist for the FBI* (1951), in which Communists usually appeared slovenly, overly fat, or effeminate—but always dangerous.[51] On the Senate floor, McCarthy unleashed vicious attacks on Acheson and Marshall. In one speech, the senator made up the story of a wounded Korean veteran, "Bob Smith, from Middleburg, Pa.," who had been trapped at the Chosin Reservoir:

> His hands and his feet are still in the hills on this side of the Yalu—a tribute to the traitorous Red Communist clique in our State Department, who have been in power ever since before the days of Yalta. I suggest that when the day comes that Bob Smith can walk, when he gets his artificial limbs, he first walk over to the State Department. . . . He should say to Acheson: "You and your lace handkerchief crowd have never had to fight in the cold, so you cannot know its bitterness. . . ." He should say to him, "Dean, thousands of American boys have faced those twin killers [of bullets and freezing] because you and your crimson crowd betrayed us."[52]

Such attacks soon drove some of the most experienced and knowledgeable officers out of the Foreign Service. Former Secretary of State James Byrnes tried to defend one victim by saying that since the officer "was reared in the state of Georgia, he could not be expected to have any Communist tendencies."[53] But that defense did not work either.

McCarthyism, the Truman-Acheson-MacArthur errors in trying to take North Korea, the Chinese invasion—all combined into a highly perilous venture. "The Korean war," historian William Stueck writes, "stands as the most dangerous armed conflict" in the entire post-1945 era. Several times between November 1950 and early 1953, Stueck notes, U.S. officials discussed expanding the war beyond Korea, "which would have made a direct confrontation with the Soviet Union difficult to avoid."[54] In 1952, Republican presidential nominee Dwight D. Eisenhower swept into the White House with the assurance that he would stop the war but protect U.S. interests. The Republican platform promised to "end neglect of the Far East which Stalin has long identified as the road to victory over the West." That proved to be a big job, even after Stalin suddenly disappeared from the scene.

NOTES

1. Margaret Truman, *Harry S. Truman* (New York, 1973), pp. 449–450.
2. Nancy Bernkopf Tucker, *Patterns in the Dust: Chinese-American Relations and the Recognition Controversy, 1949–1950* (New York, 1983).
3. Warren Cohen, "Conversations with Chinese Friends," *Diplomatic History* 11 (Summer 1987): 283–289. Parts of this argument are outlined in Cohen's widely used text, *America's Response to China*, 2d ed. (New York, 1980), pp. 200–207.
4. Jeremy Bernstein, *Hans Bethe, Prophet of Energy* (New York, 1980), p 88; *New York Times*, 14 January 1993, p. A12.
5. Oral History interview of Dean Acheson, 16 February 1955, Harry S. Truman Post-Presidential Papers, Harry S. Truman Library, Independence, Mo.
6. NSC-68 can best be found in a well-edited version, and with the important supporting documents, in U.S. Department of State, *Foreign Relations of the United States, 1950*, 8 vols. (Washington, D.C., 1977), I, pp. 234–292; Melvyn Leffler, *A Preponderance of Power* (Stanford, 1992), p. 356.
7. David A. Rosenberg, "American Atomic Strategy and the Hydrogen Bomb Decision," *Journal of American History* 66 (June 1979): 62–67; David Alan Rosenberg, "The Origins of Overkill: Nuclear Weapons and American Strategy, 1945–1960," *International Security* 7 (Spring 1983): 11–15.
8. Rosenberg, "The Origins of Overkill," 21–22.
9. Bernstein, p. 94.
10. Princeton Seminar, 10–11 October 1953, Papers of Dean Acheson, Harry S. Truman Library.
11. Stephen E. Ambrose, *Nixon: The Education of a Politician, 1913–1962* (New York, 1987), pp. 205–206.

12. Richard N. Rovere, *Senator Joe McCarthy* (New York, 1959), pp. 8, 110.
13. Gaddis Smith, *Dean Acheson, The American Secretaries of State and Their Diplomacy*, Vol. XVI, ed. Samuel Flagg Bemis and Robert Ferrell (New York, 1972), p. 135, analyzes the speech.
14. U.S. Department of State, I, pp. 206–209.
15. Princeton Seminar, Acheson Papers.
16. This story is well told in Bruce Cumings's pioneering *The Origins of the Korean War* (Princeton, 1981), esp. chs. IV–VI and X–XII, on the 1945–1947 years, and *Child of Conflict: The Korean-American Relationship 1943–1953*, ed. Bruce Cumings (Seattle, 1983), in which Cumings, Stephen Pelz, John Merrill, and James I. Matray contribute key essays on pre-June 1950 events.
17. Richard E. Neustadt and Ernest R. May, *Thinking in Time: The Uses of History for Decision-Makers* (New York, 1986), pp. 34–35.
18. Nikita Khrushchev, *Khrushchev Remembers*, ed. and trans. Strobe Talbott (Boston, 1970), pp. 367–373; the newly released documents are discussed in *Los Angeles Times*, 25 January 1993, p. A4. I am indebted to Milton Leitenberg for this reference.
19. Glenn D. Paige, *The Korean Decision, June 24–30, 1950* (New York, 1968), pp. 132–133, 174–177; Smith, pp. 185–186.
20. The important UN and U.S. documents of late June 1950 can be found in *The Record of American Diplomacy*, ed. Ruhl J. Bartlett, 4th ed. (New York, 1964), esp. pp. 768–769.
21. Steven L. Rearden, *The Evolution of American Strategic Doctrine: Paul H. Nitze and the Soviet Challenge* (Boulder, Col., 1984), p. 30; Neustadt and May, p. 43.
22. Arthur Krock, *Memoirs* (New York, 1968), p. 260.
23. Robert A. Taft, *A Foreign Policy for Americans* (New York, 1957), pp. 21–36.
24. A good recent account of the resolution is in Ronald W. Pruessen, *John Foster Dulles: The Road to Power* (New York, 1982), pp. 426–431.
25. Blanche Wiesen Cook, "Eleanor Roosevelt and Human Rights," in *Women and American Foreign Policy*, ed. Edward M. Crapol (New York, 1987), esp. pp. 107–117.
26. Arthur Vandenberg, *The Private Papers of Senator Vandenberg*, ed. Arthur H. Vandenberg, Jr. (Boston, 1952), p. 536.
27. U.S. Congress, Senate, Foreign Relations Committee, 81st Cong., 1st and 2d sess., 1949–1951, *Reviews of the World Situation: 1949–1950*, Historical Series (Washington, D.C., 1974), p. 184.
28. A useful analysis, placed within the context of the Korean War, is William W. Stueck, Jr., *The Road to Confrontation: American Policy toward China and Korea, 1947–1950* (Chapel Hill, N.C., 1981), esp. pp. 137–143, 196–198.
29. Michael Schaller, *The American Occupation of Japan: The Origins of the Cold War in Asia* (New York, 1985), pp. viii–ix, 298; Richard J. Barnet, *The Alliance: America-Europe-Japan, Makers of the Postwar World* (New York, 1983), p. 94.
30. Howard Schonberger, "Peacemaking in Asia . . . ," *Diplomatic History* 10 (Winter 1986): 73; a distinguished Japanese view is in Chihiro Hosoya, "Japan's Response to U.S. Policy on the Japanese Peace Treaty . . . ," *Hitotsubashi Journal of Law and Politics* 10 (December 1981): 15–27.
31. Pruessen, pp. 459, 494–495.
32. Robert J. McMahon, "Anglo-American Diplomacy and the Reoccupation of the Netherlands East Indies," *Diplomatic History* 10 (Winter 1978): 23; and McMahon's

fine analysis, *Colonialism and Cold War: The United States and the Struggle for Indonesian Independence, 1945–49* (Ithaca, N.Y., 1981), esp. pp. 315–316; and also an early classic account, George McTurnan Kahin, *Nationalism and Revloution in Indonesia* (Ithaca, N.Y., 1952).

33. This document can be conveniently found in *Vietnam: A History in Documents*, ed. Gareth Porter (New York, 1979, 1981), pp. 79–80.

34. Thomas McCormick, "Crisis, Commitment, and Counterrevolution, 1945–1952," in *America in Vietnam: A Documentary History*, ed. William A. Williams *et al.* (New York, 1985), pp. 97–99.

35. *Ibid.*, esp. pp. 82–87, 104–111, for the key documents on the Japan–Southeast Asia connection, with commentary and editorial notes.

36. *Vietnam: A History in Documents*, p. 86.

37. U.S. Department of State, VI, pp. 164–173; quoted and analyzed in Lloyd Gardner, *Approaching Vietnam: From World War II through Dienbienphu* (New York, 1988), ch. III.

38. Barnet, pp. 123–137.

39. *Ibid.*, pp. 57–58.

40. Dean Acheson, *Present at the Creation: My Years in the State Department* (New York, 1969), pp. 452–455.

41. David M. Oshinsky, *A Conspiracy So Immense: The World of Joe McCarthy* (New York, 1983), pp. 172–173.

42. Matthew B. Ridgway, *The Korean War* (Garden City, N.Y., 1967), p. 42.

43. Omar Nelson Bradley, *Substance of Statements Made at Wake Island Conference on October 15, 1950* (Washington, D.C., 1951), esp. p. 5.

44. Allen S. Whiting, *China Crosses the Yalu* (New York, 1960), pp. 155–159; the Chinese documents and an analysis are in *The Korea Herald*, 27 February 1992, pp. 1, 5. I am indebted to Milton Leitenberg for this reference. Also of major importance is Jian, Chen, "The Sino-Soviet Alliance and China's Entry Into the Korean War," a paper published by the Woodrow Wilson Center's Cold War International History Project (Washington, D.C., 1992).

45. Michael Kernan, "The Chosin Survivors," *Washington Post*, 1 December 1984, p. D1.

46. Rosemary Foot, *The Wrong War: American Policy and the Dimensions of the Korean Conflict, 1950–1953* (Ithaca, N.Y., 1985), pp. 114–118.

47. Rovere, p. 9; Nora Sayre, *Running Time: Films of the Cold War* (New York, 1982), p. 11.

48. Press release, statement by the president, 19 December 1950.

49. Harry Truman to Dwight Eisenhower, 12 April 1951, 1916–1952 Files, Box 108, Papers of Dwight D. Eisenhower, Dwight Eisenhower Library, Abilene, Kans.

50. U.S. Congress, Senate, Committee on Foreign Relations and Committee on Armed Services, *Hearings: Military Situation in the Far East* (Washington, D.C., 1951), pp. 32, 45, 66–68, 86–87 (esp. for MacArthur's views), and 924–926 (for Acheson's reply); Allan R. Millett and Peter Maslowski, *For the Common Defense: A Military History of the United States of America* (New York, 1984), pp. 489–490.

51. Sayre, p. 80.

52. *Congressional Record* (Senate), 82d Cong., 1st sess., 24 May 1951, 97, pt. 4, p. 5779.

53. Gary May, *China Scapegoat: The Diplomatic Ordeal of John Carter Vincent* (Washington, D.C., 1979), p. 207.

54. William Stueck, "The Korean War as International History," *Diplomatic History* 10 (Fall 1986): 291; the same point is made in Coit D. Blacker, *Reluctant Warriors: The U.S., the Soviet Union, and Arms Control* (New York, 1987), pp. 71–72; and for comments on U.S. plans to use the A-bomb in Korea, see Bruce Cumings to the editor, *New York Times*, 21 June 1984, p. A22.

For Further Reading

For further reading on specific topics, consult this chapter's notes and the General Bibliography at the end of the book; these references are usually not repeated below. Most important, begin with the well-annotated entries in *Guide to American Foreign Relations since 1700*, ed. Richard Dean Burns (1983), which is exhaustive on the pre-1981 publications. See also references in chapter 14. The following are largely post-1981 accounts.

Good overviews can be found in Melvyn P. Leffler's magisterial *A Preponderance of Power* (1992); and Warren Cohen, *America in the Age of Soviet Power, 1945–1991*, in *Cambridge History of American Foreign Relations*, ed. Warren Cohen (1993); Robert J. Donovan, *Tumultuous Years: The Presidency of Harry S. Truman, 1949–1953* (1982); the early chapters in Lawrence Freedman, *The Evolution of Nuclear Strategy* (1983); Joseph M. Siracusa, *Rearming the Cold War: Paul H. Nitze, the H-Bomb and the Origins of a Soviet First Strike* (1983); and one of the most important primary sources, U.S. Congress, Senate, Foreign Relations Committee, 81st Cong., 1st and 2d sess, *Reviews of the World Situation: 1949–1950*, Historical Series (1974), in which Acheson and others become frank behind closed doors. Excellent on the subject is Ernest R. May, ed., *American Cold War Strategy: Interpreting NSC-68* (1993), as is David McCullough, *Truman* (1992).

On Asia, especially China, a useful overview is Carol Morris Petillo, "The Cold War in Asia," in *Modern American Diplomacy*, ed. John M. Carroll and George C. Herring (1986); Nancy Bernkopf Tucker, *Patterns in the Dust* (1983), is standard on U.S.-China relations, 1949–1950; June M. Grasso, *Harry Truman's Two-China Policy, 1948–1950* (1987), is key on the Truman-Taiwan relationship and based on new documents; Leonard A. Kusnitz, *Public Opinion and Foreign Policy: America's China Policy, 1949–1979* (1984), has extensive data. Joseph Camilleri, *Chinese Foreign Policy: The Maoist Era and Its Aftermath* (1980), is most important on the Chinese policies; and William A. Walker, *Opium and Foreign Policy* (1991), is a fascinating, pioneering study. The effect on the U.S. Foreign Service and foreign policy is analyzed in *The "China Hands" Legacy: Ethics and Diplomacy*, ed. Paul Gordon Lauren (1987), especially essays by May, Iriye, Hsu, Davies, Wylie; a fine case study of a central figure is Gary May, *China Scapegoat: The Diplomatic Ordeal of John Carter Vincent* (1979).

Thomas C. Reeves, *The Life and Times of Joe McCarthy* (1982), is a good narrative. *Beyond the Hiss Case: The FBI, Congress, and the Cold War*, ed. Athan G. Theoharis (1982), is crucial for understanding both the time and U.S. government policies, as is Ronald Radosh and Joyce Milton's widely noted *The Rosenberg File* (1983).

Recent research has focused on initial U.S. commitments to Vietnam to give important insights into U.S. policy more generally in Asia (especially Japan) and, indeed, worldwide. Seminal are William S. Borden, *The Pacific Alliance: U.S. Foreign Economic Policy and Japanese Trade Recovery, 1947–1955* (1984); Andrew J. Rotter, *The Path to Vietnam: Origins of the American Commitment to Southeast Asia* (1987); Gary R. Hess, *The U.S. Emergence as a Southeast Asian Power, 1940–1950* (1986); and, for an exhaustive bibliography, *The Wars in Vietnam, Cambodia and Laos, 1945–1982*, ed. Richard Dean Burns and Milton Leitenberg (1984), with excellent cross references. One result is traced through from the Japanese perspective in Michael M. Yoshitsu, *Japan and the San Francisco Peace Settlement* (1982).

For Korea, the background is well provided in Yur-Bok Lee and Wayne Patterson, *One Hundred Years of Korean-American Relations, 1882–1982* (1986), and three indispensable books from Bruce Cumings: *Child of Conflict: The Korean-American Relationship, 1943–1953* (1983), which he edited and wrote with leading scholars, and *The Origins of the Korean War*, whose first volume on 1945–1947 appeared in 1981, and whose second volume, *The Roaring of the Cataract* (1990), is a classic study of the 1947–1952 events. Excellent on the war's diplomacy is Rosemary Foot, *The Wrong War* (1985), critical of U.S. policy. Important and useful overviews, with good bibliographical references, include Barton J. Bernstein, "New Light on the Korean War," *International History Review* 3 (April 1981); Robert Jervis, "The Impact of the Korean War upon the Cold War," *Journal of Conflict Resolution* 24 (December 1980); and Arthur A. Stein, *The Nation at War* (1980), especially useful for its suggestive approach to how the war affected U.S. society. The war's battles and attendant politics are well examined in Callum A. MacDonald, *Korea: The War before Vietnam* (1987), which ranks with the Cumings and Foot volumes as one of special importance; Bevin Alexander, *Korea: The First War We Lost* (1987), by a combat historian in the war; and Roy E. Appleman, *East of Chosin* (1987), a distinguished military history of the darkest days for U.S. forces. The role of India and Indian scholars' views on the war, U.S.-Chinese relations, and U.S.-Indian relations are central to understanding the diplomacy of the conflict and can be found in *American History by Indian Historians*, ed. Norman H. Dawes (1964); but also consult Dennis Merrill's important *Bread and the Ballot* (1990), on U.S.-Indian economic relations.

16

The Era of Eisenhower:
The Good Old Days (1953–1960)

EISENHOWER AND DULLES: AT HOME

When Dwight D. Eisenhower entered the White House in January 1953, he was better prepared to handle foreign policy than any other twentieth-century president. Texas-born son of pacifist parents, "Ike" had graduated from West Point. He then lived in Asia, Latin America, Europe, and Africa as well as in Washington during the early 1930s, where, as a lobbyist for the U.S. Army, he came to know Congress well. During World War II, he commanded the greatest amphibious invasion force in history and became a world hero by liberating much of western and central Europe from Nazism. Meanwhile, he displayed rare political talent by dealing successfully with Roosevelt, Stalin, Churchill, and de Gaulle. After the war, Eisenhower served as U.S. Army Chief of Staff, president of Columbia University, and then supreme commander of Allied forces in NATO.

He was more than certain of his own abilities, but in public he called himself just "a farm boy from Kansas," where he had grown up.[1] That approach, together with his famous grin and soldierly bearing, made him the trusted father figure of the 1950s. As television ownership expanded from 9 percent of U.S. homes in 1950 to 87 percent in 1960, Eisenhower knew how to exploit the new technology. A father figure could be politically popular when the most-watched television program, "I Love Lucy," showed the laughs and happiness enjoyed by a supposedly typical American family. Ike's low-keyed manner, his apparent preference for the golf course over the White House, led observers to consider him a "national sedative." After the frenzy of 1947–1952, however, Americans were ready for a sedative.[2]

Harry Truman, who had grown to dislike Eisenhower, growled that "The general doesn't know any more about politics than a pig knows about Sunday." But Ike's vice-president, Richard Nixon, saw a different Eisenhower—a "complex," even "devious man" who approached problems from many "lines of reasoning" and preferred to be "indirect" rather than obvious and direct.[3] Nixon knew firsthand. He was never completely trusted by Eisenhower, nor did he ever fully know where he stood with the president. Nixon also learned that Ike's grin hid a boiling temper that had moved entire armies. "My God," an aide remarked after watching one explosion, "how could you compute the amount of adrenalin expended in those thirty seconds? I don't know why long since he hasn't had a killer of a heart attack."[4] Eisenhower did suffer a severe heart attack in 1955. But despite this, Americans so trusted him that they re-elected him by a landslide in 1956 in his second race against the eloquent Democratic party nominee, Adlai Stevenson of Illinois.

Eisenhower remained popular in part because foreign-policy setbacks were usually blamed on his sour, militantly anti-Communist secretary of state, John Foster Dulles. Ike's sparkle radiated next to "Dull, Duller, Dulles." One British observer reflected widespread opinion when he concluded that Dulles was not "a likeable or well-balanced personality."[5] But as Dulles himself said, his foreign policy did not aim at "winning a popularity contest. . . . I prefer being respected to being liked."[6] He was most respected by the only one who really counted: Eisenhower. The president knew that this son of a Presbyterian minister in Watertown, New York, had been closely involved with U.S. diplomacy since the first decade of the century. "Foster has been studying to be Secretary of State since he was five years old," Ike commented.[7] The president trusted Dulles to be his agent abroad. The secretary of state spent so much time going to and from airports that critics exclaimed, "Don't do something, Foster, just stand there!" But Eisenhower always controlled the policy. For his part, Dulles recalled how his uncle, Secretary of State Robert Lansing, had been fired for crossing Woodrow Wilson, and so was careful never to repeat such a mistake with Eisenhower. When both were in Washington, they often got together privately for a late-afternoon drink at the White House to exchange views.

President Dwight D. Eisenhower (1890–1969), at right, and Secretary of State John Foster Dulles (1888–1959) formed the most experienced foreign-policy team in recent U.S. history. They presided over American power as it reached its peak and, by 1958–1960, was beginning a relative decline.

Besides Eisenhower's trust, Dulles enjoyed the confidence of both liberals and conservatives within the Republican party. Eisenhower thus used Dulles as lobbyist in Congress as well as a political lightning rod to deflect criticism from the presidency. Dulles worked hard shaping opinion. Privately, he could explain his policies by giving hard-headed geopolitical reasons. But publicly, he used the moral and religious reasons that he believed Americans preferred to hear, even though he was often laughed at by observers at home and overseas for mouthing platitudes. Dulles was the first secretary of state to allow reporters to quote him directly and, later, to allow television to cover his press conferences.

Eisenhower and Dulles dominated Congress, although they had to overcome two early problems to do so. The first problem was Senator Joseph McCarthy's shrill anticommunism. In one of the worst moments of his life, Eisenhower had refused to criticize McCarthy in the 1952 campaign, even though the senator had grossly defamed General George Marshall, the man who had championed Eisenhower's military career. In 1953–1954, the president kept his distance from McCarthy. And in mid-1954, the senator went too far by accusing Ike of being soft on communism and then by trying to conduct a witch hunt within the U.S. Army. In late 1954, with the elections safely past, the Senate finally found the political courage to censure McCarthy's conduct. His political power faded.

Eisenhower's second problem with Congress was the Bricker Amendment. This proposed addition to the Constitution, pushed by conservative Republican Senator John Bricker of Ohio, aimed at limiting the president's power to make executive agreements with foreign countries. More generally, its supporters wanted to ensure that no international agreements (such as those passed in the United Nations to improve the rights of women or blacks) could become law in the United States without congressional approval. Bricker mirrored the long Republican frustration with Roosevelt's deals at Yalta and Tehran. Eisenhower, who was not about to surrender any of his power, began to wonder if Bricker's supporters "had lost all their brains." Ike won a key Senate test by only one vote in 1954. But, by the end of the year, his hard lobbying in Congress made the amendment a dead issue.[8]

After that, Eisenhower controlled Congress. He held regular afternoon meetings with Democratic leaders, usually over a much-appreciated bourbon and branch water, and courted Republican leaders—even those, such as Senator William Knowland of California, for whom he had little respect. (In Knowland's case, Ike noted in his diary, there seemed to be no final answer to the question: "How stupid can you get?")[9] Eisenhower's popularity was such that polls revealed a majority of liberals thought him a liberal, and a majority of conservatives believed that he agreed with them. Thus, he and Dulles ably fashioned a bipartisan foreign policy. But, as is usually the case in American politics, bipartisan policy actually meant ever-greater presidential power.[10]

Eisenhower, nevertheless, had to work within some limits. McCarthy was dying (he passed away in 1957), but McCarthyism remained alive. Dulles tried to please fervent anti-Communists by allowing one of them, Scott McLeod, to oversee State Department personnel. As a result, hundreds left the Foreign Service, and morale and standards sank. (A bitter Dean Acheson said privately that "Dulles's people seem to me like [Russian] Cossacks quartered in a grand city hall, burning the paneling to cook with.") Asian policy especially suffered. The Committee of One Million, which appeared in the early 1950s, was a well-financed pressure group formed to help Chiang Kai-shek's (Jiang Jieshi's) exiles on Taiwan and to ensure that the United States never deal with the Chinese Communists. This "China lobby" included Republican conservatives such as Knowland as well as Democratic liberals such as Senator Hubert Humphrey of Minnesota. Thus, the president had to deal with China policy gingerly.[11]

The atmosphere of the 1950s was captured in *Invasion of the Body Snatchers*, a popular movie of the decade that tells of normal Americans being taken over by alien forces that duplicate the bodies but kill the emotions of their victims, thus creating a society of docile, seemingly content humanoid beings. Subtly capitalizing on Americans' fears of communism, the film drew huge audiences. A more important movie of the 1950s, however, was *High Noon*. In it, a brave frontier marshal (Gary Cooper) decides, despite great personal fear, to stand up to a band of ugly, vicious villains, although the cowardly townspeople and even his new wife (Grace Kelly) urge him to run away. The film was written by Carl Foreman, who himself became a victim of Hollywood McCarthyism.[12] Given the climate of the 1950s, however, whether Gary Cooper's brave lawman represented Dwight Eisenhower or Senator McCarthy depended on the politics of the viewer. But few doubted that a lot of ugly villains threatened American happiness, and their numbers seemed to increase dangerously as the decade wore on.

Eisenhower and Dulles Abroad: Capitalism and Nuclear Wars

The new president followed two principles in shaping his foreign policy. First, communism must not be allowed to expand. Second, capitalism must not go bankrupt in trying to contain communism.

Nothing, not even communism, seemed to obsess Eisenhower as much as his fear that capitalists would ruin their system by spending too much on defense. A sometime reader of Marx and Lenin, the president warned that those Communists might be correct: capitalists were too "selfish," too willing to spend and profit now at the cost of "long-term" interest and thus "in the long run would destroy any free economic system."[13] Military spending that leads to inflation and waste should not be thrown into budgets but into civilian goods. "Unless we can put things in the hands of people who are starving to death we can never lick Communism," he told his cabinet. Worse, a militarized U.S. economy "would either drive us to war—or into some form of dictatorial government" and perhaps even force "us to *initiate* war at the most propitious moment."[14] After beating back demands from Congress and private corporations for more military spending, Ike privately exclaimed, "God help the nation when it has a President who doesn't know as much about the military as I do."[15]

Eisenhower, therefore, searched for a cheap way to contain communism. He found it in the nation's huge nuclear superiority over the Soviets. He and his top advisers worked out the policy during mid-1953 in Operation Solarium, named for the White House sun room where the secret discussions were held. The group considered three ways to deal with the Soviet Union: continued containment largely through conventional means; telling the Soviets that nuclear weapons would be used if the Soviet Union tried to take more territory; and, finally, using all-out economic and propaganda campaigns to roll back communism. Eisenhower decided on a combination of the first two: containment and reliance on nuclear weapons, instead of fighting expensive and unpopular conventional wars (as Truman did in Korea).[16] He and Dulles also planned to build new alliance systems so that every non-Communist part of the world would be a responsibility of the United States and its allies. But above all, nuclear weapons gained new importance. As historian David A. Rosenberg concludes: "Where Harry Truman viewed the atomic bomb as an instrument of terror and a weapon of last resort, Dwight Eisenhower viewed it as an integral part of American defense, and, in effect, a weapon of first resort."[17]

This policy became known as "massive retaliation." Dulles defined it as the "free world's" ability to "retaliate, instantly, by means and at places of our own choosing." Trying to match Communists "man for man, gun for gun," he warned, meant "bankruptcy."[18] Instead, Americans should get "more bang for the buck," as the 1950s phrase went, not more expensive conventional weapons. Eisenhower, thus, had it both ways. To reduce expenditures in 1954, he cut Truman's military budget of $50 billion to $34 billion largely by reducing the number of men in the army. But to contain communism, he increased the number of nuclear warheads from 1,000 in 1953 to 18,000 by early 1961. Although U.S. superiority was already overwhelming, one additional nuclear weapon soon rolled off the American production line each day. Eisenhower also exploited new technology. In 1955, the huge B-52 bomber appeared. The eight-engine giant was the first true jet bomber designed to carry nuclear weapons (although it later became famous for destroying hundreds of square miles of Vietnam in mere minutes with conventional bombs). The two-stage ballistic missile, Polaris, capable of being fired from a submerged submarine, provided a capability in 1960 to launch a nuclear attack from deep within the oceans.

Nuclear testing by both superpowers produced an ever-larger weapon

The cold war comes home. Schools prepared for possible nuclear war in the early 1950s by having students wear "dog-tags" so they could be identified after the attack.

(equal to 400 Hiroshima-type bombs). It also produced deadly radio-active fallout. As early as 1953, milk in Albany, New York, was found to contain sixteen times the normal amount of this radiation. U.S. officials lied or hid information about the effects of testing. The world shuddered in 1954, when it learned that twenty-three members of a Japanese fishing boat, the *Lucky Dragon*, innocently sailed into a U.S. nuclear testing area in the Pacific and within days became deathly ill from radiation poisoning. Testing, nevertheless, continued on both sides. American education leaders prepared school students for possible nuclear war. Youngsters in New York City, San Francisco, and elsewhere wore identification necklaces so they could be better identified in case of attack. Schools were redesigned, and windows eliminated, to protect students against radiation and fallout from nuclear war. There was no panic; instead "the threat of atomic war was domesticated," in the words of historian JoAnne Brown, and Americans were to accept the possibility of all-out nuclear conflict as part of their daily lives. By 1958, larger bombs produced so much radiation that it could more gravely threaten Americans in a future war than could enemy weapons—or so reported a U.S. Navy commander. Overruling strong objections from the Pentagon and such scientists as Edward Teller, Eisenhower, on his own, stopped testing in October 1958. Khrushchev halted Soviet testing the next month.[19]

By 1955, the president realized that growing crises in Vietnam and the Middle East might remain limited and not escalate into a direct confrontation with the Soviets. Experts, including Henry Kissinger of Harvard University, warned that the United States would face many such crises in the Third World and had to learn to fight effective "limited wars," short of an all-out nuclear exchange with the Soviet Union. But Eisenhower was determined not to become trapped in another Korea-type war that, in historian Barton Bernstein's phrase, could "drain America's resources . . . split the NATO alliance, and impair [Eisenhower's] popularity at home."[20] In 1955, the president said it directly: nuclear bombs were to be considered conventional weapons and "used just exactly as you would use a bullet or anything else."[21]

He even claimed to have secretly followed that policy in Korea. During the 1952 campaign, Eisenhower blasted the Democrats for mishandling the war. He scored a triumph by announcing that if elected, "I shall go to Korea" (although he never said what he would do after he arrived). Eisenhower did travel to Korea and decided to get tough with China. In February 1953, he announced the so-called "unleashing" of Chiang Kai-shek, who could now threaten to attack the mainland. But the crisis peaked in early summer 1953, when Eisenhower found the peace talks tied up. South Korean president Syngman Rhee refused to surrender his dream of ruling all Korea. He tried to kill the talks by freeing thousands of Chinese prisoners whom China's government wanted returned home. The Communists broke off the talks and began a military offensive. The president and Dulles hinted, through Indian officials close to the Chinese, that unless the Communists signed a truce, the United States would "not be limited" in its use of weapons. Public-opinion polls showed that a majority of Americans wanted atomic shells used. The effect of the warning is unknown. The Chinese later denied they were frightened by it. Strong evidence exists that they and the Soviets had actually decided to end the war immediately after Stalin's death three months earlier. But U.S. officials believed that the threat broke the logjam. In any case, in mid-summer both sides signed a truce, and the war finally stopped.[22]

That was not the last time Eisenhower considered "massive retaliation." In 1955, he and his advisers agreed that if China invaded Indochina, they would ask Congress for a declaration of war and then use "new weapons" on China itself. In 1958, when the Chinese shelled the small offshore islands held by Chiang Kai-shek, Eisenhower moved "tactical" nuclear weapons into place. During the Berlin crisis of 1958–1960, U.S. fighter-bombers went on regular airborne alert. Some planes carried weapons 1,000 times more powerful than the 1945 bombs. The U.S. Navy flew bombers loaded with nuclear weapons off China's coast—partly to see how Chinese radar reacted.[23]

Supporters claimed that the threat of "massive retaliation"—or, as Dulles called it, "going to the brink of war"—made the Soviets and Chinese behave. But it did not achieve Dulles's goal of "liberating" the Soviet bloc. During the 1952 campaign, he and Eisenhower had urged such "liberation," although Eisenhower emphasized that it must be done "only by peaceful means."[24] Their chance arose in spring 1953. Stalin had suddenly died in March. Frustrated East Berlin workers seized the opportunity to strike and even riot against the Communist regime. Red flags were ripped down as the protests threatened to spread. U.S.-government-sponsored radio programs egged the workers on. But when Soviet tanks suddenly appeared to smash the riots and execute the leaders, the United States did nothing except issue protests.

British Prime Minister Winston Churchill dramatically proposed that the Big Four leaders (the United States, USSR, Great Britain, and France) meet at a summit conference to discuss—and perhaps even settle—the most dangerous problems. The new Soviet leaders were clearly trying to find more effective policies (for example, they called for a Korean peace), and Churchill thought the time ripe to work with them. Eisenhower flatly refused to meet with the Soviets unless the new leaders agreed beforehand to surrender key Soviet positions on German, eastern European, atomic-energy, and Asian issues. That demand, of course, effectively killed Churchill's plan. After all, Ike told the prime minister, "Russia was . . . a woman of the streets and whether her dress was new, or just the old one patched, there was the same whore underneath."[25]

EISENHOWER AND DULLES ABROAD: REVOLUTIONS AND THE CIA

"Massive retaliation" might control the whore, but Eisenhower and Dulles knew that her supposed children—the growing number of revolutionaries in the newly emerging nations—required other kinds of action. Eisenhower understood that using nuclear weapons to defeat these rebels was as wildly out of proportion as burning down buildings to control ants. He, therefore, devised a second policy to deal with communism: covert operations handled by the Central Intelligence Agency. The policy's attractions were many: cheapness, secrecy, speed, and no need to deal with Congress. Eisenhower alone supervised the CIA's activities, working closely with its director, Allen Dulles, the secretary of state's brother. Both the president and the director had extensive experience running such covert operations during World War II. Within eighteen months after entering the White House, Eisenhower and Dulles used the CIA to destroy supposed revolutionaries in two nations.

The first was Iran. In 1951, Mohammad Mosaddeq had risen to power in that country. Described by Dean Acheson as a "pixie" with a bald, "billiard-ball head," Mosaddeq was a shrewd politician and fervent nationalist. He challenged the monopoly over his country's oil long held by the British-controlled Anglo-Iranian Oil Company. The company had exploited Iran for decades, allowing the country to have about 20 percent of the profits from its own oil. That cozy deal, however, had been jarred in 1950, when the U.S. oil company, Aramco, gave Saudi Arabia 50 percent of the profits from Saudi oil. Mosaddeq demanded the same. The British refused. In 1952, as the Iranians moved toward seizing the British company's resources, the Truman administration tried to mediate. Acheson sympathized with Mosaddeq.[26] But U.S. policy changed sharply when Dulles replaced Acheson.

The new administration feared Mosaddeq's nationalism and agreed with British warnings that he was becoming dangerously dependent on Iran's Communist party, the Tudeh. With Washington's approval, the large international oil companies cooperated to prevent Iranian oil from reaching world markets. Mosaddeq found that he could produce oil but not sell it. In early summer 1953, he asked Eisenhower for economic help. The president responded that he would be happy to provide aid after Mosaddeq reached agreement on the oil dispute. With his power slipping, Mosaddeq called a public referendum to approve his policies, then fixed the results to gain more than 95 percent of the vote, a figure Eisenhower associated with Communist elections. Having tried and failed to remove Mosaddeq, the young Mohammad Reza Shah Pahlavi, who had replaced his father as ruler of Iran, left the country suddenly for a "rest cure." As pro-Mosaddeq mobs took to the streets, Eisenhower and the British decided to move.

CIA agents found supporters in the capital of Tehran, especially in the military, then bought off other Iranians and arranged massive street demonstrations that threw the city into chaos. Mosaddeq was arrested, and the shah returned to claim his throne. (He offered a toast to the top CIA agent: "I owe my throne to God, my people, my army, and to you.") As frosting on an already rich cake, the major U.S. oil companies forced the British company to cut them in on the production of Iran's oil. Allen Dulles declared that Iran had been saved from a "Communist-dominated regime." But historian Mark Lytle offers a more accurate judgment. Knowing "almost nothing about Iran," U.S. officials overthrew a nationalist and "revered" figure, Mosaddeq. Afterward, the shah "would always seem beholden to the United States," and so both he and Americans would become targets of nationalists and Moslem fundamentalists in Iran. It was, Lytle concludes, "interventionism of the worst kind."[27]

In the poorer Central American nation of Guatemala, the CIA again overthrew a nationalist regime in the name of anti-communism. Until 1944, the ruling Guatemalan elite made up 2 percent of the population but held more than 60 percent of the land. The poorest 50 percent of the people held only 3 percent of the land but depended on the land for their food. Half the population were Indians who earned less than $100 annually and suffered brutal discrimination. In 1944, a student–middle-class revolt overthrew a corrupt, stagnant dictatorship and installed a reform-minded government. Jacobo Arbenz Guzmán came to power in 1951 after perhaps the fairest election in the country's history. He and his wife, the beautiful and wealthy Mariá Vilanova, who was determined to aid the nation's poor, especially set out to help the landless and the Indians. Among other measures, Arbenz planned to give them land by seizing 234,000 acres from the United Fruit Company (UFCO), the Boston-based "Octopus" that controlled much of the region's fruit production, transportation, and even governments. He singled out UFCO simply because it owned 42 percent of the country's arable land but was using less than 10 percent of it. Arbenz offered to pay for the land, but UFCO demanded much more.

The Dulles brothers, whose old law firm had close ties with UFCO, were afraid that the seizure of U.S. property would be copied by other governments in Latin America. But most of all, they and Eisenhower concluded that Arbenz's action indicated that Guatamala was turning Red. The country's Communist party did grow in popularity, especially in the poor rural areas and among union workers. Only four Communists, however, sat in the fifty-six-member Congress. Arbenz and his top advisers, moreover, were not Communist, nor, certainly, were the most powerful national institutions—the Roman Catholic church and the army.

Dulles, nevertheless, flew to an inter-American conference in Caracas, Venezuela, in March 1954 and demanded the condemnation of "international Communism." He obtained the resolution. But when, in May, he asked for help from the Organization of American States in taking action, the Latin Americans refused—especially after Dulles admitted that it was "impossible to produce evidence clearly tying the Guatemala Government to Moscow."[28] Deciding to go it alone, Eisenhower ordered the CIA to train Guatemalan exiles to overthrow Arbenz. The frightened Guatemalan government accepted a shipload of arms from the Soviet bloc.

That was enough for Eisenhower. In June, the CIA-led exiles moved from bases in Honduras and Nicaragua to eliminate Arbenz. The exile army nearly failed, but at the decisive moment Eisenhower ordered American-flown planes to drop small sticks of dynamite on the capital, Guatemala City. Arbenz's army then deserted him, and that desertion was the turning point. (Learning directly from this experience, Fidel Castro in Cuba during the 1960s and the Sandinista revolutionaries in Nicaragua during the 1980s made the army and their revolutionary government a single unit so that they would not be victimized as Arbenz had been.)

As Arbenz fled, the exile leader, General Carlos Castillo Armas, became president and put hundreds of Arbenz's followers in front of firing squads until the reform movement was destroyed. In 1957, one of his own palace guard murdered Castillo Armas. He was the first in a long line of military dictators who brutalized and exploited Guatemala during the next three decades. Nevertheless, in 1954, John Foster Dulles concluded that the country had been saved from "Communist imperialism" and that Castillo Armas's victory added "a new and glorious chapter to the already great tradition of the American States." He never mentioned the CIA's role. Others disagreed. Historian Richard Immerman concludes that Arbenz's attempt to end "social and economic injustice" was stopped by CIA action that "made moderation impossible" in Guatemala.[29] Philip C. Roettinger, a U.S. Marine colonel who helped overthrow Arbenz, wrote in 1986 that it turned out to be "a terrible mistake. . . . Our 'success' led to 31 years of repressive military rule and the deaths of more than 100,000 Guatemalans."[30]

Eisenhower, nevertheless, had used the CIA to install new governments in Iran and Guatemala. The agency did not stop there, however. Although its 1947 charter forbade it from engaging in "security functions" within the United States itself, from the 1950s onward the CIA opened letters that Americans mailed overseas (some 13,000 such letters a year by 1959) and wire-tapped journalists and other private citizens.[31] Meanwhile, Eisenhower's popularity jumped. As a leading journalist wrote in 1954, "That man has an absolutely unique ability to convince people that he has no talent for duplicity."[32]

"You boys must be crazy": Eisenhower and Indochina (1953–1954)

U.S. officials had little time to celebrate the overthrow of Arbenz because, at the same moment, they were confronting a major crisis in Southeast Asia. During that crisis, they learned that in some cases neither "massive retaliation" nor the CIA could achieve U.S. policy objectives. It was the first in a long line of lessons that Vietnam taught those Americans who cared to learn.

The reasons that had moved U.S. officials to become involved in Vietnam during 1949–1950 (see p. 519) only became more powerful after 1952. Chinese communism had to be contained. With the British fighting revolutionaries in Malaya and the Philippine government facing a rebellion, U.S. leaders believed that Ho Chi Minh's Communists in Vietnam had to be defeated or no place in the region would be safe. With massive U.S. help, the Filipinos did contain their revolutionaries. The British, on their own, began winning in Malaya, thus convincing U.S. officials that Ho could also be beaten. Southeast Asia, moreover, had both the strategic materials (such as oil and tin) and locations (for air and naval bases) that the West required for its cold-war build-up. The area seemed especially important because, in American eyes, its markets and raw materials were necessary for Japan's stability. If Southeast Asia became Communist, a top-secret National Security Council paper concluded, it could mean "Japan's eventual accommodation to Communism." Eisenhower later finished that thought: "Should Japan go communist (in fact or in sympathy) the U.S. would be out of the Pacific, and it [i.e., the Pacific] would become a communist lake."[33]

The president tied all this together in a famous press conference that took place on April 7, 1954, when he speculated about the results if Indochina turned Communist:

> First of all, you have the specific value of a locality in its production of materials that the world needs. Then you have the possibility that many human beings pass under a dictatorship that is inimical to the free world. Finally, you have broader considerations that might follow what you would call the "falling domino" principle.

Ho Chi Minh (1890–1969), the father of the Vietnamese revolt against France (1946–1954), led the fight against U.S. intervention until his death. His career as a revolutionary reached back to 1919–1920, when he met with other Third World leaders in Paris while Woodrow Wilson vainly tried to create a world that was "safe for democracy."

You have a row of dominoes set up, you knock over the first one, and what will happen to the last one is a certainty that it will go over very quickly. . . .

It takes away, in its economic aspects, that region that Japan must have as a trading area or Japan, in turn, will have only one place to go—that is, toward the Communist areas in order to live.

So the possible consequences of the loss are just incalculable to the free world.[34]

In addition, the French had to be helped in Asia or they would be even weaker and less cooperative partners in western Europe. The United States poured over $4 billion into the French attempt to defeat Ho between 1950 and 1954. The money did little good. Neither French arms nor French-controlled Vietnamese governments could stop the revolution. During early 1954, France's commander decided to fight a climactic battle at Dien Bien Phu, near the northern Vietnamese border. It was one of the great errors of twentieth-century military history. The French garrison occupied the bottom of a valley while Ho's Vietminh armies bombarded the garrison by moving artillery to the heights—a feat the French did not think the shabby-looking Communist army could pull off.

Eisenhower privately called the French "a hopeless, helpless mass of protoplasm." Dulles, nevertheless, warned publicly in late March

1954 that Vietnam had to be saved even if it "might involve serious risks." He and Eisenhower secretly spelled out those risks in early April, when the president asked congressional leaders for authority to use, if necessary, U.S. forces to save the French position. Led by Democratic Senator Lyndon Johnson from Texas, the congressmen refused to go along unless the British also joined. They warned that there must be "no more Koreas with the United States furnishing 90 percent of the manpower."[35] Prime Minister Churchill, who considered the French effort a lost cause, flatly rejected any plan for intervention.

Eisenhower knew that Vietnam was pivotal, but he refused to go in alone. "Unilateral action . . . would destroy us," he later observed privately. "If we intervened alone in this case we would be expected to intervene alone in other parts of the world."[36] Both Dulles and U.S. military officials then put forward the idea of saving the French by using small nuclear weapons. "You boys must be crazy," Eisenhower replied. "We can't use those awful things against Asians for the second time in ten years. My God."[37] His army chief of staff, Matthew Ridgway, had helped convince Eisenhower that even nuclear weapons would not work without sending in a U.S. ground force afterward. And that was something neither Eisenhower nor Ridgway would seriously think of doing.

On May 7, 1954, Dien Bien Phu fell. Against Dulles's wishes, the French traveled to Geneva, Switzerland, where an international conference met to settle the war. China's sharp, urbane foreign minister, Zhou Enlai (Chou En-lai), attended. Against his will, Dulles also went, although he made it clear that he would meet with Zhou (Chou) only if their "cars collide." The Geneva Conference finally produced two agreements. The first, signed by the French and Ho's Vietminh, provided for a cease-fire, the temporary division of Vietnam along the seventeenth parallel, and regrouping French forces south of the line while the Vietminh moved north. This agreement emphasized that the seventeenth parallel was not to be seen as "constituting a political or territorial boundary." The second agreement, or Final Declaration, provided that neither north nor south would join a military alliance or allow foreign bases. General elections were to be held in 1956. Neighboring Laos and Cambodia were to be neutral. Unwilling to deal away half of Vietnam to communism and have his picture taken as he did it, Dulles refused to have the United States sign the Geneva Accords. He did issue a separate statement that agreed with the general principles and promised not to "disturb them" by the "threat or the use of force."[38]

PICKING UP THE PIECES IN ASIA (1954–1961)

But Eisenhower and Dulles then devised a dual policy to contain China and Ho Chi Minh. First, they used economic and political pressure to push out the French and bring in Ngo Dinh Diem to lead the South Vietnamese. Diem had never worked for the French, but he had collaborated with the Japanese occupation and, since 1950, had lived in Europe and the United States rather than fight in the nationalists' struggle. His Roman Catholic beliefs set him apart from the Buddhists, who made up more than 90 percent of Vietnam's population. Those beliefs, nevertheless, made him popular with many Americans. To oversee Diem, Dulles installed two U.S. advisers: General J. Lawton Collins and Colonel Edward Lansdale. Within a year Collins felt that Diem had neither the public support nor the talent to pull South Vietnam together. But Lansdale, who had played a major role in containing the Philippine revolutionaries, believed that he and Diem could repeat that triumph and make South Vietnam a nation. Eisenhower finally went along with Lansdale. From the start of Diem's rule, the United States set out to protect him by ignoring key agreements made at Geneva. The seventeenth parallel was not to be temporary (as the Geneva Accords provided), but was to become a permanent boundary between North and South Vietnam. Dulles and Diem, moreover, had no intention of holding the promised elections in 1956 because they feared Ho would win.[39] Thus, the United States not only became committed to South Vietnam, but—as the phrase soon went—to "sink or swim with Ngo Dinh Diem."

The second Eisenhower-Dulles response was to create the Southeast Asia Treaty Organization (SEATO) in September 1954. Its odd assortment of members included the United States, France, Great Britain, New Zealand, and Australia. The only Asian countries that joined were the Philippines, Thailand, and Pakistan (which hoped to use SEATO against its bitter enemy, India). Each nation agreed that in case of an armed attack against a Southeast Asian state or territory, it would respond "in accordance with its constitutional processes." Dulles clearly told the U.S. Senate: "We do not intend to dedicate any major elements of the United States Military Establishment to form an army of defense in this area."[40] In reality, the other members contributed little to SEATO either, and the organization became militarily irrelevant, although for the next dozen years U.S. officials used this supposed *col-*

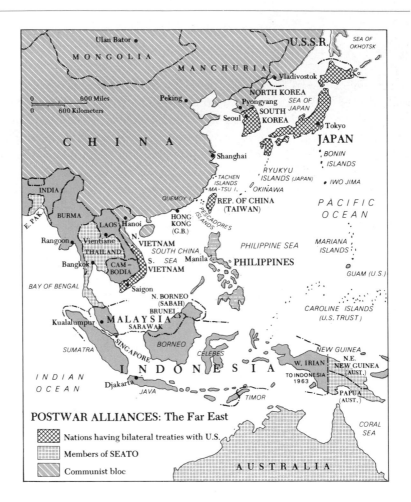

POSTWAR ALLIANCES: The Far East

- Nations having bilateral treaties with U.S.
- Members of SEATO
- Communist bloc

lective security pact to justify the *unilateral* American commitment to Vietnam.

Between 1954 and 1961, Eisenhower, indeed, committed the United States to Vietnam. U.S. Army advisers taught Vietnamese soldiers how to fight a conventional war (as in Korea), not counterrevolutionary tactics. Diem proved to be a weak ruler. He was afraid to carry out needed reforms because he would lose support of rich and powerful Vietnamese. By 1961, he was among the top five recipients of U.S. foreign aid in the world, but his economy was failing. The year before, his army had proved to be inept when fighting resumed with Ho's Vietnamese Communists or Vietminh. In 1957, the first American, Captain Harry Cramer, had died in the war. But as a U.S. expert in Vietnam wrote in 1961, "American aid has built a castle on sand." George Herring, author of the standard one-volume history on U.S. involvement in Vietnam, concludes that only by leaving office in 1961 did Eisenhower avoid suffering "the ultimate failure of his policies in Vietnam."[41]

Between 1954 and 1958, however, Eisenhower and Dulles felt that they had taught the Communists, especially the Chinese, a lesson. The Americans could point not only to holding firm in Vietnam, but also to successes in the so-called offshore-islands crises. Those islands (especially Quemoy and Matsu) were tiny spots just off China's coast but claimed by Chiang Kai-shek. In August 1954, the Communists called for liberation of the islands and began shelling them. Dulles and Chiang then signed a mutual defense alliance, but it said nothing about defending the offshore islands.

In early 1955, Eisenhower asked Congress for broad authority to use U.S. forces in the area at his discretion. In an amazing display of trust, within five days both houses of Congress overwhelmingly gave Eisenhower such power. In that short time, Congress surrendered to the president its constitutional power to decide when and for which reasons war might be declared. The resolution set a historic precedent for later grants of power by Congress to the president that Congress regretted. But the shelling of the islands quieted. In 1958, the Chinese Communists again threatened Quemoy and Matsu. This time, Eisenhower moved nuclear weapons into place in case Mao's armies tried to move toward the offshore islands and Taiwan. Fortunately, the crisis again passed.

The consequences of the offshore-islands crises were many. Congress helped build the "imperial presidency" (as it was soon known). Eisenhower further militarily allied the United States with Chiang. The president again threatened to use nuclear weapons against Asians. U.S. officials concluded that the Chinese Communists would stop their expansionism only when confronted with massive force. Finally, perhaps the crises helped widen the split developing between the Chinese and Soviets. Mao became angry when Moscow showed no interest in going to war with Americans over something as small as the offshore islands. Dulles indeed now concluded that by being tough, he could show Mao how undependable the Soviets were and thus split the two Communist powers. Historian David Mayers concludes that the U.S. military pressure seemed "to have contributed," as Eisenhower and Dulles hoped, "to the weakening" of the Sino-Soviet partnership until it finally fell apart between 1957 and 1961. But history played an interesting joke, for the split did not occur as U.S. officials had predicted. They thought Mao might be a new Tito (see p. 478) and move closer to the United States. Instead, U.S.-China relations worsened while, incredibly, U.S.-Soviet relations warmed. Observers began to suggest, only half-humorously, that a Soviet leader might be the new Tito.[42]

THE "AGONIZING REAPPRAISAL": EISENHOWER, DULLES, AND EUROPE

Those Soviet leaders were smashing into a number of problems. Stalin's death in early 1953 left them with a leadership crisis and a set of foreign policies that had grown stagnant by the early 1950s. Nikita Khrushchev gained power by 1955 and drew up fresh policies. A British official wondered, "How can this fat, vulgar man with his pig eyes and ceaseless flow of talk, really be the head" of the Soviet Empire?[43] But Khrushchev, born in a lowly miner's family, had shown ruthlessness in purging anti-Stalinists in the Ukraine during the 1930s and in trying (unsuccessfully) to improve Soviet agriculture later. As he clawed his way to the top, moreover, he shrewdly understood that Stalin's brutal policies had alienated the growing number of newly emerging peoples and had even helped the United States arm a frightened western Europe. By 1954–1955, Khrushchev was flying around the globe, trying to woo India, Burma, and other neutral countries.

As for Europe, the Soviets began to wonder whether a relaxation of tension would reassure the westerners and perhaps loosen up the NATO alliance. At one point (on April Fool's Day 1955), the Soviets even offered to join NATO to show their good will. The new approach seemed to work. In August 1954, France finally and flatly rejected the U.S. plan to rearm West Germany. Warning that the security of the Western world was at stake, Dulles announced that the United States would have to undertake an "agonizing reappraisal" of its foreign commitments if France did not change its mind. Translated, Dulles's phrase meant either that the United States would go home and leave Europe to Soviet mercies or—much more likely—go ahead and arm the Germans without French participation. A solution to the crisis finally occurred to British foreign minister Anthony Eden during his Sunday morning bath. West Germany was to be rearmed, but increased controls would be imposed, including the prohibition of German-produced nuclear weapons. To reassure the French further, Eden reversed historic British policy and pledged to station four divisions of British troops on the mainland of Europe to help protect France against aggression. In December 1954, the French accepted the deal. But Dulles

By 1955, with the rearmament of West Germany by NATO and the Soviet creation of the Warsaw Pact alliance, Europe seemed divided into two camps. But
that division became confused in 1956 with the Suez Canal affair and the anti-
Soviet uprisings in Hungary and Poland.

and Eisenhower had also compromised. They had hoped that their
plans for a new European Defense Community (EDC) would further
integrate the Europeans militarily, while allowing a cutback of U.S.
military spending in NATO. Eden's plan, however, killed the EDC
while attaching the new German military to NATO. As historian Brian
R. Duchin observes, Eisenhower's decision to accept Eden's plan "placed
security above fiscal economy."[44]

Khrushchev made the best of it. He certainly did not like West German rearmament, but he loved a divided Germany. Thus, he established diplomatic relations with the West Germans in 1955. At the
same time, he built up the Communist East German Army. Most
importantly, in May 1955, he broke a ten-year logjam by agreeing to
pull Soviet troops out of Austria and to allow that nation to regain
independence. He demanded in return that Austria remain neutral.
After signing the treaty, Molotov and Dulles—Old Ironpants and Old
Sourpuss—even appeared on a balcony to wave handkerchiefs in cel-

*Given the intensity of the cold war and their failure to hold a summit confer-
ence for ten years, the mood seemed jovial when the Big Four (Bulganin of the
USSR, Eisenhower of the United States, Faure of France, and Eden of Great
Britain) convened at Geneva in the summer of 1955. Although the photo typifies
the famous "spirit of Geneva," there were no significant diplomatic results to be
celebrated.*

ebration. That breakthrough led, in turn, to a four-power summit
meeting at Geneva in mid-1955, the first summit since the Potsdam
Conference of a decade before. The meeting produced nothing of
importance except good will. But given the events of the previous ten
years, the world gratefully accepted even that result.[45]

A TURN: SUEZ AND HUNGARY, 1956

In the following year, world affairs nearly fell apart, then regrouped,
and marched off in dramatically different directions. Crises in eastern
Europe and the Middle East, at first disconnected, suddenly came
together in November and opened a new chapter in the cold war's
history.

In early 1956, Khrushchev continued to try to reform and make more
efficient the Soviet system. He shocked the Twentieth Communist Party
Congress in Moscow by condemning Stalin's brutalities against party

members and the Communist system. (He carefully did not criticize Stalin's crimes against the Soviet people because Khrushchev himself had been involved in some of those.) The new leader then reversed Stalinist policy and urged "peaceful coexistence between states with differing political and social systems." The effect of his words was electric. The CIA director, Allen Dulles, suggested that perhaps Khrushchev was merely drunk when he made the speech. But peoples in the Soviet bloc quickly tried to pull down leaders associated with Stalin and demanded more open and democratic societies. Protesters in Poland attacked Communist party headquarters. In Hungary, street protests turned anti-Soviet. Khrushchev now appeared unsure and confused in responding to these challenges.[46]

Meanwhile, another crisis brewed in the Middle East. Egyptian army officers had begun pushing the British out of the Suez Canal area in 1954. The following year, the Egyptians turned to the Soviet bloc for a supply of arms. Eisenhower and Dulles did not approve, but they understood. Throughout 1955, Egyptian and Israeli forces had been involved in sharp border skirmishes. Moreover, Dulles had long condemned British colonialism for alienating such people as the Egyptians and driving them toward the Soviets. He decided to pull the Egyptians back by helping finance the building of the Aswan Dam on the Nile. The dream of their new leader, General Gamal Abdel Nasser, the dam was to help tame the river and create rich lands for cotton, among other crops.

But within six months, Dulles changed his mind. He had hoped that in return for the money, Nasser would move toward peace with Israel and end the dangerous fighting between Egyptian and Israeli armies. Nasser refused. To do so could be his ruin both within Egypt and throughout an Arab world that refused to recognize the existence of the Jewish state. Moreover, Congress cooled as it saw that Egyptian cotton would compete with the U.S. crop and that Nasser was becoming friendly with China.[47] In a rather crude move, Dulles announced that the United States would not fund the dam just when Nasser's foreign minister was flying to Washington to sign the contract. Furious, Nasser seized and nationalized the Suez Canal to obtain his own funds and to defy the West.

The Egyptian leader now controlled the waterway through which the West's oil supply flowed. British prime minister Anthony Eden and the French secretly decided to use force to regain the canal. Paris officials especially hoped that destroying Nasser would stop the aid going to Algerian revolutionaries who were killing many French soldiers and

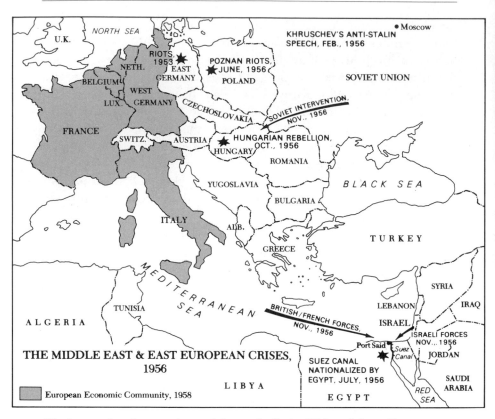

NORTH SEA
U.K.
RIOTS, 1953
NETH.
EAST GERMANY
BELGIUM
WEST GERMANY
LUX.
CZECHOSLOVAKIA
FRANCE
SWITZ.
AUSTRIA
HUNGARY
ITALY
ALB.
GREECE
MEDITERRANEAN SEA
TUNISIA
ALGERIA

• Moscow
KHRUSCHEV'S ANTI-STALIN SPEECH, FEB., 1956
POZNAN RIOTS, JUNE, 1956
POLAND
SOVIET UNION
SOVIET INTERVENTION, NOV., 1956
HUNGARIAN REBELLION, OCT., 1956
ROMANIA
YUGOSLAVIA
BULGARIA
BLACK SEA
TURKEY
BRITISH/FRENCH FORCES, NOV., 1956
SYRIA
LEBANON
IRAQ
ISRAEL
ISRAELI FORCES NOV... 1956
Port Said   Suez Canal
JORDAN
SUEZ CANAL NATIONALIZED BY EGYPT, JULY, 1956
SAUDI ARABIA
RED SEA
LIBYA
EGYPT

THE MIDDLE EAST & EAST EUROPEAN CRISES, 1956

European Economic Community, 1958

The international arena changed dramatically in 1956, and the cold war entered a new phase—in the Middle East and in eastern Europe, but also within the Western alliance itself.

destroying what remained of the French Empire. For their own reasons, Israelis agreed to cooperate with Paris and London. Although kept in the dark by the British, Dulles and Eisenhower knew from intelligence reports that something was afoot. Warning Eden to be restrained, the two Americans worked to find a compromise between the British and the Egyptians.

But it was too late. On October 29, 1956, Israel, according to plan, attacked Egypt and drove toward the Suez. Then, however, the plan collapsed. Eden and the French delayed sending in their forces. When they did so, their armies moved slowly. Eisenhower's famous temper exploded: "It's the damnedest business I ever saw supposedly intelligent governments getting themselves into." He was afraid that the Soviets would use the crisis to provide massive help to Nasser. U.S. officials angrily told the British "to comply with the goddamn cease-fire [resolution passed by the U.N.] or go ahead with the goddamn invasion. . . . What we can't stand is [the] goddamn hesitation waltz while Hungary is burning!"[48]

For as the Middle East became engulfed in war, Khrushchev had seized the chance to smash protests in Poland and Hungary with Soviet tanks. Proccupied with Suez (and the final hours of his own re-election campaign), Eisenhower did not know how to respond. He rejected sending U.S. troops or supplies because Hungary was "as inaccessible to us as Tibet." He rejected a suggestion of using atomic weapons because "to annihilate Hungary . . . is in no way to help her."[49] His only answer was to focus on the Middle East and end the war before Khrushchev moved in to help Nasser. In one phone conversation, the furious president reduced the British prime minister to tears. U.S. officials threatened to cut off oil to Great Britain and ruin the British currency unless the war stopped. By November 5, Khrushchev was proclaiming that he would use Soviet missiles for "country busting" in western Europe, unless the British and French left Egypt. Eisenhower warned him to back off and by mid-November restored some order to the Suez area as the British-French-Israeli forces retreated.

But the world would not be the same afterward. By defying Great Britain and France, Nasser helped trigger immense pride and ambitions in the newly emerging nations. By turning the screws on the Brit-

David Levine's cartoon nicely captures how, by the Suez crisis of November 1956, U.S. Secretary of State Dulles was taming and caging the once-feared British lion (here with Prime Minister Anthony Eden's face).

ish and French after they had deceived him, Eisenhower—with Eden's blundering help—badly split the Western alliance. Not just the United States suffered, however. By having to impose order and restore hard-line Communist leaders in Poland and Hungary through sheer force, Khrushchev had to admit just how fragmented and anti-Russian the Soviet bloc had become. Since 1945, the globe had been described as "two camps." But with the 1956 crises, the two camps splintered into many camps. Eisenhower faced a different world as he began his second term.

EUROPE IS EUROPEANIZED AS THE U.S. ECONOMY IS LESS U.S. (1957–1960)

The Suez disaster was followed in October 1957 by the Soviet launching of Sputnik I, the first small, human-made satellite placed in orbit around the earth. The Soviet triumph convinced most Americans that Soviet science was equal to, if not ahead of, U.S. science. It also made them believe that, indeed, Khrushchev could now "direct rockets to any part of the globe," as the Soviets bragged. In 1957, Eisenhower suffered a small stroke. His speech never fully recovered. The next year, charges of corruption riddled the White House staff. In 1959, John Foster Dulles died after a two-and-a-half-year fight with cancer. Against this background, the president had to deal with an angry Europe and a revolutionary, newly emerging bloc of nations—and do so, moreover, with a sliding U.S. economy.

Great Britain and France had been humiliated by the Suez fiasco. The episode marked the true end of the British Empire and destroyed French chances to put down the Algerian rebellion. France's failures finally led to the demand that the tall, arrogant figure of General Charles de Gaulle be returned to power in 1958. De Gaulle began to pull France out of Algeria. Then he moved to restore French authority and independence. De Gaulle told Eisenhower that the French and British should be involved in U.S. decisions about the Western alliance, especially those involving nuclear weapons. Eisenhower ignored the request. The United States was not going to give up its freedom of action, especially to down-on-their-luck colonial nations. De Gaulle responded by accelerating development of a French nuclear bomb. The British did the same with their own bomb. As a London official told an American, "Since the events of last year [in Suez] we cannot be entirely confident of America."[50]

The Europeans also moved on the economic front. In 1950, the French had proposed a European Coal and Steel Community to tie together the basic French and German industries. The French hoped, thereby, to control German recovery and to gain access to rich West German raw materials. In 1957, the French and West Germans took the next step: they formed the Common Market (the European Economic Community or EEC) in a historic agreement with four other states— Italy, Belgium, the Netherlands, and Luxembourg. The EEC aimed at eliminating tariffs between members and making the region a United States of Europe for traders and investors. Members did, however, erect a tariff against outsiders—for example, against the British, who refused to join, and the Americans.

In 1957–1958, U.S. investors began flooding the promising, rich EEC with dollars. The Americans had grown wealthy from their post-1945 trade and had money to invest abroad. U.S. corporations, moreover, flocked to Europe to get inside the new tariff wall and sell to the vast EEC market. American private investment overseas shot up from $11.8 billion in 1950 to nearly $30 billion by 1959. Historically, this investment had gone into Canada and Latin America. (U.S. business owned three-fourths of the oil and gas as well as half of the manufacturing plant of the Canadians.) But after 1957, the investment tripled in western Europe to $6 billion within three years. The United States was taking over large parts of Europe's economy in an "American invasion."

Just as suddenly, the Americans—by far the richest people in history—discovered that they were beginning to run out of money. They were not only sending billions abroad for investment, but billions overseas to contain communism. Until 1957, these vast expenses had been paid for by a large trade surplus. (Americans each year were selling about $7 billion more abroad than they bought.) After 1957, this surplus slid to under $4 billion and, for a moment in 1959, actually moved into the red as Americans bought more abroad than they sold. The moment passed, but it returned in 1971 to stay. Thus, the late 1950s marked a historic turning point in U.S. economic and diplomatic history. For the first time since the 1870s, Americans found that they could not compete as they wanted in world markets. They were suddenly spending more overseas than they earned. U.S. officials could cover this deficit in only two ways: by printing more dollars or by shipping out gold bars from their reserves. By 1960, the U.S. gold supply, which led the world in 1945 with a total of nearly $25 billion, sank to $19 billion and, by 1968, to $10 billion. Not enough gold remained to

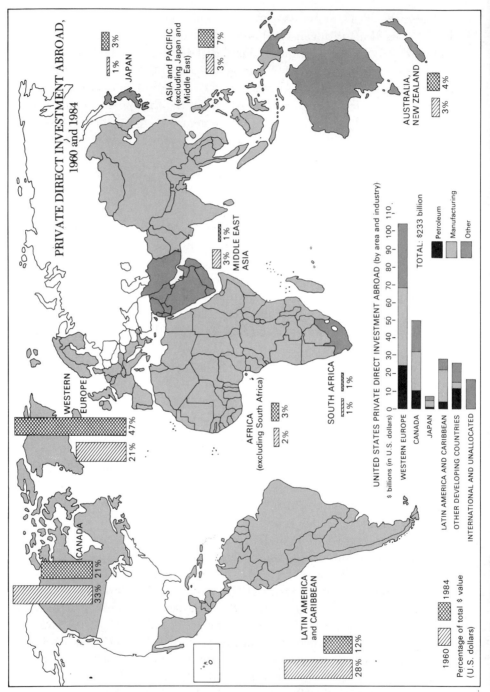

PRIVATE DIRECT INVESTMENT ABROAD, 1960 and 1984

JAPAN
3%
1%

ASIA and PACIFIC (excluding Japan and Middle East)
7%
3%

AUSTRALIA, NEW ZEALAND
4%
3%

MIDDLE EAST ASIA
1%
3%

WESTERN EUROPE
47%
21%

AFRICA (excluding South Africa)
3%
2%

SOUTH AFRICA
1%
1%

CANADA
21%
33%

LATIN AMERICA and CARIBBEAN
12%
28%

1960
1984
Percentage of total $ value (U.S. dollars)

UNITED STATES PRIVATE DIRECT INVESTMENT ABROAD (by area and industry)

$ billions (in U.S. dollars)   0 10 20 30 40 50 60 70 80 90 100 110

TOTAL: $233 billion

Petroleum
Manufacturing
Other

WESTERN EUROPE
CANADA
JAPAN
LATIN AMERICA AND CARIBBEAN
OTHER DEVELOPING COUNTRIES
INTERNATIONAL AND UNALLOCATED

Beginning in the late 1950s, U.S. private investment moved overseas more rapidly, especially into western Europe, where observers warned of an "American invasion." By the mid-1980s, however, Americans owed other nations more than foreign nations owed Americans.

support the dollar bills Americans used every day, let alone support the dollars moving overseas.

For most Americans, however, the dollar's dilemma was not the bad news. They were being flooded with cheaper and better goods from West Germany (such as Volkswagens) and Japan. The United States economy slowed and stumbled into a recession in 1958–1959. In retrospect, it is clear that these years marked part of another historic turn— the turn in the United States from an industrial (iron, steel, autos) to a service (insurance, investment, communications) economy. It was going to be a tough adjustment for many Americans. And it could not have come at a worse time. For they faced a slumping economy at home just when they were confronting challenges from Japan and western Europe, and major threats from the Soviet Union and revolutions in the newly emerging world.[51]

EISENHOWER, HIS DOCTRINE, AND CRISIS (1957–1960)

Between 1945 and 1960, approximately 40 nations with 800-million people revolted against their colonial masters. This political earthquake shook the United Nations. Its original 51 members exploded to 100 and then to 114 by 1965. The United States could no longer assume support from a majority in the UN. A growing gap appeared between the prosperous United States and the poor, newly emerging world, where only one out of seven persons earned more than $450 per year (in India the average worker got 15 cents a day), where drinkable water and medical care were rare, and where money needed for trade and development disappeared into Japanese and Western pockets because of unfavorable trade balances.

Eisenhower and Dulles emphasized that communism could not be stopped unless the West outraced the Communists economically. But the Soviets were "increasing their own productivity at the rate of about 6 percent per annum, which is about twice our rate," the secretary of state complained. In newly emerging areas such as India, Southeast Asia, and Latin America, "there is little, if any, increase. That is one reason why Communism has such great appeal" and "slogans of 'liberty, freedom' " do not. The U.S. ambassador to the United Nations, Henry Cabot Lodge, bluntly told Eisenhower's cabinet in 1959 that Americans should quit pushing "the specific word 'Capitalism' which is beyond rehabilitation in the minds of the non-white world." Lodge then asked the big question: "The U.S. can win wars but the question is can we win revolutions."[52]

Dulles hoped to solve that problem—at least in part—by bringing the new nations into a U.S. alliance system. When a top State Department official asked him if "we are opposed to any neutrals," Dulles answered, "Yes." After all, he went on, the Soviets believe that "a neutral is one who does not participate in [U.S.] collective security arrangements." Dulles wanted to try to lock the newly independent peoples into SEATO, OAS, and various Middle East arrangements (such as the Baghdad Pact). But he knew that this was not enough. Eisenhower finally enlarged the Export-Import Bank funding, agreed to easier World Bank loans to the new nations, and even set up new regional development banks (for Latin America and the Middle East) to provide economic carrots.

The president also used a stick (often held by the CIA). In Africa, Ghana's independence from the British Empire in 1957 helped trigger the appearance of a dozen new African nations over the next four years. Many had not been prepared for self-rule by their colonial governors. The Belgian Congo had long been notorious for exploiting its black subjects (see p. 172), and when it became independent in 1960, Eisenhower instantly viewed its leader, Patrice Lumumba, as a possible Communist. Lumumba was an ardent nationalist, not a Communist, but CIA agents saw little difference and prepared plans to eliminate the Congolese leader. In Indonesia, the Eisenhower team also sent in the CIA when Dulles thought that President Achmed Sukarno was turning leftward. A long-time hero and leader of Indonesia, Sukarno was also a nationalist, colorful and effective, who used Communists for his own purposes. But Allen Dulles, director of the CIA, tried to overthrow him with $10 million of support for anti-Sukarno rebels. It was a plan patterned after the 1954 CIA coup in Guatemala. Eisenhower publicly claimed that the U.S. policy was only "careful neutrality," but Sukarno's forces shot down a CIA plane, damned the U.S. involvement, and then destroyed the rebellion. Relations between the United States and Southeast Asia's largest nation sank to a new low in 1959–1960.

Eisenhower's policies worked better in the Middle East, but only in the short run. The Suez disaster set off major political changes in the region, including the rise of General Nasser to hero's status among many Arabs. He worked with Syria and Jordan to spread his pan-Arab policies, which, Secretary of State Dulles feared, had strong Soviet support. Dulles privately condemned Nasser as "an expansionist dic-

Bastian, the cartoonist for the San Francisco Chronicle, *catches the complexities of Middle Eastern politics of July 1958, when Dulles and Eisenhower landed U.S. troops on Lebanon's beautiful beaches in an effort to contain what they feared was Arab radicalism that had appeared in Egypt and Iraq.*

tator somewhat of the Hitler type" who "will get help from the Soviet Union."[53] Eisenhower asked Congress to give him authority to use force, whenever he thought it necessary, to prevent "international communism" from conquering the Middle East. Some Democratic senators protested giving such a blank check to the president, but Eisenhower, as usual, won. Congress passed the so-called Eisenhower Doctrine of 1957, which allowed him to use armed forces to help any nation resist "armed attack from any country controlled by international communism." Congress, again giving the president an enormous amount of power, never tried to define what it meant by "international communism."

The doctrine had little effect on Nasser's popularity. Jordan finally broke with Nasser (and received massive military help from the United States as a reward). But Egypt and Syria formed the United Arab Republic in early 1958. On July 13, 1958, the weak Iraqi kingdom fell to nationalist army officers who admired Nasser. Eisenhower was afraid that Lebanon would be next. That nation's Maronite Christian officials were under fire from the much larger Moslem majority. On July 14, with little hesitation or preparation, Eisenhower ordered 5,000 U.S. troops to land on Lebanon's beautiful beaches and maintain order. The president never invoked the Eisenhower Doctrine. Everyone understood that nationalism, not communism, was on the march. But the president was afraid that the dominoes were falling in a strategic area where the last to fall could land on U.S. companies that controlled the world's largest oil reserves. It was too late, however, to restore the Iraqi kingdom or the U.S.-created treaty system (the Baghdad Pact) in which Iraq was the key link. U.S. troops finally left Lebanon in October. They also left a Middle East that was greatly changed since the Suez crisis, one much less friendly to the United States.[54]

CASTRO AND THE THREAT TO THE MONROE DOCTRINE (1957–1960)

Latin America was also building up to an explosion by the late 1950s. Dulles had trouble blaming this crisis on communism. The Soviets had little interest or contact in the region. Local Communist parties sometimes had large memberships, but they were politically irrelevant, ignored by Moscow, and closely watched by powerful Latin American army officers.

The central problem was economic. With the end of the Korean War, demand and prices slumped for Latin American raw materials. The region's imports rose much more rapidly than exports. Money grew ever scarcer. Economic hard times struck as the U.S. economy slowed; the proven rule was that when the North American economy sneezed, Latin Americans got pneumonia. The slowdown hit as the area's population growth rate was 2.5 percent annually, one of the world's highest. The number of Latin Americans would double to 360 million in just thirty years. U.S. businesses moved into the region but invested mostly in Venezuelan oil. These North American companies, nevertheless, accounted for 10 percent of Latin America's gross national product and a full 30 percent of its exports, figures that set the Southern Hemisphere apart from Africa or even Southeast Asia. In those parts of the world, problems could be blamed on European colonialism. But in Latin America, where few colonial enclaves existed, the economic problems were often pinned on U.S. control of the export economies.

U.S. officials usually tried to keep the lid on these boiling problems by working with Latin American military officers. Eisenhower even awarded medals to two of the area's worst dictators: Manuel A. Odría of Peru and Marcos Pérez Jiménez of Venezuela. Pérez Jiménez was overthrown in January 1958. Four months later, Vice-President Nixon visited Caracas, Venezuela. Earlier in his trip through the region, he had encountered hostile crowds, but in Caracas mobs spit on Nixon and his wife, Pat, then stopped and tried to overturn his limousine.

One Secret Service man sitting next to Nixon pulled his revolver and said, "Lets get some of these sons-of-bitches." Nixon ordered him to "put that away," at least until the mob tried to enter the car itself. The driver finally managed to get the car to safety. Meanwhile, Eisenhower mobilized U.S. military units for a possible parachute drop to rescue the vice-president. Nixon returned to Washington shaken but unscathed.[55] He urged that new policies be pushed, but no one could think of fresh approaches that would be both non-revolutionary and cheap.

As the debate wandered on, U.S. power was suddenly challenged in the most surprising place in Latin America: Cuba, which Washington had controlled since the war of 1898. By the late 1950s, North Americans owned nearly all of its mines and cattle ranches and half of its sugar—the three products on which the nation's economy rested. After 1934, U.S. officials had stood aside as General Fulgencio Batista took control of the island. He reigned over a highly corrupt society marked by Mafia rule, rampant unemployment, and widespread prostitution. On July 26, 1953, a twenty-six-year-old lawyer-politician, well educated in Roman Catholic schools and embittered by the U.S.-Batista alliance, tried to overthrow the government.

Fidel Castro was captured, jailed (where he organized prisoners and read Shakespeare, Kant, Lenin, Einstein, novels, and books on Franklin D. Roosevelt), released in 1955, and then went to Mexico where he gathered support for another try. He and eighty other revolutionaries landed in Cuba in 1956 but were nearly wiped out by Batista's forces. The rebels were down to sixteen soldiers when their fortunes turned around. Long-suffering peasants joined them. Batista's troops could not exterminate Castro's followers. When the dictator claimed he had done so, newspapers (especially the *New York Times*) published interviews with Castro that made him an international hero. By late 1958, U.S. officials finally took Castro's threat seriously as he scored military victories. They tried to stop his Twenty-sixth of July Movement by bringing to power someone who thought like, but was more popular than, Batista. It was too late.[56] On New Year's Day, 1959, the raggedy rebel soldiers marched victoriously into Havana.

The triumphant Castro was determined to change Cuban society. That meant breaking ties with the United States so that he could control his nation's resources. He understood the special need for a massive land-reform program (0.5 percent of the population owned one-third of the land, much of which lay unused). Castro later claimed that he had been a Marxist-Leninist since he had read their works

Fidel Castro (1926–) led the Cuban revolution that deposed a pro-U.S. government in 1959. An effective guerrilla leader, Castro also proved adept at mobilizing the Cuban people with his speeches, some of which continued for hours.

years before, but the evidence is more complex. He had received little help from the inept Cuban Communist party and later used the party only to carry out his own program. When Castro visited the United States in April 1959, Eisenhower refused to meet him, but Vice-President Nixon held a long talk with Castro and came away believing that the Cuban was not a Communist.[57] Nevertheless, relations rapidly fell apart. U.S. economic help slowed. In early 1960, Castro agreed to sell sugar to the Soviets in return for oil and industrial goods. He then demanded that the U.S. oil firms in Cuba refine the oil. The companies were bitter but agreed to do so until the State Department told them to refuse. Castro seized the oil companies. Eisenhower shut off the U.S. market on which Cuban sugar had depended since the 1890s. Khrushchev moved in to buy more sugar. In March 1960, Eisenhower secretly ordered the CIA to prepare plans for overthrowing Castro. The Cuban leader rapidly moved to confiscate privately owned firms, both foreign and domestic. Eisenhower responded by cutting off all U.S. trade to Cuba except medicine and some food staples. By the time the president left office in January 1961, U.S.-Cuban relations had broken.

Historian Richard Welch believes that "Castro only became a Marxist sometime between fall 1960 and fall 1961." Welch also concludes that U.S. policy did not fully determine the course of Castro's policies, but U.S. responses gave the Cuban revolutionaries excuses for centralizing their power and accelerated "the formation of the Cuban-Russian alliance." To use Lodge's phrase, the United States had not been able to "win revolutions" even 90 miles off its own coast. In mid-1960, Khrushchev publicly boasted that the Monroe Doctrine was dead. Privately he predicted that "Castro will have to gravitate to us like an iron filing to a magnet."[58]

Sputnik versus U-2: The U.S.-Soviet Rivalry (1957–1960)

The Soviet leader had also caused Eisenhower other bad nights. In October 1957, Soviet missiles had sent Sputnik into space. A month later they sent up another satellite, this time with a dog on board. Eisenhower's public-opinion rating sank an astonishing 22 percent. The Soviets actually seemed to be beating the land of Henry Ford at the American game of technology and invention. For the first time since World War II, the United States mobilized schools and factories to fight a war, this time in technology and science instead of on battlefields. "It was Us versus Them," a journalist recalled of the post-Sputnik days. "It was the American way of life, not to mention tailfins, Wrigley's Spearmint gum, Wednesday night bowling and attending the church of your choice, going against the godless horde."[59]

Even before Sputnik mania set in, Eisenhower secretly appointed a special committee, headed by H. Rowan Gaither, Jr., of the Ford Foundation, to study U.S. security needs. In a report written largely by Gaither and Paul Nitze, the Gaither committee warned the president that the United States would lose the cold war in the near future unless he pumped up defense spending by $11 billion to some $48 billion. Using phrases that indicated that the nation's survival was at stake, Gaither's group also argued that spending such money would boost employment and help avoid economic recession. When the committee's conclusions leaked to newspapers, they worsened the panic already caused by Sputnik.[60]

But Eisenhower refused to panic. He flatly rejected most of Gaither's recommendations. When the committee urged the creation of fallout shelters to protect Americans against atomic radiation (at the cost of $100 per American, or $30 billion over five years), the president said that no defense existed against such a war. He was afraid that another $10 billion for defense would fuel inflation and undermine the economy. The retired general called military hardware this "negative stuff." Nor did he change his mind when leading Democrats, smelling the 1960 presidential race just ahead, blasted Eisenhower for letting the nation's guard down. Senators Stuart Symington of Missouri, John F. Kennedy of Massachussetts, and Lyndon Johnson of Texas led the attack. Aiming at the 1960 Democratic nomination as well as at Eisenhower, they warned of a large "missile gap" in Khrushchev's favor unless the president spent more money. Eisenhower privately called them "sanctimonious hypocritical bastards."[61]

The president felt strongly about the accusations because he knew no missile gap existed—or, more accurately, that one existed and that it overwhelmingly favored the United States. He knew this because since June 1956 he had secretly approved flights of a new plane, the U-2, piloted by CIA agents at 70,000 feet to take pictures of Soviet military installations. The plane supposedly flew too high to be shot down by Soviet missiles, although from the start Khrushchev apparently knew that the U-2s were flying over his territory. Using cameras that, from a distance of 11 miles, could photograph the license-plate numbers on a Soviet official's car, Eisenhower learned that Khrushchev had decided not to rush ahead and build missiles. The Soviet leader apparently was waiting for new missiles to be developed, meanwhile using Sputnik as a way to bluff Americans into thinking that the USSR had a massive strategic force. Knowing that it was a bluff, Eisenhower refused to listen to demands for much larger military budgets. He did, however, go along with a $2.5 billion rise, especially for the air force. Instead, Congress gave him $8 billion more in 1958. Eisenhower, meanwhile, could not make public the information gleaned by the secret U-2 flights or by the first spy satellites circulating in outer space that he authorized in 1960. Once again, politics could not keep pace with technology.[62]

Khrushchev tried to use his bluff to win a great prize: Berlin. Fearful that West Germany would obtain nuclear weapons, he floated the Rapacki Plan (named after the Polish foreign minister) to create a nuclear-free zone in central Europe. In the United States, George Kennan supported such a disengagement, only to be bitterly attacked by Dean Acheson (Kennan's boss in the State Department during 1949–1950), who wanted no part of negotiations with Moscow: "Mr. Kennan has never . . . grasped the realities of power relationships, but takes a rather mystical attitude toward them." (Columnist James Reston observed: "Next to the Lincoln Memorial in moonlight the sight of Mr. Dean G. Acheson blowing his top is without doubt the most impressive view in the capital.") Dulles privately thanked Acheson for blasting Kennan. The Rapacki Plan consequently had a short life, so in late 1958 Khrushchev issued an ultimatum. Calling West Berlin a "malignant tumor" inside the Communist bloc, he demanded the Western powers evacuate the city within six months. Believing that abandoning 2 million Germans in West Berlin would ruin the entire U.S. position in Europe, the president said the United States would not leave. He then underlined his point by warning that he had no intention of fighting a ground war against the massive Soviet army in central Europe. The war would be nuclear. He would, however, be happy to talk with Khrushchev about it, if Moscow removed its six-month ultimatum.[63]

Khrushchev, who lusted after an invitation to visit the United States for the first time, quickly accepted. His trip to the president's retreat at Camp David, Maryland, and to a midwestern farm went well. (A visit to Hollywood to see the filming of *Can-Can* went less well; Khrushchev was shocked by the brief costumes and sexy dancing.) A "spirit of Camp David" emerged. The Soviets announced a cut in their army by 1 million men, and a thaw began to melt the cold war. A summit conference was scheduled in Paris for May 1960, after which Eisenhower planned to make a triumphal tour of the Soviet Union.

On the eve of the summit, the Soviets finally shot down a U-2 plane. Eisenhower, believing the pilot had died, lied, saying that it was only a weather plane that had gone off-course. With great glee Khrushchev then produced the live pilot, Francis Gary Powers, who had already confessed to the spy mission. Humiliated, Eisenhower told his secretary that he was "very depressed" and "would like to resign." Khrushchev went to Paris, attacked Eisenhower, and short-circuited the summit. The Soviets again upped the pressure on West Berlin. The cold war returned in force. But the question remains: Why, in the midst of the most promising era of U.S.-Soviet relations since 1945, did someone in the CIA or the White House allow the U-2 to make this final, fateful mission? That question has never been answered.[64]

THE EISENHOWER ERA AS FANTASY AND FACT

In looking back, the 1950s seem one of the happiest, most stable, and most secure eras in American history. At the time, however, the United States was a troubled nation, made nearly paranoid by McCarthyism, revolutions in the newly emerging world, and imagined "missile gaps," as well as by the shadow of economic recession. Hope seemed to lie in the military, CIA, and FBI. Hollywood's science-fiction films (which were new in postwar movie making) mirrored the great fear of technology, communism, and the unknown. In *The Thing*, for example, scientists were ignorant or evil (if not pro-Soviet), while the military personnel knew that the only way to deal with the creature from outerspace was to kill it. The memorable last line of the film could be understood as a political warning: "Tell the world—Watch the skies, everywhere—Watch the skies!"[65]

Eisenhower, however, seemed a center of calm and reason. His popularity, journalist James Reston wrote in 1955, had become "a national phenomenon, like baseball." The president tried to use his great appeal to control defense spending and, above all, to protect the U.S. economy. In truth, by early 1961 the U.S. nuclear stockpile had tripled in just two years to 18,000 weapons. The Pentagon's plans were now aimed at striking not the twenty to thirty Soviet targets picked out in 1948, but more than 2,500 such targets in 1960. U.S. nuclear weapons were stationed in at least four overseas countries. As for the economy, in 1960, the head of the Federal Reserve Board warned that gold and dollars were so rapidly exiting the country that "this is the first time in my lifetime that the credit of the United States has been questioned." Eisenhower meanwhile set important precedents by using the CIA to try to overthrow nationalist, popular governments in Iran, Guatemala, and Indonesia. Dulles fashioned a far-flung network of alliances that, in Eisenhower's words, committed Americans "to support the defense of almost every free area . . . facing the Sino-Soviet complex."[66]

With these foreign policies, Eisenhower helped transform the Republican party from one led by conservative senator Robert Taft— who feared overextended commitments, mistrusted presidential power, and especially disliked NATO—to one led by Richard Nixon and Ronald Reagan, who believed that such global commitments and increased presidential power were both necessary and natural. Eisenhower's popularity and prestige helped make possible Nixon's and Reagan's expansive policies.

But Eisenhower is especially remembered for his farewell speech of January 1961. About to turn the White House over to John F. Kennedy, the old soldier, on national television, warned his audience that there would be "a recurring temptation" to solve crises through "some spectacular and costly action" that promised to be "the miraculous solution to all current difficulties." Such a miracle cure, Eisenhower declared, did not exist, nor could "a huge increase" in defense spending find it. He was worried that the nation would, nevertheless, bow to the pressures of vast powers "new in American experience": the "immense military establishment and a large arms industry." Americans "must guard against the acquisition of unwarranted influence, whether sought or unsought, by the military-industrial complex. The potential for the disastrous rise of misplaced power exists and will persist."[67]

Eisenhower, thus, left some interesting advice to his young successor. But he also left a powerful CIA, nuclear superiority based on a huge stockpile of weapons of mass destruction, and global commitments that depended on that "military-industrial complex." In the words of historian H. W. Brands, Jr., by emphasizing anticommunism and increased collective security, Eisenhower left "a debt of commitments that would outstrip American capabilities"; and by waging the cold war "by covert and admittedly repugnant means," and by failing to take "serious steps toward disarmament," Eisenhower left behind a record that could "eventually damage America's interests."[68] It was now up to Kennedy to choose.

NOTES

1. Stephen E. Ambrose, *Eisenhower*, Vol. II: *The President* (New York, 1984), pp. 18–19.
2. Robert Wright, "Eisenhower's Fifties," *Antioch Review* 38 (Summer 1980): 277–290.
3. Douglas Brinkley, *Dean Acheson: The Cold War Years, 1953–71* (New Haven, Conn., 1992), pp. 8–9; Fred I. Greenstein, *The Hidden-Hand Presidency: Eisenhower as a Leader* (New York, 1982), pp. 9, 69.
4. Paul Boller, Jr., *Presidential Anecdotes* (New York, 1981), p. 292.
5. Sir Maurice Peterson to N. M. Butler, 10 April 1947, FO 371 AN 1480/28/45, British Public Record Office, Kew, Eng.; Ambrose, p. 21.
6. *U.S. News & World Report*, 24 January 1958, p. 104.
7. Robert J. Donovan, *Eisenhower: The Inside Story* (New York, 1956), p. 162.
8. A good and slightly different view is Duane A. Tananbaum, "The Bricker Amendment Controversy: Its Origins and Eisenhower's Role," *Diplomatic History* 9 (Winter, 1985): 73–93; "Legislative Leadership Meeting, Jan. 11, 1954, Supplementary Notes," Legislative Meetings, January–February 1954 File, Box 1, Ann Whitman File, Papers of Dwight D. Eisenhower, Dwight Eisenhower Library, Abilene, Kans.
9. Michael R. Beschloss, *Mayday: Eisenhower, Khrushchev, and the U-2 Affair* (New York, 1986), p. 83.
10. Anna K. Nelson, "John Foster Dulles and the Bipartisan Congress," *Political Science Quarterly* 101 (Spring 1987): pp. 43–44, 64.
11. Brinkley, p. 17; Stanley D. Bachrack, *The Committee of One Million: "China Lobby" Politics, 1953–1971* (New York, 1976).
12. Nora Sayre, *Running Time: Films of the Cold War* (New York, 1982), pp. 176, 201.
13. Diary entry of 2 July 1953, from the personal diaries of Dwight D. Eisenhower, made available by Francis L. Loewenheim, professor of history, Rice University, who found it at the Eisenhower Library.
14. Lloyd C. Gardner, *A Covenant with Power: America and World Order from Wilson to Reagan* (New York, 1984), p. 51; Donovan, pp. 3, 9.
15. Beschloss, p. 153.

16. William B. Pickett, "The Eisenhower Solarium Notes," *Society for Historians of American Foreign Relations Newsletter* 16 (June 1985): 1–8; Robert A. Divine, *Eisenhower and the Cold War* (New York, 1981), pp. 33–39.

17. David Alan Rosenberg, "The Origins of Overkill: Nuclear Weapons and American Strategy, 1945–1960," *International Security* 7 (Spring 1983): 27.

18. Samuel F. Wells, Jr., "The Origins of Massive Retaliation," *Political Science Quarterly* 96 (Spring 1981): 31–52; John Foster Dulles, "A Policy of Boldness," *Life*, 19 May 1952, p. 151.

19. JoAnne Brown, "A is for Atom, B is for Bomb: Civil Defense in American Public Education, 1948–1963," *Journal of American History* 75 (June 1988), pp. 80–88; Robert A. Divine, *Blowing on the Wind: the Nuclear Test Ban Debate, 1954–1960* (New York, 1978), esp. pp. 4–11, 100–101, 182–193, 281–295; *Washington Post*, 27 December 1983, p. A9; Robert Divine, "Early Record on Test Moratoriums," *Bulletin of Atomic Scientists* 42 (May 1986): 24–26.

20. Barton J. Bernstein, "Foreign Policy in the Eisenhower Administration," *Foreign Service Journal* 50 (May 1973): 30.

21. Lawrence Freedman, *The Evolution of Nuclear Strategy* (New York, 1983), pp. 77–78.

22. The standard account of the war is now Burton I. Kaufman, *The Korean War* (New York, 1986), esp. pp. 251–342, on ending the conflict; also see Ambrose, pp. 51–52; and especially Michael Carver, "Across the Dividing Line," *Times Literary Supplement*, 11–17 December 1987, p. 1368.

23. Walter Pincus, "Early Postwar Era . . . ,"*Washington Post*, 22 January 1985, p. A8; Wells, 37.

24. Divine, *Eisenhower and the Cold War*, ch. I, details the debate over "liberation."

25. John Colville, *Winston Churchill and His Inner Circle* (New York, 1981), p. 139; the best account of the debate in the summer of 1953 is M. Steven Fish, "After Stalin's Death: The Anglo-American Debate over a New Cold War," *Diplomatic History* 10 (Fall 1986): esp. 343,353.

26. Dean Acheson, *Present at the Creation: My Years in the State Department* (New York, 1969), pp. 652–659.

27. Mark Hamilton Lytle, *The Origins of the Iranian-American Alliance, 1941–1953* (New York, 1987), pp. 192–203, 205–218; Barry Rubin, *Paved with Good Intentions: The American Experience and Iran* (New York, 1980), pp. 45–90. A remarkable firsthand account by the key CIA agent is Kermit Roosevelt, *Countercoup* (New York, 1979).

28. Blanche Wiesen Cook, *The Declassified Eisenhower* (New York, 1981), pp. 269–270, 276.

29. Richard H. Immerman, *The CIA in Guatemala: The Foreign Policy of Intervention* (Austin, Tex., 1982), pp. 190–201; Robert J. McMahon, "Eisenhower and Third World Nationalism: A Critique of the Revisionists," *Political Science Quarterly* 101, no. 3 (1986): 467. The Dulles quote is in Peter Lyon, *Eisenhower, Portrait of the Hero* (Boston, 1974), p. 627.

30. Philip C. Roettinger, "For a CIA Man, It's 1954 Again," *Los Angeles Times*, 16 March 1986, pt. V, p. 5; an important recent account, put in the 1944–1985 context, is Robert Trudeau and Lars Schoultz, "Guatemala," in *Confronting Revolution*, ed. Morris J. Blachman (New York, 1986), esp. pp. 25–28.

31. Jonathan Schell, *The Time of Illusion* (New York, 1976), p. 59.

32. Beschloss, p. 104.

33. "Legislative Leadership Meeting, June 21, 1954, Supplementary Notes," Legislative Meetings Series, Box 4, Eisenhower Library; *The Pentagon Papers*, Senator Gravel ed., 4 vols. (Boston, 1971), I, pp. 83–84.

34. U.S. Government, *Public Papers of the Presidents of the United States: Dwight D. Eisenhower, 1954* (Washington, D.C., 1958), pp. 382–383.

35. George C. Herring and Richard H. Immerman, "Eisenhower, Dulles, and Dienbienphu," *Journal of American History* 71 (September 1984): 356–357; Colville, p. 140.

36. Divine, *Eisenhower and the Cold War*, pp. 45–51.

37. Ambrose, p. 184. The most thorough and useful analysis of the 1953–1954 U.S. decisions is now Lloyd Gardner, *Approaching Vietnam: From World War II through Dienbienphu* (New York, 1988), esp. chs. IV–VIII

38. The Geneva agreements and the U.S. statement are in Department of State, *American Foreign Policy, 1950–1955: Basic Documents* (Washington, D.C., 1957), pp. 750–788; a good brief discussion is in George Herring, *America's Longest War: The United States and Vietnam, 1950–1975*, 2d ed. (New York, 1986), pp. 37–42.

39. George McT. Kahin, *Intervention: How America Became Involved in Vietnam* (New York, 1986), pp. 70–81.

40. The U.S. creation of SEATO as a means for containing communism is a central theme in Gardner, *Approaching Vietnam;* U.S. Congress, Senate, Committee on Foreign Relations, 83d Cong., 2d sess., 1954, *Hearings . . . on the Southeast Asia Collective Defense Treaty* (Washington, D.C., 1954), pt. I, pp. 16–17; important documents and commentary are in Lloyd Gardner, "Dominoes, Diem, and Death, 1952–1963," in *America in Vietnam*, ed. William Appleman Williams *et al.* (New York, 1985), esp. pp. 172–179.

41. Herring, pp. 71–72; Kahin, p. 88, has the 1961 quote by the U.S. expert.

42. David Mayers, "Eisenhower's Containment Policy and the Major Communist Powers, 1953–1956," *International History Review* 5 (February 1983): 83; and Mayers's detailed analysis in his *Cracking the Monolith* (Baton Rouge, La., 1986), esp. pp. 135–150; Gordon H. Chang, *Friends and Enemies* (Stanford, 1990), p. 144.

43. Beschloss, pp. 103–104.

44. Anthony Eden, *The Memoirs of Anthony Eden: Full Circle* (Boston, 1960), pp. 60–71, 167–194; Brian R. Duchin, "The 'Agonizing Reappraisal,' " *Diplomatic History* 16 (Spring 1992), p. 220.

45. Richard J. Barnet, *The Alliance: America-Europe-Japan, Makers of the Postwar World* (New York, 1983), pp. 574–596; an authoritative French view is Pierre Mélandri, *Les États-Unis face à l'unification de l' Europe: 1945–1954* (Paris, 1980).

46. Adam B. Ulam, *Expansion and Coexistence: The History of Soviet Foreign Policy, 1917–1967* (New York, 1968), pp. 574–596.

47. Nelson, 58; Chester L. Cooper, *The Lion's Last Roar: Suez, 1956* (New York, 1978), p. 94.

48. Cooper, pp. 181–182; Beschloss, p. 137.

49. Ambrose, p. 367. The best detailed analysis of the Suez (and eastern bloc) crisis is Donald Neff, *Warriors at Suez* (New York, 1981), esp. pp. 342–414, on how events in the two regions collided.

50. Cooper, pp. 259–260.

51. A superb analysis of the change in the late 1950s is Burton Kaufman, *Trade and Aid* (Baltimore, 1982), esp. pp. 152–182; Harold Vatter, *The American Economy in the 1950s: An Economic History* (New York, 1963), pp. 259–264.

52. "Minutes of Cabinet Meeting, November 6, 1959," p. 2, Cabinet Meetings of President Eisenhower (microfilm), Eisenhower Library; H. W. Brands, Jr., "Blueprint for Quagmires, or Keeping the SOBs on Our Side," *Society for Historians of American Foreign Relations Newsletter* 17 (March 1986): 5.

53. "Remarks of the Secretary," Opening Session, Western European Chiefs of Mission Meeting, Paris, 9 May 1958, Conference Dossiers, Papers of John Foster Dulles, Princeton; off-the-record remarks to U.S. ambassadors to Europe, Paris, 9 May 1958, NATO Ministers' Meeting, Conference Dossiers, *ibid.*

54. Steven L. Spiegel, *The Other Arab-Israeli Conflict: Making America's Middle East Policy, from Truman to Reagan* (Chicago, 1985), pp. 82–93; documents on the doctrine and the invasion are in *The Record of American Diplomacy*, ed. Ruhl J. Bartlett 4th ed. (New York, 1964), pp. 842–848.

55. Stephen E. Ambrose, *Nixon: The Education of a Politician, 1913–1962* (New York, 1987), pp. 476–477.

56. Tad Szulc, *Fidel: A Critical Portrait* (New York, 1986), pp. 284, 314–315, 381; Wayne S. Smith, *The Closest of Enemies: A Personal and Diplomatic Account of U.S.-Cuban Relations since 1957* (New York, 1987), esp. ch. I.

57. Jeffrey J. Safford, "The Nixon-Castro Meeting of 19 April 1959," *Diplomatic History* 4 (Fall 1980): 425–431; Saul Landau, "Asking the Right Questions about Cuba" (1987), manuscript in author's possession.

58. Richard E. Welch, Jr., *Response to Revolution: The United States and the Cuban Revolution, 1959–1961* (Chapel Hill, N.C., 1985), pp. 10, 26; Arkadi Shevchenko, *Breaking with Moscow* (New York, 1985), p. 105.

59. Unnamed *Washington Post* columnist quoted in the *Nation*, 21 December 1985, p. 687.

60. Ambrose, *Eisenhower: The President*, p. 434; the text is available in U.S. Congress, Joint Committee on Defense Production, 94th Cong., 2d sess., 1976, *Deterrence and Survival in the Nuclear Age* [the Gaither Report of 1957] (Washington, D.C., 1976), esp. pp. 12–23.

61. Beschloss, p. 154; a sample of Johnson's criticism is in *U.S. News & World Report*, 17 January 1958, pp. 100–102.

62. Beschloss, pp. 5, 392; Douglas Kinnard, *The Secretary of Defense* (Lexington, Ky., 1980), pp. 60–61.

63. Brinkley, p. 82; Barry M. Blechman and Stephen S. Kaplan, *Force without War: U.S. Armed Forces as a Political Instrument* (Washington, D.C., 1978), pp. 374–377; Beschloss, pp. 162, 378.

64. Beschloss, pp. 254, 317.

65. Sayre, pp. 191–198.

66. Dwight D. Eisenhower, *The White House Years*, 2 vols. (Garden City, N.Y., 1963–1964), II, pp. 364–365; Rosenberg, p. 66; Godfrey Hodgson, *America in Our Time* (New York, 1976), p. 7, a useful and readable survey of the post-1945 years.

67. The text is in *Eisenhower as President*, ed. Dean Albertson (New York, 1963), pp. 162–163.

68. H. W. Brands, Jr., *Cold Warriors: Eisenhower's Generation and American Foreign Policy* (New York, 1988), p. 211, also 195, 199–200.

For Further Reading

Materials for further reading on specific topics may be found in the notes of the relevant sections of this chapter and also in the General Bibliography at the end of this book. The best place to look next is *Guide to American Foreign Relations since 1700*, ed. Richard Dean Burns (1983), more helpful on pre-1981 works than any textbook could be. References that follow are consequently mostly post-1981 publications. References in the notes and General Bibliography are generally not repeated below.

A useful bibliographical source is R. D. Bohanan, *Dwight Eisenhower: A Selected Bibliography of Periodical and Dissertation Literature* (1981). For overviews of the 1950s and more references (other than the Ambrose and Divine volumes listed in the notes), helpful are Jeff Broadwater, *Eisenhower and the Anti-Communist Crusade* (1992), an important analysis that stresses Ike's anti-communism even after McCarthy was discredited; Gary W. Reichard, *Politics as Usual: The Age of Truman and Eisenhower* (1987), especially good for interpretations; *Reevaluating Eisenhower: American Foreign Policy in the Fifties*, ed. Richard A. Melanson and David Mayers (1987), with interpretive essays; John Lewis Gaddis, *Strategies of Containment* (1982), critical and places the 1950s in a larger containment context; Frederick C. Mosher, David W. Clinton, and Daniel G. Lang, *Presidential Transitions and Foreign Affairs* (1987), good case studies on 1952 and 1960; Burton I. Kaufman's important and pioneering *Trade and Aid: Eisenhower's Foreign Economic Policy, 1953–1961* (1982); Walt W. Rostow, *Eisenhower, Kennedy and Foreign Aid* (1985), an insider's account.

The Eisenhower Presidential Library at Abilene, Kansas, has been an exemplary leader in declassifying and making available its rich resources. University Publications of America has microfilmed many of these resources. Subjects include the Dulles-Eisenhower telephone conversations, NSC meetings, cabinet meetings, and, of particular interest, twenty-eight reels (with printed guide) of *The Diaries of Dwight D. Eisenhower, 1953–1961*. Two sets of important letters are available in published form in *Ike's Letters to a Friend, 1941–1958*, ed. Robert W. Griffith (1984); and Peter G. Boyle, *The Churchill-Eisenhower Correspondence, 1953–1955* (1990).

Good work has appeared on specific subjects and geographical regions. On Korea, Edward C. Keefer, "President Dwight D. Eisenhower and the End of the Korean War," *Diplomatic History* 10 (Summer 1986), provides both synthesis and interpretation; on Vietnam (in addition to the key volumes by Gardner and Herring cited in the notes), the dean of U.S.–Southeast Asia scholars, George McT. Kahin, has published *Intervention: How America Became Involved in Vietnam* (1986); Louis A. Peake's *The United States in the Vietnam War, 1954–1975: An Annotated Bibliography* (1984), has 1,200-plus well-organized entries, along with a chronology; and David L. Anderson's *Trapped by Success* (1991) is good on Vietnam policy, 1953–1961. On the Offshore Islands crises, Thomas E. Stolper, *China, Taiwan, and the Offshore Islands* (1985), is especially important for the Chinese side.

For U.S.–Western European relations, see especially Frank Costigliola, *France and the United States* (1992); Frank Ninkovich, *Germany and the United States* (1988); *The*

Special Relationship: Anglo-American Relations since 1945, ed. William Roger Louis and Hedley Bull (1986), is crucial on the English-speaking partners; Alfred Grosser, *The Western Alliance: European-American Relations since 1945* (1980), gives a distinguished western European viewpoint; a French view is in Bernard Lewidge, *De Gaulle et les Americains* (1984); Robert Rhodes, *Anthony Eden: A Biography* (1987), exploits Eden's private papers and, along with David Carlton's biography of Eden, can be used to gain insight into the decline of British power from 1935 to 1956; Diane B. Kunz's important *Economic Diplomacy of the Suez Crisis* (1991); Evelyn Shuckburgh, *Descent to Suez: Foreign Office Diaries, 1951–1956*, ed. John Charmley (1986), gives a British insider's view of the sad story; and Peter L. Hahn, *The U.S., Great Britain and Egypt, 1945–1956* (1991), is the standard account. The historic agreement on Austria is well analyzed in Audrey Kurth Cronin, *Great Power Politics and the Struggle over Austria, 1945–1955* (1986). A too-often-overlooked analysis is Bennet Kovrig's important and provocative *The Myth of Liberation: East-Central Europe in United States Diplomacy and Politics since 1941* (1973). On the Middle East, other than the volumes dealing with Suez noted above, William J. Burns, *Economic Aid and American Policy toward Egypt, 1955–1981* (1985), is especially good on U.S. domestic politics, as is Steven L. Spiegel, *The Other Arab-Israeli Conflict: Making America's Middle East Policy, from Truman to Reagan* (1985); and Cheryl Rubenberg, *Israel and the American National Interest* (1986), which is more critical of those domestic politics. Two key accounts are David W. Lesch, *Syria and the United States* (1992), and Douglas Little, "Cold War and Covert Action, The U.S. and Syria, 1945–1958," *Middle East Journal* 44 (Winter 1990). On Africa, Martin Meredith, *The First Dance of Freedom: Black Africa in the Postwar Era* (1985), is a starting point, as is Peter Duignan and L. H. Gann, *The United States and Africa: A History* (1984), important for its sweeping historical framework; Madeline Kalb, *The Congo Cables: The Cold War in Africa from Eisenhower to Kennedy* (1982); and for a revealing case study, see Harold G. Marcus, *Ethiopia, Great Britain, and the United States, 1941–1974: The Politics of Empire* (1983), rich in its use of British materials and questioning of Western policies. On the Cuban Revolution and on U.S. policy in Latin America more generally, Morris Morley's *Imperial State and Revolution: The United States and Cuba, 1952–1985* (1987) is important, as is Louis A. Perez, Jr., *Cuba and the United States* (1990). W. LaFeber, "Thomas C. Mann," in *Behind the Throne*, eds. T. McCormick and W. LaFeber (1993)—essays in honor of Fred Harvey Harrington—gives an overview on Latin American policy. A standard account is now Piero Gleijeses, *Shattered Hope* (1991), which is on U.S.-Guatemalan relations.

Nuclear strategy in the 1950s has received much attention. In addition to the Divine volumes listed in the notes, and Divine's *Eisenhower and Sputnik* (1993), a good overview is provided in George T. Mazuzan, "American Nuclear Policy," in *Modern American Diplomacy*, ed. John M. Carroll and George C. Herring (1986); Walter A. McDougall's magisterial and prize-winning *The Heavens and the Earth: A Political History of the Space Age* (1985); Samuel F. Wells, Jr., "The Origins of Massive Retaliation," *Political Science Quarterly* 96 (Spring 1981), which traces the roots back to Truman; *The Structure of the Defence Industry: An International Survey*, ed. Nicole Ball and Milton Leitenberg (1983), especially Judith Reppy and David Holloway on the United States and the USSR since 1945; Howard Ball, *Justice Downwind: America's Atomic Testing Program in the 1950s* (1986); Milton S. Katz, *Ban the Bomb: A History of SANE, the Committee for a Sane Nuclear Policy, 1957–1985* (1986), provides important social as well as political history; Richard Pfau, *No Sacrifice Too Great: The Life of Lewis L. Strauss* (1984), a fine biography that focuses on the *Oppenheimer* case; and Barton J. Bernstein's view of the same subject in "Sacrifices and Decisions: Lewis L. Strauss," *Public Historian* 8 (Spring 1986). In addition to the work of David Holloway and Adam Ulam, George W. Breslauer, *Khrushchev and Brezhnev as Leaders* (1982), is important for a glimpse inside the Kremlin; and T. Michael Ruddy, *The Cautious Diplomat: Charles E. Bohlen and the Soviet Union, 1929–1969* (1986) examines a key figure, if sometimes a distant one. An important interpretive overview is Lloyd C. Gardner, "The Atomic Temptation," in *Redefining the Past: Essays in Honor of William Appleman Williams*, ed. Lloyd C. Gardner (1986). A key perspective is Stuart W. Leslie, *The Cold War and American Science: The Military-Industrial-Academic Complex at MIT and Stanford* (1992).

17

JFK and LBJ: From the New Frontier through the Great Society to Vietnam (1961–1969)

KENNEDY

The 1960s were characterized by violence, domestic rioting, near-nuclear war, assassinations, and economic failure. The decade also was a time of unmatched progress in civil rights; in peaceful relations between Soviets and Americans; in long-needed programs to help schools, the sick, and the elderly; and in music (the Beatles) and technology (the first person, Neil Armstrong, walked on the moon in 1969). One view of the 1960s was recalled a quarter of a century later by a distinguished American historian: "Unparalleled power, unprecedented wealth, unbridled self-righteousness—it all struck me as an ominous combination full of potential dangers to the republic."[1]

Another view emerged from a 1979 public-opinion poll revealing that 33 percent of Americans wished that John F. Kennedy, of all U.S. presidents, "were President today." JFK received more than twice the support given the second choice (Franklin D. Roosevelt).[2] Remembered as "decisive," no doubt he was also recalled as a handsome man with a beautiful wife and family who perfectly used the relatively new medium of television. He represented in his own career the American-dream marriage between the glamor of Hollywood (where his father invested in movies and JFK dated actresses) and the power of Washington.

Born in 1917, raised in both Boston's Irish-Catholic neighborhoods and high society's vacation spots in Florida and Cape Cod, Kennedy first gained attention in 1940, when he published his Harvard senior thesis, *Why England Slept.* He argued that deep forces in democracy and capitalism had paralyzed the West in the 1930s. Democratic leaders, in his view, had disastrously failed to meet Hitler's challenge. During World War II, he became a hero when Japanese ships destroyed his torpedo boat and he rescued other sailors before the survivors were found by U.S. vessels. Elected to the House of Representatives in 1946 and the Senate in 1952, Kennedy was not a Democratic party power. His votes on economic issues earned him his reputation as a liberal, but he was more conservative on civil liberties (his public attitude toward Senator Joseph McCarthy was not critical) and on many foreign-policy issues. He condemned a "sick" Roosevelt for giving away too much at the 1945 Yalta Conference, blasted Truman for supposedly losing China to the Communists, and urged always higher defense spending.[3] Between 1956 and 1960, he used his family's great wealth to help set up an organization outside the Democratic party's machine, whose senior members considered his youth and his Roman Catholicism to be handicaps in a presidential race.

A City on the Hill on the New Frontier

Kennedy, nevertheless, won the nomination and faced Vice-President Richard Nixon in the 1960 campaign. Each man took a hard line on foreign policy. Kennedy was tougher on Castro than was Nixon, and the vice-president was more adamant about defending the Chinese offshore islands than was Kennedy. Neither impressed Harry Truman or Dean Acheson, who considered Nixon too sleazy and Kennedy too young and more concerned with image than substance. "The best campaign cheer," Acheson wrote friends, is that "anyway, they can't elect both of them."[4] But Nixon's poor appearance in the first televised debate between two presidential candidates, an economic downturn, and southern votes gathered by JFK's vice-presidential nominee, Lyndon B. Johnson of Texas, had more to do with Kennedy's paper-thin margin of victory than did foreign-policy issues.

The new president saw himself as a man of action. His movie hero was John Wayne, his favorite reading included Ian Fleming's novels about superagent James Bond. His campaign theme was "the New Frontier" on which he believed Americans must embark. In his inaugural address, the key line was "And so, my fellow Americans: ask not what your country can do for you—ask what you can do for your country." He believed that Americans would "bear any burden" to win "the freedom of man."[5] Scholars had recently predicted that the technological society would put an end to ideological debates (such as communism versus capitalism), and Kennedy believed that the nation was moving beyond them as well to form a new consensus on national— and especially foreign—policies.

He had good reasons for reaching such a conclusion. In 1961, a commission funded by the Rockefellers (led by Nelson Rockefeller, the Republican governor of New York) published *Prospects for America*,[6] which called for a rapid military build-up to close the supposed missile "gap" that favored the Soviets, more money and men needed to fight expensive conventional (not just nuclear) wars, and more resources poured into newly emerging nations before the Soviets could obtain footholds. Republicans shaped the Rockefeller report (the staff director was a young Harvard professor, Henry Kissinger). But Democrats, including Dean Rusk, also signed it. From now on, the cold war was to be waged against communism abroad, not argued about at home.

Or so many on the New Frontier believed. Leaving Boston in 1961 to move into the White House, Kennedy quoted the famous words of John Winthrop to the Massachussetts Bay settlers in 1630: "We must always consider that we shall be as a city upon a hill—the eyes of all people are upon us." Such overblown rhetoric was too much for one Republican. Kennedy is making a "frightful call to arms," while building a huge government "that is Big Brother to us all." "Under the tousled boyish hair cut it is still old Karl Marx." Thus wrote Hollywood actor Ronald Reagan to Richard Nixon.[7]

THE CONSENSUS PRESIDENCY

The new administration believed that a strong, popular, glamorous presidency supported by key Republicans would allow Kennedy to ignore such critics as Reagan and dismiss—or control—public opinion. As the president's top aide, Theodore Sorensen, phrased it, public opinion "is frequently hampered by myths and misinformation." It is "promiscuous and perfidious in its affection, and always difficult to distinguish. For it rarely speaks in one . . . united voice."[8] Voices that did emerge in 1961 strongly supported their own version of anti-communism. For example, the Committee to Warn of the Arrival of Communist Merchandise on the Local Business Scene was formed that year in Miami and quickly spread to forty-six states. It attacked merchants who sold communist-made products (such as hams from Poland) by posting signs saying, "Always buy your Communist products at _____."[9]

Kennedy moved to cement the anti-Communist consensus by reappointing the ultraconservative J. Edgar Hoover as director of the Federal Bureau of Investigation (FBI) and Allen Dulles as director of the Central Intelligence Agency (CIA). After consulting extensively with Republicans, he appointed Dean Rusk as secretary of state. Rusk was not a Republican, but a quiet Democrat who had been president of the Rockefeller Foundation. Between 1949 and 1953, he had served as Dean Acheson's top assistant for Far Eastern affairs and was known as violently anti-Chinese—or, as he put in in a 1951 speech, he believed that the Maoist "regime may be a colonial Russian government. . . . It is not the government of China."[10] Rusk was a secretive, capable bureaucrat who was rightly proud of his rise to power from a childhood spent in the poor Georgia back country.

Rusk's State Department had quadrupled from 6,200 persons in 1941 to over 24,000 in the 1960s. It had to act on some 1,300 incoming telegrams every day and send out over 1,000.[11] The cautious Rusk and his careful professionals moved too slowly for the on-the-move Kennedy crowd that relaxed by playing bruising games of touch football. The president appointed McGeorge Bundy to head the National Security Council (NSC). A Harvard professor and member of a well-connected New England family, Bundy had long been close to Republicans. With Kennedy's approval, he changed the NSC until it became a small, fast-acting State-Department-in-the-White-House that could immediately respond to the president's desires. And, unlike Rusk, Bundy could not be called before Congress to testify. The NSC could act more secretly as well as more rapidly.

To head the Defense Department, Kennedy named Robert McNamara. A Republican and the young president of the Ford Motor Company, McNamara had a mind like a computer and the firm belief that if you could find the right numbers, you could find the right foreign policy. To make the Pentagon more efficient, McNamara brought in "whiz kids" from leading universities. These experts from "think tanks" of M.I.T., Columbia, Princeton, California, and Harvard had worked closely with the military to develop a more efficient generation

President John F. Kennedy (1917–1963) confers with Secretary of Defense Robert S. McNamara (center) and General Maxwell Taylor (left) as the two advisers brief the president on the war in Vietnam. The resulting instability in the nations involved forced American diplomacy to focus increasingly on the so-called Third World.

of technology for U.S. forces as well as computerized accounting methods so that the Pentagon could deliver more bang for the buck. Foreign policy was to be removed as far as possible from politics and made more scientific.[12]

THE CONSENSUS ECONOMY

The president gave the key Treasury position to C. Douglas Dillon, another Republican and head of one of the world's most powerful investment banking houses. Kennedy worried that unless the economy was pumped up, his foreign policy would collapse. "If we cannot keep up our export surplus," he warned, dollars would not be available "to meet our overseas military commitments." And if Americans had to "pull back," they might repeat the tragic story of the ancient Romans, whose success "depended on their will and ability to fight successfully at the edges of their empire." Kennedy was not certain that "we were yet in a position" to fight on those edges of the American Empire.[13] He ordered Dillon to strengthen the economy.

But the new Treasury secretary hoped to do it without radical measures. Neither of the two great drains on the economy—military spending and private overseas investment—was to be cut. Indeed, Kennedy asked that both be jumped to ever-higher levels. The new costs were to be paid by cutting and reforming the tax structure so that the economy would speed up and produce more government revenue. The export of gold to pay for U.S. trade deficits was to be stopped by a variety of economic tinkering. And, above all, world markets were to be opened to U.S. goods. In 1962, Congress passed the most far-reaching trade bill since the 1930s. It gave the president the power to cut U.S. tariffs 50 percent for nations that would welcome more American goods. It also established under the president a special trade representative who was to open more international markets for U.S. producers. This measure led to a "Kennedy round" of trade talks in which other nations did, indeed, agree to open global trade, although the prosperous European Economic Community, under French president Charles de Gaulle's prodding, never opened itself to American goods as Washington officials had hoped.

The Kennedy team also tried to find dollars by setting up an office in the Defense Department to sell weapons abroad for profit. *Forbes* business magazine noted that, in the 1930s, such salesmen of weapons were called "merchants of death," but "times have changed." The government itself now helped sell arms to assist "non-communist countries . . . and also to close the dollar gap." Unfortunately, as *Forbes* admitted, arms sometimes also went to non-Communists who hated each other—such as India and Pakistan, who used the weapons to fight against one another. Nevertheless, such giant firms as General Dynamics and Lockheed sold about $1 billion worth of arms abroad each year.[14]

The Kennedy policies helped create a U.S. economic boom between 1961 and 1967. But it was not enough. American overseas commitments and costs rose faster than even the booming economy could pay for. By mid-1963, despite growing political troubles worldwide, Kennedy told a French visitor that he was most worried about the dollar's weakness.[15] The greenback was less and less able to pay for defending the free world. The president's attempt to create a political consensus also stumbled. He had brought experts to power, and "they may be every bit as intelligent as you say," the salty, powerful Speaker of the House, Sam Rayburn, told Vice-President Johnson, "but I wish just one of them had run for sheriff once."[16]

THE CHALLENGE: LATIN AMERICA AND THE ALLIANCE FOR PROGRESS

A series of crises quickly challenged Kennedy's ability to fight the cold war. The first arose in the less-industrialized world. The president was especially sensitive to these nations because, in January 1961, Nikita Khrushchev delivered a ringing declaration that revolutions in such countries were the wave of the future; the Soviet system—not the American—was best able, he proclaimed, to ride that wave.

The new nations in Asia, Africa, and Latin America helplessly watched the prices of their raw materials sink 22 percent between 1950 and 1964 as compared to the prices of manufactured goods they bought from Europeans, Japanese, and Americans.[17] The rich were getting richer, the poor poorer—and more numerous. The world population of 2.8 billion in 1960 was projected to reach 7.0 billion by the year 2000. John Spanier estimated that India's population increase each year equaled a city the size of New York, and the Asians were doubling their birth rate over that of Europeans, while Latin Americans were roughly doing the same over that of North Americans.[18]

In his January speech, Khrushchev pointed to Castro's victory in Cuba as a sign that the "onslaught of the imperialists" was being destroyed with a triumphant "war of national liberation."[19] Kennedy was not pleased. During the presidential campaign, he had blasted Eisenhower for losing Cuba and urged military intervention by U.S.-supported Cuban exiles to remove Castro. But the president realized, too, that parts of Latin America were, indeed, ripe for Castroism. Poverty multiplied, and U.S. aid was insignificant. Between 1946 and 1960, the United States gave about $60 billion in foreign aid, but less than 7 percent of it went to Latin America, and most of that directly benefited U.S. corporations operating in the region.[20] On March 13, 1961, Kennedy proposed to Latin American ambassadors the Alliance for Progress. Over the next ten years, $100 billion ($20 billion from North Americans and $80 billion from Latin Americans) had to be made available for development. U.S. aid would thus multiply many times. But, in return, Kennedy asked for land and tax reforms so that the money would benefit the poor and middle classes. In 1962, he warned of the consequences if the alliance failed: "Those who make peaceful revolution impossible will make violent revolution inevitable."[21]

The alliance was organized at Punta del Este, Uruguay, in August

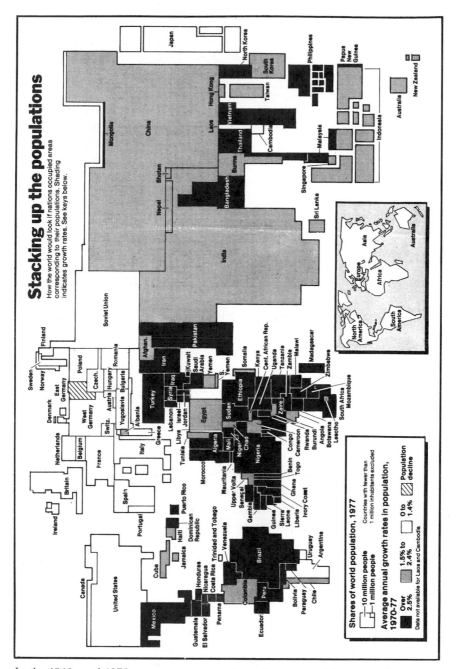

Stacking up the populations

How the world would look if nations occupied areas corresponding to their populations. Shading indicates growth rates. See keys below.

Shares of world population, 1977

□ —10 million people
☐ —1 million people

Countries with fewer than 1 million inhabitants excluded

Average annual growth rates in population, 1970-77

- ■ Over 2.5%
- ▨ 1.5% to 2.4%
- ☐ 0 to 1.4%
- ▨ Population decline

Data not available for Laos and Cambodia

In the 1960s and 1970s, awareness grew about the impact of the increasing population on dwindling resources. The U.S.'s Alliance for Progress was a key program created to handle the problem. (Source: *Michael Kidron and Ronald Segal,* The State of the World Atlas. *Used by permission, Simon & Schuster.*)

1961, when the hemisphere's nations—except for Cuba, which abstained—pledged to make the reforms in return for the billions. But the plan soon broke down, and by 1970 Latin America was worse off than in 1961. The reasons for the failure were many. First, most southern nations were ruled by small, rich elites, or oligarchs, who controlled the best lands. They had little intention of giving up their land to the landless or heavily taxing themselves. The oligarchs, thus, took the dollars but also kept their wealth. To make the alliance work first required political change to remove these elites. But U.S. officials wanted nothing to do with throwing out or weakening these stable, pro-Washington oligarchs.

Second, Congress directly ordered no U.S. funds to be used to carry out the heart of the program—that is, land redistribution to the poor. Taking from the rich and giving to the poor may have sounded good to Robin Hood, but it sounded too much like socialism to Congress.

Third, most Roman Catholic Latin Americans rejected birth-control methods needed to curb the population increase. They were supported by Latin American politicians, who warned that birth control was a Yankee plot to keep southern nations weak. And with high infant mortality as well as the need for many cheap hands in the villages, southern Americans believed they needed large families to survive.[22]

Fourth, the Latin elites put alliance funds not into staple foods (such as beans) to feed the poor, but into export crops (such as cotton and coffee). Thus, the elites profited from their export trade, while the poor starved.

Fifth, U.S. officials were never able to create a plan or an organization to resolve these problems. The officials wanted slow reform and believed that measures proven effective under the Marshall Plan (1948–1952) in western Europe (see p. 479) could work in Latin America. But Latin American economies were radically different from democratic European societies that only needed capital to rebuild war-devastated industries. In Latin America, fundamental change, not just money, was needed.

By the mid-1960s the alliance did reach its target of an annual 5.5 percent growth rate in the region. But of every $100 of new income produced, only $2 went to the poorest 20 percent of the people. Anger and frustration grew until terrorism and revolution burst out in Venezuela, Colombia, Bolivia, and Guatemala. Latin American military forces often responded brutally. By 1970, military rule had replaced thirteen constitutional governments since 1960, usually by forceful overthrow. Kennedy was rarely downbeat, but just before his death in November

1963 he admitted he was "depressed" by the alliance's sad turn of affairs.[23]

THE CHALLENGE: THE BAY OF PIGS

One month after announcing the Alliance for Progress, Kennedy launched an invasion of Cuba at the Bay of Pigs to overthrow Castro. In 1960, Eisenhower had ordered the CIA to train several hundred Cuban exiles for a military offensive. The agency believed that a small invasion would trigger an uprising against Castro, just as the invasion of Guatemala in 1954 caused the overthrow of that government (see p. 546). By April 1961, the invasion force had grown to 1,500, but Kennedy had decided not to provide U.S. air cover. He feared that if the United States became directly involved, Khrushchev would perhaps retaliate by invading West Berlin.[24]

Nevertheless, the president pressed ahead, despite warnings from his military advisers, because the CIA believed that there would be an anti-Castro uprising. Moreover, Kennedy did not want to kill Eisenhower's plan, especially after he had condemned Eisenhower for being too soft on Castro. In early April, White House aide Arthur Schlesinger, Jr., wrote a public white paper to justify an invasion on the ground that Castro had betrayed the Cuban Revolution. The white paper was mostly propaganda, especially since Castro himself had largely defined that revolution. Meanwhile, a CIA agent refused to tell the anti-Castro underground inside Cuba when the invasion would begin, thus revealing another weakness in the plan. "I don't trust any goddamn Cuban," the agent declared. The leader of the CIA operation, Richard Bissell, knew little about Cuba and its people, and, as it turned out, even less about the Bay of Pigs (where the CIA thought that photos of sharp coral reefs that wrecked landing craft revealed only seaweed). When Kennedy told Dean Acheson of the plan, even this crusty old Cold Warrior was astounded: you didn't need to consult such accountants as "Price Waterhouse to discover that 1,500 [invading] Cubans weren't as good as 250,000 [Castroite] Cubans," Acheson told the president.[25]

Without air cover, without a historical justification, without trust, and without intelligence, the invasion began on April 17. Within hours, it was wiped out by Castro's forces. No uprising occurred. Castro had learned the real lesson of the 1954 Guatemala operation—he made the government and the army one and the same. Thus, his army, unlike

Guatemala's, never deserted his government. In all, the Bay of Pigs invasion was the perfect failure. Kennedy was humiliated. But the consensus held. Public-opinion polls gave him the highest ratings of support during his entire presidency immediately after this disaster. "It's just like Eisenhower," Kennedy joked. "The worse I do the more popular I get."[26] But he knew that one more such failure and his presidency could be finished.

He and his brother, Attorney General Robert Kennedy, secretly set up a $100 million plan—code-named Operation Mongoose—employing several thousand people to wage a covert war against Castro. The president ordered the CIA to sabotage the Cuban economy. The agency also planned to kill Castro, plans apparently worked out in cooperation with U.S. mob figures. One plan was to give Castro exploding cigars. Another plan was to spread the word in Cuba that the Lord's Second Coming was about to occur, but that the Lord hated Castro. On the day of the Lord's supposed appearance, a U.S. submarine would surface along the coast, set off fireworks, and so frighten the Cubans that they would then overthrow Castro. One CIA agent labeled this bizarre plan "Elimination by Illumination."[27]

To paraphrase Shakespeare, however, the problem was not in the stars but in Kennedy's foreign policy. He and the CIA actually made Castro more popular and powerful than ever. In a televised speech of April 20, 1961, the president took full responsibility for the invasion fiasco and called on Americans to rally around him to fight a new kind of cold war in, among other places, Vietnam.[28]

THE CHALLENGE: VIETNAM (1961–1963)

In 1961, Southeast Asia seemed to be swinging like a huge pendulum, slowly but surely toward neutralism, perhaps communism. The British had largely destroyed a Communist rebellion in their former colony of Malaya, but newly independent (and renamed) Malaysia remained weak and vulnerable. India and Indonesia also seemed open to Communist-bloc pressure. The three former French colonies of Indochina—Vietnam, Laos, and Cambodia—appeared to be falling slowly to Communist rebels despite nearly $1 billion in U.S. aid that poured into the area between 1955 and 1961, and despite 658 U.S. advisers in Vietnam and 300 more in Laos.

Even before the Bay of Pigs embarrassment, Kennedy had determined to stand firm in Southeast Asia. Vividly recalling the vicious attacks (including his own) against Truman for "losing" China, Kennedy did not plan to become a similar political victim in the 1960s. Moreover, the need of Japan (by far the most important U.S. ally in Asia) for Southeast Asian markets and raw materials rose along with the skyrocketing Japanese economy. But the picture in Vietnam itself was grim. As elderly General Douglas MacArthur told the young president in late 1961, "The chickens are coming home to roost, and you live in the chicken house."[29]

Kennedy's most pressing problem was in Laos, the narrow, strategically located nation that the 1954 Geneva Conference had supposedly neutralized. But Laos became a vital highway (the Ho Chi Minh Trail) along which Ho's North Vietnamese Communist forces moved covertly into South Vietnam. Moreover, by 1961, the United States had ignored the Geneva agreement and established a friendly regime of General Phoumi Nosavan. Laos's Communists, the Pathet Lao, and neutralist forces countered by seizing key areas. As he left the White House, Eisenhower emotionally warned Kennedy that Laos was the gateway to all of Southeast Asia, and if it fell, the new president could forget about saving the rest of the region.[30] (See map, p. 552.)

In April 1961 (amid the Bay of Pigs failure), Kennedy sent the U.S. Seventh Fleet and a helicopter force to the area. He obtained a cease-fire between Phoumi and the Communists, but far-right forces—supported by the CIA—kept on fighting. The Communists retaliated and seemed on the brink of a major victory. Kennedy sent air power and U.S. Marines into areas bordering Laos. Both sides then agreed to talk and, in July 1962, made a pact that again neutralized Laos. All foreign troops were to leave. But the Pathet Lao continued to seize territory, and the North Vietnamese continued to protect the Ho Chi Minh Trail. Americans both armed the neutralist right-wing government and bombed Communist forces. In 1964, a right-wing faction seized control of the government. The CIA returned to Laos in force.[31]

Throughout his ordeal, Kennedy's allies refused to give much help. They believed that the West's power in Laos was small, almost nonexistent. One day on a yacht cruising down the Potomac, the president tried to convince the elegant, cool British prime minister, Harold Macmillan, to send help. Macmillan refused to waste scarce British resources in Laos. Amid the argument, they saw a local college team rowing a small racing scull down the river. "What have we here?" asked Macmillan. "The Laotian Navy?"[32]

By the end of Kennedy's presidency, Vietnam had become more important than Laos. When he entered the White House, the president found Vietnam still governed by the authoritarian, inefficient regime of Ngo Dinh Diem. Reforms, especially crucial land reform, had stopped. Between 1958 and 1960, Ho Chi Minh's northern Communists had begun organizing revolts against Diem and had discovered that many of the South's peasants were willing to join. With Ho's help, the National Liberation Front (NLF or Vietminh) became the rebels' political arm in 1960. It included non-Communist as well as Communist leaders. China helped by accelerating economic aid to Ho.

In April 1961, a special U.S. military mission told Kennedy that Diem only controlled 40 percent of South Vietnam. Shortly after this report (and the Bay of Pigs invasion), the president sent 500 more U.S. advisers to help Diem. The president especially took a strong personal interest in the new Special Forces, or Green Berets, that he had helped develop (he even paid special attention to such details as the design of their uniform) to fight revolutionaries in such places as Vietnam. Kennedy broke the 1954 Geneva agreement, which provided that no more than 685 military advisers were to be in South Vietnam. As historian Stephen Pelz concludes, "Between January and May [1961] Kennedy had committed the United States to save South Vietnam."[33]

At this point, the president dispatched Vice-President Johnson to examine the growing crisis. Johnson publicly called Diem the "Churchill of today," but Diem rejected the U.S. request that American troops be sent in to help fight the war. Determined to keep control of his own army, Diem only wanted U.S. advisers to train his soldiers. But, as Kennedy's top military adviser, General Maxwell Taylor, recalls, "We eventually broke down [Diem's] resistance."[34] In October 1961, a mission led by Taylor and Walt Rostow of the State Department reported back to the president that only a major increase in the U.S. effort could save Diem. Kennedy took their report seriously. Taylor had belonged to a group known as the Never Again Club—top military officers experienced in the Korean War who swore that U.S. troops should never again be sent to fight in Asia without, if necessary, nuclear weapons. But Kennedy also knew that sending more troops could be dangerous. "The troops will march in," he said privately, "the bands will play; the crowds will cheer; and in four days everyone will have forgotten. Then we will be told we have to send in more troops. It's like taking a drink. The effect wears off and you have to take another." Historian Lloyd Gardner comments: "Prompted by the advisers he had appointed . . . , Kennedy took the first drink. How could he do otherwise?"[35]

Rejecting one U.S. military request that 40,000 men be sent, he nevertheless ordered in 10,000 troops during 1962–1963. By 1963,

Kennedy had placed more than 16,000 U.S. soldiers in South Vietnam and had tripled military aid to the area to $185 million. But it was not nearly enough. Diem's regime continued to flounder, especially when powerful Buddhist leaders protested the war as well as Diem's governmental policies. As more U.S. soldiers died, the American media began to pay attention. Kennedy and the military tried to restrict media coverage and to remove critical journalists, but with little success.[36]

Even his acclaimed win in the Cuban missile crisis of October 1962 (see p. 597) did not help Kennedy. He, indeed, concluded that while that victory taught the Soviets a lesson, the Chinese—now bitter enemies of the Soviets—would want to humiliate both superpowers by gaining control of Southeast Asia. "The Chinese are perfectly prepared, because of their lower value of human life," he privately told a French official in 1963, "to lose hundreds of million [of people] if necessary . . . to carry out their militant and aggressive policies." It is now clear that Kennedy became so obsessed with his fear that China was developing a nuclear weapon that, after the Cuban missile crisis, he approached Khrushchev with the suggestion that military strikes might be used to destroy the Chinese nuclear facilities. As he phrased it in instructions to the U.S. diplomat (W. Averell Harriman) who was to discuss this with the Soviet leader: "You should try to elicit Khrushchev's view of means of limiting or preventing Chinese nuclear development and his willingness either to take Soviet action or to accept U.S. action aimed in this direction." As the historian of this remarkable episode, Gordon Chang, concludes, "The Kennedy administration came dangerously close to answering in the affirmative the question . . . : 'Should we bomb Red China's bomb?' " Only Khrushchev's cold response to Kennedy's approach perhaps prevented a U.S. attack on China.[37]

But as the president became more fixated on the Chinese threat to Asia, he seemed to become more confused, at least publicly, about how to deal with his collapsing policy in Southeast Asia. In a television interview of September 1963, Kennedy declared, "In the final analysis it is their [the Vietnamese'] war." A week later, however, the president told another television audience that "I believe" in the domino theory. China (which "looms so high") could seize the region, so "I think we should stay" in Vietnam. "We should not withdraw."[38]

Washington officials saw Diem as the problem. After eight years of U.S. training, his much larger army was humiliated by a mere battalion of Vietminh at a key battle in the village of Ap Bac during 1963. Three Americans died in the fight. Diem's army then fired into a crowd

Dismissed as a mere "barbecue show" by the sister-in-law of South Vietnam's leader, Ngo Dinh Diem, the self-immolation by Buddhist monks who protested Diem's rule created a major crisis for Kennedy's policy in Vietnam in mid-1963.

of Buddhists who were defying a government ban on parading religious banners. Riots erupted in mid-1963. In protest, Buddhist monks burned themselves to death while U.S. television cameras rolled. Americans were doubly shocked when Diem's sister-in-law, Madam Nhu, described the scene as a "barbecue show." The U.S. policy of "Sink or Swim with Ngo Dinh Diem and Let's Have No Poo about Madam Nhu" now began to change. Kennedy demanded that Diem hurry reforms and listen to U.S. advice. Frustrated South Vietnamese generals saw their chance and prepared to overthrow Diem. U.S. officials did nothing to stop the coup and, indeed, gave signals that the generals interpreted as a green light. On November 1, 1963, Diem and his brother Ngo Dinh Nhu were captured and killed by the generals. (Madame Nhu was out of the country.) Three weeks later, President Kennedy was assassinated in Dallas, Texas.

Historians have since argued whether, as some of his aides have claimed, Kennedy intended to pull U.S. troops out of Vietnam once he was safely re-elected in 1964. Filmmakers have also entered this argument, led by Oliver Stone, whose highly popular movie, *JFK*, starred Kevin Costner. Stone's Kennedy intended to leave Vietnam, and, as a result, was assassinated by right-wing conspirators who intended to put Lyndon Johnson in the White House so the United States would remain in Southeast Asia. The evidence for Stone's argument is, to say the least, weak. If Kennedy had any thoughts about getting out, he had to drop them after Diem's murder because, after that, the military situation in Vietnam fell apart, U.S.–South Vietnamese forces were faced with defeat, and the United States now had heavy responsibility for the new South Vietnamese regime it had helped put in power. The number of U.S. advisers continued to grow on the battlefields, and in Washington Kennedy placed great faith in the very advisers who later pushed Johnson to increase the American commitment. Kennedy's closest aide, Theodore Sorensen, later said that the president viewed the war as "this nation's severest test of endurance and patience," and that "He was simply going to weather it out, a nasty, untidy mess to which there was no other acceptable solution." But it was now Lyndon Johnson's war. The warning given by U.S. Department of State official Chester Bowles to Kennedy in 1961 seemed prophetic: "We are headed full blast up a dead end street."[39]

THE SUPERPOWERS: FROM VIENNA AND TANKS IN JULY

Vietnam was not the only "chicken" that came "home to roost" in Kennedy's White House during 1961. Khrushchev renewed his 1958 demands that the Allies turn West Berlin over to the Communist East German regime. Kennedy was determined not to give way on the German question. He agreed with a top adviser that without West Germany, "Western Europe is an eggshell."[40]

The two leaders met in Vienna during June 1961. It was a frosty affair. (When a frustrated JFK asked the Soviet leader whether the latter ever admitted to having made a mistake, Khrushchev only replied, "Certainly"—in 1956 "I admitted all of Stalin's mistakes.")[41] Kennedy warned that neither side should try to upset the balance of power, especially in the newly emerging world. Khrushchev retorted that the Soviets would continue to support "wars of national liberation." The two men engaged in a heated ideological debate. Kennedy returned home worrying that it was "going to be a long winter."

But the president also knew by mid-1961 that the so-called missile gap did, indeed, exist—overwhelmingly in his favor. The U.S. Samos II spy satellites revealed that instead of the 400 intercontinental ballistic missiles (ICBMs) that Kennedy feared the Soviets possessed, a mere

4 existed. The president dug in his heels when Khrushchev threatened in July to move on Berlin. On national television Kennedy warned that the United States would tolerate no changes. To make his point, he ordered 150,000 reservists to active duty, tripled the number of draft calls for young men, and asked for an immediate $3.2 billion to spend on defense. (Eisenhower's arms budget of nearly $46 billion in 1960 was on its way to becoming $54 billion by the end of 1963.) Most ominously, the president demanded $207 million for more civil defense in anticipation of possible nuclear war. "In the coming months," Kennedy told Americans, "I hope to let every citizen know what steps he can take without delay to protect his family in the case of attack." As historian Douglas Brinkley comments, "JFK had made the Berlin crisis a test of both his and America's courage and determination."[42] And the president had overwhelming superiority in nuclear weaponry to back him up in the test.

As tension thickened in early August 1961, East Germans (especially the better educated) left their Communist home in ever-greater numbers. On August 13, Khrushchev suddenly solved the problem by building a cement-block wall, topped with barbed wire and sentry houses, to seal off East Berlin (and, later, most of East Germany) from the West. No longer could skilled East Germans leave for work in western Europe. The wall was built on Soviet-controlled territory. Kennedy could only have destroyed it by invading East Germany. He instead sent Vice-President Johnson to buck up West German morale. West German officials angrily demanded more and better U.S. protection. Talks between Kennedy and aged Chancellor Konrad Adenauer were so bitter that they agreed to burn the record of their meeting. In June 1963, the president nevertheless made a triumphant visit to West Berlin. Before the wall he told a huge crowd, "All free men, wherever they may live, are citizens of Berlin, and, therefore, as a free man I take pride in the words, *'Ich bin ein Berliner'* [I am a Berliner]."

Despite American rhetoric, the wall stood and the military build-up accelerated on both sides. Kennedy's NSC adviser, McGeorge Bundy, told him during the 1961 crisis that if force had to be used, "the current plan calls for shooting off everything we have in one shot."[43] To gain flexibility, the president ditched Eisenhower's plan to depend on nuclear weapons. Instead he listened to Paul Nitze, whose NSC-68 in 1950 (see p. 504) had urged a conventional force build-up. Kennedy, thus, could make a "flexible response." But he and McNamara also continued developing their nuclear stockpile of ICBMs. The United

States was running the arms race against itself, for Khrushchev had decided to await new technology.

By 1962, Kennedy and top Pentagon officials realized the extent of their force superiority. They began to discuss openly the possibilities of a U.S. first strike (to which the Soviets could not respond) or making nuclear war more attractive by using their new, more accurate weapons to hit only military targets (a "counterforce" strategy) instead of civilian targets. Furious Soviet officials denied that such targets could be so neatly separated. Khrushchev halted his three-year nuclear test ban in September 1961 by exploding huge (if primitive) weapons. Kennedy also resumed testing, despite the U.S. lead and pleas from the British that he not do so. Meanwhile Khrushchev angrily asked his advisers, "Why [do] Americans have so many bases around the Soviet Union and we have no bases near the United States?"[44]

... To the Cuban Missile Crisis (1962)

Resembling the U.S.-USSR nuclear relationship, U.S.-Cuban relations had also worsened since the Bay of Pigs. In early 1962, Kennedy was able to have Cuba expelled from the Organization of American States (OAS) and an economic embargo imposed on the island. Castro moved closer to Khrushchev. By mid-1962, estimates placed more than 20,000 Soviet advisers inside Cuba. Reports circulated that Soviet missiles and IL-28 jet bombers were in place. Sensing a political victory in the 1962 congressional elections, Republicans cried that Kennedy stood by while missiles were being placed in Cuba to level "the American heartland." The president responded that defensive missiles (that is, ground to air) were acceptable, but ground-to-ground weapons were not. He believed that the Cubans had the former but not the latter missiles. In truth, Kennedy was finding himself cornered. His CIA Director, John McCone, had warned the president in August 1962 that Khrushchev might move missiles and bombers into Cuba. McCone was the only Kennedy adviser who gave the warning, but the president became so worried about the political implications that he ordered McCone to change the wording of his report. McCone believed that Kennedy feared if information of the arrival of Soviet bombers in Cuba "got into the press, a new and more violent Cuban issue would be injected into the [1962 political] campaign and this would seriously affect his independence to act." When in September, the CIA warned

A U.S. reconnaissance spy-plane photo of Soviet missile sites in Cuba during the tensest moments of the October 1962 crisis.

Kennedy that a surface-to-surface missile system might be moving into Cuba, the White House ordered the information kept completely away from the American public.[45]

On October 14, 1962, however, a U-2 plane filmed medium-range (1,000 mile) missiles on Cuban launching pads. Intermediate (2,000 mile) missiles also appeared to be under construction. Documents released nearly thirty years later in Moscow revealed why Khrushchev took the gamble of his life. To his closest advisers, he gave two reasons: first, the Americans intended to invade Cuba with their own forces ("we had good information on this account"); and second, "since the Americans have already surrounded the Soviet Union with a ring of their military bases and various types of missile launchers, we must pay them back in their own coin . . . so they will know what it feels like to live in the sights of nuclear weapons." There was also a third reason: Castro so strongly wanted nuclear protection against the United States that, ultimately, he was willing to incinerate his island if only Khrushchev would strike the United States first. In June, Fidel's brother, Raul, had flown to Moscow to work out the plan. By October 14, missiles and warheads were in Cuba when the U-2 spotted the sites.[46]

Two days later, Kennedy convened a special group of top officials, soon known as the ExComm (Executive Committee), to discuss policy in strict secrecy. One member (Sorensen) doubted that the missiles "significantly alter[ed] the balance of power." McNamara agreed with Sorensen, but the top military officials (the Joint Chiefs of Staff) argued that the power balance was substantially changed. The usually cautious Rusk decided at one point that instead of going "down with a whimper," it might be "better to go down with a bang." ExComm finally sorted out four possible options: handle the issue diplomatically and make no military response; trade off U.S. missiles in Turkey for the removal of Soviet missiles in Cuba; attack the missile sites by air and, if necessary, follow up with a U.S. invasion; or set up a blockade (or "quarantine") that would cut off Cuba and squeeze Khrushchev and Castro into removing the missiles. President Kennedy finally chose the last option, in part because if it did not work he could then escalate to a military option. Dean Acheson (brought in as a special adviser), was so bitterly disappointed that Cuba and the Soviet bases were not going to be bombed immediately that he resigned from ExComm.[47]

The ExComm (Executive Committee) group that advised President Kennedy during the missile crisis of 1962. Secretary of State Rusk stands at the right, the president bends down in front of Rusk, Vice-President Johnson is across the table from the president, Attorney General Robert Kennedy paces at left. The president's top aide, Theodore Sorensen (seated third from the left), later wrote: "I saw first-hand how brutally physical and mental fatigue can numb the good sense as well as the senses of normally articulate men."

In a dramatic television speech of October 22, the president announced the naval "quarantine," demanded the removal of the missiles, and warned that if any of the weapons were launched against the United States, he would fully respond—against the Soviet Union itself. Within forty-eight hours, the western European allies endorsed his policy. The OAS unanimously supported the blockade. The U.S. Strategic Air Command (SAC) went on its biggest airborne alert, with part of the B-52 bomber force, loaded with nuclear bombs, in the air at all times. Five army divisions prepared to invade Cuba. Unknown to McNamara, the SAC commander raised his forces to the next-to-highest level of alert in a clear, uncoded order so the Soviets could read it (which they did). The commander, as a later observer phrased it, rubbed "the Soviets' noses in their nuclear inferiority." Khrushchev never ordered his forces to go on alert. "We had a gun at his head and he didn't move a muscle," a U.S. Air Force general recalled.[48] On October 24, twelve of the twenty-five Soviet ships headed for Cuba changed course to return home. The remaining vessels carried no missiles.

But the most dangerous moments of the crisis lay ahead. In a rambling letter of October 26, Khrushchev indicated that he would dismantle the missiles in return for Kennedy's pledge never to invade Cuba. When told of the message, Acheson declared that the Soviet leader was "either tight or scared" and urged that the president get even tougher with Khrushchev. On the twenty-seventh, a quite different note arrived from Moscow: a demand that fifteen U.S. Jupiter missiles be removed from Turkey in return for dismantling the Cuban weapons. Kennedy had, months before, moved to take out the old, unneeded Jupiters; but any removal now could appear to give Khrushchev a major public victory. And just as Khrushchev's tougher note arrived, Kennedy learned that one of his U-2 planes had been shot down over Cuba and its pilot killed. McNamara believed that new orders had been given to Soviet and Cuban soldiers on the island, perhaps in preparation for war. At that moment, Kennedy received yet another piece of bad news: the Soviet technicians had moved the warheads closer to the missiles, possibly in preparation for a strike. That Saturday, the twenty-seventh, ExComm held a bitter meeting. Its members were exhausted as they approached a decision about attacking Cuba, a strike that would obviously kill many Soviets and perhaps provoke a response. McNamara realized, as he later said, that one missile "directed at Miami or New York or even Washington might have killed a million or 2 million people."[49]

Kennedy finally accepted a suggestion from his brother, the attorney general, to ignore the last note from Moscow and accept Khrushchev's suggestion of October 26. A virtual ultimatum cabled to Moscow demanded that the Soviets immediately stop work on the missiles. But Kennedy also gave vague assurances that there would be no invasion of Cuba. Moreover, he sent Robert Kennedy to inform a Soviet diplomat privately that the president had ordered the removal of the Jupiter missiles at NATO bases in Turkey and Italy. The attorney general further told the diplomat that if the Cuban missiles were not dismantled in forty-eight hours, the United States would take military action. Then, as Rusk revealed a quarter-century later, the president apparently moved to make certain there would be no war. He gave UN Secretary General U Thant a statement that the Jupiters would be removed if the Cuban weapons were dismantled. The statement was to be made public if Khrushchev rejected the ultimatum. "I am not," Kennedy said privately, "going to go to war over worthless missiles in Turkey." U Thant never had to use the statement. Khrushchev was ready to deal. On the twenty-sixth, the Soviet leader received a secret letter from Castro begging Khrushchev to launch a nuclear strike on the United States if Kennedy tried to invade Cuba. Castro seemed prepared to go down in flames. Khrushchev further learned of incidents that were erupting between Soviet and Cuban military. He considered the shooting down of the U-2 dangerously irresponsible. It was time to end the crisis. On October 28, he accepted Kennedy's public offer of taking out the missiles in return for a no-invasion pledge. The world stepped back from nuclear annihilation. Castro angrily castigated Khrushchev, refused to receive the Soviet ambassador to Cuba, and did his best to prevent a UN team from verifying that the missiles had indeed been taken down.[50]

How close the two superpowers came to the ultimate war became clear only a quarter-century later when American and Soviet documents began to be declassified. It was then revealed that Khrushchev had also placed in Cuba Luna missiles with nuclear warheads that had a range of twenty-five miles. If U.S. forces invaded, and communications with Moscow were cut, the Soviet commander in Cuba had the authority, on his own, to use these nuclear weapons against the invaders. When McNamara heard this in 1992 he was deeply shaken: "No one should believe that U.S. troops could have been attacked by tactical nuclear warheads without the U.S. responding with nuclear warheads. And where would it have ended? In utter disaster." Instead of utter disaster, Kennedy escaped with a spectacular victory. It later became apparent that he had even left a loophole in his no-invasion pledge: he promised no invasion if the missiles were removed and if "Cuba itself commits no aggressive acts against any of the nations of the Western Hemisphere." That loophole could have allowed his successors in the White House to invade Cuba in the 1960s, 1970s, and 1980s, given the belief of many Americans that Castro was indeed stirring up revolution in the hemisphere. In Moscow, Khrushchev's power never recovered. In early 1963, he dolefully complained in a secret, rambling, thirty-page letter to Castro that the Chinese were attacking him for not treating the United States like "a paper tiger, dung." As the Sino-Soviet split widened and Soviet-Cuban relations worsened, Khrushchev's Politburo finally removed him from power in October 1964 for public failures both abroad and at home (especially in collective agriculture). Meanwhile, Kennedy drew the most important lesson from the missile crisis: "Domestic issues can only lose elections, but foreign policy issues can kill us all."[51]

THE FALLOUT FROM THE MISSILE CRISIS

The effects of the crisis were felt far into the future. First, the Soviets made up their minds that "you Americans will never be able to do this to us again," as a top Soviet diplomat declared in late 1962.[52] The Moscow government launched a massive military build-up that within a decade pulled it close to U.S. nuclear strength. Khrushchev was replaced by a new group led by Leonid Brezhnev and Aleksei Kosygin—conservative, unimaginative, but usually predictable bureaucrats who jacked up military budgets.

Second, at home, the Democrats won the 1962 elections, but the missile crisis contributed little to the win. Kennedy came under strong attack from such Republicans as Arizona Senator Barry Goldwater and columnist William F. Buckley, Jr., for supposedly selling out the Monroe Doctrine with a no-invasion pledge that allowed Soviet influence to remain in the Western Hemisphere. The issue continued to boil. Twenty years later, conservatives urged the repudiation of the supposed 1962 pledge because the Communists brought in new jets and used Cuba as a base for supporting revolution in the region.[53]

Third, during the weeks after the missile crisis, the Western alliance, oddly, nearly shattered. European leaders had publicly supported Kennedy in the dark days of October, but, in President Charles de Gaulle's words, they were "informed" rather than "consulted" about U.S. policy. Europeans feared that they had gotten uncomfortably close to annihilation without representation. The snub was compounded when

Kennedy pushed a "grand design," one that would integrate U.S.-European economic and political policies so that the partners could pay more of the U.S. defense costs. When the Europeans saw that he had no intention of allowing them to help shape U.S. nuclear decisions, they blotted out the "grand design." But even worse occurred in late 1962, when Kennedy told London officials that they would not receive the U.S.-built Skybolt missile for use in British jet bombers. Eisenhower had promised them the Skybolt, and Great Britain had planned its air force around it. Now it was suddenly gone because the Americans thought the weapon not cost-efficient. The British then accepted other arms that made them even more dependent on the Americans.

De Gaulle had seen enough. He had long agreed with a British official who spit out, "The United States didn't want a partner. They wanted a satellite." He built up his own nuclear arsenal so that France would be independent of U.S. plans. De Gaulle never believed that in a future crisis the United States would risk nuclear war merely for French interests. He also announced that France would formally leave NATO by 1966. Then came his final blow: in early 1963, the stumbling British economy tried to find help by joining the European Common Market, but de Gaulle killed London's application. The British, he declared, were a "Trojan horse" for Washington, which, he feared, would use the horse to take over the entire Common Market. De Gaulle, one frustrated U.S. official complained, "is the most goddamn undealable-with human being that's ever existed."[54] Kennedy left the Western alliance much weaker than he had found it.

A fourth result of the missile crisis was the growing American fear that others would copy de Gaulle. The crisis revealed that at the moment of truth, neither superpower consulted its allies nor wanted to go to war. Thus, the stand-off allowed the allies—especially the newly emerging nations—to have more freedom from the superpowers. Washington officials privately warned that U.S. policy had to stop this fragmentation, this splintering of Western cooperation, by stepping up American commitments.[55] This reasoning led to greater involvement in Vietnam during 1963, and also to Kennedy's determination to contain China's influence in the newly emerging nations.

Fifth, one part (perhaps the most important) of U.S. foreign policy markedly improved. Both Americans and Soviets had learned the horror of teetering on the brink of nuclear war. In a June 1963 speech at American University in Washington, D.C., Kennedy asked that the cold-war rhetoric and policies be changed so such crises could be avoided. Khrushchev responded cooperatively. In August 1963, the two nations signed their first arms-control pact, an agreement in which the above-ground testing that was causing lethal radiation in milk and other foods was prohibited. The two powers also wanted a deal that would discourage nuclear testing by new competitors (such as the French and Chinese). Besides, weapons for Kennedy's new "flexible response" military plans could be tested below-ground. Indeed, below-ground testing went on at an ever-faster rate. But at least a first step had been taken in arms control. Kennedy took that step, however, only after fighting and compromising with those Pentagon, CIA, and Senate opponents who feared any arms deal at all with Communists. When the president next made a major wheat sale to the Soviets, Richard Nixon (now practicing law while raising himself from the political dead) warned that "the [Soviet] bear is always most dangerous when he stands with his arms open in friendship."[56]

Finally, after the crisis, Kennedy secretly entered into indirect talks with Fidel Castro, even as the CIA's Operation Mongoose tried to destroy Castro's regime and as the president showed warm support for the anti-Castro Cuban exiles in Miami. Castro opened the exchange, Kennedy responded, and both sides wrote out an agenda for the talks just before Kennedy was shot in Dallas on November 22, 1963.[57]

Henry Kissinger suggested a dozen years later that "the Kennedy period will be seen as the last flowering of the previous era rather than as the beginning of a new era."[58] Between 1961 and 1963, confidence in U.S. power and in a glamorous, active presidency had never been higher. That confidence resembled a star that beamed brightest just as it began to burn out.

LBJ: AT HOME AND THE GULF OF TONKIN

Many believed the new chief executive, Lyndon Baines Johnson of the Texas hill country, would never burn out. He seldom saw movies because he "didn't like to be alone in dark places," an aide said. "Talking on the telephone was the way he unwound." On the phone or in person, LBJ was usually giving someone "the treatment." As described by one Texas politician, "Lyndon got me by the lapels and put his face on top of mine and he talked and talked and talked. I figured it was either getting drowned or joining." His vice-president, Minnesota Democrat Hubert Humphrey, was often poked in the chest and once pulled his trouser leg up to show cuts where Johnson had kicked him while yell-

Walter Lippmann (1889–1974), at left in the picture, was perhaps the most influential American journalist in the twentieth century. As a young man he was a leading theorist of Progressivism; later he became a theorist of American conservatism. Refusing to serve in government after his disillusionment with Woodrow Wilson (see p. 325), he nevertheless was an intimate of many presidents, including Lyndon Johnson, sitting here for a bust of himself in April 1965. But as Lippmann became a key conservative critic of the Truman Doctrine in 1947 (see p. 483), so he became an early and leading critic of Johnson's policies in Vietnam, until the two men became bitter enemies in 1966–1967.

ing, "Get going now!" Despite, or because of, "the treatment," and because of a rare political intuition, Johnson had become perhaps the most powerful majority leader in the U.S. Senate's history before Kennedy asked him to run as vice-president. With his aggressiveness came immense pride and possessiveness in his state's, his nation's, and his own power. When he invited dignitaries to his Texas ranch, they were met by a fleet of large cars and helicopters, including, one foreign leader recalled, one "helicopter for the liquor—the United States is a great power." "You will never work for or with a more complicated mind than Lyndon Johnson so long as you live," Robert McNamara told a White House aide.[59] One way or another, the new president believed he could control any person, any situation.

He grew up politically in the 1930s, when Munich was a bad name (see p. 386). World War II seemed to be proof that Americans could, when they put their minds to it, run world affairs. He attacked Harry

Truman for not destroying the Chinese in the Korean War and condemned Dwight Eisenhower for allowing a supposed "missile gap." Within hours after becoming president, he pledged, "I am not going to be the President who saw Southeast Asia go the way China went."[60] Sometimes, however, he scored with remarkable patience. When Fidel Castro shut off the water supply to the U.S. base in Guantánamo Bay, many screamed for retaliation. Johnson only dispatched equipment so that the base could purify its own water. The crisis ended; the base remained. In Panama, the Panamanians' demand to fly their flag with the American banner in the canal zone led to riots and bloodshed in early 1964. In December 1964, LBJ agreed to negotiate a historic pact to replace the 1903 treaty that divided Panama in half. The new pact needed fourteen more years of talk, but Johnson had taken the crucial first step.

During the 1964 presidential campaign, however, Johnson was less patient. This was partly due to conservative Republican nominee Barry Goldwater, who demanded tough military responses. And it was partly due to the weakness of the post-Diem governments in South Vietnam. Regime replaced regime as if they were in a revolving door. The war could not be waged effectively because of this weakness. Nor—of special importance—could Johnson think of negotiating a settlement with Ho Chi Minh's Communist regime in North Vietnam while holding such a weak hand. Amid this frustration, North Vietnamese torpedo boats attacked a U.S. warship on August 2 in the Gulf of Tonkin. Two days later, another attack supposedly occurred.

Johnson's response proved historic. He ordered U.S. planes to bomb the north's ships and bases. Then LBJ asked Congress to pass a Gulf of Tonkin resolution giving him the right "to take all necessary measures to repel any armed attack against the forces of the United States and to prevent further aggression." The resolution sailed through the House by a vote of 416 to 0 but encountered trouble in the Senate from Oregon Democrat Wayne Morse and Alaskan Democrat Ernest Gruening, who warned that the measure gave the president a blank check to use force as he wished in Southeast Asia. This charge was denied by Arkansas Democrat J. William Fulbright, chairman of the Senate Foreign Relations Committee, who urged that the president be trusted. The Senate then passed the resolution 88 to 2 on August 7, 1964. Over the next four years, evidence appeared that the Gulf of Tonkin attack was not unprovoked. The U.S. ships were accompanying sabotage operations against North Vietnam. Moreover, the second attack had probably never occurred.[61]

Johnson, nevertheless, had it both ways in 1964. He lambasted
Goldwater as a dangerous fanatic and pledged that "we are not about
to send American boys 9 or 10,000 miles away from home to do what
Asian boys ought to be doing for themselves."[62] Meanwhile, he ordered
air attacks on North Vietnam. As usual, foreign policy mattered little
in most voters' minds. (One survey showed 25 percent of Americans
did not know that China was a Communist country or that U.S. soldiers were fighting in Vietnam.)[63] Johnson, emphasizing the need for
a "Great Society" at home made up of government programs for helping the young, old, poor, and minorities, buried Goldwater in a political landslide.

LBJ AND LATIN AMERICA: THE JOHNSON DOCTRINE IN ACTION

Johnson knew that he was dealing with a boiling furnace in trying to
handle the newly emerging world. But he could figure out neither how
to escape to a safe distance nor how to turn the fire down. The president noted in 1966 that eight years before, thirty-four important conflicts had erupted in the world, but in 1965 some fifty-eight had
occurred—more than half in nations whose people earned less than
$100 annually. In Latin America, the Alliance for Progress was creat-
ing an immense foreign debt, military rulers, and revolutions, not
progress. LBJ continued to support publicly the alliance and change,
but his speechwriter thought that LBJ's words seemed like "a lot of
crap to me."[64] Johnson feared revolution and had grown to mistrust
the alliance. He wanted stability and order. U.S. training for Latin
American police and military was increased.

"I know my Latinos," said Thomas Mann, LBJ's top adviser on Latin
America. "They understand only two things—a buck in the pocket and
a kick in the ass."[65] Johnson used the bucks in Brazil and the kicks in
Peru and the Dominican Republic. Throughout the twentieth century,
huge, rich, strategically located Brazil had been Washington's closest
Latin American partner. By 1964, however, the government of João
Goulart, like its neighbors, was in deep economic trouble. When Gou-
lart could not carry through internal belt-tightening, Johnson cut off
U.S. aid. Inflation went out of control. Goulart then moved to seize
U.S. properties. Encouraged by officials from the U.S. Embassy, the
Brazilian military overthrew Goulart, while Washington ordered its fleet
to stand off the coast in case it were needed. But the Brazilian military
required no help and established a brutal twenty-year dictatorship.

Ironically, once in power, the generals often defied the United States by dealing with revolutionary African regimes and refusing to promise Washington that they would not build nuclear weapons.[66]

But Johnson continued to send aid to the generals while cutting off money to Peru's civilian government. The Peruvians were trying to gain control of their country's major oil company, a firm owned by Standard Oil of New Jersey. Robert Kennedy, now a senator from New York, observed: "What the Alliance for Progress has come down to then is that you can close down newspapers, abolish congress, jail religious opposition [such as in Brazil] . . . and you'll get lots of help, but if you fool around with a U.S. oil company, we'll cut you off without a penny." A State Department official agreed, "That's about the size of it."[67]

LBJ also delivered a kick to the Dominican Republic. Since the 1930s a U.S. Marine-trained dictator, Rafael Trujillo, had ruled the country and supported Washington's policies. In 1956–1958, however, his brutal police agents carried out kidnappings and murders of Trujillo's opponents in the United States. His methods at home seemed to be creating conditions for another Castro to come to power. President Eisenhower sent weapons to the Dominican military who opposed Trujillo. In May 1961, they gunned down the elderly dictator as he drove to visit his twenty-year-old mistress. Juan Bosch, a moderate, won election to the presidency. By 1963–1964, the military had deposed Bosch and regained power.

The Dominican military, however, divided into factions. Bosch's group also maneuvered to regain power. In April 1965, one military group tried to overthrow the government. Civil war erupted. Bosch's supporters gained strength, a turn that frightened U.S. officials, who wrongly believed that Bosch was a mere front for communism. On April 28, 1965, a panicked U.S. Embassy told Johnson that "Castro-type elements" might win. If that occurred, a top aide told LBJ, "it will be the worst domestic political disaster any administration could suffer." The president sent 22,000 U.S. and OAS troops to the Dominican Republic to stop the fighting and install a conservative regime. He claimed on television on May 2, 1965, that a "communist dictatorship" threatened—a threat "the American nations cannot, must not, and will not permit."[68]

This Johnson Doctrine (the president could use military force whenever he thought communism threatened the hemisphere) caused an angry uproar in both Latin America and the United States. The doctrine directly contradicted the nonintervention clause in the OAS char-

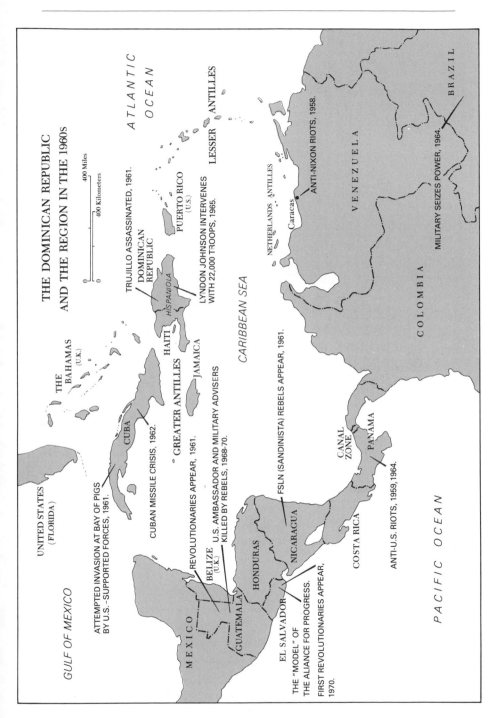

THE DOMINICAN REPUBLIC
AND THE REGION IN THE 1960s

ter signed in 1948 by the United States. The roar grew louder in Washington when reporters discovered that the dozen or so inept, isolated Communists in the Dominican Republic posed no danger. If they were Marxists, they seemed closer to Groucho than Karl. Congress (now including the powerful Senator Fulbright) and other Americans concluded that LBJ had deceived them. Their anger increased between 1965 and 1972, when the new government in the small nation could neither stop hundreds of political killings each year nor curb rampant corruption. But for Johnson, much worse lay ahead.

LBJ AND VIETNAM: THAT "BITCH OF A WAR"

In December 1963, Defense Secretary McNamara declared, "We have every reason to believe that [U.S. military] plans will be successful in 1964." By late 1964, however, the South Vietnamese government and army were falling apart, while Americans were killed by terrorists in the South Vietnamese capital of Saigon. Johnson had not yet decided how to respond. He passionately wanted his Great Society at home more than a war 10,000 miles away. But he wondered whether Americans would support him in Washington if he appeared weak in Vietnam. His closest advisers, led by McNamara and NSC director McGeorge Bundy, believed that an escalated response by the world's greatest power would compel Ho Chi Minh's Communist forces to retreat. They also argued that LBJ had to move rapidly or the chaotic Saigon government would collapse.

These arguments moved Johnson to action in February 1965, when communist guerrillas killed 7 Americans and wounded 109 at the U.S. base at Pleiku. He first ordered air strikes against North Vietnam. Then he announced in April a $1 billion aid program and, in May, dispatched two U.S. Marine combat divisions. Only American soldiers, he believed, could now pump life into South Vietnam. In July, U.S. troop numbers jumped from 75,000 to 125,000. By late 1965, Americans had found two military leaders who promised to provide the needed political stability: Premier Nguyen Cao Ky and President Nguyen Van Thieu. Neither had the nationalist, anti-French background of Ho Chi Minh, but they were the most acceptable leaders whom U.S. officials could find. By the end of 1965, 160,000 U.S. troops were in Vietnam.

Johnson made this Far Eastern commitment for many reasons, reasons that tell us much about the entire course of post-1945 U.S. foreign policy. First, he believed that every president since Roosevelt had made

THE VIETNAM WAR

a commitment to protect Vietnam. American "credibility" was, therefore, at stake worldwide. If Communists won in Asia, he said in 1966, they can "succeed anywhere in the world."[69]

Second, he believed that China posed the great threat. Quoting Theodore Roosevelt, that Americans now lived in the "Pacific era," Johnson declared that "over this war—and all Asia" lay "the deepening shadow of Communist China," which "is helping the forces of violence in almost every continent." China was to be contained by Americans fighting in Vietnam. U.S. fear grew as Chinese scientists exploded a first, small atomic bomb in 1964 and, within three years, set off a hydrogen bomb one hundred times larger than the first bomb.

Third, his view of history appeared when Johnson raised the ghost of the 1930s: "We learned from Hitler at Munich that success only feeds the appetite of aggression."

Fourth, Johnson increasingly saw links between winning "the only woman I really loved" (the Great Society programs at home) and the "bitch of a war" in Asia. Losing could be costly. Truman's problems at home with the McCarthyites and witch hunts after the fall of China in 1949, LBJ believed, "were chickenshit compared with what might happen if we lost Vietnam."

Fifth, Johnson assumed that the incredible U.S. power could do the job—and do it alone, if necessary. Merely by picking up the phone, he could send hundreds of thousands of soldiers across the ocean. They would be accompanied by the genius of American technology. Helicopters, experimented with in France as early as 1914, had only run medical missions in the Korean War, but they now gave U.S. soldiers battlefield mobility and protection never before known. The air force and scientists united to defoliate huge jungle areas, where guerrillas liked to hide. ("Only we can prevent forests," ran one air unit's motto.) When critics noted how the French had failed to win in Indochina, a Pentagon official shot back, "The French also tried to build the Panama Canal."

Finally, Johnson believed that if he escalated slowly and did not demand too much of Americans and their economy, they would support his policy. The president, therefore, refused to ask for a congressional declaration of war that could justify a full-scale effort. With good reason, he believed that Americans would support a strong president who fought communism. "We did not put on big bond drives or [have] movie actors going around the country whopping up war-fever," Rusk later said, "because there's too much power in the world to let the American people become too mad." The plan, Rusk declared, "was not to let the situation go down the chute—the chute into a larger war."[70] Johnson, thus, tried to find a middle way that gained Americans' support but avoided war with China and the Soviets.

LBJ AND VIETNAM: THE MISCALCULATIONS

By 1966–1967, each of these reasons had crumbled. First, allies, indeed, began to doubt U.S. "credibility." But they did so because LBJ insisted on pouring resources into a bottomless war that these partners did not believe could be won. Moreover, many observers doubted that any links existed between Communist advances in Asia and those in, say, Latin America. Each region had its own peculiar conditions.

Second, experts on Asia noted that for a thousand years Vietnamese nationalists such as Ho had fought (not embraced) China. In 1946, Ho had even preferred to work with France: "It is better to smell the French dung for awhile than eat China's all our lives." Mao's government,

moreover, had sunk into bitter infighting followed by a "cultural revolution" in 1966–1967 in which young Chinese tried to restore revolutionary fervor in the nation. Instead, they nearly drowned China in
chaos. At the same time, nationalists in a number of newly emerging
nations (even Castro's Cuba) killed or drove out pro-Chinese Communist factions. On the other hand, China did move 50,000 men into
North Vietnam, partly to operate base complexes but mostly to warn
Johnson that an invasion of the North could (as in Korea) lead to a
larger war. Johnson and McNamara admitted that if U.S. power was
not limited, it could "trigger Chinese intervention on the ground."[71]
Having gone to war to contain China, Johnson now found that Chinese
threats were being limited around the world—except in a pocket of
North Vietnam, where the Chinese effectively contained U.S. power.

Third, Ho's (or Mao's) nationalism was not the same as Hitler's worldwide ambitions. The rugged peasants in the Communist army hardly
compared with Hitler's armored divisions, and the 1930s bore little
resemblance to the nuclear world of the 1960s.

Fourth, the Great Society sank as war expenses rose. Johnson and
Vice-President Humphrey repeatedly said that the U.S. economy could
produce "both guns and butter." But by 1967, it could not turn out as
many guns and as much butter as the Johnson policies demanded
without imposing new taxes (which the president feared for political
reasons) or creating severe weaknesses in the economy. War costs shot
upward from $8 billion in 1966 to $21 billion in 1967. Dollars flew out
of the United States to pay for both the war and growing American
private investments abroad (which rose from $49 billion in 1960 to
$101 billion in 1968). The nation's export trade could not pull those
dollars back. Instead, U.S. producers were finding that they could no
longer compete with Japanese and German products. Americans were
spending so much money abroad that the dollar, the backbone of the
world's financial system, began to weaken. Confidence in that backbone started to disappear. The long U.S. economic slide had begun,
and it had been heavily greased by the Vietnam War's costs.[72]

Fifth, the power of American technology proved to be less potent
than the willingness of the North Vietnamese to die for their cause. As
Johnson sent in more troops, Ho moved about 1,000 of his soldiers
into the south each month in 1964, but 4,500 per month in 1965, and
5,000 each month in 1966. Secretary of State Rusk noted in 1971 that
the Communists suffered the loss of over 700,000 (the equivalent, given
the size of the two populations, of killing 10 million Americans), but
"they continue to come." Johnson and the U.S. military could come

up with no better policy. Journalist Walter Lippmann condemned LBJ for "conducting the war like a gambler who, when he loses one round, doubles his bet in the hope of recovering what he has lost." McNamara's faith in statistics was undercut by figures that were misleading or cooked up to please Washington officials. U.S. troops in Vietnam called such statistics MEGs—Mostly Exaggerated Guesses. American ignorance of Vietnamese history and customs seemed so limitless that it could never be made up by U.S. technology. For example, when the Communists destroyed much of the South's rice harvest, the United States rushed in California and Louisiana rice, only to find that the Vietnamese hated American rice so much that they used it instead of dirt to fill their sandbags.[73]

LBJ AND VIETNAM: AT HOME

Johnson certainly had problems but they did not include his power as president. In 1966, columnist James Reston marveled at LBJ's incredible authority: not even the leader of the Soviet Union enjoyed "such freedom of action in foreign affairs." Power over Vietnam policy was centralized in a Tuesday luncheon group that included the president, Rusk, McNamara, and NSC director Walt Rostow and that, one macabre joke went, began with prayer and ended with selecting bombing targets. When Congress complained that the Constitution gave it, not the president, the authority to declare war, Assistant Attorney General Nicholas Katzenbach told Congress flatly that the constitutional clause was "an outmoded phraseology." That remark, Minnesota Democratic Senator Eugene McCarthy declared, was "the wildest testimony I have ever heard. There is no limit to what he says the President could do." As a result of this exchange, McCarthy decided to challenge Johnson for the 1968 presidential election.[74]

An anti-war movement in colleges was soon marked by "teach-ins" conducted by faculty and outside lecturers. A "new Left" bloomed, differing from the "old Left" of the 1930s by being less ideological, less interested in economics, and more devoted to community and social changes as well as to opposing the war. A counterculture appeared that cared more about music and political activism than about shaving and being well dressed. These groups thought critically about subjects long uncriticized by most of American society. A landmark was Stanley Kubrick's film, *Dr. Strangelove*, in which the U.S. presidency, nuclear war, and the American military (in the figure of "General Jack D. Rip-

President Johnson discusses his policy on Vietnam with his top advisers. Johnson sits at center right. Secretary of Defense McNamara is to his left and Secretary of State Rusk to his right.

per") were made to appear as foolish as the Soviet characters. All authority seemed open to question.[75]

Johnson had once courted college students, but by 1967–1968 their protests made it impossible for him to visit campuses and some cities safely. "To him," one aide said, these students "appeared to be extraterrestrial invaders—not only non-American but nonearthly."[76] Some 250 students from twenty-five medical schools signed a pledge that they would not serve in Vietnam. The protests gained a new dimension when students joined forces with civil-rights demonstrators to obtain full rights for blacks and other minorities. Johnson had worked hard for civil rights, but it was too late. Urban riots began in mid-1964. In 1965, the Los Angeles black ghetto of Watts erupted in violence, and thirty-four persons were killed. By 1968, Tampa, Newark, Cincinnati, Atlanta, and Detroit (where forty-three died) had burned, and finally the nation's capital itself exploded in flames during April 1968, after civil-rights and anti-war leader Martin Luther King, Jr., was assassinated.

The war had come home. U.S. military vehicles moved onto Capitol

A marine, despite his wounds, reaches out for another marine during a lull in the bloody battle of October 1966 over Hill 484 in South Vietnam. This stunning photo was taken after U.S. soldiers had barely driven back North Vietnamese troops.

Hill and the grounds of the White House to protect the government's leaders from the violence. Violence seemed to breed more violence. From July 1965 to December 1967, U.S. planes dropped more bomb tonnage on Vietnam than the Allies dropped on Europe during all of World War II. More than 344,000 of Ho's forces were killed in these months, but their strength actually rose from 187,000 to 261,000. The war's frustrations, especially the inability to tell a Vietnamese peasant from a deadly enemy, led to wholesale destruction. After the village of Ben Tre was burned, a U.S. officer declared, "It became necessary to destroy the town in order to save it." The war abroad and at home also linked up when the veterans began to return. As one medical aide put it, "It's not at all like a John Wayne movie. The most distressing, the most grotesque are those with an arm or a leg blown off," and "you realize what despair, what deformity, what suffering they're going to have."[77]

Leaders such as George Kennan and Senator Fulbright (chairman of the Senate Foreign Relations Committee) also opposed the war. So did retired military leaders such as Generals Matthew Ridgway (hero of the Korean War) and David Shoup (former Marine Corps commandant). Johnson grew furious at allied leaders who took advantage of visits to the United States to condemn the conflict. When Canadian prime minister Lester Pearson did so in 1965, LBJ got Pearson alone, grabbed him by the shirt collar, and yelled, "You pissed on my rug!"[78] But the attacks continued, especially after the 1967 national election in South Vietnam, which was obviously rigged. Political opponents were imprisoned so that Thieu and Ky could retain their hold on the government.

But Johnson continued to hope. He could be encouraged because, until early 1968, U.S. television largely reported the war uncritically and gave weight to the administration's views.[79] In January 1968, both LBJ and his top commander in Vietnam, General William Westmoreland, said with good evidence on their side that the war was being won. Then, in late January 1968, it all changed. Taking advantage of a holiday lull during the lunar New Year (Tet), the Communists launched

---

I went to Vietnam to heal
and came home silently wounded.
I went to Vietnam to heal
and still awaken from nightmares
about those we couldn't save.
I went to Vietnam to heal
and came home to grieve for those
we sent home blind, paralyzed,
limbless, mindless.
I went to Vietnam to heal
and discovered I am not God.

To you whose names are on this wall
I am sorry I couldn't be God.
If I were God, if there were a God,
there would be no need for such a wall.

But I am not God, and so I go on
seeing the wounded when I hear a
chopper, washing your blood from my hands,
hearing your screams in my sleep, scrubbing
the smell of your burned bodies from my clothes,
feeling your pain, which never eases,
fighting a war that never ends.
                              —*Dusty [a former nurse in
                              Vietnam 1966–1968]*

A poem written by a survivor of Vietnam in memory of eight U.S. nurses who did not survive. The poem captures the feelings of many veterans who returned from the war but could never leave it behind.

a massive offensive in which hand-to-hand combat actually occurred in the U.S. Embassy compound in Saigon. Ho's troops took tremendous losses (probably 30,000 dead), and after being repulsed they were again devastated when they tried a second offensive. But U.S.–South Vietnamese losses were also high.

Americans were stunned that the Communists could launch such a massive campaign after Johnson and Westmoreland claimed that the war was being won. The U.S. positions in the cities and villages had clearly been weakened. American television, led by the country's most respected newsman, Walter Cronkite of CBS News, now publicly questioned whether the conflict could ever be won. Critics zeroed in on ineffective South Vietnamese troops, who, a U.S. military adviser declared, "are leaderless and gutless."[80]

General Westmoreland publicly claimed a great victory, but news then leaked that he had asked the president for 206,000 more U.S. troops. Badly shaken, Johnson called in a group of "Wise Men," senior retired officials led by Dean Acheson and McGeorge Bundy. At first strong supporters of the war, by March 1968 they believed that the cost had soared too high. They received strong support from Clark Clifford, the new secretary of defense. Clifford and the Wise Men especially feared the effect of a prolonged war on a stumbling U.S. economy. When a top U.S. general argued that the Americans must never retreat, but admitted that a "classic military victory" was impossible, Acheson roared, "Then what in the name of God are five hundred thousand men doing out there? Chasing girls?" Acheson reviewed the evidence and told Johnson that he (the president) had been badly misled by his military advisers. Some officials opposed sending more troops overseas because of the fear that the troops would be needed to put down uprisings within the United States itself.[81]

On March 31, 1968, LBJ declared on national television that he was limiting the bombing of North Vietnam as part of an appeal for peace talks with Ho Chi Minh. The president then stunned the country by announcing that in order to concentrate on ending the war, he would not be a candidate for re-election. The war claimed the Johnson administration as its ultimate victim.

OTHER COSTS OF VIETNAM: U.S. RELATIONS WITH AFRICA, THE MIDDLE EAST, AND THE SOVIET UNION

Johnson had become obsessed with the war. Unable to sleep, he visited the White House War Room in the middle of the night to learn whether

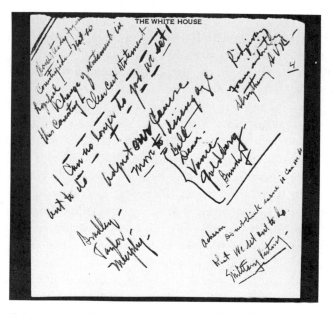

President Johnson's doodling during the crucial March 25, 1968, meeting with his "wise men" on Vietnam. Note Johnson's highlighting of Acheson's comment to the group that the United States "can no longer do job we set out to do."

the bombers he had ordered out had returned safely. Such obsession prevented the administration from dealing more effectively with other troubles—and opportunities—in the world.

Along with Southeast Asia and Latin America, Africa was transformed between 1958 and 1968. Dominated by European colonial powers in the mid-1950s, within a decade it was a huge continent of independent nations (see map, p. 664). As usual, the United States publicly supported this anticolonial movement. President Kennedy spent much time greeting heads of the new states and obtaining aid for them.

There was, however, a glaring, embarrassing contradiction at the center of U.S. policy in Africa. It was South Africa, where a white minority of 4 million oppressed some 20 million blacks through a system of apartheid (rigid, legal, police-enforced racial separation.) Apartheid had begun in 1948 when the white Nationalist Party responded to the worldwide explosions of anticolonialism and demands for racial equality, which appeared during and after World War II, by turning inward and brutally putting down any talk of racial moderation in South Africa. Under Harry Truman and Dwight Eisenhower, U.S. policy accepted apartheid because officials cared much more about South Africa's strategic location and, above all, its rich uranium mines so necessary to the making of nuclear weapons. Moreover, the segregation of the races was accepted by Americans in the late 1940s and early 1950s. As historian Tim Borstelmann explains the growing U.S.– South African partnership in trade and military planning, "A country in which white people held the preponderance of power and people of color were widely disenfranchised, impoverished, and physically intimidated could not have seemed strange to representatives of the United States" at that time. U.S. racism and anticommunism meshed together perfectly in the relationship with South Africa. That tie did not begin to loosen until nearly a decade after the 1954 U.S. Supreme Court decision, *Brown* v. *Board of Education,* that finally outlawed racial segregation in the United States. President Kennedy, understanding the contradiction in professing democracy and supporting South African apartheid, finally cut off arms sales and government loans to the white government. It would, however, be another quarter-century before Washington's policies finally helped pull down apartheid.[82]

But Kennedy and Johnson also used the CIA and other weapons to fight black nationalists whom they believed to be pro-Communist. The Congo became the example. In June 1960, this West African nation (later renamed Zaire), finally broke free of an especially incompetent, ruthless, and exploitative Belgian colonialism. Strategically located, the Congo was rich in tin, copper, gold, cobalt, and diamonds. Its Katanga Province (later Shaba Province) produced the tantalum the United States needed to build aircraft. Prime Minister Patrice Lumumba was a charismatic socialist who kicked out remaining Belgian troops and frightened the 100,000 remaining Europeans. With Belgian support, however, Moise Tshombe declared Katanga and its riches an independent province. Although Eisenhower sympathized with the Belgians, he supported the United Nations team that tried to work out peace terms. The UN group was led by Ralph Bunche, a black American who had won the Nobel Peace Prize for his extraordinary diplomacy in the Middle East. The Soviets then tried to enter the scene by accusing Bunche of being a mere frontman for U.S. interests. Soviet military advisers appeared to help Lumumba as the Congo fragmented.

With CIA help, Colonel Joseph Mobuto's soldiers captured and killed Lumumba in January 1961, just as Kennedy moved into the White House. The new president sympathized with African nationalism but was in no mood to watch the Soviets make any gains in Africa. Through CIA and U.S. military aid, he helped Mobutu gain power. When rebels seized some 3,000 foreigners as hostages in late 1964, U.S. and Belgian troops rescued them and helped crush the rebellion. By 1965, the United States had replaced Belgium as the dominant foreign power.[83]

Ralph Bunche (1904–1971), the grandson of a slave, was born in Detroit, was educated at UCLA and Harvard, became a teacher at Howard University, joined the State Department, then gained fame as the United Nations official who successfully mediated the 1949 Arab-Israeli War, a success that brought him the Nobel Peace Prize. He led the UN effort to find peace in the Congo in the early 1960s. This photo was taken during his service with the United Nations.

Mobutu took his place as a virtual (if elected) dictator whose regime became increasingly corrupt but more pro-Western. Johnson wanted to augment U.S. aid to Mobutu and other new African leaders, but Vietnam's costs prevented it.

Kennedy and Johnson could do even less to help preserve peace in the Middle East. JFK hoped to follow an "even-handed" approach in dealing with the bitter dispute between Egypt and Israel. He did not want to give up the advantage of Israel's military power or the support of Jewish voters at home, but he did want to work with Egypt's General Gamal Abdel Nasser so that the general would not look to the Soviets for help. Kennedy's plan, however, fell apart in 1962–1963. When the small Middle East kingdom of Yemen became embroiled in revolution, Nasser sent 75,000 troops to help the revolt. Saudi Arabia (the region's greatest oil producer and Washington's closest Arab friend) quickly intervened in Yemen to stop Nasser. The United States first pressured Nasser to step back but then decided not to oppose his policy. The Saudis quickly squeezed U.S. oil firms. Israel and Great Britain protested Kennedy's tilt toward Egypt. The president reversed course, declared Nasser untrustworthy, and sent air power to defend the Saudis. By the time of his death, JFK had fully moved U.S. policy to a pro-Israel, pro-Saudi, anti-Egypt position.[84] Kennedy pledged to use the U.S. Sixth Fleet to protect Israel, if necessary, and for the first time sold a large amount of arms (antiaircraft missiles) to the Israelis.

Johnson, long a close friend of American Jewish groups, moved even closer to Israel. The first U.S. shipments of tanks and Skyhawk bombers went to the Israelis in 1965–1966. But intensifying problems in Vietnam and at home forced LBJ to stand on the sidelines in 1967, when Nasser moved to cut off a vital ocean route to Israel. Egypt ordered a UN peacekeeping team out of the Sinai Peninsula, then moved 100,000 troops close to Israel's borders. The most Johnson could do—and did do—was to tell the Israelis that if they struck Egypt, he would not restrain them as Eisenhower had done at Suez in 1956. The Israeli troops suddenly attacked on June 5, 1967. In the spectacular Six-Day War, they destroyed much of Nasser's army and air force. They also crippled Egypt's allies, Jordan and Syria. Israel then seized the West Bank of the Jordan River (claimed by Jordan), the Sinai, and the Gaza strip, as well as all of the great city of Jersualem. Israel had won near-total victory, but the question of whether more than half a million Palestinian Arabs on the West Bank would have to remain in Israel now haunted Middle Eastern diplomacy. For the next six years, the United States could do little to help solve that explosive issue.

Nor could Johnson do as much as he had hoped to improve U.S.-USSR relations. After the Cuban missile crisis, the United States continued its nuclear build-up, while the Soviets built up even faster to catch up with the Americans. By 1967, the president, and especially Defense Secretary McNamara, feared that the race was getting out of hand. The United States had 1,054 ICBMs, and the Soviets approached 900 in their arsenal. Also ominous was a Soviet antiballistic missile (ABM) system that could possibly make Communist cities less vulnerable to U.S. missiles. Johnson accelerated U.S. development of an ABM, and the Americans also stepped up work on Multiple Independent Reentry Vehicles (MIRVs)—nuclear warheads that were launched on a single missile and, in flight, separated to fly off in as many as ten different directions to hit targets. Thus, two new arms races threatened.

In a speech at Montreal in 1967, McNamara warned that "bridges" had to be built to Moscow, even to Beijing (Peking), to stop the arms build-up. He was worried that the growing number of conflicts in the newly emerging world could dangerously escalate and begged that money for arms be spent instead on erasing the poverty that produced these conflicts. He, Johnson, and Soviet president Aleksei Kosygin met for a hastily planned summit conference at Glassboro, New Jersey, in 1967. McNamara again passionately argued for controls on arms and especially on ABM development (which, he feared, could lead to the building of more offensive weapons that would simply overwhelm any ABM system).

Kosygin refused to agree with McNamara, but the two sides signed a historic treaty to halt the proliferation of their nuclear weapons (to third powers such as China or the two Germanies, for example). In 1968, fifty-seven other nations also signed the nonproliferation pact. Direct air service opened between New York and Moscow. Johnson planned to visit Moscow in 1968 to help continue thawing the cold war. Before he could do so, however, in August 1968 the Soviets invaded Czechoslovakia.

The Czechs had begun economic and political reforms that frightened the conservative, military-based Communist governments of eastern Europe. If they were not stopped, the reforms could sweep through the bloc like a warm, unwelcome breeze. Soviet leader Leonid Brezhnev justified using force to stop the "Prague spring" (as it became known in the West) with a "Brezhnev Doctrine": Communist governments were justified in using force to preserve communism where it was already established. Johnson canceled his trip. Cold-war temperatures dropped dangerously. The arms races sped on.

JFK, LBJ, *Bonnie and Clyde*

John Kennedy did not leave behind a bitterly divided society. "Our country is not divided today, not split into warring groups—thank goodness," President Johnson said in June 1964.[85] The tall, dynamic Texan tried to ensure national unity (and compassion) with his Great Society programs.

Despite his successes, however, by 1969 the nation was ripped apart by anti-war and pro-civil-rights riots. In April 1968, Martin Luther King was murdered in Memphis, Tennessee, and cities exploded. Smoke from blocks of burning buildings curled above the Capitol. King had become the victim of the violence he had spent his life exposing—both in the United States and more recently Vietnam. For by 1966–1967, he believed that "racism and militarism" were interrelated problems in America that could not be solved while "the heart of the administration is in that war in Vietnam."[86] Senator Robert Kennedy had reached the same conclusion, but in June 1968 he was also assassinated in Los Angeles just after winning the California Democratic primary election. Street protests at the Democratic convention in Chicago and brutal retaliation by the city's police prevented Johnson from attending his party's nomination of Vice-President Hubert Humphrey for the top job.

Artists reflected the effects of these divisions on American society.

Writer Susan Sontag called the white race the cancer of history. In 1967, Hollywood produced a highly popular film, *Bonnie and Clyde*, the story of two uneducated bankrobbers whom the film portrayed as more innocent than the unjust, violence-ridden society that drove them to crime.[87] Violence seemed the only effective response to a violent society that devastated square miles of Southeast Asia and square blocks of American cities.

Kennedy, however, had left behind much of the foreign policy that led to this devastation. The "most important decision" Kennedy made, Secretary of State Rusk recalled, was breaking the troop limits set by the 1954 Geneva Accords and committing "about seventeen- or eighteen-thousand [U.S. troops] before his death."[88] Kennedy's decision in 1961–1962 to build on the tremendous U.S. nuclear superiority, rather than negotiating arms agreements, led to an accelerated arms race in which the Soviets would catch up to America within a decade. JFK's glamor, the "Camelot" of the Kennedy White House, enlarged and added purple hues to an already "imperial presidency" in foreign policy. Johnson carried on these Kennedy legacies until the Tet offensive in Vietnam and the rioting at home forced a reassessment. Then, as historian Larry Berman puts it, the war had become "at once, a human and a national tragedy in the United States."[89] Johnson finally

President Lyndon Johnson buries his head in his arm at the cabinet table as he sits alone listening to his son-in-law's taped descriptions of the death and destruction witnessed during his tour of duty in Vietnam. Taken by Jack Knight-linger on July 31, 1968, the photo caught not only the feelings of the president, but those of many Americans after nearly four years of intensified war.

decided to restrict the bombing, but he never wavered in his determination to keep South Vietnam non-Communist.

LBJ's decision to open peace talks came too late to save Hubert Humphrey. In a tight race, Republican Richard Nixon defeated the vice-president by 0.7 percent of the popular vote. Vietnam played a major, but not decisive, part in Humphrey's defeat. More important, polls revealed, was the desire of the average American ("the housewife in Dayton, Ohio," as one pollster said) to be able to walk down a street without crime and violence—and to live again in a country of law and order, not Bonnies and Clydes.[90] Nixon had solemnly promised to end the war in both Vietnam and on American streets.

NOTES

1. C. Vann Woodward, *Thinking Back: The Perils of Writing History* (Baton Rouge, La., 1986), p. 103.
2. Thomas E. Cronin, "Looking for Leadership, 1980," *Public Opinion* 3 (February–March, 1980): 18.
3. James MacGregor Burns, *John Kennedy: A Political Profile* (New York, 1960), pp.

40–42, 79–84, 88–95; John F. Kennedy, *Why England Slept* (New York, 1940), esp. pp. 215–216, 224–231.

4. Douglas Brinkley, *Dean Acheson: The Cold War Years, 1953–71* (New Haven, 1992), p. 112.

5. Henry Fairlie, *The Kennedy Promise: The Politics of Expectation* (Garden City, N.Y., 1973), p. 116; *Washington Post*, 29 August, 1976, p. E3. The New Frontier and related concepts and phrases are placed in context in Arthur Schlesinger, Jr., *A Thousand Days* (Boston, 1965), pp. 4–5, a detailed, highly favorable biography of Kennedy.

6. Rockefeller Brothers Fund, *Prospects for America* (Garden City, N.Y., 1961).

7. Stephen E. Ambrose, *Nixon: The Education of a Politician, 1913–1962* (New York, 1987), p. 546.

8. Theodore Sorensen, *Decision-Making in the White House* (New York, 1963), pp. 45–48.

9. Bruce W. Jentleson, "From Consensus to Conflict: The Domestic Political Economy of East-West Energy Trade Policy," *International Organization* 38 (Autumn 1984): 640.

10. Dean Rusk, "Chinese-American Friendship," *Department of State Bulletin*, 21 May 1951, pp. 846–847.

11. Barry Rubin, *Secrets of State* (New York, 1985), p. 95.

12. David Halberstam, "The Programming of Robert McNamara," *Harper's* 242 (February 1971): 44; *National Observer*, 6 December 1965, p. 1.

13. Frank Costigliola, "The Failed Design: Kennedy, de Gaulle, and the Struggle for Europe," *Diplomatic History* 8 (Summer 1984): 229.

14. *Forbes*, 1 February 1966, pp. 15–16.

15. Oral History interview of Couve de Murville, 20 May 1964, John F. Kennedy Presidential Library, Boston, Mass.

16. *Newsweek*, 19 November 1973, p. 90.

17. *New York Times*, 22 November 1965, p. 43.

18. John Spanier, *American Foreign Policy since World War II* (New York, 1965), pp. 176–177.

19. W. W. Rostow, *The Diffusion of Power* (New York, 1972), p. 52.

20. *New York Times*, 12 July 1960, p. 7.

21. U.S. Government, *Public Papers of the Presidents of the United States: John F. Kennedy, 1962* (Washington, D.C., 1963), p. 223. Documents on the Alliance for Progress and its implementation are in *The Record of American Diplomacy*, ed. Ruhl J. Bartlett, 4th ed. (New York, 1964), pp. 868–874.

22. Pat M. Holt, "The Political Aspects," in U.S. Congress, Senate, Committee on Foreign Relations, 91st Cong., 1st sess., 1969, *Survey of the Alliance for Progress* (Washington, D.C., 1969), pp. 14–16.

23. Theodore C. Sorensen, *Kennedy* (New York, 1965), pp. 535–536.

24. Barton J. Bernstein, "Kennedy and the Bay of Pigs Revisited Twenty-four Years Later," *Foreign Service Journal* 62 (March 1985): pp. 535–536.

25. Review of Peter Wyden's *Bay of Pigs* (New York, 1979), in *Business Week*, 23 July 1979, p. 17; Brinkley, p. 127.

26. Michael R. Beschloss, *Mayday: Eisenhower, Khrushchev, and the U-2 Affair* (New York, 1986), p. 303; Schlesinger, p. 292.

27. *Washington Post*, 12 September 1976, p. L5.

28. Speech excerpts and analysis can be found in Lloyd Gardner, "Dominoes, Diem, and Death, 1952–1963," in *America in Vietnam*, ed. William Appleman Williams *et al.* (New York, 1985), pp. 189–191.

29. Paul Boller, Jr., *Presidential Anecdotes* (New York, 1981), p. 301; *New York Times*, 14 February 1965, p. E9.

30. Stephen E. Pelz, " 'When Do I Have Time to Think?': John F. Kennedy, Roger Hilsman, and the Laotian Crisis of 1962," *Diplomatic History* 3 (Spring 1979): 223, quoting Clark M. Clifford, "A Viet Nam Reappraisal: The Personal History of One Man's View and How It Evolved," *Foreign Affairs* 47 (July 1969): 604.

31. Gareth Porter, "After Geneva: Subverting Laotian Neutrality," in *Laos: War and Revolution*, ed. Nina S. Adams and Alfred W. McCoy (New York, 1970), pp. 179–212.

32. *Washington Post*, 28 November 1980, p. C4.

33. Stephen E. Pelz, "John F. Kennedy's 1961 Vietnam War Decisions," *Journal of Strategic Studies* 4 (December 1981): 370–371.

34. Maxwell D. Taylor, *Responsibility and Response* (New York, 1967), p. 57.

35. Gardner, p. 143.

36. James Aronson, *The Press and the Cold War* (New York, 1970), pp. 182–183.

37. Oral History interview of William Tyler, 7 March 1964, John F. Kennedy Presidential Library; Chester L. Cooper, *The Lost Crusade: America in Vietnam* (New York, 1970), p. 171; Gordon H. Chang, *Friends and Enemies* (Stanford, 1990), pp. 240–252.

38. Gardner, pp. 198–201, has the interviews; Leslie H. Gelb, "Kennedy and Vietnam," *New York Times*, 6 January 1992, p. A31.

39. Pelz, "Kennedy's Vietnam Decisions," p. 378.

40. W. Averell Harriman quoted in Frank Costigliola, "The New Atlantic Community" (1987), manuscript in the author's possession, p. 13.

41. Boller, p. 303.

42. Brinkley, p. 147; Kennedy's speech in Berlin is in U.S. Government, *Public Papers of the Presidents of the United States: John F. Kennedy, 1963* (Washington, D.C., 1964), pp. 524–525; Costigliola, "The Failed Design," pp. 240–241.

43. Scott D. Sagan, "SIOP-62: The Nuclear War Plan Briefing to President Kennedy," *International Security* 12 (Summer 1987): 23n.

44. *New York Times*, 14 October 1987, p. A10.

45. Walter Pincus, "CIA Records Offer Behind-the-Scenes Look at Cuban Missile Crisis," *Washington Post*, 19 October, 1992, pp. A10–A11.

46. Foreign Broadcast Information Service, *Daily Report Annex: Soviet Union*, 17 January 1989, pp. 6–11.

47. Marc Trachtenberg, "The Influence of Nuclear Weapons in the Cuban Missile Crisis," *International Security* 10 (Summer 1985): 148–149; Elie Abel, *The Missile Crisis* (Philadelphia, 1968), pp. 70, 81, 118–119.

48. J. Anthony Lukas, "Class Reunion: Kennedy's Men Relive the Cuban Missile Crisis," *New York Times Magazine*, 30 August 1987, p. 51; Trachtenberg, p. 161; Laurence Chang and Peter Kornbluh, eds., *The Cuban Missile Crisis, 1962: A National Security Archive Documents Reader* (New York, 1992), pp. 150–154.

49. Chang and Kornbluh, eds., *The Cuban Missile Crisis*, pp. 197–199; Lukas, p. 58; Walter Pincus, "Standing at the Brink of Nuclear War," *Washington Post*, 25 July 1985, pp. A1, A10.

50. The recorded discussion of the 27 October meeting is in McGeorge Bundy, transcr., and James G. Blight, ed., "October 27, 1962: Transcripts of the Meetings of the ExComm," *International Security* 12 (Winter 1987–1988): esp. 48, 58, 87–88; Chang and Kornbluh, eds., *The Cuban Missile Crisis*, pp. 226–229, 230–232; the Castro letter was originally printed in *Le Monde*, and then reprinted in the Louisville *Courier-Journal*, 2 December 1990, pp. D1, D4.

51. Letter to the editor from Bruce J. Allyn and James G. Blight, *New York Times*, 2 November 1992, p. A18; *Washington Post*, 7 January 1992, p. A12; *New York Times*, 22 January 1992, p. A30. *New York Times*, 14 October 1987, p. A10; Rubin, p. 98.

52. Charles E. Bohlen, *Witness to History, 1929–1969* (New York, 1973), p. 495.

53. Gaddis Smith, "The Legacy of the Monroe Doctrine," *New York Times Magazine*, 9 September 1984, p. 128; Thomas G. Paterson and William J. Brophy, "October Missiles and November Elections . . . ," *Journal of American History* 73 (June 1986): 87–93, 112–119; Stephen S. Rosenfeld, "That Cuban Missile Understanding," *Washington Post*, 2 April 1982, p. A17.

54. Costigliola, "The Failed Design," 234–235, 237; Stewart Alsop, "The Collapse of Kennedy's Grand Design," *Saturday Evening Post*, 6 April 1963, pp. 78–81; Alexander Werth, *De Gaulle, a Political Biography* (New York, 1966), pp. 331–333.

55. Walt W. Rostow, "Domestic Determinants of U.S. Foreign Policy: The Tocqueville Oscillation," *Armed Forces Journal* 27 June 1970, p. 16D.

56. Theodore Draper, *Present History* (New York, 1983), pp. 197–198; U.S. Congress, Senate, Committee on Foreign Relations, 88th Cong., 1st sess., 1963, *Nuclear Test Ban Treaty* (Washington, D.C., 1963), pp. 422–427.

57. Oral History statement by William Attwood, 8 November 1965, John F. Kennedy Presidential Library; Terence Ripmaster, "The Kennedy Assassination in U.S. History Books," *The Third Decade: A Journal of Research on the John F. Kennedy Assassination* 3 (May 1987): 4–6.

58. *Department of State Bulletin*, 12 May 1975, p. 606.

59. Robert Divine, "The Johnson Literature," in *Exploring the Johnson Years*, ed. Robert Divine (Austin, Tex., 1981), pp. 3–4, 13; *Washington Post*, 29 August 1976, p. E3; Boller, p. 310; Lawrence Martin, *The Presidents and the Prime Ministers* (Toronto, 1982), p. 220.

60. *Who We Are: An Atlantic Chronicle of the United States and Vietnam*, ed. Robert Manning and Michael Janeway (Boston, 1969), pp. 16, 216.

61. The documents may be found in *America in Vietnam*, pp. 234–239; U.S. Congress, Senate, Committee on Foreign Relations, 90th Cong., 2d sess., 1968, *The Gulf of Tonkin: The 1964 Incidents* (Washington, D.C., 1968).

62. U.S. Government, *Public Papers of the Presidents of the United States: Lyndon B. Johnson, 1964* (Washington, D.C., 1965), pp. 1390–1391, 1441.

63. Barry Hughes, *Domestic Context of American Foreign Policy* (San Francisco, 1978), p. 57.

64. Oral History interview of Harry McPherson, tape #4, p. 13, Lyndon B. Johnson Presidential Library, Austin, Tex.; U.S. Government, *Public Papers of the Presidents of the United States: Lyndon B. Johnson, 1966* (Washington, D.C., 1968), p. 936.

65. Samuel Baily, *The United States and the Development of South America, 1945–1975* (New York, 1976), pp. 58, 118–119, 215–216.

66. Phyllis Parker, *Brazil and the Quiet Intervention, 1964* (Austin, Tex., 1979), pp. xi, 58, 63, 68–70, 81, 92–99, 102–103; Thomas E. Skidmore, "U.S. Policy toward Bra-

zil: Assumptions and Options," in *Latin America: The Search for a New International Role*, ed. Ronald G. Hellman and H. John Rosenbaum (New York, 1975), pp. 198–200.

67. Arthur Schlesinger, Jr., "The Alliance for Progress: A Retrospective," in *Latin America*, p. 80.

68. *New York Times*, 3 May 1965, p. 10; "Report for the President" from Jack Valenti, 30 April 1965, CO 1-8, White House Central Files, Lyndon B. Johnson Library.

69. Sources of the quotations in this and the next four paragraphs can be found in (in order): U.S. Government, *Public Papers of the Presidents, 1966*, p. 762; *New York Times*, 13 July 1966, p. 2; U.S. Government, *Public Papers of the Presidents of the United States: Lyndon B. Johnson, 1965* (Washington, D.C., 1966), pp. 395, 794; George C. Herring, "The War in Vietnam," in *Exploring the Johnson Years*, p. 27; Richard E. Neustadt and Ernest R. May, *Thinking in Time: The Uses of History for Decision-Makers* (New York, 1986), p. 86; Michael Herr, *Dispatches* (New York, 1977), p. 154; Neustadt and May, p. 86.

70. Oral History interview of Dean Rusk, recorded in 1969, released in 1987, Lyndon B. Johnson Library; a splendid detailed analysis of the crucial 1965 decision can be found in Larry Berman, *Planning a Tragedy* (New York, 1982), esp. pp. 31–129, and also in George McT. Kahin, *Intervention: How America Became Involved in Vietnam* (New York, 1986), pp. 286–401.

71. Oral History interview of Rusk; Allen S. Whiting, *The Chinese Calculus of Deterrence: India and Indochina* (Ann Arbor, Mich., 1975), pp. 182–189.

72. William S. Borden, *The Pacific Alliance: U.S. Foreign Economic Policy and Japanese Trade Recovery, 1947–1955* (Madison, Wis., 1984), pp. ix, 3–17, 37–41, 218–222; "Economic Report of the President," *Department of State Bulletin*, 26 February 1968, p. 280.

73. Murray Fromson, "The American Military in Vietnam: 1950s," in *Vietnam Reconsidered: Lessons from a War* ed. Harrison E. Salisbury (New York, 1984), p. 39; John E. Mueller, "The Search for the 'Breaking Point' in Vietnam," *International Studies Quarterly* 24 (December 1980): 497, has the Rusk quote, *New York Times*, 23 April 1965, p. 42, on the "MEGs"; *New York Herald Tribune*, 28 December 1965, p. 18, has the Lippmann quote.

74. *New York Times*, 18 August 1967, p. 14; *ibid.*, 2 February 1966, pp. 7–8; David C. Humphrey, "Tuesday Lunch at the Johnson White House," *Diplomatic History* 8 (Winter 1984): 81–101, a helpful overview.

75. Nora Sayre, *Running Time: Films of the Cold War* (New York, 1982), pp. 218–219.

76. George Reedy, *The Twilight of the Presidency* (New York, 1970), pp. 96–97.

77. *New York Times*, 3 March 1968, p. 6.

78. Martin, p. 2.

79. Daniel C. Hallin's *The "Uncensored War": The Media and Vietnam* (New York, 1986) is a full, critical account.

80. *New York Times*, 28 February 1968, p. 27.

81. *Vietnam: A History in Documents*, ed. Gareth Porter (New York, 1979, 1981), pp. 354–357; for U.S. business opposition by 1967, there is a good account in Bruce M. Russett and Elizabeth C. Hanson, *Interest and Ideology: The Foreign Policy Beliefs of American Businessmen* (San Francisco, 1975), pp. 59–96; Brinkley, p. 261.

82. Thomas Borstelmann, *Apartheid's Reluctant Uncle* (New York, 1993), esp. pp. 195–202.

83. *New York Times*, 5 July 1966, p. 15; Henry Jackson, *From The Congo to Soweto* (New York, 1982), pp. 25–45.

84. Douglas Little, "From 'Even-Handed' to 'Empty-Handed': JFK, Nasser, and U.S. Policy in the Middle East, 1961–1963" (1985), manuscript in the author's possession; *Egypt, a Country Study*, ed. Richard Nyrop (Washington, D.C., 1982).

85. U.S. Government, *Public Papers of the Presidents . . . 1964*, p. 777.

86. David J. Garrow, *Bearing the Cross* (New York, 1986), pp. 551–573.

87. Richard Dorfman, "Conspiracy City," *Journal of Popular Film and Television* 7, no. 4 (1980): 435–436.

88. Oral History interview of Rusk.

89. Berman, p. xiii.

90. *Washington Post*, 1 October 1969, p. A23; Richard M. Scammon and Ben J. Wattenberg, *The Real Majority* (New York, 1970), pp. 38–49; William L. Lunch and Peter W. Sperlich, "American Public Opinion and the War in Vietnam," *Western Political Quarterly* 32 (March 1979): 21–44.

FOR FURTHER READING

Begin with *Guide to American Foreign Relations since 1700*, ed. Richard Dean Burns (1983), which no text can match for pre-1981 references. (Consequently the listing below notes post-1981 references almost entirely.) Also consult the chapter's notes and the General Bibliography at the end of this book for specific topics; those references are usually not repeated below.

An important overview and bibliography are in Warren Cohen, *America in the Age of Soviet Power, 1945–1991*, in *The Cambridge History of American Foreign Relations* series, which Cohen edited (1993). Good surveys on Kennedy include James N. Giglio, *The Presidency of John F. Kennedy* (1991), with a useful bibliography; Herbert S. Parmet's *JFK: The Presidency of John F. Kennedy* (1983), and Warren Cohen's *Dean Rusk* (1980), a searching biography of an enigmatic man; the enigmatic man's own remembrances, Dean Rusk as told to Richard Rusk, *As I Saw It* (1990); Lloyd Gardner's essay on McGeorge Bundy in *Behind the Throne*, eds. T. McCormick and W. LaFeber (1993), essays in honor of Fred Harvey Harrington; Montague Kern, Patricia Levering, and Ralph B. Levering's *The Kennedy Crisis: The Press, the Presidency, and Foreign Policy* (1983), an excellent analysis; David P. Calleo's *The Imperious Economy* (1982), perhaps the best available examination of international economic policy from 1960 to 1980; Charles Lipson's *Standing Guard: Protecting Foreign Capital in the Nineteenth and Twentieth Centuries* (1985), especially provocative on the 1960s; Michael R. Beschloss, *The Crisis Years: Kennedy and Khrushchev, 1960–1963* (1991), the major account of the Soviet-American rivalry during those years; Desmond Ball's *Politics and Force Levels* (1981), a powerful argument that Kennedy unnecessarily escalated the arms race; Bernard J. Firestone's *The Quest for Nuclear Stability: John F. Kennedy and the Soviet Union* (1982), which focuses on the nuclear test ban.

On specific topics and regions, C. J. Bartlett's useful survey, *The Special Relationship* (1992) explores how U.S.-British relations deteriorated in the 1960s; Frank Costigliola's

The Cold Alliance (1992) is the standard, and highly readable, account of post-1945 U.S.-French relations. On Asia (besides the separate Vietnam accounts noted below), Timothy P. Maga's *John F. Kennedy and the New Pacific Community, 1961–1963* (1990) is a succinct account that deemphasizes Vietnam in the regional context; Harold A. Gould and Sumit Ganguily, eds., *The Hope and the Reality: U.S.-Indian Relations from Roosevelt to Reagan* (1992), is important on Kennedy. On Cuba and Latin America, Graham H. Stuart and James L. Tigner's *Latin America and the United States*, 6th ed. (1975), is an encyclopedic account that is a superb starting place; W. Michael Weiss, *Cold Warriors and Coups D'état* (1992), is important for the U.S.-Brazil relationship to 1964; Bruce Palmer, *Intervention in the Caribbean: The Dominican Crisis of 1965* (1989), is a standard account; Trumbull Higgins's *The Perfect Failure* (1987) is fine on the Bay of Pigs; Morris Morley's *Imperial State and Revolution: The United States and Cuba, 1952–1985* (1987) provides a highly critical context for the missile crisis and after. On the missile crisis itself, Robert A. Divine, ed., *The Cuban Missile Crisis*, 2nd ed. (1988), is a good place to start for further references and interpretations; Raymond L. Garthoff, *Reflections on the Cuban Missile Crisis*, rev. ed. (1989), is by a former U.S. official and an expert on Soviet affairs; James G. Blight, *On the Brink* (1990), superbly brings together the then-latest U.S. and Soviet recollections; Dino A. Brugioni, *Eyeball to Eyeball* (1992), is by a technician who interpreted the U-2 pictures; James A. Nathan, ed., *The Cuban Missile Crisis Revisited* (1992), is a set of especially important essays (notably Barton Bernstein's and Philip Brenner's); and Chang and Kornbluh, eds., *The Cuban Missile Crisis, 1962* (1992), cited in the footnotes, is the authoritative set of correspondence and documents published by the National Security Archive. On Africa, Zaki Laidi, *The Superpowers and Africa: The Constraints of a Rivalry, 1960–1990* (1990), is a useful interpretive overview; while Peter Duignan and Lewis H. Gann's *The United States and Africa: A History* (1984) provides a historical context; and Richard D. Mahoney's *JFK: Ordeal in Africa* (1983) is important for the early 1960s; Thomas J. Noer's *Cold War and Black Liberation: The U.S. and White Rule in Africa, 1948–1968* (1985) is now the standard on the entire era; William Attwood's *The Twilight Struggle: Tales of the Cold War* (1987) is important for both its African and Cuban sections. On the Middle East, Seth P. Tillman's *The United States and the Middle East* (1982) is a thoughtful and important analysis; James W. Harper's "The Middle East, Oil, and the Third World," in *Modern American Diplomacy*, ed. John M. Carroll and George C. Herring (1986), is both a good overview that sees a decline in the U.S. ideological drive and useful for its bibliography; Steven L. Spiegel's *The Other Arab-Israel Conflict* (1985) critically looks at domestic policy making.

For the Johnson presidency, in addition to materials given in the notes and in the paragraph above on specific geographical areas, a most useful place to begin for further reading is Staff of the Lyndon Baines Johnson Library, *Lyndon B. Johnson: A Bibliography* (1984); Clark Clifford's *Counsel to the President* (1991); Vaughn D. Bornet's *The Presidency of Lyndon B. Johnson* (1983) is an overview with a chapter on Vietnam; Göran Rystad's *Prisoners of the Past?: The Munich Syndrome and Makers of American Foreign Policy in the Cold War Era* (1982) is good on both JFK and LBJ, but especially the latter; Glenn T. Seaborg, with Benjamin S. Loeb, *Stemming the Tide: Arms Control in the Johnson Years* (1987), provides most useful information from an insider; Michael McGwire's *Military Objectives in Soviet Foreign Policy* (1987) is important for its emphasis on the 1966–1967 Soviet changes; Karen Dawisha's *The Kremlin and the Prague Spring* (1984) is now the standard account of the Soviet intervention in 1968. A fascinating interpretation of the 1965 Dominican Republic intervention is put in a larger and provocative context in Frank Brodhead and Edward S. Herman's *Demonstration Elections* (1984), which compares that intervention with Vietnam.

Vietnam materials are overwhelming in number and variety of topics. Useful places to begin (other than entries cited in the notes of this chapter and in the General Bibliography) include George C. Herring, "The Vietnam War," in *Modern American Diplomacy*, ed. John M. Carroll and George C. Herring (1986); Herring's abridged edition of *The Pentagon Papers* (1993); *The Wars in Vietnam, Cambodia and Laos, 1945–1982*, ed. Richard Dean Burns and Milton Leitenberg (1984), with over 6,200 entries for further reading; Benjamin R. Beede, *Intervention and Counterinsurgency: An Annotated Bibliography of the Small Wars of the United States, 1898–1984* (1985); *Vietnam As History*, ed. Peter Braestrup (1984), papers and discussions by fifty experts; Loren Baritz's *Backfire: A History of How American Culture Led Us into Vietnam and Made Us Fight the Way We Did* (1985), the best social history of the conflict; Larry Berman's fine *Lyndon Johnson's War* (1991); Gabriel Kolko's *Anatomy of a War* (1985), especially important for its analysis of U.S. economic policies; Ellen J. Hammer's *A Death in November: America in Vietnam, 1963* (1987), a definitive account of Ngo Dinh Diem's overthrow; Andrew F. Krepinevich, Jr.'s *The Army and Vietnam* (1986), which contradicts Harry Summers, Jr.'s *On Strategy: A Critical Analysis of the Vietnam War* (1981), a much discussed critique of U.S. military (and political) strategy; William Rust, *Kennedy in Vietnam* (1985); David DiLeo's excellent *George Ball, Vietnam. . . .* (1991); Ronald Spector, *After Tet* (1992); and David W. Levy, *The Debate over Vietnam* (1991).

Dissenters are discussed and exemplified in Kenneth Heineman, *Campus Wars: The Peace Movement at American State Universities in the Vietnam Era* (1993); Todd Gitlin's *The Sixties* (1987); James Miller's *Democracy Is in the Streets* (1987); George Ball's *The Past Has Another Pattern* (1982); William C. Berman's *William Fulbright and the Vietnam War* (1988), which uses Fulbright papers; Eugene Brown's *William Fulbright: Advice and Dissent* (1984), another good biography; Melvin Small's *Johnson, Nixon, and the Doves* (1988); Lawrence S. Wittner's *Rebels against War: The American Peace Movement, 1933–1983* (1984), an updated edition of a fine work; *Peace Heroes in Twentieth-Century America*, ed. Charles DeBenedetti (1986), especially on Martin Luther King and the Berrigans; David J. Garrow's *Bearing the Cross: Martin Luther King and the Southern Christian Leadership Conference* (1986); Steven M. Gillon's *Politics and Vision: The ADA and American Liberalism, 1947–1985* (1987), on the dilemma of the Democrats' liberal wing; and Douglas Pike's *Vietnam and the Soviet Union* (1987), which surveys the entire relationship. In a category by itself as an account of the war is Neil Sheehan, *A Bright Shining Lie: John Paul Vann and America in Vietnam* (1988).

18

Coming to Terms with History:
The Nixon-Kissinger Years
(1969–1976)

OF OUTHOUSES AND COWBOYS

Richard Nixon, most so-called experts concluded in the early 1960s, was politically dead. After losing the races for the presidency in 1960 and the California governorship in 1962, he angrily told reporters that they would not "have Nixon to kick around anymore." But private law practice did not calm this most restless and fascinating of post-1945 politicians. By 1968, he was back at the top of the political heap. His determination was never in doubt. While attending Whittier College, he decided to win a contest to find the largest outdoor wooden toilet to throw into the flames of the annual bonfire rally. The all-time champion had been a three-holer, but Nixon had somehow located a four-holer and hauled it to the rally. "Picture the systematic intensity that went into this achievement," biographer Garry Wills suggests.[1]

The young Nixon also played a fair, if risky, game of poker. In the navy during World War II, he won thousands of dollars, which helped him launch his political career as a California congressman. In 1950, he won election to the Senate. After serving as Dwight Eisenhower's vice-president (1953–1961) and spending the 1960s on the "rubber chicken circuit," speaking at endless Republican dinners for local candidates, Nixon was the best known and most owed of the party's candidates. With his wide experience and contacts, he should have been superbly equipped to rebuild the national consensus destroyed by the Vietnam War and to govern the country effectively.

But throughout, as Henry Kissinger later observed, there was the problem of how this true loner, who had few close friends, could "become .a politican. He really dislikes people."[2] Nixon admired films made by Clint Eastwood and John Wayne about strong, lonely, one-of-a-kind men. His all-time film favorite was *Patton*, in which (according to him) a brash but brave and brilliant U.S. general accomplished what better-liked military officers could not. (Some critics felt that the film only showed how war allowed a mentally unbalanced person to gain life-and-death power over others.)[3] Nixon's instincts for politics, resembling George Patton's for battles, were well developed, if flawed. By the late 1960s, he understood that the Vietnam War signaled the breakdown of U.S. postwar domination. Other powers—the Soviet Union, China, Japan, even newly emerging states—were creating a new world arena in which Americans faced tough competition. Nixon especially believed that, during the 1960s, Americans "saw a break-down in frankly what I could call the leadership class of this country."[4] He concluded that history had taken a sharp turn and that he was now the most capable person to steer the U.S. system around that turn.

The vehicle for making the turn had to be foreign policy. Domestic affairs were petty and boring—simply "building outhouses in Peoria," as Nixon once phrased it.[5] Foreign relations, unlike internal affairs, also allowed the president much freedom of action. He ensured his control over diplomacy by placing an equally secretive Harvard professor, Henry Kissinger, at the head of his National Security Council (NSC). Kissinger later liked to picture himself as a "lone cowboy" who bravely rode into town to battle evil international forces. In reality, he had risen to power by working closely with Harvard's international-affairs groups, New York's prestigious Council on Foreign Relations, and the rich, ambitious governor of New York, Nelson Rockefeller, who had challenged Nixon for the Republican nomination. Kissinger exemplified the "eastern establishment" that had long controlled U.S. foreign policy. Resembling many others in that "establishment," he had disliked and mistrusted Nixon. When Rockefeller lost the nomination, however, Kissinger moved easily into the victor's camp. "Nixon had a consuming need for flattery and Kissinger a consuming need to provide it," one journalist recalled.[6]

But Nixon also picked Kissinger for other, more important reasons. Both agreed that they alone should control foreign policy. In their view, neither the State Department nor Congress had the imagination or will to take the daring new initiatives needed. Nixon appointed an old friend (and distinguished lawyer), William Rogers, as secretary of state, precisely because Rogers knew little about diplomacy. He could be counted on to be loyal and keep the State Department preoccupied with minor matters while Nixon and Kissinger conducted policy. Both men also feared the right wing of American politics more than the left wing. Nixon had been identified with that right wing in the 1950s, but to protect himself from it further, he named the former governor of Maryland, Spiro Agnew, as his vice-presidential running mate. In the 1968 campaign, Agnew blasted Democratic candidate Hubert Humphrey as having been "soft on Communism and soft on law and order over the years." Between 1969 and 1973 (when he had to resign his office due to charges of corruption and fraud), the vice-president delighted in attacking the supposed "liberal" media.

For his part, Kissinger quickly cut everyone but the president out of policy making. He loved to conduct supersecret, so-called "back channel" diplomacy with leaders of the other major powers, especially the Soviets. In a secret report of June 12, 1969 (only released in Russia in 1993), Soviet Ambassador to the United States Anatoly F. Dobrynin described Kissinger to Kremlin officials:

> Kissinger himself, an intelligent and erudite man, is at the same time vain and prone in conversations with me . . . , especially when we have dinner alone, to brag of his influence. At our last conversation, for example, he declared without excess modesty that in all Washington only two people can answer precisely at any given moment about the U.S. position on this or that issue: President Nixon and he, Kissinger.

Determined to monopolize policy making, and with "absolutely paranoid suspicions" about the bureaucracy, as one aide described it, the NSC director even wire-tapped the telephones of his own staff. While Agnew and Nixon wanted to treat reporters "with considerably more contempt" (in the president's words), Kissinger cultivated and shaped stories written by leading journalists. His abilities, as well as an intellectual background that too often awed his listeners, enabled him to sell the administration's policies through the media from the top down— even as Agnew regularly condemned the media. It all was brilliantly orchestrated.[7]

If, then, as Kissinger wrote, "the acid test of a policy . . . is its ability to obtain domestic support,"[8] he and Nixon seemed to control the levers necessary to obtain that support—at least during their first term in power.

. . . AND WOODROW WILSON AND ELEPHANTS

Nixon had another reason for naming Kissinger to head the NSC. Both men thought in broad, conceptual terms. Both believed the United States had reached a historic turn. Both agreed on the outlines of a new, workable foreign policy. In mid-1970, Kissinger placed the American crisis in perspective. During a private discussion with reporters, he declared that after Vietnam, no president would again repeat John F. Kennedy's inaugural address that had asked Americans to "fight any foe, support any friend." Instead, Kissinger continued, "a new phase" of policy had to begin, one which assumed that Americans would no longer rush out to stop "aggression wherever it occurred."[9] At the same time, however, U.S. interests would somehow have to be protected. It was a terrible tightrope to walk.

One answer was simply to reduce U.S. overseas interests and commitments. By 1969, Americans had 302 major and 2,000 secondary military bases abroad. Perhaps those incredible numbers could be cut. Nixon and Kissinger, however, did not want to reduce those commitments drastically. They believed that to retreat would, among other things, fly in the face of four hundred years of American history. As a German-Jewish émigré in the 1930s, and as a scholar of European history, Kissinger knew that "in Europe the frontier repelled; in America it beckoned." Citing "the great historian [Frederick Jackson] Turner," Kissinger declared that Americans' experience with their frontier gave them a sense of triumph over nature that held meaning for "all mankind. America was not itself unless it had a meaning beyond itself. This is why Americans have always seen their role in the world as the outward manifestation of an inward state of grace."[10] In other words, Americans now had the world as their frontier (much as they once had the Ohio River or Rocky Mountains as their frontier), and to retreat from it meant that they would be the first Americans to fail, the first to deny the greatness of their own past. Obviously, a great deal was suddenly at stake.

Nixon believed that Woodrow Wilson ("our greatest President of this century") provided "the greatest vision of America's world role." Wilson "wasn't practical enough" in conducting diplomacy, Nixon added, but clearly understood how the United States had to lead a

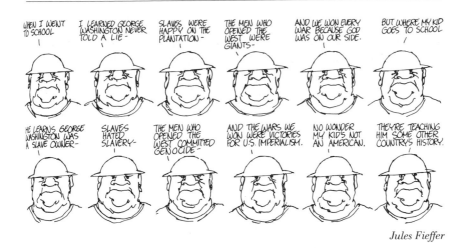

Jules Fieffer

collective effort (in Wilson's famous phrase) to make the world safe for democracy. In a 1967 essay, Nixon had sketched out his plans to lead such an effort. First, Asians were to help themselves more and rely on the United States less. But Americans had to play a great role by reaching "westward to the East" and by working with Japan to build "a Pacific community." Second, after more changes occurred inside China, it, too, could help build this community. That was a stunning proposal from the man who, since 1949, had damned "Red" China (and those U.S. officials who had "lost" China).[11]

Kissinger and Nixon began to see that (in the professor's words) "the greatest need of the contemporary international system is an agreed concept of order," and that China—after a decade of turmoil and major economic and diplomatic failures—might be ready to support such order. The two Americans most feared not communism, but disorder—especially revolutionaries who wanted to destroy order. Kissinger even thought order more important than justice. After all, he argued, order could lead to justice, but justice did not necessarily lead to order. He and Nixon believed that the Soviets and Chinese were both interested in peace and order as well as better relations with the United States (especially to obtain U.S. technology and wheat). The real enemies to world peace were North Vietnam, Cuba, and revolutionaries in Africa and other newly emerging areas that wanted to destroy the order that the United States had created and had benefited from since 1945.[12]

Nixon and Kissinger concluded that U.S. interests could be protected (and with less expense to financially squeezed Americans) by having Japan, China, and even the Soviet Union work with the United States—especially against revolutionaries. The country had gone through a kind of hell in the 1960s, but it had hung on to remain the world's greatest power, although that power was slipping. "Living next to you is in some ways like sleeping with an elephant," Canada's prime minister Pierre Trudeau told Americans in 1969. "One is affected by every twitch and grunt."[13] If Nixon succeeded, the elephant would sleep more soundly but roam more widely when awake, especially in a world viewed as a frontier for American opportunity. But first the Vietnam War had to be resolved.

VIETNAM AND THE NIXON DOCTRINE (1969–1972)

As early as 1966, Kissinger publicly admitted that the Vietnam conflict could not be won militarily. In his first day in office in 1969, top-secret studies informed Nixon that the United States could not win the war. The Pentagon believed that, under the best of conditions, it would take eight to thirteen years just to control all of South Vietnam. Those "best of conditions" had never been found in the region. U.S. troop strength stood at 543,000. The war's cost to Americans had leaped to $30 billion annually.[14] Some 14,600 U.S. troops had died in 1968 alone. Nixon decided to withdraw—but slowly and on his terms. By the time he finished in 1973, another 26,000 Americans and at least 1 million more Southeast Asians had perished in the conflict.

Nixon's plan rested on Vietnamization and the Nixon Doctrine. Through Vietnamization, the president planned to withdraw his forces slowly, replacing them with well-supplied Vietnamese. The idea had first appeared in the 1950s, when U.S. officials wanted "good Asians" to fight "bad Asians." It had not worked, but Nixon now determined to support Vietnamization with other strategies. He wanted to sit down with the Communists and negotiate a cease-fire and mutual U.S.–North Vietnamese withdrawal from South Vietnam, Cambodia, and Laos. Then he planned to launch massive bombing raids on the North until the Communists agreed to withdraw. It seemed to be an offer they could not refuse.

The president placed this approach into a much broader policy. The Nixon Doctrine, presented at Guam in mid-1969, indicated that the United States would help "the defense and development of allies and friends" but "cannot—and will not—conceive all the plans, design all the programs, execute all the decisions and undertake all the defense of the free nations of the world." Others would have to grab the oars

TABLE 3

PRINCIPAL WARS IN WHICH THE UNITED STATES PARTICIPATED: U.S. MILITARY PERSONNEL SERVING AND CASUALTIES

War/Conflict	Branch of service	Number serving	Casualties		
			Battle deaths	Other deaths	Wounds not mortal
Korean Conflict	*Total*	5,720,000	33,643	20,617	103,284
(25 Jun. 1950–27 Jul. 1953)	Army	2,834,000	27,709	9,429	77,596
	Navy	1,177,000	466	4,043	1,576
	Marines	424,000	4,268	1,261	23,744
	Air Force	1,285,000	1,200	5,884	368
Vietnam Conflict	*Total*	8,744,000	47,312	10,703	153,303
(4 Aug. 1964–27 Jan. 1973)	Army	4,368,000	30,899	7,269	96,802
	Navy	1,842,000	1,605	919	4,178
	Marines	794,000	13,070	1,749	51,392
	Air Force	1,740,000	1,738	766	931

Source: Department of Defense.

and help row. By announcing that he would begin to pull U.S. troops out of Vietnam, Nixon showed that he meant business with his doctrine. He also planned to cut back the inflated military budget by ordering American forces to have only the capability to fight 1.5 wars (for example, a major conflict in Europe and a lesser one in a newly emerging area) instead of the present capability to wage 2.5 wars. By late 1972, he had pulled out all but 3,000 U.S. troops from Vietnam as well as one-third of the 60,000 American soldiers in South Korea, 12,000 from Japan, and 16,000 from Thailand.

But, in Kissinger's words, "we could not simply walk away from an enterprise involving two administrations, five allied countries, and thirty-one thousand dead as if we were switching a television channel." Nor, as the president vowed privately, would he bow to New York's Wall Street and legal communities who advised "scuttling Vietnam at any price." Nixon combined the troop withdrawal with an incredible bombing campaign that, on average, dropped a ton of bombs each minute on Vietnam between 1969 and early 1973. Democratic Senator J. William Fulbright from Arkansas agreed with the *Washington Post* that Nixon had become "the greatest bomber of all time."[15] Meanwhile, the CIA's Phoenix program weakened the Communists by killing at least 21,000 supposed enemy civilians who worked in the villages of South Vietnam. The North's government, however, continued to refuse to accept a divided Vietnam.

Kissinger flew secretly to Paris to talk with the North's negotiator, Le Duc Tho—"gray-haired, dignified," as the American described him, with perfect manners and "large luminous eyes [that] only rarely revealed the fanaticism" that had led him at the age of sixteen to fight the French. Nixon decided that the North's representative was stalling in the talks until the Communists could rebuild their forces. The president discussed the bombing of harbors and even considered using nuclear weapons. He pulled back at the last minute from expanding the bombing in October 1969, when a massive anti-war rally marched on Washington. Nixon announced that he had ignored the marchers and had coolly watched a televised Ohio State football game. In truth, the frightened president had ordered 300 troops armed with light machine guns to protect him in the White House.[16]

CAMBODIA, LAOS, AND KENT STATE

Vietnamization was not working. Nixon was furious that the Communists used trails through Cambodia and Laos to supply their troops in the south. The 6.5 million people of Cambodia, a beautiful country the size of Oklahoma, had been spared most of the war's horrors. Although its leader, Prince Sihanouk, had broken relations with the United States in 1965, he said nothing when Nixon bombed the Communist bases in Cambodia. Nixon did so secretly—a secret kept, that is, from Congress and the American people but not from Southeast Asians who were the targets. The air strikes forced the Communists farther inside Cambodia, and the nation became more unstable. In March 1970, Sihanouk was overthrown by his prime minister, General Lon Nol, who was more willing to work with the Americans.

The new regime was corrupt and incompetent, but Nixon seized the chance and launched an invasion of eastern Cambodia on April 30, 1970, to destroy the camps of some 40,000 Communists. It was a sudden, highly risky expansion of the war. Even the old cold warrior, Dean Acheson, had his doubts. Nixon, Acheson told a friend, was the only horse he knew who would run back into a burning barn.[17] On national television, the president warned that when "the chips are down," the United States must not act "like a pitiful helpless giant." But the invasion failed. U.S. and South Vietnamese troops could not find and destroy the Communist forces. By late 1970, those forces had grown until they spread over at least one-third of Cambodia. By early 1974, they controlled the entire country—or what remained of a starving population that soon became virtually enslaved by the brutal, Communist Khmer Rouge.[18]

Nixon failed at home as well. The Cambodian campaign, known as a "sideshow" to the main event in Vietnam, triggered a massive protest when American students in nearly 450 colleges went on strike. Many students marched on Washington to lobby both the administration (some of Nixon's advisers, but not Kissinger, sympathized with the protesters) and Congress. The president called the students "bums" who are "blowing up the campuses." Then, in early May, the Ohio National Guard fired on anti-war protesters at Kent State. Four students died. Ten days later, two black students were shot to death by Mississippi state police during protests at Jackson State College. The nation went into shock. On the night of the Kent State shootings, Nixon could not sleep, made fifty-one phone calls, and led Kissinger to conclude that the president was "on the edge of a nervous breakdown."[19] Amid the chaos, several thousand hard-hat construction workers paraded in New York City to support the president and beat up members of anti-war groups. But other New Yorkers, including Wall Street banking leaders, flew to Washington to warn Nixon that the threat of a wider war was threatening a stock-market collapse and a possible financial panic.[20]

This photograph captures the horror of the shootings at Kent State University on May 4, 1970, when the campus erupted in protest against President Nixon's invasion of Cambodia. A young woman screams over the body of Jeffrey Glenn Miller.

The president announced that the U.S. soldiers in Cambodia would be out by June 30, 1970. Congress voted to prohibit U.S. combat troops or advisers from re-entering Cambodia. Sixteen years after the United States had become enmeshed in Southeast Asia, Congress, for the first time, had been able to find the votes to limit the president's power to make war in the region.

That ability, nevertheless, remained awesome. Nixon grew frustrated as he continued to withdraw U.S. troops from Vietnam, but the Vietnamese soldiers could not fill the gap left by the Americans. He decided to try to buck up his collapsing Vietnamization policy by attacking neighboring Laos, along whose supposedly neutral territory the Communists marched their troops into South Vietnam. The size of Oregon and with only 3 million people, Laos had been promised neutrality by both sides since 1954; both sides had repeatedly broken the promise. Since 1964, and especially 1968, giant U.S. B-52 bombers secretly bombed the Ho Chi Minh Trail in massive attacks. The CIA covertly armed 15,000 Meo tribesmen to fight 30,000 Laotian Communist troops. The Communists, nevertheless, continued to gain ground. Laos became a case study of how bombing did not have the desired effect on peasant revolutionary forces. The attacks only produced thousands of dead Laotians and hundreds of thousands of desperate refugees. In February 1971, Nixon tried to drive back the Communists with an invasion of Laos. This time only South Vietnamese troops, not Americans, went in. Vietnamization, however, failed miserably. The South Vietnamese broke and retreated before Communist attacks. By late 1971, the pro-Communist groups held more of Laos than before.

THE GREAT TURNAROUND:
THE DRAFT PROVIDES POLITICAL ROOM

By February 1971, when Laos was invaded, Nixon faced failure on nearly every side. In addition to problems with Vietnamization, he endured riots at home, Democratic victories in the 1970 elections, defeats in attempts to obtain conservative Supreme Court appointments, and rapid decline in public support. In mid-1971, the *New York Times* obtained 7,000 pages of secret documents, the so-called Pentagon Papers, that revealed the innermost decisions that had led to deepening U.S. involvement in Vietnam between the 1940s and 1968. Ordered in 1967 by Secretary of Defense Robert McNamara, who was determined to learn from this tragic past, the Pentagon Papers did not include documents from the Nixon years. But the record revealed enough embarrassing errors in policy and blatant attempts to lie to the American people that the anti-war movement received additional fuel.

Nixon and Kissinger, moreover, were terrified that new leaks would reveal their own secrets, especially the bombing of Cambodia and Laos. The Pentagon had even falsified computer records to ensure that Americans would remain ignorant of the bombing. When the *New York Times* published a story about the bombing in May 1969, Kissinger quickly placed secret wiretaps on his own assistants to uncover the leak. He never did discover who was leaking the information to the media, but by 1971 the president had set up a White House "plumbers" unit that used former and present CIA agents to discover and stop leaks. In 1972, one plumbers group was arrested when it broke into the Watergate Hotel office complex in Washington to tap Democratic party telephones. The discovery led to the downfall of Richard Nixon in 1974, after he tried to cover up the crime. It all seemed to prove correct a

Chinese official's remark to Kissinger: "One should not lose the whole world just to gain South Vietnam."[21]

Between 1971 and 1974, however, the president opened a startlingly new chapter in U.S. foreign policy, a chapter that historian Lloyd Gardner has entitled "The Great Nixon Turnaround."[22] The president began by correctly estimating that he could stop much of the anti-war protesting. As one of his aides phrased it, "If there is one thing the Americans are more sick of today than fighting in the jungles abroad, it is fighting in the streets and campuses at home."[23] Many polls showed that Americans did not want to lose Vietnam, but neither did they want to send thousands of their sons and daughters to die for such a country. The U.S. military agreed. Its morale and fighting ability were being destroyed by the war. One general later recalled walking through a train station "when a well-dressed, middle-aged woman came up, called me names I couldn't repeat and spit on me."[24] Nixon went far in stopping such protests by announcing that the draft was to end in 1973. A much reduced military would find its soldiers through a lottery system and volunteers. College campuses began to quiet down. The president had created some political breathing space. To help Vietnamization, he increased the bombings. Americans now said little.

THE GREAT TURNAROUND: THE ECONOMY

They were complaining loudly, however, about the rising rates of inflation and unemployment in 1971. The U.S. economy seemed about to collapse. True, its annual gross national product (GNP) had passed the $1 trillion mark in 1970 for the first time. True, U.S. exports incredibly quintupled between the 1950s and 1970s to $107 billion, excluding services, and now accounted for the sale of nearly 20 percent of U.S. factory and farm production. But not even those staggering figures were enough to pay for global U.S. defense commitments and overseas investment. Americans were spending more than they could produce and sell.

Since the Bretton Woods agreements of 1944 (see p. 431), the world's economy had largely rested on the dollar because Americans could back up the dollar with their dynamic economy and $15 billion to $24 billion in gold. By 1970–1971, however, they had spent too many dollars. Some $40 billion was held overseas, but only $10 billion in gold remained in the United States to support it. Foreigners began to doubt that the dollars they held were truly "as good as gold." That doubt

U.S. Merchandise Trade Balance, 1967–1984

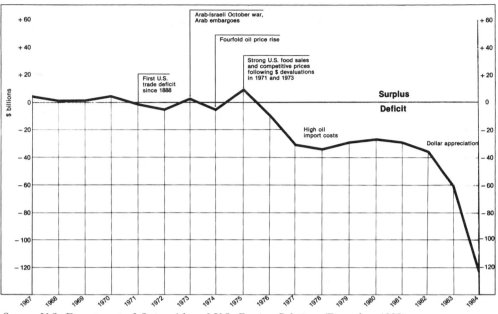

Source: U.S. Department of State, *Atlas of U.S. Foreign Relations* (December 1985).

turned to near panic in 1971, when figures revealed that, for the first time since 1893–1894, the United States had imported more goods (such as oil and automobiles) than it had been able to sell abroad. It marked a moment of historic importance. Foreigners and Americans alike started to cash in their dollars for gold and other securities. Nixon recalled that, in 1958, the United States had "all the chips" in the "great poker game" of international economics, and that no one else could play unless the Americans passed out some of their chips. By the early 1970s, he sorrowfully noted, "the world [was] a lot different."[25] Others were now building up their pile of chips as the American pile disappeared.

The president had several choices. First, he could save dollars by reducing U.S. defense commitments even below the level promised by the Nixon Doctrine. He and Kissinger, however, were determined to expand, not reduce, the nation's influence. Second, he could limit U.S. investment abroad. Between 1958 and 1968, American manufacturers had moved into the new European Common Market, or had sought cheap labor in Asia, by increasing their overseas capacity by an amazing 471 percent, compared with a 72 percent expansion at home. (Ford, for example, made 40 percent of its cars abroad.) American multinational corporations were reshaping the world but bringing too few dollars back to the United States. Nixon, however, refused to interfere in this marketplace. He knew that if he tried, the corporations could ignore him and continue to operate out of overseas offices, where they would be out of his reach.

He decided upon a third choice: he would force allies to help the U.S. economy. At Kansas City in mid-1971, Nixon declared that the world now contained "five great economic superpowers"—the United States, Japan, USSR, China, and the European Common Market. (As historian Alan Henrikson notes, "This was an admission [by Nixon] of the descent of the United States from superiority to parity, from being *the* center to being *a* center.")[26] Because "economic power will be the key to other kinds of power" in the late twentieth century, Nixon warned, Americans had to get their economic act together or they would go the way of ancient Rome. In August 1971, he tried to stop the erosion of U.S. power by placing ninety-day controls on wages, prices, and rents. But that was only a Band-Aid. As the election approached, he could not safely demand more from Americans. Indeed, he even slashed income taxes. So he demanded more from allies who depended on U.S. goods and military protection. He turned the job over to a tough Texan, Secretary of the Treasury John Connally. "My basic approach," Connally declared, "is that the foreigners are out to screw us. Our job is to screw them first."[27]

Nixon's and Connally's "new economic policy" imposed a 10 percent surcharge on U.S. imports. Japan and Canada quickly felt the shock. So did western Europeans and newly emerging nations. Nixon did not care. He privately condemned the Japanese because, he believed, they had cheated on a deal that he had made with them: they were to get back the Pacific island of Okinawa (which U.S. bombers had used as a major base since 1945) and, in turn, were to reduce the flood of their textile exports to the United States. But the Japanese government did not deliver on its end of the deal. By early 1971, a secret U.S. analysis reflected Nixon's fury by concluding that Japan had to be considered a potential enemy. As for the western Europeans, they were making political and economic deals with the Soviets but not lowering their tariffs on U.S. goods. Nixon determined to keep their feet to the fire until they promised to help support the dollar.

In an agreement made at Washington's Smithsonian Institution in late 1971, the allies finally agreed to accept a cheaper dollar (a dollar that also cheapened U.S. goods and so made them more competitive) and more expensive Japanese and European currencies. Nixon typically called it the "greatest monetary agreement in the history of the world." But the following year, the dollar again sank. A second deal was needed to prop it back up. The U.S. economy had contracted a fundamental sickness. The Smithsonian agreement, however, did help improve conditions enough to aid Nixon's re-election victory in 1972. It also enabled him to deal from greater economic strength as he made historic journeys to China and the Soviet Union.

THE GREAT TURNAROUND: CHINA

In July 1971, Nixon told an astonished world that he planned to travel to China. According to opinion polls, 56 percent of Americans continued to see China as the world's most dangerous nation.[28] Moreover, some 50,000 U.S. lives had been lost in Vietnam supposedly to contain Chinese Communist power. Few Americans, however, could challenge Nixon from the right. Since 1949, he had led the attacks on Democrats for "losing China." He could travel to Beijing (Peking) without political fears. As for Vietnam, the rationale for the U.S. commitment had gone through a strange, little-noted change. By 1971, the Soviets were becoming the great ally of the Communist Vietnamese (who historically feared the Chinese anyway). The greatest hatred in the region was not between Communists and U.S.-supported "dominoes," but between the Communists themselves as the Chinese tried to block growing Soviet influence on their southern borders. Instead of using Vietnam to contain China, Nixon concluded that he had better use China to contain Vietnam.

The Chinese had been through a kind of hell and were ready to change policies. In 1966, Mao had ordered a "cultural revolution" to shake up the society. Wild teen-aged Red Guards killed suspected conservatives and sent intellectuals and government officials to work in the fields with fertilizers (urine and feces). By 1969, when Mao finally put a brake on the Red Guard, the society and his foreign policy were in chaos. Moreover, a massive million-man build-up by the Soviet and Chinese armies along their common border of some 5,000 miles erupted in shooting and the death of both Chinese and Soviet troops in 1969. Hatred between the two Communist powers became red-hot. ("Who do they think they are!" exclaimed Soviet Ambassador to the United Nations Yakov Malik. "We'll kill those yellow sons of bitches!") If John F. Kennedy had contemplated attacking Chinese nuclear facilities in 1963 only to have the Soviets refuse to cooperate, now the Soviets seemed

Richard Nixon (1913–   ) surprised the world and began to reorient U.S. foreign policy toward China when, in 1972, he flew to Beijing (Peking) and shook hands with a man he had long attacked—Mao Zedong (Tse-tung) (1893–1976), the leader of the Chinese Revolution.

ready to attack while the United States pulled back. Assessing the crisis, Mao and his brilliant prime minister, Zhou Enlai (Chou En-lai), decided to reverse their policies toward the United States. They sent friendly signals to Nixon. The president responded during the border fighting by publicly signaling to the Soviets to back off. He even privately considered the use of nuclear weapons in case the Soviets tried to invade China. Premier Zhou (Chou) invited a U.S. table-tennis team to play Chinese teams. Nixon then relaxed the trade embargo and stopped military flights over China. In another border war of 1971, the United States publicly "tilted" toward Pakistan, which was pro-Chinese, and against Pakistan's enemy, India, which had moved closer to the Soviets. Nixon even stood with Pakistan when its army overthrew an elected government and unleashed a brutal attack against East Pakistan (which, with India's help, became the independent nation of Bangladesh). In return for U.S. support, the Pakistanis helped Kissinger travel secretly to Beijing (Peking) to plan the president's visit.

In February 1972, Nixon became the first U.S. president to step on Chinese soil. He seemed awestruck by what he was doing (when visiting the Great Wall of China he could only say, "This is a great wall"). At a state banquet, he told Zhou (Chou) in a public toast that "our two peoples tonight hold the future of the world in our hands"—which, no doubt, was news to the Soviets. But the final Shanghai communiqué, issued by Nixon and Zhou (Chou) on February 27, was indeed a turning point. In a thinly veiled reference to Soviet power, they declared that they would oppose anyone trying "to establish hegemony" in "the

Asia-Pacific region." They also agreed to broaden their relations through scientific, cultural, and economic exchanges as well as some political ties. (Full diplomatic recognition did not occur until 1979). On the most divisive point of Taiwan, the Chinese continued to claim the island, and the United States carefully announced it would "reduce its forces and military installations on Taiwan as the tension in the area diminishes."[29] In the meantime, U.S. ties with the island remained.

Between 1971 and late 1973, U.S.-China trade made a great leap forward from $5 million to $900 million annually. Excluding special grain deals, it even surpassed U.S.-Soviet trade. Thus, Nixon had also successfully moved to block Japan's attempts to monopolize China's foreign concessions. But most of all, as a watchful French official said, the president "wanted to show the Russians. This was the biggest purpose of the trip [to China], and it was very successful."[30]

The Great Turnaround: The Soviets and Vietnam

The president thus approached his second historic meeting in 1972 from a good position. As Soviet leader Leonid Brezhnev openly admitted the year before, the Soviets' badly run economy had slowed to a crawl. It needed a jump-start from foreigners, especially from U.S. technology and American-built ("turnkey") truck and car factories. For its part, the United States could use the Soviet Union's rich mineral resources. (Americans, Nixon's secretary of commerce complained, used up their own resources "like a drunken sailor" who now begins to feel "the hole in the bottom of his pocket.") Brezhnev also needed some arms controls so that more money could go into the basic economy. By 1972, the United States and the USSR had enough nuclear weapons to explode 15 tons of radioactive TNT on every man, woman, and child on earth. World military expenses ran $200 billion annually, a figure greater than the combined gross national product of Africa and southern Asia. Governments spent two-and-one-half times the amount on arms that they spent on health.[31]

Nixon had his own reasons for meeting Brezhnev. Besides wanting to ease the growing American economic strain by making trade and arms deals, he hoped for a television spectacular on the eve of the 1972 presidential campaign. He also hoped to regain the diplomatic initiative and put Vietnam behind him. In 1969–1972, for example, he had lost that initiative in central Europe when West Germany's popular chancellor, Willy Brandt, ended a quarter-century-long argument by recognizing the existence of the East German Communist government. Brandt also signed pacts that finally accepted eastern European boundaries drawn by the Red Army in 1945. The chancellor believed that Communist rule could better be penetrated—and all Germany reunited—by a policy of détente, or a lessening of tension, than by aggressive anticommunism. Nixon and Kissinger did not like Brandt's play to the Soviet Union (for one thing, the Americans had little control over it), but they did not try to stop him. Nixon just decided to make his own deals with Brezhnev. In the president's view, the West Germans and others (including Middle Eastern and Asian governments) too easily played off Americans against Soviets.

Unlike Eisenhower and Kennedy, Nixon and Kissinger held power when the United States could no longer build up to such military superiority that it could simply face down the Soviets. The Soviet nuclear force approached parity with the American, and Brezhnev used this new power to extend his influence into such areas as Egypt and Vietnam. The two Americans believed that a new means for controlling the Communists had to be found. In their hands, détente was to be the containment of Soviet power by different—and cheaper—means.

Nixon also hoped that Brezhnev would help him escape from Vietnam with some honor. It was a badly misplaced hope. Although the Soviets heavily supplied Vietnam, they had little control over the Hanoi government. Documents discovered in Moscow in the early 1990s indeed showed that the Vietnamese ruthlessly used the Soviets—not least when Vietnam's gunboats positioned themselves next to Soviet vessels as the gunboats blasted away at U.S. planes. The Vietnamese dared the Americans to bomb them when the bombs could well hit Soviet ships instead. Brezhnev (like Stalin and Khrushchev before him) simply could not fully control smaller members of their supposed "fraternal socialist camp." Indeed, on March 30, 1972, as Nixon prepared for his Moscow trip, North Vietnam launched a massive attack against South Vietnamese and what remained of U.S. troops. The president viewed the attack, led by Soviet-built tanks, as a direct challenge to his entire policy and, more personally, as an attempt to embarrass him before the world. He responded with a renewed bombing campaign (code-named Operation Linebacker, reflecting Nixon's love for football) that devastated targets never before hit. Using laser-guided bombs of 500 to 3,000 pounds, the planes destroyed bridges, railroads, and other military and civilian targets with great precision. On May 8, U.S. planes dropped mines in Haiphong harbor, where Soviet ships were anchored. The Soviets made no response. At home, telegrams poured into the White House supporting Nixon's action. (Later, however, his aides admitted they had used about $8,400 from CREEP—the Committee to Re-elect the President—to send the telegrams to themselves and to place a phony advertisement in the *New York Times* congratulating the president.)[32] Abroad, Brezhnev never let out a peep of protest. Soviet interests overrode North Vietnamese lives.

Brezhnev did show his displeasure by giving Nixon a cool reception when the president arrived in the Soviet Union on May 22, 1972. And, of course, the Soviets bugged the U.S. delegation's hotel with listening devices. When Nixon casually mentioned to a secretary he'd like an apple, in ten minutes a hotel maid appeared with the fruit. But the two leaders got along well personally. Brezhnev, like nearly all Soviets, was terrified of a potentially powerful China on his border. He tried later to convince Nixon that "we the whites" and "we Europeans" should control the Chinese before they became "a superpower."[33] Nixon rejected that approach but used the USSR's fear of China as a high card in his negotiations.

The discussions produced four historic agreements at the summit. The first was SALT I (Strategic Arms Limitations Talks), which limited the number of offensive intercontinental ballistic missiles to 1,410 land-based missiles and 950 submarine-launched missiles on the Soviet side, and, for the United States, 1,000 land-based missiles and 710 submarine-launched weapons. The Americans more than made up the gap with their allies' nuclear deterrents in western Europe, the greatly superior fleet of U.S. bombers (450 to 150 USSR planes), and especially with the astonishing MIRVs (Multiple Independent Re-entry Vehicles). Hoping to take advantage of U.S. technology, Nixon refused to accept any limits on these "space buses," as Pentagon officials called them. His refusal proved to be a crucial mistake. The Soviets not only soon produced MIRVs of their own, but had larger missiles (such as their huge SS-18) on which they could place as many as ten warheads.

A second agreement (actually a part of SALT I) involved defensive antiballistic missile systems (ABMs). Since the late 1960s, U.S. officials had warned the Soviets not to continue to deploy such systems because it would force the United States to build more and larger nuclear weapons to overcome these defenses. Thus, ABMs would speed up—not slow—the arms race. Brezhnev finally accepted the reasoning. In the ABM treaty, both sides agreed to limit themselves to one defensive system for their capitals and a second to defend an area containing ICBM launchers. Both powers abided by the deal (indeed, the United States never even bothered to build a system to protect Washington) until the 1980s. Then President Ronald Reagan tried to destroy the ABM pact so that he could test his Strategic Defense Initiative (SDI or Star Wars) that he hoped would form a defensive shield.

The third agreement was the "Basic Principles of U.S.-Soviet Relations." Not a treaty, it attempted to set up ground rules to make superpower competition less dangerous. Both sides pledged to avoid confrontation and to coexist peacefully. They also promised to renounce claims to privileges in other regions (which U.S. officials—but certainly not Brezhnev—interpreted to mean the end of the Brezhnev Doctrine [see p. 623]).

Nixon and Kissinger not only hoped to tie the Soviets closer to U.S. interests, but to pressure Brezhnev to observe the other agreements. Thus, they presented him with a fourth deal: new U.S.-Soviet economic exchanges. As Kissinger later noted, U.S. trade and technology "would be a carrot for restrained [Soviet] political behavior."[34] This "carrot" became known as "linkage"—that is, telling the Soviets that progress in one area of diplomacy was linked to their behavior in another area. U.S.-Soviet trade did triple between 1971 and 1973 to about $650 million (with American exports accounting for a rich $546 million of the total). But in 1972–1973, half the trade occurred when the Soviets cleverly and secretly entered the American grain market to buy up at low prices wheat and corn that U.S. taxpayers had paid farmers high subsidies to produce. As U.S. grain dealers made a fortune and Brezhnev obtained shiploads of cheap farm products, Nixon did nothing. American bread prices increased. U.S. politicians grew furious at the way Americans had been taken by Communist buyers. When the president agreed to give the Soviets favored-trade treatment in a new reciprocity deal, the U.S. Senate rebelled.

The Senate, despite reservations by anti-Soviet "hawks," had accepted both SALT I and the ABM accord by an 88-to-2 vote. But in 1974, led by "superhawk" Washington Democrat Henry Jackson, the Senate tied the Jackson-Vanik Amendment to the reciprocity treaty. The amendment stated that most-favored-nation status would be extended to the Kremlin only when it allowed more Jews to leave the Soviet Union. Working quietly, Nixon and Brezhnev had increased the number of Jewish emigrants (usually to Israel or the United States) from 400 annually in 1968 to 35,000 in 1973. Human-rights advocates worldwide, including such prominent Soviet citizens as Nobel Prize–winning physicist Andrei Sakharov, demanded that the remaining thousands of Jews who wanted to leave should now have their wish granted. Suddenly, in 1973, Brezhnev imposed a tax, making emigra-

Soviet leader Leonid Brezhnev met with President Nixon in 1972, 1973, and 1974 (when this photo was taken, with Secretary of State Kissinger in the foreground). The meetings opened the first important era of U.S.-USSR détente but did not save Nixon's presidency. Kissinger recalled Brezhnev as "quintessentially Russian" in that he combined "crudeness and warmth," and was both "brutal and engaging. . . . Having grown up in a backward society nearly overrun by Nazi invasion, he . . . seemed to feel in his bones the vulnerability of his system." (Henry Kissinger, White House Years [Boston, 1979], p. 1141.)

tion from the Soviet Union more difficult. The Jackson-Vanik Amendment followed. Democratic senator Adlai Stevenson, Jr., from Illinois attached another amendment to the treaty sharply limiting the credit that U.S. agencies (such as the Export-Import Bank) could provide to increase U.S.-Soviet trade. The Soviets angrily denounced the entire treaty. The number of Jewish émigrés dropped 40 percent in 1975.

The results of the first major effort at détente were mixed. Of the 105 treaties that the United States and Soviet Union made between 1933 and 1980, 41 were drawn up between May 1972 and May 1974. Several were historic in slowing the arms race. But in the United States, the Pentagon demanded more money to build more efficient and destructive Trident submarines, new bombers, and better missiles. In the Soviet Union, Brezhnev also modernized his forces and cracked down on dissent until one lonely critic cried that "we [in the Soviet Union] are living on a moonscape. There is no one left. We are all alone on the moon."[35] Americans grew embittered, and Kissinger saw one reason for it: "It is an uncomfortable experience for Americans to deal with a country of roughly the same strength. We have never had to do this in our history."[36] In the short run, however, Nixon profited. As he rolled over Democrat George McGovern in the 1972 presidential election, eight of ten Republicans believed that Nixon's greatest achievements in office were his foreign policies. "You would argue that [the president] is not a moral leader," Kissinger told novelist Norman Mailer, a loud Nixon critic, ". . . but perhaps you go along with me that he has political genius." Mailer replied, "Absolutely."[37]

DÉTENTE'S TURNAROUND: CHILE

In 1973–1974, Nixon's political skills were put to the ultimate test and failed. The U.S. Congress held hearings on the Watergate break-in. At the same time, a series of foreign-policy events began to undermine the president's authority.

The key events occurred not in U.S.-Soviet relations, but in relations with the newly emerging nations, those outer edges of U.S. power where that power was most easily eaten away. Kissinger was ultrasensitive to the danger. "The peace of the world will be threatened, when it is threatened," he observed, "not primarily by strategic forces [of the superpowers] but by geopolitical changes, and to resist those geopolitical changes we must be able to resist regionally."[38] This fear had led to the "Basic Principles" agreement at the summit in which the United States tried to obtain Brezhnev's pledge to accept the *status quo* in the world. For their part, the newly emerging nations, eager to develop and gain control over their own destinies, were determined to change the *status quo* as fast as possible.

The first post-summit challenge occurred in Chile. In 1970, Salvador Allende Gossens, a middle-aged, experienced politician, used his Popular Unity party (a coalition of his own Socialist party and other Marxist groups) to run for the presidency. Determined not to have a second Cuba and intent on showing Brezhnev that the United States could control its own hemisphere, Kissinger saw Allende as "a challenge to our national interest."[39] Just before the election, Nixon ordered the CIA to prevent the Socialist's victory, even if it cost $10 million.[40] A two-track policy was launched. Track 1 cut off outside aid to Chile, with the aim of squeezing the nation's economy until it "screamed," to use Nixon's word. Track 2 secretly put the CIA into contact with extreme right-wing army officers who would use force to prevent an Allende victory.[41] But it was too late. Allende, with 36 percent of the vote, won by a paper-thin margin. The U.S. ambassador cabled home: "Chile voted calmly to have a Marxist-Leninist state, the first nation in the world to make this choice freely and knowingly." U.S. officials then turned to overthrowing the newly elected president. They systematically cut off international as well as American aid. By September 1973, the CIA had reported spending $8 million in anti-Allende activities, much of this money used in cooperation with the Chilean military. Allende did not help himself. Mismanagement worsened an already declining economy. He was unable to counter either his opponents' or the CIA's success with both the army and the middle class (especially housewives), who took to the streets to protest shortages. In September 1973, the army attacked the president's offices. Allende, the U.S. ambassador to Chile claimed, apparently committed suicide during the struggle.[42] But the circumstances of his death remain murky. Many, including his closest family members, believe he was murdered.

The United States had again helped overthrow an elected government. Nixon did so for many reasons. Several of his closest supporters, including Donald Kendall of Pepsi-Cola and Harold Geneen of International Telephone & Telegraph, urged the president to get rid of Allende before their extensive Chilean holdings were nationalized. U.S. intelligence and military agencies also feared the loss of their stations in Chile. But, above all, Nixon and Kissinger saw Allende as a threat to their order in the hemisphere. "I don't see why we have to let a country go Marxist just because its people are irresponsible," Kissinger was quoted as exclaiming.[43]

But the price turned out to be high. Word spread of the deep CIA involvement, a congressional investigation was held, and the result was a scathing indictment of the Nixon-Kissinger policies. In Chile itself, the brutal dictatorship of General Augusto Pinochet Ugarte locked into power. Pinochet's brutality even bloodied the streets of Washington, D.C., in 1976, when his agents killed Orlando Letelier, Allende's foreign minister and an outspoken critic of the new dictatorship. An American woman was also killed in the bomb attack.

Pinochet's legacy for North Americans was explored in the popular film, *Missing*, of 1982. The leading character, a U.S. citizen played by actor Jack Lemmon, discovers that his son has been one of some 10,000 victims of Pinochet's police. The son apparently knew too much about plans drawn up by the Chilean military and U.S. advisers to topple Allende. Until that point, Lemmon's character uncritically accepted the American way of life: "I can no longer abide the young people of our country who live off their parents and the fat of the land and then they find nothing better to do than whine and complain." But when he concludes that U.S. officials have tried to cover up the killing of his son, he confronts the U.S. ambassador. The official, however, tells Lemmon: "We're here to protect American interests. Over 3,000 U.S. firms do business here and that is your, our interest. . . . I'm concerned with the preservation of a way of life. . . . You can't have it both ways."[44]

Elsewhere in the hemisphere, Nixon did (and apparently cared) little. With his attention fixed on the Soviet Union and China, the aid he sent Latin America was mostly supplies to the armies that maintained order by force. Many South American nations, led by Argentina and Brazil, turned against these policies and increased trade with Europe and Japan. Soviet trade, especially in the Argentine wheat market, leaped forward. Despite (or because of) Allende's overthrow, Nixon and Kissinger faced losing control of a most important region.

DÉTENTE'S TURNAROUND: THE MIDDLE EAST

Both the Soviets and Americans nearly lost control of their allies in the Middle East during 1973. The result was a military alert that brought the world closer to nuclear war than at any time since 1962.

The crisis began on October 6, 1973, when Egyptian and Syrian forces launched a devastating surprise attack against Israel in an attempt to regain the land lost to Israeli armies in the 1967 war (see p. 622). Both attacking forces received massive supplies and military intelligence from the Soviet Union, although Brezhnev carefully kept the Soviet military out of any direct involvement. He did not have to urge on Anwar el-Sadat, who became Egypt's leader after Nasser suffered a fatal heart attack in 1970. Sadat was determined to avenge Egypt's 1967 humiliation. But he had also grown fearful of Soviet involvement in his country and had expelled 10,000 Soviet advisers in 1972. He clearly wanted to move closer to the United States. Nixon and Kissinger ignored the signals until Sadat took matters into his own hands by invading Israel on Yom Kippur, the most solemn Jewish holy day.

After suffering severe losses, the Israeli army counterattacked and, by October 20, was driving toward Egypt. Kissinger and the Soviets arranged a cease-fire. But Israel surrounded and began to starve out

Sadat's best troops. Brezhnev, mistakenly believing that Kissinger had tricked him with the cease-fire policy, supported Sadat's plea for joint U.S.-USSR intervention to stop the fighting. Nixon coldly turned down the offer. He was not about to allow the Soviet Union to become a power broker in the Middle East. Brezhnev then threatened to move unilaterally to save Sadat's troops. On the night of October 24, Kissinger and other senior officials responded by telling the Soviets to stay out of the region. They made the point clear by ordering U.S. forces worldwide to move to a stage 3 alert—halfway up the ladder to launching a nuclear attack. With the Watergate scandal engulfing him, a nearly broken-down Nixon isolated himself in another part of the White House but was apparently kept informed. After some anxious hours had elapsed, it became clear that Soviet forces were not going to go on alert or try to move into the Middle East.[45]

Kissinger, however, did not desire a total Israeli victory. By manipulating U.S. supplies, he pressured Israel into breaking its encirclement of the Egyptian army. Kissinger, whom Nixon had made secretary of state in September 1973, now had what he wanted: a Middle East in which neither side—Israel or the Arab nations—had won total victory but in which both depended on him to mediate a peace. His peace efforts received help at the United Nations, where Israelis, Arabs, and other members agreed on UN resolutions 242 (passed in 1967) and 338 (passed in 1973), which called for direct talks, Israeli withdrawal, and recognition of "the territorial integrity of every state in the area." In return for withdrawing, Israel was to be recognized by the Arabs. But withdraw from where? That was the question that Kissinger had to answer while assuring Israeli officials that their nation's security would not be endangered by withdrawal.

In several rounds of exhausting "shuttle diplomacy," Kissinger flew between the Egyptian and Israeli capitals until his plane was known as the "Yo-Yo Express" because it was up and down so often. By the end of 1975, he had persuaded the Israelis to give up strategic passes and oil fields in the Sinai desert (located between Israel and Egypt). In return, Sadat promised to deal with Israel peacefully. It marked a historic breakthrough: the Israelis retreated from land gained by military conquest for the first time, and Egypt recognized Israel's right to exist. Kissinger also negotiated the Israelis' withdrawal from Syrian territory, although they remained in the strategic Golan Heights. The Syrians, with extensive Soviet aid, became the leading anti-Israeli power in the Middle East. Tensions soon rose as Kissinger failed to move Israel from its occupation of the West Bank of the Jordan River, where 1 million

David Levine caricatures the Henry Kissinger of 1974 as a card dealer who keeps both a gun and carrots in reserve. At the time, the secretary of state was trying to settle critical problems in the Middle East, Africa, Southeast Asia, and the North Atlantic alliance, even as the Nixon administration collapsed.

Palestinian Arabs lived. The Israelis had seized the land from Jordan in their 1967 triumph. In 1968, the Palestine Liberation Organization (PLO) was formed under the leadership of Yasir Arafat. The PLO was dedicated to an Arab state in Palestine, which the Israelis interpreted as meaning the destruction of their own homeland. In 1974, Arab states recognized the PLO as the sole representative of the Palestinians. The West Bank problem became a festering boil that soon infected internal Israeli, as well as broader Middle Eastern, politics.

The Israelis had, nevertheless, gained much, including the U.S. pledge to send billions of dollars each year in military aid and to protect their security. But relations also warmed between Washington and Cairo, where Sadat began receiving U.S. aid. Relations between Washington and Moscow, however, grew worse by the day.

DÉTENTE'S TURNAROUND: THE ARAB OIL EMBARGO

For Americans, the most dramatic result of the Yom Kippur War of 1973 was a quick doubling, and then a near-doubling again, of the price that they paid for gasoline and oil. Costs shot up, and inflation soared as Arab oil producers cut back production in an effort to pressure Israel to meet their demands for a return to the pre-1967 boundaries. Because Washington was Israel's strongest supporter, the Arabs tried to cut off oil completely to the United States.

In perspective, the oil embargo marked an important turn in U.S. economic and diplomatic history. Resembling other such turns, it had deep roots. Just twenty years before, in the early 1950s, Americans had produced at home all the oil they needed. By 1960, however, their booming factories and wasteful automobiles made them dependent on foreign sources for one of every six barrels of oil they used. By 1973, one of every three barrels they consumed came from abroad. Few worried. Supply seemed assured, and Arab or Venezuelan oil was cheaper then the U.S. product. But signs had appeared. In 1959–1960, the U.S.-dominated petroleum companies (the so-called "Seven Sisters") were awash in oil and tried to cut back prices paid to producers. Led by Venezuela, Iran, and Saudi Arabia, the producers formed OPEC (Organization of Petroleum Exporting Countries) in 1960 to restore higher prices. They failed to obtain more money. But one of OPEC's members, Libya, scored a breakthrough in 1970.

The year before, a group of young army officers, led by Mu'ammar al-Qadhafi, had overthrown the disorganized pro-U.S. Libyan monarchy. Qadhafi and his followers disliked U.S. military bases (although many of the men had been trained in the United States) and especially Western influences. (As Moslems, they condemned drinking, smoking, gambling, and prostitutes—all of which were known to appear around U.S. bases.) A major oil producer, Libya also had large cash reserves. Qadhafi knew that U.S. consumers, U.S. companies, and U.S. allies needed his petroleum. He succeeded in squeezing a higher price from the American companies pumping Libyan oil.[46] Thus, an OPEC member had forced the once all-powerful companies to pay producers higher prices.

When OPEC successfully enforced the embargo of 1973–1974, the

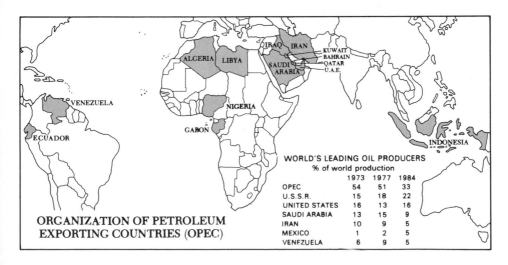

ORGANIZATION OF PETROLEUM
EXPORTING COUNTRIES (OPEC)

WORLD'S LEADING OIL PRODUCERS
% of world production

	1973	1977	1984
OPEC	54	51	33
U.S.S.R.	15	18	22
UNITED STATES	16	13	16
SAUDI ARABIA	13	15	9
IRAN	10	9	5
MEXICO	1	2	5
VENEZUELA	6	9	5

West and Japan were, nevertheless, surprised and badly shaken. As a result, first, the United States appeared highly vulnerable—not to the pressures of the other superpower, but to the oil-producing machines of small Middle Eastern countries. Second, Nixon and Kissinger found some relief from the shah of Iran, who quietly shipped large amounts of oil to Americans. Since 1972, Nixon had depended on the shah to be the guardian of U.S. interests in the Persian Gulf region. Until the late 1960s, that guardian had been the British, but they had to pull back. Nixon then went to the shah in 1972 and simply pleaded, "Protect me."[47] The astonished shah was delighted to do so. He came through handsomely in the 1973 crisis but demanded several pounds of flesh in return, including much higher prices for his petroleum and massive U.S. arms shipments. Those shipments amounted to over $9 billion between 1973 and 1977. The Americans and the shah had become intimate allies.

Third, as enormous amounts of money moved to the Middle East producers, the West's bankers gladly moved in to help the producers invest these billions. Huge amounts were lent to oil consumers (Argentina, the Philippines, Peru, South Korea), to countries intent on rapid industrialization (Poland, Brazil), and even back to the oil producers themselves (Mexico, Venezuela). When the world economy slowed between 1975 and 1982, many of these nations were buried under an unpayable debt that threatened the world's financial system.

Finally, the oil crisis helped sink détente. The Soviets actually exported ten times more oil to the United States in 1973 than they had in 1972 (and, of course, charged top price). But they had also worked closely with the Egyptians, whose attack on Israel triggered the crisis. U.S. officials angrily believed that in the spirit of détente Brezhnev should at least have warned Washington about the attack. Nor did the U.S. move to a stage 3 nuclear alert improve relations. Détente could not prevent either superpower from acting in its own interest in the newly emerging world, whether the opportunity lay in Egypt or Chile.

DÉTENTE'S TURNAROUND: THE ALLIES AND A BAD "YEAR OF EUROPE"

Kissinger believed that during the 1973 crisis, the closest U.S. allies had acted like traitors. He deeply feared the western Europeans' warmer relations with the Soviets. The once-formidable NATO alliance, he later wrote, was so bogged down in disputes that it was merely "an acciden-

tal array of forces in search of a mission."[48] U.S. and European producers, especially farmers, tore into each other for alleged trade
discriminations. Kissinger knew that he and Nixon had ignored Europe
to follow their own agendas in Vietnam, Moscow, and Beijing (Peking).
So in mid-1973, he announced that it was to be "the year of Europe."
The historic relationship was to be restored. The western Europeans,
however, believed that little substance lay below his rhetoric. Since
1963–1965 (if not since the Suez fiasco of 1956), U.S. attention had
been diverted from the Atlantic and Japan, and toward the newly
emerging nations and the superpowers' concerns. As the president of
France sarcastically informed Nixon, "For Europeans every year is the
year of Europe."[49]

Then, during the 1973 Mideast crisis, Nixon asked the NATO allies
to make their military bases available to U.S. planes flying supplies to
Israel. All except Portugal refused. Even West Germany turned Nixon
down. The Europeans, who received 80 percent of their oil from the
Arab producers, and the Japanese, who received over 95 percent, openly
defied the president. In the most serious break in the post-1949 alliance system, these allies made their own deals to obtain Middle East
oil. "I don't care what happens to NATO," Kissinger reportedly blurted
out, "I'm so disgusted."[50] Anti-Tokyo feelings also rose as the ever-
efficient Japanese increased their exports to ever-eager U.S. buyers until
the trade balance in Japan's favor more than quadrupled between 1973
and 1977 to $8.1 billion.

The alliance's slide continued in 1974–1975, when the long-lived
dictatorships of Franco in Spain and Salazar in Portugal ended in death.
Strong Socialist and Communist factions appeared in both nations.
Kissinger, assuming the worst, concluded that without secret CIA help,
the two nations would swing toward Moscow. Western European moderates, led by Christian Socialists and Social Democrats, disagreed.
Believing the Spanish and Portuguese peoples capable of finding their
own way to democracy, the European leaders checked Kissinger's moves.
The Europeans were proven correct as moderates came into power in
both Spain and Portugal, although not without overcoming threats from
both the military right wing and the Communist factions. Kissinger
refused to raise his estimate of the allies: "All of Europe will be Marxist within a decade," he reportedly declared in 1976.[51]

Canada, neighbor and leading trading partner of the United States,
also turned bitter. In 1968, Pierre Trudeau became prime minister. A
playboy bachelor, Harvard-educated, wealthy, and athletic, he would
have been a perfect match for John Kennedy but was an ill-fit for Rich-

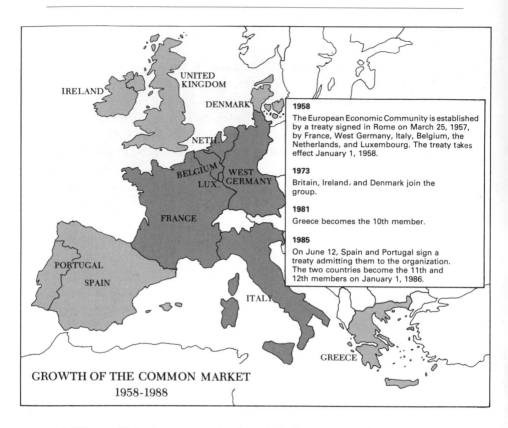

1958

The European Economic Community is established by a treaty signed in Rome on March 25, 1957, by France, West Germany, Italy, Belgium, the Netherlands, and Luxembourg. The treaty takes effect January 1, 1958.

1973

Britain, Ireland, and Denmark join the group.

1981

Greece becomes the 10th member.

1985

On June 12, Spain and Portugal sign a treaty admitting them to the organization. The two countries become the 11th and 12th members on January 1, 1986.

GROWTH OF THE COMMON MARKET
1958-1988

ard Nixon. Relations soured when Washington, without consulting Ottawa, set off a nuclear device in the Aleutian Islands that threatened to spread (but did not) a radioactive cloud over much of Canada. When the unattached Trudeau met Nixon, the president publicly greeted "the Prime Minister and his lovely wife." But nothing shook the relationship like Nixon's 1971 import tax. With 70 percent of their exports going to Americans, Canadians were hurt more severely than any other people by Nixon's actions. For its part, Canada had taken in thousands of American men who moved north to resist the military draft. Trudeau, faced with a difficult economy and a declining NATO, next cut back his nation's commitment to the military alliance.[52] By 1976, U.S.-Canadian relations approached a twentieth-century low.

DÉTENTE'S TURNAROUND: AFRICA

The Nixon-Kissinger view held that Africa, like the allies, had to play second fiddle to the more important U.S. relations with China and the

Soviet Union. Black Africa was so unimportant (and racism so strong in the Nixon White House) that at one point the president told Kissinger, "Henry, let's leave the niggers to Bill [Secretary of State William Rogers] and we'll take care of the rest of the world."[53] In 1970, this attitude was made policy in the National Security Council's secret paper, National Security Study Memorandum 39 (or NSSM 39). It declared that the United States should help the many new black African nations but place primary emphasis on relations with the white government of South Africa and the white colonial government of Portugal. This approach was labeled the "Tar-Baby option" by a State Department dissenter who believed (correctly) that it would stick Americans to a lost Portuguese cause.

South Africa's attractions were its highly effective military force, its rich holdings of minerals, its strong economy (where the rate of return on U.S. investment was above 17 percent annually), and its strategic location at the tip of Africa. These lures overcame U.S. qualms about South Africa's brutal apartheid policy under which 22-million blacks and 5 million other nonwhites were now forcefully segregated and discriminated against by 5 million ruling whites. Portugal's value was its bases in the eastern Atlantic, for which Washington paid nearly $500 million each year. The Portuguese spent the money trying to stop anticolonial wars in Angola, Mozambique (where a Marxist government soon came to power), and Guinea.[54]

Nixon and Kissinger had again bet on the wrong horse. By 1974, the Portuguese had lost the fight in the key nation, Angola. Some 170,000 whites could no longer rule 4.6 million blacks. The African nation became a case study of how local problems in emerging countries were turned into a global confrontation between the Americans and the Soviets. Three factions, all black, fought to rule the newly independent Angola. Agostinho Neto's MPLA had long received Soviet and Cuban aid. That aid, however, was reduced after 1972, and Neto vowed to protect the U.S.-owned Gulf Oil Company, which produced the revenues on which the economy rested. Opposed to Neto were the FNLA (supported by the United States and China) and Jonas Savimbi's UNITA (backed by South Africa). In early 1975, the three factions agreed to settle differences through an election. But since at least mid-1974, the CIA had bankrolled the FNLA; and now the FNLA, with secret U.S. support, destroyed the agreement by attacking the stronger MPLA. Kissinger later said that he had intended to show China how to be tough with Soviet-backed groups. But the Soviets and Cubans responded with 230 military advisers to help Neto, who seized power. The fighting

FOREIGN INFLUENCE IN AFRICA
Political affiliation — 1952

Belgium | Spain
France | Union of South Africa
Italy | United Kingdom
Portugal | Independent country

0 — 1000 Miles
0 — 1000 Kilometers

escalated until South African troops, CIA agents, and over 20,000 Cubans were involved. Some of the Cuban troops protected Gulf Oil property. The Chinese decided to make a quick escape from the entire mess.

Kissinger insisted that the United States had to respond to the Communists' escalation. Massive arms shipments flowed from both superpowers—Soviet aid to Angola, Uganda, and Somalia; American aid to Kenya, Zaire, and Ethiopia. Africa became a bloody arena for superpower confrontation and brutal wars. But there seemed to be little understanding of, or concern about, the local causes of the wars. In Ethiopia, for example, a radical regime came to power and, for its own domestic reasons, switched to the Soviet side in 1976 even though the United States had just delivered $100 million worth of advanced jet fighters. As in a game of musical chairs, Kissinger then clutched Ethiopia's enemy, Somalia, as a U.S. ally, although Somalia had just been supported by Moscow.[55]

The U.S. Congress was shocked. Vietnam had made it leery of Third-World wars. And, in 1974, it passed a law (the Hughes-Ryan Amendment) that tried to curb CIA activities. The agency obviously had paid little attention to the law during the Angolan affair. So Congress next passed the Clark Amendment, which prohibited U.S. military assistance to either side in Angola. Kissinger railed against the law, but Congress held fast. Since 1970, Kissinger and Nixon had chosen whites over blacks, a military policy over a negotiated settlement, and a focus on superpower rivalry over a focus on local conditions. Kissinger could no longer convince Congress that U.S. policy made sense. Unlike the Tar Baby of Uncle Remus's famous story, Congress seemed to be freeing itself from the Angolan (if not South African) Tar Baby. But because of African affairs, the superpowers had become more tightly locked into a new cold war.

DÉTENTE'S TURNAROUND: THE LAST DAYS OF THE VIETNAM WAR AND NIXON'S IMPERIAL PRESIDENCY

"America's longest war," as historian George Herring calls the conflict in Vietnam, meanwhile ended with a series of bangs. The first and biggest bang went off in late 1972. After nearly three years of talks, Kissinger believed that he had an agreement with North Vietnam to end the conflict. "Peace is at hand," he announced in late October 1972. But the South Vietnamese government refused to accept the deal because it was afraid that the Communists would obtain even more power in the South. Nixon, in the last days of his re-election fight, deserted Kissinger's agreement so that it would not appear that he (Nixon) was deserting South Vietnam. When Kissinger returned to the talks after the election and demanded nearly seventy changes, the North Vietnamese refused.[56]

The president then decided to show his willingness to use force. He unleashed the heaviest bombing raids of the war. Nixon declared that he "did not care if the whole world thought he was crazy" dropping so many bombs, because "the Russians and the Chinese might think they were dealing with a madman and so [they] had better force North Viet-

Henry Kissinger and North Vietnam's envoy, Le Duc Tho, walk together in Paris in February 1972 during their protracted talks to end the war. The two men shared the Nobel Peace Prize in 1973 for their efforts. But because the war continued, Le Duc Tho refused to accept his share of the prize.

nam into a settlement before the world was consumed in a larger war." Only 24 percent of Americans polled opposed this "madness." Congress did nothing to stop Nixon.[57]

In January 1973, Kissinger and the North Vietnamese finally reached an agreement. In the view of some experts, the settlement could have been obtained months—perhaps even years—earlier.[58] First, a cease-fire went into effect, and Nixon agreed to pull out all U.S. combat forces in sixty days. Meanwhile, the Communists were to withdraw from Laos and Cambodia. Second, all U.S. prisoners were to be released. Third—and of special importance—the United States recognized the "unity and territorial integrity of Vietnam," but South Vietnam's "right to self-determination" was also recognized by both sides. Finally, the pro-U.S. Thieu government was to remain in power pending an election in which Communists could participate. To obtain Thieu's acceptance this time, Nixon secretly told him that if the Communists violated the pact, "You can count on us" to protect the South.[59]

Congress was not told of Nixon's secret assurance, but that legislative body had long since quit trusting the president. In 1971, it had finally repealed the 1964 Gulf of Tonkin Resolution (see p. 606). In early 1973, the House and Senate forbade Nixon to bomb Indochina after July 1 of that year. In the War Powers Resolution of late 1973,

Congress passed a law that (1) asked the president to consult with Congress before committing troops to combat areas, and (2) required that if he did send troops, he must withdraw them within ninety days unless Congress expressly approved the commitment. Nixon angrily vetoed the act, but Congress passed it over his veto.

Congress had finally begun curbing the powers of King Richard. With the 1972 Watergate break-in and his attempt to cover up that criminal act, Nixon was personally guilty for the loss of his power. But the changing nature of the presidency went much deeper. Cold-war issues were developing less in the military arena (where the president as commander in chief can take the lead) and more in the economic arena (where the Constitution gives Congress greater control). The changing nature of the cold war produced a changing relationship between a once-all-powerful president in foreign policy and a now more active Congress. House and Senate attempts at limiting the CIA and military ventures in Africa also signaled this change.

Despite Nixon's pledge to Thieu, South Vietnam fell on April 30, 1975, twenty-one bloody years after Eisenhower had tied the United States to the anti-Communist regime. In March 1974, the last U.S. combat troops had left. In August 1974, Nixon, facing impeachment,

As David Levine illustrates in this cartoon, Nixon's most serious problem by late 1972 was no longer with the North Vietnamese (who had largely agreed to peace terms), but with his ally, Nguyen Van Thieu, leader of South Vietnam, who disliked the terms and forced Nixon to re-enter negotiations. The president finally stopped the biting and clawing by secretly guaranteeing Thieu in 1973 that the United States would use force, if necessary, to protect Thieu's regime under the peace agreement.

became the first U.S. president to resign his office. In October, North Vietnam's leaders concluded that even if the Americans re-entered the war, Thieu's government could not be saved. The Communists launched a major offensive in March 1975. They believed that a two-year war would follow. Instead, the South Vietnamese army, now left on its own, melted away. Kissinger and the new president, Gerald Ford, pleaded that Congress had a "moral obligation" to send $300 million more in military aid. Congress refused. It was afraid that the money would only be wasted or end up in Communist hands. Moreover, Congress knew that, according to CIA estimates, the Thieu regime had already received $3.3 billion in 1973–1974—as opposed to the North's $730 million from its Communist partners—but was no longer able to use aid effectively.[60] The Communists ended the war with the capture of Saigon, the South's capital (now renamed Ho Chi Minh City).

Kissinger blamed the Watergate scandal, congressional opposition, and the Communist breaking of the 1973 agreements as the reasons for the final collapse. "If we didn't have this damn domestic situation," he complained in 1973, "a week of bombing would put this Agreement in force."[61] But in quieter moments, Kissinger admitted that there was another reason for the North's triumph: "Because there were always more Vietnamese prepared to die for their country than foreigners, their nationalism became the scourge of invaders and neighbours alike."[62]

By the end, the costs of the civil war had become enormous. About 58,015 Americans died (more than half after 1968), and 150,303 more were wounded. Some groups suffered more than others. Hispanics, who made up 7 percent of the U.S. population, suffered 20 percent of the battle deaths. African Americans, with 11 percent of the population, also suffered 20 percent of the deaths. The largest number of U.S. deserters were minorities and blue-collar whites who knew little about Vietnam until they arrived there. The middle class, especially whites, used lawyers and college deferments to escape the war. On the other side, 2 million Vietnamese died. Twice that number were wounded. The U.S. government, moreover, had broken numerous laws during the conflict. Although the CIA charter forbids it from conducting covert activities within the United States, the agency (acting on presidential orders) infiltrated college student groups and other organizations suspected of not being sufficiently patriotic. By 1971, the CIA was opening nearly 8,000 private letters. In Operation Chaos, the agency kept secret computer files on 7,500 Americans (and indexes on 300,000 more),

Dear 'Smitty,

Perhaps, now I can bury you; at least in my soul. Perhaps, now, I won't again see you night after night when the war re-appears and we are once more amidst the myriad hells that Vietnam engulfed us in.

We crept 'point' together and we pulled 'drag' together. We lay crouched in cold mud and were drenched by monsoons. We sweated buckets and endured the heat of dry season. We burnt at least a thousand leeches off one another and went through a gallon of insect repellent a day that the bugs were irresistibly attracted to.

When you were hit, I was your medic all the way, and when I was blown 50 feet by the mortar, you were there first. When I was shaking with malaria, you wiped my brow.

We got tough, 'Smitty. We became hired guns, lean and mean and calloused. And after every ambush, every firefight, every "hot" chopper insertion you'd shake and get sick.

You got a bronze star, a silver star, survived 18 months of one demon hell after another, only to walk into a booby trapped bunker and all of a sudden you had no face or chest.

I never cried. My chest becomes unbearably painful and my throat tightens so I can't even croak, but I haven't cried. I wanted to, just couldn't.

I think I can, today. Damn, I'm crying now.

> 'Bye Smitty,
> Get some rest

A letter left by a Vietnam veteran at the Vietnam Veterans Memorial in Washington, D.C.

despite the CIA director's knowledge that it was illegal. These operations marked "a step toward the dangers of a domestic secret police," in the words of a Senate report.[63]

The war did produce a victor other than North Vietnam: the Soviet Union. Fearful of its ancient enemy China, North Vietnam turned increasingly to Moscow for help. By the late 1970s, the Soviet navy had taken over the strategic Vietnamese bases built in the 1960s by the United States. Moscow's power leapfrogged over much of Asia to become a presence in Southeast Asia, as well as to surround further with Red Army might the nervous Chinese. To obtain all this, the Soviets lost few lives and little money. "Somewhere in the world," a U.S. official groused in 1974, "there must be a school where foreign governments learn to con Americans."[64] The problem, however, lay much closer to home, where Americans were ignorant of their own and others' histories, and, consequently, ignorant of the limits of their own power.

DÉTENTE'S TURNAROUND:
THE FORD PRESIDENCY (1974–1977)

Gerald Ford had to pick up the tattered remnants of a failed foreign policy. A graduate of the University of Michigan, where he had been a star football player, Ford was a likable, unpretentious, ardent Republican who, without displaying excess talent, rose to the leadership of the House of Representatives. In mid-1973, Nixon tapped him to replace the disgraced Agnew as vice-president. One observer wrote that "few men are better qualified than Ford for a job that demands practically nothing of the man who holds it."[65] In August 1974, he suddenly became president. If the departing Nixon liked the movie *Patton*, Ford's favorite was the cotton-candy *That's Entertainment, Part 2*. When pressed to explain the declining U.S. economy, the new president declared, "Things are more like they are now than they've ever been."[66]

But the new chief executive also showed an openness, an ability to identify with the person on the street, that sharply separated him from Nixon. Americans had finally grown suspicious of power, even their own. That suspicion was made evident in the popularity of such movies between 1969 and 1976 as *Z, All the President's Men,* and *Three Days of the Condor,* which showed society's most powerful figures engaged in secret conspiracies (such as the Watergate scandal) to overturn democratic systems.[67] Ford's apparent innocence and directness restored some confidence in White House authority. His attempt to use that authority in foreign policy, however, produced few successes.

First, he and Kissinger made a last-ditch attempt to save South Vietnam in April 1975. When that try failed, Ford traveled to Hawaii and announced a Pacific Doctrine. Despite the tragedies in Vietnam, he declared, the United States remained a Pacific power. In a new variation of Frederick Jackson Turner's frontier thesis (see p. 185), the president declared, "The center of political power in the United States has shifted westward. Our Pacific interests and concerns have increased." He demanded an "equilibrium" of power to protect U.S. interests in the region. Ford focused on the growing American "commercial involvement" in Asia, thus acknowledging the rising commitment to Pacific rim markets. For the first time in four hundred years, U.S. economic interests in Asia were becoming larger than those in Europe. Yet Ford's doctrine also acknowledged that U.S. power was much less than it had been a generation earlier. Americans needed help from partners in Indonesia, Japan, and the Philippines.[68] That need had

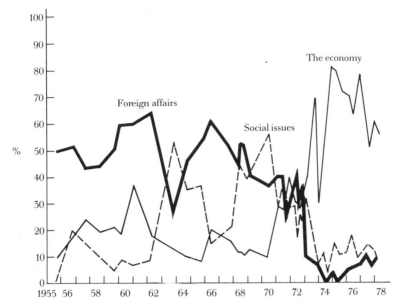

This graph from Public Opinion *(May / June 1978) illustrates what Americans considered to be their "most important problem facing the country today" (between 1955 and 1978). Note the sharp changes in 1964–1968, when the Vietnam War reached its peak, and then the increasing concern over the economy with the Arab oil embargo of 1974.*

been one reason why Nixon and Ford said nothing after Philippine ruler Ferdinand Marcos imposed a corrupt martial-law regime on his people in 1972. Of special importance, the economic relationship along the Pacific rim was being defined by Japanese efficiency, not by Americans.

Second, Ford and Secretary of State Kissinger made a major effort at reviving détente. They met with Brezhnev in the Soviets' Pacific coast city of Vladivostok during November 1974. Building on the last two Nixon-Brezhnev summits of 1973–1974, the Americans and Soviets agreed to place a ceiling on the number of strategic nuclear missiles and big bombers. A later meeting was to turn this general agreement into a treaty with specific numbers. In 1975, U.S. and Soviet astronauts worked together for the first time in a dramatic Apollo-Soyuz space flight. Later that year, thirty-five nations (led by the United States and the USSR) met at Helsinki, Finland, to make historic agreements in four areas (called "baskets"). One basket provided that force would not be used to change frontier boundaries, an agreement the Soviets had wanted to make with the United States since the Red Army redrew

President Gerald Ford (1913–   ) points during a meeting held to discuss the Mayaguez *crisis in 1975. The president talks with Secretary of Defense James Schlesinger. Secretary of State Kissinger is at left.*

European boundaries between 1944 and 1948. In return, the Soviets had to agree to a basket that recognized the right of peoples to enjoy human freedoms, including the freedom to move across national borders. When, however, "Helsinki Watch" groups appeared in the Soviet Union to ensure that these rights would be respected, they were brutally beaten and imprisoned. The Helsinki baskets, which seemed to offer hope for détente, turned into another reason to believe that détente was dying, if not dead. As he ran for election in 1976, Ford outlawed the use of the word *détente* by his staff. Kissinger lamented that it "is a word I would like to forget."[69]

Third, Ford effectively revived the president's commander-in-chief power during a crisis in 1975. On May 12, Communist Cambodian vessels captured a U.S. freighter, the *Mayaguez*, and imprisoned its thirty-nine-member crew. Determined to show their muscle, Ford and Kissinger ordered the bombing of a Cambodian port, then dispatched troops to rescue the crew. Unknown to them, the Cambodians were already releasing the prisoners. An accidental explosion killed forty-one of the U.S. troops. Ford had, indeed, made his point: the Vietnam failure did not lessen U.S. willingness to use force. He did so, moreover, while refusing to recognize formally that Congress's 1973 War

Powers Act in any way limited his power to dispatch troops without consulting Congress. But Americans had paid a high and unnecessary price for the Ford-Kissinger adventure.

ADJUSTING TO A NEW WORLD

After an era of unequaled U.S. dominance in world affairs between 1945 and the 1960s, Americans began to discover the limits of their power. The unfavorable international trade balances of the late 1950s and early 1960s flashed a first sign. The Vietnam tragedy became the clearest indication that the tide had turned. Nixon and Kissinger faced the task of gently convincing Americans that the 1945-to-1960s years were unnatural. No people have ever taken readily to the idea that they had to give up power. Many Americans, whose ignorance of history especially left them unprepared to face such a challenge, not surprisingly refused to accept the realities of the new world.

Nixon failed in part because of the corruption, indeed crime, that undermined his presidency. Tapes on which he recorded White House conversations revealed a man who had no hobbies and no real friends except Miami businessman Bebe Rebozo, who would spend hours drinking with Nixon while feeding his ego and paranoia ("You're doing a great job," or "Your enemies are out to get you.") Two drinks could spin the president off into a slurred, sometimes reckless speech; once he simply fell asleep while in the middle of a phone conversation with a close aide. He covered insecurity with racism; in private conversation (but recorded on tape), Jews were "kikes" and blacks were "niggers," while the detested journalists were "press pricks." Believing himself surrounded by enemies, by 1973–1974 the president seemed to feel closer to the enemies in Moscow than the enemies in Washington. As for Kissinger, he had publicly warned that, in a democracy, obtaining public support was a statesman's "acid test." Historian Robert Beisner concludes that "Kissinger failed the 'acid test' . . . because he stepped outside the constraints imposed by the American political tradition without reshaping that tradition itself."[70] The same conclusion applies to Nixon.

These personal and political failures became especially disastrous for Nixon and Kissinger because through détente, they had planned to contain Soviet power, but at lower cost than in the past.[71] Détente, however, required that Americans no longer view the Soviets simply as evil aggressors, but as friendly enough to be negotiated with—but dangerous enough to be guarded against. After thirty years of a fierce cold war, this subtle policy turned out to be too much to ask from a society whose historic dealings with Indians, Mexicans, Spaniards, Chinese, and Russians had hardly been subtle. Nor was U.S. tolerance helped by Brezhnev's policies, which stressed détente with the United States, military support for "wars of liberation," and, at home, the exiling of dissenters to Siberian prisons.

Many Americans, disappointed with Nixon and détente, and tired of helping such ungrateful people as the western Europeans and Vietnamese, began to retreat to a position that critics termed "neo-isolationism." The respected conservative journalist Walter Lippmann gave his view of the problem: "Well, neo-isolationism is the direct product of foolish globalism. If you think you can run the world and then you find out you can't, you withdraw to what you can run." In 1975, the governor of Louisiana heard Kissinger describe how Americans were going to help developing countries around the world and retorted: "I hope we can do it for them a helluva lot better than we have been able to do it for ourselves, because we haven't done it in this country yet. And I think Americans and the world ought to come to grips with that reality."[72]

It was not unlike the late 1920s, when a postwar world structure, carefully constructed under U.S. guidance, rested on American economic power. When that power buckled, the structure began to collapse. Nixon and Kissinger had worked to prop up the structure, but the foundations—the U.S. economy and their domestic support—crumbled under their touch. It was now left for Jimmy Carter and Ronald Reagan to design fresh policies for this different world or to try to go *Back to the Future* (as a popular film of the 1980s was entitled) in an attempt to retrieve the lost American power of the 1950s.

NOTES

1. Garry Wills, *Nixon Agonistes* (Boston, 1970), p. 160.
2. Lawrence Martin, *The Presidents and the Prime Ministers* (Toronto, 1982), p. 259.
3. Ralph H. Wolfe quoting Ted Sennett in "Review Essay," *Journal of Popular Film and Television* 12 (Summer 1984): 89.
4. Interview of Richard Nixon, *Washington Star*, 10 November 1972, p. 1.
5. Garry Wills, *Reagan's America* (New York, 1987), p. 344.
6. Seymour Hersh, *The Price of Power* (New York, 1983), p. 40.

7. Dobrynin's 1969 report is in *New York Times*, 8 February 1993, p. A8. *New York Times*, 31 May 1987, p. 24; *ibid.*, 26 January 1974, p. 19; Theodore Draper, "Kissinger's Apologia," *Dissent* 27 (Spring 1980): 253.

8. Henry A. Kissinger, *A World Restored: Castlereagh, Metternich, and the Problems of Peace, 1812–1822* (London and New York, 1957, 1964), pp. 326–330.

9. *New York Times*, 6 July 1970, p. 2.

10. Henry A. Kissinger, *American Foreign Policy*, exp. ed. (New York, 1974), pp. 182–183.

11. Richard M. Nixon, "Asia after Vietnam," *Foreign Affairs* 46 (October 1967): 111–125; Wills, *Nixon Agonistes*, pp. 20–21.

12. Kissinger, *American Foreign Policy*, p. 57; J. L. S. Girling, " 'Kissingerism': The Enduring Problems," *International Affairs* 51 (July 1975): 325n; the justice-versus-disorder reference is in John G. Stoessinger, *Henry Kissinger: The Anguish of Power* (New York, 1976), pp. 12–14.

13. Martin, p. 241.

14. Henry Kissinger, *White House Years* (Boston, 1979), p. 235; Hersh, pp. 50–51; Theodore Draper, *Present History* (New York, 1983), p. 153.

15. The Kissinger quote is in Kissinger, *White House Years*, pp. 227–228; Douglas Brinkley, *Dean Acheson: The Cold War Years, 1953–1971* (New Haven, 1992), p. 269; J. William Fulbright, *The Crippled Giant* (New York, 1972), p. 74.

16. Hersh, p. 130; Kissinger, *White House Years*, p. 441.

17. Garry Clifford, "Present before and after the Creation," *SHAFR Newsletter* 16 (March 1985): 2–3.

18. The best account is William Shawcross, *Sideshow: Kissinger, Nixon, and the Destruction of Cambodia* (New York, 1979), esp. pp. 128–160.

19. Jonathan Schell, *The Time of Illusion* (New York, 1976), pp. 100–101.

20. Leonard Silk, *Nixonomics* (New York, 1972), p. 144.

21. Draper, "Kissinger's Apologia," 248.

22. Lloyd C. Gardner, *The Great Nixon Turnaround: America's New Foreign Policy in the Post-Liberal Era (How a Cold Warrior Climbed Clean Out of His Skin)* (New York, 1973).

23. *Washington Post*, 28 February 1971, p. B3.

24. *Wall Street Journal*, 17 November 1986, p. 17.

25. *Department of State Bulletin*, 5 November 1973, p. 555.

26. Alan K. Henrikson, "America's Changing Place in the World: From 'Periphery' to 'Centre,' " in *Centre and Periphery: Spatial Variation in Politics*, ed. Jean Gottmann (Beverly Hills, Calif., 1980), p. 92. Nixon's five-bloc speech is in U.S. Government, *Public Papers of the Presidents of the United States: Richard Nixon, 1971* (Washington, D.C., 1972), pp. 805–813.

27. Quoted by Frederick Adams in "Why Certain Ideas Count," *Reviews in American History* 11 (September 1983): 440.

28. Leonard A. Kusnitz, *Public Opinion and Foreign Policy: America's China Policy, 1949–1979* (Westport, Conn., 1984), p. 138.

29. A good succinct background, including the Malik quote, is in Gordon H. Chang, *Friends and Enemies* (Stanford, 1990), esp. p. 285. The text of the communiqué and Kissinger's press conference are in *New York Times*, 28 February 1972, p. 16.

30. André Malraux, quoted in C. L. Sulzberger, *The World and Richard Nixon* (New York, 1987), p. 7.

31. *Washington Post*, 1 June 1972, p. F2.

32. *Los Angeles Times*, 25 January 1993, p. A4; Carl Bernstein and Bob Woodward, *All the President's Men* (New York, 1974), pp. 265–266.

33. Sulzberger, pp. 199–200. A superb overview of these agreements and the talks leading to them is U.S. Congress, Senate Committee on Foreign Affairs, 96th Cong., 1st sess., 1979, *Special Studies Series on Foreign Affairs Issues*, Vol. I: *Soviet Diplomacy and Negotiating Behavior: Emerging New Context for U.S. Diplomacy* (Washington, 1979), pp. 444–491. This study was prepared by Dr. Joseph G. Whelan of the Congressional Research Service.

34. Kissinger, *White House Years*, p. 1250.

35. *New York Times*, 23 December 1974, p. 16.

36. *Department of State Bulletin*, 1 March 1976, p. 269.

37. Norman Mailer, *St. George and the Godfather* (New York, 1972), p. 119. The term "détente" comes from the Latin *tendere*, meaning "to stretch," by way of the Old French *destente*, which was a device that held and then released the tensed string of cross-bows. When bows gave way to guns, *détente* became the modern French word for "trigger." In both French and English, it came to signify a relaxation of tension. (*New York Times*, 28 June 1974, p. 2.)

38. Interview of Henry Kissinger in *U.S. News & World Report*, 15 March 1976, p. 28.

39. Kissinger, *White House Years*, pp. 653–654.

40. *Ibid.*, p. 673.

41. Hersh, pp. 275–276.

42. Nathaniel Davis, *The Last Two Years of Salvador Allende* (Ithaca, N.Y., 1985), pp. 278–306.

43. Kissinger, *White House Years*, p. 673; Hersh, pp. 260, 267–269 (on Kendall and Geneen); Roger Morris, *Uncertain Greatness* (New York, 1977), pp. 240–241.

44. Stephen Prince, *Visions of Empire* (New York, 1992), pp. 90–93.

45. Scott D. Sagan, "Lessons of the Yom Kippur Alert," *Foreign Policy* no. 36 (Fall 1979): 160–174.

46. Carl Solberg, *Oil Power* (New York, 1976), pp. 203–204; James E. Akins, "The Oil Crisis: This Time the Wolf Is Here," *Foreign Affairs*, 51 (April 1973): 462–465, 470–472.

47. Gary Sick, *All Fall Down: America's Tragic Encounter with Iran* (New York, 1985), pp. 16–17.

48. Draper, *Present History*, p. 81.

49. Richard J. Barnet, *The Alliance: America-Europe-Japan, Makers of the Postwar World* (New York, 1983), p. 320.

50. *Ibid.*, pp. 324, 328; *Washington Post*, 27 October 1973, p. A7.

51. Quoted by Flora Lewis in the *New York Times*, 16 February 1976, p. 1.

52. Martin, pp. 236–237, 242–243.

53. Hersh, p. 111.

54. *The Kissinger Study of Southern Africa/NSSM 39/(SECRET)*, ed. Mohamed A. El-Khawas and Barry Cohen (Westport, Conn., 1976), esp. pp. 19–54, 86–100.

55. The superb analysis is John A. Marcum's *The Angolan Revolution*, Vol. II: *Exile Politics and Guerrilla Warfare (1962–1976)* (Cambridge, Mass., 1978); and for a fine, succinct analysis by a leading expert on the region, see Gerald J. Bender, "Angola, a Story of Stupidity," *New York Review of Books*, 21 December 1978, pp. 26–36.

56. *Vietnam: A History in Documents*, ed. Gareth Porter (New York, 1979, 1981), pp.

419–420; George Herring, *America's Longest War: The United States and Vietnam, 1950–1975*, 2d. ed. (New York, 1986), esp. pp. 250–256.

57. Barry B. Hughes, *The Domestic Context of American Foreign Policy* (San Francisco, 1978), p. 39; the Nixon quote is in Thomas L. Hughes, "Foreign Policy: Men or Measures?" *Atlantic Monthly* 234 (October 1974): 56.

58. Leslie Gelb, "The Kissinger Legacy," *New York Times Magazine*, 31 October 1976, pp. 82–83; the terms are outlined in the *New York Times*, 28 January 1973, p. E1.

59. *Washington Post*, 7 January 1979, p. A25.

60. *Vietnam: A History in Documents*, p. 445.

61. Henry Kissinger, *Years of Upheaval* (Boston, 1982), pp. 302, 318–319, 326, 338.

62. *Ibid.*, p. 12.

63. *New York Times*, 19 May 1976, p. 14; Lyman B. Kirkpatrick, Jr., "Intelligence and Counterintelligence," in *Encyclopedia of American Foreign Policy*, ed. Alexander DeConde, 3 vols. (New York, 1978), I, pp. 426–427; casualties suffered by minority groups are analyzed in comments by Frank Walker and Ruben Treviso in *Vietnam Reconsidered: Lessons from a War*, ed. Harrison E. Salisbury (New York, 1984), esp. pp. 184, 206.

64. *Washington Post*, 28 July 1974, p. A7.

65. Richard Rovere in the *New Yorker*, 3 December 1973, p. 173.

66. Mark Green, "Presidential Truth and Consequence," *Nation*, 29 October 1983, p. 385; on the film preferences, see the *Washington Post*, 29 August 1976, p. E3.

67. Richard Dorfman, "Conspiracy City," *Journal of Popular Film and Television* 7, no. 4 (1980): 436–437.

68. *Department of State Bulletin*, 29 December 1975, p. 914.

69. *Ibid.*, 1 December 1975, p. 767; Richard W. Stevenson, *Rise and Fall of Détente* (Urbana, Ill., 1985), p. 172.

70. Robert Beisner, "History and Henry Kissinger," *Diplomatic History* 14 (Fall 1990), p. 526; Seymour Hersh, "Nixon's Last Coverup: The Tapes He Wants the Archives to Suppress," *The New Yorker*, 14 December 1992, pp. 93–94.

71. *Department of State Bulletin*, 12 May 1975, p. 609.

72. *Washington Post*, 10 October 1971, p. C5; *Department of State Bulletin*, 6 October 1975, p. 522; two useful French views on the U.S. problems are Michel Tatu, *Eux et nous: Les relations est-ouest entre deux détentes* (Paris, 1985), by a distinguished journalist, and Denise Artaud, *La Fin de l'inocence: Les États-Unis de Wilson à Reagan* (Paris, 1985), which provides the larger framework.

For Further Reading

For specific topics, also consult the notes of this chapter and the General Bibliography at the end of the book. For sources published before 1981, use *Guide to American Foreign Relations since 1700*, ed. Richard Dean Burns (1983), whose exhaustive annotated lists of reading cannot be matched by any text and makes possible noting mostly post-1981 publications below. References listed in the notes usually are not repeated here.

For general analyses of the Nixon years, Kissinger's two volumes of memoirs and

Seymour Hersh's detailed critique of Kissinger's policies (all listed in the notes) can be supplemented with Richard Nixon, *RN: The Memoirs of Richard Nixon* (1978); Stephen E. Ambrose, *Nixon*, 3 vols. (1987–1992); Walter Isaacson, *Kissinger* (1992), which is the most detailed biography; Franz Schurmann, *The Foreign Politics of Richard Nixon: The Grand Design* (1987), focusing on Nixon himself and critical of his Third-World policies; Harvey Starr, *Henry Kissinger: Perceptions of International Politics* (1984); Robert D. Schulzinger, *Henry Kissinger* (1989), a fine study; David P. Calleo, *The Imperious Economy* (1982), which remains the best critical overview of the post-1960 economic policies; John S. Odell, *U.S. International Monetary Policy: Markets, Power, and Ideas as Sources of Change* (1982), stressing post-1965 years; and Terry L. Deibel, *Presidents, Public Opinion and Power: The Nixon, Carter, and Reagan Years* (1987), a helpful brief account.

On Soviet relations, the place to begin is Raymond L. Garthoff's detailed *Détente and Confrontation* (1985); Alexander L. George et al., *Managing U.S.-Soviet Rivalry: Problems of Crisis Prevention* (1982), with excellent essays (especially George Breslauer's on détente); Richard Pipes, *U.S.-Soviet Relations in the Era of Détente* (1981), a conservative, critical argument; Robert S. Litwak, *Détente and the Nixon Doctrine* (1984), a more balanced analysis; Robert C. Gray and Stanley J. Michalak, Jr., *American Foreign Policy since Détente* (1984), a series of essays, especially useful on the world economic context; Philip J. Fungiello, *American-Soviet Trade in the Cold War* (1988); Gerard Smith, *Doubletalk: The Story of SALT I* (1985), by the U.S. negotiator of SALT I, who is highly critical of Kissinger; Paul B. Stares, *The Militarization of Space: U.S. Policy, 1945–1984* (1985), by far the best on the subject; Philip Hanson, *Trade and Technology in Soviet-Western Relations* (1981), which can be used with *The Politics of East-West Trade*, ed. Gordon B. Smith (1984), good on technology and agriculture. For Soviet policy and motivations, along with Garthoff, noted above, start with Jonathan Steele, *Soviet Power: The Kremlin's Foreign Policy—Brezhnev to Andropov* (1983), a superb survey; Harry Gelman, *The Brezhnev Politburo and the Decline of Détente* (1984); Adam Ulam, *Dangerous Relations: The Soviet Union in World Politics, 1970–1982* (1983), readable and critical; *Soviet Decisionmaking for National Security*, ed. Jiri Valenta and William C. Potter (1984), especially Garthoff's essay on SALT and Golan's on the 1973 war; and Galia Golan, *Soviet Policies in the Middle East* (1990).

For Asian affairs, a brief, suggestive essay by a professional diplomat is Leslie H. Brown, *American Security Policy in Asia*, Adelphi Papers No. 132 (1977), focusing on the Nixon Doctrine; Robert G. Sutter, *The China Quandary: Domestic Determinants of U.S. China Policy, 1972–1982* (1983), based on over one hundred interviews of officials; David Shambaugh *Beautiful Imperialist: China Perceives America, 1972–1990* (1991); *Soviet Policy in East Asia*, ed. Donald S. Zagoria (1984); Thomas R. H. Havens, *Fire across the Sea: The Vietnam War and Japan, 1965–1975* (1987), a first-rate study on Japan's turn, and also its anti-war movement; I. M. Destler, Haruhiro Fukui, Hideo Sato, *The Textile Wrangle: Conflict in Japanese-American Relations, 1969–1971* (1979), excellent on perhaps the pivotal event; Kunio Muraoka, *Japanese Security and the United States*, Adelphi Papers No. 195 (1973), a Japanese diplomat's view of the Nixon 1971 shocks.

On Vietnam, Gabriel Kolko's *Anatomy of a War* (1985) is a richly researched book on the entire post-1945 era; Harry G. Summers, Jr., *On Strategy: The Vietnam War in Context* (1981), one of the more widely discussed critiques of U.S. military policy; Timothy J. Lomperis, *The War Everyone Lost—and Won* (1984), viewing the war as both revolution and conventional war; Ole Holsti and James R. Roseneau, *American Leadership in World Affairs: Vietnam and the Breakdown of Consensus* (1984), much quantitative evidence to provide the context; John Hellmann, *American Myth and the Legacy of Vietnam* (1986), on U.S. self-image in novels, films, and memoirs; Nguyen Tien Hung and Jerrold Schecter, *The Palace File* (1986), important for the Nixon-Thieu correspondence; Truong Nhu Tang with David Chanoff and Doan Van Toai, *A Vietcong Memoir* (1985), by a North Vietnam insider; Melvin Small, *Johnson, Nixon, and the Doves* (1988), quantitative evidence on the anti-war movement's influence; and Anthony Campagna, *The Economic Consequences of the Vietnam War* (1991).

Other specific topics and areas are analyzed in the following accounts. On Latin America, Stephen G. Rabe, *The Road to OPEC: U.S. Relations with Venezuela, 1919–1976* (1982), is standard on U.S.-Venezuela, most helpful on OPEC's rise; James E. Petras and Morris Morley's *The United States and Chile* (1975) remains a most powerful critical account; Seymour Hersh's *The Price of Power*, listed in the notes, which is detailed in condemning the Kissinger approach to Chile; William F. Sater, *Chile and the United States* (1990), for an overview; and John Dinges and Saul Landau, *Assassination on Embassy Row* (1980), the best account of the Letelier assassination and the Chilean government's (and some Americans') complicity in the event. On Canada, Charles F. Doran, *Forgotten Partnership: U.S.-Canada Relations Today* (1984), key on the oil-gas question; William Diebold, "Canada and the United States: Twenty-five Years of Economic Relations," *International Journal* 39 (Spring 1984). On the Middle East, see William R. Polk, *The Arab World*, 2nd ed. (1991), an overview with a useful bibliography; Seth P. Tillman, *The United States in the Middle East* (1982), an authoritative, critical analysis, especially good on Arab relations; Daniel Yergin, *The Prize* (1991), on the U.S., oil, and the Middle East; Steven L. Spiegel, *The Other Arab-Israeli Conflict* (1985), emphasizing U.S. domestic ideas and background; James W. Harper, "The Middle East, Oil, and the Third World," in *Modern American Diplomacy*, ed. John M. Carroll and George C. Herring (1986); Noam Chomsky, *The Fateful Triangle: The U.S., Israel, and the Palestinians* (1984), a provocative critique of U.S. policy toward the Palestinians. The *Mayagüez* crisis is analyzed in Richard G. Head, Frisco W. Short, and Robert G. McFarlane, *Crisis Resolution* (1978). On Africa, two good (and critical) overviews are Henry Jackson's *From the Congo to Soweto: U.S. Foreign Policy toward Africa since 1960* (1982) and Ali A. Mazrui's *Africa's International Relations* (1977).

The best overall view of the Ford presidency can be found in the Schulzinger, Korb, and Finger essays in *Gerald R. Ford and the Politics of Post-Watergate America*, 2 vols, ed. Bernard J. Firestone and Alexej Ugrinsky (1993).

19

Back to the Future:
The Carter-Reagan Years (1977–1988)

Jimmy Carter: The Search for a Foreign-Policy Consensus

By 1976, Americans had learned firsthand every day how their power had relatively declined since the 1950s. They could do little about having to pay Arab sheiks and other foreign producers four times more for gasoline. U.S. prices doubled between 1968 and 1978, not only driving up the cost of their groceries, but making their goods less competitive in the tough global marketplaces. Thousands of American workers faced unemployment in such old "rust belt" industries as steel and autos. Their nuclear forces continued to be superior to the Soviets, but Brezhnev was closing the gap, and, in any case, gaps meant little when a nuclear exchange could trigger nearly 50,000 warheads. Traditional cold-war alliances with western Europe and Japan were tattered. Many African and Latin American countries moved toward revolution. The strong and respected (if not always liked) presidency of Truman and Eisenhower collapsed into Nixon's forced resignation and Ford's confusion.

To reverse such a flow of history was like trying to change the flow of a great river. Jimmy Carter, who had been educated at the U.S. Naval Academy as an engineer, believed he could do it. After all, few had thought this little-known former governor of Georgia could win the White House. When he had told his mother that he was going to run for president, even she asked, "President of what?"[1] With brilliant organization, dogged work, and the message that he, as a Washington outsider, could best clean up the mess in the Capital, the Georgian had won it all. Carter was helped by Republican nominee Ford's major errors (in one televised debate, Ford even made the astounding remark that "no Soviet domination" of Poland existed), but the Georgian also made his share of mistakes. Perhaps the best known occurred when this born-again Baptist tried to win *Playboy* readers by telling the magazine that "I've committed adultery in my heart many times."[2] After losing a lead of thirty points in early public-opinion polls, Carter won by attacking Republican economic policy and by riding on the coattails of Democratic candidates running for the House and Senate.

Thus, from the start, the new president found himself in a weak position. Members of Congress owed him little. He had, moreover, run against the Washington power blocs. Now he found that he had to work with those blocs. He also discovered that the Democratic party was of little help. No "party loyalty or discipline" existed, Carter later wrote. "It was every member for himself, and the devil take the hindmost."[3] It was partly his own fault. His campaign had been too "Jimmyist" and not enough "Democratic," as one observer noted. But the president's dilemma also came from a long decline in political-party institutions—and their replacement by special-interest-group politics—that posed special dangers. In 1977, some political scientists grew so concerned that they held a rally at Washington's Jefferson Memorial and warned: "Our political party system, first inspired by Thomas Jefferson, is in serious danger of destruction. Without parties, there can be no organized and coherent politics. When politics lacks coherence, there can be no accountable democracy."[4]

Carter had won the election but now found that he had trouble governing effectively. The new president tried to help solve this dilemma by appointing as his top foreign-policy advisers two respected members of the New York–Washington "establishment." Cyrus Vance became secretary of state. A New York City lawyer, Vance had served with distinction at sub-cabinet positions in earlier Democratic administrations. A low-keyed, colorless, intelligent, and experienced diplomat, he concluded that the Nixon-Kissinger détente policy had collapsed because, by focusing so much on the Soviet Union and China, that policy had failed to understand, in Vance's words, "the explosive forces of change in the developing world." Problems in that world, he stressed, had to be dealt with "on their own terms and not through the prism of East-

West competition."[5] Vance had learned this the hard way: he had been involved in making Vietnam policy during the 1960s, when U.S. officials thought that they were dealing with Chinese or Soviet expansionism but were really facing Vietnamese nationalism. As far as the Kremlin was concerned, Vance emphasized arms control. Although human rights and economic relations were important, reducing nuclear arsenals was "a life or death" issue, in his words. It had to be handled by itself, not "linked," as many Americans wanted, to Soviet good behavior on human-rights questions or Third-World issues.

Carter named another New Yorker, Zbigniew Brzezinski of Columbia University, as the National Security Council director. The two had known each other since 1973, when Brzezinski and New York banker David Rockefeller set up the Trilateral Commission, a private group of American, western European, and Japanese businesspeople, officials, and academicians who, Rockefeller hoped, could coordinate the capitalist world's policies in the face of the newly emerging nations' challenges. Carter was brought into the commission as a representative southerner and soon considered Brzezinski "my teacher" in foreign policy.

Brzezinski differed with Vance over two key points. First, unlike the reserved secretary of state, the NSC director was brash, colorful, and happy to talk with reporters—much to the displeasure of Vance, who believed that he (Vance) should be the president's sole foreign-policy voice. Second, Brzezinski's gut response to foreign-policy difficulties often was to blame the Soviets. The son of a prewar Polish diplomat, his family had little love for Russians. He believed that the Soviet system was doomed to stagnation and was afraid that Kremlin leaders would try to save themselves through adventurism and expansion abroad. When problems erupted in Africa or Asia, therefore, he (unlike Vance) saw Moscow's hand at work and often urged direct military responses. Brzezinski became highly infatuated with China and the possibility of using the "China card" against the Soviets.[6] Vance thought this a bad bet. He already had suffered through one disaster in the 1960s, when Americans tried to pit Asians against Soviets.

JIMMY CARTER: THE SEARCH FOR A FOREIGN POLICY

As the final decision maker, Carter had placed himself between two men with quite different foreign-policy views. The president had little experience in overseas questions. He tried to decide policy through incredibly hard work (Brzezinski noted with amazement how Carter would turn a short briefing into an intense seven-hour session) and by mastering every detail. One experienced Washington observer believed that "Carter's an engineering officer" and, thus, has "to know how every single engine or pump works. . . . He looks upon government as machinery to be improved, to be lubricated."[7] This implied that Carter had no larger framework, no set of fundamental beliefs (such as Nixon's détente or Acheson's "positions-of-strength") that he could use to make decisions. He lacked "a historical memory," one official noted, that was needed to judge. Carter realized this weakness. In 1979, he told a reporter that he had read more history since becoming president than in all his earlier life.[8] But by then, it was too late.

As a result, he seemed to go in many directions at once. In the 1976 campaign, he condemned Kissinger as a "Lone Ranger" who acted without regard for Congress or allies. But Carter also consulted with few in Washington and handled western European and Japanese problems so inconsistently that the alliances were gravely weakened. He pledged to reduce expensive U.S. commitments to such peripheral (and increasingly wealthy) areas as South Korea; but after pulling out 6,000 troops, he reversed course and reaffirmed the commitment to South Korea. He promised to cut defense spending by $5 billion to $7 billion; but after six months in office, he moved to increase it. In a remarkable speech at the University of Notre Dame in 1977, Carter memorably said: "Being confident of our own future, we are now free of that inordinate fear of Communism which once led us to embrace any dictator who joined us in that fear." He asked instead that U.S. policies stress human-rights, environmental, and development issues, not simple anticommunism. Within twenty-four months, his own policy increasingly revolved around anticommunism. A veteran journalist wrote as early as February 1977 that Carter acted less like the captain of a ship of state than like a "frantic . . . white-water canoeist."[9]

The president tried to make his policies more coherent in two ways. First, he toyed with the Trilateral Commission approach. Besides Brzezinski and Vance, the president employed twenty other members (or nearly one-third of the entire U.S. membership on the commission) in his administration. After the trauma of Vietnam, Carter hoped that trilateralism would restore the confidence of American leaders and renew cooperation within the Western-Japanese capitalist community. But trilateralism proved an empty dream. As U.S. officials condemned Japan's huge $12 billion trade surplus with the United States, the Japanese belittled the Americans' refusal to save and make their economy

Time *magazine's cover of August 8, 1977, catches Jimmy Carter's early—and many—foreign-policy dilemmas. Clockwise from the lower left, the "lions" surrounding the pious Carter are Mao Zedong of China, Helmut Schmidt of West Germany, Leonid Brezhnev of the Soviet Union, Menachem Begin of Israel, and Anwar el-Sadat of Egypt. Note that some of the "lions" are eying each other (not Carter) for attack.*

more competitive. Some Americans responded by slitting tires on Japanese-made automobiles or by reverting to World War II racism in calling them "those little Yellow people," to use the words of one Michigan congressman. When the Japanese and West Germans most reluctantly agreed to try to help the sliding U.S. economy in 1977, the operation was termed Coordinated Reflation Action Program (or, appropriately, CRAP) and utterly failed. Each nation's domestic pressure groups prevented such international teamwork. West German chancellor Helmut Schmidt bluntly declared that the Americans had given up their economic leadership in the early 1970s, and he saw no one in New York or Washington "training for the job." Carter recorded privately that in a "bitter" discussion of economic issues, Schmidt "got personally abusive toward me."[10]

Trilateralism also came apart in the Middle East, where the United States tried to take a tough line against Arab oil producers and anti-Israeli forces. The Europeans and Japanese—who had great need for oil but had no Jewish political pressure groups at home—refused to follow Washington's line. Trilateralism collapsed as well in the handling of East-West issues. Carter dealt with Brezhnev bilaterally, using increasingly tough economic sanctions against the Soviets. The western Europeans, however, grew deathly afraid whenever Russians and Americans began talking alone behind closed doors. But both Europeans and Japanese continued their profitable trade with Moscow and refused to cut off the new financial arrangements (especially those for developing oil and gas fields) that they made with the Soviet bloc.

Most significantly, Americans and Europeans wrangled over nuclear defense. Since the 1950s, the Soviets, who could not hit the United States with precision, had aimed nuclear missiles at Europe to hold it hostage against a possible U.S. attack on the Soviet Union. Americans promised to defend Europe with U.S.-based missiles and, after 1962, with small "tactical" nuclear weapons in Europe itself. As Brezhnev's military closed the nuclear gap, however, western Europeans grew uneasy—especially West Germany, which was banned from having its own nuclear weapons. They were no longer certain that a U.S. president would defend Hamburg if it meant the obliteration of Chicago. Their unease grew in the mid-1970s, when Moscow began deploying 180 mobile, more precise SS-20 missiles, each with three independently targeted warheads aimed at Europe. Pressured at home and personally disdainful of Carter ("who knows everything and under stands nothing"), Chancellor Schmidt warned that European security was being undermined.

Carter responded in part by announcing that he would develop a neutron bomb. It could counter a Soviet conventional attack by killing people with radiation but not destroying property. A top German official called the bomb a "symbol of mental perversion," but Schmidt reluctantly promised to support Carter. The president then changed his mind and ditched the neutron bomb, apparently for moral reasons. Schmidt was furious. So were Washington hawks such as the Committee on the Present Danger, led by Paul Nitze, who warned that Carter's indecisiveness was giving the Soviets a nuclear advantage. The president then promised to install 572 Pershing II and ground-based cruise missiles in Europe to counter the SS-20s. These missiles had little effect on the military balance. The United States already had 7,000 tactical nuclear weapons in Europe; Carter made the commitment for political reasons—and especially to appease Schmidt. Massive antinuclear protests erupted in Europe in 1980–1981. To blunt the protests, Carter and other Western leaders announced that they would install the Pershing IIs but also open talks with the Soviets in the hope that the intermediate weapons on both sides would be mutually withdrawn. The withdrawal would not occur for a decade.

Long before, in early 1978, one U.S. official announced the obvious: "The trilateral idea is dead."[11] At its postwar low in 1973–1974, the Western alliance had sunk even lower by 1981.

Carter also attempted to give coherence to his foreign policies by declaring in his inaugural address that he had an "absolute" commitment to human rights. The president condemned the U.S. policy that supported "right-wing monarchs and military dictators" as long as they were anticommunist. (He doubtless had in mind Kissinger's backing of Chile's military rule and Africa's conservative white-minority governments.) By stressing "moral principles," he believed that repressive governments could be reformed before left-wing revolutionaries replaced them.[12] Carter concluded, moreover, that this emphasis could help restore Americans' confidence in their own idealism, which had been lost in the muck of Watergate and Vietnam. Congress approved. It had, indeed, begun demanding improved human rights in the Communist bloc and Third-World nations as early as 1973–1974. Brzezinski agreed because he saw that preaching human rights could put the Soviets on the defensive.

Carter appointed a talented, feisty human-rights activist, Pat Derian, as assistant secretary of state for human rights and humanitarian affairs. She worked near-miracles in pushing repressive military regimes in Argentina and Brazil toward democracy, but elsewhere her efforts often hit stone walls. Some of the walls were built by Carter himself. Demands that the South Korean dictatorship allow more human rights were largely silenced when the president realized that the demands might destabilize or alienate such a strategically located country. China's government regularly imprisoned dissidents. But instead of effectively protesting, Carter (at Brzezinski's urging) sent new technology to the Chinese. When El Salvador's military butchered opponents, Carter cut off military aid. The Salvadorans ignored him. When their regime was threatened by revolutionaries in 1980–1981, he turned aid back on despite evidence that four U.S. churchwomen had been raped and killed by Salvadoran military in 1980.

Carter's commitment to human rights was, therefore, not "absolute." "The real problem," a U.S. diplomat noted, "was that the human rights policy was not a policy but an attitude."[13] When the "attitude" threatened to undercut governments important to U.S. strategic or economic interests, it was dropped. Brzezinski, however, used the policy more consistently against the Soviets. When they jailed leading dissidents, the White House temporarily stopped the sale of computers to Moscow. The Soviets, who naïvely believed that Carter was using human rights only as a "bargaining chip" to obtain other concessions from them, became angry and condemned the policy as mere "propaganda." Such allies as West Germany and France also disapproved. They saw no profit intervening in Soviet internal affairs and disrupting their growing trade with the Soviet market.[14]

Carter never solved these contradictions in his trilateral and human-rights approaches. He did score two diplomatic triumphs, however, through hard work and by following Vance's advice to deal with the newly emerging world on its own terms.

A VICTORY: THE PANAMA CANAL TREATIES

Almost from the moment in 1903 that the United States claimed complete control over the Canal Zone that cut their country in half, Panamanians had tried to share, if not remove, that control. Their efforts intensified as U.S. officials established camps for training Latin American police and military, and built large air-force bases. Bloody anti-U.S. riots led Lyndon Johnson to take the first step toward sharing power in 1964–1967. Despite loud complaints (one conservative senator objected to having "a country with one-third the population of Chicago kick us around"), Henry Kissinger, in 1974, agreed in principle to transfer ultimate control of the canal to Panama. He realized that the great waterway, beautifully engineered and still durable, was also highly vulnerable to sabotage and other kinds of stoppages. It was also being bypassed by huge oil tankers and container ships that could not pass through the Canal locks and often did not need to use it anyway given alternative ship-train routes.

Carter had the political courage to complete the treaties in September 1977 and then push them through the Senate in the spring of 1978. He spent much of his small political capital in the effort—so much, some observers believed, that his influence over Congress, which was never great, became almost invisible. He won the fight despite bitter opposition of conservatives led by former California governor Ronald Reagan, who claimed that the treaty was "appeasement" and proved that the United States was collapsing like a corrupted ancient Roman Empire. Carter received strong support from other conservatives, including columnist William Buckley, Jr., and film star John Wayne, who regularly sailed his yacht in Panamanian waters. In addition, State Department officials spanned across the country on over 1,500 occasions to sell the treaties in an intense, nationwide debate.

The first treaty, which outlined U.S. rights after the year 2000, when Panama will assume control of the canal, passed with one vote to spare, 68 to 32, in early 1978. The second pact, stipulating how Panama was gradually to obtain authority over the waterway during the next twenty-two years, passed by the same vote. But the Senate accepted the agreements only after inserting a "reservation" proposed by Arizona Democrat Dennis DeConcini. It stated that if the canal were to close after 2000 for any reason, the United States had the right to intervene to open it. Panamanians rioted, and their government declared that it would never grant such a right. The Senate then rewrote the DeConcini reservation: the United States could intervene to keep the canal open, but Americans did not have the right of intervention.[15] With that wondrous word magic, both sides accepted the treaties. It had been the second-longest treaty debate in the Senate's history. But Carter and the Senate leadership had avoided more bloodshed and the possible closing of the canal. He scored the most significant victory in U.S.–Latin American relations since Franklin D. Roosevelt's good-neighbor policies four decades earlier.

A VICTORY: THE CAMP DAVID ACCORDS

The president pulled off an even more remarkable diplomatic feat in the Middle East. Kissinger's diplomacy had produced a delicate truce in 1975. That same year, however, Lebanon began to be torn apart by the terrorist acts of the Palestine Liberation Organization (PLO), which claimed to represent millions of homeless Palestinians. As the country fell apart, Syria (which received large amounts of Soviet supplies), Egypt, and Israel jockeyed dangerously for control of Lebanon. Meanwhile, PLO-Egyptian-Syrian fury grew as Israel's hard-line government of Menachem Begin consolidated its power over the Jordan River's West Bank, where the Palestinians hoped either to have their own homeland or settlements linked to Jordan. (See map, p. 727.)

Carter angered Begin by calling for a Palestinian homeland. Israel saw such a homeland on the West Bank as a grave threat to its existence, especially if that homeland came under PLO control. Carter then frightened Egypt's leader, Anwar el-Sadat, by agreeing with the Soviets to sponsor a Mideast peace initiative. Sadat was afraid that

Before the flags of the three nations, Jimmy Carter celebrated his greatest diplomatic triumph as president: Prime Minister Anwar el-Sadat of Egypt (at left) and Prime Minister Menachem Begin of Israel clasp hands after signing the Camp David Accords in September 1978.

Egypt would be isolated as the Soviets supported Syria and other Arab states while the United States backed Israel. In a dramatic and historic decision, Sadat personally flew to Israel and talked with Begin, whose nation Egypt had never fully recognized. Sadat's and Begin's refusal to deal with the Soviets undercut Carter's peace plan. The region then threatened to go up in flames when Begin sent troops into Lebanon to secure Israel's borders and destroy the PLO. Washington pressured the Israelis to retreat, but everyone feared another, greater explosion.

The President boldly—and desperately—invited Sadat and Begin to discuss a settlement at his Camp David retreat in Maryland. Both Israel and Egypt depended on U.S. aid, but Sadat also faced threats of retaliation by other Arab states if he gave away too much to the Israelis. Begin was restrained by his view of his nation's security needs, including the West Bank and Gaza. At different times, Carter prevented both men from walking out of the talks with threats of cutting aid or promises of more concessions (and sometimes even by holding long, quiet discussions about the Bible with Begin). In March 1979, Israel and Egypt signed their first peace agreement in history. Sadat agreed to recognize Israel's government; Begin pledged to turn the Sinai desert region over to Egypt. Carter and Sadat believed that they also had an Israeli pledge to freeze Jewish settlements on the West Bank and negotiate a deal on this explosive area. But Begin later denied that those vaguely worded provisions promised any such thing. He refused to retreat from the West Bank, and the issue continued to fester. The three men had, nevertheless, achieved a great deal, if perhaps not enough.

Defeat: Carter, Africa, and Andrew Young

Carter enjoyed a high point of his presidency in early 1979 with the Camp David Accords. His last two years in office were pockmarked by a series of devastating setbacks. He had not discovered how to stop the leakage of U.S. power or, especially, how to bring order to disorderly— even revolutionary—areas. Nor had he discovered how to reconcile Vance's and Brzezinski's differing policies.

African problems centered on two areas: the Horn (or the central eastern coast) and southern Africa. The Horn is a key strategic region controlling the Indian Ocean–Suez Canal route sailed by giant oil tankers. It encompasses five countries containing 70 million of the world's poorest people. Between 1974 and 1977, a Marxist regime had risen to power in Ethiopia. Neighboring Somalia saw the chance to seize disputed territory in the Ogaden desert region long held by Ethiopia. The Ethiopians turned to the Soviets, who airlifted in supplies and 13,000 Cuban troops. Somalia, holding the most valuable strategic location, asked for U.S. aid. Carter demanded that it first retreat from the Ogaden, which Somalia did. But guerrilla warfare and the Cubans remained. Brzezinski urged Carter to send a U.S. fleet to the area to tell the Soviets to pull out the Cubans or else U.S.-USSR arms talks would stop. Vance hotly disagreed. He wanted no such "linkage," and he was supported by the U.S. ambassador to the United Nations, Andrew Young, the highest-ranking black man in the administration and a close friend of the president. Carter dispatched NSC officer David Aaron to Ethiopia to stop a possible Ethiopian counterattack. (Aaron recalled that the Ethiopian leader, Mengistu Haile Mariam "kept lions, live lions, right under his office. Each time my voice rose to make a point, it was drowned by the roar of beasts beneath my feet. With my eyes glued to the floor, searching for a trap door, I almost missed his offhand assurance that Somalia would not be invaded.")[16] But nothing else worked out: the war continued; the Soviet-Cuban presence was

Andrew Young (1932–   ) served as Carter's ambassador to the United Nations until he was dismissed for talking with PLO representatives. A native of New Orleans, educated at Howard University, Young worked closely in the 1960s with Martin Luther King, Jr., and was notably successful in quietly negotiating agreements with the white power structure in cities that Dr. King pushed to desegregate. Eloquent, skilled in negotiations, Young brought strong black support to Carter's presidency and greatly improved U.S. relations with black African nations.

firmed up by a twenty-year USSR-Ethiopian alliance; and the episode further poisoned the superpower relationship.

Young did score some victories. Nigeria, an African power and the second largest exporter of oil to America, had refused to deal with Kissinger because of his Angolan policies (see p. 663). But the Nigerians cooperated with Young. The UN ambassador, however, could not persuade Carter to recognize the Angolan government, especially after Cuban troop strength rose to 20,000 to help the Angolans put down a rebellion. Nor could he toughen U.S. policy toward South Africa's white apartheid government. Carter's tongue-lashing of South Africa's human-rights abuses against the majority black population did not help the blacks, but did make the white South Africans determined not to help the president in handling other regional questions. Historian Thomas J. Noer has concluded that Carter's record "in southern Africa was one of naiveté and failure." By late 1979, Young was gone. He broke a U.S. policy of not dealing with the PLO in any manner when he met secretly with PLO observers at the UN. Protests, led by pro-Israeli voices, erupted. The protests sharpened because Young and TransAfrica (a leading black political action group in Washington) had pointedly condemned growing Israeli–South African relations. With Young forced out, Vance lost one of his most important allies in the battle against Brzezinski.[17]

DEFEAT: SOMOZA FALLS, SANDINISTAS RISE, SALVADORANS KILL

Proud of his Spanish-language ability and some trips south of the border, Carter hoped to pull U.S.–Latin American relations out of the quicksand of the previous decade. The 1977 treaties with Panama were a major step forward. Also in 1977, he and Fidel Castro agreed to thaw U.S.-Cuban ties by lifting some travel and economic restrictions. Diplomatic "Interests Sections" opened in Havana and Washington, although no formal diplomatic recognition occurred. By 1979, however, the relationship had again cooled, and Carter's policies turned sharply toward a renewed cold-war stance (as they had in Africa).

Most notably, the United States and Nicaragua were becoming deadly enemies. This seemed odd. Since the 1930s, the Somoza dynasty had made Nicaragua a warm friend of Washington's. But the Somozas also milked their country until they controlled its most profitable industries as well as 5 million acres of fine land (an area roughly equal to El Salvador). As the peasants and middle class lost out, revolutionaries taking their name from the martyred Augusto Sandino (see p. 360) began organizing with Castro's support in 1961. Originally consisting of only three men, the Sandinistas made little headway until Kennedy's Alliance for Progress sharpened class divisions, the government's response to a terrible 1972 earthquake revealed Anastasio ("Tacho") Somoza's incompetence and corruption, and several daring raids into the capital city of Managua demonstrated the power and rising popularity of several hundred Sandinistas. In early 1978, Tacho's troops foolishly gunned down Pedro Joaquín Chamorro, a respected newspaper publisher and Somoza critic. Working from a strong rural base, the Sandinistas expanded their authority. They were joined by moderate middle-class leaders who were sick of Somoza's greed, use of torture on political prisoners, and air bombing of barrios (slum areas) to root out Sandinista sympathizers. (See map, p. 722.)

Carter could not decide what to do. His top State Department experts urged the removal of Somoza. They wanted to install moderate leaders

In mid-June 1979, Bill Stewart, an ABC-TV reporter, was covering the Sandinista revolt in Nicaragua when troops of dictator Anastasio Somoza stopped him. Kneeling, he held his hands out to show he was unarmed, but the soldiers shot him in cold blood. They did not know that Stewart's colleagues were filming the atrocity. The pictures finally led many Americans to understand the nature of the Somoza regime and why the Sandinistas had waged a nearly twenty-year revolution that finally triumphed the following month. (Courtesy ABC News NYT Pictures)

before the revolutionaries seized power. That advice, however, was countered by Tacho's powerful friends in the U.S. Congress and Carter's hope that somehow elections could bring in a new, friendly regime. How legitimate elections could be held amid a revolution and after the Somozas had corrupted every balloting for thirty years was difficult to figure out. As usual, most people in the United States paid little attention and took Central America for granted. This began to change on June 20, 1979, when Somoza's troops seized an ABC-TV reporter, Bill Stewart, made him kneel in the street, then shot him in the head. The cold-blooded murder was captured on film by other reporters, and the scenes horrified U.S. viewers. (In the popular, important film, *Under Fire* [1983], actor Gene Hackman plays a reporter whose murder resembles Stewart's. In the film, Hackman's one-time lover, Joanna Cassidy, breaks down and cries. A Nicaraguan nurse reminds Cassidy that thousands of Nicaraguans had been murdered by the Somozas, then adds bitterly, "Maybe we should have killed an American journalist fifty years ago.") Carter nevertheless continued to equivocate, and as he did so, the Sandinistas launched their "final" offensive in May 1979. In June, Carter asked the Organization of American States to intervene and establish a moderate government. Not one Latin

American nation supported the U.S. plan. On July 19, the Sandinistas completed their "triumph" by marching into Managua. Tacho and his mistress escaped to Miami, then to Paraguay, where he was obliterated in a car bombing.[18]

About 50,000 Nicaraguans had died (equivalent to 4.5 million U.S. citizens), and Somoza had stolen nearly all of the national treasury. Carter moved to reconcile the Sandinistas by asking Congress to send $75 million in economic aid. Congress, however, refused to act on the request until spring 1980. The Sandinistas, meanwhile, looked for help (in health and educational as well as military aid) to Castro, who had long backed them. The new leaders also declared their independence in the cold war by refusing to vote for U.S. resolutions at the UN. They opened relations with western Europe, Canada, and the Soviet bloc. The Sandinistas held tightly to power. Promised elections were pushed back to 1984. Moderate leaders quit the government. Nicaragua was not a Communist nation; 60 percent of the economy remained in private hands, and the Roman Catholic church remained strong and loudly critical of the Sandinistas. But neither was the nation any longer an unquestioning friend of Washington's.

Next door, El Salvador threatened to follow in Nicaragua's revolutionary footsteps. Since the 1930s, the Salvadoran oligarchs (or "the fourteen families") had formed an alliance with the military to preserve their monopoly of Salvadoran wealth. In one of the region's richest and most efficient nations, 10 percent of the 4.6-million Salvadorans had to migrate to other countries to find land and food for survival. Eighty percent of children under five years of age suffered from serious malnutrition. A revolutionary movement took root in the 1960s, but the military had kept it in check with "death squads" that killed suspected critics. When Carter condemned the brutalities and cut off military aid, the Salvadorans went elsewhere for equipment. By 1979, however, five revolutionary groups expanded their control and formed the Farabundo Martí National Liberation Front (FMLN). More moderate military officers tried to institute reforms after seizing power in 1979, but the oligarchs and conservative military reasserted themselves. In 1980, José Napoleón Duarte, educated at the University of Notre Dame in Indiana, returned from exile to head the government. A moderate who had been tortured by the military in 1972, the popular Duarte now tried to stop both the FMLN on the Left and the death squads on the Right.

But he found himself depending on the military for his own survival. Death squads had murdered the archbishop of San Salvador while he was saying mass in March 1980 and, in December, raped and murdered four U.S. churchwomen. Carter cut off aid to Duarte. The rebels announced their own "final" offensive. Duarte appealed for help, and Carter now responded. The Salvadoran military stopped the FMLN drive. The war became a low-intensity struggle marked by incredible brutality. It wrecked the Salvadoran economy in a Central America that had suddenly become an arena for a new cold war.

DEFEAT: CARTER, THE SHAH, AND THE AYATOLLAH

By 1980, U.S. control of Central American affairs was at its lowest point in a century. U.S.-Iranian relations had also reached their nadir. Since the end of World War II, and especially since 1973, the ruling shah had been the central U.S. military and economic partner in the region. But he also alienated his own people by westernizing and overmilitarizing Iranian society. Powerful fundamentalist Shiite Moslems, led by their religious leaders, the ayatollahs, bitterly objected. The shah used force to keep the fundamentalists in line. After they tried to seize power in 1963, he exiled their leader, Ruhollah Khomeini, to Iraq and then Paris, where the shah hoped Khomeini would be forgotten. It was the shah, however, who had forgotten the wonders of telephones and audio cassettes, which Ayatollah Khomeini used to mobilize his millions of supporters. The shah had also forgotten an old saying: "Stepping on an ayatollah is like stepping on a Persian rug: it only increases in value."

The Iranian ruler was sitting on a powder keg. Two-thirds of the population was under age thirty; the urban settlements had quadrupled to 20 million after 1955; 15 percent of the nation tried to live around the capital of Tehran, where slums lacked proper sewage or water facilities; vast oil wealth was not trickling down, especially not to a restless student generation; and the government bureaucracy was bloated and corrupt. Even the military was losing status, despite the shah's squandering of $18 billion on arms purchases (mostly from the United States) between 1974 and 1978. As the Shiite leaders gained support, the shah's secret police, Savak, imprisoned 50,000 people.[19] Iranians flocked to the security and absolute beliefs of the ayatollahs for refuge.

Most U.S. officials knew or cared little about these changes. Accepting Brzezinski's awkward description of Iran as a "regional influential," the president said nothing about Savak's brutality and reaffirmed

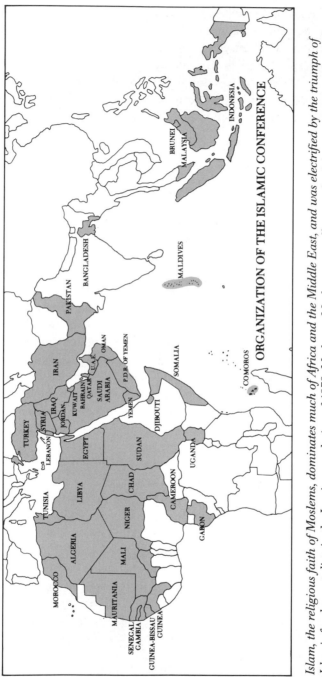

ORGANIZATION OF THE ISLAMIC CONFERENCE

Islam, the religious faith of Moslems, dominates much of Africa and the Middle East, and was electrified by the triumph of Islamic fundamentalists in the Iranian revolution of 1979. Moderate Moslems, as well as much of the rest of the world, worried that the fundamentalism might spread into neighboring states.

Richard Nixon's dedication to the shah. In a New Year's Eve toast in 1977, Carter praised the shah for making Iran "an island of stability" and also for "the admiration and love which your people give you."[20] U.S. intelligence agents had obeyed the shah's wishes that they maintain little contact with his opposition; so as strikes and street protests grew to fever pitch in 1978, neither the shah nor U.S. officials understood what was happening.

As his reign wobbled, the shah hesitated, in part because of growing ill-health from a cancer that had struck him in 1974. He especially feared ordering the Shiite-infiltrated military to fire on other Shiites. Carter also hesitated as his advisers were bitterly divided on the issue. Vance and the U.S. ambassador to Iran, William Sullivan, opposed any use of force. They wanted to work with the opposition to effect a transitional government. Brzezinski, however, opposed any deals with revolutionary religious fanatics. He urged working with the military to keep the shah in power. During the last days of the shah's rule, Carter told Sullivan to follow Brzezinski's plan. The ambassador wired back that the president of the United States must be "insane." The revolution had moved far past the point where Americans could set its course. In February 1979, the military made its deal with the ayatollahs, the shah fled, and the nearly eighty-year-old Khomeini took power.[21]

In mid-1979, the shah asked to enter the United States for treatment of his cancer. His close friends, Henry Kissinger and David Rockefeller, as well as Brzezinski, pressured Carter to approve the request. Carter prophetically observed that he "did not wish the Shah to be here playing tennis while Americans in Tehran were being kidnapped or even killed." But the president took pity and allowed the shah in.[22] Within a month, Khomeini's followers seized the U.S. Embassy in Tehran and held fifty-three Americans hostage. As the Iranians paraded and mocked the hostages before worldwide television, U.S. officials were helpless. American anger riveted on Khomeini, even to the point of creating ABC-TV's popular late-night program, "Nightline," originally aired to keep daily watch on the crisis. Allies condemned the seizure but refused to use force to free the Americans. Vance assured them that only negotiations, not force, would be employed. In April 1980, however, the cornered, frustrated Carter—in the middle of a bitter re-election campaign and urged on by Brzezinski—ordered a daring helicopter rescue of the hostages. Vance resigned. He was the first secretary of state to resign on a matter of principle in sixty-five years. On their way into Tehran, two helicopters had mechanical problems. Another hit a U.S. C-130 plane and crashed in the Iranian desert. Eight Americans perished. The Iranians displayed the burned corpses for television. Khomeini finally released the hostages on January 20, 1981, and timed the release so it occurred several minutes after Carter left office. After thirty-five years, U.S. influence over a pivotal Middle East nation had ended.

Iran's turmoil drove up the price of oil 60 percent in 1979. U.S. infla-.tion, running at a dangerous 7 percent annual rate since 1975, nearly doubled to 13 percent. The world economy threatened to spin out of control as oil-poor nations went ever-deeper in debt. Amid this chaos, Carter found himself at flashpoint with the Soviets.

DEFEAT: CARTER, SALT II, AND AFGHANISTAN

That crisis did not come out of the blue. Both Brezhnev's aged regime and the Soviet economy were slowing down like an unwound clock. Soviet economic growth had sunk toward an actual 0 percent in 1979–1980. Brezhnev suffered foreign-policy reverses in relations with southern Asia and especially China and the Middle East. The appearance of the violently anti-Communist Khomeini on their boundary must have given top Moscow officials very long nights, especially as religious fundamentalism threatened to infect the large Moslem population inside the Soviet Union. Communism produced no new ideas to deal with these problems. One Soviet scholar believed, "You can read any book [on ideology] in 20 minutes" because it merely repeated all other books on the subject. The Soviets, however, did excel at building military equipment and space programs. "This place is like a banana republic," a U.S. journalist declared privately in Moscow, "but this one can incinerate us."[23]

Carter and Brezhnev had hoped to expand détente. But the president's human-rights policy defending Soviet dissidents and Moscow's involvement in Angola and Ethiopia had stalled the relationship. In 1977, moreover, Carter, pushed by Brzezinski and other "hawks," tried to go beyond the SALT II agreement made by Brezhnev and Gerald Ford in 1975. Carter's proposal to reduce nuclear weapons was mostly aimed at reducing the heaviest missiles (on which Soviet forces relied), and Brezhnev bitterly rejected the deal. As tempers cooled, Brzezinski again seized the initiative and persuaded Carter to establish formal diplomatic relations with China, now the Soviet Union's archenemy. Over Vance's objections about the timing, Carter did so on New Year's Day, 1979. A new trade agreement gave China economic privileges not granted the Soviets, and Sino-American trade boomed to $4 billion in 1980 (with three-fourths being profitable U.S. exports).

Both leaders, however, needed a new SALT deal—Brezhnev for economic reasons, Carter for a badly needed political push toward the 1980 elections. At the Vienna summit in June 1979, they struck a SALT agreement. It capped strategic nuclear launchers at 2,400 (with a future reduction to 2,250), and no more than 1,320 were to be MIRVed. To help obtain the U.S. Senate's consent, Brezhnev allowed 50,000 Jews—the highest number ever—to leave the Soviet Union in 1979. But the United States did not respond cooperatively. U.S. officials refused to give Moscow the same trade privileges that they had just given Beijing (Peking). More important, SALT II came under scathing attack. Led by the Committee on the Present Danger and its best-known spokesman, Paul Nitze, the opponents warned that the treaty allowed the Soviets to keep 300 missiles and warheads that were much larger than the Americans' weapons. Defenders of the deal, led by Carter's arms negotiator, Paul Warnke, responded that only the treaty's limits on numbers of actual warheads could prevent the Soviets from using their big missiles as Nitze feared. Such arguments as Nitze's convinced the Senate to move slowly in debating SALT II.[24]

The formal debate, indeed, never occurred. On December 25–27, 1979, 80,000 Soviet troops invaded neighboring Afghanistan. Soviet influence had long been dominant there, but the fiercely independent 14 million Moslems who lived in the mountainous country the size of Texas had no intention of becoming another Bulgaria. A coup in 1973 and another in 1978 threw into turmoil the pro-Communist faction that ruled the country. Soviet involvement rapidly grew. When U.S. ambassador Adolph Dubs was kidnapped by rebels in 1978, Afghan forces, advised by Soviet officers, killed Dubs in an attack on the kidnappers. Washington strongly protested to Moscow. But neither the Afghan regime nor Brezhnev's officials could restore order. In the later view of both Vance and Brzezinski, the Soviets had probably concluded by this time that they had more to gain in Afghanistan than in the rapidly souring U.S.-USSR relationship.[25] When Red Army troops finally invaded Afghanistan, Brezhnev claimed that the Afghan leader, Hafizullah Amin, had invited them in. But they quickly killed Amin and tried to overrun the country. The Russians ran straight into a fanatical Islamic resistance of the mujahedeen, Afghan peasant fighters who were as brutal as they were effective. Soon, 115,000 Soviet troops found themselves enmeshed in a costly war that could not be won.

U.S. IMPORT DEPENDENCE AND IMPORT SOURCES IN THE 1970s
(1977 estimates except where noted)

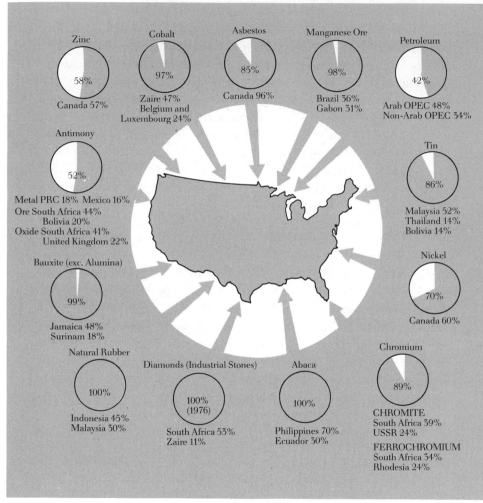

Zinc
58%
Canada 57%

Cobalt
97%
Zaire 47%
Belgium and
Luxembourg 24%

Asbestos
85%
Canada 96%

Manganese Ore
98%
Brazil 36%
Gabon 31%

Petroleum
42%
Arab OPEC 48%
Non-Arab OPEC 34%

Antimony
52%
Metal PRC 18% Mexico 16%
Ore South Africa 44%
Bolivia 20%
Oxide South Africa 41%
United Kingdom 22%

Tin
86%
Malaysia 52%
Thailand 14%
Bolivia 14%

Bauxite (exc. Alumina)
99%
Jamaica 48%
Surinam 18%

Nickel
70%
Canada 60%

Natural Rubber
100%
Indonesia 45%
Malaysia 30%

Diamonds (Industrial Stones)
100%
(1976)
South Africa 53%
Zaire 11%

Abaca
100%
Philippines 70%
Ecuador 30%

Chromium
89%
CHROMITE
South Africa 39%
USSR 24%

FERROCHROMIUM
South Africa 34%
Rhodesia 24%

Source: U.S. State Department, *The Trade Debate* (May 1978).

THE CARTER RESPONSE AND DEFEAT (1980)

The president declared that the invasion was "the gravest threat to
peace" since 1945. It was estimated that the Soviets had used military
force as an instrument of foreign policy at least 190 times since 1945.
(The same estimate concluded that the United States had done so on
over 200 occasions.)[26] But now Soviet forces had actually moved beyond

the boundaries established between 1944 and 1948. Carter struck back by shutting off grain and high-tech exports that had been flooding into the Soviet Union. He ordered young men to register for a military draft and requested that U.S. athletes not participate in the 1980 Summer Olympic Games in Moscow.

Most dramatically, in his January 1980 State of the Union Address, he announced a Carter Doctrine: "An attempt by any outside force to gain control of the Persian Gulf region" would "be repelled by any means necessary, including military force." Brzezinski helped convince Carter to follow this policy by emphasizing that it would be modeled on the historic 1947 Truman Doctrine—a doctrine that had long enjoyed almost automatic support from Americans (see p. 476). Critics such as Richard Betts warned that the similarity was slight and, above all, that Carter, unlike Truman, might have to reach "for the nuclear crutch" even as Nitze and others warned of a growing U.S. inferiority.[27] U.S. military and medical aid, nevertheless, began flowing directly to the Afghan rebels.[28]

Carter now seemed to abandon any idea of military parity with the Soviets. He wanted to obtain superiority: "The United States will remain the strongest of all nations." Even earlier, he had made a pivotal decision to produce and deploy the MX, a new and supposedly more accurate intercontinental missile with ten warheads, and to protect the new weapons by placing them on two hundred huge "race tracks" around which they would continually move so that the Soviets could not have a fixed-site target. And even while he was asking the Senate to accept SALT II, he was also asking approval for the largest new U.S. weapons program in nearly thirty years. In 1980, he signed Presidential Directive 59, drawn up mainly by Brzezinski and Defense Secretary Harold Brown. PD-59 planned to give U.S. officials the massive arms needed to fight a controlled, prolonged nuclear war and to win the exchange on every level of escalation that would probably occur over a period of months, not days or hours. After cutting $36 billion in domestic spending, Carter added $47 billion in new weapons systems. The Pentagon budget jumped from $170 billion in 1976 to $197 billion in 1981 (in 1986 dollars). To buck up both the allies and the stumbling U.S. economy, Carter also nearly doubled arms sales between 1977 and 1980 to $15.3 billion. Historian Gaddis Smith calls Carter's policies of 1979–1980 the "return to militarism."[29]

Carter's defense budgets formed the roots of Ronald Reagan's policies in the 1980s. But that did not save Carter from scathing attack. Allies in western Europe and Japan continued their rich trade with the

Soviets and ignored Carter's pleas for economic sanctions. Argentine and Canadian wheat farmers sold to the Soviet Union the wheat it needed. As U.S. farmers and companies lost direct access to USSR markets, George Shultz (once Nixon's Treasury secretary and soon to be Reagan's secretary of state), damned Carter for "light switch" diplomacy that made international trade so unpredictable. By mid-1980, in a public-opinion poll, 75 percent of Americans gave Carter an overall negative rating, and 82 percent disliked his foreign-policy record. Much of this anger came from his handling of Iran, but it also arose from his decision to allow into the country 100,000 Cuban refugees—a decision that especially infuriated American blacks, Hispanics, and southerners, who were having economic troubles of their own. The president, one politician declared, "couldn't get the Pledge of Allegiance through Congress."[30]

Historian Burton Kaufman summarized Carter's position in 1980: "His domestic and foreign policies were largely in ruin; the economy seemed incurable; the hostage crisis was dragging on with no end in sight; major differences had surfaced between the United States and its allies over Iran and Afghanistan; a Congress controlled by his own party had rebuked him; . . . and he had the lowest approval rating of any president ever." *Business Week* drew a conclusion: The "Pax Americana that shaped modern history since World War II is fast disintegrating. . . . Even America's closest allies in Europe and Asia are now its fiercest competitors."[31]

REAGAN

The Republican presidential nominee in 1980, Ronald Reagan—former movie actor and California governor—rode Carter's troubles and the nation's pessimism to victory. Americans must ask themselves, Reagan declared, "Is the United States stronger and more respected than it was 3½ years ago? Is the world today a safer place in which to live?"[32] He not only captured the White House, but, for the first time in twenty-eight years, Republicans gained control of the Senate (although not the House).

Reagan's triumph had many sources. The politics of key Western nations (especially Great Britain and West Germany) responded to the shocks of the 1970s by polarizing between Right and Left, and then giving majorities to the Right. Many in the United States especially were alienated by the results of the counterculture and Great Society programs of the 1960s. Such experiences had caused "a social-political hangover," one prominent left-wing critic argued in 1980.[33] To regain their confidence that the nation had a unique role to play in world affairs (the need for "a new Wilsonianism," as one Reaganite referred to the revival of Woodrow Wilson's old dreams), Americans supported much larger military budgets and more CIA operations.[34]

Many observers considered Reagan dangerous. He knew little about foreign policy and seemed lazy and easily confused. He introduced Liberia's head of state, Samuel Doe, as "Chairman Moe." He had little curiosity or apparently little interest in mastering details. The respected journalist, Lou Cannon, who had followed Reagan since the 1960s, wrote that no one could recall when the president had last read a book. He cited Reagan's own joke: "It's true hard work never killed anybody, but I figure, why take the chance?" No one, however, denied the president's talent in keeping his several central beliefs before Americans, and his political brilliance and determination in making them accept his ideas. With "strength, patriotism, and charm," Cannon noted in 1987, Reagan "remains . . . secure in his convictions as well as his ignorance."[35]

Some of these convictions produced serious problems. As a television pitchman for General Electric in the 1950s, Reagan had a standard speech that warned of "encroaching government control." His hero became Calvin Coolidge, who cut income taxes in the 1920s. But Reagan also intended to increase military spending sharply and to impose a conservative social agenda. One result was that the government's debt rose by more than $1 trillion between 1981 and 1987 (or more debt in 6 years than the U.S. government had accumulated during the previous 190 years). Another result, in the *Washington Post*'s words, was a "steady infiltration of the Defense Department into U.S. factories and laboratories." Research programs in many industries and universities increasingly depended on the national government to give thumbs up to their requests.[36] The government's share of the gross national product rose, not fell.

Nevertheless, Reagan's popularity remained high. He knew he was going to succeed, he told a reporter in 1980, "for one simple reason. . . . The American people want somebody in command." Moreover, he believed he knew one way to command. Once, he recalled, he believed because he was "only an actor" he could not be a politician. Now he wondered "how you could be President and not be an actor." Since the time of John F. Kennedy, Hollywood's illusions and Washington's politics had seemed to be converging. In Reagan's presidency, they met. They would never again be easily separated.[37]

THE REAGAN FOREIGN-POLICY STRUCTURE: FOUR CORNERSTONES

The first cornerstone of Reagan's overseas policies rested on his insight that Americans wanted someone who appeared to be in command. Extending presidential powers to the fullest, he swamped the imperial Congress of 1973 to 1980 with a revived imperial presidency. As an accomplished actor, he did this by using his considerable talents on television and radio. But he also gained power by defining U.S. policies in military terms (in which case he could use his constitutional commander-in-chief authority) rather than in economic terms. As the military budget soared, economic foreign aid dropped. Congress seldom fought back successfully, even though public opinion on such issues as arms talks and Central American policy often supported congressional positions. Congress was too fragmented, its members too frightened of being fingered by Reagan as the villains if their alternative policies did not work out. When a presidential spokeswoman claimed that "there are some in Congress who would actually welcome a Marxist victory in El Salvador," she was revealing not the truth, but a well-tested tactic that pushed frightened fence-sitters in Congress over to the president's side. Like his predecessors, Reagan refused to recognize the restraints placed on him by the 1973 War Powers Act (see p. 666). In 1983, the Supreme Court helped him by issuing a decision that declared unconstitutional one of those congressional restraints.[38]

A second cornerstone of his foreign policies was an ardent, outspoken anticommunism that focused on Soviet power. Since at least 1917— and especially since the Truman Doctrine of 1947—anticommunism had been a most potent political medicine when presidents spooned it out in large doses. If that medicine had lost some of its punch during Nixon's détente years, it had regained its strength in 1978–1981. Reagan went further than any recent president in administering it. In a 1980 interview, he declared that "the Soviet Union underlies all the unrest that is going on. If they weren't engaged in this game of dominoes, there wouldn't be any hot spots in the world." In his first presidential press conference, he said that Moscow rulers reserved "the right to commit any crime, to lie, to cheat." He later told a West Point audi-

"I DIDN'T REALIZE HE'D HAVE SUCH A COMPREHENSIVE
APPROACH TO FOREIGN AFFAIRS"

During the President's first term in office, Washington Post *cartoonist "Herblock" (Herbert Block) caught President Ronald Reagan's single-minded focus on fighting and destroying the "evil empire," as Reagan called the Soviet Union. The second term was to be quite different.*

ence that the Soviet Union was "an evil force" and repeated to a Christian fundamentalist gathering that the Soviets were "the focus of evil in the modern world . . . an evil empire."[39]

Until 1982, Reagan also defined China as an enemy of the United States. He opposed talks with Beijing (Peking) and condemned Nixon and Carter for moving closer to China or for implying that the Chinese should have something to say about Taiwan's fate. Reagan had to retreat from this position by 1983, however. U.S.-Soviet relations were so bad, and the American need for Chinese cooperation and markets so great, that he swallowed his earlier words and traveled to the People's Republic in 1984 to strengthen U.S.-Chinese ties. His anticommunism thus focused on the Soviets. The highly popular *Rambo* movies captured the moment as the make-believe hero single-handedly, and with the use of awesome fire power, destroys Communists (especially in Vietnam) who are backed by the Soviets. The Soviets responded with their own Rambo, a Soviet commando leader in the highly popular film, *Solo Voyage,* who stops a group of supersecret and slightly crazy U.S. agents from starting a nuclear war between the two superpowers. Neither side lacked imagination in defining the other side as evil or in making money from such work.

A third cornerstone was a distinction between "authoritarian" governments (which Reagan supported in South Africa, the Philippines, and Argentina) and "totalitarian" regimes (which he opposed in the Soviet Union and China). The distinction had been drawn for him by Jeane J. Kirkpatrick in a 1979 essay, and it led to her appointment as the U.S. ambassador to the UN in 1981. Kirkpatrick argued that although "authoritarians" suppressed freedoms in the political area, they were stable, had demonstrated the possibility of evolving into more democratic regimes, kept their economy open to foreign investors, and usually supported the United States. "Totalitarians," however, were Communists (or Fascists), demonstrated little likelihood of becoming more democratic, hated American-style capitalism, and opposed U.S. interests. If Jimmy Carter had acted on these insights, Ambassador Kirkpatrick believed, he would have kept the shah of Iran and the Somoza dictatorship in Nicaragua in power. Her neat formula allowed Reagan to support right-wing systems and oppose those on the Left. It also allowed him to reverse Carter's human-rights policies. Carter had stressed the sanctity of human life and freedom from starvation and torture. Reagan said that he also supported human rights, but he meant such political freedoms as the right to vote in elections. Authoritarian regimes were often glad to allow meaningless votes, but they had not wanted to listen to Carter's protests about the mistreatment of their people.

Kirkpatrick's distinction, however, soon appeared to have fatal problems. In 1982, "authoritarian" Argentina (whose military leaders she strongly supported) attacked the nearby Falkland Islands (or Malvinas), which Great Britain had colonized in 1830. To her dismay, Reagan decided to work with the closer and more democratic British ally, which did succeed in holding on to the islands. Contrary to her formula, moreover, U.S. officials discovered that it was necessary to work more closely with totalitarian China. And when authoritarian regimes in the Philippines and Haiti began to topple, Reagan at first tried to shore them up and then—despite Kirkpatrick's warnings—followed the advice of Secretary of State George Shultz and helped both countries remove the authoritarian rulers in an effort to create more represen-

President Ronald Reagan (1911–) was educated at Eureka College in Illinois, broadcast Chicago Cubs baseball games, became a notable Hollywood actor, served as governor of California, and then won the presidency in 1980. In this photo, the new president visits the United Nations to introduce his closest for- eign-policy advisers who are standing behind him: (from left) Jeane Kirkpatrick (1926–), U.S. ambassador to the UN; Mrs. and Secretary of State Alexander Haig (1924–); Nancy Reagan (1923–).

tative and stable regimes. By 1985, Kirkpatrick's ideology had proven to be both unworkable and unpopular, especially because it placed U.S. support behind some of the world's most oppressive rulers in South Africa, the Philippines, and Latin America.[40]

The final cornerstone of the Reagan foreign policies was the most obvious and, in dollar terms, most costly. He pledged to "rearm" the United States by jacking up military spending over five years from Carter's projection of $1.1 trillion to $1.5 trillion. The plans included a massive nuclear build-up that threatened to destroy the limits set in 1979 by Carter's and Brezhnev's SALT II agreement. The administra- tion also planned to create a 600-ship navy that revolved around 13 to 15 aircraft-carrier battle groups. The navy, which would be of little use in all-out war with the Soviets, was clearly being planned for actions in the newly emerging nations. The fleet, along with expensive Rapid Deployment Forces, was particularly aimed at winning low-intensity conflicts (or LICs) in such Third-World regions as Central America and the Middle East. In the words of one leading study by Michael T. Klare and Peter Kornbluh, the new forces and the LIC plans represented "a strategic reorientation of the U.S. military establishment, and a renewed commitment to employ force" against "Third World revolutionary movements and governments."[41]

Reagan increased military spending 40 percent between 1980 and 1984, while cutting taxes. He had also promised to balance the budget, a claim that his 1980 Republican rival and later vice-president, George Bush, had called "voodoo economics." But Bush was proved correct as the administration's spending fastened the trillion dollars of debt on the country. That spending, moreover, came under sharp questioning by 1984–1985, as the Central Intelligence Agency admitted that it had far overestimated Soviet defense expenditures after 1976. It also became clear that even when Carter had left office in 1981, the United States was the equal of—and usually superior to—the Soviets in nearly every important defense category.[42]

By 1985, defense spending finally slowed, but resources were also being shifted to high-cost research for the president's Strategic Defense Initiative (SDI or Star Wars, as some critics derided it). Announced in a surprise presidential speech of March 1983, Reagan hoped that SDI would be a space-based defense system forming a high-tech defensive shield over Americans and their allies against incoming missiles. Defense Secretary Caspar Weinberger revealed a major objective of SDI (and, indeed, a major reason for the entire defense build-up): a hope that Americans could return to the more secure days of the 1940s, when they had absolute nuclear superiority. "If we can get a system which is effective and which we know can render their weapons impotent," he told Congress, "we would be back in the situation we were in, for example, when we were the only nation with the nuclear weapon and we did not threaten others with it."[43]

Critics of SDI argued that such absolute security could never be scientifically achieved. Nor did they believe that Americans wanted their existence turned over to hair-trigger, novel computers that would have to operate Star Wars just seconds after a supposed Soviet attack. Many feared that if one side mounted a defensive shield, the other side would plan simply to overwhelm it with vast numbers of missiles—a planned response that could set off a limitless arms race. Others drew back when they concluded that the massive military spending distorted the economy and made U.S. goods less competitive in the world marketplace. Many Americans were especially dismayed that Reaganites seemed to treat even nuclear war lightly. T. K. Jones, a Defense Department official, declared that if such a war broke out, Americans only had to "dig a hole, cover it with a couple of doors, and then throw three feet of dirt on top. . . . If there are enough shovels to go around," he believed, "everybody's going to make it." But even the president sometimes seemed confused about the protection that SDI would provide for its $1-trillion cost: "My concept of the strategic defense system has been one that, if and when we finally achieve what our goal is, and that is a weapon that is effective against incoming missiles, not a weapon system that is effective against incoming weapons, missiles."[44] Or so the president said in 1985.

THE GREAT DEBATE OVER THE USE OF FORCE

Perhaps, then, it was not surprising that the military build-up produced bitter debates inside as well as outside the administration. The most important erupted between Weinberger and Shultz. The secretary of defense spoke for the U.S. military that certainly wanted more modern weapons. But the military also wanted no more involvements such as Vietnam, which had nearly destroyed the morale of, and public trust in, the military. In a November 1984 speech, Weinberger consequently asked that U.S. forces not be sent into conflict unless six criteria were met: (1) the war was vital for U.S. or alliance interests; (2) it was to be fought "wholeheartedly, and with the clear intention of winning"; (3) objectives were to be clearly defined; (4) reassessments of the commitment were constantly to be made; (5) popular and congressional support of the commitment were reasonably certain; and (6) use of arms was the last resort to protect U.S. interests.

Secretary of State Shultz attacked such thinking. Believing that "diplomacy not backed by military strength is ineffectual," he warned that at critical moments, foreign policy might require quick military action without the six assurances. Indeed, such moments had already arisen in 1982 when Shultz persuaded Reagan to back U.S. policy with force in the Middle East, and in 1983 when the administration overthrew the government on the Caribbean island of Grenada. In both instances, the Pentagon was reluctant to commit forces, much to Shultz's frustration. On the other hand, the two secretaries also clashed over arms talks with the Soviets. Weinberger feared such talks. He preferred trying to outspend and outarm the Soviets. Shultz, however, pushed hard after 1983 for a deal to reduce nuclear arms. He believed

Secretary of Defense Caspar Weinberger (1917–   ) and Secretary of State George Shultz (1920–   ) are shown here briefing the press in 1986 after the U.S. raid in Libya. The two men were not always this close. Indeed, after Shultz replaced Haig as secretary of state in mid-1982, he and Weinberger often strongly disagreed over foreign policy. When Weinberger resigned in 1987, Shultz had become the most powerful foreign-policy official in the Reagan administration.

that such an agreement would reassure allies who feared the nuclear build-up and would also cut some defense spending. The two men never resolved their differences. Weinberger resigned in 1987 before he had to support a treaty, negotiated by Shultz, that eliminated the U.S. and Soviet intermediate-range missiles stationed in Europe. The president joked that "sometimes in our administration, the right hand doesn't know what the far-right hand is doing."[45]

The debate over whether and how the United States should use military force naturally used the Vietnam War as a reference point. Reagan and others who wanted to use force condemned the preoccupation with the Vietnam defeat. This fundamental, historic debate was, as usual, reflected in films. In 1968, *The Green Berets,* starring John Wayne, had shown a Vietnam conflict that more resembled the so-called "good war" of 1941–1945 than the actual savage, complex struggle then occurring in Southeast Asia. By the mid-1980s, however, a series of films, led by *Apocalypse Now, The Deer Hunter, Coming Home, Platoon,* and *Full Metal Jacket,* among others, showed the horror, brutalities, and personal consequences of the U.S. involvement in Vietnam. Unfortunately, these films were notably weak in picturing Vietnam and Vietnamese. They viewed the war narrowly as about people and values in the United States, while usually ignoring the millions of people in Vietnam who had perished in the thirty-year conflict. But within their narrower focus, many popular films for the first time began to raise questions about the use of U.S. power abroad—and the price that might have to be paid at home.[46]

SHIFTING SANDS: THE ECONOMY

Historian Paul Kennedy noted an especially disturbing result of the arms build-up when he traced the rise and inevitable decline of empires over the past five hundred years: "Great Powers in relative decline instinctively respond by spending more on security, thereby diverting potential resources from investment and compounding their long-term dilemma."[47] That insight applied to the relative decline of both U.S. and Soviet economic power in the 1970s and 1980s. But it seemed especially ominous for the future of the U.S. system and the international capitalist order to which it had given birth after 1945.

Even as the stock market soared between 1982 and 1987, Americans found their economy shifting beneath them in dangerous, even historic, ways. For fifteen of the sixteen years between 1970 and 1986, they suffered trade deficits (that is, they bought more goods from abroad than they sold abroad). This development was historic because between 1894 and 1971 they had always sold more than they bought from other nations. (See the graph on p. 645.) Nevertheless, until 1981, this dangerous trend was disguised because U.S. investments overseas (in foreign businesses, stocks, and branches of U.S. corporations) had produced so much income that it helped wipe out the merchandise trade problem.

But in 1981, that changed. As the Reagan budget deficits climbed to an unheard-of $200 billion each year, Americans had to borrow from foreigners to pay for the deficit. By 1985, their borrowing, especially from the Japanese and western Europeans, became so heavy that, for the first time since 1914, Americans actually owed more money overseas than they were owed from abroad. After seventy-one years, they had become a debtor nation—like Mexico, Brazil, and many Third-

World countries. Indeed, by 1988, they had borrowed until they owed more than $400 billion to foreign lenders and were the world's most indebted people. "It will be recorded of us in the 1980s," New York Democratic Senator Daniel Patrick Moynihan wrote, that "America borrowed a trillion dollars from the Japanese and gave a party." The nation's top banker, Paul Volcker, chairman of the Federal Reserve Board, warned that "we are obviously in danger of losing control over our own economic destiny." As the U.S. domestic debt soared toward another trillion dollars in the 1990s, young Americans faced a lifetime of paying Japanese and other non-U.S. creditors, while cutting back not only on their own spending, but on spending for their national defense.[48]

This washing away of the economy had many causes. Americans spent far more than Japanese and western Europeans on military power (in part, to defend the Japanese and western Europeans), and so had less to spend on improving their civilian productivity. Americans only saved about one-third as much as did Japanese, so Japan had more money for new investment (and for investment in land, factories, and apartment houses in the United States). Reagan slashed taxes in 1981, supposedly so Americans could save more, but they instead spent more on themselves while their savings rate dipped 25 percent. For 350 years, farm exports had been the backbone of U.S. trade. But those exports sank from $43.7 billion in 1981 to $26.3 billion in 1986. Foreign buyers were too deeply in debt themselves or working hard to become self-sufficient in food to buy American goods. The United States could no longer compete in key sectors of the world economy.

Reagan tried to stimulate the economy in part by reducing trade barriers between the United States and Canada, who were already the world's largest trading partners. He envisioned a massive free-trade community of Canada, the United States, and Mexico. He finally signed a preliminary agreement with Canada in 1987, and in 1989 a giant free-trade area of the United States and Canada began to take shape. Nevertheless, bitter debate erupted on both sides of the border over the question of whether all North America and Mexico would become a giant common market.[49]

The Reagan military plans became a prime target for those who hoped to discipline spending. The Pentagon budget was reduced in real dollars during the later 1980s. In the words of Alexander Haig, who in 1981–June 1982 had been Reagan's first secretary of state, "This administration threatens in eight years to be the largest defense spender and the largest defense cutter simultaneously, and that's the worst kind

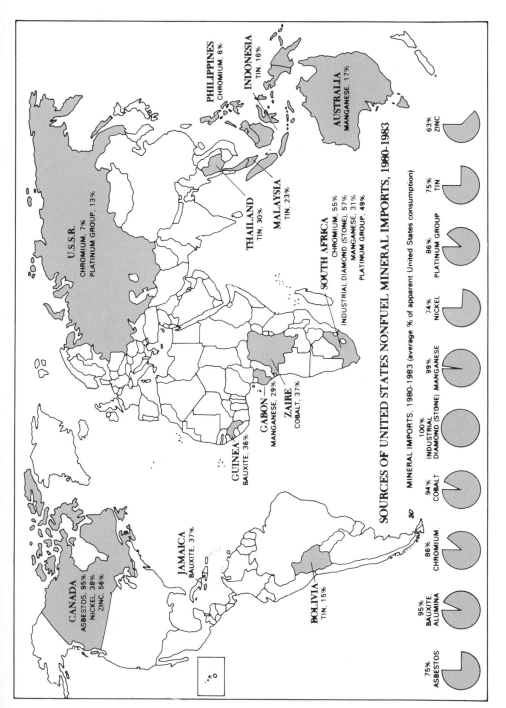

SOURCES OF UNITED STATES NONFUEL MINERAL IMPORTS, 1980–1983

PHILIPPINES
CHROMIUM, 6%

INDONESIA
TIN, 16%

AUSTRALIA
MANGANESE, 17%

U.S.S.R.
CHROMIUM, 7%
PLATINUM GROUP, 13%

THAILAND
TIN, 30%

MALAYSIA
TIN, 23%

SOUTH AFRICA
CHROMIUM, 55%
INDUSTRIAL DIAMOND (STONE), 57%
MANGANESE, 31%
PLATINUM GROUP, 49%

GABON
MANGANESE, 29%

ZAIRE
COBALT, 37%

GUINEA
BAUXITE, 36%

JAMAICA
BAUXITE, 37%

BOLIVIA
TIN, 15%

CANADA
ASBESTOS, 95%
NICKEL, 38%
ZINC, 56%

MINERAL IMPORTS, 1980–1983 (average % of apparent United States consumption)

63% ZINC

75% TIN

86% PLATINUM GROUP

74% NICKEL

99% MANGANESE

100% INDUSTRIAL DIAMOND (STONE)

94% COBALT

86% CHROMIUM

95% BAUXITE, ALUMINA

75% ASBESTOS

By the 1980s, Americans were heavily dependent on other nations for the essential minerals that made the U.S. economy go. Note especially the American dependence on minerals from South Africa and the Soviet Union.

of defense policy there is." Nevertheless, military spending remained near $300 billion. The Defense Department was the nation's largest purchaser of goods and services. It employed one-quarter of American scientists and engineers. An "iron triangle" of the Pentagon, defense industries, and members of Congress whose constituents depended on military spending kept arms budgets at near-record levels despite the cuts and the effects on the economy.[50]

THE SUPERSTRUCTURE: THE REAGAN DOCTRINE (OR WILSONIANISM UPDATED)

The administration, indeed, required new, expensive military power to reach a prized foreign-policy goal: the so-called Reagan Doctrine. The president best defined it in his 1985 State of the Union message:

> Freedom is not the sole prerogative of a chosen few; it is the universal right of all God's children. . . . [Peace and prosperity flourish] where people live by laws that ensure free press, free speech, and freedom to worship, vote, and create wealth. Our mission is to nourish and defend freedom and democracy, and to communicate these ideals everywhere we can. . . . We must stand by all our democratic allies. And we must not break faith with those who are risking their lives—on every continent, from Afghanistan to Nicaragua—to defy Soviet-supported aggression and secure rights which have been ours from birth. . . . Support for freedom fighters is self-defense.[51]

The doctrine's roots went back at least to Woodrow Wilson's faith that the world could "be made safe for democracy" by direct United States involvement. Now, U.S. officials told the Soviets that the 1968 Brezhnev Doctrine (which stated that Soviet socialist regimes must be considered permanent and guaranteed by force, if necessary) was dead and that "it's a new ball game." The Soviets concluded that traditional U.S. containment policy was out and that a rollback policy was in.[52]

It sounded attractive. Americans were to go on the offensive in the newly emerging nations by supporting indigenous anti-Communist groups. Thus, there would not be a costly Vietnam but, instead, cheap supplying of the "freedom fighters," probably with covert CIA aid. Large U.S forces would supposedly not be needed. With this approach, U.S. political debate could also be quieted. Out of sight meant out of mind, Reaganites hoped. The new CIA director, William Casey, took on the

During the 1980s, a vigorous debate erupted over whether the Soviet Union and the United States had entered an era of inevitable "decline." Some argued that on the basis of their severe economic problems and their overspending on military budgets, the two great powers, and especially the Soviets, were following the examples of the Dutch, Spanish, French, and British who had created great empires and then had become overextended until they finally lost their empires and global power. Washington Post *cartoonist "Herblock" (Herbert Block) raises the question of whether U.S. political leadership had declined in the 200 years after the decisive 1781 victory of the American revolutionaries at Yorktown, Virginia.*

job with gusto. A Republican party power and self-made millionaire, Casey had probably been happiest during World War II, when he was operating spy missions inside Nazi Europe.[53] Casey believed that Congress did not need to know about some of his operations (despite laws requiring such disclosures), and he apparently did not even at times inform the president. Critics pointed out other problems with the Reagan Doctrine as well. Both George Kennan and Robert W. Tucker (who had advised Reagan in 1980), warned that it was too open-ended and ideologically explosive. It could deeply involve Americans in a country where they had few interests.[54]

The Reaganites disagreed. They were willing to engage in an ideological—even a covert military—war for the sake of democratic "universalism and moralism," as one phrased it. The president and Secretary of State Shultz, moreover, were furious and frustrated because of terrorist attacks on U.S. citizens, including the killing of an American and a Turkish citizen in a West Berlin nightclub bombing. When Reagan claimed to have evidence linking the bombing to Libya's leader, Mu'ammar al-Qadhafi, the president ordered fifty-five U.S. planes to bomb Libyan shore facilities and Qadhafi's living quarters in April 1986. Qadhafi escaped, but the casualties were not light. Two American flyers and at least thirty-seven Libyans lost their lives. (Later evidence indicated that Syria, not Libya, had instigated the nightclub explosion.) But the Reagan Doctrine's key targets became Afghanistan, Angola, Kampuchea (Cambodia), and Nicaragua.

The greatest success appeared in Afghanistan. Some 115,000 Soviets troops could not control the country after their 1979 invasion. The Soviets suffered at least 40,000 casualties in fighting against the mujahedeen by 1987. Many survivors returned home as drug addicts and alcoholics. U.S. support of the rebels leaped upward (nearly doubling to at least $400 million in 1984–1985 alone) and included Stinger missiles with which the mujahedeen rebels shot down Soviet helicopters. After three aged Soviet leaders died in power between 1982 and 1985, Mikhail Gorbachev assumed the top job in Moscow. Gorbachev had supported the invasion, but he saw that the conflict was draining resources required for his top priority: revitalizing the slowing, inefficient Soviet economy. The war threatened to have no end. In early 1988, he declared that Soviet troops planned to leave Afghanistan, although a pro-Moscow regime and Red Army advisers were to remain.

Reagan's policy in Afghanistan enjoyed strong congressional support, but such a consensus did not exist on Angola. Having tried to overthrow the Marxist Angolan government since 1975 (see p. 663), U.S. officials found themselves supporting Jonas Savimbi's guerrilla forces. In 1985, the president had successfully pushed Congress to repeal the Clark Amendment, which had prohibited U.S. involvements in the quarrel. But then the Reagan Doctrine ran into problems. For one, the Angolan government continued to work closely with U.S. oil companies (especially Chevron and Texaco), welcomed Western investment, and modified its socialist controls. For another, Savimbi made little headway on his own, but he was embarrassingly successful in blowing up U.S.-owned oil facilities in 1986, just one month after he had received American military aid. Perhaps most important, Savimbi's main support came from the white South African government. It repeatedly used the continent's most powerful military to attack neighboring black states that supported the blacks inside South Africa who fought to end the apartheid system.

The white South Africans were hated throughout the region. U.S. interests were not helped by being allied with them and Savimbi. Nevertheless, the Reaganites asked Congress for funds to help Savimbi and also to follow a policy of "constructive engagement" toward the South African regime. Reagan's policy condemned apartheid, but it also condemned Jimmy Carter's attempts to use political and economic pressures to change the apartheid system. Reagan hoped instead

---

SULLIVAN PRINCIPLES

In 1977, Reverend Leon Sullivan—a Baptist minister in Philadelphia and General Motors Corp. director—formulated a set of principles for fair employment practices in South Africa. He encouraged U.S. companies with investments in South Africa to implement these principles in their South African facilities and thus break down the apartheid regulations.

- Nonsegregation of the races in all eating, comfort, and work facilities;
- Equal and fair employment practices for all employees;
- Equal pay for all employees doing equal or comparable work for the same period of time;
- Initiation and development of training programs that will prepare blacks, coloreds, and Asians in substantial numbers for supervisory, administrative, clerical, and technical jobs;
- Increasing the number of blacks, coloreds, and Asians in management and supervisory positions;
- Improving the quality of employees' lives outside the work environment in such areas as housing, transportation, schooling, recreation, and health facilities.

In 1987–1988, after more than 150 U.S. corporations in South Africa adopted the Sullivan Principles, Reverend Sullivan concluded that South African society had not sufficiently changed and urged the corporations to withdraw from South Africa.

---

to work quietly with South Africa to provide it with economic and political security so that the whites would be willing to give the blacks (who formed 72 percent of the population) more freedom to move, live, and work as they pleased. By 1984, however, the whites proposed a new constitution that gave no significant new rights to blacks. When protests erupted, the government imposed martial law, killed more than a thousand blacks over a period of fifteen months, and threw out foreign television crews when they tried to report the events.

A storm of protest erupted in American corporate stockholders' meetings and on college campuses, where pressure built to force large U.S. firms working in South Africa to "divest" and quit cooperating with the white government. A number of firms (including Ford and IBM) did pull out, but their plants kept running, often under South African white management. Of the 350 American companies operating in South Africa in 1980, nearly 200 remained by 1988. In 1986, an angry U.S. Congress began replacing Reagan's policy with tough economic sanctions against the South African government.[55] Within four years these sanctions seemed to have an effect. The white government began to ease apartheid and even to release the leading black leader, Nelson Mandela, from a long jail term.

In other trouble spots, the Reagan Doctrine proved irrelevant. In 1986, after fourteen years of dictatorship, Ferdinand Marcos lost his grip on the Philippines. He could not stop a growing pro-Communist insurgency on the nation's outlying islands—at least not without further oppressing a people from whom he had already stolen over $1 billion. U.S. officials had said little. They believed that they needed the huge American bases at Subic Bay and Clark Field. Marcos happily leased the bases for an annual rent of $500 million. In 1981, Vice-President George Bush toasted Marcos: "We love your adherence to democratic principle and to the democratic processes." Many Filipinos disagreed, especially after Marcos's military gunned down leading political opponents. By February 1986, Marcos could no longer deal with either the rebels or rising demands for a fair election. Running against Corazon Aquino (the wife of one of his murdered opponents), Marcos won, but the vote was so corrupt that street demonstrations and—at the last minute—White House pressure forced him to leave the country. Reagan had supported the dictator nearly to the end. Aquino won power, but she proved ineffective in blunting the growing rebel movement that by 1987 operated in sixty-three of the nation's seventy-three provinces. U.S. financial problems prevented Reagan from giving her the aid she needed to breathe life into the devastated Philippine economy.[56] The Reagan Doctrine's determination to roll back Communist gains oddly seemed to be failing in a nation that had been closely allied with the United States since 1898.

THE REAGAN DOCTRINE, LATIN AMERICA, AND THE TICKING TIME BOMB

The doctrine's most hotly debated action occurred in Central America. The president tried to keep leftist guerrillas from seizing power in El Salvador, while he attempted to prevent the Sandinista government from remaining in power in Nicaragua. But these crises were only two of many dangerous developments that threatened U.S.–Latin American relations.

Tiny El Salvador presented Reagan with his first test case. The revolutionary FMLN offensive had miserably failed in early 1981 (see p. 695), and the rebels wanted to discuss a settlement. The president rejected any such deal. As his new NSC adviser, Richard Allen, put it, U.S. military force in the hemisphere "has always been the basis for the development of a just and humane foreign policy, and it's some-

El Playón, a lava bed outside of El Salvador's capital, San Salvador, has been used for years as the dumping grounds for those seized, tortured, and killed by Salvadoran police, security squads, and right-wing vigilantes. Between 40,000 and 50,000 Salvadorans (equivalent to nearly 3 million U.S. citizens) have been murdered in this manner. They have been critics, or merely suspected critics, of the military-dominated Salvadoran government and have especially been targeted by large landowners who are determined to hold on to their wealth. The Reagan administration strongly supported the Salvadoran government while trying—unsuccessfully—to stop the torture and killing. The picture on the left shows masks at El Playón once worn by death-squad members. The picture on the right shows the remains of one of the nearly 50,000 victims.

thing we can be proud of." Reagan's first secretary of state, Alexander Haig, assured him, "Mr. President, this is one you can win."[57] With enough military help, the 17,000-man Salvadoran army could not only destroy the 4,000 guerrillas, but show the Soviets that the Reagan administration did not intend to be the "wimp" that Reagan had accused Carter of being. U.S. advisers and the CIA moved into El Salvador in large numbers, while thousands of Salvadoran soldiers were brought to the United States for training.

But the president's policy floundered. Guerrillas more than doubled in number, controlled large sections of the country, carried out attacks within the capital of San Salvador, and wrecked key sectors of the economy. Reagan's approach stressed the need for democratic elections in a nation that had never known democracy. When elections were held in 1982, right-wing military factions, closely associated with the secret "death squads" that had slaughtered tens of thousands of Salvadorans, nearly seized the presidency. They were stopped only when U.S. officials intervened to nullify the election results and install a more moderate politician as president. In 1984, new elections, more closely supervised by the United States and financed by as much as $1.5 million in CIA funds, brought the U.S.-educated José Napoleón Duarte back to power. Duarte was the one figure both Salvadorans and North Americans could rally around, and the U.S. Congress was willing to trust him with funds. By 1988, Washington pumped $1.5 million per day into El Salvador to keep Duarte and the decimated Salvadoran economy afloat.

The effort resembled rolling a huge boulder uphill. The money built little, especially as the richest Salvadorans sent their money to safe overseas banks. Duarte's key reform—land redistribution to the peasant masses, who depended on but had no land—stopped as the right-wing death squads killed officials and peasants who tried to carry out the reform. In 1985–1986, the FMLN lost ground to the U.S.-supplied military, but they then carried out daring raids, including the murder of four U.S. soldiers in San Salvador. Duarte, whom the constitution prevented from running again in 1989, lost much of his control. In late 1986, hundreds of university students burned the U.S. flag and threw rocks at Duarte in one of the largest anti–United States protests in years. On the other side, the death squads stepped up their work. Frightened Salvadoran courts released military figures implicated in the murder of North Americans and Salvadorans. In 1988, right-wing groups linked with the death squads won nationwide legislative elections as Duarte's party went down to a crushing defeat. The war intensified, the people suffered, the dying continued.[58]

Reagan focused his Central American effort on Nicaragua, where the revolutionary Sandinistas had seized power in 1979 from the U.S.-supported Somoza dictatorship. The Sandinistas kept nearly 60 percent of the economy in private hands, but they were determined to carry out fundamental reform and break the long North American grip on their country's affairs. They nationalized banks and some land (mostly Somoza's old holdings), as well as foreign trade. They also set up neighborhood committees to carry out the revolution and, according to critics, to intimidate those who questioned the revolution. The Sandinistas rapidly improved both literacy and health conditions, but they also lost support of more moderate (especially business) groups that had backed the revolution. The new government turned to Cuba, then

the Soviet bloc, for military supplies, advisers, and health and education aid—although western Europe, other Latin Americans, Japan, and
Canada also sent much economic help.

From the start, Reagan's policy seemed to aim at either overthrowing the Sandinistas (make them cry "uncle," as the president said at
one news conference) or forcing them to share power with U.S.-financed
"Contras," who had begun fighting the government in 1981. Key Contra military leaders had belonged to Somoza's regime, but the United
States—contrary to its own laws—allowed them to train in Florida to
prepare to overthrow a government that Washington itself recognized.
In November 1981, the president signed a secret order permitting the
CIA to spend at least $19 million to train and lead the Contras. The
United States also built large bases in Honduras from which the Contras could launch attacks and where up to 30,000 U.S. soldiers and
sailors carried out maneuvers after 1983 to frighten the Sandinistas.
The president called the Contras "freedom fighters" and compared
them to the "founding fathers" of 1776. The *Boston Globe*, noting the
many reports of how Contras destroyed health facilities and killed women
and children in their attacks, called them "an unlikely collection of
cattle rustlers, terrorists, members of a discredited dictatorship, profiteers [whose leaders lived comfortably in Miami] and mercenaries."
The CIA privately called them its "unilaterally controlled Latin assets."[59]

But the CIA and the Contras could not deliver a victory. Bitter disputes erupted within the Reagan administration between State
Department area experts, who believed that Sandinista power could be
better (and certainly more cheaply) contained through diplomatic
negotiations, and other civilians—especially in the Pentagon and the
White House—who favored escalating the fighting. The U.S. military,
fearing another Vietnam and considering Nicaragua a small sideshow,
mostly agreed with the State Department. In 1983, Reagan tried to
quiet this fight in Washington by appointing a special commission,
headed by Henry Kissinger, to investigate the problem. The commission recommended increased aid to the Contras, continued support of
the Salvadoran government (but tied to demands that the Salvadorans
quit killing political opponents), and a massive aid program to rebuild
the war-devastated Central American nations. Reagan followed the first
recommendation, tied aid to human rights only after Congress forced
him to do so, and failed to work out any effective economic-aid program. The CIA finally took matters into its own hands in late 1983 by
mining Nicaraguan harbors and attacking oil and airport facilities. An
angry Congress responded by cutting off military aid to the Contras in

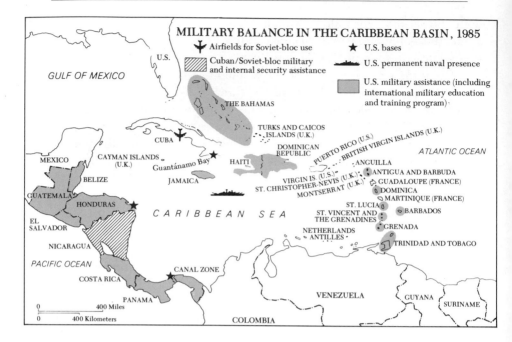

MILITARY BALANCE IN THE CARIBBEAN BASIN, 1985

✈ Airfields for Soviet-bloc use

▨ Cuban/Soviet-bloc military and internal security assistance

★ U.S. bases

⚓ U.S. permanent naval presence

▦ U.S. military assistance (including international military education and training program)·

1984. Reagan officials retaliated by publicly encouraging private Americans to send money for the overthrow of the Nicaraguan government and by diverting CIA and other funds to the same effort.

Nevertheless, the Sandinistas stopped the Contras in the field and held an election in 1984 that many observers (but not U.S. officials) considered open and fair. Sandinista leader Daniel Ortega Saavedra was elected president. In 1985, Ortega imposed martial law on the land, held as many as 4,000 political prisoners (critics claimed that there were 12,000 such prisoners), and closed opposition media. Washington's policy seemed to be at a dead end. "None of our options hold much promise," a U.S. official gloomily concluded in 1985.[60] But Reagan doggedly continued to pressure Congress for Contra military aid, and in 1986 he won. As the Nicaraguan economy suffered from Sandinista mismanagement and U.S. strangulation (Reagan succeeded in cutting off nearly all international lending to Managua, except for Soviet-bloc aid), the Contras' numbers grew. They, nevertheless, had little chance of defeating the well-trained, experienced Sandinista army, and suffered 400 dead and wounded each month by 1987.

One hope for peace suddenly appeared in mid-1987, when President Oscar Arias Sanchez of Costa Rica convinced the other four Central American presidents (including Ortega) to sign a peace plan. It included (1) a cease-fire throughout the region; (2) negotiations between governments and rebels, especially in El Salvador and Nicaragua; (3) a cutoff of aid from outside sources to rebel forces (that is, a cutoff of U.S. aid to the Contras and Soviet-bloc aid to the FMLN in El Salvador); and (4) the promise that all nations would move toward elections and "political pluralism." Arias won the 1987 Nobel Prize for Peace, but Reagan was much less impressed. He objected that the plan allowed the Soviets to continue helping the Sandinista government. (It also allowed him to continue helping the Salvadoran government.) He believed that the Sandinistas would never accept real political pluralism. When Reagan consequently insisted on more military aid for the 10,000 to 12,000 Contras, Arias warned that such aid could destroy all hopes for peace because the Sandinistas would never allow more freedom within if they were so threatened from without. Arias announced that "the contras . . . are the problem, and not the solution."[61]

The peace process edged along, but Reagan and other Contra supporters determined to keep the rebels alive and fighting—by private gifts, if necessary. Meanwhile, the war that had already taken 40,000 Nicaraguan lives between 1981 and 1987 stopped in early 1988 as the Contras and Sandinistas began peace talks. North Americans now faced the question of whether they would continue to try to impose their policies on their "backyard" as they had throughout the twentieth century, or whether—since those policies had not prevented the worst death and destruction in 350 years of the region's history—they would allow, for the first time in the twentieth century, Central Americans such as Arias and Ortega to determine Central American affairs.

U.S. officials' fixation on Nicaragua gave them little time to deal with other dangers in the region. Reagan's policy turned Honduras into a huge staging base for U.S.-Contra operations. The second poorest nation in the hemisphere, this one-time "banana republic" lived less by bananas than by U.S. aid (which soared from $3 million annually to over $100 million in seven years) and by catering to the American military's need for places of relaxation and prostitution. Terrorism and anti-U.S. protests broke out for the first time in the 1980s, but the Honduran army maintained order. Elsewhere, the Reaganites bragged that ten Latin American military rulers gave way to democratic governments during the 1980s. Such rushes of democracy were not new: they had appeared in the late 1950s, only to revert to military control within a decade. Credit was, nevertheless, due in the 1980s to Carter's human-rights policies, Reagan's preaching about the need for democracy, and the Latin American military's realization that it could no longer govern the economically sick system in such pivotal nations as Brazil and Argentina.

But this apparent turn toward democracy hid the time bomb that was ticking throughout the region. Latin American nations (led by the giants Brazil, Argentina, and Mexico) owed hundreds of billions of dollars for debts that had piled up during the 1960s and 1970s. To pay the debts meant taking resources out of their own populations and perhaps causing revolts. Not paying the debts threatened the U.S. banks and international lenders that made the loans. Per-capita Latin American income sank 10 percent between 1980 and 1988. Inflation raged at over 150 percent annually in Mexico, Brazil, and Argentina. Growth rates plummeted as population (especially of those under age sixteen) rose. The Reagan administration at first trusted the marketplace to find solutions. When that failed, it could come up with nothing else to turn off the ticking bomb. One of Brazil's solutions was to become a leading arms dealer, making fat profits by selling weapons to nations (such as Libya) that Reagan strongly disliked.[62]

In one tiny Caribbean island, however, Reagan had his way. Grenada had become independent of Great Britain in 1974, then was ruled by a highly corrupt anti-Communist regime until 1979, when Maurice Bishop forcefully replaced it with a leftist government that soon cooperated with Fidel Castro. Between 1981 and 1983, Bishop opened secret talks with the United States. He offered to call elections and discuss Washington's concerns, but Reagan finally refused to talk with Bishop in mid-1983. When a more radical Bernard Coard overthrew and killed Bishop, then fired into pro-Bishop protesters, U.S. officials determined to invade. The official reason for the October 25, 1983, invasion was to protect 595 U.S. medical students supposedly endangered by Coard's forces. The more important reason was the opportunity to use U.S. fire power quickly and successfully on behalf of the Reagan Doctrine—especially after 241 U.S. troops had been killed by terrorists two days before in Lebanon. The invasion, however, suffered embarrassing problems of logistics and a failure of the Eighty-second Airborne Division (supposedly the crack U.S. fighting force) to overcome 700 Cuban engineers who fought back. American troops even discovered that they had to use 1977 tourist maps that had such points of interest as nutmeg factories on it instead of the grid coordinates needed in battle. After the invasion force was increased from 1,900 to 6,000, had lost 19 dead (116 wounded), and had killed 24 Cubans and 45 Grenadan soldiers, it finally conquered the island.[63]

By the late 1980s, the good-neighbor policy was only a historical memory. As historian Mark T. Gilderhus observes, "Unlike Carter administration officials who understood the [Latin American] problem as a North-South issue pitting the less-developed against the developed world, the Reagan administration presented the turmoil as an East-West issue. Indeed, [to Reagan] it appeared as a classic Cold War confrontation conducted by surrogates in which the Communists sought strategic advantage by destabilizing countries on the southern flank of the United States. . . ." Twenty-five years after the Alliance for Progress had begun in 1961, the head of the Organization of American States declared, "On the whole, the region is worse off than it was 25 years ago."[64]

THE REAGAN DOCTRINE, THE MIDDLE EAST, AND THE IRAN-CONTRA AFFAIR

U.S. policy struggled in Latin America. But "in the history of the American Republic it is unlikely that any issue of foreign relations has confounded and frustrated the nation's policy makers more completely, repeatedly, and over a longer period of time than the problems of the Middle East in the years since World War II," as historian Seth Tillman observes.[65] Washington officials had never been able to figure out how to achieve all—or even any—of their objectives: Israel's security; Egypt's stability and acceptance as a leader by other Arab nations; self-determination and a territorial settlement accepted by millions of displaced Palestinians; placating the strong anti-Israeli feelings in oil-rich Arab kingdoms, especially Saudi Arabia; and containment of Soviet influence, particularly as it worked through Syria, which disliked Egypt and hated Israel. It was a minefield of religious, racial, and national rivalries that could explode instantly.

One explosion had occurred in 1982. The Palestine Liberation Organization (PLO) had finally settled in Lebanon. The PLO was involved in skirmishes along the border with Israel, then shot the Israeli ambassador to Great Britain. In June 1982, Israel invaded Lebanon, drove out the PLO, and tried to establish a friendly Maronite Christian regime. But Lebanese politics collapsed, and brutalities escalated. Secretary of State Shultz and President Reagan sent in U.S. troops to work with western Europeans in enforcing a cease-fire. The Israelis found themselves entrapped. They were attacked by Shiite Moslems and then shocked by bloody Christian massacres of Palestin-

U.S.-SOVIET MILITARY BALANCE, 1985

	U.S.	Soviet	
Soviet-bloc combat troops	⚓	⚓	Use of docking facilities
Soviet-bloc military assistance personnel	✚	✚	Use of air facilities
U.S. military assistance personnel			Naval presence

ians in Israeli-controlled camps. A shaken Menachem Begin resigned as Israel's prime minister.

Afraid that the chaos and Israeli withdrawal would permit Syria to move into Lebanon, Reagan—who had said in early 1983 that he wanted to "expedite" the departure of the U.S. forces in the region—implied that the troops would remain as long as necessary to restore order. In April 1983, despite (or because of) their presence, a powerful bomb wrecked the U.S. Embassy in Beirut, killing 46 people, including 16 Americans. Reagan had condemned earlier presidents for sending U.S. troops into Vietnam "with one hand tied behind them." But he now placed the Marines in a virtually indefensible position on the outskirts of Beirut. On October 23, 1983, Moslem terrorists drove a vehicle packed with explosives into the marines' barracks and killed 241 men. Reagan declared that "the United States will not be intimidated by terrorists" and later announced that Americans would never "cut and run."[66] But the marine position could not be defended, U.S. policy was bankrupt, and the president faced a re-election campaign. In early 1984, he pulled out the troops. Lebanon became a chaotic battlefield.

Another explosion in the region had occurred in 1980, when Iraq's Sunni Moslem government attacked Khomeini's Shiite Moslems in neighboring Iran. The United States sympathized with Iraq, but neither side could defeat the other despite exceptionally brutal and bloody fighting. By 1985, however, Iranian-backed terrorists had seized a number of U.S. hostages in the Middle East, including State Department and CIA personnel. In 1979–1981, Carter had negotiated with the Iranians to gain the release of U.S. hostages. But Reagan swore loudly and often (especially when running against Carter in 1980 and Carter's former vice-president, Walter Mondale, in the 1984 election) that he would never "be intimidated by terrorists" or negotiate with them. His passion rose higher as Americans died in terrorist attacks on airplanes, airports, and even cruise ships.

In August–September 1985, however, the president worked through Israel to send TOW antitank missiles and other military equipment to

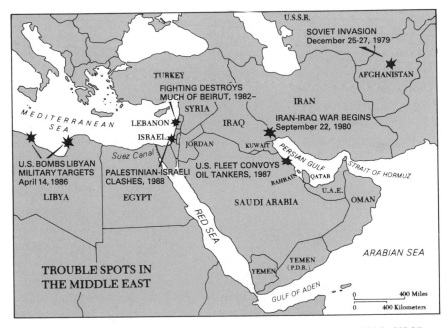

The Middle East became the focal point of U.S. foreign policy and U.S.-USSR competition in the 1980s, much as central Europe and then Asia had been such focal points in the 1940s, 1950s, and 1960s.

Khomeini's regime in a highly secret operation. Clearly, the shipments were sent to gain the release of hostages. As the weapons continued to flow to Iran in several shipments over the next fourteen months, some hostages were released. But new ones were then seized. Under Reagan's orders, his NSC adviser, Robert McFarlane, secretly went to Tehran (carrying, for some reason, gifts of a chocolate cake and a Bible) to negotiate with the Iranians. Nothing resulted. When the weapons shipments and mission were revealed in November 1986 by a Lebanese journal, Reagan told stunned Americans that the policy was aimed at opening contact with Iranian "moderates," although who the moderates might be in Khomeini's fundamentalist regime was never made clear. It turned out, moreover, that the president had followed the arms-for-hostages policy despite strong protests from Secretary of State Shultz and Secretary of Defense Weinberger.

Three weeks after this revelation, Attorney General Edwin Meese announced that money obtained from the arms sales to Iran had been secretly sent to the Contras for use in Nicaragua. This diversion of funds had occurred in 1985–1986 despite Congress's ban on the sending of lethal aid to the Contras. The scheme was apparently the brainchild of William Casey, head of the CIA, whose budget was rising even faster than the Defense Department's budget. The CIA was literally out of both the president's and Congress's control. Casey worked through Lieutenant Colonel Oliver North, an aide in the White House NSC who had fought in Vietnam and was haunted by the U.S. failure.[67] North determined that such a failure would never occur in Central America. Working with Casey as well as with General Manuel Antonio Noriega, head of the Panamanian government (and later indicted as a leading international drug trafficker), North directed secret supply missions to the Contras. Some equipment was paid for by Iranian arms sales, others by North's effective multimillion-dollar fund-raising among conservative Americans.

During the summer of 1987, joint Senate and House special committees conducted nationally televised hearings on the schemes. As they organized, a special commission headed by former Texas Republican Senator John Tower, which Reagan had asked to investigate the role of the White House in the Iran-Contra affair, made its report. The Tower commission concluded that the NSC staff was responsible for the chaotic policy and that the president was out of touch with the foreign policies of his own White House. The House-Senate investigation confirmed much of the Tower commission's report. North testified that he had largely worked under Casey's direction, but he had also kept the new NSC director, Admiral John Poindexter, informed of the plan. Poindexter testified that he never told the president about the diversion plan. Casey never testified at all. He had died of a brain tumor months earlier and took to the grave whatever he had told his close friend Ronald Reagan about the plan.

North became a hero to much of the television audience for his defense of the Reagan Doctrine, even if the defense meant breaking the law. His attractiveness wore off, however, as second thoughts appeared. North, after all, admitted that he had illegally destroyed government documents that might have contained damning evidence. He also admitted that he had made statements to Congress that were "false," "evasive and wrong." The *Army Times* condemned North for having "paraded a travesty of military values before a credulous national television audience." Retired Colonel Harry Summers damned North and the others for selling weapons to Iran that might well be used against U.S. soldiers, and for starting down the "slippery slope" by placing their wishes above those of Congress or the president—"for at the bottom of that slope is military dictatorship" in the United States.[68]

The State Department's point man on Central America, Assistant Secretary of State Elliott Abrams, had also lied to Congress when he told it, in November 1986, that no third-party funds were going to the Contras, even though he personally had begged for some of those funds from the sultan of Brunei. Abrams became an outcast on Capitol Hill (Minnesota Republican Senator David Durenberger said that he would trust Abrams no further "than I can throw Oliver North"), but Reagan and Shultz kept him in the State Department. Democratic congressman Lee Hamilton from Indiana, chairman of the House investigation committee, summarized the affair by declaring that the "policy was driven by a series of lies— . . . lies to our friends and allies, lies to the Congress, and lies to the American people." Hamilton concluded that "the policy achieved none of the goals it sought. The Ayatollah got his arms, more Americans are held hostage today [and] subversion of U.S. interests throughout the region by Iran continues."[69] Reagan's confusion throughout the three-year affair was exemplified when reporters asked him if the late William Casey had engaged in secret CIA activities without the president's knowledge. Reagan replied, "Not that I know of." In the end, 11 members of the Reagan administration were convicted or pleaded guilty. Two of these convictions (including North's) were overturned on technical grounds. Several others were saved from trial by presidential pardons issued by George Bush.[70]

But he was not finished with the Middle East. In early 1987, his administration concluded that Iran threatened the oil exports of Kuwait (which was pro-Iraq in the Iran-Iraq war). The Kuwaiti exporters depended on free movement of their tankers through the Persian Gulf. The president put Kuwaiti tankers under the American flag and used a U.S. fleet to protect them against attacks by Iranian gunboats. Behind that decision lay Reagan's and Shultz's determination to reassert their power in the region as well as to try to intimidate Khomeini. Reagan had been told that the nine U.S. warships in the area were sufficient for the job. Within two months, however, he had to send forty-one combat vessels to the region and spend $10 million to $20 million each day on the operation. Even then, the Iranians disabled a number of U.S. and non-U.S. flagships. Americans and Iranians were virtually at war with each other. In 1987, a missile from Iraq—which Reagan was supporting in its war with Iran—killed 37 sailors on a U.S. ship. In mid-1988, a U.S. naval commander mistook an Iranian airliner for an attack jet and shot it down, killing 290 innocent civilians. The passageway was kept open, and the U.S. Navy, with the help of a few allies, continued to carry off a difficult and dangerous task. Critics believed that, given Iranian policy and naval strength, the passage would have remained open without such a U.S. commitment.[71]

REAGAN, THE SOULLESS EMPIRE, AND THE INF TREATY

The president viewed all foreign policy through the telescope of the U.S.-Soviet conflict. Like nearly all Americans, he despised and belittled the Soviet system. "Sometimes I think Adam and Eve must have been Russian," he repeatedly told audiences. "They didn't have a roof over their heads, nothing to wear, only one apple between them, and they called it paradise." In more serious moments in the 1960s he said he would refuse even to negotiate with them because "how do you compromise with men who say we have no soul, there is no hereafter, there is no God?" Critics replied that talks were necessary simply because although each side had the nuclear weapons to incinerate the other, neither had the power or resources to impose its will on the other.

Reagan received little contrary advice from his closest advisers. William Clark served as NSC adviser during much of the president's first term, and while he was a close personal friend, Clark knew little about foreign policy and had even less experience in it. His one conviction was that the Soviet Union was "a bizarre and evil episode of history whose last pages are even now being written."[72] Another powerful official, Assistant Secretary of Defense Richard Perle, had more sophisticated views, but they ended up at the same place: the Soviets could be handled through a major arms build-up; no serious talks should be held on arms control and little talk held on anything else except human rights inside the Soviet Union. Not one top Reagan official between 1981 and 1984 had significant experience dealing with the Soviet Union.

By 1983, Reagan's policies were beset by at least two contradictions. If, as he planned, he did exert immediate short-term pressure against Moscow, he had to do it through economic sanctions. Military build-ups took time, and no responsible official considered threatening Brezhnev with nuclear war. To exert economic pressure effectively, however, required extensive government controls in the marketplace—exactly the kind of controls that Reagan had promised to avoid. Condemning Carter's grain embargo and turnoff of some high-technology items in 1980, Reagan promised American voters that he would impose no such restraints. After hesitating, he did lift the grain embargo. When, however, the Communist government in Poland imposed martial law in late 1981 to control economic crisis and loud political dissent from the Solidarity labor movement, Reagan stopped food shipments to the Poles. He found himself fattening the Soviets and starving the Poles. When he did allow goods to go into Poland again, the president's right-wing supporters damned him for trading with the Communists. Reagan discovered that he could not fight communism without compromising his free-enterprise principles.

But a second contradiction also existed. When he tried to pressure the Soviets by stopping the sale of U.S. high-tech and oil-gas drilling equipment to them, his closest allies in western Europe and Japan continued to send these items to the Soviets. These allies considered the Soviets' gas and oil supplies to be more dependable than the Middle East's. Furious, Reagan tried to stop the trade by intervening in the internal affairs of the allies and met angry reaction. After he replaced Haig in mid-1982, Secretary of State Shultz finally began to change Reagan's and Clark's policies by lifting many of the trade restraints and no longer bothering the allies about the issue. The alliance not only strengthened, but, in 1987, U.S. business was selling new items such as personal computers to Moscow, and, in turn, the Soviets signed a long-term agreement to buy American grain.

As he began running for re-election in 1984, Reagan had not scored one important diplomatic success. During the previous year, his announced intention of building SDI (Star Wars) and, in September 1983, the Soviet shooting-down of South Korean Airliner 007, which

Major reasons for détente. The dot in the center square represents all of the fire power used in World War II, including the atomic bombs dropped on Hiroshima and Nagasaki. The 6,000 dots in the rest of the squares represent the comparative destructive power of the nuclear weapons that existed in the 1980s. Just two squares on the chart represent enough fire power to destroy all of the large- and medium-sized cities of the world.

killed 269 including a U.S. congressman, poisoned superpower relations. The Soviets claimed that the airliner, which was 350 miles off course, had intentionally strayed over some of their most sensitive military installations for the purposes of U.S. intelligence. The president countered that it was not an intelligence mission, and even if it had strayed off course, the Soviets should never have fired on a civilian airliner. U.S.-USSR relations reached their lowest point since the worst days of the cold war in the early 1950s.

Then, as both sides began to worry about rushing down a dead-end road that ended in a superpower confrontation, they searched for side exits. Reagan began softening his rhetoric. "The fact that neither of us likes the other system is no reason to refuse to talk," he noted in early 1984, which he then defined as "a year of opportunities for peace."[73] Not wanting to frighten Americans during an election year, the president also declared that his military build-up had reached the point where negotiations could now be profitably held. (He, doubtless, also realized that major budget problems prevented any such future arms build-up.) Shultz's State Department fought endless battles to check Perle and others in the Pentagon and White House who wanted to ignore the informal SALT II arms limits (signed in 1979) and to force the allies to get tough with Moscow. On at least two occasions, Shultz kept Reagan on the path to negotiations by threatening to resign if the president ditched efforts to cap the arms race.

By 1985, the Soviets were also ready to talk. During the three years after Brezhnev's death in 1982, they had endured two more elderly, ill leaders. After they died, fifty-four-year-old Mikhail Gorbachev came to power in early 1985. Trained as a lawyer and an agricultural expert, he had no personal ties to the Stalinist years (as had his three predecessors) and slowly but surely brought to power others of his age and outlook. Gorbachev's policy was driven by several insights. He realized that the Soviet economy could not continue business as usual. It had fallen behind Japan as well as the United States and was slipping so badly that it had begun to resemble a poor African economy—"an Upper Volta with missiles," as even Gorbachev allegedly remarked. Few worked hard or imaginatively, drunkenness abounded, productivity dived. Industry had been denuded of investment capital to pay for the military build-up during the 1960s and 1970s. Gorbachev determined not to tinker, but to begin fundamental restructuring (or *perestroika*). He planned to do it by lessening tensions, curbing military deployments, and opening the society to outside competitiveness (or *glasnost*). These decisions led to Gorbachev's second insight: the United States had also declined in economic power and no longer served (as it had during the Nixon years, for example) as the single source of high technology and expertise needed by the Soviets. He could find better and more dependable sources of such technology in Japan and West Germany. But even a declining America could offer something no one else could match: a break in the arms race and overall improvement in super-power relations so that Gorbachev could concentrate on the top priority of reviving the Soviet economy and society.[74]

In 1983, the Soviets had walked out of arms talks in Geneva because Reagan had insisted on continuing to deploy intermediate Pershing IIs and cruise missiles in western Europe (see p. 685). By early 1985, however, the Kremlin returned to the talks. In April, Gorbachev made the first of several proposals to cap, then cut back, the intermediate missile forces on both sides in Europe. At Geneva during November 1985, in the first summit meeting in six years, the two men agreed in principle on an intermediate-force (INF) deal, renewed cultural and academic exchanges, created a Risk Reduction Center to analyze how to avoid risks of a nuclear war, and decided to cooperate to prevent the spread of nuclear forces. The summit marked a giant step forward for both sides. At a hastily convened second summit in Reykjavík, Iceland, in October 1986, an INF deal was nearly struck until Gorbachev wanted it linked to some limits on the SDI program. Reagan refused; the talks collapsed. Gorbachev was bitter, especially as relations threatened to refreeze. The Soviet leader believed he had been misled by the Americans. In a Politburo meeting (whose minutes were only declassified in 1993), Gorbachev declared, "Yes, Reagan appears a liar." But he nonetheless urged his Soviet colleagues not to "stop before [taking] the most decisive measures."[75] Gorbachev, however, needed immediate relief for an economy staggering under Communist inefficiency, and that meant, in turn, imposing some kind of controls on military spending.

In early 1987, he dropped the linkage between limiting INF and his demand for limits on Reagan's beloved SDI program. The two superpowers agreed to a heretofore unimaginable deal: a "double-zero option"—that is, the elimination of both intermediate missiles (600 to 3,400 miles) and short-range missiles (300 to 600 miles). Perle and other hard-liners had actually suggested the "double-zero option" during 1981–1982 negotiations in the firm belief that the Soviets would never accept it. Gorbachev not only accepted it, but agreed to historic verification measures in which, for the first time, officials and scientists on each side were to inspect the other side's highly sensitive military and scientific installations.[76]

At a third summit, in Washington during December 1987, Gorbachev and Reagan signed the historic agreement. It marked the first time that the actual number of nuclear weapons had been reduced (about 4 percent of all such missiles) and that an entire class of arms had been dismantled. The Soviets took out about 1,500 of their warheads from Europe; the United States, less than half that number. The two leaders made much of the completed INF treaty at their summit meeting in Moscow in May 1988. The summit produced no other major result, although it was the leaders' fourth such meeting in just three years.

Hope also rose that superpower clashes in the newly emerging nations would now cool. As a top State Department official noted, Gorbachev had told the Twenty-seventh Party Congress earlier in 1987 that Soviet friends in the Third World must build socialism "mainly by their own efforts." Gorbachev made no specific offers of military and economic help to those nations.[77] The Soviet leader clearly wanted to get out of Afghanistan (while protecting USSR security interests). At the Washington summit, he even told Reagan that he was willing to discuss a

*Soviet leader Mikhail Gorbachev (1931–   ) flew to Washington in December
1987, worked the press and U.S.-citizens-in-the-street like a talented American
politician, then shook hands with President Reagan after the two men signed
the INF (Intermediate Nuclear Force) treaty that removed both nations' intermediate nuclear weapons from central Europe.*

cutoff of Soviet aid to the Sandinistas in Nicaragua. Reagan made no
response to the offer.

LEGACIES OF THE 1980s

The post-1985 events were the most hopeful in years. If the ardent
anti-Communist wing in American politics (represented by Reagan)
and a younger Soviet leadership realizing the necessity of reconciling
foreign hopes to domestic needs (as represented by Gorbachev) could
strike such deals, the future could be more promising and exciting for
young Americans and Soviets than ever before in the history of U.S.-
Soviet competition. But the obstacles seemed huge. For more than a
century, Americans had not gotten along with Russians, whether those
Russians were under Communist or tsarist rule. Moreover, the earth
was a revolving powder keg. Its inhabitants spent $930 billion—or $1.8
million per minute—on military goods in 1987. Americans accounted
for $293 billion of this amount, the USSR $260 billion. A single U.S.
Trident submarine, armed with twenty-four missiles, alone carried the
destructive force of eight World War II conflicts.[78] In other parts of the

This photo, taken while President Reagan met with Gorbachev in Moscow during the May–June 1988 summit, nicely captures both the progress of U.S.-Soviet relations in the mid-1980s and the irony of the nuclear competition between the superpowers. Lieutenant Commander Woody Lee is manacled by a leather strap to the briefcase (known as "the football") that contains the codes to be used by President Reagan if he decides to launch nuclear weapons. Lee, whose job it is to be close to the president at all times and to protect "the football" with his life, is standing in Moscow's Red Square—on which, presumably, many of the U.S. nuclear missiles are targeted.

world, and even in the United States, the gap widened between rich and poor.

As the world's leading power, Americans had their own problems in dealing with this complex, explosive planet. When Americans celebrated the bicentennial of their Constitution (the world's oldest such written charter), they suffered the embarrassment of watching an inept imperial executive out of control in the Iran-Contra scandal and a Congress unable to supervise foreign policy because of the splintering of the entire political-party system. And although Americans depended increasingly on foreign nations for goods and even economic survival, polls showed them to be abysmally ignorant of national and international affairs. In 1925, Walter Lippmann had predicted that Americans would fail in this task: "The public will arrive in the middle of the third act and will leave before the last curtain, having stayed just long enough perhaps to decide who is the hero and the villain of the piece."[79]

But Americans faced another problem as well. After enjoying the luxury of applying their unchallenged economic resources to dealing with both their internal and external problems throughout the twentieth century, they suddenly found this power wasting away in the 1970s and 1980s. The world's great moneybags between 1914 and 1970, the United States, after 1971, lost much of its ability to compete in the world marketplace and then, between 1981 and 1987, shockingly turned into the world's greatest debtor.[80] The legacies of the Reagan years were both hopeful and ominous.

NOTES

1. Paul Boller, Jr., *Presidential Anecdotes* (New York, 1981), p. 340.
2. The quote and a good analysis of the effect is in Gerald Pomper *et al.*, *The Election of 1976* (New York, 1977), p. 68.
3. Jimmy Carter, *Keeping Faith* (New York, 1982), p. 80.
4. *New York Times*, 14 November 1978, p. 14; the best analysis of interest-group politics is Theodore Lowi's *End of Liberalism* (New York, 1979); William Lee Miller, *Yankee from Georgia: The Emergence of Jimmy Carter* (New York, 1978), pp. 82–83 for the "Jimmyist" reference.
5. Cyrus Vance, *Hard Choices* (New York, 1983), esp. pp. 23–24.
6. Zbigniew Brzezinski, *Power and Principle* (New York, 1982), pp. 8, 42–44; Richard Burt, "Zbig Makes It Big," *New York Times Magazine*, 30 July 1978, p. 20; Stanley Hoffmann, "In Search of a Foreign Policy," *New York Review of Books*, 29 September 1983, p. 51.
7. Quoted in Hedrick Smith, "Problems of a Problem Solver," *New York Times Magazine*, 8 January 1978, pp. 30 ff.
8. Interview of Don Oberdorfer, *Washington Post*, 18 February 1979, p. C4.
9. Richard E. Neustadt and Ernest R. May, *Thinking in Time: The Uses of History for Decision-Makers* (New York, 1986), p. 68; the Notre Dame speech is in U.S. Government, *Public Papers of the Presidents of the United States: Jimmy Carter, 1977*, Book 2 (Washington, D.C., 1978), pp. 954–962.
10. Carter, p. 112; *Washington Post*, 16 March 1979, p. 1; Richard J. Barnet, *The Alliance: America-Europe-Japan, Makers of the Postwar World* (New York, 1983), pp. 385–386, 388–390.
11. *New Yorker*, 1 May 1978, p. 109; Barnet, pp. 372–377; for a good overview of early trilateralism, see the *Washington Post*, 16 January 1977, p. A1; a useful background

on the Pershing II decision is Fred Kaplan's "How Politics Led to the Euromissiles," *Boston Globe*, 8 March 1987, p. 1.

12. Carter, pp. 142–143.

13. *New York Times*, 13 February 1981, p. A8.

14. Tom J. Farer, "Reagan's Latin America," *New York Review of Books*, 19 March 1981, p. 15; Banning Garrett and Mark Paul, "Trading on Human Rights," *Inquiry*, 18 September 1978, pp. 1–15.

15. J. Michael Hogan, *The Panama Canal in American Politics* (Carbondale, Ill., 1986), pp. 6–7, 194–195; Carter, pp. 161–162.

16. David Aaron, "Playing with Apocalypse," *New York Times Magazine*, 29 December 1985, p. 26.

17. Thomas J. Noer, *Cold War* and *Black Liberation* (Columbia, Mo., 1985), p. 249; *New York Times*, 14 June 1978, p. A3; Henry Jackson, *From the Congo to Soweto* (New York, 1982), pp. 152–162.

18. Stephen Prince, *Visions of Empire* (New York, 1992), p. 104; the contradictions and hesitations of the Carter policies are revealed by an insider in Robert Pastor's *Condemned to Repetition* (Princeton, 1987), esp. pp. 13–14, 50–66, 74–79, 153–176.

19. Useful overviews are in Gary Sick's *All Fall Down: America's Tragic Encounter with Iran* (New York, 1985), pp. vii–49; Abul Kasim Mansur, "The Crisis in Iran," *Armed Forces Journal International* 116 (January 1979): 27–33.

20. U.S. Government, p. 2221; Vance, p. 323.

21. Brzezinski's view can be found in *Power and Principle*, esp. pp. 355, 388–393; Vance's in *Hard Choices*, esp. pp. 340–341; an insider's expert view is given in Sick, pp. 99–101, 138–140, 160–161.

22. Brzezinski, pp. 474–475; Carter, pp. 452–453.

23. Author's conversation in Moscow, 12 November 1980; *New York Times*, 29 June 1979, p. A6; *New York Times*, 6 November 1977, p. E5; William Pfaff, "Reflections," *New Yorker*, 16 August 1976, p. 58.

24. Both sides are argued succinctly in *Newsweek*, 21 May 1979, p. 43; Fred Kaplan, *The Wizards of Armageddon* (New York, 1983), pp. 377–384; Adam Ulam, *Dangerous Relations: The Soviet Union in World Politics, 1970–1982* (New York, 1983), pp. 236–241.

25. Vance, pp. 388–389; Brzezinski, p. 353; especially important is Melvyn P. Leffler, "From the Truman Doctrine to the Carter Doctrine," *Diplomatic History* 7 (Fall 1983): 245–266; *New York Times*, 22 February 1979, p. A7.

26. *Washington Post*, 2 March 1981, p. A5.

27. Richard K. Betts, *Nuclear Blackmail and Nuclear Balance* (Washington, D.C., 1987), p. 11; Brzezinski, pp. 443–446.

28. Tad Szulc, "Putting Back the Bite in the CIA," *New York Times Magazine*, 6 April 1980, p. 28; Milton Leitenberg, "United States Foreign Policy and the Soviet Invasion of Afghanistan," *Arms Control* 7 (December 1986): 271–290.

29. Gaddis Smith, *Morality, Reason and Power: American Diplomacy in the Carter Years* (New York, 1986), pp. 9, 81–84; *Washington Post*, 27 February 1986, p. A11; *ibid.*, 29 March 1981, p. 82; Jeffrey Richelson, "PD-59, NSDD-1 and the Reagan Strategic Modernization Program," *Journal of Strategic Studies* 6 (June 1983): 125–146. I am especially indebted to Max Miller and Milton Leitenberg for analyses of PD-59 and its links to the Reagan policies.

30. *Washington Post*, 30 July 1980, p. A12, has the polls; Business Week Team, *The*

Decline of U.S. Power (Boston, 1980), p. 15; Boller, p. 344; *Economist*, 14 June 1980, p. 73.

31. Burton I. Kaufman, *The Presidency of James Earl Carter, Jr.* (Laurence, Kan., 1993), p. 179; Business Week Team, pp. 1–2.

32. Text of Reagan's 1980 acceptance speech, *New York Times*, 18 July 1980, p. A8.

33. Irving Howe, quoted in the *New York Times*, 28 December 1980, p. E5.

34. *New York Times*, 14 December 1980, p. E5; Charles Krauthammer columns, *New Republic*, 4 March 1985, p. 25, and 8 September 1986, pp. 17–24.

35. *Boston Globe*, 24 August 1987, p. 15.

36. *Washington Post*, 1 March 1985, p. A7.

37. Terry Deibel, *Presidents, Public Opinion and Power: The Nixon, Carter and Reagan Years* (New York, 1987), p. 48; George F. Custen, *Bio-Pics* (New Brunswick, N.J., 1992), p. 205.

38. I. M. Destler, "Dateline Washington: Life after the Veto," *Foreign Policy* no. 52 (Fall 1983): 181–186; I. M. Destler and Eric Alterman, "Congress and Reagan's Foreign Policy," *Washington Quarterly* 7 (Winter 1984): 91–101; Theodore Lowi, *The Personal President* (Ithaca, N.Y., 1985), pp. 15–20.

39. Strobe Talbott, *The Russians and Reagan* (New York, 1982), pp. 32–33; *Wall Street Journal*, 3 June 1980, p. 1.

40. Jeane J. Kirkpatrick, *Dictatorship and Double Standards* (New York, 1982), esp. pp. 2–52 for the essay; Judith Elwell, "Barely in the Inner Circle: Jeane Kirkpatrick," in *Women in American Foreign Policy*, ed. Edward P. Crapol (New York, 1987), pp. 153–171; John Pearson, "Flawed Rationale," *Business Week*, 6 September 1982, p. 10; an Argentine view is in J. R.-Lallemant, *Malvinas, Norteamèrica en guerra contra Argentina* (Buenos Aires, 1983).

41. *Low Intensity Warfare*, ed. Michael T. Klare and Peter Kornbluh (New York, 1988), p. 3.

42. *New York Times*, 10 January 1984, p. A23. An early, thorough critique of Reagan's defense expenditures is in the various papers in Ronald V. Dellums with R. H. Miller and H. Lee Halterman, *Defense Sense* (Cambridge, Mass., 1983).

43. Union of Concerned Scientists, *The Fallacy of Star Wars* (New York, 1984), p. 28.

44. Jeremy Bernstein, letter, *New York Times Book Review*, 1 December 1985, p. 44; Kaplan, *Wizards of Armageddon*, p. 88; Robert Dallek, *Ronald Reagan: The Politics of Symbolism* (Cambridge, Mass., 1984), pp. 146–147.

45. *Washington Post*, 29 September 1986, p. A2; *New York Times*, 30 November 1984, p. 86; News Release, Office of Assistant Secretary of Defense (Public Affairs), "The Uses of Military Power," 28 November 1984, no. 609–84.

46. Prince, *Visions of Empire*, pp. 117–151.

47. Paul Kennedy, "The (Relative) Decline of America," *Atlantic* 254 (August 1987): esp. 34.

48. *New York Times*, 21 December 1986, p. E11; *New York Times*, 20 May 1987, p. D2; *Washington Post*, 18 June 1985, p. E1.

49. *Washington Post*, 21 May 1987, p. F4; *Economist*, 25 October 1986, p. 13; *New York Times*, 2 February 1986, p. E4.

50. *Washington Post*, 20 October 1987, p. A4; *Washington Post*, 17 January 1986, p. 50.

51. U.S. Government, *Weekly Compilation of Presidential Documents*, XXI, 11 February 1985, pp. 145–146.

52. Talbott, pp. 72–73.

53. Bob Woodward, *Veil: The Secret Wars of the CIA, 1981–1987* (New York, 1987), pp. 50–53.
54. Stephen S. Rosenfeld, "The Guns of July," *Foreign Affairs* 64 (Spring 1986): 701–705; *New York Times*, 21 February 1986, p. A14.
55. Thomas J. Downey, "Reagan's Real Aims in South Africa," *Nation*, 8 February 1986, pp. 138–140; *Washington Post*, 31 July 1986, p. A2.
56. *New York Times*, 26 February 1986, p. A16; a good account of post-1972 U.S. involvement is Raymond Bonner's *Waltzing with a Dictator* (New York, 1987).
57. Garry Wills, *Reagan's America* (New York, 1987), p. 47; Penny Lernoux, "El Salvador's Christian Democrat Junta," *Nation*, 1 December 1980, p. 63; *Washington Post*, 14 October 1981, p. A14.
58. *Washington Post*, 4 January 1988, p. A21, on the return of the death squads; *ibid.*, 12 November 1986, p. A21, on the protests; *ibid.*, 25 January 1982, p. A1; *New York Times*, 5 March 1983, p. 4.
59. *Boston Globe*, 15 May 1987, p. 14; *New York Times*, 28 December 1981, p. A16.
60. The quote is in the *Boston Globe*, 25 January 1985, p. 19; also James Chace, "The End of the Affair," *New York Review of Books*, 8 October 1987, p. 28.
61. *Washington Post*, 10 December 1987, p. A48.
62. Abraham F. Lowenthal, *Partners in Conflict: The U.S. and Latin America* (Baltimore, 1987), pp. 103–130; *New York Times*, 4 January 1988, p. 17; *Washington Post*, 16 June 1985, pp. C1, C4.
63. *New York Times*, 28 October 1983, p. A9, contains the text of Reagan's speech on the invasion; Max Holland's "The Origins of the Problem," *New York Times*, 30 November 1986, p. E15, has important background.
64. *Washington Post*, 19 March 1986, p. A30; Mark T. Gilderhus, "An Emerging Synthesis?" *Diplomatic History* 16 (Summer 1992), 149–150.
65. Seth P. Tillman, *The United States in the Middle East* (Bloomington, Ind., 1982), pp. 275–276.
66. *New York Times*, 9 February 1984, p. A12, has a useful record of Reagan's quotes, 1982 to 1984.
67. Sidney Blumenthal, "Dateline Washington: The Conservative Crackup," *Foreign Policy* 69 (Winter 1987–1988): 183–184.
68. The *Army Times* is quoted in the *Washington Post*, 6 August 1987, p. A20; Summers's views are inserted by Congressman Ronald Dellums in the *Congressional Record*, 100th Cong., 1st sess., 14 July 1987, 133, p. E2885.
69. U.S. Congress, House and Senate Select Committees, 100th Cong., 1st sess., 1987, *Report of the Congressional Committees Investigating the Iran-Contra Affair with Supplemental, Minority, and Additional Views* (Washington, D.C., 1987), esp. pp. 11–22, 195–209, 352–353, 375–384. I am deeply indebted to Max Miller for the copy of this complete report.
70. *Washington Post*, 5 October 1987, p. A2; Scott Spencer, "Laurence Walsh's Last Battle," *New York Times Magazine*, July 4, 1993, pp. 28–33.
71. Michael H. Armacost, "U.S. Policy in the Persian Gulf and Kuwaiti Reflagging," U.S. Department of State, *Current Policy*, no. 978, 16 June 1987; *New York Times*, 2 August 1987, p. 1.
72. The Reagan quotes are in George W. Ball's "White House Roulette," *New York Review of Books*, 8 November 1984, p. 5. The Clark quote is in Steven R. Weisman,

"The Influence of William Clark," *New York Times Magazine*, 14 August 1983, pp. 17–20.

73. *New York Times*, 17 January 1984, p. A9.

74. This section has been especially informed by Paul Marantz's "Gorbachev's Road to Reykjavík and Beyond," ms. in the author's possession (1987), esp. 6–8; and the analysis in the U.S.Congress, Joint Economic Committee, 100th Cong., 1st sess., 1987, *Gorbachev's Economic Plans*, 2 vols. (Washington, D.C., 1987), esp. chs. I, II, IV, VII, and X. I am, again, indebted to Max Miller for making these volumes available.

75. *New York Times*, 8 February 1993, p. A8.

76. *Treaty between the United States of America and the Union of Soviet Socialist Republics on the Elimination of Their Intermediate-Range and Shorter-Range Missiles* (Washington, D.C., 1987), pp. 4–6, 12–18.

77. Michael Armacost, "U.S.-Soviet Relations: Coping with Conflicts in the Third World," U.S. Department of State, *Current Policy*, no. 879, 26 September 1986, p. 3.

78. Ruth Leger Sivard, *World Military Expenditure, 1987–1988*, 12th ed. (Washington, D.C., 1987), pp. 5–9; Coit D. Blacker, *Reluctant Warriors: The United States, the Soviet Union and Arms Control* (New York, 1987), p. 1.

79. Quoted in Steven R. Weisman, "Can the Magic Prevail?" *New York Times*, 29 April 1984, p. 54.

80. Stanley Hoffmann, "The New Orthodoxy," *New York Review of Books*, 16 April 1981, p. 26.

FOR FURTHER READING

See also the notes to this chapter and the General Bibliography at the end of the book; references in those sections are usually not repeated here. *Guide to American Foreign Relations since 1700*, ed. Richard Dean Burns (1983), has some useful sources for the late 1970s. Recent overviews include Warren Cohen, *America in the Age of Soviet Power*, in *The Cambridge History of American Foreign Relations* ed. Warren Cohen (1993); Saul Landau, *The Dangerous Doctrine* (1988); *Estrangement: America and the World*, ed. Sanford J. Ungar, (1986), especially the David Watt essay; Fred Halliday, *The Making of the Second Cold War*, 2d ed. (1986), a critical view; Robert O. Keohane, *Neorealism and Its Critics* (1986), a stimulating framework; two books on the economic dilemmas: Alan Wolfe, *America's Impasse* (1981), and Bernard D. Nossiter, *The Global Struggle for More* (1987); David Green's imaginative *Shaping Political Consciousness: The Language of Politics in America from McKinley to Reagan* (1988); Edmund Muskie *et al.*, *The President, the Congress, and Foreign Policy* (1986).

On the Carter administration, a starting place for a fine overview (and excellent bibliography), is Burton I. Kaufman, *The Presidency of James Earl Carter, Jr.* (1993). Other than the Carter, Brzezinski, and Vance memoirs listed in the notes, David S. McLellan's *Cyrus Vance* (1985) should be read along with Gaddis Smith's work that is noted. *Tri-*

lateralism ed. Holly Sklar (1985), is an important, critical set of essays; Strobe Talbott's *Endgame* (1979) is crucial for the politics of SALT II.

On the Reagan years, Lou Cannon's *President Reagan: The Role of a Lifetime* (1991) is standard; Robert Dallek's *Ronald Reagan* (1984) gives an interpretive overview, as does Michael Schaller's *Reckoning with Reagan* (1992); Michael P. Rogin's *Ronald Reagan: The Movie* (1987) analyzes provocatively the relationship between films and politics; Thomas Ferguson and Joel Rogers's *The Hidden Election . . . 1980* (1981) is special, most notably for Bruce Cumings's essay; Alexander M. Haig, Jr.'s *Caveat* (1984) is a bitter memoir by Reagan's first secretary of state. David K. Kyrig, ed., *Reagan and the World* (1990), has good essays on geographical areas.

On U.S.-Soviet competition and the arms race, Raymond L. Garthoff's *Détente and Confrontation* (1985) is a standard, encyclopedic reference; a respected journalist's view is in Michel Tatu, *Eux et nous: Les relations est-ouest entre deux détentes* (1985); Alexander L. George *et al.*, *U.S.-Soviet Security Cooperation* (1988), provide twenty-one case studies on maintaining balance of power; *The Making of America's Soviet Policy*, ed. Joseph S. Nye (1984), goes far beyond bureaucratic politics; Stephen A. Garrett's *From Potsdam to Poland* (1986) is important, especially in noting the influence of ethnic groups on U.S. policy; Don Oberdorfer, *The Turn* (1991) is by a correspondent with access to top officials; *U.S.-Soviet Relations: The Next Phase*, ed. Arnold L. Horelick (1986), provides analyses by leading experts on key areas of contention. Anthony Arnold's *Afghanistan* (1981) places the invasion in post-1919 perspective; Bruce Jentleson's *Pipeline Politics* (1986) is a pivotal study on the declining U.S. ability to use economic sanctions. Ronald E. Powaski's *March to Armageddon* (1987) surveys the arms race since the outbreak of World War II; Strobe Talbott's *Deadly Gambits* (1984) is a fascinating analysis of nuclear-arms politics inside the early Reagan administration; Stephen J. Cimbala's *The Reagan Defense Program* (1986) has useful statistics and analyses; Ronald V. Dellums, R. H. Miller, and H. Lee Halterman's *Defense Sense* (1983) provides essays with an alternative policy to Reagan's; Robert Scheer's *With Enough Shovels* (1982) contains eye-popping interviews with Reagan and his civil-defense officials; Paul Stares's *Space and National Security* (1987) is standard for SDI and its background; Sidney Drell *et al.*, *The Reagan Strategic Defense Initiative* (1985), gives a useful, critical overview; and Dan Caldwell, *The Dynamics of Domestic Politics and Arms Control* (1991), is on the SALT II debate.

On other specific regions, *Perspectives on a U.S.-Canadian Free Trade Agreement*, ed. Robert M. Stern (1987), is important for an often-overlooked part of U.S. foreign policy. U.S.-European relations are studied in *The Atlantic Alliance and Its Critics*, ed. Robert W. Tucker and Linda Wrigley (1983); Diana Johnstone, *The Politics of Euromissiles* (1985); Antony J. Blinken's *Ally versus Ally* (1987), studies in depth the 1982 gas-pipeline dispute. On the Middle East, William B. Quandt's *Camp David* (1986) and Shibley Telhami, *Power and Leadership . . . : The Path to the Camp David Accords* (1990), are excellent accounts; *The Middle East since Camp David*, ed. Robert D. Freedman (1984), is a valuable overview on all the players; Itamar Rabinovich's *The War for Lebanon* (1984, 1986), is a most useful and important account that stresses the historical context; Cheryl A. Rubenberg's *Israel and the American National Interest* (1986), takes a critical look; Edward Tivnan's *The Lobby: Jewish Political Power and American Foreign Policy* (1987), is on a most effective foreign-policy pressure group; Seymour M. Hersh, *The Samson Option* (1991), is on U.S. policy and Israel's nuclear bomb; R. K. Ramazani's *The U.S. and Iran* (1982), is short but superb, especially on the shah's manipulation of Americans; *The Iranian Revolution and the Islamic Republic*, ed. Nikki R. Keddie and

Eric Hooglund (1986), has important essays on U.S. policies; Robert Huyser's *Mission to Tehran* (1987), is by Carter's last emissary; but start with Michael A. Palmer's overview, *Guardians of the Gulf* (1992), which is on U.S. policy in the Persian Gulf from 1833–1991. On China, Robert G. Sutter's *The China Quandary* (1983) studies 1972 to 1982 with the help of many interviews; Leonard A. Kusnitz's *Public Opinion and Foreign Policy* (1984) ends with 1979 and sees public opinion as crucial in shaping key approaches to China. Robert Shaplen's *The Unfinished Revolution* (1987) should be used with Raymond Bonner's *Waltzing with a Dictator* (1987) to understand U.S.-Philippine relations since the 1960s. There are some excellent studies on U.S.-African relations: Sanford J. Ungar's *Africa* (1985), is a superb overview; Gerald J. Bender *et al.*, *African Crisis Areas and U.S. Foreign Policy* (1985); *Politics and Government in African States*, ed. Peter Duignan and Robert H. Jackson (1987), are on key African nations; Christopher Coker's *The United States and South Africa, 1968–1985* (1986), is a succinct, helpful interpretive survey; Anthony Sampson's *Black and Gold* (1987), is a readable analysis focusing on U.S. corporations in South Africa; David A. Korn's *Ethiopia, the United States, and the Soviet Union* (1986), is on a key problem area, as is Jeffrey A. Lefebvre, *Arms for the Horn: U.S. Security Policy in Ethiopia and Somolia, 1953–1991* (1991).

The material on Latin American relations is rich. Three special studies have informed this chapter: Abraham F. Lowenthal's *Partners in Conflict* (1987) and two books by Lars Schoultz—*Human Rights and U.S. Policy towards Latin America* (1981) and *National Security and U.S. Policy toward Latin America* (1987). *The United States and Latin America in the 1980s*, ed. Kevin J. Middlebrook and Carlos Rico (1986), has Latin American as well as North American views presented; Henry Kissinger's *The Report of the President's National Bipartisan Commission on Central America* (1984) is the administration's view, for the most part; *Central America: Anatomy of Conflict*, ed. Robert S. Leiken (1984), is a detailed criticism of the Kissinger commission's assumptions; PACCA, *Changing Course* (1984), criticizes the Kissinger commission and offers a "blueprint" for an alternative policy; Walter LaFeber's *Inevitable Revolutions: The United States in Central America* (1984, 1993) tries to put Central American policies in the context of two hundred years of U.S. relations with the region; Karl Bermann's *Under the Big Stick* (1985) is a superb volume on the United States and Nicaragua since 1848, as is John Booth's *The End and the Beginning* (1982, 1985); Mary B. Vanderlaan's *Revolution and Foreign Policy in Nicaragua* (1986) beautifully relates internal Nicaraguan change in the 1980s to U.S. policies; *Reagan versus the Sandinistas*, ed. Thomas W. Walker (1987), has excellent essays and is only the latest from Walker, who has also published other important studies in the 1980s on the Sandinistas; E. Bradford Burns's *At War in Nicaragua* (1987) is a readable overview by a dean of U.S. scholars of Latin America; *Trouble in Our Backyard*, ed. Martin Siskin, (1984), has important critical essays, especially those by Womack and Montgomery; *El Salvador: Central America in the New Cold War*, ed. Marvin Gittleman *et al.* (1982), is a valuable collection of documents and essays on the entire region; Tommie Sue Montgomery's *Revolution in El Salvador* (1982) has the best account; David N. Farnsworth and James W. McKenney's *U.S.-Panama Relations, 1903–1978* (1983) is especially strong on Panamanian politics; William J. Jorden's *Panama Odyssey* (1984) is a detailed account by the U.S. ambassador in the 1970s; Michael L. Conniff's *Panama and the United States* (1992) gives a fine overview; Tom Barry *et al.*'s *The Other Side of Paradise: Foreign Control in the Caribbean* (1984) provides an excellent critical perspective; Morris Morley's *Imperial State and Revolution* (1987) is the standard (and provocative) study of the United States and Cuba since the early 1950s; Louis A. Perez, Jr.'s

Cuba and the United States gives the best one-volume overview (1990); Carla Anne Robbins's *The Cuban Threat* (1983) is by a journalist who knows Cuba well; *American Intervention in Grenada*, ed. Peter M. Dunn and Bruce W. Watson (1985), has excellent overview essays, especially by George Quester; Hugh O'Shaughnessy's *Grenada* (1985) is a most valuable critique by a British journalist who was there; Reynold A. Burrowes's *Revolution and Rescue in Grenada* (1988) provides a good account and is kinder to U.S. policy than most; Peter H. Schuck and Rogers M. Smith's *Citizenship without Consent* (1985) has an important legal and historical analysis on illegal aliens. Latin American views are in *Estados Unidos: Una visión latinoamericana*, ed. Luis Maira (1984); *La Política de Reagan y la crisis en Centroamérica*, ed. Luis Maira (1982), a good collection of papers; SELA (Sistema Económico Latinoamericano), *América Latina/Estados Unidos* (1983, 1986), a series on economic relations during the debt crisis; Francisco López Segrera, *El Conflicto Cuba–Estados Unidos y la crisis Centroamericana* (1985), for a larger context. A good account is George D. Moffett III's *The Limits of Victory* (1985), which is on the Panama treaties.

On the Iran-Contra debacle, Theodore Draper's *A Very Thin Line* (1991) is a superb starting place; Malcolm Byrne and Peter Kornbluh, eds., *The Iran-Contra Affair* (1993), has key documents; Joseph E. Persico's *Casey* (1990) is the biography of the CIA director; Caspar Weinberger's autobiography, *Fighting for Peace* (1990), is bland, but George Shultz's autobiography, *Turmoil and Triumph* (1993), is detailed and highly important on the range of 1980s foreign policies as well as on Iran-Contra, which Shultz opposed.

On the growing debate over immigration, starting points include Bill Ong Hing's *Making and Remaking Asian America Through Immigration Policy, 1850–1990* (1992); Barbara M. Yarnold's *Refugees Without Refuge* (1990), which is on U.S. asylum policy; Roger Daniels's *Asian America: Chinese and Japanese in the United States Since 1850* (1988).

20

New World Order to World Disorder: Bush and Clinton (1989–1993)

From Dorothy to Lula

"We meant to change a nation, and instead we changed a world," Ronald Reagan declared in his televised "farewell address" on January 11, 1989. "Countries across the globe are turning to free markets and free speech." The outgoing president placed this remark into historical context: "I've thought a bit of the shining 'city on a hill.' The phrase comes from John Winthrop, who wrote it [in 1630] to describe the America he imagined. . . . And how stands the city on this winter night? More prosperous, more secure and happy than it was eight years ago."[1]

Some observers were not as certain. *Commonweal*, a Roman Catholic journal, noted that in the president's "farewell" there were "No warnings here . . . . Nothing about racism. Nothing about the global environment. Nothing about national addictiveness, nuclear mismanagement, homelessness, the financial IOU's we are leaving to our children. And certainly nothing about corruption in government or the growing gap between rich and poor." The respected "TRB" column in the sometimes liberal *New Republic* agreed: the last years of Reagan's rule were marked by "an ongoing struggle among advisers for the soul of a man who was virtually brain dead. The fact that things worked out no worse than they did is either a tribute to the institutional sturdiness of the presidency or proof of the existence of God."[2]

These bitter assessments of the most popular president of the previous quarter-century symbolized the mixed legacy of his policies. The oldest person ever to serve as chief executive, Reagan belonged to a cold-war era that began to end after Mikhail Gorbachev gained power in the Soviet Union in 1985–1986. The world suddenly became more complex, unpredictable, even strange—as when Americans and their vigorously anti-Communist president began cooperating with the Soviets on issues that had once bitterly divided them. Popular films again captured some of the transition in American history from an earlier era when, even on the verge of world war, Americans seemed to be more optimistic and certain than they were in the late 1980s. In *The Wizard of Oz*, released in 1939, Dorothy, the Scarecrow, the Tin Man, and the Cowardly Lion journeyed through danger down "the yellow brick road" to find their search fulfilled, their hopes realized. The story was as old and as upbeat as the white settlers' quest for land and political sufficiency in the West during the several previous centuries. Sam Shepard (one of the country's most popular playwrights and actors) and David Lynch (director of the widely watched television show "Twin Peaks" and of several well-known films, especially *Wild at Heart*) showed a much different American character between 1988 and the early 1990s. *Wild at Heart* revealed the former western frontier region now full of characters such as Sailor and Lula, who lacked aim or values and moved through a society that was breaking down. Sailor laments that it is too bad a person "can't just visit that old Wizard of Oz and get some advice." Lula later observes, "Seems we sort of broke down on the yellow brick road."[3] The popularity of Lynch and Shepard seemed difficult to reconcile with President Reagan's confidence that it "is morning in America."

Reagan's successor in the White House, George Bush, did come to symbolize some of the confusion and, finally, the lost hope that Lynch's characters portrayed. George Herbert Walker Bush grew up in a prominent Connecticut family (his father was a wealthy banker and U.S. Senator) during the late 1930s and early 1940s when *The Wizard of Oz* and the political commitments of *Casablanca* were popular. Just turned eighteen when he entered Naval Flight School in 1942, he survived a plane crash in 1944 and continued to fight the Japanese. His historical hero was that most all-American of presidents, Theodore Roosevelt. Bush said he admired TR because Roosevelt had left (as did Bush) a comfortable life in the East to live, and make much of his political fortune, on the frontier, and because he (like Bush), loved "the strenuous life" of outdoor activity and athletics. One of the new president's first acts in 1989 was to hang Roosevelt's portrait in the Cabinet Room of the White House.[4]

Also resembling TR, Bush paid special attention to foreign policy. Few came to the job with a better diplomatic background. After successfully building a fortune in Texas oil, and helping create a Republican party in hostile Texas politics, Bush served in Congress, directed the U.S. Liaison Office in China, was head of the Central Intelligence Agency, and then became Reagan's vice-president—a position from which he helped shape U.S. policy, especially in Latin America and Asia.

One of the few people who could approach the broad political experience Bush brought to the presidency was his new secretary of state, James Baker. A wealthy lawyer from an old Texas family, Baker had helped Bush build the Texas Republican party. He managed Reagan's spectacular 1980 electoral victory, then served as a highly skillful White House chief of staff, secretary of the Treasury, and the brains behind Bush's come-from-behind victory in 1988 over Democratic nominee Michael Dukakis. In the State Department he surrounded himself with a small, young, fiercely loyal staff, only a few of whom had any diplomatic experience. The question became whether, for all their great political abilities, Baker and his young staff had the necessary sense of history and broad vision to deal with the new, incredibly complex, post–cold-war world that suddenly began to take shape.

Despite his experience, Bush proved to be of little help to Baker in working out what the new president called "the vision thing." His first, much-awaited foreign-policy statement in the spring of 1989 only asked for more of the same U.S. policies. A product of the cold-war era, he would be the last president who had served in World War II; he seemed almost reluctant to see the post-1941 era end. Such reluctance was part of a natural caution that restrained Bush from making commitments to fresh policy departures. Part of that reluctance was probably rooted in 1975–1976, the years of Gerald Ford's presidency, when Bush was director of the CIA. His national-security adviser, General Brent Scowcroft, was Ford's NSC adviser, and his secretary of defense, Richard Cheney, served as Ford's White House chief of staff. Bush, Scowcroft, and Cheney never forgot how Ford was associated with the Nixon-Kissinger détente policy toward the Soviets, then lost the 1976 election as détente became a dirty word in American politics (see p. 672). Bush never wanted to repeat that political disaster. A tough, cold-war-like approach seemed safest. "I will never apologize for the United States of America, ever. I don't care what the facts are," he declared in 1988.[5]

"THE END OF THE MIDDLE AGES" IN CENTRAL AMERICA?

In one bloody area, however, Bush did break free of, while learning from, cold-war history. He and Baker realized that Reagan's tough military policies had not resolved the long, terrible wars in Nicaragua, El Salvador, and Guatemala. Those conflicts indeed threatened to infect the other two Central American nations of Costa Rica (the most democratic and literate society in Latin America), and Honduras. Moreover, Americans polled in the 1980s consistently opposed Reagan's use of force. Even Congress had grown tired of this failed approach by the mid-1980s. When Reagan officials tried secretly to avoid Congress's restraints on them, the result—the Iran-Contra debacle (see p. 725)— set off a U.S. political, constitutional, and diplomatic crisis.

Bush and Baker wanted to resolve these Central American problems so they could move on to more profitable and popular diplomatic ventures. They suddenly were doubly blessed in 1989. The peace plan of Costa Rican President Oscar Arias picked up speed. The Nicaraguan Sandinista government accepted the peace plan's key provisions: a military cease-fire, a de-escalation of military-force numbers, and the holding of open elections. The Sandinistas fully expected to win such elections over their Contra foes and more moderate opponents led by popular newspaper publisher Violeta Chamorro. Then Mikhail Gorbachev tired of throwing scarce Soviet resources into bottomless Central American wars. He also reduced his help to Fidel Castro's Cuba, which had long supported the region's revolutionaries. Bush and Baker proposed a deal: They agreed to accept the results of the Nicaraguan election in early 1990 if Gorbachev would cut aid to the Sandinistas and warn them that they too had to accept the results. It seemed to be a highly risky deal for Bush.[6]

But he won. The Sandinistas lost the 1990 elections—the victims of their inability to create a growing economy amid civil war, and also of Gorbachev's deal with the Americans. It became clear later, moreover, that the United States had not only spent $9 million openly during the election, but the CIA had spent millions more covertly to ensure Mrs. Chamorro's victory.[7] The Sandinistas surrendered power to Chamorro's National Opposition Union (UNO). The Contras, with U.S. aid, dismantled their bases. After nearly a decade of war, peace broke out. The people, however, found little comfort. When Chamorro tried to create a consensus by allowing the Sandinistas to continue to control the army and police, she was harshly attacked by her own supporters and the United States. Bush and the Congress cut back on economic aid. Political murders began again. Some six hundred Contras returned to northern jungle areas to prepare for a new civil war. As Chamorro's hold weakened and the economy slid, the Sandinistas' well-organized party hoped to regain power in the 1996 elections.[8]

Bush also profited when Arias, and then the United Nations, brokered a truce in El Salvador's decade-long bloodbath. The war had stalemated as the revolutionary FMLN obtained less support from the disintegrating Soviet bloc, and the United States finally pressured its Salvadoran military allies to make peace in January 1992. The army was reduced, and the FMLN slowly laid down its arms. Most dramatically, a commission studying the brutalities of the war forced the removal of thirty-four army officers, including the minister of defense. A UN Truth Commission verified that while both the FMLN and the military had committed horrible crimes, the U.S.-supported and trained military was especially guilty of uncivilized acts, including the murder of an archbishop while he said mass in 1980, the rape-murders of 4 U.S. churchwomen in 1980, the massacre of 200 civilians in 1981, and the killing of 6 Jesuit priests in 1989. U.S. officials had lied throughout the 1980s to cover up these crimes so Congress would continue to send nearly $5 billion of aid to the Salvadoran military. Reporters who had written accurately about the crimes, and were then attacked as liars by the Reagan administration, were now vindicated by the UN Commission.[9]

Guatemala, after thirty years of war in which the United States had fully supported the military government, had suffered 150,000 dead, another 50,000 "disappeared" (that is, unaccounted for), and one million displaced (many of whom had gone to the United States). In 1990, this war also wound down, although fighting between the revolutionaries and the army continued. Bush cut off $3.2 million in U.S. aid after an American was killed in 1990, probably by government forces. World attention focused on Guatemala when Rigoberta Menchú won the Nobel Peace Prize in 1992. Born to a peasant Indian family, she saw two of her brothers die of malnutrition, a not-uncommon occurrence in Guatemala. Her father had been burned to death by the army when he peacefully protested the military's repression. Her mother was tortured, raped, and killed; her body, the daughter recalled, was found "tied to a tree and partially devoured by animals." Menchú refused to become directly involved on either side in the war, but instead she eloquently condemned the atrocities while living in exile. The Guatemalan military and U.S. officials denounced her actions as supporting

After winning the 1992 Nobel Peace Prize for her opposition to the militaristic Guatemalan regime, Rigoberta Menchú placed her Nobel medallion in a Mexico City museum where it would remain, she announced, until her native Guatemala became peaceful. President Carlos Salinas de Gortari and Cecilia Ocelli de Gortari watched Menchú, who had been forced by the Guatemalans to seek refuge in Mexico City.

the revolutionaries. The Nobel citation declared she was "a vivid symbol of peace and reconciliation."[10]

A Salvadoran leader hoped that "it is the end of the Middle Ages in El Salvador." Nearly all Central Americans prayed they could say the same for their own nations. A historical verdict for U.S. foreign policy was given by Honduran President Rafael Callejas: "Most of the U.S. money came to sustain the wrong policies. We lost a decade."[11]

THE INVASION OF PANAMA

In another part of the region during late 1989, Bush sent not U.S. money, but 24,000 troops to overthrow the Panamanian dictatorship of General Manuel Antonio Noriega. On the surface, such massive use of force was puzzling. Since 1903, the United States had dominated Panama. Since the mid-1970s, Bush, first as director of the CIA and then as vice-president, had personally worked closely with Noriega.

The Panamanian had cooperated with Bush in providing intelligence and by fighting against Central American revolutionaries. Not that Noriega was a nice man. A sadist who tortured and assassinated political opponents, he also cooperated with major drug traffickers (who profited enormously from U.S. buyers), and openly corrupted elections to maintain his power. The Reagan administration was nevertheless willing to overlook Noriega's crimes—until 1986–1987, when he quit cooperating so fully with U.S. military policies in Central America. By 1989, Bush and Noriega taunted each other publicly. Often derided as a "wimp" for his indecision, Bush seemed to live up to the term in the autumn of 1989, when he moved too slowly to help Panamanian military officers who were trying to overthrow Noriega. Noriega smashed the revolt.

Tension thickened between Noriega's forces and the 13,000 U.S. troops stationed in Panama, supposedly to protect the canal. In mid-December, Panamanian forces killed an American soldier who, they claimed, tried to run a roadblock in front of Panama's military headquarters. Then a U.S. naval officer and his wife were attacked and abused. Bush decided to show that he was not a wimp. On December 19–20, 11,000 more U.S. troops flew in and overthrew, then finally captured, Noriega. At least 300 Panamanian civilians died in the bombardment, 3,000 were wounded; 23 U.S. servicemen were killed, 324 more wounded; 18,000 Panamanians lost their homes.[12]

Bush gave four major reasons for the invasion: first, the threat to U.S. personnel in Panama; second, the danger Noriega posed to the Panama Canal's security; third, the general's deep involvement in drug traffic headed for North American streets; and fourth, the need to create democracy in Panama. As a former naval officer, Bush seemed to feel especially strong about the first point.

Critics quickly raised questions about these reasons. As to the first, special investigating committees of the New York City Bar Association concluded that Bush could have removed the threat to U.S. personnel by moving or isolating them (as often was done in other countries when Americans were threatened), instead of ordering an invasion that caused many civilian casualties. As to the second, the Bar Association and other investigators discovered no threat posed by Noriega to the canal. He had carefully avoided threatening it. As to the third point, Noriega's involvement with the drug trade was real, but less so than Bush alleged. Moreover, despite the capture of Noriega, by 1991–1992 more cocaine than ever was moving through Panama's so-called "trampoline" route that acted as a springboard for flying drugs into the United

States. Packets of cocaine washed up on Panamanian beaches. Those who lived along the ocean in Panama City itself observed "Little boats . . . with the stuff and then fine cars, sometimes Mercedes-Benzes, come to take it away." If the Bush administration cared about this traffic in 1989, it seemed to care much less in 1991. Finally, instead of a functioning democracy, Panamanian politics seemed headed toward chaos and corruption by 1992. The civilian government installed by Bush was threatened with destruction by its own military and was finally saved again by U.S. troops. Noriega meanwhile was taken to Florida. After a lengthy and highly criticized trial, he was sentenced to long terms in a U.S. jail for his drug trafficking.[13]

A central reason for Bush's strong action seemed to be his determination to escape both Noriega's taunting and the wimp label. The president also demonstrated to other possible opponents that he was not reluctant to use massive military power. The effect of the invasion on Panama is less clear. As New Year's Day of the year 2000 approaches (that is, the moment when, according to the 1977–1978 treaties, the United States will turn over the great canal to Panamanian control), the passageway's importance declines. Larger warships cannot use it, and alternative carriers (such as oil pipelines and giant railway container cars) have become more popular. But the canal's strategic and economic usefulness remains significant, even as its future remains endangered.

THE HISTORIC TURN OF THE LATE TWENTIETH CENTURY: BUSH AND GORBACHEV

The president was finally decisive, awesomely so, in destroying Noriega. He was less decisive in dealing with his greatest foreign-policy problem—indeed, the most historic event in the last half of the twentieth century: the collapse of the Soviet Union and, consequently, the end of the cold war.

As Bush entered the White House, Soviet leader Mikhail Gorbachev knew he was burdened by an increasingly weak economy and, indeed, a disintegrating society. Generations of Communist rigidity and corruption had taken a heavy toll, but Gorbachev and his foreign minister, Eduard Shevardnadze, were the first Soviet leaders to act on those facts. After signing historic agreements with Reagan (see p. 734), in late 1988 Gorbachev announced major cuts in the Soviet military, began pulling troops out of the eastern European Communist bloc, and moved to end the disastrous ten-year intervention in Afghanistan. For these acts, he won the Nobel Peace Prize in 1990.

The scene was set for a dramatic response by Bush. But the new president spent the first half of 1989 making an extensive, and finally bland, policy analysis of U.S.-Soviet relations. Having known only the cold war in their lives, the president and his top advisers (NSC adviser Brent Scowcroft and Secretary of State James Baker) feared chaos and dangerous unpredictability if the cold war suddenly ended. They also feared what Scowcroft called "the clever bear syndrome," that is, that Gorbachev was lulling the West to sleep while secretly preparing to launch a new, more devastating cold war. Bush and Baker even privately condemned Reagan for having made too many deals with Gorbachev. In other words, they believed Ronald Reagan had been too soft on communism. Having little knowledge of, or apparent interest in, the broad historical background, Bush, Scowcroft, and Baker became limited by the only history they knew—that of the cold war. Vice-President Dan Quayle ridiculed Gorbachev as just a Stalinist "in Gucci shoes." Bush's press secretary called the Soviet leader, "a drugstore cowboy." (That remark led a knowledgeable State Department official to comment, "Some cowboy. Some drugstore!")[14]

Gorbachev, however, believed he had no alternative but to continue putting an end to the cold war. In mid-1989, the Soviets agreed to U.S. positions on key arms disputes. Gorbachev also suddenly and dramatically refused to send Soviet troops into Poland, Hungary, or Czechoslovakia to prop up falling Communist regimes. He told the Polish Communists in the summer of 1989 that they had to make their own deals with their political opposition. Soon, to the West's surprise, Poland's anti-Communist Solidarity party won open elections and began claiming power. Gorbachev, it is clear, was also surprised. He remained a devout Communist. But he believed that good Communists in the USSR and its East European satellites saw the light as he did—that is, they would scale down the cold war, reform their inefficient economies, revitalize their societies, and continue to hold power. Poland's experience, however, proved that Gorbachev was a dreamer.

His, and Bush's, greatest shock lay just ahead. By October 1989, Hungary and Czechoslovakia had followed Poland in overthrowing Communist rulers. Romania's dictatorship fell, as well, in late 1989. East Germany's hard-line Communists, however, tried to crack down on internal dissenters, only to find that East Germans were escaping in large numbers to West Germany through the Hungarian and Czech gaps in the iron curtain. At 11:17 P.M., on November 9, 1989, a new

East German government decided, with Gorbachev's support, to recognize new realities by opening the Berlin Wall. Within seventy-two
hours this blood-stained, twenty-eight-year-old symbol of the cold war
was being battered down by giant jackhammers, and also by small
hammers wielded by aspiring capitalists who sold small pieces of the
wall to eager U.S. and European buyers.

The changes in Poland forced the president to believe that "There's
big stuff, heavy stuff going on here." As he watched the Berlin Wall
come down, he finally concluded that the Soviets have "got to be really
serious—more serious than I realized." Bush now fully embraced Gorbachev and, in skillful diplomatic strokes, helped the Soviets prepare
for the unthinkable: the reunification of the powerful 62 million West
Germans with the 16 million East Germans. Gorbachev fought against
German reunification, for, among other things, it would be the ultimate humiliation for the Soviets who had sacrificed so greatly (including 20 million lives) to win World War II. Since the late 1940s, Western
leaders had said they supported a united Germany, but now that it
suddenly became a real possibility, they had second thoughts. West
German Chancellor Helmut Kohl was nevertheless determined to make
his place in history, despite estimates that it would cost his people a
half-trillion dollars over ten years to raise the East German living standards. Realizing the inevitable, Bush helped bring Gorbachev around
to accepting unification, and even the inclusion of the new Germany
in NATO, by assuring him that U.S. troops would remain in Europe to
help keep Germany under control, if such restraint were needed. He
also pieced together a $24 billion aid package for Gorbachev, although
the Soviets received only a small fraction of it. It was Kohl, however,
who controlled the unification process in early 1990. While Bush (like
most Americans and western Europeans who had vivid memories of
World War II) had qualms about a new, united, powerful Germany,
and while the British and French governments actually pleaded with
Gorbachev not to allow unification, the German Chancellor flew to
Gorbachev's summer home and negotiated the pivotal deals. Kohl
accepted a long-term U.S. military presence in Europe, gave Gorbachev $15 billion, and—most important—guaranteed the new Ger-
many's acceptance of the boundaries imposed by the triumphant Allies
in 1945. The Chancellor, that is, gave up all claims to parts of Poland
that had once belonged to Germany.[15]

As these agreements took effect in mid-1990, Bush finally admitted
that the cold war had ended. Gorbachev agreed: "We are no longer
adversaries." The events were mind-boggling. For decades, the Soviets
had tried to push the United States out of Europe. But Gorbachev,

faced with a rising Germany and a declining Soviet military power, now told the president, "It's important for the future of Europe that you are in Europe, so we don't want to see you out of there." Bush agreed; he knew that NATO was one of the few remaining points through which the United States could influence European affairs. Nevertheless, the 300,000 U.S. troops in Europe declined to 180,000 by 1993 and seemed to be headed toward 100,000. The Soviet retreat from eastern Europe was even more rapid. In early 1991 Gorbachev issued the stunning announcement that the Warsaw Pact—the Moscow-directed military alliance through which the Red Army had policed eastern Europe since 1955—would be dissolved in April 1991. The Communist bloc's economic alliance, Comecon, also disappeared.[16]

For obvious reasons, Bush now saw Gorbachev as "really the best hope" for U.S. policies. The president had become convinced that without Gorbachev, the Soviet Union, with its 30,000 nuclear weapons, would fragment and finally split apart. He seemed as terrified of this possibility as were Soviet leaders. At a press conference, Bush declared that the "enemy" was not Germany (or the Soviet Union, or Japan, as many Americans believed). "No, the enemy is unpredictability. The enemy is instability." This view took Bush to dangerous ground. The three Baltic states (Latvia, Lithuania, and Estonia) had been conquered by Stalin in 1939–1940, although the United States had never formally recognized Soviet control. In 1990–1991, the Baltic peoples moved toward independence. Gorbachev resisted. In early 1991, fifteen Lithuanian protesters were killed by Red Army units. Bush refused to condemn the Soviet action or undercut Gorbachev. At the same time, several other of the fifteen republics making up the Soviet Union also demanded their independence. They were led by Ukraine and Georgia. In August 1991, Bush flew to Ukraine's capital, Kiev, to lecture the parliament that it should remain under Gorbachev's guidance. Critics, who wanted to seize this golden opportunity to dismantle the Soviet empire, condemned what they labeled Bush's "Chicken Kiev" speech.[17]

Three weeks later, Gorbachev was nearly destroyed by a right-wing coup. He was saved, temporarily, by his political enemy, Boris Yeltsin.

The Historic Turn in the Late Twentieth-Century: Bush and Yeltsin

Yeltsin was the tall, white-haired, rough-edged Russian who was strongly reform-minded—in part because he came from a poor peasant family

*The map of central and eastern Europe radically changed three times during
the twentieth century: 1919, 1945, and 1990–1991. This map shows the vital
region in 1993. Note the newly united Germany. Estonia, Latvia, Lithuania
(the three Baltic States), Belarus, Ukraine, and Moldova had—along with the
giant republic of Russia—been part of the Soviet Union before 1989 but now
moved toward independence. Note also Croatia and Bosnia and Herzegovina,
once part of Yugoslavia but now areas for brutal wars in 1992–1993 among
Croatian Christians, Muslims (especially in Bosnia), and Serbian Eastern
Orthodox Christians. Prague (Czech Republic) and Budapest (Hungary) were
becoming cultural and business centers of eastern Europe.*

(which for warmth had slept on their hut's floor with the farm animals). His father was arrested during Stalin's bloody purges in the
1930s.[18] In 1987, Gorbachev threw Yeltsin out of the Soviet government for being too reform-minded. The two men became bitter oppo-

nents. Yeltsin clawed his way back. In early 1990 he won election to the new Russian Parliament. In June 1991, he won 57 percent of the vote to become the Russian Republic's first elected president in its history. He enjoyed much stronger democratic credentials than did Gorbachev, whose election to the Soviet presidency had been by votes of the old Communist party hacks who were now trying to stop his programs of change.

Yeltsin was becoming a hero in Russia, but not in Washington. In 1989, Scowcroft reluctantly agreed to talk with Yeltsin, brought him quietly into the White House through a side door so few would notice, then fell asleep while Yeltsin talked at length. Rumors spread that the Russian was publicly drunk. Bush agreed with Scowcroft that Yeltsin was a "boor" and that Gorbachev seemed so much more civilized. Bush, however, relied too much on his taste for personality. Several overriding events proved to be more important. Yeltsin had a strong democratic base, and Gorbachev did not. Yeltsin, moreover, realized that the Soviet Union was coming apart and was willing to make deals with the emerging republics. Gorbachev meanwhile worked to keep the old Soviet Empire together. When the Red Army killed the fifteen Lithuanians in 1991, Yeltsin flew to the scene to sympathize with the victims. "That son of a bitch," Gorbachev cried—and Yeltsin had to return secretly to Moscow after fears spread that his plane was to be sabotaged. Finally, Yeltsin wanted to dismantle the Soviet military more rapidly than did his rival. As Yeltsin built his democratic base, Gorbachev tried to save his power by appointing old Communists and militarists. These were the people who then tried to overthrow him in August 1991.[19]

Bush nevertheless stuck doggedly with Gorbachev, even as the Soviet leader's popularity sank with the economy. Without an economic plan, and unable to deal with a mushrooming "Moscow Mafia" (one Russian likened the situation to that in Chicago during gangster Al Capone's days in the 1920s), Gorbachev floundered as inflation soared and the people lost the security they at least had received from the old, stagnant, Communist regime. A Soviet economist found "it strange to hear Americans talk about the 'possibility' of an economic crash. The crash has already happened when, as now, there are deep shortages of 95 percent of all goods." Experts on Soviet affairs in both the Pentagon and the CIA warned Bush and Scowcroft that they were on the wrong side of a historic turn. These experts urged that the United States and its allies at least push Gorbachev and Yeltsin to work together so the strongest possible political team could ease the USSR's political and economic tensions. Bush and Scowcroft refused. They compared Gorbachev to Lincoln in 1861 heroically trying to keep the Union together. Not so, the Pentagon and CIA responded; he resembled those in 1776 who fought vainly against revolutionary change and the overriding need for a new constitution in the United States.[20]

In April 1991, the CIA warned that an anti-Gorbachev coup by right-wing hard-liners could occur. Scowcroft dismissed the warning as "simplistic" and believed the agency was a hotbed of Yeltsinistas. On August 19–20, the hard-liners struck. They put Gorbachev under house arrest, although he refused to sign a letter of resignation as they demanded. Key elements of the army, however, refused to follow the coup-plotters' orders. Yeltsin and his followers held out in the "white house" a short distance from the Kremlin. New technology helped undermine the plotters: CNN televised the events, and Yeltsin's determined opposition, throughout the world. American culture also played a small part; McDonald's, with its largest outlet in the world in Moscow, trucked hamburgers and coffee to the "white house." Disorganized, often quite drunk, unsupported by enough of the military, the plotters finally quit. One committed suicide. Gorbachev returned to Moscow, but as Bush said privately, "I'm afraid he may have had it." Yeltsin was the hero. The reformer took power, stripped Gorbachev of his office, launched an economic reform program and—in a historic moment on December 25, 1991— decreed that the Soviet Union ceased to exist. Yeltsin nevertheless controlled an impressive nation: Russia, whose vastness stretched across ten time zones and some of the world's richest mineral resources. He hoped to work out new relationships, moreover, with the eleven other increasingly independent republics.[21]

The Soviet Union was dead at age seventy-four. Gorbachev and Bush had been unable to control its final illness. Bush quickly moved to work with Yeltsin. The two men signed the Start II treaty that cut their nuclear weapons by two-thirds so that each held 3,500 warheads and bombs. The United States continued to work on the $24 billion aid package. It was, however, again too late. Three years had been lost. As Yeltsin tried to push Russia's huge bureaucracy-burdened economy into a free-market system, prices skyrocketed 350 percent in weeks. Inflation began to soar toward a 2,000 percent annual level (Americans worry when their inflation rate goes above 4 percent). Food and other necessities grew scarce. Even with the $24 billion and another $12 billion that the new, French-created European Bank for Reconstruction could invest, the West on its own could not significantly help turn around the Russian economy.[22]

The smiles of President George Bush and President Boris Yeltsin were appropriate. The U.S. and Russian leaders had just signed in Moscow a historic START-II treaty that for the first time sharply reduced the strategic nuclear weapons on both sides. The smiles, however, also hid a personal relationship between the two men that had in 1989–1991 been tense and even bitter as Bush had strongly supported Yeltsin's rival in Moscow, Mikhail Gorbachev. The picture was snapped on January 3, 1993—less than three weeks before Bush was due to leave office.

One Western banker complained that trying to start a business in Moscow was "like trying to irrigate a desert with a garden hose." Throughout the cold war, the CIA and military intelligence, for their own budgetary purposes, had consistently overestimated Soviet economic capacity—which, it turned out, on a per capita basis was more equal to Mexico's than to the economies of the United States or western Europe. Although many Western businesses (such as McDonald's, Pizza Hut, Pepsi-Cola, and several oil companies), found profits, others, in the words of a U.S. newspaper, "go away complaining about unappetizing meals that cost $75 and shabby $200-a-night rooms in [Moscow] hotels where 25-watt bulbs and prostitutes are part of the decor." The number of homeless and beggers increased dramatically.[23] Some of the more ambitious Russians seized the opportunity to find (or steal) Western goods and become rich by charging exorbitant prices. Russians, whose history was filled with such (indeed, worse) crises, nevertheless still found humor in their situation: a Moscow mother asks what her small child hopes to be after growing up. The child replies, "A foreigner."

THE POST–COLD-WAR DISORDER: WAR WITH IRAQ

With the Soviet Union (or much of it) now calling itself the Commonwealth of Independent States, the State Department's Soviet Desk retitled itself EUR/ISCA—that is, "Europe—Office of Independent States and Commonwealth Affairs." Some critics believed a better title for Bush's Soviet advisers was EUR/OBE, or "Europe—Overtaken By Events."[24] During the 1990–1991 conflict with Iraq, however, the president's cultivation of Gorbachev paid off.

Since the 1970s, Soviet military advisers had trained and helped supply Iraqi dictator Saddam Hussein's military. In 1980–1981, when Iraq began one of the bloodiest, most brutal, and longest twentieth-century wars by attacking Iran, the United States and some of its allies (notably West Germany and France) also began sending aid to the Iraqi dictator. Informed estimates of this aid between 1983 and 1988 run as high as $34 billion, with half coming from the Soviets. The Reagan administration also gave Saddam Hussein valuable intelligence information. By 1988, with the Iranians and Iraqis exhausted, the war halted. Nearly bankrupted by the conflict, Saddam Hussein pushed his fellow Arab oil producers to cut production and thus increase both oil prices and his income. Led by Saudi Arabia and Kuwait, they refused. The dictator did not take opposition kindly. He had slaughtered his political opponents in cold blood, sometimes with his own hand, as he moved toward power after 1968. Now he demanded that Kuwait give him strategic islands and oil fields that had been in dispute since British colonial officials (who then controlled the region) had drawn arbitrary boundaries between Kuwait and Iraq in 1922. Kuwait also refused these demands.[25]

Saddam Hussein prepared again for war. He apparently believed, with good reason, that the Soviets would continue to support him. He thought the Americans were paralyzed by memories of Vietnam. In any case, as he prepared to launch the attack on August 2, 1990, the U.S. ambassador to Iraq, April Glaspie, assured him the United States "had no opinion" on these boundary struggles. She said this on direct instructions to her from the Bush-Baker State Department. (Later, she unfairly became the scapegoat for this disastrous policy and suffered severely professionally and personally.) The Iraqi dictator was already on record as declaring he hoped to see all Israel in flames. He also had used poison gas in trying to destroy the Kurds, a minority people concentrated in northern Iraq. Bush, however, was so determined to have normal relations with Saddam Hussein that when the U.S. Congress moved to impose economic sanctions on Iraq in response to the dictator's brutalities on his own people, Bush blocked the attempt. If Bush had not blocked the sanctions, U.S. farmers, as well as arms merchants, would have been upset. American rice growers, for example, sold one-fifth of their exports to Iraq as part of an overall $1 billion in U.S. agricultural shipments to that country.[26]

On August 2, 1990, Iraq seized Kuwait in a lightning military operation. Saddam Hussein now controlled about 20 percent of the world's known oil reserves. U.S. officials feared he was poised to conquer Saudi Arabia; he then would have 40 percent of the reserves, as well as control of a close U.S. military ally. A surprised Bush hesitated, then (pushed especially by Britain's tough Prime Minister, Margaret Thatcher, whose nation depended heavily on Kuwaiti money), the president vowed to defend Saudi Arabia and liberate Kuwait. Over the next six months, Bush gave various reasons for this commitment: the naked Iraqi seizure of territory (he compared Saddam Hussein to Hitler); the threat posed to world oil prices; the opportunity to destroy Iraq's growing capacity to produce nuclear and chemical weapons; the need to uphold the UN's pledge to resist aggression; and the bitter personal betrayal he felt after trying to work with the Iraqi leader. Bush notably argued that with the end of the cold war "a new world order" was emerging, but that it could be stillborn, with a more dangerous world appearing unless aggressors such as Saddam Hussein learned their lessons now.[27] (In reality, neither Bush nor any of his advisers was ever clear about what this "new world order" meant. The term had been mentioned in an informal discussion by NSC Adviser Scowcroft shortly after the Iraqi invasion. When Pam Olson, of CNN television, asked a Bush adviser what was going on, he responded that "the new world order" was at stake. She used the term on television and it promptly became identified with Bush's policy and worldview—although neither then nor later did he ever bother to define it. It became one of those terms that many people used, but none knew exactly what it meant.)

The most spectacular successes of Bush's presidency followed. He pieced together an effective alliance of nations, including some (such as Israel on the one hand, and Saudi Arabia and Syria on the other) that were violent political enemies. He gained full support from the United Nations which, for the first time in its history, acted as its founders of 1944–1945 had planned. It could resist Iraqi aggression because for the first time the Soviets, under Gorbachev, cooperated with rather than blocked UN action. Bush's personal diplomacy paid dividends, for Gorbachev rejected advice from his pro-Iraqi military (which predicted a great victory for Saddam Hussein over the U.S. forces). Gorbachev tried to work out a peace plan and delay the start of the U.S. offensive, but he never directly opposed Bush's actions. The president was also shrewd, if rather devious, at home. He shipped 250,000 men and women to Saudi Arabia and other bases immediately after the Iraqi invasion, but then waited until after the November congressional elections before he doubled those forces. The doubling of the troops signaled an early military confrontation. Having avoided a divisive political debate in the election campaign, he went to Congress in January 1991 and demanded that it pass a resolution supporting his use of force. Bush was the first president since Franklin D. Roosevelt in 1941 to honor, however loosely, the Constitution's requirement that Congress must declare war. Intense debate followed. Opponents argued that by sending in a half-million troops, Bush had put them in an impossible position to debate a war resolution; clearly, war was inevitable anyway. They also argued that economic pressures would force Saddam Hussein to give in without the need to go to war. The resolution authorizing the president to use force narrowly passed the Senate (52–47) and more easily passed the House (250–183).[28]

The great question became whether U.S. and allied forces could destroy Iraq's battle-hardened troops without suffering heavy casualties. Such casualties could lead, as they had in the Vietnam conflict, to Americans demanding an immediate peace. Secretary of Defense Richard Cheney told a Middle East official, "The military is finished in this society, if we screw this up."[29] U.S. military officers, however, had closely studied and learned from the Vietnam debacle. By using overwhelming force at the start, and by aiming at definite objectives, they believed U.S. forces could achieve quick victory and avoid a political backlash.

This strategy was best argued by General Colin Powell, chairman of the Joint Chiefs of Staff. The first African American to hold this highest of military positions (and the first as well to hold the job of NSC adviser—from 1987–1989), Powell had been educated at City College of New York and George Washington University. He served two tours in Vietnam. When not rapidly moving up the military ladder (or pursuing his hobby of restoring Volvos), Powell studied Vietnam's lessons.[30] He steadily opposed committing U.S. forces unless (as in Panama,

General Colin Powell and Secretary of Defense Richard Cheney (behind Pow-
ell's arm) visited a U.S. base in Saudi Arabia during February 1991—just
before the all-out ground assault against Iraqi forces. Powell, the first African
American to serve as the President's National Security Adviser and then as
Chairman of the Joint Chiefs (1989–1993), proved to be a brilliant strategist in
fighting the war, but in other instances also acted as a restraint on both Presi-
dents Bush and Clinton when they considered the use of U.S. forces in later
crises.

and now in Iraq), he believed a quick, relatively cost-free victory that
achieved specific targets (such as the liberation of Kuwait), could be
won. Bush agreed both to commit overwhelming power and not to
second-guess Powell once fighting began.

On January 16, 1991, U.S. planes and missiles, many launched from
ships in the Persian Gulf, massively attacked Iraq. The Iraqis responded
with Soviet-built Scud missiles that caused fatalities in Israel and Saudi
Arabia. U.S.-built Patriot missiles destroyed some of the Scuds (often
captured in spectacular television pictures instantly shown in the United
States via satellites), although apparently not more than twenty-four of
the eighty-six Scuds that Iraq launched were actually hit. Overall, the
U.S. air and missile attacks were less effective than the Bush administration claimed during the conflict.[31] Saddam Husscin's installations
for developing nuclear and chemical weapons, for example, were not
destroyed. Nevertheless, the Iraqi military suffered severe damage. A

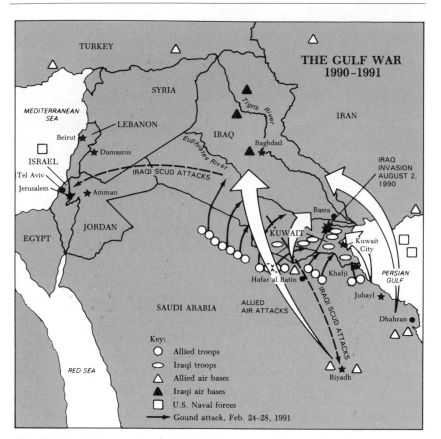

After U.S. battleships and amphibious forces in the Persian Gulf made a feint at landing at Kuwait City, the half-million troops in the coalition forces moved along the ground out of Saudi Arabia to cut off Iraqi forces in Kuwait and southern Iraq. The war lasted less than 100 hours in February 1991, although U.S. airpower failed to destroy one of its key targets: chemical and nuclear plants in central and northern Iraq.

month later, the allied ground forces attacked Kuwait and southern Iraq. Saddam Hussein had promised to wage "the mother of all battles," but in only a hundred hours his troops were either destroyed or retreating to the capital of Baghdad.

Kuwait was freed, but it turned out that many of the dictator's best troops survived. In one of several miscalculations at the end of the fighting, U.S. officers allowed Iraqi helicopter forces to escape. These forces were later used again to attack the Kurdish people in northern Iraq.[32] Bush and Powell had no intention of widening the war's objectives by driving to Baghdad and destroyng Saddam Hussein's regime, nor would any of their Arab allies have approved such a drive. Many of the Arab people on the streets of such nations as Jordan, Egypt, and even Saudi Arabia sympathized with Saddam Hussein's struggle against the Western forces. A direct attempt to overthrow him could lead to severe political disturbances within those and other Middle East nations. The Iraqi dictator therefore was able to intensify efforts to build nuclear weapons, hold off UN teams that tried to inspect his nuclear plants, and launch new attacks on the Kurds and other internal enemies until U.S. and UN forces finally had to try to protect these victims. Meanwhile, the United States moved to implement the "new world order" in the Middle East by building the region's greatest military presence. That power rested on new base agreements with Kuwait and other Arab countries to support the long-term stationing of 24,000 U.S. troops,

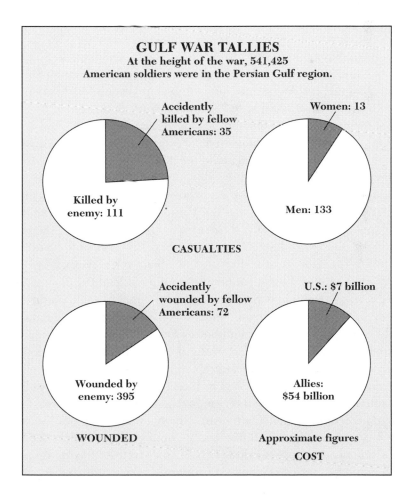

GULF WAR TALLIES
At the height of the war, 541,425
American soldiers were in the Persian Gulf region.

Accidently
killed by fellow
Americans: 35

Women: 13

Killed by
enemy: 111

Men: 133

CASUALTIES

Accidently
wounded by fellow
Americans: 72

U.S.: $7 billion

Wounded by
enemy: 395

Allies:
$54 billion

WOUNDED

Approximate figures

COST

26 warships, and more than 150 planes.[33] These agreements marked a long step since 1946, when U.S. officials had debated whether to put even one U.S. warship in the eastern Mediterranean.

The New Disorder: Bush to Clinton

George Bush thought of himself as the foreign-policy president, much as Richard Nixon had thought of himself twenty years earlier. And like Nixon, Bush was removed from office before he wanted to leave, albeit in a more regular process of election. Bush was justly proud of many foreign-policy accomplishments: triumphing over Iraq; initiating the first comprehensive peace process to end the nearly half-century war between Israel and its neighbors; pushing negotiations that established the world's richest free-trade area comprising Canada, Mexico, and the United States; handling the Soviet collapse and German unification; signing the most radical nuclear-arms reduction agreements in history; improving, in a controversial move, relations with China even after Communist officials killed pro-democracy protesters in Beijing's Tiananmen Square in 1989; and helping bring an end to several bloody Central American revolutions. In a speech at Texas A & M University in late 1992, he boasted that many of "these once seemed a dream. Today they are concrete realities."[34]

Critics, as usual, nevertheless found weaknesses. When Bush and other Republicans claimed that the United States (or, more precisely, the Republican party) "won" the cold war, George Kennan—the father in 1947 of the tough U.S. "containment" policy toward the Soviets— called the claims "intrinsically silly." To believe Americans had such power over another "great country on another side of the globe is simply childish," Kennan wrote. In truth, he concluded, "Nobody—no country, no party, no person, 'won' the cold war. It was a long and costly political rivalry, fueled on both sides by unreal and exaggerated estimates of the intentions and strength of the other party." It resulted in the weakening, if not near-bankruptcy, of both sides.[35] Others believed that the true victors were not U.S. foreign policies, but U.S. political institutions, which absorbed technological changes and overcame the lies and corruption of McCarthyism, Nixon's Watergate, and Reagan's Iran-Contra scandal. The Soviet Union, on the other hand, rotted from the inside out. Some critics attacked Bush as well for having no policy for handling Americans' greatest economic competitor, the Japanese;

for being too kind to the Chinese totalitarians; and for largely ignoring world environmental problems.[36]

Bush's challenger in the 1992 presidential campaign, Democratic governor Bill Clinton of Arkansas, attacked the president on all these issues. He emphasized, however, the weak U.S. economy that, Clinton claimed, Bush had mishandled and ignored. A talented politician, Clinton was single-minded, even cynical, in his pursuit of power. Among his "laws of politics," he said, were "There's no such thing as enough money," and "When someone tells you it's nothing personal, it means they're fixing to screw you." He promised "to focus like a laser beam" on the economy. This approach shaped his foreign-policy plans, Clinton declared, because now that "the Cold War is won," "we have entered a global economy." After defeating Bush and third-party candidate Ross Perot of Texas, Clinton observed in his January 1993 Inaugural Address: "There is no longer division between what is foreign and what is domestic—the world economy, the world environment, the world AIDS crisis, the world arms race—they affect us all."[37]

Clinton also echoed Woodrow Wilson: Americans must "organize and lead a long-term Western strategy" to advance "democracy," especially in the former Soviet Union. He, like Wilson, also stressed the need to use military power, if necessary, to advance this cause. He attacked Bush for being too reluctant to commit U.S. forces to stop the brutalities and starvation of the Muslim population in a disintegrating Yugoslavia controlled by Christian Serbs. He also stressed that stronger governmental action was needed to help Americans prepare themselves for intense competition in the new global marketplace. In 1972, the young Bill Clinton, fresh from a Rhodes Scholarship at Oxford, England, had worked for George McGovern's presidential campaign. In 1992, however, Clinton's aides made clear that he had then worked only for the end of the U.S. involvement in Vietnam, not for broader "isolationist" foreign policies that McGovern had been accused of supporting.[38]

CLINTON'S WORLD: THE PROBLEM OF ASIA

The world, of course, had changed considerably since Woodrow Wilson preached the need for Americans to support international democracy. Just how complicated the globe had become was shown when the new president and his top advisers—Secretary of State Warren Christopher and National Security Adviser Anthony Lake—turned toward

Bill Clinton, at right, had won the presidency in 1992 by promising to focus on domestic issues. But once he entered office in January 1993, he found that he had to work closely with his secretary of state, Warren Christopher (at left) to deal with crises in Russia, Yugoslavia, U.S.-Japan relations, the planned U.S.-Canada-Mexico common market, Somalia, Haiti, and Angola—among others. The American economy was now so tightly integrated within the world economy that Clinton could not improve conditions at home (for example, find more jobs for U.S. workers) without dealing with foreign policy.

Asia. In that region Japan's economic powerhouse had tormented key U.S. producers for more than twenty years. China was emerging as an economic and major military force, complete with nuclear weapons; an unpredictable Communist North Korea hurriedly built its own nuclear weapons. And the world's largest democracy, India, erupted again in a murderous struggle between the majority Hindus and the minority Muslims. Christopher had been a successful Los Angeles lawyer, an able deputy secretary of state in the Carter administration, and a masterful negotiator who gained the release of the U.S. hostages in Iran during 1980–1981 (see p. 698). But he had little experience in Asian affairs.

Lake, once a professional Foreign Service officer, had served courageously in Vietnam and had resigned when Nixon expanded the war in 1970–1971. After working in the Carter State Department, he spent the 1980s teaching at Mount Holyoke College and raising beef cattle.

Lake was the idea man, the conceptualizer, among Clinton's closest advisers. The NSC director believed the foreign-policy debate in the 1990s was between those (such as George Bush) who saw the world in traditional balance-of-power terms, and those (such as Clinton and himself) who had a "neo-Wilsonian view" that led to using U.S. power to promote democracy around the world. Indeed, in President Carter's State Department, Lake had worked successfully to use economic pressure against white-ruled Rhodesia until that African nation was finally governed by the black population that had a huge majority. But Lake was also greatly affected by the misuse of power in Vietnam, and—like General Powell and other military leaders—swore never to make that kind of mistake again. Lake wrote that the Vietnam Veterans Memorial in Washington, with its list of 58,000 dead, "perfectly represents America's collective memory of its longest war." This memory of Vietnam shaped the Clinton administration's response to crises in Yugoslavia, Africa, and elsewhere.[39]

Asia was explosive largely because, as historian Bruce Cumings noted, while Europe had entered the post–cold war era, "East Asia remains decidedly" in the cold-war era.[40] China and North Korea remained Communist controlled. China, however, was more dangerously complicated. Its Communist leaders had built the nation's economy in the 1980s by encouraging free-market enterprise. The nation's annual economic growth rate soared toward 12 percent. Even Japan's rate had slowed to about half of China's. U.S.-Chinese trade boomed, although China enjoyed a large favorable balance. This growing gap led U.S. critics to demand that China open itself to more American goods, and that its Communist leaders allow more democracy and personal expression. Beijing officials, however, wanted no part of political democracy. It threatened their own power and also threatened to fragment their vast country. Clinton and his advisers had to decide whether to push for more democracy and possibly lose valuable trade just as the long-mythical "China market" seemed to materialize, or push for more trade and give up Clinton's emphasis on democracy.

The new president also faced another dangerous choice because China was rapidly building its military forces to the level, one expert declared, of a "regional superpower." It was developing a modern navy while buying advanced fighter planes and missiles from Russia. Neighbors, such as Taiwan, South Korea, and Indonesia, grew nervous. Even as the Taiwanese, once a part of China (which the Chinese still claimed as part of their empire), invested heavily on the Communist mainland, they also rushed the building of their own military. Japan, long reluctant to overcome its "nuclear allergy" and again become a military power, boosted its spending until it possessed the region's best navy and air force—although both were to be used only for the close defense of the home islands. Uneasiness grew in the region as the United States, faced with tighter defense budgets and Philippine nationalism, abandoned its advanced naval and air bases in the Philippines. Americans had maintained them since 1898. U.S. forces now moved back to Guam. Clinton thus faced the problem of protecting U.S. interests in an explosive, dynamic Asia with fewer American resources.[41]

Asia also exemplified another danger for Clinton. A growing consensus of scientists concluded that the world's delicate environmental balance was gravely threatened by a rapidly rising population, increased carbon emissions that caused global warming (and thus melted icecaps that could raise the oceans to dangerous levels), depletion of the ozone layer (and a consequent rise of skin cancers), the mass destruction of valuable forests, and the erosion of topsoil until farming in such areas as Haiti, parts of Africa, and Central American regions was impossible. These dangers haunted the entire globe, even the relatively prosperous United States. But as the huge populations of China (1.5 billion), India (1 billion), and Indonesia (150 million) grew and developed economically, Asian environmental problems increasingly became a worldwide threat. Merely putting modern refrigerators in each Chinese home, for example, could drive up the release of ozone-destroying chlorofluorocarbons to extremely dangerous levels.[42] How Clinton and other world leaders could meet demands for rapid economic development from Asia, Africa, and Latin America, yet protect human life (and the crops and animals needed to help sustain that life), stood at the center of post–cold war problems.

Finally, since 1947 the Washington-Tokyo relationship had been the most important in U.S.-Asian policy. The rapid economic and military changes of the 1980s, especially the rise of China and the declining importance of American military power, placed a heavy strain on that relationship, as did the intense, often bitter economic competition between Americans and Japanese. The new U.S. leaders had to figure out how to strengthen this relationship—or create a fundamentally different policy toward Asia.

CLINTON'S WORLD: THE PROBLEM OF THE BLOCS

Since 1945, the world had been neither peaceful nor unchanging. It nevertheless retained a kind of order and predictability because two superpowers dominated its military and economic life. Each super-power had learned to fear and, to some extent, understand the other. After 1990, that order was gone. Nationalist, ethnic, and religious con-flict, once held in check by the superpowers, now erupted. Such con-flict even broke out with a dangerous intensity inside the former Soviet Union itself.

The new order seemed not to be orderly at all. Instead, it seemed to be going off in two quite different, perilous directions. One direction was growing regional economic blocs. That is, as the military and eco-nomic blocs of the two superpowers disappeared, they were being replaced by three major economic blocs: the twelve-nation European Community (EC), the U.S.-Canada-Mexico free-trade area being negotiated to create a huge American common market, and the less-formal-but-nevertheless-potent Asian development area powered by Japanese capital. These units were soon called the Deutsche-mark bloc (because of Germany's enormous economic power in the EC), the dol-lar bloc, and the yen bloc.

By the time Bill and Hillary Rodham Clinton entered the White House in 1993, however, they found each of the blocs in trouble. In Europe, the new, united Germans threatened to grow so powerful and indepen-dent that first Denmark, then Great Britian, pulled away. A top British official charged that the EC was merely "a German racket designed to take over the whole of Europe," with the French acting as Germany's "poodles." The EC was supposed to be largely unified by 1993, but instead it was bogged down amid nationalist disputes. In the Americas, Canadians believed they were being exploited by their 1989 free-trade treaty with the United States. They even forced out of power the prime minister who had negotiated the treaty. U.S. citizens, especially in organized labor, meanwhile condemned the proposed U.S.-Mexican agreement because it allowed too many industries to move to Mexican regions where wages were low (Mexican laborers received in a day the wages U.S. laborers received in an hour) and environmental standards were below those in the United States. Pro-treaty forces estimated that by opening Mexico to U.S. goods, a net of 175,000 jobs would be cre-ated in the United States.[43] But Clinton insisted that he would accept the U.S.-Mexico treaty only after safeguards were added to help Amer-ican labor and protect the environment. Japan's bloc meanwhile was hurt by a Japanese economic downturn and rising power centers in Taiwan and China.

Hopes that the new economic world would be more orderly seemed to be disappearing as the blocs ran into trouble. Of equal importance, the long-running talks (begun in Uruguay in 1986), among more than a hundred nations for the purpose of opening world markets to greater international trade also seemed to have hit a dead end. Just as Americans depended increasingly on the global marketplace for their jobs, that marketplace was threatened with the specter of trade wars that reminded some observers of the terrible 1930s.

CLINTON'S WORLD: THE NEW WORLD DISORDER

Hence the post-1990 world headed off in another, more dramatic direction: toward fragmentation, intense nationalism, and deeply scarred and bloody ethnic and religious wars. Freed of Stalinist restraints, not only did the fifteen former Soviet republics move toward independence, but such major republics as Armenia, Georgia, and Russia began to split apart themselves. Where one nuclear power once stood, now four (Russia, Belarus, Ukraine, Kazakhstan) housed these weapons, although the Russian military supposedly continued to control all the triggers. The former Soviet military disintegrated until its ability to restart a long cold war disappeared. Some 60 to 70 percent of young men ordered to report for service simply refused to show up. But danger remained amidst the disorder: the Russian military "can do nothing much in Moscow," one expert believed, "but they can wipe out New York."[44]

In Yugoslavia, Africa, and parts of the former Soviet Union, the spreading conflicts posed a critical foreign-policy problem for Clinton: Should he intervene in these struggles if they threatened to spin out of control? And if so, how capable would U.S. military power be in solving such crises? After all, the military, led by General Powell and his Vietnam-trained generation, willingly fought only wars that promised quick victories. As many foreign armies had discovered over the centuries, quick victories were not to be found in Russia or Yugoslavia. As for Africa, the United States paid little attention to the great continent after the white South African government finally, after forty years, began to end apartheid and treat the black majority better, although by no means equally. Analyst Marguerite Michaels noted that the end of the cold war "set America free to pursue its own interests in Africa—and found that it did not have any." U.S. investments between 1985 and 1993 tripled in Latin America, quintupled in East Asia, but actually declined in Africa.[45]

So why, on December 4, 1992, did President Bush, with President-elect Clinton's strong support, suddenly send 21,000 U.S. troops into

A New World Order? After the collapse of the Soviet empire in 1989–1991, many hoped for "a new world order," as President Bush phrased it in 1991. Instead, nationalist, ethnic, and religious wars erupted in parts of the globe. The worst occurred in Yugoslavia during 1992, when the country splintered and religious groups (especially Eastern Orthodox Christians and Muslims) fought each other. As the casualties mounted into the tens of thousands in the Bosnian capital of Sarajevo, this soccer field had to be turned into a ceme-tary—and a place where an elderly man mourned the death of his wife of some fifty years. She had been killed by the random shelling and sniper fire. Neither the United States nor the Europeans could figure out how to end the horror without sacrificing their own soldiers. U.S. Secretary of State Warren Christopher called Yugoslavia a "problem from hell."

the East African nation of Somalia? This episode exemplified the kinds of questions that promised to plague (and tax) Americans in the new era of disorder.

In the 1980s, first Moscow, then Washington poured weapons into this poor, but strategically located, nation of 5 million souls in order to keep Somalia's dictator, Mohamed Siad Barre, friendly. In 1991, the cold-war aid dried up and Siad Barre fled. He left behind enough U.S. and Soviet arms "to fuel hostilities for 100 years" in Somalia, one Pentagon official noted. In early 1991, two factions used these weapons to kill each other as each tried to seize power. The country spiraled downward into banditry, wholesale looting, mass destruction, and finally spreading starvation. United Nations personnel who tried to feed the people were repeatedly attacked. U.S. television crews soon showed American viewers fly-covered, starving children with rail-thin legs and bloated stomachs. Some 300,000 people died, with 2 million more starving. Demands rose that Bush and other world leaders act. The United Nations seized the moment and, for the first time in its history, became directly involved militarily in a nation's internal affairs without that nation's consent. It was a historic turn. Bush thus dispatched the U.S. troops (joined by 2,000 French soldiers and military units from a dozen other nations.)[46]

Bush aimed to end the starvation by protecting food supplies from the many armed bandits. (One puzzled U.S. soldier was told how to tell friends from enemies: the "good guys" were very thin and the "bad guys" were fat.) It was a mission of mercy, the arrival of "the cavalry" as in movie westerns, declared General Powell. Questions, however, plagued Bush and Clinton. First, should U.S. forces be used for such missions when no direct American strategic or political interest was involved? That question became more pressing as U.S. soldiers were killed and a planned two-month mission stretched far longer. Second, how could Americans and other UN members decide when intervention was necessary? Starvation was not limited to Somalia. It was perhaps worse in parts of the Sudan, Liberia, and Yugoslavia. Some critics believed Somalia was singled out because it was defenseless and easy for U.S. forces to reach. Critics also believed Somalia gained attention simply because television highlighted the starvation there. U.S. policy and lives, in other words, were becoming dependent on decisions made in the offices of CNN, ABC, NBC, and CBS. When the troops waded ashore, they fought their way, not through Somali resistance, but through hundreds of reporters, cameras, and giant strobe lights that turned the night into day.[47]

Another question involved the United Nations. Freed of Soviet-bloc opposition, the UN took on some fourteen peacekeeping operations (including Somalia), with its blue-helmeted forces that represented many nations. These operations had even received the Nobel Peace Prize in 1988, especially for efforts in the Middle East and Africa. The question became whether Americans, who historically have greatly mistrusted an international organization unless they controlled it, would accept such peacekeeping responsibilities if future UN policies ran against U.S. interests. China, after all, held a veto in the UN, as did the Russians. Secretary of State Christopher, moreover, believed that Germany and Japan would become the sixth and seventh permanent members of the Security Council, and thus also would hold veto power.

Raeside's cartoon caught the influence that the media exerted on U.S. policy toward Somalia and, in particular, on the military landings—landings that occurred in December 1992 amid ranges of television cameras and lights controlled by scores of reporters who occupied the landing sites ahead of the troops.

United Nations power could fragment, much as power was already fragmenting in the world the UN represented. Indeed, by mid-1993, UN efforts in Somalia were threatened by disputes among the U.S., French, Pakistani, and Italian forces that made up the UN peacekeepers. When Somali strongmen, angry at the UN presence, killed thirty-five peacekeepers, U.S. gunships strafed and bombed the strongmen's bunkers—only to have the Italians condemn Clinton's use of force as resembling "Rambo's" and demanding that diplomacy replace force.[48]

Clinton's World: The American Age

Answering these questions assumed that Americans can respond meaningfully and rationally to the problems of the growing disorder in the world. Americans are, after all, the only remaining superpower. Only they can militarily intervene nearly anywhere on the globe. They enjoy an economy that is twice the size of its nearest competitor. Their culture of films, fast food, jeans, sports, music, and language permeates other important countries, even those, such as Japan and France, that are intensely protective of their own national cultures. It would seem, therefore, that Americans should indeed be worldly wise, careful, and rational.

Shrewd observers, however, have expressed doubts about this assumption. Perhaps the shrewdest, the French visitor Alexis de Tocqueville, wrote in the 1830s that the American democratic system was splendid for developing a continent, but he did not believe the individualistic, open, rapidly changing society could conduct an effective foreign policy.[49] In the 1920s, Walter Lippmann, agreed (see p. 737).

Between 1947 and 1990 Tocqueville's and Lippmann's fears were removed by the Truman Doctrine. This 1947 doctrine created such a strong anti-Communist consensus that U.S. officials could simply assume public support when they confronted the Soviet bloc. In 1990–1991, however, the consensus disappeared along with the Soviet bloc. George Bush could not build a new consensus. The Republican party, which had brilliantly used anticommunism to paper over its internal disputes on such domestic issues as abortion, began to divide. Clinton played on those divisions by stressing domestic issues in his campaign.

The question nevertheless remained whether the new president could build a consensus for his foreign policies. He made two early attempts. First, he urged Americans to rally behind the advancement of democracy and self-determination. When Secretary of State Robert Lansing had heard Woodrow Wilson's cry for self-determination in 1918, he worried that "the phrase is simply loaded with dynamite. It will raise hopes that can never be realized. It will, I fear, cost thousands of lives. What a calamity that the phrase was ever uttered!" Lansing's fears were borne out in eastern Europe after 1990. Even Secretary of State Christopher warned in 1993 that unless something was done, "We'll have 50,000 countries rather than the hundred plus we now have."[50]

Clinton's second attempt to build a consensus arose from his economic policies. He declared that, contrary to Reagan's and Bush's beliefs, government had to play a strong role in supporting U.S. economic interests. The new president found, however, that many such interests existed, and some bitterly clashed with others. For example, industrialists and investors, as noted above, supported the free-trade treaty that allowed them to build plants in Mexico, but U.S. laborers fought the treaty.

President Clinton's hope that Americans would support active economic policies overseas also hit other obstacles. There was, for instance, a question of how far Americans could even shape such policies. The world economy was increasingly dominated by giant multinational

A handshake marked a high point of early post–cold war history and symbolized the hope to end generations of war in the Middle East. In September 1993 Prime Minister Yitzhak Rabin of Israel (on left) and Yasir Arafat, chairman of the Palestinian Liberation Organization (PLO) gingerly shook hands on the sun-drenched White House lawn after their foreign ministers signed a historic peace treaty. President Bill Clinton helped pull the once-mortal enemies together for the handshake. The treaty provided that Israel withdraw its troops from Gaza and the West Bank city of Jericho, then later from other populated West Bank areas. Palestinians in these areas would move toward more self-government. Israel would retain military supremacy in surrounding territory. The PLO's one-time pledge to destroy Israel would be replaced by joint PLO-Israeli groups to work out common problems. Clinton promised to tackle the pivotal problem of raising some $4 billion (mostly from allies) to ease the West Bank– Gaza economic crises. Rabin's eloquence captured the moment: "We who have seen our relatives and friends killed before our eyes; we who have attended their funerals and cannot look into the eyes of their parents . . . we say to you [Palestinians] today, in a loud and clear voice: enough of blood and tears. Enough."

corporations (Honda, General Motors, Nike, Sony, Ford, IBM) that easily moved across national boundaries. Many a multinational produced more goods than did dozens of nations. Over a trillion dollars a day moved through world financial markets. A nation, even the United States, would try to control that tide of money only at its own financial peril.

Such private economic power could help develop countries, but it could also help push them into disorder. Most notably, as the cold war's vast military needs ended, producers and merchants of military arms sold their weapons in regions where the new wars erupted. In 1987, the United States sold $6.5 billion in arms abroad. By 1992, the figure nearly quadrupled to $24 billion. Taiwan, Kuwait, Saudi Arabia, and South Korea were among the heavy buyers. China and Russia also sold massive amounts of arms, especially to such anti-U.S. countries as Iran. As one U.S. banker put it, "We're unlikely to sacrifice economic interests to take the moral high ground in curbing arms sales."[51]

Americans liked stability. But they also liked modern capitalism, and they wanted other peoples to emulate their economic system. They had problems, however, in seeking both stability and capitalism. Modern, multinational capitalism could be quite disorderly. As the conservative journal, the *Economist* of London, phrased it, in 1993 Russia again "is convulsed by a revolutionary idea imported from the West. The idea this time is not Marxism but the market. Yet the upheaval could end once more in disaster."[52] A disaster had already occurred in China. Dynamic fresh ideas, especially private enterprise, clashed with the government's Communist ideology. One result was the government's killing of protesters in Tiananmen Square in 1989. As noted earlier in this book, Americans had actually experienced similar disasters themselves. Between the 1840s and 1900 a new U.S. industrial and financial capitalism had produced strikes that were put down with armed force, massive social dislocation, violent protests in major cities, and, some would argue, the Civil War. In the 1990s, President Clinton dealt with an even more dynamic and independent capitalism that breached national boundaries—just as ethnic and religious hatreds exploded within those boundaries.

Clinton represented a new generation, the Vietnam generation, that now took the reins of government. But key problems seemed to resemble less the 1960s than the 1920s, or the late nineteenth-century-to-1914 era. After forty years of cold war, history seemed to be beginning again. Americans had to come to terms with that history. What we are and what we would like to be, the conservative British philosopher Michael Oakeshott warned, is a creature of what we have been.[53] Understanding and building on that past is necessary, or else a famous American conservative, Henry Adams, might have the last word:

> Modern politics is, at bottom, a struggle not of men but of forces. The men become every year more and more creatures of force, massed about central power-houses. The conflict is no longer between the men, but between

the motors that drive men, and the men tend to succumb to their own motive forces.[54]

James Madison and other founders raised grave doubts about Adams's pessimistic view that individuals could not control the "motors" of their own society. Out of a fragmented country, Madison and his colleagues created a more coherent and prosperous nation. In 1829, Madison wrote that he did not expect the system he helped create to last forever. But to note the way he and others went about their work in 1787, especially how they studied and learned from history, is an appropriate way to end as well as begin the story of the American age.

NOTES

1. Paul Boyer, ed., *Reagan as President* (Chicago, 1990), pp. 264–267.
2. *Ibid.*, pp. 270–281.
3. This is drawn especially from Caryn James, "Today's Yellow Brick Road Leads Straight to Hell," *New York Times*, 19 August 1990, p. H1.
4. *New York Times*, 22 March 1989, p. A25.
5. George Bush, *Bushisms*, compiled by the editors of *The New Republic* (New York, 1992), p. 60.
6. Michael R. Beschloss and Strobe Talbott, *At the Highest Levels* (Boston, 1993), p. 193; Walter LaFeber, *Inevitable Revolutions*, 2nd ed. (New York, 1993), pp. 339–353.
7. William I. Robinson, *A Faustian Bargain: U.S. Intervention in the Nicaraguan Elections and American Foreign Policy in the Post-Cold War Era* (Boulder, Colo., 1992), pp. 111–119.
8. *Washington Post*, 15 November 1992, p. A31; *New York Times*, 16 February 1993, p. A1.
9. *New York Times*, 16 March 1993, p. A20; *Washington Post*, 16 December 1992, p. A1; *Washington Post*, 13 March 1993, p. A1; *Washington Post*, 14 March 1993, p. C1.
10. *New York Times*, 17 October 1992, p. 5; *Washington Post*, 17 October 1992, p. A18; Rigoberta Menchú, *I, Rigoberta Menchú . . .* (London, 1984).
11. *Washington Post*, 16 December 1992, p. A24.
12. *Ibid.*, 22 November 1992, in *Central America NewsPak*, 16–29 November 1992, p. 2.
13. The background is in Michael L. Conniff, *Panama and the United States* (Athens, Ga., 1992), esp. pp. 149–168; and Andrew Zimbalist and John Weeks, *Panama at the Crossroads* (Berkeley, Calif., 1991), pp. 142–156. The most thorough investigation is the New York Bar Association Committees' report in *The Record of the Association of the Bar of the City of New York* 47 (October 1992), esp. pp. 607–609, 634–

651, 674–678, 692–693; also *New York Times*, 13 August 1991, p. A1, on later drug traffic; *Washington Post*, 10 April 1992, p. A35, for a summary of the Noriega trial.

14. Beschloss and Talbott, *At the Highest Levels*, pp. 9–13, 27–28, 34, 43–45; Don Oberdorfer, *The Turn* (New York, 1991), pp. 333–334; David Remnick, "Dumb Luck; Bush's Cold War," *The New Yorker*, 25 January 1993, p. 106.

15. Frank Costigliola, "German Reunification, NATO, and the Problem of U.S. Leadership, 1989–1990," forthcoming, in *Contemporary European History*, 1994; Beschloss and Talbott, *At the Highest Levels*, pp. 169–170, 184–187; Stephen F. Szabo, *The Diplomacy of German Unification* (New York, 1992), pp. 41–51, 62–65, 95–112; *Newsweek*, 25 December 1989, p. 33; *Washington Post*, 14 September 1990, p. A18; *New York Times*, 1 July 1990, p. 6.

16. Oberdorfer, *The Turn*, p. 381; *New York Times*, 7 July 1990, p. A1.

17. Beschloss and Talbott, *At the Highest Levels*, pp. 176–177, 192.

18. John Morrison, *Boris Yeltsin* (New York, 1991), pp. 33–35.

19. Beschloss and Talbott, *At the Highest Levels*, pp. 296–309; also Morrison, *Yeltsin*, pp. 56–73, for background.

20. Beschloss and Talbott, *At the Highest Levels*, p. 349; author's interviews in Moscow, June 1989, March 1991; *Washington Post*, 30 May, 1990, p. A8.

21. *Washington Post*, 22 March 1993, p. A12; *Washington Post*, 17 February 1993, p. A42; Beschloss and Talbott, *At the Highest Levels*, pp. 421–441; Remnick, "Dumb Luck," pp. 106–108.

22. *Washington Post*, 22 March 1993, p. A12.

23. *Ibid.*, 6 June 1990, p. A17; *New York Times*, 4 February 1991, p. D6.

24. Christopher Madison, "Catch-up Diplomacy," *National Journal*, 22 February 1992, p. 448.

25. Judith Miller and Laurie Mylroie, *Saddam Hussein, The Crisis in the Gulf* (New York, 1990), esp. chaps. 1–4; Daniel Yergin, *The Prize* (New York, 1991), pp. 770–775; Theodore Draper, "The Gulf War Reconsidered," *New York Review of Books*, 16 January 1992, pp. 46–51; *Washington Post*, 7 August 1990, p. A14.

26. Micah L. Sifry and Christopher Cerf, eds., *The Gulf War Reader* (New York, 1991), pp. 119–133 for the Glaspie-Saddam Hussein exchange; Draper, "Gulf War Reconsidered," pp. 51–53; *New York Times*, 9 August 1990, p. D19.

27. Yergin, *The Prize*, pp. 775–779.

28. A good contemporary analysis is Elizabeth Drew, "Letter from Washington," *The New Yorker*, 4 February 1991, pp. 86–88; representative views can be found in Sifry and Cerf, *The Gulf War Reader*, pp. 234–264, 269–289, which also gives the joint resolution's text of January 12, 1991.

29. Michael A. Palmer, *Guardians of the Gulf: A History of America's Expanding Role in the Persian Gulf, 1833–1991* (New York, 1992), p. 196.

30. *New York Times*, 17 August 1990, p. A1; the best analysis of Powell, and his reluctance to use force in Iraq, is Bob Woodward, *The Commanders* (New York, 1992).

31. *Economist*, 2 May 1992, pp. 53–54.

32. Laurie Mylroie, "Iraq's Real Coup," *Washington Post*, 28 June 1992, p. C1.

33. *Washington Post*, 20 January 1993, p. A4; *Washington Post*, 5 September 1992, p. A15.

34. The text is in *New York Times*, 16 December 1992, p. A25.

35. *New York Times*, 28 October 1992, p. A21.

36. Wade Huntley, "Point of View," *Chronicle of Higher Education*, 31 March 1993, p. A40; *New York Times*, op-ed by James Webb, "What Foreign Policy?," 1 December 1991; *New York Times*, 14 June 1992, p. 10.

37. *Washington Post,* 19 September 1992, p. A10; *Washington Post,* 6 November 1992, p. A11; *Washington Post,* 21 January 1993, p. A26, for the inaugural address.
38. "Remarks Prepared for Delivery. Governor Bill Clinton. Foreign Policy Association. New York—April 1, 1992," unpublished; *New York Times,* 4 October 1992, p. 28.
39. *New York Times,* 3 January 1993, p. 16; Lake, "Vietnam War," in Joel Krieger, et al., eds., *The Oxford Companion to the Politics of the World* (New York, 1993) p. 958.
40. Bruce Cumings, "Trilateralism and the New World Order," *World Policy Journal* 8 (Spring 1992), p. 210.
41. *Washington Post,* 1 December 1992, p. A30; *Economist,* 20 February 1993, pp. 19–22; *New York Times,* 18 March 1993, p. A23; *New York Times,* 11 January 1993, p. A1.
42. *Washington Post,* 3 May 1992, p. A1; *Washington Post,* 15 May 1990, p. A4.
43. Gregory F. Treverton, *America, Germany, and the Future of Europe* (Princeton, 1992), pp. 180–181; *Washington Post,* 11 October 1992, p. C7.
44. *Washington Post,* 24 March 1993, p. A24.
45. *New York Times,* 7 March 1993, p. E4.
46. *Washington Post,* 4 December 1992, p. A20; *Washington Post,* 1 December 1992, p. A1; Richard J. Barnet, "Still Putting Arms First," *Harper's Magazine* (February 1993), pp. 59–65.
47. Stephen John Stedman, "The New Interventionists," *Foreign Affairs* 72 (No. 1, 1992–1993), esp. pp. 2–4; *New York Times,* 13 December 1992, p. E3; *New York Times,* 8 December 1992, p. C20; *Washington Post,* 4 December 1992, p. A24.
48. Samuel W. Lewis, "Point of View: The Decade of the 1990s," *United States Institute of Peace Journal* III (March 1990), p. 2; *New York Times,* 9 December 1992, p. A17; *New York Times,* 22 July 1993, p. A23.
49. Alexis de Tocqueville, *Democracy in America,* 2 vols. (New York, 1948), I, pp. 234–236.
50. *New York Times,* 7 February 1993, p. 1; *New York Times,* 22 September 1993, p. A13.
51. *Ibid ,* 4 October 1992, p. F5.
52. *Economist,* 13 March 1993, p. 17.
53. Quoted in Henry Jackson, *From the Congo to Soweto* (New York, 1982), p. 39.
54. Henry Adams, *The Education of Henry Adams* (Boston, 1918), p. 421.

For Further Reading

Begin by consulting the footnotes for this chapter and the General Bibliography at the end of the book. References given in those two places are usually not repeated here. A number of useful overviews have been published on the end of the cold war and possible consequences: Michael J. Hogan, ed., *The End of the Cold War* (1992); Nicholas X. Rizopoulos, ed., *Sea-Changes* (1990), especially the McNeill, Strange, Hoffmann essays for background; James Chace, *The Consequences of the Peace* (1992), good notably on economic consequences; William G. Hyland, *The Cold War Is Over* (1991), by an experienced expert on Russia; Robert Jervis and Seweryn Bailer, eds, *Soviet-American Relations after the Cold War* (1991), especially the Dallek essay on U.S. responses; John Lewis Gaddis, *The United States and the End of the Cold War* (New York, 1992), which gives more credit to Reagan than do many observers.

For Russian-American relations, a key source is U.S. Congress, House Committee on Foreign Affairs, *Special Studies Series on Foreign Affairs Issues.* Volume III: *Soviet Diplomacy and Negotiating Behavior—1988–1990: Gorbachev-Reagan-Bush Meetings at the Summit* (1991). Also very helpful are Fred Halliday, *From Kabul to Managua* (1989), on the background; Lubomyr Hajda and Mark Beissinger, eds., *The Nationalities Factor in Soviet Politics and Society* (1990); Timothy Garton Ash, *The Magic Lantern* (1990), wonderful on the opening of eastern Europe; Charles Gati, *The Bloc That Failed* (1990), by a respected scholar on eastern Europe; Michael A. Freney and Rebecca S. Hartley, *United Germany and the United States* (1991), with helpful documents as well as commentary; John R. Lampe, *et al., Yugoslav-American Relations Since World War II* (1991), for background to the tragedy; Francis Fukuyama, *The End of History and the Last Man* (1992), the widely read argument on what it all means.

On specific regions, the following are helpful as starting points: Jan S. Adams, *A Foreign Policy in Transition: Moscow's Retreat from Central America and the Caribbean, 1985–1992* (1992); John Booth and Thomas Walker, *Understanding Central America* (1993); Brenda Gayle Plummer, *Haiti and the United States* (1992), a superb, concise background for understanding the immigrant question and Haiti's upheaval in 1990–1993; Kevin Buckley, *Panama: The Whole Story* (1991), to be used with Conniff, noted in the footnotes; Michael Clough, *Free at Last? U.S. Policy Toward Africa and the End of the Cold War* (1992); Zaki Laidi, *The Superpowers and Africa, 1960–1990* (1990). For the trade relationships, as well as the political relationships, Frank Costigliola, *The Cold Alliance* (1992), is an excellent analysis of U.S.-western European economic developments since 1945, and the best account of U.S.-France relations during the cold war and after; René Schwok, *U.S.-EC Relations in the Post–Cold War Era* (1991), has good background; Sidney Weintraub, *A Marriage of Convenience* (1990), is excellent on U.S.-Mexico relations; Sidney Weintraub, *et al., U.S.-Mexican Industrial Integration* (1991), is an excellent overview; Robert Bothwell, *Canada and the United States* (1992), examines the political effects of economic ties; Kenneth B. Pyle, *The Japanese Question* (1992), is an excellent and concise discussion of the historical background; Paul Krugman, ed., *Trade with Japan* (1992), is a thorough analysis; Akio Morita and Shinturo Ishihara, *The Japan That Can Say "NO"* (1990), is a widely noted, controversial Japanese view; William Dietrich, *In the Shadow of the Rising Sun* (1991), well analyzes why the United States faces such tough Japanese competition.

On the Persian Gulf War, the best overviews are Stephen R. Graubard, *Mr. Bush's War* (1992), and Jean Edward Smith, *George Bush's War* (1992), which is also quite critical; Michael A. Palmer, *Guardians of the Gulf* (1992), is an excellent history of 1833–1991; Kenneth R. Timmerman, *The Death Lobby* (1991), brilliantly reveals how Saddam Hussein was armed by the West; Abdul-Reda Assiri, *Kuwait's Foreign Policy* (1990), is a Kuwaiti view of a nation that was not especially friendly to the United States until August 1990; General Norman Schwarzkopf, with Peter Petrie, *It Doesn't Take a Hero* (1992), is the U.S. general's best-selling account; Alexander George, *Forceful Persuasion* (1992), beautifully explores nonmilitary alternatives in the Iraqi and other crises.

Warren Cohen, *America in the Age of Soviet Power*, in *The Cambridge History of American Foreign Relations*, ed. Warren Cohen (1993) is superb on the pre-1992 background and has an excellent bibliography.

For the Clinton administration. Charles F. Allen, *The Comeback Kid* (1992), is an initial start on a biography of Clinton.

U.S. Presidents and Secretaries of State

Presidents	Secretaries of State
George Washington of Virginia (1789–1797)	Robert R. Livingston of New York (1781–1783 under Continental Congress)
	John Jay of New York (1784–1789 under Continental Congress)
	Thomas Jefferson of Virginia (1789–1793)
	Edmund Randolph of Virginia (1794–1795)
John Adams of Massachusetts (1797–1801)	Timothy Pickering of Pennsylvania (1795–1800)
	John Marshall of Virginia (1800–1801)
Thomas Jefferson of Virginia (1801–1809)	James Madison of Virginia (1801–1809)
James Madison of Virginia (1809–1817)	Robert Smith of Maryland (1809–1811)
	James Monroe of Virginia (1811–1817)
James Monroe of Virginia (1817–1825)	John Quincy Adams of Massachusetts (1817–1825)
John Quincy Adams of Massachusetts (1825–1829)	Henry Clay of Kentucky (1825–1829)
Andrew Jackson of Tennessee (1829–1837)	Martin Van Buren of New York (1829–1831)
	Edward Livingston of Louisiana (1831–1833)
	Louis McLane of Delaware (1833–1834)
Martin Van Buren of New York (1837–1841)	John Forsyth of Georgia (1834–1841)

William Henry Harrison of Ohio (1841)

Daniel Webster of Massachusetts (1841–1843)

John Tyler of Virginia (1841–1845)

Abel P. Upshur of Virginia (1843–1844)

John C. Calhoun of South Carolina (1844–1845)

James K. Polk of Tennessee (1845–1849)

James Buchanan of Pennsylvania (1845–1849)

Zachary Taylor of Louisiana (1849–1850)

John M. Clayton of Delaware (1849–1850)

Millard Fillmore of New York (1850–1853)

Daniel Webster of Massachusetts (1850–1852)

Edward Everett of Massachusetts (1852–1853)

Franklin Pierce of New Hampshire (1853–1857)

William L. Marcy of New York (1853–1857)

James Buchanan of Pennsylvania (1857–1861)

Lewis Cass of Michigan (1857–1860)

Jeremiah S. Black of Pennsylvania (1860–1861)

Abraham Lincoln of Illinois (1861–1865)

William H. Seward of New York (1861–1869)

Andrew Johnson of Tennessee (1865–1869)

Ulysses S. Grant of Illinois (1869–1877)

Hamilton Fish of New York (1869–1877)

Rutherford B. Hayes of Ohio (1877–1881)

William M. Evarts of New York (1877–1881)

James A. Garfield of Ohio (1881)

James G. Blaine of Maine (1881)

Chester A. Arthur of New York (1881–1885)

Frederick T. Frelinghuysen of New Jersey (1881–1885)

Grover Cleveland of New York (1885–1889)

Thomas F. Bayard of Delaware (1885–1889)

Benjamin Harrison of Indiana (1889–1893)

James G. Blaine of Maine (1889–1892)

John W. Foster of Indiana (1892–1893)

Grover Cleveland of New York (1893–1897)

Walter Q. Gresham of Indiana (1893–1895)

Richard Olney of Massachusetts (1895–1897)

William McKinley of Ohio (1897–1901)

John Sherman of Ohio (1897–1898)

William R. Day of Ohio (1898)

John Hay of the District of Columbia (1898–1905)

Theodore Roosevelt of New York (1901–1909)

Elihu Root of New York (1905–1909)

Robert Bacon of New York (1909)

William Howard Taft of Ohio (1909–1913)

Philander C. Knox of Pennsylvania (1909–1913)

Woodrow Wilson of New Jersey (1913–1921)

William Jennings Bryan of Nebraska (1913–1915)

Robert Lansing of New York (1915–1920)

Bainbridge Colby of New York (1920–1921)

Warren G. Harding of Ohio (1921–1923)

Charles Evans Hughes of New York (1921–1925)

Calvin Coolidge of Massachusetts (1923–1929)

Frank B. Kellogg of Minnesota (1925–1929)

Herbert C. Hoover of California (1929–1933)

Henry L. Stimson of New York (1929–1933)

Franklin D. Roosevelt of New York (1933–1945)

Cordell Hull of Tennessee (1933–1944)

Edward R. Stettinius of Virginia (1944–1945)

Harry S. Truman of Missouri (1945–1953)

James F. Byrnes of South Carolina (1945–1947)

George C. Marshall of Pennsylvania (1947–1949)

Dean G. Acheson of Maryland (1949–1953)

Dwight D. Eisenhower of New York (1953–1961)

John Foster Dulles of New York (1953–1959)

Christian A. Herter of Massachusetts (1959–1961)

John F. Kennedy of Massachusetts (1961–1963)

Dean Rusk of New York (1961–1969)

Lyndon B. Johnson of Texas (1963–1969)

Richard M. Nixon of California (1969–1974)

William P. Rogers of Maryland (1969–1973)

Gerald R. Ford of Michigan (1974–1977)

Henry A. Kissinger of the District of Columbia (1973–1977)

Jimmy Carter of Georgia (1977–1981)

Cyrus R. Vance of New York (1977–1980)

Edmund Muskie of Maine (1980–1981)

Ronald Reagan of California (1981–1989)

Alexander Haig of Maryland (1981–1982)

George Shultz of California (1982–1989)

George Bush of Texas (1989–1993)

James A. Baker of Texas (1989–1993)

William Clinton of Arkansas (1993–   )

Warren Christopher of California (1993–   )

General Bibliography

AFGHANISTAN: Anthony Arnold, *Afghanistan* (1981); Stanley Wolpert, *Roots of Confrontation in South Asia* (1982).

AFRICA: *Africa Contemporary Record: Annual Survey and Documents* (1968–   ); Peter Duignan and Lewis H. Gann, *The United States and Africa* (1984); Henry F. Jackson, *From Congo to Soweto* (1982). (See also individual countries.)

ANGOLA: John A. Marcum, *The Angolan Revolution*, 2 vols. (1969, 1978). (See also AFRICA.)

ARGENTINA: Joseph Tulchin, *Argentina and the United States* (1990); Arthur P. Whitaker, *The U.S. and the Southern Cone* (1976). (See also LATIN AMERICA.)

ATLASES: Gerard Chaliand and Jean-Pierre Rageau, *Strategic Atlas* (1985); Michael Kidron and Dan Smith, *The State of the World Atlas* (1981); Harry F. Young, *Atlas of U.S. Foreign Relations* (1983).

AUSTRALIA: Glen St. John Barclay, *Friends in High Places: The Australian-American Security Relationship since 1945* (1985).

BIBLIOGRAPHY: *Guide to American Foreign Relations since 1700*, ed. Richard Dean Burns (1983); Linda Killen and Richard L. Lael, *Versailles and After: An Annotated Bibliography of American Foreign Relations, 1919–1933* (1982). (See also individual topics.)

BRAZIL: Frank D. McCann, *The Brazilian-American Alliance, 1937–1945* (1972); Robert Wesson, *The U.S. and Brazil* (1981). (See also LATIN AMERICA.)

CAMBODIA: William Shawcross, *The Quality of Mercy* (1984); William Shawcross, *Sideshow* (1979). (See also VIETNAM.)

CANADA: Charles Doran, *Forgotten Partnership* (1985); *Canada and the United States*, ed. Charles F. Doran and John H. Sigler (1985); Seymour Martin Lipset, *Continental Divide* (1990); Lawrence Martin, *Presidents and the Prime Ministers . . . 1867–1982* (1982).

CENTRAL AMERICA: John Booth and Thomas Walker, *Understanding Central America* (1993); *The Central American Crisis*, ed. Kenneth M. Coleman and George C. Herring (1991); Walter LaFeber, *Inevitable Revolutions* (1993); Thomas M. Leonard, *Central America and U.S. Policies, 1820s–1980s* (1985). Ralph L. Woodward, *Central America* (1986). (See also individual countries.)

CENTRAL INTELLIGENCE AGENCY: John Ranelagh, *The Agency* (1987); Bradley F. Smith, *The Shadow Warriors* (1983); Gregory F. Treverton, *Covert Action* (1987).

CHILE: James Petras and Morris Morley, *The U.S. and Chile* (1975); William F. Sater, *Chile and the United States* (1990).

CHINA: Warren Cohen, *America's Response to China* (1990); John K. Fairbank, *The U.S. and China* (1983); Michael H. Hunt, *The Making of a Special Relationship: The U.S. and China to 1914* (1983); Arnold Xiangze Jiang, *The U.S. and China* (1988); Michael Schaller, *The U.S. and China in the Twentieth Century* (1990).

COLOMBIA: Richard Lael, *Arrogant Diplomacy . . . 1903–1922* (1987).

COMMUNISM: Hoover Institution, *Yearbook on International Communist Affairs* (1966–   ). (See also individual countries.)

CONGRESS: John Rourke, *Congress and the Presidency in U.S. Foreign Policymaking* (1983); *Congress and American Foreign Policy*, ed. Göran Rystad (1982); *To Advise and Consent*, 2 vols., ed. Joel Silbey (1990).

CONSTITUTION: Louis Fisher, *Constitutional Conflicts between Congress and the President* (1985); Louis Henkin, *Foreign Affairs and the Constitution* (1975); Charles A. Lofgren, *Government from Reflection and Choice* (1986); John H. Sullivan, *The War Powers Resolution* (1982).

CONTAINMENT: *Containment*, 2 vols., ed. Terry L. Deibel and J. L. Gaddis (1986); J. L. Gaddis, *Strategies of Containment* (1982).

CUBA: Philip S. Foner, *A History of Cuba in Its Relations with the U.S.* (1962–   ); Morris H. Morley, *Imperial State and Revolution* (1987); Louis A. Perez, Jr., *Cuba: An Annotated Bibliography* (1988); Louis A. Perez, Jr., *Cuba and the United States* (1990); Robert F. Smith, *The U.S. and Cuba* (1969).

CULTURE AND PHILANTHROPHY: Edward H. Berman, *The Influence of the Carnegie, Ford, and Rockefeller Foundations on American Foreign Policy* (1983); Morrell Heald and Lawrence S. Kaplan, *Culture and Diplomacy* (1977); Frank A. Ninkovich, *The Diplomacy of Ideas . . . 1938–1950* (1981); Ron Robin, *Enclaves of America; The Rhetoric of American Political Architecture Abroad, 1900–1965* (1992).

DEPARTMENT OF STATE: Robert U. Goehlert and Elizabeth Hoffmeister, *The Department of State and American Diplomacy* (1986) [bibliography]; Barry Rubin, *Secrets of State* (1985); Richard H. Werking, *The Master Architects: Building the U.S. Foreign Service, 1890–1913* (1977).

DICTIONARIES: John E. Findling, *Dictionary of American Diplomatic History* (1980).

DOCUMENTS: Ruhl Bartlett, *The Record of American Diplomacy* (1964); U.S. Department of State, *Foreign Relations of the United States* (1861–   ); U.S. Superintendent of Documents, *Monthly Catalog of U.S. Government Publications* (1895–   ).

DOMINICAN REPUBLIC: Rayford W. Logan, *Haiti and the Dominican Republic* (1968).

ECONOMICS: *Economics and World Power*, ed. William H. Becker and Samuel F. Wells, Jr. (1984); Joan Edelman Spero, *The Politics of International Economic Relations*, (1981); *Economic Coercion and U.S. Foreign Policy*, ed. Sidney Weintraub (1982); Mira Wilkins, *The Emergence of the Multinational Enterprise* (1970); Mira Wilkins, *The Maturing of the Multinational Enterprise* (1974); William A. Williams, *The Tragedy of American Diplomacy* (1988).

EGYPT: William J. Burns, *Economic Aid and American Policy toward Egypt, 1955–1981* (1985). (See also MIDDLE EAST.)

EL SALVADOR: Cynthia Arnson, *El Salvador* (1982); Raymond Bonner, *Weakness and Deceit* (1984); *El Salvador*, ed. Marvin E. Gettleman *et al.*, (1981); Tommie Sue Montgomery, *Revolution in El Salvador* (1982). (See also CENTRAL AMERICA.)

ENCYCLOPEDIAS: *Political Handbook of the World*, ed. Arthur S. Bank (1975–   ); *Ency-*

clopedia of American Foreign Policy, 3 vols., ed. Alexander DeConde (1978).
ETHIOPIA: David A. Korn, *Ethiopia, the U.S., and the Soviet Union* (1986). Jeffrey S. Lefebvre, *Arms for the Horn . . . 1953–1991* (1991). (See also AFRICA.)
ETHNIC GROUPS: *Ethnic Groups and U.S. Foreign Policy*, ed. Mohammed E. Ahrari (1987); Paul Findley, *They Dare to Speak Out* (1985); Edward Tivnan, *The Lobby* (1987); Stephen A. Garrett, *From Potsdam to Poland* (1986) [on Polish ethnic groups]. (See also RACE AND ETHNICITY.)
EUROPE: Richard Barnet, *The Alliance* (1984); *American Historians and the Atlantic Alliance*, ed. Lawrence Kaplan (1991); Pierre Mélandri, *Les États-Unis face à l'unification de l'Europe: 1945–1954* (1980); *The Dissolving Alliance*, ed. Richard L. Rubenstein (1987). (See also individual countries.)
EXECUTIVE AGREEMENTS: Diane Shaver Clemens, "Executive Agreements," in *Encyclopedia of American Foreign Policy*, ed. Alexander DeConde (1978); Lawrence Margolis, *Executive Agreements and Presidential Power in Foreign Policy* (1986). (See also CONSTITUTION.)
FRANCE: Frank Costigliola, *The Cold Alliance* (1992); Julian G. Hurstfield, *America and the French Nation* (1986).
GERMANY: Manfred Jonas, *U.S. and Germany* (1984); Frank Ninkovich, *Germany and the United States* (1988); *Germany and America*, ed. Hans L. Trefousse (1981).
GREAT BRITAIN: *The Special Relationship . . . since 1945*, ed. William R. Louis and Hedley Bull (1986).
GREECE: *Greek-American Relations*, ed. Theodore A. Couloumbis and John O. Iatrides (1980); Lawrence S. Wittner, *American Intervention in Greece, 1943–1949* (1982).
GRENADA: *American Intervention in Grenada*, ed. Peter M. Dunn and Bruce W. Watson (1985); Gordon K. Lewis, *Grenada* (1987).
GUATEMALA: Jim Handy, *Gift of the Devil* (1985); Richard Immerman, *The CIA in Guatemala* (1982). (See also CENTRAL AMERICA; LATIN AMERICA.)
HAITI: Tom Barry et al., *The Other Side of Paradise* (1984); Brenda Gayle Plummer, *Haiti and the United States* (1992). (See also LATIN AMERICA.)
HUMAN RIGHTS: Natalie Kaufman, *Human Rights Treaties and the Senate* (1990); A. Glenn Mower, *The U.S., UN, and Human Rights* (1979); Lars Schoultz, *Human Rights and U.S. Policy toward Latin America* (1981).
IMPERIALISM: Philip Darby, *Three Faces of Imperialism . . . 1870–1970* (1987); Michael W. Doyle, *Empires* (1986); *Imperialism and After*, ed. Wolfgang J. Mommsen and Jurgen Osterhammel (1986); Vivian Triás, *Historia del imperialismo norteamericano*, 3 vols. (1975–1977).
INDIA: H. W. Brands, *India and the United States* (1990); Gary R. Hess, "Global Expansion and Regional Balances . . . ," *Pacific Historical Review* 56 (May 1975): 159–195 [a valuable bibliographical essay]; Dennis Merrill, *The United States and India . . . 1947–1962* (1990); Kilaru Ram Chandra Rao, *India, U.S. and Pakistan* (1985).
INDIANS (NATIVE AMERICANS): Brian W. Dippie, *The Vanishing American* (1982); Francis Paul Prucha, *The Indians in American Society* (1985).
INDONESIA: Michael Leifer, *Indonesia's Foreign Policy* (1983).
INTELLIGENCE: *Knowing One's Enemies*, ed. Ernest R. May (1985). (See also CENTRAL INTELLIGENCE AGENCY.)
INTERNATIONAL LAW: Calvin D. Davis, *The U.S. and the First Hague Peace Conference* (1962); Calvin D. Davis, *The U.S. and the Second Hague Peace Conference* (1976); *International Law: A Contemporary Perspective*, ed. Richard Falk et al. (1985); Daniel

Patrick Moynihan, *The Law of Nations* (1990); D. P. O'Connell, *The International Law of the Sea* (1982).

IRAN: James A. Bill, *The Eagle and the Lion* (1988); Mark H. Lytle, *The Origins of the Iranian-American Alliance, 1941–1953* (1987); R. K. Ramazani, *The United States and Iran* (1982).

IRAQ: See MIDDLE EAST; OIL; PERSIAN GULF.

IRELAND: Donald H. Akenson, *The U.S. and Ireland* (1973).

ISOLATIONISM: Wayne S. Cole, *Roosevelt and the Isolationists* (1983); Justus D. Doenecke, *Anti-Intervention: A Bibliographical Introduction to Isolationism and Pacifism from World War I to the Early Cold War* (1987); Manfred Jonas, *Isolationism in America* (1966).

ISRAEL: Cheryl Rubenberg, *Israel and the American National Interest* (1986); David Schoenbaum, *The U.S. and Israel* (1993); (See also MIDDLE EAST.)

ITALY: Alexander DeConde, *Half-Bitter, Half-Sweet* (1971); H. Stuart Hughes, *The U.S. and Italy* (1979).

JAPAN: *The U.S. and Japan in the Postwar World*, ed. Akira Iriye and Warren Cohen (1989); Charles E. Neu, *The Troubled Encounter* (1975); William L. Neumann, *America Encounters Japan* (1963).

KOREA: *One Hundred Years of Korean-American Relations*, ed. Yur-Bok Lee and W. Patterson (1986); Chae-Jin Lee and Hideo Sato, *U.S. Policy toward Japan and Korea* (1982).

LABOR: Philip S. Foner, *U.S. Labor . . . and Latin America (1846–1919)* (1988); Ronald Radosh, *American Labor and U.S. Foreign Policy* (1969).

LATIN AMERICA: Cole Blasier, *The Hovering Giant* (1975); Lester Langley, *America and the Americas* (1990); Lester Langley, *Americans and the Caribbean in the Twentieth Century* (1980); John T. Reid, *Spanish-American Images of the U.S., 1790–1960* (1977); Harold Molineau, *U.S. Policy toward Latin America* (1986); (See also CENTRAL AMERICA; individual countries.)

LAW: See INTERNATIONAL LAW.

LEBANON: Itamar Rabinovich, *The War for Lebanon* (1986). (See also MIDDLE EAST.)

LIBERIA: Katherine Harris, *The U.S. and Liberia* (1985); Hassan B. Sisay, *Big Powers and Small Nations* (1985).

LIBYA: P. E. Haley, *Qaddafi and the U.S. since 1969* (1984).

MALAYSIA: *The United States and Malaysia*, ed. Pamela Sodhy (1988).

MANIFEST DESTINY: Albert K. Weinberg, *Manifest Destiny* (1935).

MEXICO: George W. Grayson, *The U.S. and Mexico* (1984); Lester Langley, *Mexico and the United States* (1991); W. Dirk Raat, *Mexico and the United States* (1992); Alan Riding, *Distant Neighbors* (1984); Josefine Zoraida Vazquez and Lorenzo Meyer, *The U.S. and Mexico* (1985). (See also LATIN AMERICA.)

MIDDLE EAST: L. Carl Brown, *International Politics and the Middle East* (1984); Thomas Bryson, *U.S.–Middle East Diplomatic Relations, 1784–1978* (1979) [an annotated bibliography]; William R. Polk, *The Arab World Today* (1991); Steven L. Spiegel, *The Other Arab-Israel Conflict* (1985); William Stivers, *America's Confrontation with Revolutionary Change in the Middle East, 1948–1983* (1986); Seth Tillman, *The U.S. in the Middle East* (1982). (See also individual countries.)

MILITARY: Benjamin R. Beede, *Intervention and Counterinsurgency . . . 1898–1984* (1985) [annotated bibliography]; *The Wars in Vietnam, Cambodia, and Laos, 1945–1982*, ed. Richard D. Burns and Milton Leitenberg (1984) [annotated bibliography]; John Whiteclay Chambers, *To Raise an Army: The Draft Comes to America* (1987); *A Bibli-*

ography of American Naval History, ed. Paolo E. Coletta (1981); Kenneth J. Hagan and William R. Roberts, *Against All Enemies* (1986); *American Historians and the Atlantic Alliance*, ed. Lawrence Kaplan (1991); Ariel E. Levite, Bruce W. Jentleson, Larry Berman, *Foreign Military Intervention* (1992); Peter Maslowski and Richard Millett, *The Common Defense* (1984); Paul B. Stares, *The Militarization of Space* (1985).

MISSIONS: William R. Hutchison, *Errand to the World* (1987); James Reed, *The Missionary Mind and American East Asia Policy, 1911–1915* (1986).

MONROE DOCTRINE: Dexter Perkins, *A History of the Monroe Doctrine* (1963).

NETHERLANDS, THE: *A Bilateral Bicentennial: A History of Dutch-American Relations, 1782–1982*, ed. J. W. Nordholt *et al.* (1982).

NICARAGUA: Karl Bermann, *Under the Big Stick* (1986); Peter Kornbluh, *Nicaragua, the Price of Intervention* (1987); Thomas W. Walker, *Nicaragua* (1991). (See also CENTRAL AMERICA; LATIN AMERICA.)

NORWAY: Sigmund Skard, *The U.S. in Norwegian History* (1976).

NUCLEAR ARMS: Coit D. Blacker, *Reluctant Warriors* (1987); Lawrence Freedman, *The Evolution of Nuclear Strategy* (1983); Institute for Strategic Studies (London), *The Military Balance* (1959–); Ronald Powaski, *March to Armageddon* (1987); Gordon C. Schloming, *American Foreign Policy and the Nuclear Dilemma* (1987). (See also MILITARY.)

OIL: David S. Painter, *Oil and the American Century* (1986); Stephen J. Randall, *U.S. Foreign Oil Policy, 1919–1984* (1985); Michael B. Stoff, *Oil, War, and American Security* (1980); Daniel Yergin, *The Prize* (1991).

PAKISTAN: *U.S.-Pakistan Relations*, ed. Leo E. Rose and Noor A. Husain (1985); M. S. Venkataramani, *The American Role in Pakistan, 1947–1958* (1982). (See also INDIA.)

PANAMA: Michael L. Conniff, *Panama and the United States* (1992); David N. Farnsworth and James W. McKenney, *U.S.-Panama Relations, 1902–1978* (1983); George D. Moffett III, *Limits of Victory* (1985); Walter LaFeber, *The Panama Canal* (1990). (See also LATIN AMERICA.)

PEACE MOVEMENTS: *Peace Heroes in Twentieth-Century America*, ed. Charles DeBenedetti (1986); Charles DeBenedetti, *The Peace Reform in American History* (1980); Justus D. Doenecke, *Anti-Intervention* (1987) [annotated bibliography]; Lawrence S. Wittner, *Rebels Against War . . . 1933–1983* (1984).

PERSIAN GULF: *The Persian Gulf States*, ed. Alvin J. Cottrell (1980); Charles A. Kupchan, *The Persian Gulf and the West* (1987); Michael A. Palmer, *Guardians of the Gulf: A History of America's Expanding Role in the Persian Gulf, 1833–1992* (1992); *The Gulf War Reader*, ed. M. L. Sifry and C. Serf (1991). (See also MIDDLE EAST; OIL.)

PERU: Frederick B. Pike, *The U.S. and the Andean Republics* (1977). (See also LATIN AMERICA.)

PHILIPPINES: Raymond Bonner, *Waltzing with a Dictator* (1987); H. W. Brands, *Bound to Empire* (1992); *Reappraising an Empire*, ed. Peter W. Stanley (1983).

POLAND: Stephen A. Garrett, *From Potsdam to Poland* (1986); Piotr Wandycz, *The U.S. and Poland* (1980).

PRESIDENT: E. S. Corwin, *The President* (1957); Theodore Lowi, *The Personal President* (1985); Edmund Muskie *et al.*, *The President, the Congress and Foreign Policy* (1986). (See also CONGRESS; CONSTITUTION.)

PUBLIC OPINION AND THE PRESS: Bernard C. Cohen, *The Public's Impact on Foreign Policy* (1973); W. A. Dorman and Mansour Farhang, *The U.S. Press and Iran* (1987); Ralph B. Levering, *The Public and American Foreign Policy, 1918–1978* (1978).

Puerto Rico: Raymond Carr, *Puerto Rico* (1984); *Time for Decision*, ed. George Heine (1983).

Race and Ethnicity: Alexander DeConde, *Ethnicity, Race, and American Foreign Policy* (1992); Paul Gordon Lauren, *Power and Prejudice (1988)*.

Russia and the Soviet Union: Michael Beschloss and Strobe Talbott, *At the Highest Levels* (1993) [covers 1988–1992]; John L. Gaddis, *Russia, the Soviet Union and the United States* (1990); Raymond L. Garthoff, *Détente and Confrontation* (1985) [covers 1969–1984]; Colin White, *Russia and America* (1988).

Saudi Arabia: Irvine H. Anderson, *Aramco, the U.S. and Saudi Arabia* (1981); Benson Lee Grayson, *Saudi-American Relations* (1982); David E. Long, *The U.S. and Saudi Arabia* (1985). (See also Middle East; Oil.)

Somolia: Jeffrey A. Lefebvre, *Arms for the Horn . . . 1953–1991* (1991).

South Africa: Thomas Borstelmann, *Apartheid's Reluctant Uncle* (1993); Christopher Coker, *The U.S. and South Africa, 1868–1985* (1986); *The Anti-Apartheid Reader*, ed. David Mermelstein (1987); Thomas J. Noer, *Cold War and Black Liberation . . . 1949–1968* (1985); Anthony Sampson, *Black and Gold* (1987). (See also Africa.)

Terrorism: Augustus Norton and Martin Greensburg, *International Terrorism* (1980) [annotated bibliography].

Thailand: Robert J. Muscat, *Thailand and the United States* (1990).

Turkey: Theodore A. Couloumbis, *The U.S., Greece and Turkey* (1983). (See also Middle East.)

United Nations: Seymour M. Finger, *American Ambassadors at the UN* (1987); Thomas M. Franck, *Nation against Nation* (1985); Evan Luard, *A History of the UN* (1982); Edmund Jan Osmanczyk, *The Encyclopedia of the UN and International Agreements* (1985); Giuseppe Schiavone, *International Organizations: A Dictionary and Directory* (1983).

Uruguay: Arthur P. Whitaker, *The U.S. and the Southern Cone* (1976). (See also Latin America.)

Venezuela: Sheldon B. Liss, *Diplomacy and Independence* (1978); Stephen G. Rabe, *The Road to OPEC: U.S. Relations with Venezuela, 1919–1976* (1982). (See also Latin America; Oil.)

Vietnam: Loren Baritz, *Backfire* (1985); *The Wars in Vietnam, Cambodia, and Laos, 1945–1982*, ed. Richard Dean Burns and Milton Leitenberg (1984) [an annotated bibliography of 6,200 entries]; Lloyd Gardner, *Approaching Vietnam* (1988); George Herring, *The Longest War* (1986); George Kahin, *Intervention* (1986); Paul M. Kattenburg, *The Vietnam Trauma in American Foreign Policy, 1945–1975* (1980); Gabriel Kolko, *Anatomy of a War* (1985); Gareth Porter, *Vietnam* (1980) [extensive documents]; Neil Sheehan, *A Bright Shining Lie: John Paul Vann and America in Vietnam* (1988); William A. Williams *et al.*, *America in Vietnam* (1985) [documents and introductions].

Acknowledgments for the
First Edition

Along with the usual but ever more sincere thanks to Sandra, Scott, and Suzanne LaFeber for making the past years and the writing of this book worthwhile, I am deeply indebted to Ed Barber of W. W. Norton & Company and Gerry McCauley for the encouragement that made the book possible. The growing length of the manuscript was unforeseen, but not Ed Barber's patience, sound advice, and humor, and they made the enterprise bearable. I am also indebted to Linda Puckette and Carol Flechner of Norton for special help in preparing the manuscript for publication, and to indexer Anne Eberle.

Lloyd Gardner of Rutgers University critiqued the entire manuscript and continues to set the example as both a committed scholar and friend. Robert Divine of the University of Texas also read all the pages, as he has of much else I have drafted, and his friendship has been especially important during the past several years. The historical profession lost what it cannot afford to lose when R. H. Miller left it to join Congressman Ron Dellums's staff. Max Miller not only read all of this book, but conducted a private four-year seminar by providing detailed comments and volumes of research materials. I am much indebted to Diane Clemens of the University of California and William Widenor of the University of Illnois, both of whom gave large sections of the manuscript close and most helpful readings. Milton Leitenberg, whether in Sweden or Washington, provided important studies of his own and others on East-West relations. Despite the Carter-Reagan attempts to close off documents from scholars, there remain some to whom we owe a huge debt for their professionalism and practicing belief that a democracy can survive only when the government's actions can be examined. These persons include David Langbart of the National

Archives, David Humphrey of the Lyndon Johnson Presidential Library, and Dennis Bilger of the Harry S. Truman Presidential Library.

Eric Edelman and Dan Fried of the Department of State, and John Greer, now a lawyer, are scholars, valued friends and detached critics. The best ideas in this book are probably largely stolen from those named above or from Fred Harvey Harrington and Tom McCormick, both of the University of Wisconsin, and William Appleman Williams of Oregon State; those three are very special as scholars and friends.

Persons associated with Cornell University have, as always, been irreplaceable. Marie Underhill Noll's encouragement is even more valued now because she is also a neighbor. David Maisel, Arthur Kaminsky, Peter Schuck, Jeff Bialos, David Wechsler, Laurie Keenan, Stephen Arbogast, Dan Weil, Mark Lytle, Eric Alterman, Douglas Little, Frank Costigliola, Fred Adams, Frederick Drake, Bob Seidel, David Green, Gayle Plummer, Rich Johnston, and Kathy Harris are former students who now enjoy much success in their various professions but are never too busy to provide valuable advice and reading materials. Rick Mandel, David Jackson, Colleen Curtin, Agnes Sagan, and Jessica Wang have been imaginative research assistants. Cathy Hendley typed the final draft carefully and against deadlines. Jackie Hubble kindly helped with the typing when the deadlines were pressing. The Cornell University Libraries continue to be unsurpassed in resources and accessibility; I owe Alain Seznec, David Corson, Caroline Spicer, Janie Harris, and Martha Hsu particular thanks.

Five friends in the History Department read much of this book in various forms and provided important materials which often resulted from their own scholarship. This book is dedicated to them. They first came to Cornell to help teach the introductory American history course, and they have remained to become distinguished scholars, noted teachers, superb colleagues, and—of special importance—close friends. They and other friends who are Americanists—Margaret Washington, Stuart Blumin, Paul Gates, Fred Somkin, Dan Usner, Glenn Altschuler, Nick Salvatore, Bob Harris, and, in a special category, Ted Lowi—have made Ithaca a stimulating place in which to study American history.

Walter LaFeber
March 1988

Photo Credits

P. 13: National Portrait Gallery, Smithsonian Institution; p. 20: Bibliothèque Nationale, Paris; p. 22: New-York Historical Society, New York; p. 31: Department of State; p. 44: American Philosophical Society; p. 49: Warder Collection; p. 53: Historical Pictures Service; p. 59: Metropolitan Museum of Art; p. 60: Courtesy Department of Library Services, American Museum of Natural History; p. 64: Library of Congress; p. 72: Metropolitan Museum of Art, Gift of I.N. Phelps Stokes, Edward S. Hawes, Alice Mary Hawes, Marion Augusta Hawes, 1937 (37.14.34); p. 77: National Archives; p. 83: Pennsylvania Academy of Fine Arts; p. 102: National Portrait Gallery, Smithsonian Institution; p. 103: Library of Congress; p. 115: National Archives; p. 128: Metropolitan Museum of Art, Gift of I.N. Phelps Stokes, Edward S. Hawes, Alice Mary Hawes, Marion Augusta Hawes, 1937 (37.14.2); p. 128: Metropolitan Museum of Art; p. 130: National Archives; p. 131: National Archives; p. 139: UPI-Bettmann; p. 151: *Public Opinion*, January 17, 1901; p. 156: Granger Collection; p. 160: State Historical Society of North Dakota; p. 161: State Historical Society of North Dakota; p. 164: Library of Congress; p. 169: Public Archives of Hawaii; p. 176: Warder Collection; p. 183: National Portrait Gallery, Smithsonian Institution; p. 186: Brown Brothers; p. 187: New-York Historical Society, New York; p. 193: Charles Musser, *The Emergence of Cinema: The American Screen to 1907* (New York: Scribner's, 1990); p. 199: *Literary Digest*, January 26, 1901; p. 201: Smithsonian Institution; p. 203: Library of Congress; p. 207: Library of Congress; p. 220: Library of Congress; p. 228: Library of Congress; p. 231: *Public Opinion*, September 1, 1904; p. 241: Library of Congress; p. 245: Library of Congress; p. 255: Franklin D. Roosevelt Library; p. 258: National Portrait Gallery, Smithsonian Institution; p. 260: Library of Congress; p. 263: Library of Congress; p. 271: *The New York Times*; p. 280: UPI-Bettmann; p. 288: National Archives; p. 297: National Portrait Gallery, Smithsonian Institution; p. 305: *Daily Herald*; p. 308: Warder Collection; p. 311: Library of Congress; p. 317: Department of State; p. 318: National Portrait Gallery, Smithsonian Institution; p. 321: Wide World Photos; p. 337: Historical Pictures Service; p. 338: Cesare, *Outlook*; p. 343: National Archives; p. 352: Franklin D. Roosevelt Library; p. 354: National Portrait Gallery, Smithsonian Institution; p. 361: UPI-Bettmann; p. 365: C. D. Batchelor, © 1936 New York News Inc., reprinted with permission; p. 381: Franklin D. Roosevelt Library; p. 383: National Archives; p. 384: Franklin D. Roosevelt Library; p. 394: Franklin D. Roosevelt Library; p. 404: Franklin D. Roosevelt Library; p. 407: Franklin D. Roosevelt Library; p. 417: Franklin D. Roosevelt Library; p. 419: National Archives; p. 423: U.S. Army, courtesy of Harry S. Truman Library; 427: UN Photo, 149433; p. 442: Warder Collection; p. 436: Archives of Harry S. Truman Presidential Library, Independence, Missouri; p. 448: Wide World Photos; p. 450: Library of Congress; p. 457: Department of State; p. 461: U.S. Information Agency; p. 480: Drawing by David Levine, reprinted with permission from The New York Review of Books, © 1964–74; p. 485: UPI-Bettmann; p. 500: UPI-Bettmann; p. 502: Roche in the *Buffalo Courier Express;* p. 511: UPI-Bettmann; p. 514: Advertisement reproduced from *School Executive,* August 1951, p. 92, and noted in JoAnne Brown, "A is for Atom, B is for Bomb: Civil Defense in American Public Education, 1948–1963," *Journal of American History* 75 (June 1988), pp. 68–90, p. 521: European Picture Service; p. 528: dpa-Bild; p. 531: Drawing by David Levine, reprinted with permission from The New York Review of Books, © 1964–74; p. 537: Bastian, *San Francisco Chronicle;* p. 541: Magnum; p. 555: Wide World Photos; p. 558: © 1981 by Pluto Press Limited, reprinted by permission of Simon & Schuster, Inc.; p. 564: AP–Wide World; p. 567: U.S. Air Force; p. 568: Cecil Stroughton; p. 582: Lyndon B. Johnson Library; p. 584: Life Picture Service; p. 586: Lyndon Baines Johnson Library Handwriting File, Austin, Texas; p. 587: UPI-Bettmann; p. 590: Brooks, *Birmingham News;* p. 591: Lyndon B. Johnson Library; p. 603: © Jules Feiffer; p. 608: *Valley News Dispatcher;* p. 611: Department of State; p. 614: UPI-Bettmann; p. 618: UPI-Bettmann; p. 623: Drawing by David Levine, reprinted with permission from The New York Review of Books, © 1964–74; p. 631: UPI-Bettmann; p. 632: Drawing by David Levine, reprinted with permission from The New York Review of Books, © 1964–74; p. 636: *Public Opinion,* Vol. 1, no. 2, May/June 1978; p. 637: White House Official Photograph; p. 649: © 1977, Time, Inc., all rights reserved, reprinted by permission from Time; p. 654: AP Photo; p. 656: UN Photo; p. 664: U.S. State Department; p. 670: AP–Wide World; p. 673: UPI-Bettmann; p. 682: Susan Moeller; p. 697: UPI-Bettmann; p. 699: UPI-Bettmann.

Index

Italicized page numbers refer to drawings and photographs.